ART DECO JEWELRY

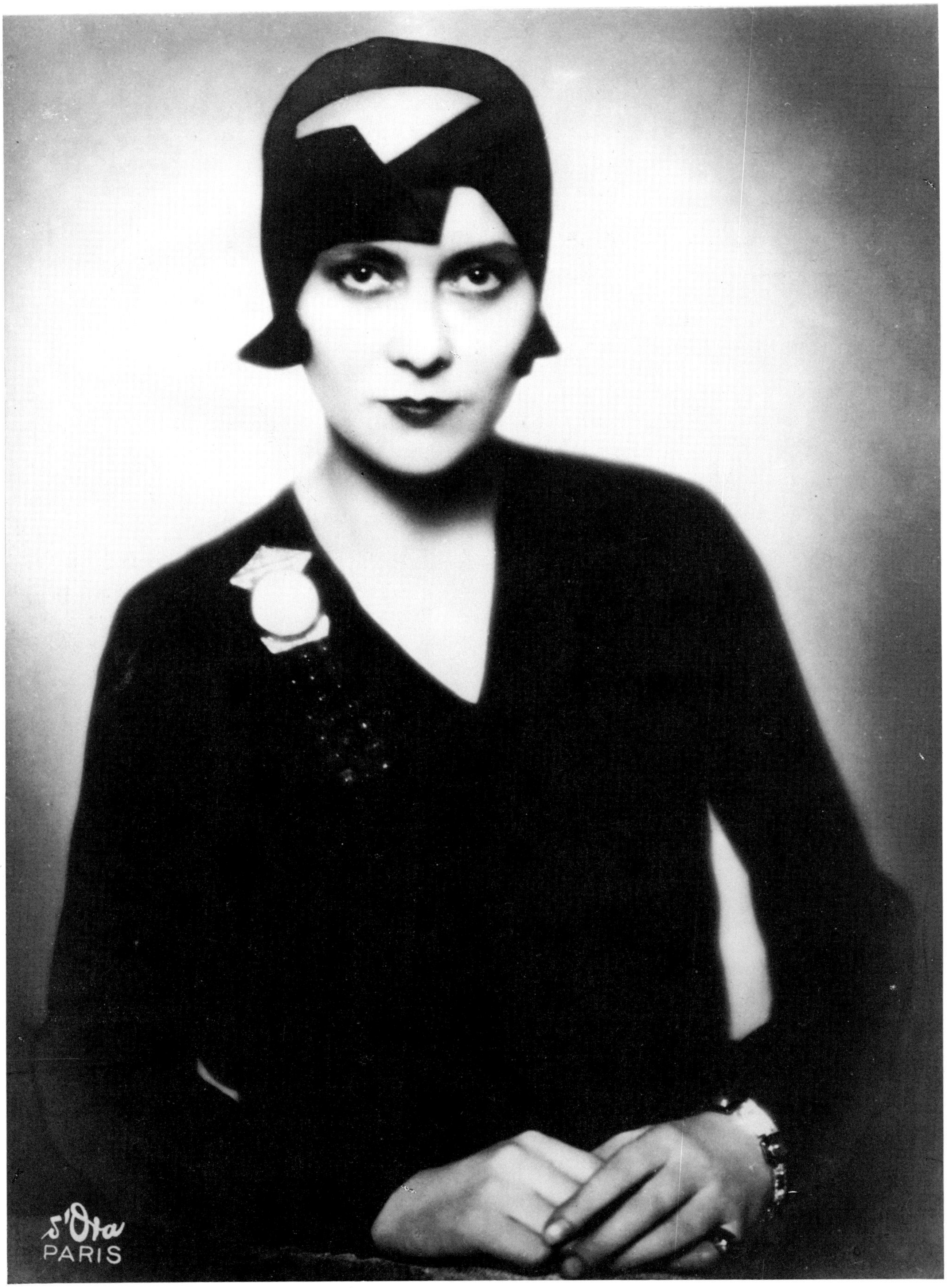

Arletty wearing jewelry by Fouquet, January 1929.

ART DECO JEWELRY

SYLVIE RAULET

with 792 illustrations, 261 in colour

THAMES AND HUDSON

Translated from the French
Bijoux Art Déco
by Lucinda Gane

First published in Great Britain in 1985
by Thames and Hudson Ltd, London

Printed and bound in Italy
by GEA S.p.A. - Milan

CONTENTS

For J. B.

AUTHOR'S NOTE

A PIECE OF JEWELRY is the symbolic object *par excellence*, appreciated as much for its aesthetic qualities as for its intrinsic value. After the First World War, all the arts participated in an unprecedented cultural revolution. From Paris, which was its centre, Maurice Sachs wrote: 'I remember that decade as a perpetual fourteenth of July. It was a tricolour age.' It is true that the 1920s, nicknamed the 'Golden Twenties', witnessed an exceptional alliance of taste, talent and money: '. . . couturiers, barmen, snobs, wealthy art lovers, intellectuals and society figures strove with one frantic accord to reveal and perfect the bold aesthetic impulses of the age . . .' (Jean Cassou, *Panorama des Arts Plastiques*, 1960). At the time of the 'Exposition Internationale des Arts Décoratifs' in 1925, Pierre Contreau remarked that 'the works of these artists seem the logical conclusion of labours destined to form a style for which our descendants will find a name. . . .' (in *Le Grand Négoce* – special number devoted to the 1925 Exhibition). The style was not, in fact, to be christened until 1966, following an exhibition at the Musée des Arts Décoratifs in Paris, first entitled 'Les Années 25', then 'Art Déco'.

In order to demonstrate clearly the sculptural aspect and the powerful sense of rhythm and balance inherent in these creations, it has been thought useful to illustrate them sometimes larger than their actual size, in the same way as an enlarged detail may be used to facilitate the proper understanding of a work of art.

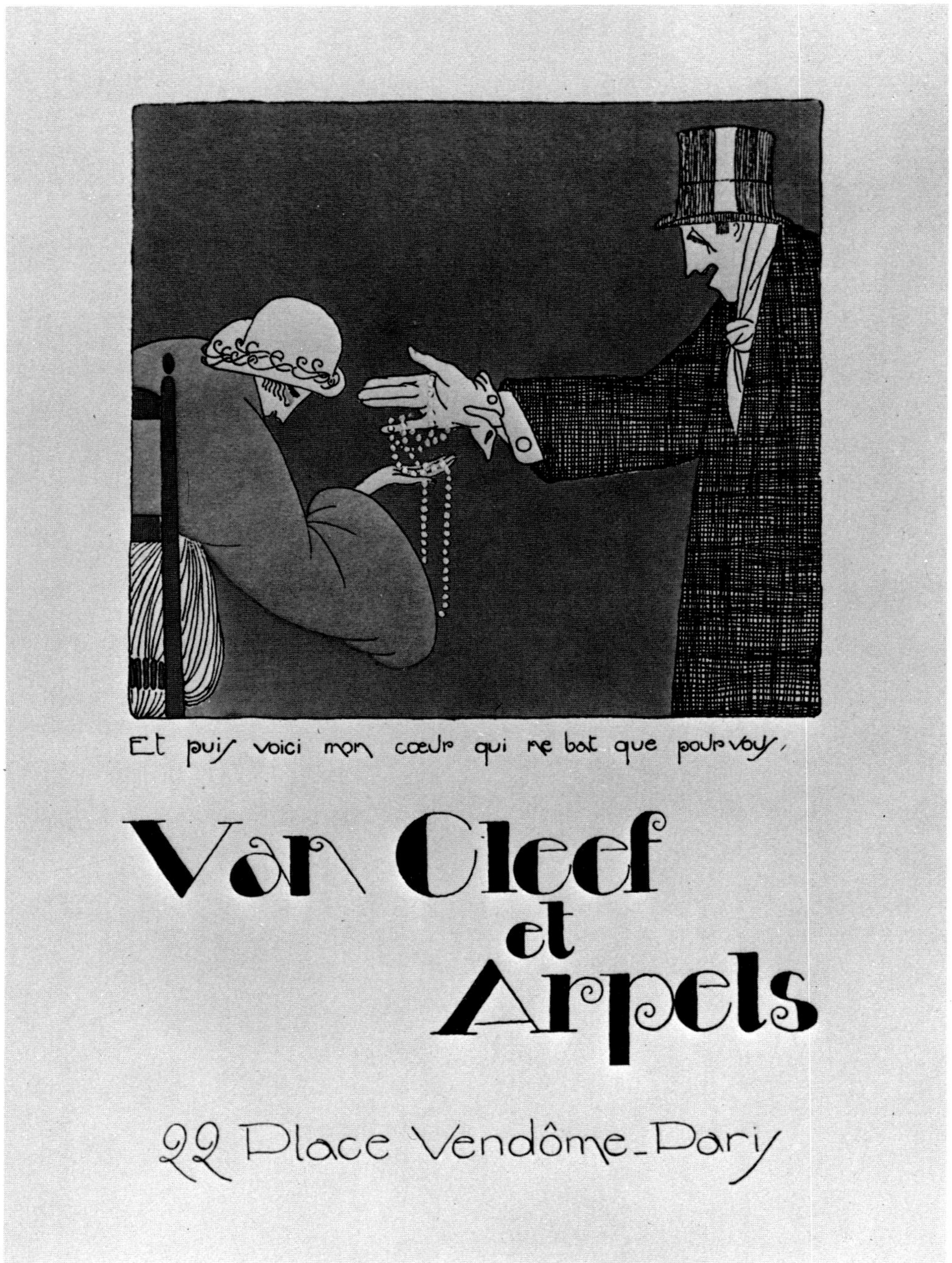
Et puis voici mon cœur qui ne bat que pour vous,
Van Cleef
et
Arpels
22 Place Vendôme - Paris

THE BIRTH OF ART DECO

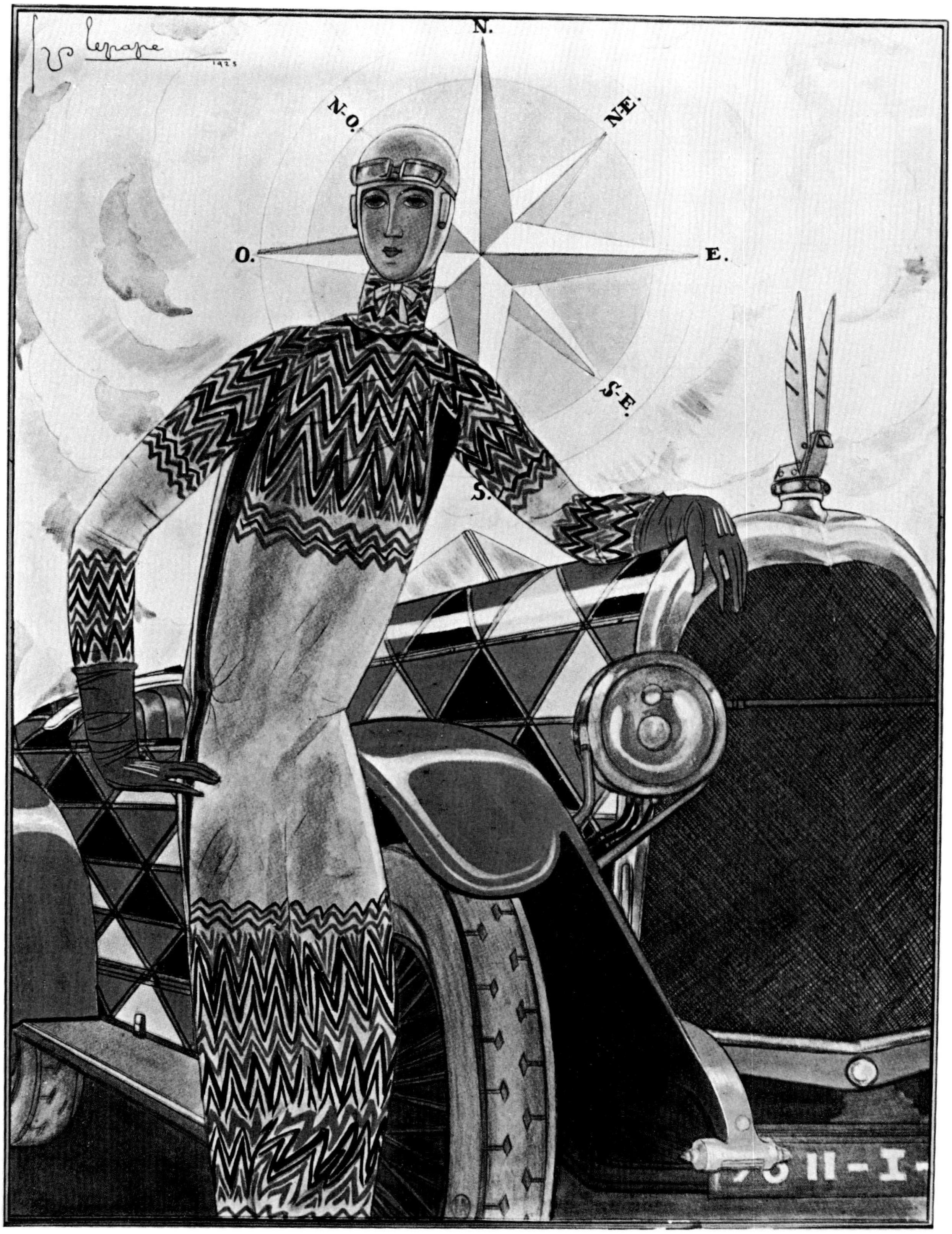

Georges Lepape: original gouache for the cover of Vogue France, *1 November 1925. 36.5 × 27.5 cm. Photo: Edimedia.*

As the nineteenth century drew to an end, a new artistic phenomenon took hold of the decorative arts and dominated the creative desires and the aesthetic impulse of the age: Art Nouveau. Everyone swore by the 'modern style'; naturalism held sway; animals, flowers and female silhouettes invaded the language of ornament. 'From a gourd', wrote Mr Robert de la Sizeranne, 'a library emerges, from a thistle a bureau, from a water-lily a ballroom.' Applying their skill and enthusiasm to these new sources of inspiration, jewelers were given the opportunity to see their talents admired and recognized at the 'Exposition Universelle' in Paris in 1900: names like Falize, Aucoc, Chaumet, Boucheron, Lalique, Templier and Sandoz vied with one another in imaginative virtuosity. Paul Soufflot, reporting on the *bijouterie-joaillerie* section, recorded the extent to which the dimensions of a piece had become a surprising feature, raised to the status of an integral element of the composition. The excessive size of brooches, tiaras and corsage ornaments could not be reduced, it appeared, without endangering the harmony of their creation, while the delights in the design of other – miniature – pieces of jewelry could only be fully appreciated with the aid of a magnifying glass.

The scale of jewelry, a decorative accessory to dress, became completely out of proportion to its intended function. On brooches and pendants, flowers, snakes and bindweed were entwined, insects bared their stings and fish plunged. The most absurd scenes were depicted on these pieces of jewelry: on one pendant, a giant spider loomed over a fly imprisoned in a silver web; a design for a pendant by Grasset for the Maison Vever represented two women holding hands, raising above their heads laurel garlands tied with a whimsically fluttering ribbon; necklaces were composed of baroque pearls clasped by writhing seaweed. Georges Fouquet invented the idea of the *harnais* (harness) – huge fastenings worn over a dress, attached to the shoulders – and created for Sarah Bernhardt, from a design by Alphonse Mucha, a bracelet-ring consisting of a winged serpent whose head was flattened against the back of the hand. Modelled in gold and set with emeralds and rubies, this piece was iridescent with enamel and opals and hung with fine chains. Boucheron and Chaumet produced two corsage ornaments, veritable jeweled corselets, for la Belle Otero and the lovely Fagette, irresistible *demi-mondaines*, who were proud to display, in the guise of a corsage ornament, a gem-studded breastplate – gorgeous creations which were, admittedly, conceived more as exhibition pieces. Such jewelry tended to favour combinations of pale, shimmering colours and pastel cameos of translucent enamel.

The French art of 1900, which accorded too much importance to ornament and too little to colour, was condemned to go out of fashion and disappear. To be sure, this frantic passion for representations of flowers and animals gave the artist rein to express languor, voluptuousness and ecstasy, in the form of arabesques, scrolls and intertwinings, but it excluded pure lines and the vigour of architectural structures. As early as 1904, Maurice Dufrêne published *Les Bijoux*, a collection of twenty-four illustrations of models, while Paul Follot brought out a pamphlet reproducing six illustrations of designs for modern jewelry in half-tone watercolour, both publications demonstrating a tendency towards the geometricization of forms. A vision of nature, transposed literally and literally translated, could not fulfil the demands of the object and the material. To copy nature in its fantastic aspect without studying its laws was an error.

By 1910, Art Nouveau was discredited, victim of a certain mannered academicism. The floral image lost ground, the bindweed became untangled, good sense replaced impetuosity. A desire for severity and simplicity emerged, the representational image and the soft focus disappeared gradually, giving way to stylization and geometric shapes. In accordance with what seems to be a general rule, decorative art describes a perpetual pendulum swing, ceaselessly passing from natural forms to those of abstraction. It has often been said, in diverse civilizations, that art, as it asserts itself, frees itself from tortured lines, then reverts to them again as it degenerates. It was essential, however, during these years to free jewelry from pastiche and historical retrospection, as Lalique, Georges Fouquet, Henri Vever and Eugène Grasset were attempting to do.

Shortly after the 1900 'Exposition Universelle', the decline in Art Nouveau left a void in the decorative arts which was temporarily filled by a return to eighteenth-century themes. In 1902, the magazine *Les Modes* echoed a general sentiment when it published words addressed to the critic Gabriel Mourey by an elegant young woman of the time: 'The song is becoming monotonous. When shall we be done with peacock feathers, swans, irises, orchids and that sort of thing? Mark my words, we would be only too happy, frankly, to return quite simply to the styles of times past, to that exquisite Louis XV, to that delicious Louis XVI and even to that icy Empire style which was thought hideous only ten years ago and which fashion is now reviling.' This pessimistic and backward-looking confession postponed any hope of a revival in the applied arts and in 1914 the outbreak of the First World War rang the death knell of the luxury industries.

EFFECTS OF THE WAR

It is normal for years of suffering and privation to be followed by years of frenzied exaltation. The only password was 'forget the past', erasing everything that reminded one of it, creating a new art of living, a reborn world that would push aside the traditions established by a pre-war society. The pleasure in being alive became a rage to live and to change laws according to one's imagination and conviction. Some achieved this by means of provocation, others by energetic debate, precipitating changes in what had hitherto been reined in by the force of convention. A rapid and radical transformation thus took place which, in a few years, was to engender more innovations and inventions than there had been in the forty years leading up to the First World War. It was France – impoverished, destroyed and ravaged – that to a large extent supported the cause of the innovators who were to build the new world, repeating after Apollinaire, 'After all, you're tired of this old world.' The most audacious ideas, ignored ten years earlier, won the support of a large section of society whose aspirations were changing rapidly. If the traditional middle classes frowned on novelty, a new well-to-do class, which had emerged from the conflict, made up of both aristocrats and aesthetes, people who followed fashion and people who set it, decided to join the new generation, with its energetic rhythm and its thirst for life. Paris was imbued with a frantic sense of liberty and if she didn't know how far she could go, as Cocteau said, at least she would tolerate no limit. If pre-war France had been thrifty, comfortably living off her income, in the Twenties she blazed, throwing her money about – money which was losing its value with each passing day. There was galloping inflation and the dollar, which was worth 5.45 F in January 1919, reached 50 F in July 1926. The accession to power, in 1924, of a parliamentary majority which proposed the introduction of a tax on capital sent a wave of panic through the business world. Capital funds were taken out of the country, foreign currency was bought and demands for reimbursement of Crédit National and Treasury Bonds exceeded new subscriptions. Inflation led people to invest in objects which could be converted into ready money and which would hold their value, such as pictures, jewelry and works of art. A whiff of scandal in the world of high finance – culminating in the Stavisky, Oustric, Hanau affair – tainted the political world and reduced confidence in it. Raymond Poincaré appeared like a saviour and, from 1925 to 1929, projected the image of a prosperous, golden France, living in opulence on the edge of a precipice. The flowering of the artistic avant-garde which had been working in obscurity since 1900 was accelerated by social changes, most particularly in the position of women in society.

THE TRANSFORMATION OF THE FEMALE SILHOUETTE

Jewelry fashions have always been closely linked to fashions in dress. The outbreak of the First World War in 1914 was to bring about a radical transformation in the female silhouette. During these four years, the absence of able-bodied men at the front forced women to take up activities which had previously never involved them. Documents of the period show them working in munitions factories, labouring in the fields, in workshops or in offices, as nurses at the front or in hospitals, even carrying sacks of coal. All such occupations obliged them to discard the corset which constricted the bust, distorted the waist and compressed the stomach; the skirt which fitted the hips and ballooned out to the ground or hobbled the calves and ankles, inhibiting walking; and the wide hats fixed to heavy and voluminous chignons. To give themselves more freedom, they adopted shorter skirts, exposed their arms, cut their hair and took on a boyish appearance; the change was spectacular. Between the Bourbon Restoration of 1814–48 and the

First World War, women's dress, if it varied, had nevertheless always followed a similar aesthetic. For almost a hundred years, changes in fashion were barely perceptible compared with those that took place in the Twenties. Paul Poiret and, following him, Coco Chanel, created a new woman: Poiret with his straight little dresses in the Directoire style, scarcely punctuated by a ribbon under the breast, freeing the body and created in light fabrics such as gauze or muslin; Chanel with fabrics and styles traditionally reserved for men, such as tweeds, woollens, tailor-mades and sweaters which she made into simple, elegant and functional clothes. Emancipated, in effect, by the war, women resolved to remain so and when peace returned they took an interest in sport. If, in the past, it had been in good taste to treat sport with disdain, like Beau Brummell who dreaded physical exercise because its violent movements disarranged one's clothes and hair and made one assume ridiculous positions, society women, leading the fashion, now threw themselves into sport whole-heartedly and discovered the joys of the open air. For readers of the fashion magazines, *Fémina* or *Vogue*, photographers immortalized the elegant woman, racquet in hand, striding along a golf course or wearing a bathing suit on a fashionable beach. A caption under one photograph described 'Mrs Joubert dressed entirely in white jersey, hitting a tremendous drive . . . .' They spoke of nothing but seasons on the Riviera, at Biarritz and at Deauville. Women acquired their sea-legs for scampering along the gangways of yachts, they posed in front of motor cars at stylish rallies. The more daring took the steering-wheel of sports cars and limousines. High society kept low company on country excursions and *Vogue*, for example, discussed nothing but *l'Elégance et du Confort* (elegance and comfort), *Sans Cérémonie* (casual wear) and even *Mode Active* (sportswear). The engravings and photos depicted the new type of woman for whom dresses and tailor-mades were intended: never had the silhouette been so long, so flat, the natural curves of the body suppressed as much as nature would permit. Armand Lanoux in *Paris 1925* sketched the new woman: 'From shoulders to hips, woman is a rectangle. From waist to knees, a trapezium, narrowing towards the base. Close-cropped hair reveals the shaven nape of the neck. Heavy imitation jewel pendants hang from her ears. The cloche hat hides the cap of hair except for one lock which hangs over the left eyebrow.' A contemporary jingle completed the portrait: 'The women of today – Are always coming up with the most astonishing tricks – They play the banjo – They drink cocktails, drive cars – Not content with cutting their hair – They show us their calves – Right to the top, to the top, if you please.' The fashionable young girls imitated their mothers, and devoured Victor Marguerite's *La Garçonne* which was a great success, selling more than 100,000 copies. Like its heroine, they liberated themselves, used too much make-up, giving themselves black-ringed eyes and crimson lips, and smoked in public, flourishing long amber or tortoiseshell cigarette holders. For this new tubular-shaped woman, the great couturiers – Madeleine Vionnet, Jeanne Lanvin, Jean-Charles Worth, Callot,

Jenny, Coco Chanel and Heim – presented models with evocative names: *200 à l'heure* (200 km an hour), *A toute vitesse* (at top speed), *T.S.F.* (radio), or Patou's *Je ne crains rien* (I fear nothing). The shirt-dress, after undergoing various transformations, gave way to afternoon dresses, tailor-mades and wide, quilted coats which constricted neither movement nor gait. For dynamic women, in love with speed, who passed from the tennis court to a *thé dansant*, a different sort of jewelry had to be devised. It is difficult to imagine a brooch in the form of a bouquet of flowers in diamonds, or a heavy Art Nouveau corsage ornament on a straight dress or a tweed suit. The forms of the day required jewelry with simple lines, spare design and vivid colours to underline the detail of an outfit or to complete it. The Twenties thus offered creators the opportunity to renew their repertoire of forms in conjunction with fashion styles in dress. One only has to compare the silhouette of a woman in a crinoline, bustle or padded hips with that of a Twenties woman with her androgynous looks, to understand logically one of the principal causes of the renaissance of *bijouterie-joaillerie*.

TECHNICAL INNOVATIONS

Two principal factors determine the creation of a piece of jewelry: the imagination of the designer and the range of technical possibilities. The first is not in itself sufficient to account for the innovative richness of Twenties jewelry. It is true that, if technique can inhibit creativity, it can also act on it dynamically by bringing in new resources, by contributing new gemstone cuts or by allowing a greater flexibility in metalworking. Thus, at the beginning of the twentieth century, important technical advances gave a free rein to the imagination of artists and facilitated novel combinations of surfaces and colours.

Gem cutters obtained hitherto unknown effects from precious stones. To the classic cuts – rose, brilliant and demi-brilliant – were added new combinations: in tables, baguettes, prisms and trapeziums, facilitating the execution of creator-designers' projects and breaking once and for all the invariable rigidity of traditional cuts. Playing with this inexhaustible variety of cuts – unknown to the masters of earlier times – the modern gem cutters revolutionized jewelry and obtained a diversity of refractions and brilliant oppositions of light. A panel set with diamonds was no longer simply a luminous expanse, it was a dazzling mosaic.

Craftsmen, in 1925, did not hesitate to cut into the range of hardstones – jade, onyx, lapis lazuli, malachite, turquoise, amber and coral.

Around 1900, the discovery of platinum revolutionized the art of setting and platinum took the place of gold and silver. Unlike silver, platinum does not oxydize and, because of its great strength, far less of the metal is needed to set a stone. Without mechanical intervention, using only a burnisher, pliers and a hammer, the gem mounter is able to obtain the maximum solidity and lightness from platinum. Because of its tremendous adaptability, mounts were achieved with invisible settings: real works of art revealing the stone in all its brilliance, the harmony of the design and the purity of forms and colour. The ease with which platinum is worked facilitated the production of pieces of jewelry with no gap between the stones; no unevenness was apparent, the support which held the stones together beneath the mosaic was scarcely visible and necklaces and bracelets took on the appearance and suppleness of ribbons of light. The supple strength of these invisible armatures far outstripped the creations of jewelers of preceding centuries with their heavy, blatant settings. Some stones, simply held by the culasse, appeared to be suspended in thin air.

Platinum, though it reigned supreme, was expensive and rare: to fulfil manufacturing needs, a substitute had to be found. In 1918, an alloy under the name of Osmior, Plator or Platinor was discovered and would be used a great deal by artists such as Jean Fouquet.

Another important discovery lay in the cultivation of pearl-bearing oysters, developed by the Japanese scholar Mikimoto to make up for the scarcity of natural pearls. The pearl merchants, supported by the Chambres Syndicales de la Bijouterie-Joaillerie, rose up in arms against these products of biological trickery. To mollify them, a law was passed establishing a difference in name to distinguish the two products: only those pearls found fortuitously by oyster fishermen could be called pearls, the others were to be called cultured pearls. Cultured pearls took over the European market and became the typical jewel of the Twenties.

Thanks to the latest research into metals, jewelry

makers had greater scope than ever before for experimenting with ingenious designs. A varied look could be obtained from gold, silver and platinum by burnishing them, texturing them, changing their colours and by producing grey gold and white gold.

Mention should also be made of the preparation and development of synthetic or plastic materials derived from raw materials which were predominantly organic in origin. It was in the 1890s that a patent appeared for a thermosetting semi-synthetic substance called casein, made industrially from milk, whose name differed from country to country: 'Erinoid' in England, 'Galalith' in Germany, 'Aladdinite', 'Kyloid' or 'Ameroid' in the United States. Between 1925 and 1930, there was a rapid development in the manufacture of Bakelite (a synthetic resin named after its discoverer, Leo Baekeland of Ghent, but also frequently applied to a variety of other plastics), which was to be one of the costume jewelers' favourite materials. Regarded at first only as a substitute for the rarest materials, it was used to simulate wood, marble, horn and amber, but was soon to be appreciated in its own right.

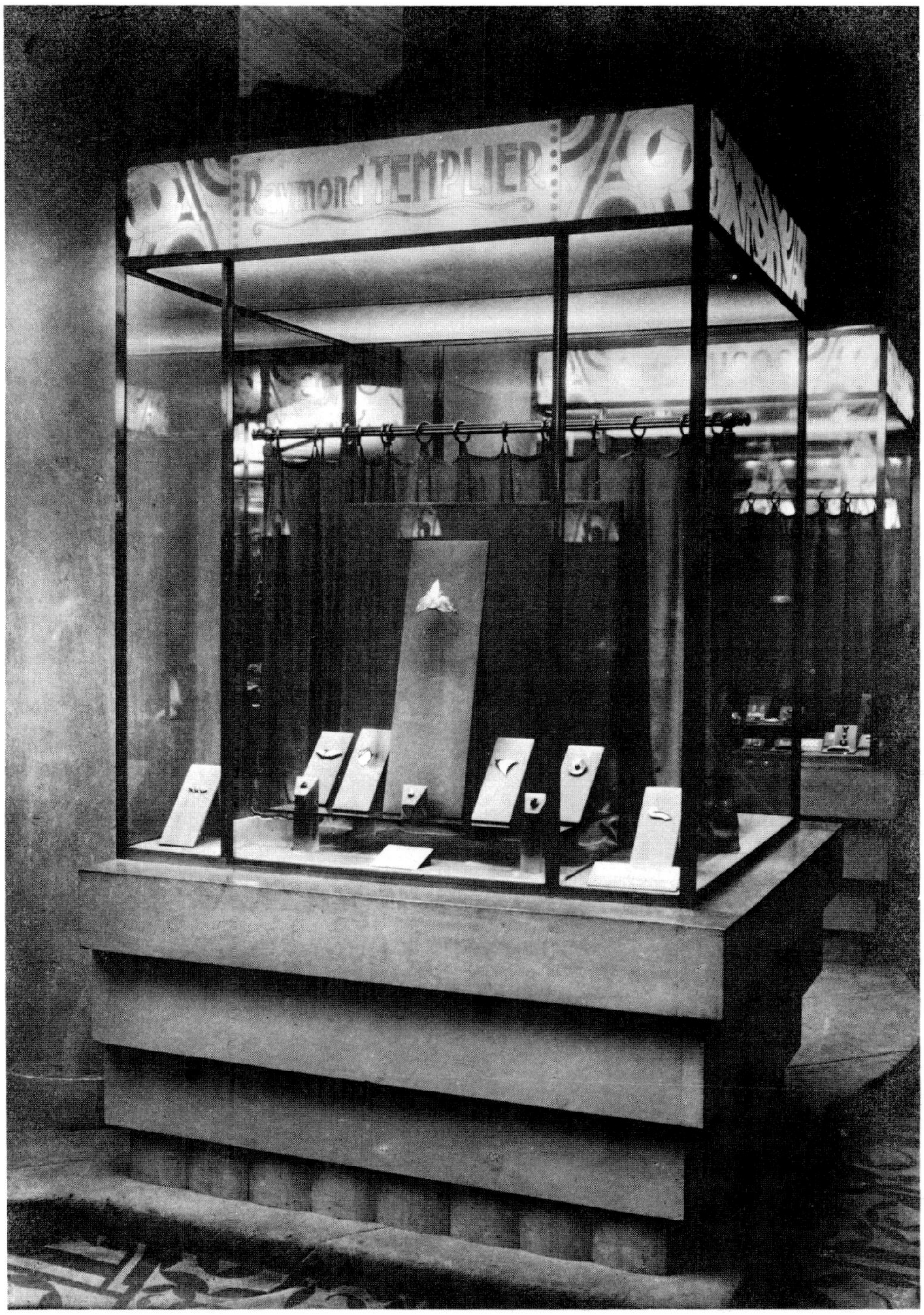

Raymond Templier's showcase at the 1925 Exposition in Paris.

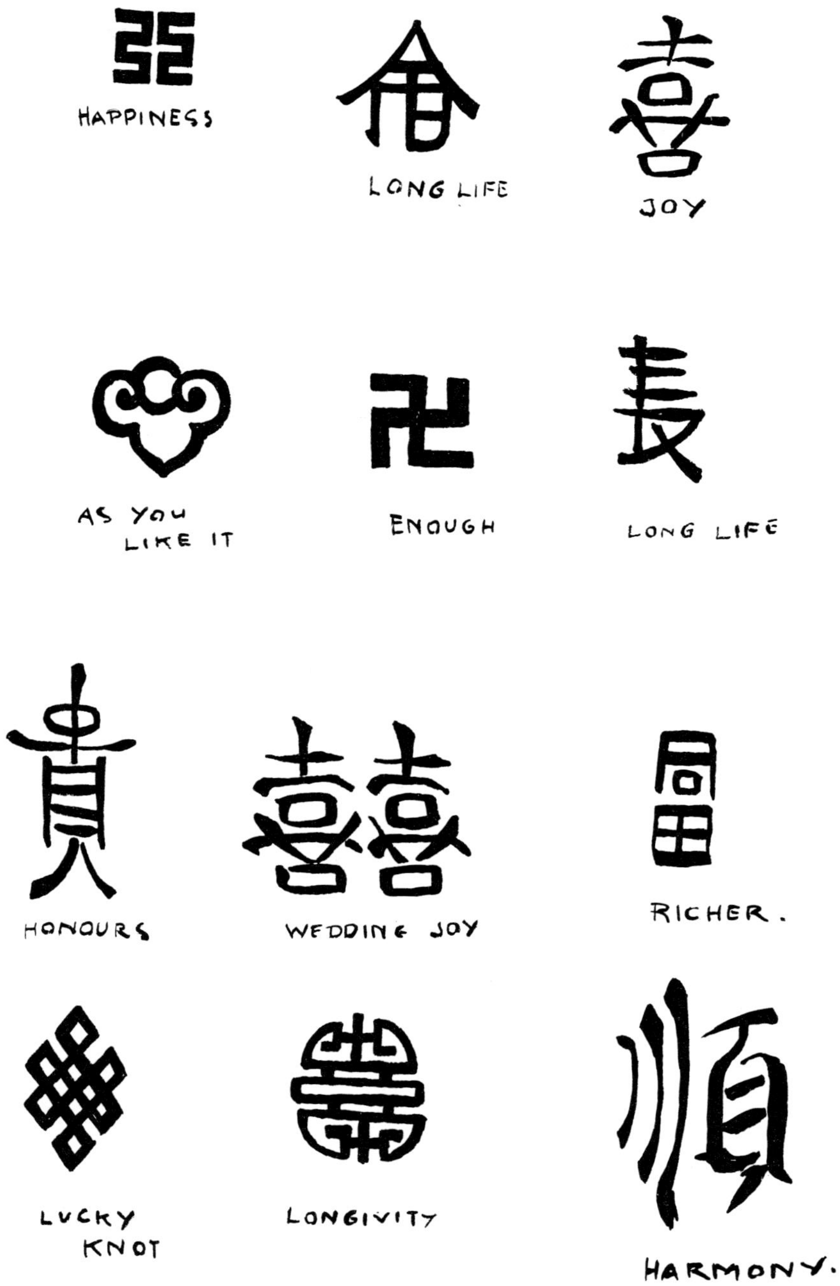

HAPPINESS
LONG LIFE
JOY
AS YOU LIKE IT
ENOUGH
LONG LIFE
HONOURS
WEDDING JOY
RICHER.
LUCKY KNOT
LONGIVITY
HARMONY.

INFLUENCES
ON
JEWELRY

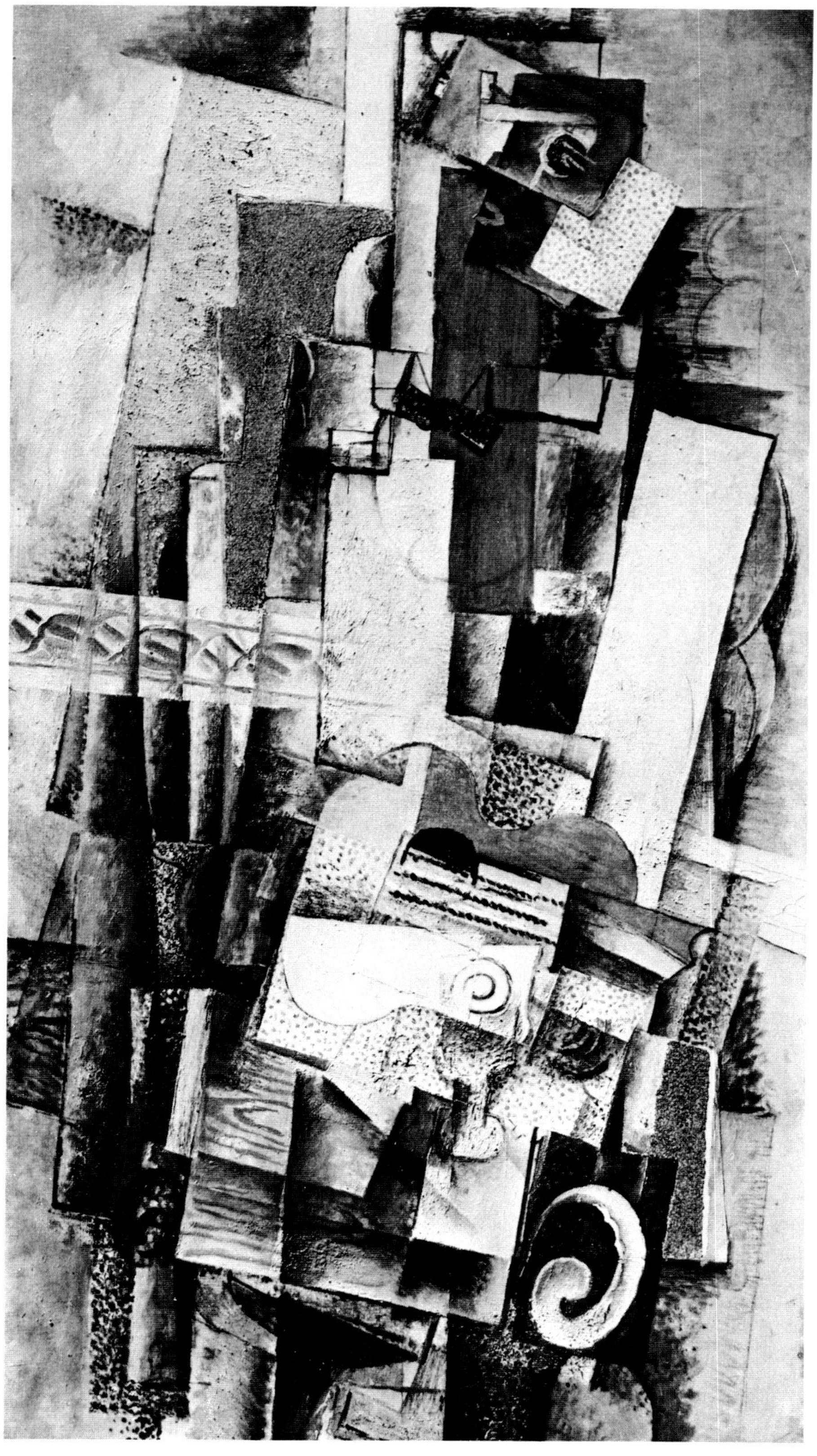

Georges Braque: Man with a Guitar, *oil and sand on canvas, 1914. 130 × 73 cm. Musée National d'Art Moderne, Paris.*

IN THE FIRST QUARTER of the twentieth century, ideas travelled with the speed of motor cars and planes. The newest and most daring found the largest number of supporters. A whirlwind blew up from nowhere and either scattered or smashed yesterday's notions. Manifestos followed one after another, electrifying the atmosphere and prompting interminable discussions. The same, at times excessive, passion that had taken hold of everyday attitudes, animated the field of artistic expression. It was during these ten years fixed by Maurice Sachs, for purely subjective reasons, between 1922 and 1932, and called by him 'the decade of illusion', 'that the game was played and lost' (Armand Lanoux, *Paris 1925*, 1957). The frontiers opened and manifestos flew across Europe: Fauvism, Expressionism, Cubism, Futurism, Neo-Plasticism, Constructivism, Suprematism and Dadaism were the artistic roots from which the Twenties grew. Rarely has there been a period so fruitful in endeavour, in discoveries, in meetings, in exchanges, and culminating in a revolution whose repercussions were felt throughout Europe and in all the art forms. The arts of *parure*, jewelry and clothing, were enriched by these currents. More than ever, the innovations in the major arts profited the applied arts and exercised a profound influence on jewelry designers. The susceptibility of jewelry to the currents which passed through the intellectual and artistic atmosphere was remarkable and undoubtedly unique.

Describing jewelry which he qualifies as *actuel* (contemporary), a writer of the time affirmed 'that a piece of jewelry, that product of vision and matter, of sensibility and emotion, of precision, of virtuosity and technique, participates in the questionings, the tendencies and the general evolution of the aesthetic of the age.' Of all the trends which went to make up this aesthetic, only those which influenced the creativity of artists in the field of *bijouterie-joaillerie* will be mentioned here.

A critical role in the move towards new art forms was played by the Vienna Secession. While an overblown ornamental style flourished elsewhere, in Vienna the decline of the Habsburg Empire was producing a sense of instability and a growing uncertainty. New aspirations challenged accepted artistic canons and questioned the language of conventional art forms. In 1895, Otto Wagner, in his inaugural speech to the Academy (given under the title 'Moderne Architektur') declared that 'modern problems' required 'modern solutions' and that 'all modern forms must reflect the new materials and new requirements of our age. . . .' In 1897, the revolt of the anti-conformists broke out – Josef Hoffman, Josef Maria Olbrich, Koloman Moser, Otto Wagner and Adolf Loos, under the aegis of the painter Gustav Klimt – and the break with the conservative establishment was accomplished. The Secessionists decided to set up on their own and the House of Secession was built in the immediate vicinity of the Academy of Fine Arts. On its pediment was engraved 'To each art its time, to each time its liberty.' The review *Ver Sacrum* was the organ through which the painters, poets, architects and sculptors expressed themselves, rejecting eclecticism and baroque excess. In an age of industrial progress, the Secessionists promoted a utilitarian style which paid heed to the function of an object without thereby suppressing harmony of form.

Out of these rationalist theories a new austere style emerged, which expressed itself in decorative motifs of a stylized, sinuous or geometric design. In 1903, the Wiener Werkstätte were founded: craft workshops which brought together artists and craftsmen from all disciplines under the artistic direction of Josef Hoffmann and Koloman Moser; and in 1908, Adolf Loos published 'Ornament and Crime'. Inveighing against the excessive use of ornament, Loos maintained that: 'The more civilized a people becomes, the more decoration disappears.' The Vienna Secession was not alone in promoting this view: to its annual exhibition in Vienna in 1900, it invited the Glasgow School under the leadership of Charles Rennie Mackintosh, whose ideas bore a close resemblance to those of the Vienna School. Like the Vienna School, Mackintosh favoured an austere art, based on straight lines and cubes.

In England at this time William Morris was setting up Morris and Company and promoting the Arts and Crafts movement. Alarmed at what he saw as the modern invasion of industrially produced goods – whose mediocrity was exemplified at the London exhibitions of 1851 and 1862, and the Paris exhibitions of 1855 and 1867 – Morris advocated a return to manual labour by craftsmen as opposed to manufacture by machines. Other, less extremist, movements, meanwhile, recognized the necessity for collaboration with industry.

In 1909 an event occurred in Paris which dazed critics and artists alike and overturned accepted theories of colour. This was the sudden explosion of colour produced at the Ballets Russes by the hand of Sergei Diaghilev – a Russian bored with the insipid realism of French theatre scenery. If Anna de Noailles is to be believed, the Ballets' success was prodigious: 'Everything that could dazzle, intoxicate, seduce and allure had been drawn there, as with a drag-net, and spilled onto the set and it blossomed there as naturally as the plant world, growing in splendour under the influence of the climate.'

Diaghilev applied to the Ballets Russes contemporary theories on the synthesis of the arts, combining music, dance and painting. Several painters made their contribution: Golovin brought his scintillating play of colours, Korovin his glowing red images, Dobuzhinsky his symbolism, Roerich a barbaric realism and Benois a nostalgic love for the French *Grand Siècle*. But the painter Léon Bakst outshone them all and became the star of the *Saisons Russes* and high priest of this enchanted world. Through expressive stylization he was able to evoke every age, with the atmosphere that imbued it: he swooped from the hieratic Egypt of *Cléopâtre* to the voluptuous orgy of *Schéhérazade*, from the Caucasian barbarity of *Thamar* to d'Annunzio's decadence in the *Martyre de Saint Sébastien*, transforming Ada Rubinstein from disquieting odalisque into mysterious ephebe. A whole spectrum of brilliant, rich, oriental colours – yellow, orange, carmine, vermilion, ultramarine and Prussian blue, emerald green, with highlights of gold and silver – deliberately juxtaposed with a boldness that set the teeth on edge, invaded the stage and swept aside the evanescent shades of Art Nouveau.

This explosion of colour led the critic Vaudoyer to say of Bakst's harem in *Schéhérazade* that 'its strident polychromy makes one think of a bar on the Ivory Coast or in Honolulu.' All the productions which followed one another until the war – *Schéhérazade*, *Le Spectre de la Rose*, *Thamar*, *L'Oiseau de Feu*, *Pétrouchka*, *L'Après-Midi d'un Faune*, *Le Sacre du Printemps*, *Le Coq d'Or* – set their mark on the artistic milieus and modified existing conceptions of the theatre, fashion and the decorative arts. Gabriel Mourey reported that 'the influence of the Ballets Russes, not only on the theatrical arts but also on those of printing and of textiles, in fact on the entire range of the decorative arts, seems to have been as dominant as that of Japanese art on the preceding age.'

The enthusiasm for colour was contagious and spread like a trail of powder from the stage to the picture galleries where the Fauves exhibited in a group for the first time at the 1905 'Salon d'Automne'. Marquet, Dufy and Matisse presented canvases whose composition rejected perspective and chiaroscuro, organizing space simply through the interaction of pure colours, eliminating detail and reducing line to the essential. 'A pot of paint has been thrown in the public's face', declared the critic Camille Mauclair indignantly. These gaudy colours filtered down to the man in the street and the public gradually became familiar with a new artistic universe. Decoration, the arts of *parure*, jewelry and clothing all jumped on the bandwagon. After his meeting with Poiret in 1909, Dufy abandoned painting and began, instead, to design fabrics for dresses and furnishings. This was a field where he could make full use of his colourist's palette, combining it with forms derived from the Cubist movement, recently emerged in France.

Rejecting the decorative and representational, Cubism – in a manifesto published in 1912 by Gleizes and Metzinger – proposed an analytical, realistic and objective vision of form. Picasso, Braque, Léger, Juan Gris and Delaunay produced paintings entirely lacking illustionistic effects, where the subject was flattened and the volume fragmented on the canvas. Here was a new source of inspiration for the decorative arts, for fashion and jewelry. They, in turn, renounced flora and fauna for the play of geometric shapes juxtaposed or superimposed on one another. Cassandre, a jewelry designer for Georges Fouquet, used on his pendants one of the Cubists' favourite motifs: the guitar. Sonia Delaunay produced *tissus simultanés* (simultaneous fabrics), fabrics printed from a plate, whose simple, repetitive, geometric designs seem surprisingly modern even today. She designed dresses, produced exclusively by the House of Jacques Heim, and bearing, in 1923, the revealing name *Mots croisés* (Crosswords), and she noted in passing that 'if painting has become part of life, it is because women are dressed in it.' And certain geometric motifs, appearing in designs by Madeleine Vionnet and Jeanne Lanvin, came straight out of Fernand Léger's canvases.

The close relationship between French and Russian artists mutually influenced artistic experiment in both countries. In Russia, Malevich founded Suprematism, derived from both Cubism and Fauvism and based on the geometric abstraction of the rectangle, the circle and the triangle together with the use of primary colours. The influence of Russian art on Paris culminated in the 1914 'Salon des Indépendants' in which seventy-eight Russian artists were represented; alongside the Cubists there were canvases by Malevich, Exter, Matiushin and the Burliuk brothers. For evidence of a formal link between these canvases and certain pieces of Art Deco jewelry, one need look no further than Jean Dunand's black, red and white combinations or Gérard Sandoz' 'semaphore' brooch.

In 1917, shortly after his departure from Paris, where his painting had undergone a complete revision under the influence of Cubism, Mondrian met, in Holland, the architect Theo van Doesburg and founded with him an association of painters, architects, sculptors and interior designers assembled under the banner of a review entitled *De Stijl*. Variant of Cubism, Neo-Plasticism confined itself exclusively to the use of horizontal and vertical lines intersecting at right angles to form squares and rectangles, and the three primary colours, to which were added the three non-colours, white, black and grey. Piet Mondrian's theory, according to which 'least is best', clearly expressed his desire for simplification through the exploration of fundamental form and the rejection of superfluous decoration which he called, not without a certain pejorative nuance, 'ornamental accidents'. Affirming that 'colour is not an ornamental value but an elementary means of architectonic expression', Theo van Doesburg defended the Neo-Plasticists' aim to replace decoration superimposed on the structure of an object by colour organically assimilated into the structure itself. The volume of an object had to be reduced to an arrangement of planes from which the essential, expressive form of the object would emerge. These theories, which were intended to encompass all forms of plastic expression, influenced artists such as Jean Fouquet and Raymond Templier who were to favour the juxtaposition of visually bold geometric forms and the use of vivid colours, rejecting all superfluous ornament which would detract from the purity of an object.

Yet another aesthetic revolution was taking place in Germany, in the town of Weimar. Here Walter Gropius assembled a group of architects, painters and sculptors and in 1919 founded the Bauhaus. Bauhaus teaching included all the various crafts, which were practised in workshops under the direction of prominent figures such as Klee, Kandinsky, Moholy-Nagy in painting and Mies van der Rohe in architecture. The Bauhaus connection with French applied arts was not immediately established but, some years later, the German movement would influence the pioneers of modern art such as the members of the UAM: Gérard Sandoz, Raymond Templier and Jean Fouquet.

While echoes of the Dutch De Stijl group were making themselves heard across the border, in Italy a new movement emerged, bearing the evocative name of Futurism. Its spokesman was the poet Marinetti. On 20 February 1909, the *Figaro* published Marinetti's 'Le Manifeste du Futurisme', which exalted urban life, speed and the machine. 'We affirm', says Marinetti, 'that the world's magnificence has been enriched by a new beauty: the beauty of speed. A racing car whose hood is adorned with great pipes, like serpents with fiery breath; a roaring car, that seems to ride on grapeshot, is more beautiful than the *Victory of Samothrace*. . . .' It was no accident that this manifesto originated in Italy and was published in France, Marinetti explaining it thus: 'It is from Italy that we launch through the world this violently disturbing, incendiary manifesto of ours. With it, today, we establish Futurism, because we want to free this land from its smelly gangrene of professors, archaeologists, ciceroni and antiquarians.' Movement – broken down into its different phases – was what fired the Futurists' imagination. For them, plastic and dynamic expression were synonymous, as the 'Speeding Locomotive', executed at the Institute of Decoration in Leningrad and published in the review *Art et Décoration* in 1926, amply demonstrated. The message broadcast by the Futurists spread throughout Europe via a series of exhibitions which took place after 1911 in Paris, Brussels and London. Futurism found devotees among all the 'moderns', in all walks of artistic life. The manifesto of Futurist architects, drawn up by Antonio de Sant'Elia, who joined the group in 1913, served the cause of pioneers in the art of *parure*. According to Antonio de Sant'Elia: 'The decorative must be abolished. We must find . . . inspiration in the elements of the utterly new mechanical world we have created . . . Oblique and elliptic lines are dynamic. . . .' A significant parallel may be drawn between these words and an important text by Gérard Sandoz, creator of avant-garde jewelry: 'Let us speak first of all of the ideal aesthetic of our age; a powerful and clear aesthetic which guides us purposefully. Let us open our eyes wide to: the cinema, distorted images of things seen at high speed, the beauty of machine parts skilfully made; the severity and grandeur of smooth surfaces, the transatlantic liner, modern painting; aviation, percussive and syncopated music, the servo-brake, the cocktail shaker, the telephone switchboard, polished steel, matt nickel, light and shade, the mechanical and the geometric. We are all of this. We see it, we live it every day. Let us quite simply live our age. This is the modern basis of everything we create and of everything we are yet to create. I don't go about in a sedan chair and I do use the telephone. It's all there.' (*Parures*, no 29).

If jewelry designers were inspired by all the manifestos being broadcast across Europe, they also drew fresh sources of inspiration from distant civilizations. The taste for the exotic and the fascination exerted by the East were not recent phenomena; but the number of magazines and books now available on the subject offered the opportunity for increasing familiarity with foreign modes of artistic expression. In November 1922, the archaeologist Howard Carter discovered the tomb of Tutankhamun and for ten years, between 1922 and 1932, the newspapers regularly reported on the progress of excavations under Lord

Carnarvon's direction; and so the 'Egyptian' vogue was launched anew in the decorative arts. Europe's interest in the Nile civilization went back to the late eighteenth century. In 1798 Bonaparte embarked on his Egyptian campaign: not just with a military force but with a whole retinue of archaeologists and scholars, who were to produce an abundance of architectural accounts and sketches. Among them was Vivant-Denon, the publication of whose lavishly illustrated *Le Voyage en Haute et Basse Egypte*, on his return in 1802, became a source of inspiration for the applied arts. Under the Consulate and in the first years of the Empire, women wore jewelry inspired by Ancient Egypt. Furniture, bronzes and porcelain were decorated with Egyptian motifs and in December 1808 Napoleon offered Josephine a tea service decorated in the Egyptian manner and produced by the Manufacture de Sèvres from Vivant-Denon's illustrations. A series of discoveries of temples throughout the nineteenth century and the building of the Suez Canal from 1859 to 1869 sustained this enthusiasm for Egyptian archaeology. Egyptian motifs were employed at the end of the nineteenth century by Mellerio, Boucheron, Baugrand and Lalique, but it was the first quarter of the twentieth century that really confirmed the vogue. Jewelers derived an entire ornamental vocabulary from figurative Pharaonic motifs: the god Horus, the Falcon-God, lotuses, scarabs, sphinxes and imitations of hieroglyphs, chosen purely for their graphic qualities and stripped of symbolic significance. Designers, visiting the Egyptian galleries at the Louvre to sketch these motifs, were likewise concerned not with archaeological fidelity, but with exotic and aesthetic qualities. They borrowed unheard-of combinations of stones to enrich the Art Deco palette: cornelian and lapis; cornelian and turquoise; turquoise, lapis and gold. Van Cleef et Arpels created a series of brooches and bracelets representing scenes of Pharaohs, lotus flowers and birds; Lalique a necklace of scarabs; and Boucheron, in 1928, a tiara in *cloisonné* enamel representing the Falcon-Sun. Louis Cartier and Charles Jacqueau were particular enthusiasts of Egyptian art; and the firm of René Boivin, established until 1931 in the rue des Pyramides, had its Maison's letterhead decorated with Egyptian symbols.

If China and Japan remained distant and mysterious for the public at large, Western artists had long been drawing inspiration from these mines of aesthetic ideas which renewed the European repertoire. Between 1850 and 1860, a lapsed interest in Japanese art was once more revived and offered European artists a new source of stylistic motifs. The latter freely adapted oriental decorative elements transposed from nature or the use, peculiar to Asia, of jade, coral, enamel, lacquer and pearls. Lucien Gaillard's creations, exhibited for the first time in Paris in 1902, illustrated this desire to effect a personal synthesis of form, at the same time as representing certain oriental conventions. The range was extensive, from the straight imitation of images, such as the fire-breathing dragon, the pagoda, or Chinese characters, to the freest interpretation of motifs transcribed 'in the oriental manner'.

Persia was another far-Eastern civilization which cast its spell on the West. Paul Poiret invited Parisian society to transport itself for a 'Thousand and Second Night', which was attended, on 24 June 1911, at the Hôtel du Faubourg Saint-Honoré, by three hundred would-be 'Persians'. This occasion gave women of fashion the opportunity to dress *à la mode de Poiret*, donning very wide trousers in sumptuous brocades in the style of Sultanas, crowned with turbans and aigrettes, and leaving in their train a heady, intoxicating perfume blending sandalwood, oriental rose, patchouli and cloves. From Persian carpets and miniatures, designers borrowed motifs of plants and flowers, whose arabesques and curvilinear forms reappeared on jewelers' vanity cases. Subtle effects were likewise obtained from the delicate, fresh range of rose-pinks, jonquil-yellows, greens, cherry-reds and mauves, and from the combinations of colours such as blue and green: emerald and sapphire or lapis and jade.

The art of another continent – African art – was also exerting its pull. For a long time the province of a small circle of artists and astute collectors, African art was now arousing the interest of a wider public thanks to books published on the subject, exhibitions, and the jazz music vulgarized by Doucet and Wiener. In 1925, Josephine Baker, in the *Revue Nègre*, drew fashionable Paris to the Théâtre des Champs-Elysées, where she fascinated the audience with her jerky rhythms and revived the success of the Ballets Russes. Artists such as Jean Dunand were regular visitors to the Musée du Trocadéro, and the motifs of masks, statuettes and totems were beginning to emerge from the spirals and broken lines of certain pieces of jewelry. In 1924–25, the painter André Léveillé created for Georges Fouquet a pendant and a brooch in the form of an African mask copied detail for detail from a museum exhibit. Also for Georges Fouquet, Jean Lambert-Rucki, sculptor, mosaicist and fresco-painter, created brooches, clips, rings and bracelets on which African masks were mounted. The 'Negro' fashion was confirmed by the 1931 'Exposition Coloniale' in Paris when a number of artists and costume jewelry makers sought to instil a taste for the barbaric and encourage women to wear African heads in sculpted ebony on their tailor-mades.

This craze for what was called in the Thirties *l'Art de l'Afrique Noire* (the art of Black Africa) was to continue for several years and symbolized the recognition of a civilization and culture that had long been misunderstood.

European manifestos and oriental imagery exercised a dominant influence on jewelry designers of the Twenties and Thirties, whose work the public were to judge at the annual Salons, both in France and abroad.

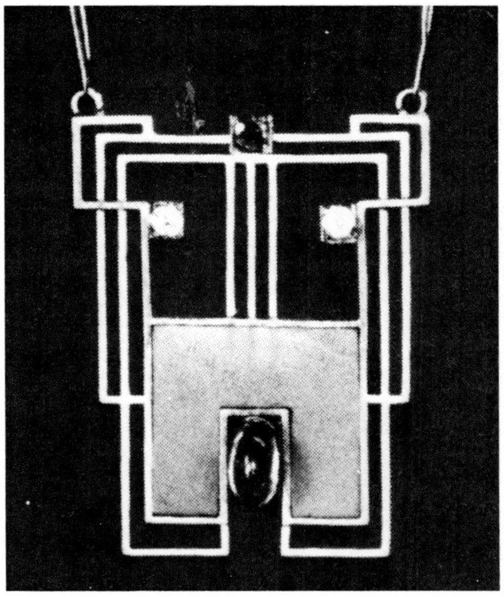

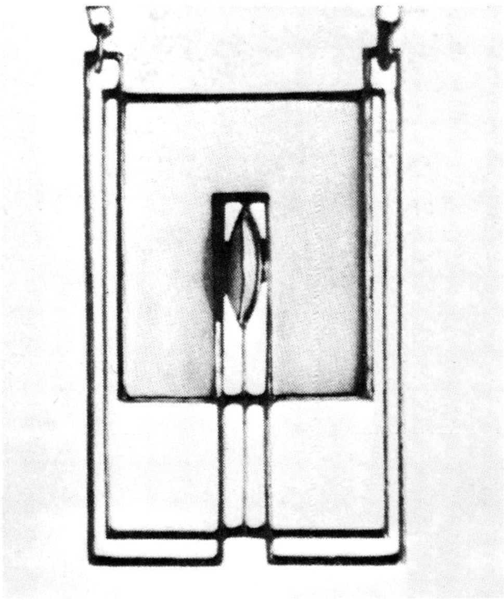

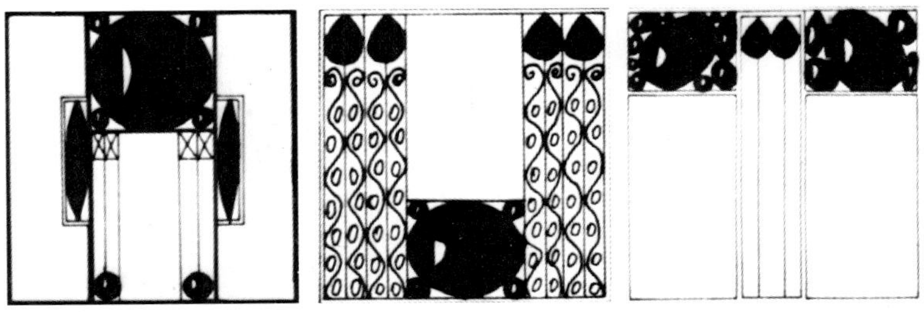

Anonymous: gold, agate and amethyst pendant, c. *1905. Germany.*

Anonymous: silver and coral pendant, c. *1905. Germany.*

Josef Hoffmann: jewelry designs for the Wiener Werkstätte, Vienna.

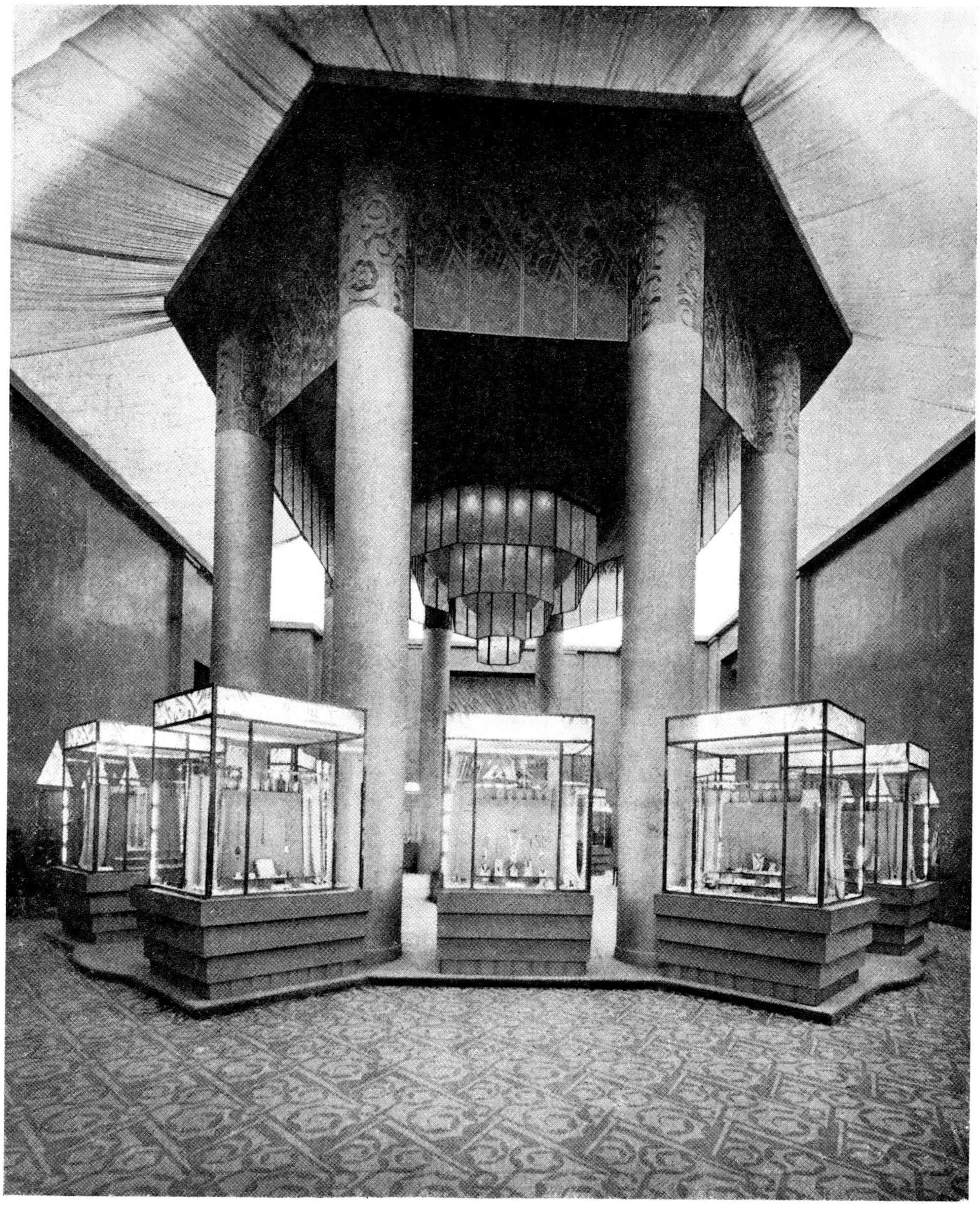

Entrance to the Bijouterie-Joaillerie *Pavilion at the 1925 Exposition in Paris.*

SALONS AND EXHIBITIONS

ANNUAL SALONS and international exhibitions played an essential role in the development of the applied arts. They stimulated creative energies and affirmed their existence and, at the same time, brought the latest creations to the notice of a wider public, both French and foreign. The 1925 'Exposition Internationale des Arts Décoratifs' in Paris remains an unprecedented event in the annals of jewelry, and was followed in 1929 by an 'Exposition de Joaillerie et Orfèvrerie' at the Palais Galliéra. The idea of organizing an 'Exposition Internationale des Arts Décoratifs' in Paris – originally planned for 1916 – was already being discussed as early as 1907. Mr Roger Sandoz, *horloger-bijoutier-joaillier*, took up its cause, but the project was brought to an abrupt halt by the outbreak of the First World War. After the War, and partly in an attempt to forget those four intervening years of nightmare, the idea of mounting the exhibition was revived once more. Roger Sandoz brought all his pre-war enthusiasm to bear and the organizers drew up and elaborated a programme of preparation and publicity designed to give the exhibition international status. In the years leading up to 1925, 'répétitions générales' (rehearsals) were organized: a 'Salon du Goût Français' in 1922 and a 'Concours de Dessinateurs', as well as the regular annual Salons. In 1924, the principal French Maisons made a trial run in New York where an exhibition of French art was held. Boucheron, Mauboussin, Van Cleef et Arpels, Cartier, Sandoz and Henry Frères all contributed, together with designers from Rubel Frères, Maynier et Pinçon, Desmarès and Verger Frères. This same year, the sixteenth 'Salon des Artistes Décorateurs' was also held and helped to pave the way for the major Exposition of April 1925, at which twenty nations, excluding only Germany and the United States, would be assembled. The 1925 Exposition was divided into five categories, of which *Parure* was one. The exhibition stretched across both banks of the Seine, between the Place de la Concorde and the Grand Palais on the Right Bank and along the Esplanade des Invalides on the Left Bank. The *Parure* section was launched at a gala where Mistinguett appeared in costume as a Solitaire Diamond, leading the girls of the Casino de Paris decked out in jewels and velvet ribbons, while Ida Rubinstein, dressed in costumes designed by Bakst, each evening attracted throngs of admirers to the *Martyre de Saint Sébastien*. Each evening Paris was dazzled with light, in celebration of the *Années Folles*: Lalique's crystal fountain sparkled; the Eiffel Tower, thanks to Citroën, was garlanded with electric lights, like a huge, bright arrow pointing to the sky; glittering cascades, whose colours changed every week, fell from the Alexander III bridge; and for the evening celebration on 1 June, after a procession of small boats disguised as butterflies and dragonflies along the Seine, there was a burst of fireworks whose brilliance recalled the splendours of Versailles.

Category Twenty-four (*Bijouterie-Joaillerie*) formed, with Category Twenty (Clothing), Twenty-one (Clothing Accessories), Twenty-two (Fashion, Flowers, Feathers) and Twenty-three (Perfume), the third group in the general class, *Parure*, to which the right-hand side of the nave of the

Grand Palais was given up. The precise ruling was that 'only those works of new inspiration and real originality, excluding all copying, inspiration from or imitation of ancient or past styles' would be selected. An exceptional but specific clause in the case of jewelry ruled 'that it will not be penalized for deriving inspiration from works in related domains, or for using motifs from other countries and other times, provided they are interpreted, transposed, reworked and adapted to their object.' It was decided that projects or pieces would be submitted to a Selection Committee under strict anonymity so that selection would be focused on the work alone. A competition was set up for the design of the Pavilion, and was won by the architect Eric Bagge.

Under a lamé awning, stretched over eight silver columns picked out in gold, a dais was erected on which the jewelers' display cases, uniformly lined with a warm beige crêpe-de-chine, were arranged. The pieces of jewelry were exhibited with a strong accent on sobriety and particular attention was paid to the lighting. Around the dais, along the walls, the work of the costume jewelers was displayed. France was a significant contributor to the *Bijouterie-Joaillerie* section, with no fewer than thirty exhibitors, the most famous of whom were Aucoc, Boucheron, Chaumet, Dusausoy, Lacloche, Linzeler et Marchak, Marzo, Mauboussin, Van Cleef, Fouquet, Sandoz and Templier. Cartier preferred to keep its distance and was installed in the Pavillon de l'Elégance, next to the great couturiers, thus establishing a fresh alliance between the two professions.

Mr Jacques Guérin, the reporter on Category Twenty-four, was full of admiration for the overall effect created by the French section: 'The most ignorant visitor,' he wrote, 'standing at the centre of the ellipse where the greatest names in Parisian jewelry were collected, was struck by the obvious kinship between pieces of jewelry which were the work of quite different establishments.' For the first time, the names of the designer-creators who were employed by the great Maisons appeared. Once again the Maison Cartier stood aloof and mentioned no names. The prize-giving jury was there to do justice to these designer-creators so often unacknowledged by the public, but a Maison as famous as Cartier, represented on one of the juries, was declared a law unto itself.

The 1925 Exposition brought to fruition all the new ideas which had been germinating for years and in the works of the exhibitors the outline of a prevailing aesthetic could be discerned: only with the passing of time would this emerge as a distinctive period style. The preference for spare volumes, clean angles, smooth surfaces and geometric lines triumphed and figurative decoration, when it did occur, was stylized. The word 'Cubism' was used again and again to define this style. The unexpected contrasts between vivid and sometimes clashing colours, the use of stones or materials which had long been forgotten but were now selected purely for their ornamental value, this was what characterized jewelry in 1925.

But, beyond the shared tendencies at the 1925 Exposition, the astute observer could distinguish at once

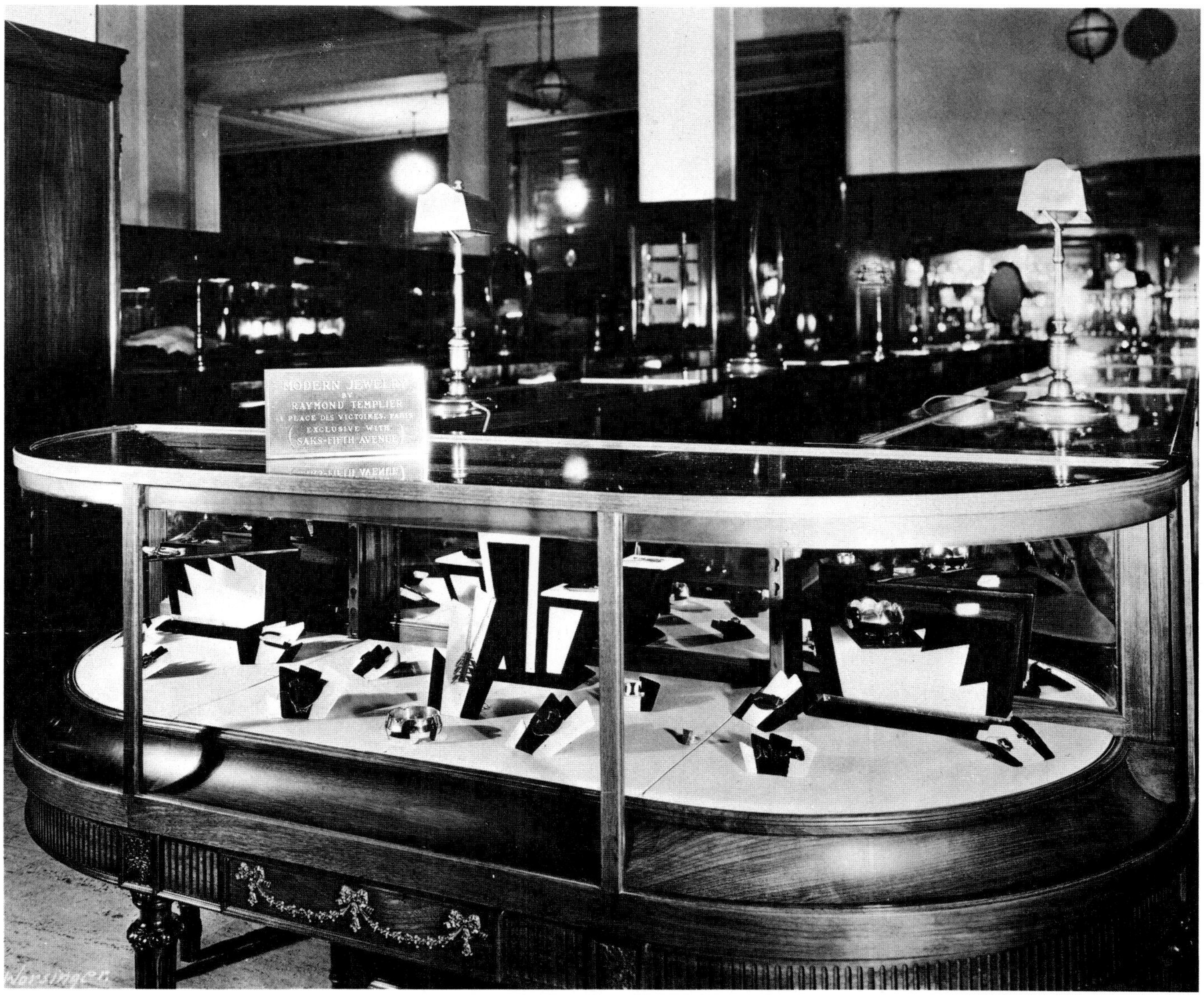

Raymond Templier's showcase at Saks in New York.

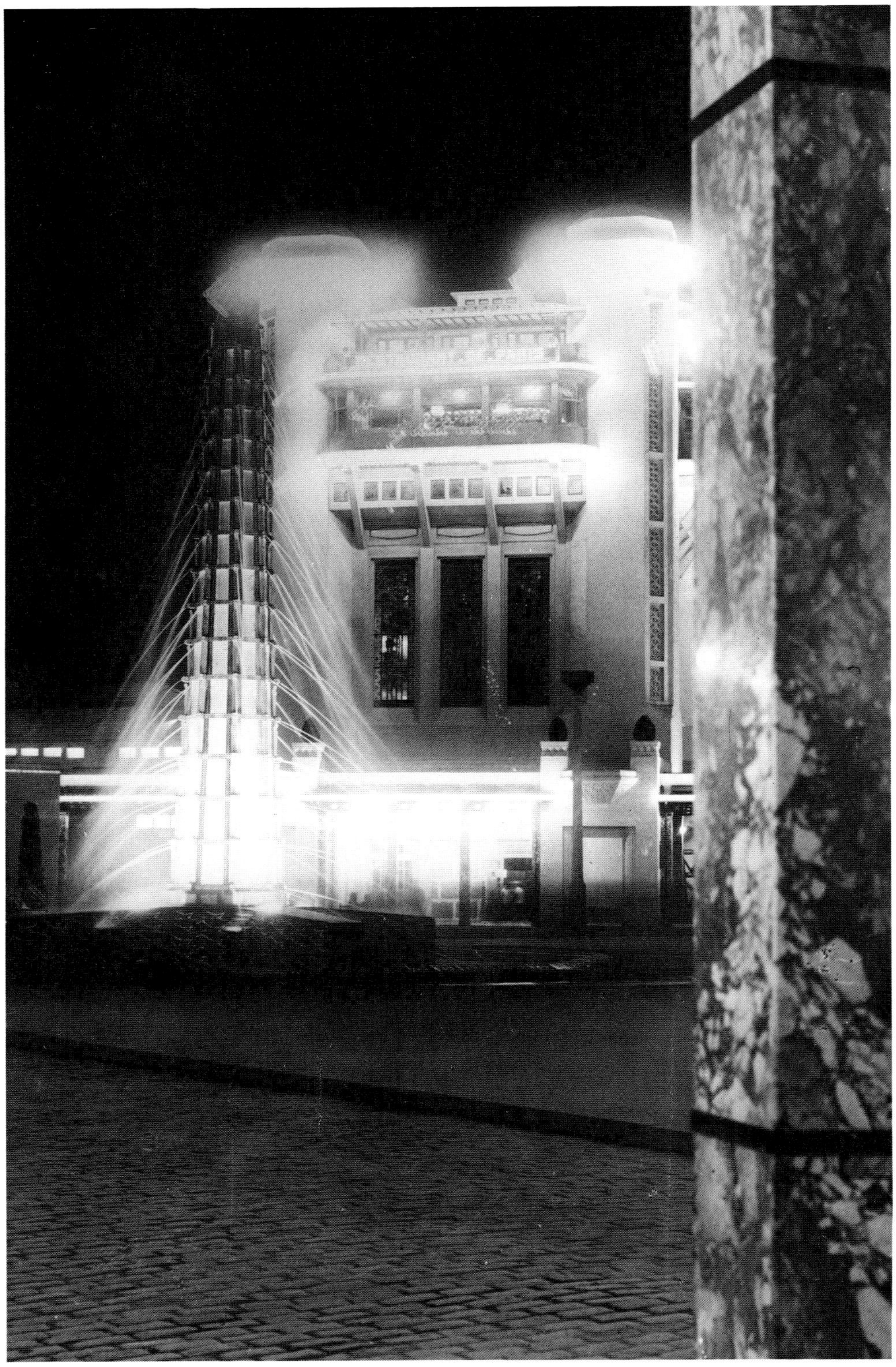

René Lalique's illuminated crystal fountain at the 1925 Exposition in Paris. Photo: R. Viollet.

between the various French exhibitors: between the *Haute Joaillerie* and the avant-garde or innovators, or, as a critic called them at the time, the 'contemporaries' and the 'moderns'. Thus Jean Fouquet was classed with decorative artists such as Paul Bablet, Boès, Jean Desprès and René Robert, while his father, Georges Fouquet, was a member of the old aristocracy of jewelry. This dividing line between the *Anciens* and the *Modernes* (the Old School and the Moderns), the *Tempérés* and the *Radicaux* (the Moderates and the Radicals) prefigured the ultimate breach and subsequent creation of the Union des Artistes Modernes (UAM) in 1930. With its African imagery, the jewelry of the Pavillon des Diamantaires and of the Joaillerie, Mallet-Stevens' trees of reinforced concrete, Ruhlmann's Hôtel du Collectionneur, the Grands Magasins and their studios, the 1925 Exposition reflected the creativity of an epoch that was still hesitating to step out of the nineteenth century – with its traditions and constraints, its technical and stylistic limitations – and head for the future.

If one looks through the press reviews of the period, discounting, as is only fair, the opinion of certain critics who were frightened by a novelty which goaded them into ironic reflections, the French section of the *Bijouterie-Joaillerie* was recognized as the 'pearl' or 'high point' of the Exposition, outshining the exhibits of the foreign sections through its lavishness and originality, and attracting hordes of curious and fashionable *croqueuses de diamants* (diamond-eaters) who lost their heads when confronted with such temptation. France was unrivalled in the world of jewelry.

Encouraged by the success of this exhibition and the support of the public, jewelry enjoyed an unprecedented era of prosperity between 1926 and 1928. The annual 'Salons des Artistes Décorateurs' and the 'Salons d'Automne' witnessed an increasing vitality in the creations of the jewelers. Whole-hearted public support inspired and encouraged a greater independence from the past, and a greater boldness of approach: the timidity still displayed in the creations of 1925 had gone for good. Parisian designers decided to repeat the 1925 experiment to prove just how far their ingenuity and imagination could stretch. Georges Fouquet initiated and was elected as President of an Exposition of *Bijouterie-Joaillerie* and *Orfèvrerie* organized by the profession's Chambre Syndicale at the Musée Galliéra from May to July 1929. The exhibition was mounted in the same spirit and with the same programme as the 1925 Exposition: once more Eric Bagge was the architect and overall designer; once more severity and simplicity characterized the décor and the showcases, and light seemed to radiate from the exhibits themselves: 'You stepped across the threshold into a vast grey jewelcase, all silver and gold.' The reviews celebrating the opening of the exhibition left a dazzling memory of its gorgeous elegance. A retrospective on 'La Parure de la Femme il y a cent ans', organized by Henry d'Allemagne, Dusausoy and Vever, threw into relief the modern, bold aspects of the latest creations and showed just how far jewelry had advanced. The great credos of modern jewelry, defended in 1925, still held in the main, but certain modifications allowed room for innovation and surprise. While the use of colour characterized the 1925 Exposition, the 'Exposition de Galliéra' was set *dans la note blanche* (in white). The diamond reigned supreme and the rainbow colours of the jewelry exhibited in 1925 gave way to the colours of half-mourning: the silver-grey of platinum, the white of diamonds, the black of jet, onyx and lacquer. The Exposition was a great success with both the French public and visitors from abroad, who flocked to Paris at this season. In the same year, the Chambre Syndicale de la Bijouterie, de la Joaillerie et de l'Orfèvrerie organized, on Georges Fouquet's initiative, an international exhibition and sale of jewelry, in which non-specialist artists, painters, sculptors and architects were invited to participate. Seven foreign nations responded to the invitation: Austria, Germany, Norway, Spain, Sweden, Switzerland and the United States. The work presented by students from the Boulle School or the Union Centrale des Arts Décoratifs demonstrated the dynamism of the new generation. Paris was unquestionably setting the tone for the elegant women of Europe and America, in jewelry as in all areas of *parure* and fashion. It was to Paris they came each season, to look, to dream, to lay themselves open to temptation, and to buy *ce qui se porte* – what was being worn.

But the great economic crisis, which shook the United States in 1929 and spread abroad like a tidal wave, struck a fatal blow to the luxury industries. From 1930 onwards far fewer luxury goods were being produced and, in 1931, in the face of the troubled financial situation, manufacturers were hesitant about participating in the

'Exposition Coloniale' in the Bois de Vincennes. Twenty-three jewelers and manufacturers were in fact represented there. Some selected for the occasion brooches and pendants recalling Negro masks and heavy bracelets with motifs borrowed from African pots, others simply contributed the major pieces from their collections. Administrative bungles provoked angry protests from the jewelers, whose stand had been relegated to the back of the metropolitan palace: 'in an out-of-the-way room, next to the boilers and central heating installations, a gallery with a low ceiling and no architectural merit, at best suitable for an exhibition of home crafts', as Henri Clouzot reported in 'Les Arts Précieux à l'Exposition Coloniale'.

The jewelers held to the principles which had emerged at the 1925 Exposition and the Galliéra Exposition in 1929, and exercised subtle variations on all the current themes. Amongst the motifs inspired by the colonial theme were tiger and panther claws, eagles' talons and lions' teeth, attached with gold links or combined with black enamel or onyx and made into bracelets, belt-buckles and brooches. These marked the invasion of the jungle into feminine attire. More modest examples comprised a necklace of gold discs composed of concentric circles alternating with plaques decorated with blue enamel triangles, or a necklace where brilliants were combined with ivory, the symbol of colonial wild life.

The 1925 Exposition was the embodiment of all the various trends which, between 1909 and 1930, combined to define the style of the age. The overall picture was at times a contradictory one, as when a Cubist rose was placed next to constructivist geometry, or the brilliant colours of the Ballets Russes were juxtaposed with the black and white theme. The 'Moderns', dissatisfied with the 1925 Exposition, founded the UAM – the Union des Artistes Modernes – and exhibited for the first time in 1930 at the Pavillon de Marsan. Jean Fouquet, Gérard Sandoz and Raymond Templier joined forces with the architects Chareau, Mallet-Stevens, Le Corbusier, Walter Gropius, René Herbst, Charlotte Parriand, Djo-Bourgeois and the sculptor Csaky with the aim of promoting an art that would be both strictly modern and strictly rational.

FOREIGNERS AT THE 1925 EXPOSITION

The foreign exhibitors in the *Parure* category were dispersed throughout the Exposition, some in the galleries of the Grand Palais, others in the national pavilions in the Cours-la-Reine. Austria received a special mention for its *orfèvrerie* through the efforts of the Wiener Werkstätte. Though Austria was scarcely represented in *bijouterie-joaillerie*, the importance of these Werkstätte, which had emerged at the beginning of the century and provided a model for French artistic conception, must nevertheless be stressed. The architect and director of the craft workshops, Josef Hoffmann, had been inspired by the Glasgow School to create his first pieces of jewelry in 1903. On brooches and pendants he arranged cabochon-cut stones in strongly contrasting combinations, held in a metal grid, thus employing two fundamental elements of Art Deco style: polychromy and geometry. Using the same inspiration he created a series of bags and pochettes which anticipated the designs of Jean Fouquet. Koloman Moser, another director of the workshops and a painter and decorative designer, designed numerous projects in the linear style, set against the luminous intensity of precious or semi-precious stones. Mention should also be made in passing of Otto Prutscher and Hans Ofner, pupils of Josef Hoffmann at the Vienna School of Decorative Arts. The workshops, thanks to their dynamism and the quality of their teaching, became a nursery for talent, facilitating the creation of original works which were nevertheless marked by certain stylistic similarities. The close relationship between all the artistic disciplines taught at the workshops perhaps explains the interest which architects took in jewelry. Other members of the workshops made names for themselves in the field of *parure*: Eduard Josef Wimmer who became a member in 1907 and remained until the break-up of the workshops in 1932; Dagobert Peche, architect and painter; Carl Otto Czeschka, who was at the workshops from 1904 to 1910 and was afterwards appointed to the Hamburg Kunstgewerbeschule.

Belgium was very successful at the Exposition and the reviews remarked on certain general similarities with France. A *grand prix* was bestowed on Wolfers Frères et Coosemans for a large pendant in lapis and brilliants representing a ship's anchor, and the firms of Altenloh and Leysen each received honorary mention.

Spain upheld tradition through its representatives Masriera y Carreras and Jaime Mercade, among a number of other Barcelona jewelers. Emilio Store, on the other hand, exhibited jewelry that was totally modern in style.

Great Britain was represented in the Grand Palais by a single firm: Wright and Hadgkiss. In the British Pavilion, the showcases harked back to the Arts and Crafts exhibition at the Pavillon de Marsan in the spring of 1914, and British designers were still working in the style promoted by William Morris. Henry Wilson, a member of the jury, deserves mention for his exhibition of exquisitely executed jewelry. Modern English decorative art was following a very different path from that of French modern art: its taste and traditions were more closely allied to the florid style of Gothic cathedrals and to the creations in precious metals produced by the Middle Ages, and some of the jewelry exhibited in 1925 revealed almost literal representations of Gothic metalwork, sculpted flowers, strawberry leaves and fourteenth and fifteenth-century capitals.

Italy was torn between the Liberty style inspired by French or Belgian Art Nouveau and the more recent movements generated by Central Europe and deriving from such centres of inspiration as Vienna and Munich. Though Italy was at pains to renew its decorative arts, its artistic production was restricted, by regional particularities, to tradition and folklore. The first international exhibition entirely devoted to the Decorative Arts in Italy had been organized in 1923 at the Villa Reale de Monza (Biennale). The firm of Giacomo Ravasco in Milan, mentioned in reviews, and that of Borelli-Vitelli, which specialized in traditional parures in coral, should be singled out for mention here.

Denmark exhibited a few pieces of jewelry in the Grand Palais, scattered among pieces of *orfèvrerie* which attracted a great deal of interest. We owe to Evald Nielsen a number of pieces in scalloped and engraved gold with fine chains decorated with small flowers, but the firm of Georg Jensen, founded in 1866 in Copenhagen and famous for its *orfèvrerie* and silver jewelry, was regrettably absent. The creations of this firm, famous thanks to the regular collaboration of a number of artists, share features with Carl Christian Fjerdingstad's superb pieces in silver, set with amber and stones, while a disciple of Jensen, Kay Bojesen (1886–1958) created jewelry of remarkable purity. Several years were to pass, however, before Scandinavia joined the proponents of the modern and functional.

Switzerland had no *joaillier-bijoutier* representing it in this section and only a few pieces of enamelled jewelry were sent by independent artists. The main attraction were the Swiss watchmakers, specialists in a long tradition, who were installed in a room nearby. The showcases at the Grand Palais reserved for Holland displayed jewelry in hammered or repoussé silver such as those created by Laurewick or Zwollo Père et Fils in the shape of triangles or lozenges set with coloured cabochons, or the filigree jewelry of M.I. Citroën and Sheltman.

The few exhibits from Japan could scarcely give an adequate impression of that country's creativity. All eyes were drawn, however, to one isolated showcase which – with no attempt at artistic arrangement – Mikimoto had flooded with cultured pearls. The jury abstained from passing judgment on them: necklaces of pearls, simply threaded together, and rings consisting of a pearl set on a band could not compete for prizes which were designed to reward creative efforts.

The decorative arts continued to flourish in Germany, a significant absentee from the 1925 Exposition. Around 1870, when schools of decorative art and academies of design were springing up on all sides, a professional School of Metalwork and a Museum of Decorative Arts were founded at Pforzheim. Pforzheim fostered, in particular, jewelry of geometric design. Like the founders of the Vienna workshops, Georg Kleemann, who taught at the Professional School at Pforzheim, renounced the Jugendstil and looked for new sources of inspiration in linear abstraction. His book, *Moderner Schmuck* (Modern Jewelry), remains a major work on the evolution of jewelry, and anticipated the ideas which burgeoned in France in the Twenties. A number of pieces of jewelry designed by artists were executed by the firms of Theodor Fahrner and Zerrenner. While these firms specialized in the use of precious metals, combining manual labour with machine work, other firms produced jewelry in multiple series. The success of metal-plating – whereby a layer of base metal was covered by a thin layer of precious metal – was such that in 1905 there were at least thirty firms specializing in this field. The list of artists and workshops active in Pforzheim in the

Twenties and Thirties is a long one, but the most famous were Kurt Heinzelmann, Kurt Baer, Wilhelm Oehler, Fritz Stabler, Zunft Turm, Erwin Holzle, Erwin Murle, Zunft Jungkunst, Theodor Wende, Elizabeth Treskow, Fritz Schwerdt and Karl Schmidt-Rottluff.

Bijouterie-joaillerie may have been of secondary importance next to other artistic disciplines at the Bauhaus at Weimar, but the latter's functional and sober style was influential throughout Germany. From 1919, Naum Slutzky directed the workshop in charge of work in precious stones, a section of the metal workshop. Slutzky, who had studied first at the Academy of Plastic Arts in Vienna and rounded out his experience in metalworking at the Wiener Werkstätte, embodied the aesthetic connections between Vienna and the Bauhaus at Weimar. Hanau, renowned for its work in precious metals, following in the great German tradition, trained artists in the influence of Cubism and the Bauhaus. Munich assembled another colony of artists who produced work along similar lines; among them were Max Olofs, Eugen Sherer, Lorenz Durner and Franz Valentin. These few examples are sufficient to indicate the quality of the creative and technical training given throughout Germany and the tremendous creative richness of that country.

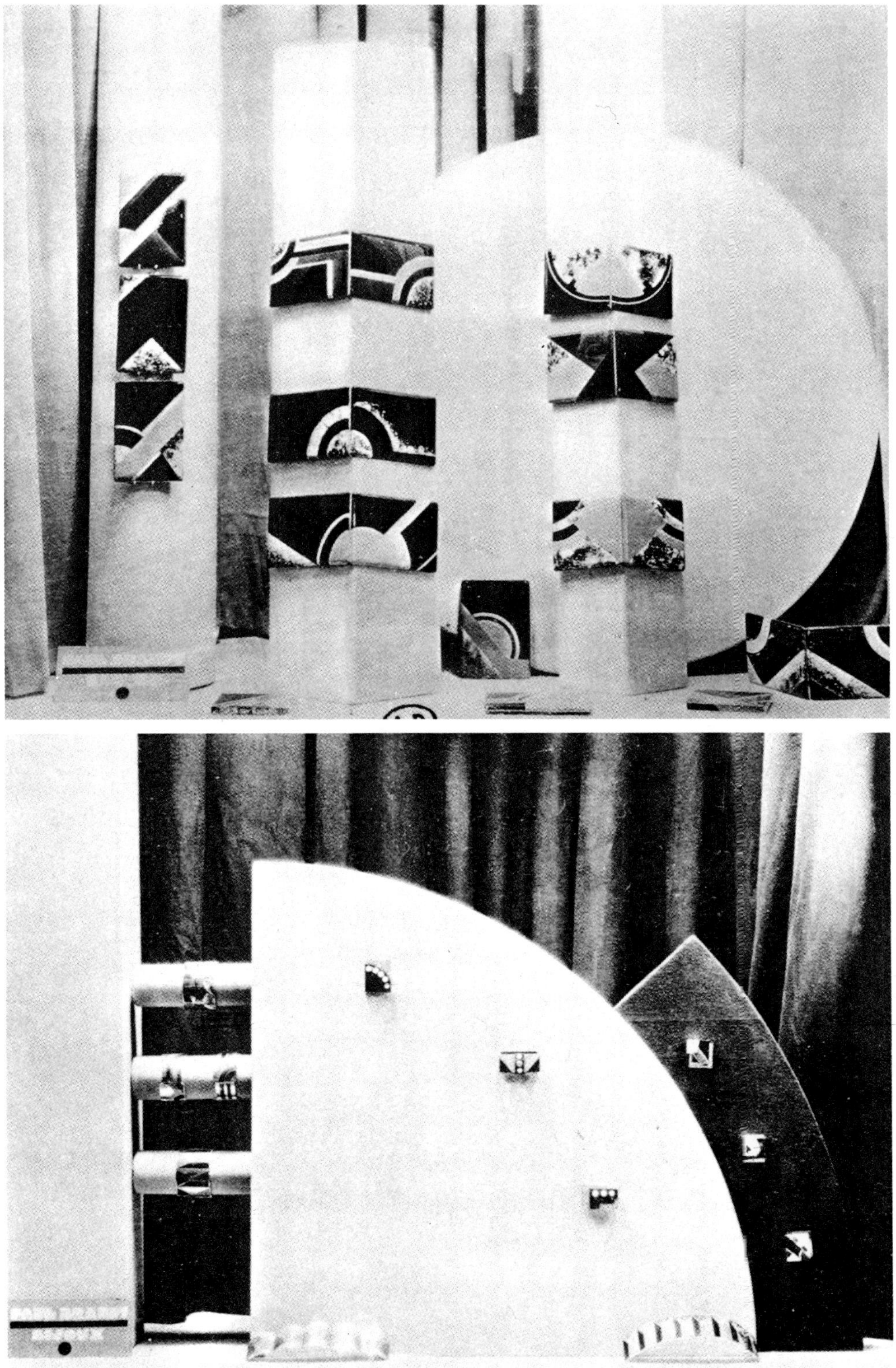

Showcases displaying Paul Brandt's jewelry arranged by René Herbst, reproduced in Jean Fouquet's Bijoux et Orfèvrerie, *1931.*

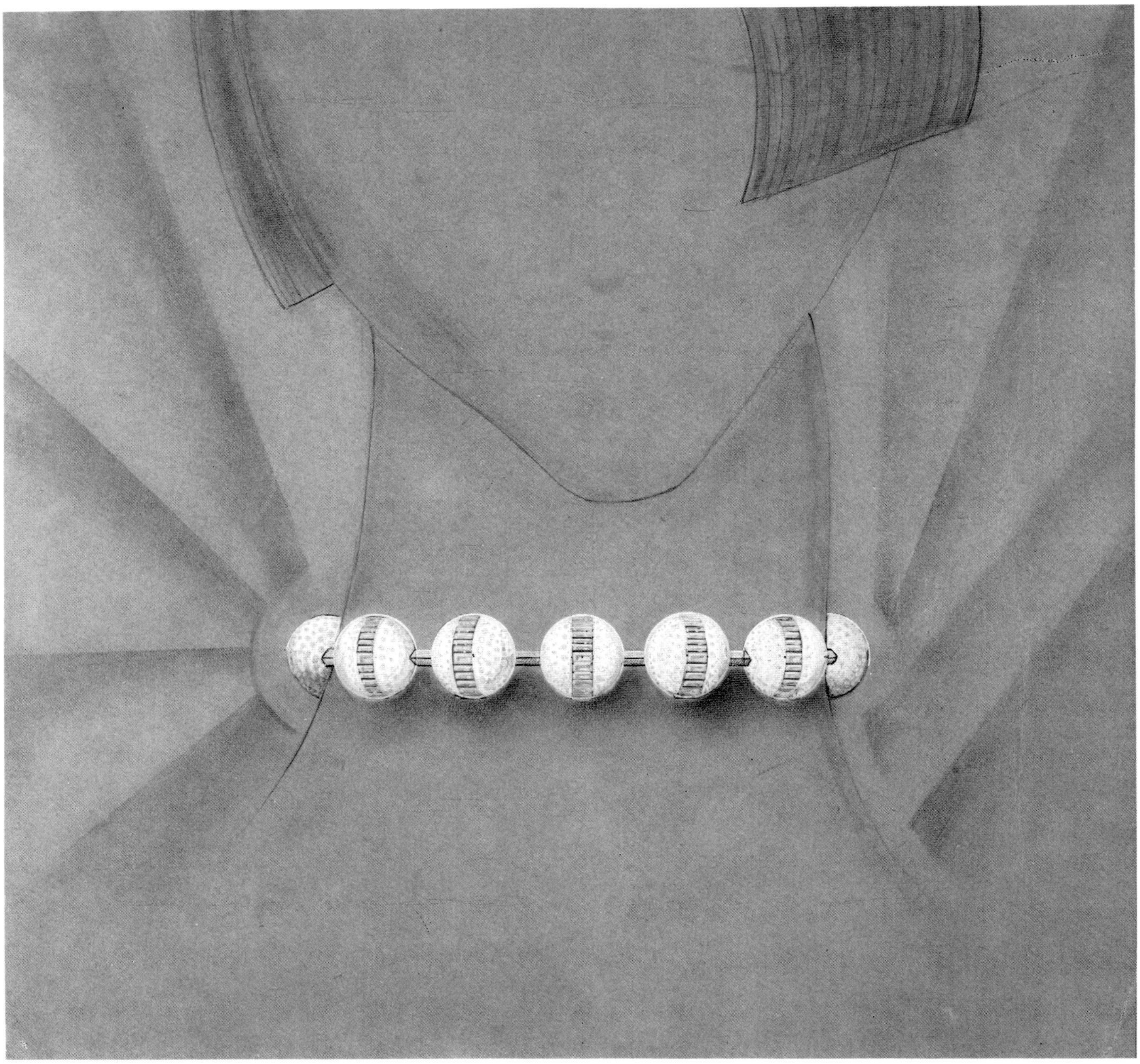

Mauboussin: design for a necklace.

THE AESTHETIC OF ART DECO JEWELRY

THE 1925 INTERNATIONAL EXPOSITION, by 'eliminating designs that imitated jewelry of bygone ages and reminiscences of the ornamental style in vogue after 1900', did a great service to French jewelers. The latter were obliged to imagine, invent and seek out inspiration in the modern world and to combat nostalgia – a challenge which was taken up by the champions of Art Nouveau. Beyond the contradictions, a number of similarities characterized the various jewelry of this period, from the most severe to the most ornate, and today we can pick out its most significant characteristics. In 1925, the work of the jeweler no longer consisted in merely showing off precious stones to advantage: the colours were now valued for themselves, and the jeweler played with them like a painter with his palette. Jewelers discovered stones which had for a long time been unfashionable or neglected, such as topaz, aquamarine, amethyst, rock crystal, turquoise and tourmaline, all of which could add an ornamental touch to the design of a piece of jewelry. The boundless enthusiasm for the East reinstated enamel, mother-of-pearl, coral, onyx and Chinese jade, materials which were purposely chosen and combined to produce exotic and original decorative effects.

Designers were fond of juxtaposing transparent faceted stones which reflected the light, with matt stones, which offered rare or unconventional contrasts through their opacity: emerald and turquoise, onyx and diamond, rock crystal and red coral; sapphire and emerald; ruby and emerald; sapphire, emerald and ruby.

Following a principle already established by Art Nouveau, the hierarchy of stones was overthrown and, on the same piece of jewelry, precious stones vied with semi-precious stones and often even coloured stones. On brooches, Jean Fouquet assembled aquamarine, topaz, brilliants and blue enamel or amethyst, topaz, brilliants and blue enamel, while Raymond Templier juxtaposed amber, diamonds, platinum and black enamel in the tiara which he created for Brigitte Helm in Marcel L'Herbier's film *L'Argent*. The UAM's manifesto waxes eloquent regarding the multiple possibilities which this wide range of materials, both rare and humble, put at the artist's disposal. Theorizing on the experience of ten years of creation, it states: 'But one thinks above all of the innumerable combinations of carefully chosen materials, employed, worked and juxtaposed at will. . . . Of all the joys to be found in a work of art, there is one of which the contemporary artist is becoming more and more aware: the visual effect he can obtain from the material he uses. Aesthete and art lover alike have today a primitive man's eye for material. Every time they come across intractability or limitations in it, they should measure its imaginative possibilities, comparing, where possible, the new and the old, and if they understand the struggle which the artist has to engage with his material, then to the satisfaction that they will derive from the so-called forms will be added an almost physical delight, a pure sensual joy. . . . No other age has loved, as ours has, all materials without exception, for themselves, for their nature, for their resistance to the artist's tools.'

The entire range of stones and new metals on which he could draw served the artist's imagination and helped him to design geometric forms in which were organized planes and colours, lines and volumes, as well as stylized figurative compositions of fruit and flowers. Explorations into linear, vertical and horizontal ornamentation, softened by curves, multiplied to infinity the variations that were possible on this favourite theme and produced embroideries in metal and stones which recall certain motifs from Persian mosaics. Georges Fouquet, in an article entitled 'La Bijouterie et la Joaillerie Modernes', which appeared in the *Figaro*'s *supplément artistique* on 13 June 1929, explained the reason for this attraction to jewelry with sharp angles and kaleidoscopic shapes: 'Speed is the characteristic of present-day life. The composition of a piece of jewelry must be readily understood and it must be constructed of simple lines, free from all affectation and superfluous detail. As its point of departure it must have a principle of construction in which the harmonious rhythm of lines, masses and colours manifests itself.' In its structure and design, Art Deco jewelry is also characterized by the explosion of colour: abandoning the diaphanous, evanescent colours of Art Nouveau, it was invaded by an intense, vibrant polychromy. Inspired, as mentioned earlier, by the Ballets Russes, the Fauves and the Orient, the creators of Art Deco indulged in a riot of crude colours and explosive combinations. And even with the vogue for black and white – supreme duo at the 'Exposition de Galliéra' in 1929 – threatening the supremacy of colour, the latter held its own without subsiding into the tedium which often goes with extremes. During Art Deco's black and white phase, the diamond reigned supreme. In March 1929, a *Vogue* journalist expressed the opinion that diamonds were always and everywhere appropriate: 'to black and to dark blue they impart brilliance, while they enhance the brilliance of white.' Panels set with diamonds were assembled in geometric shapes on onyx or black enamel with polished plaques of platinum or white gold. If it was of exceptional size or colour, the diamond was used on its own. Thanks to advances in gem cutting, jewelers could assemble stones cut in a variety of ways: baguette, trapezium, barrel or square. The baguette-cut, which was particularly favoured, reinforced the tonalities of the stone and could be combined with or opposed to the rose-cut or table-cut, according to which effects of luminous reflection were sought. These variations of cut resulted in compositions of crystallographic Cubism or, to quote Georges Fouquet: 'A harmony is revealed through the judicious combination of baguette-cut and round-cut brilliants. Varied, almost coloured, effects can be obtained by the felicitous use of different cuts and the interplay of the different stones.' Gems and semi-precious stones, emeralds, lapis lazuli, jade and coral were engraved following the oriental inspiration, or used in irregular-shaped cabochons, in the style of maharajahs' jewelry. A whole series of necklaces and bracelets, composed of irregular-shaped stones – sometimes even emeralds – uncut and strung together like cheap beads, were presented by jewelers such as Cartier, who remodelled in this way the crown jewels of the Maharajah of Patiala and displayed them to a dazzled public and audience of critics. Apart from platinum, three other supports were favoured by jewelers: rock crystal, lacquer and enamel. Frosted rock crystal presented a velvety aspect and constituted a subtle support for gold and coloured stones, as well as achieving a neutral harmony with diamonds. The use of lacquer, and also of enamel in jewelry and accessories, was another characteristic of the Twenties. Almost all the jewelers used black or coloured enamel which provided a luminous counterpoint for precious stones. Till then, lacquer had been admired in Europe without any attempt having been made, except in the Far East, to use it in jewelry. In 1900, the Maison Gaillard had brought Chinese workers over to France to teach lacquerwork to Parisian *orfèvres*, but they left Paris without having succeeded: their lacquerwork techniques had proved noxious to European skin. The malleability of lacquer, however, its perfect adherence, its resistance as well as its elasticity, predestined it to replace enamel. Influenced by the East, jewelers discovered in lacquer an ideal support which would show stones off to advantage. So they called in the help of Chinese and Annamite workers, employed during the war in lacquering aeroplane propellers, and brought together in improvised studios whole colonies of Chinese and Indochinese specialists, to whom were confided the manufacture and polishing of lacquer objects – chiefly jewelry, but also cigarette cases, lighters and dressing-cases.

Women have always tried to match clothes with hair styles and jewelry and, so, to present a coherent ensemble, as Jacques Guérin, reporting on the *Bijouterie-Joaillerie* Category at the 1925 Exposition noted: 'The complete parures which women wore at the end of the Second Empire did, undoubtedly, harmonize with their crinolines, their décolleté necklines revealing the shoulders . . . and the jeweled sprigs of flowers and leaves, copied with an admirable technical skill from nature, were undoubtedly intended for the lace corsages of thirty years ago, as aigrettes were for high-piled and bouffant hair styles.' The First World War produced a different kind of woman who wanted a different kind of jewelry. Both the range of jewelry, and the style of wearing it, changed. If some items were abandoned, others, like the pearl *sautoir* – unanimously adopted – aroused fresh interest among women of fashion. Cultured pearls had taken over the European market since the Japanese scholar Mikimoto discovered the secret of cultivating pearl-bearing oysters – until then found only by rare chance. Long *sautoirs*, wound several times round the neck, worn like a breastplate or sometimes hung down the back to emphasize the plunging neckline of an evening dress, were the principal emblem of the Twenties woman. This fashion was encouraged by the press which never tired of repeating that pearls complemented the skin, that they symbolized 'chic' and that they were as suited to daywear as to evening dress. As *Vogue* put it: 'Pearls are never wrong.' They vied with crystal which was often used in ring motifs trimmed with coral, turquoise or onyx; or even harmonized with diamonds, as in the *sautoir* made by Chaumet for the Comtesse de Breteuil. The craze for the *sautoir* was such that it produced the most astonishing creations from the jewelers: crystal gambling dice and pearls were threaded on to a cord ending in a fringed tassel; or the *sautoir* might be worn over a woman's smoking jacket in the style of a chain of office.

The most characteristic piece of jewelry of this period was undoubtedly the pendant, which was conceived to complement the short tunic dresses, belted at the hips and worn by fashionable women as both day and evening wear. The pendant could be worn in various ways: on the lapel of a jacket; as a brooch pinned to an article of clothing; but, above all, swaying at the end of an interminably long *sautoir*, below the stomach and sometimes even at knee-height, elongating still further the tubular line of the dress. The designs on these pendants ranged from figurative stylized motifs to the most rigorous geometric asbraction. Most characteristic and undoubtedly most readily available was the fringed silk tassel, twisted or braided with minuscule pearls. More expensive pendants were made up entirely of stones: coral, onyx, diamonds and pearls. Mauboussin's pendant, created in 1929, in the form of an engraved emerald vase bearing a bouquet of diamond branches with ruby leaves and emerald spheres, strung on a diamond chain, was taken up with variations by a number of jewelers. Other frequetly used motifs – of which Mauboussin's tiara is an outlandish example – were fountains and fringes, in baguette diamonds or other precious stones. The most daring pendants, on the other hand, were inspired by the world of the machine and were devised by members of the avant-garde: Jean Fouquet, Raymond Templier, Jean Després and Paul Brandt. Cleverly constructed, these clusters of stones, metals and enamel call to mind machine parts, artillery shells, whistles and harmonicas.

Jean Fouquet devised 'discs' of white gold or platinum, ringed and striped and engraved with circles, on which large stones (usually the less costly ones such as citrine, topaz or aquamarine) were placed, constituting the focal point around which the piece of jewelry was constructed. If the notoriety of Jean Fouquet, Gérard Sandoz or Raymond Templier bore witness to the success of these pieces of jewelry, there were nevertheless strong reactions in the disconcerted traditional press. Roger Nalys, echoing several alarmed critics, wrote: 'We refuse to accept these shapeless blocks which certain people put before us, speaking to us of rhythm, volume and synthesis. Maybe our lives do take place under the banner of the mechanical world, but that doesn't make a woman a machine. It is true that a mechanical component, precisely manufactured, possesses a beauty of its own which we would not dream of denying, but everything in its place. Graceful shoulders, delicate throats, fine wrists demand other caresses than those of nails, screws and bolts, even if they are in precious metal . . .' ('Le Bijou compagnon de la grâce féminine' in *L'Officiel de la Culture*, June 1929). With the retreat of the long sleeve, the arm exposed to the shoulder, the fashion for bracelets took off as never before. Two different types of bracelet shared the task of adorning the wrist: flexible, narrow bracelets like embroidered ribbons of stones, and wide bangles. The *Haute Joaillerie* were responsible for the 'embroideries' in metal and stone, incorporating the two favourite Art Deco motifs: stylized flowers and geometric shapes, to which were added more exotic decorative elements inspired by Egypt or Persia. The lightness and flexibility of these bracelets – the result of eliminating the divisions between the stones – sometimes inspired women with the idea of wearing several at a time. Broad bangles, like armillas, on the other hand, adorned the upper arm, emphasizing, by force of contrast, the fragility of the wrist. Devised by Jean Fouquet, Gérard Sandoz, Raymond Templier, Jean Desprès and Jean Dunand, these bangles combined various coloured metals and stones set off against polychrome enamels in geometric designs.

To balance the 'mannish' fashion of cropped hair and to give the face a feminine touch, ears were adorned with very long pendant earrings in the form of drops, pears and cascades of diamonds, and bunches of fruit in engraved stones. Jewelers rang the changes by combining unusual colours and materials: jade, onyx and diamonds; coral, onyx and diamonds. This fashion was accepted so unanimously that very few ear clips of the period are to be found.

Combs which had been required to support the heavy pre-war chignons, went out of favour before an increasing vogue for short, cropped hair. The same fate was reserved for hat pins which had been worn in pairs to the right and left to keep the vast, broad-brimmed hats in place. These long pins adorned with large pearls fell victim to the little cloche hat, one of the symbolic accessories of the Twenties. Aigrettes, which had given Parisian women the look of Sultanas before the war, were no longer seen in the evening. The 'mannish' hair style did not suit tiaras which were replaced by ribbons of stones worn flat, or clips, accentuating the curl of a lock of hair and reflecting light at night.

Rings tended to be massive, in the style of signet rings, and were composed principally of solid blocks: a platform of displaced planes, decorated with stones and often of imposing size, arranged on the shank itself. Nevertheless, in spite of their large dimensions, there was nothing to prevent several rings being worn on the same hand. 'Our rings', observed the critic Robert de la Sizeranne, 'look like taximeters and our brooches like the square on the hypotenuse.' The hand accustomed to handling a tennis racquet or a golf club did not suit fine, fragile rings. Rings are, without doubt, the easiest items of jewelry to dismantle. A large number of those created in the Twenties and Thirties have disappeared and only reproductions in magazines of the period and designs in jewelers' archives can give us an idea of their diversity. An innovation for the shank was the use of crystal or ivory, and Georges Fouquet created ivory rings set with light-coloured sapphires or aquamarines, while Chaveton produced a series of rings in frosted crystal on which sapphires, emeralds and lapis chips surrounded a shimmering mass of diamonds.

Jewelers found unlimited possibilities for the exercise of their imagination and ingenunity in the brooch with its multiple uses, and ensured this piece of jewelry an essential role in every wardrobe. Brooches were attached capriciously to the cloche hat, to the shoulder, to straps or to the belts which outlined the hips. The designers' fancy engendered a host of shapes and decorative elements, from abstract compositions, where circles balanced rectangles and polygons, to figurative, allusive motifs like the Scotch terriers 'Ric and Rac', jockeys on horseback, golfers and, for exotic effect, buddhas, Japanese temples and sphinxes, all set with precious stones. All the jewelers, without exception, offered variations on the theme of the bouquet of stylized flowers in a vase of geometric design or the basket of fruit, as well as the fountain motif – a favourite of Mauboussin's. Polychromy was the rage. Boucheron's brooch of 1929 offers one example among many. Depicting a vase with a bouquet of emeralds, diamonds, rubies and sapphires, it was set off with the yellow of a few jonquil-coloured diamonds. The vast range of Twenties and Thirties brooches can be grouped into easily recognizable types: the double barrette, composed of two linked parts which could be worn together or separately like twin clips; the brooch-buckle whose central motif, a ring of coral, onyx or crystal, either in a circle or an ellipse, was decorated with stylized floral motifs, and which could be attached to a belt; a variant of this in the shape of an open circle with a sliding pin; the fibula-brooch, one of the oldest forms of the clasp, and the jabot pin, worn on the lapel or the hat – all these competed for the favour of fashionable women and appeared in a thousand original and fantastic forms in the designers' sketchbooks. The plaque-shaped brooch was frequently to be found in the repertoire of the Maison Fouquet. There was the plaque brooch, for example, where squares of closely packed small diamonds alternated with flat surfaces in unpolished platinum, on which sparkled three magnificent diamonds, or another model, where black, red and blue enamel were bordered with gold, platinum and diamonds. Since brooches were frequently used as belt ornaments, artists such as Georges Fouquet devised pieces of jewelry in the form of very long tassels of mixed coloured stones, destined to adorn a belt.

WATCHES

The men and women of the Twenties were obsessed with the passing of time. 'Live fast', the leitmotiv of the *Années Folles*, gave the watch a role of primary importance. Jewelers instantly understood the capital they could made out of this useful object. The mechanisms were made by the specialized watchmaking industries of the Franche-Comté in France, or in Switzerland, and the jewelry designers then took charge of transforming this object into a piece of jewelry or a luxury object. The fate of the watch was thus closely linked with the art of *bijouterie-joaillerie*.

Mechanical advances and the miracles accomplished by the watchmaking craftsmen furnished the jewelers with infinitely small and curiously *calibré* movements which they then took pleasure in decorating. While in the eighteenth century, the watch, with its chatelaine and hanging ornaments, had offered large surfaces for decoration with enamel, diamonds and gemstones, the inverse occurred with the production of miniaturized mechanisms. Ladies' watch-bracelets, invented towards the end of the eighteenth century, were launched anew by jewelers at the beginning of this century. They became more popular, along with bracelets, when feminine fashion no longer required long sleeves and when participation in sport required a more functional jewelry. From the first watch-bracelets on their moiré or figured patent leather straps, to those sparkling with stones; from the most modest to the most lavish, the designer-creators devised an infinite number of variations whose vast range is an indication of the support of their clientele. If the watch-bracelet was to be acceptable with evening dress it had to be gorgeous enough to take its place next to other bracelets. The watch case, often very narrow, was set with precious stones, diamonds or pearls, and the dial was reduced to microscopic dimensions. The Maisons created diamond bracelets at the centre of which a tiny watch was concealed: the movement was in platinum and the crystal which covered the dial was emerald-cut to look like a large gem. Other models took the form of supple straps of gold or jewels whose central part opened like the lid of a box to reveal the dial.

Competing, between 1925 and 1930, with the watch-bracelet, the pendant- or chatelaine-watch was all the rage at a time when evening dresses were short on one side and long on the other. They were one of the most popular creations of Van Cleef et Arpels and Lacloche. The forms of these watches were fanciful in the extreme and the dial was often invisible, sometimes hidden in a pearl tassel, as in the case of one of Cartier's models.

Another variation was the watch-brooch. Only the owner of this piece of jewelry knew that it was a brooch that told the time, for the dial remained hidden. The motifs of these brooches were often figurative, but always typical of Art Deco, as, for example, in a design by Marchak which took the form of a vase of flowers in diamonds and coloured stones whose front opened to reveal the watch. Another model by Bourdier represented a diamond mill whose façade tipped up when the catch was released to reveal the minuscule dial. The watch, symbol of the active life, invaded other objects: it nestled in cigarette boxes, in lipstick cases, in powder compacts, in dressing cases or vanity cases. And inventive richness went into the design not only of ladies' watches, but also of mens', the watch being one of the few pieces of jewelry, together with tie-pins and cuff links, to which men were entitled. The wrist watch arrived and, practical as it was, began to take preference over the pocket watch. The list of watch creations by Cartier and Boucheron over the years reveals their imaginativeness and their astonishing capacity for renewing forms and combining new materials. When little shuttered watches appeared, disguised in a gold watch case in the form of a lighter, the fob watch was, literally, liberated from its chain. The movement of these watches was revealed when the two shutters were opened and the watch thus became a miniature bedside or desk clock. The watches were decorated with lacquer or with mother-of-pearl encrusted with coral. Cartier created a similar model, the slide-action pocket watch, where the rectangular enamelled watch case, which covered the dial, opened as pressure was applied at the sides. If the growing demand for watches brought with it mass-production by the watchmaking industries – Lip, Longines and Auricoste – the jewelers' watches were, nevertheless, distinguished by the refinement and luxury of their materials and by the fact that certain models were unique, designed and conceived for a single client, or produced in limited editions.

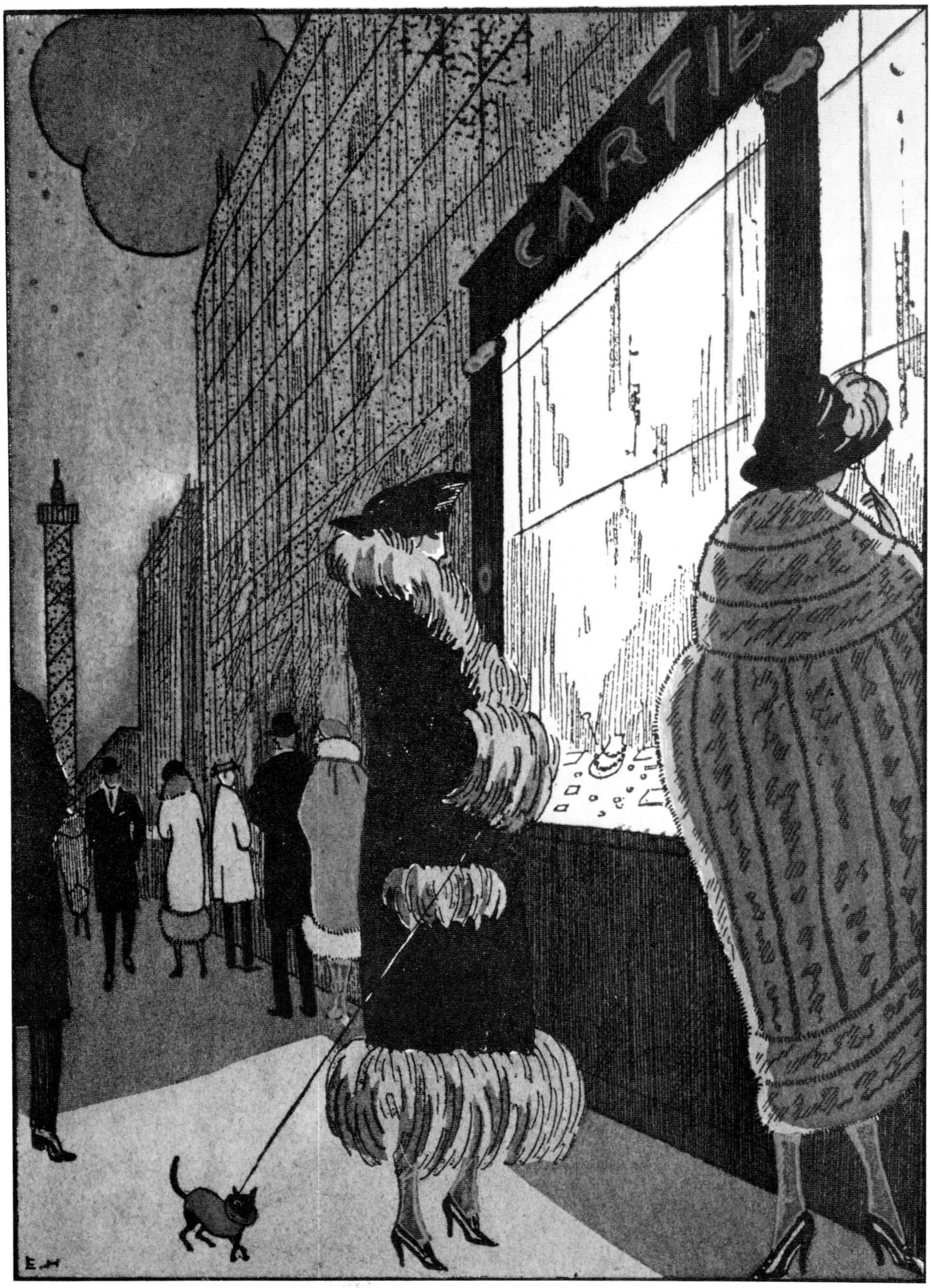

Cartier, 13 rue de la Paix.

THE HAUTE JOAILLERIE

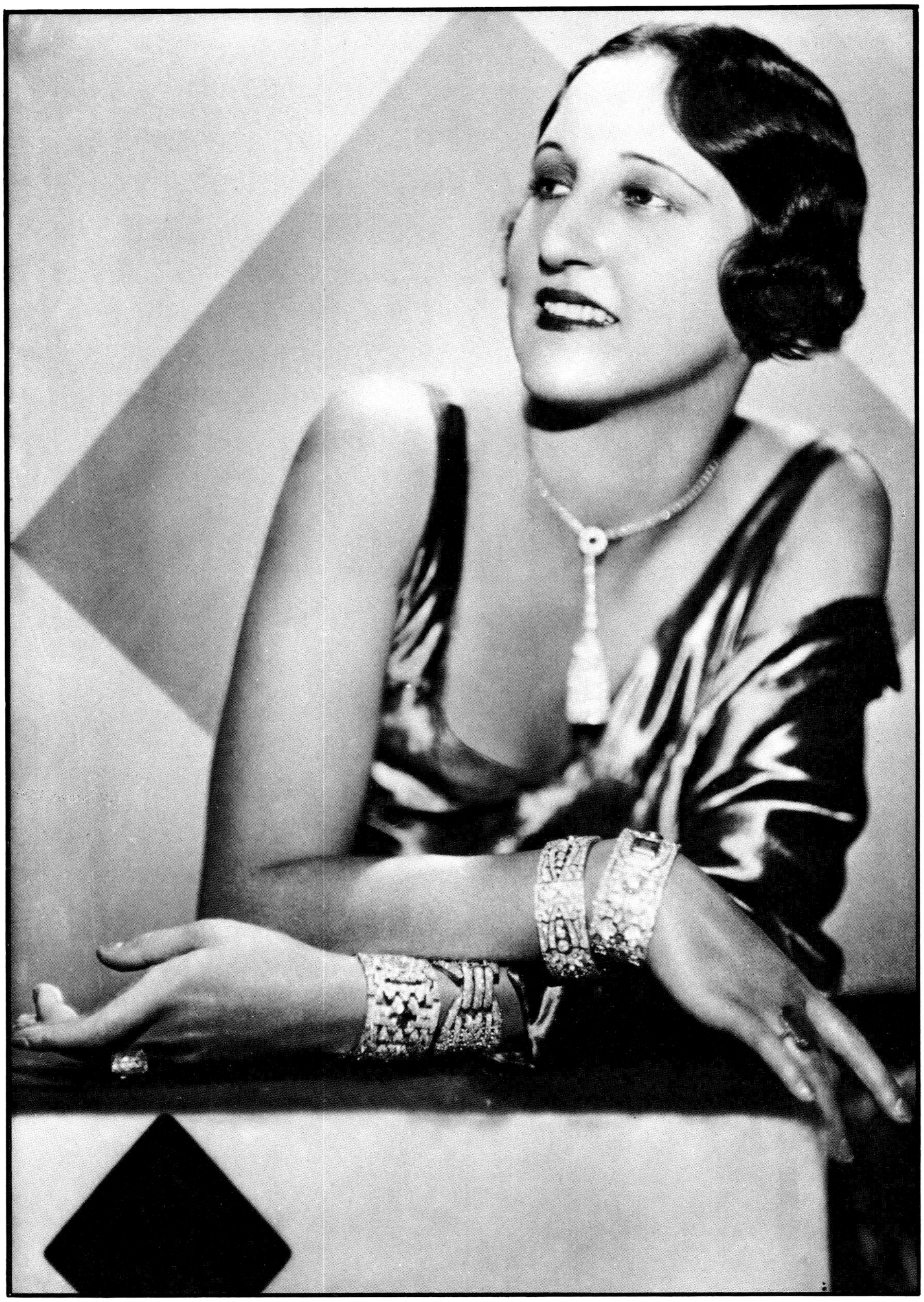

Scaïonni: portrait of Mademoiselle Duby, Paris, c. 1930. Gérard-Lévy Collection.

SO FAR AS THE WORLD JEWELRY SCENE was concerned, the spotlight had long been focused on Paris. At the beginning of the twentieth century, the great jewelers formed a colony in the rue de la Paix and the Place Vendôme, a domain which was reserved for them as the Petit-Pont district had been in the Middle Ages, the rue Saint Honoré in the eighteenth century and the Galeries du Palais Royal in the nineteenth century.

A large number of jewelers chose to take up residence in the rue de la Paix: Rozanès at no 2; Cartier at no 13; Vever at no 14; Lacloche at no 15; Mellerio at no 26; Fontana at no 7; Linzeler et Marchak at no 4; André Aucoc at no 6; Berlioz Leroy et Cie at no 19; Janesich at no 19; Morgan, successor to Jacta who had moved in in 1862, at no 17; Laillet at no 5; E. David at no 20; Henri Lyon at no 12; Marzo at no 22; Spaulding at no 23; Polak aîné at no 18; Tiffany at no 25. Others were situated in the Place Vendôme: Boucheron at no 26; Chaumet at no 12; Van Cleef et Arpels at no 22; Lalique at no 24. A few streets away, Dusausoy was at 41 boulevard des Capucines; Mauboussin at 3 rue de Choiseul; Friedmann at 38 rue de Châteaudun. However, 'if you are really modern', advised the magazine *Vogue*, 'you must go to the rue Royale or to the rue de Choiseul': to Fouquet, 6 rue Royale; Sandoz, 10 rue Royale, or, again, to Chaveton Frères, 14 rue du Quatre Septembre or to Raymond Templier, 3 Place des Victoires. Their plush salons, furnished with little tables, were like *salons de thé* (tea rooms) where the visitor was awed into silence by the inexhaustible selection of diamonds, pearls and precious stones. People came from all over the world to these meeting places to take in their heady splendours. 'It is very gratifiying to think that several times a year buyers come to Paris from every country to see what is being made and what is being worn, and they only leave after paying homage to our creators.' (G. Fouquet, 'La Bijouterie et la Joaillerie Modernes', 1942).

The distinction between *bijouterie* and *joaillerie* is often glossed over, but the terms imply clearly defined activities and the two professions are governed by entirely separate laws, which in turn affect the artistic and intrinsic value of their creations. According to Jean Lanllier, 'in a general way, *bijouterie* can be defined as the art of making objects from gold, silver or platinum, which are destined for decoration, the precious or non-precious metal alone translating the artist's conception. In contrast, the art of *joaillerie* consists in seeking the decorative effect of a piece of jewelry through the exclusive use of precious stones, the metal being used only as necessary. Deriving from both of these, a hybrid order combines the use of metal and gemstone in the composition of a piece of jewelry. Its craftsmen are designated under the name of *bijoutier-joailliers*.' (*Fouquet*, 1934).

According to regulations in force, each piece of jewelry must be marked with a hall-mark and a maker's mark. Legislation on the making and sale of objects in precious metals is almost as old as the trade of the goldsmith itself and, from earliest times, there has been the need to establish an official standard which would ensure fair dealing in transactions involving gold and silver. In France, it is not until the middle of the thirteenth century that one finds the first signs of a regulation on the standard of precious metals – that is, the quantity of precious metal contained in a gold or silver alloy. In 1275, in the reign of Philippe III, 'the Bold', a ruling specified the official standard of silver, guaranteed by a hall-mark at 958 *millièmes* (thousandths); in 1313 Philippe IV, 'the Fair', extended this practice to works in gold. The law of the nineteenth Brumaire, year six (9 November 1797) currently in force, fixed new standards for gold and silver: the eagle's head hall-mark guaranteed the legal standard of (750/1000ths) for objects in gold, the boar's head hall-mark being used for silver. After 1905, objects containing mixtures of gold and silver were marked with a hall-mark with the eagle's head and boar's head juxtaposed.

At the beginning of this century, a law dated 8 April 1910, taking into account the increasing use of platinum in jewelry, classed this metal in the rank of precious metals and guaranteed its quality by the use of a dog's head hall-mark. In 1927, a range of hall-marks was added for objects combining gold and platinum. Works in all kinds of precious metals destined for export were not subject to guarantee and were marked by the maker with a special hall-mark in the form of an irregular, equal-sided pentagon representing a square surmounted by a triangle, known as an *obus* (artillery shell) hall-mark. The hall-mark seems to have been preceded by the maker's mark, which served as a signature. In 1355, Jean II, 'the Good', had ruled that every *orfèvre* must mark all objects made by him with a hall-mark representing a crowned fleur-de-lis with the addition of a personal symbol. The maker's mark permitted a closer surveillance and a check on frauds, protecting the makers from forgeries which would threaten their livelihood and their reputation. Later, a lozenge-shaped hall-mark enclosing the initial letter of the maker's surname following a personal symbol was introduced, often with the initial of his first name in front of the symbol. The usage of the signature in full has not been properly clarified. Opinions are divided and it seems that, at the time of which we are speaking, this usage was not systematic. Several years were to pass before jewelers submitted to it. Unlike the Maisons of Cartier, Boucheron, Van Cleef et Arpels and Chaumet, who were signing their work in the Twenties, firms such as Mauboussin and Boivin did not make a rule of it. In the absence of a signature, only the maker's mark renders it possible to establish the origin of a piece of jewelry. Important pieces remain unidentified either because it is impossible to recognize maker's marks or because the latter have quite simply become illegible with the wearing and polishing of the piece of jewelry. The only way to discover their origin is to find the design in the jeweler's archives. The recent interest of jewelers in their historical past and their desire to rediscover long-neglected treasures may result in the unearthing of untold riches.

If many of the creations of the *Haute Joaillerie* remain unidentified, even more have been dispersed thanks to the market-value of their materials. A piece of jewelry which is displayed as a symbol of social status is above all a secure asset, readily converted into money. It is remarkable, and indeed regrettable, that a buyer generally places more importance on the value of the stones than the artistic merit of a piece of jewelry. He thereby risks discouraging all creative impulses on the part of the artist, constrained as the latter must be to prove that his work will survive the changing fashions and retain its intrinsic value. The artistic quality of the *Haute Joaillerie*'s work tends to be discreet as a result, subtly blending tradition and innovation. The recent alliance, however, between couturiers and *joailliers*, inaugurated by Cartier at the time of the 'Exposition Internationale des Arts Décoratifs', required that jewelry be in perfect accord with dress. Georges Fouquet created jewelry to accompany Jean Patou's 1927 and 1928 collections, and the review *Parures* presented a selection of pieces by Gérard Sandoz to complement Suzanne Talbot's evening dresses. This exercised a strong influence over the art of *joaillerie* and broadened its inspiration. In fact, if the products of each *joaillier* are examined in isolation, they do reveal considerable variations. The daring of certain designs, evoking Cubist canvases, enhanced the reputation of the *Haute Joaillerie* and their work at times shared the qualities of creations by such pioneers as Jean Fouquet, Gérard Sandoz and Raymond Templier. The following examples chosen in 1925 from different *joailliers* give an impression of the originality of their ideas. Dusausoy set gems, lapis or malachite in slabs of rust-coloured or red jasper and created brooches with diamonds combined with malachite or onyx in parallel lines bearing, at the centre, a sapphire or diamond. Mauboussin simulated the transparency of water by placing diamonds against iridescent mother-of-pearl; decorated a mother-of-pearl bracelet with three motifs in diamonds and black enamel; created a brooch consisting of a rectangular diamond surrounded on three sides by emeralds and sapphires in a chequer-board pattern; and even made a sly reference to the tool: a barrette in the form of a diamond covered nail. From Lacloche came a scene from La Fontaine, depicted in stones, on a pendant and bracelet. Van Cleef et Arpels devised bracelets and brooches with lightly stylized flowers in rubies and diamonds; Cartier, using the oriental style, made necklaces of engraved emeralds and sculpted coral and a bracelet composed of little diamond and black enamel kegs; and Aucoc produced rings of square-bezelled lapis and emeralds or fluted coral and diamonds. Chaumet, also inspired by the East, composed a necklace of ribbed emerald spheres threaded with olive-shaped rubies, diamonds and onyx. From Vever came a ribbon necklace in openwork, recalling a Persian hunting scene. Other bracelets combined diamonds with jade shuttles and onyx circles, or onyx commas punctuating a ground of small diamonds. Georges Fouquet, imitating a Cubist design by the painter André Léveillé, produced coloured stones which punctuated a panel of diamonds on a crystal pendant. The architect Eric Bagge designed rectangular and circular pendants in frosted crystal, onyx and diamonds; a gold bangle on which regular designs were inscribed in black enamel, jade and diamonds, and an

African mask in black enamel. Linzeler et Marchak devised a brooch of transparent rock crystal, darkened by a delicate tracery of leaves drawn on the underside, and on which rested a large flower in sculpted amber. Boucheron created a bracelet of large, equal-sized diamonds between two rows of small diamonds, bordered with onyx, and a tiara of stylized flowers in onyx and diamonds on a chequer-board of coral, onyx and coloured stones. Marzo devised a pair of *girandole* (cluster) earrings with lozenge and baguette diamonds, a bracelet of crystal and amethyst rings and a brooch consisting of a black enamel grille surrounded by diamonds, with diamond scrolls set off against coloured stones. After 1910, Lalique produced fewer of the lavish single pieces which had made his reputation at the beginning of the century and his Maison began to produce, instead, a series of pendants in moulded glass engraved with flowers, suspended from *sautoirs* of glass cabochons threaded on to cords and braided tassels. Argy-Rousseau was also highly successful with pendants executed in this style.

The fruit of patient endeavour, as the project albums show, each piece of jewelry was derived from multiple variations on an initial theme. Accordingly, each Maison had a studio-workshop to which designer-creators, specializing in jewelry design, were attached. External artists were sometimes also employed who, by the very fact of their ignorance of the technical difficulties of the craft, brought to it a new breath of creativity. This was made possible by a close collaboration with the technician, the head of the Maison or studio, in the course of which the decorative conception of a project would be adapted to the constraints of manufacture. Certain names are, thus, associated with the Maisons to whose reputations they contributed: Louis Fertey with Georges Fouquet, Hirtz and Massé with Boucheron, Madeleine Chazel with Dusausoy, Pierre-Yves Mauboussin and Maurice Velay with Mauboussin, Suzanne Belperron with Boivin, Charles Jacqueau and Jeanne Toussaint with Cartier. The latter, making the most of her inability to draw, both offered creative inspiration and acted as an exacting judge of the designs submitted to her for approval.

The 'Exposition Internationale des Arts Décoratifs' in 1925 was the first occasion on which the names of the designers figured in all the showcases next to the name of the Maison – with the exception of Cartier. The subtle and constant exchanges of creative ideas between jewelers and designer-craftsmen established reciprocal influences which benefited the quest for new designs. Projects conceived outside the Maison, once submitted and accepted, were generally executed in the workshop attached to the Maison; sometimes, when the designer was himself a craftsman, they were done outside. The individual character of each Maison dictated its choice in the selection of designs. Many designer-craftsmen worked on occasion for different Maisons: Verger collaborated with the Maisons of Boucheron, Van Cleef et Arpels, Linzeler et Marchak, Cartier and Marzo; Pinçon with Boucheron, Linzeler et Marchak and Marzo; Rubel with Van Cleef et Arpels, Lacloche, Linzeler et Marchak, Boucheron and Marzo.

Strauss, Allard et Meyer and Desmarès also worked for several jewelers. The Maison Aucoc collaborated occasionally with Basset, Dumont, Jolly and Sellier. Maynier worked for several Maisons; as, it appears, did Dubret, Grebel, Trahand, Sasportas, Becker and Chamson.

Georges Fouquet explained in 1929: 'that it is necessary to interest the artist in his creative work by allowing him to follow his pieces through the various phases of their creation, so that he can explain in advance to the craftsman in charge of the actual production the ideas behind his conception. That is the secret of success. It is not enough to put a design in front of a craftsman for the object to be produced; that leaves too much open to chance.' Once the projects had been prepared, accepted and costed, they passed to the workshop; metal chasers, enamellers, gem cutters and gem setters then took charge of their execution. We should stress here the long tradition which lay behind those craftsmen who, from father to son and from one country to another, established the flawless reputation of luxury craftsmanship.

The *Haute Joaillerie* sought new modes of expression – both in the ultimate form of a piece of jewelry created and the techniques used – which would be neither a contradiction nor an imitation of previous forms, but a logical development of them. As such, it subscribed to Gino Severini's motto: 'to create a work which contains all past art in combination with the modern spirit.' If, in 1930, Iribe was alarmed at the thought 'that there are any number of artists for whom the flower is not less necessary than the machine. We must sacrifice the flower on the altar of Cubism and the machine', we need not share his melancholy.

Jewelers overwhelmed the lovers of jeweled flower motifs with a choice wide enough to satisfy all tastes, and Armand Lanoux' laconic formula wittily sums up the style of 1925: 'the synthesis of Cubism in line and 1900 in ornamentation: convolvuluses squeezed into shapes drawn with a ruler.'

In the window displays of the less well-known Maisons, pendants and bracelets shone with a richness rarely seen before and symbolized a general prosperity.

All the Paris Maisons opened branches in the large foreign capitals, or in watering-places frequented by a rich and cosmopolitan clientele. The worldwide fame of the great jewelers was so well established that when, in 1929, Jacques Cartier was received by King Fuad on the occasion of an Exposition in Cairo, the king granted the Maison the royal warrant of Purveyor to the Court of Egypt. In 1930 the Shah of Iran received Louis Boucheron and appointed him as expert valuer of the 'Thousand and one Nights' treasure. Encouraged by the success achieved by the French section at the 1925 Exposition, numerous jewelers abroad took up the Art Deco style.

If, in 1925, differences of opinion and belief separated the partisans of the *Haute Joaillerie* from those of the avant-garde, the passing of time has enabled us to stand back and see beyond their differences, and the characteristics common to all their creations emerge to constitute a single style.

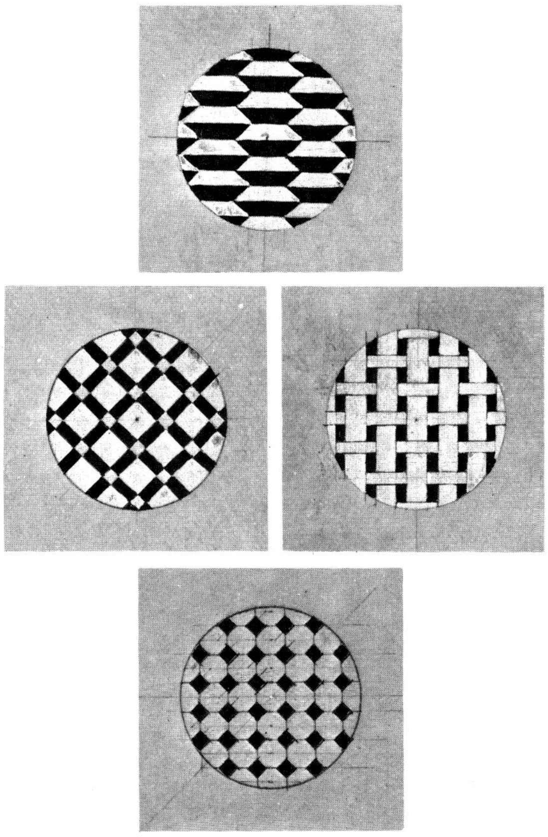

Designs for cuff-links.

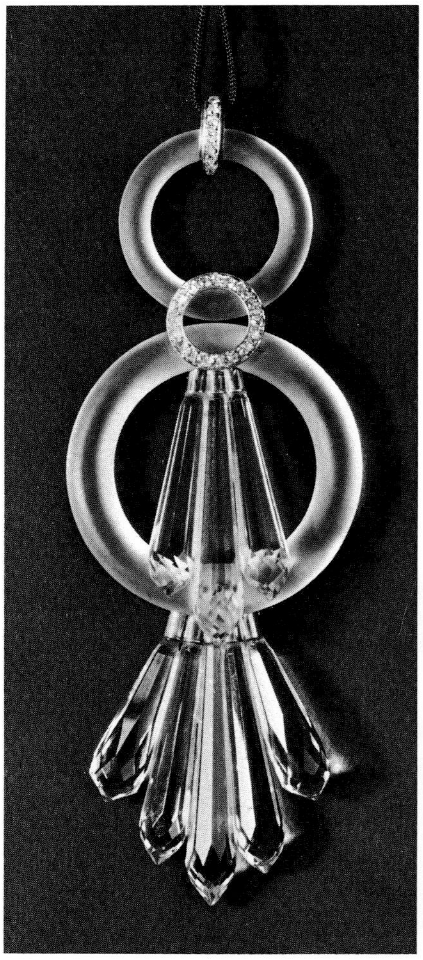

Georges Fouquet: pendant in transparent rock crystal, frosted rock crystal and diamonds, mounted on platinum. A. Lesieutre Collection. Photo: L. Sully-Jaulmes.

Georges Fouquet: pendant in frosted rock crystal, topaz and platinum. A. Lesieutre Collection. Photo: L. Sully-Jaulmes.

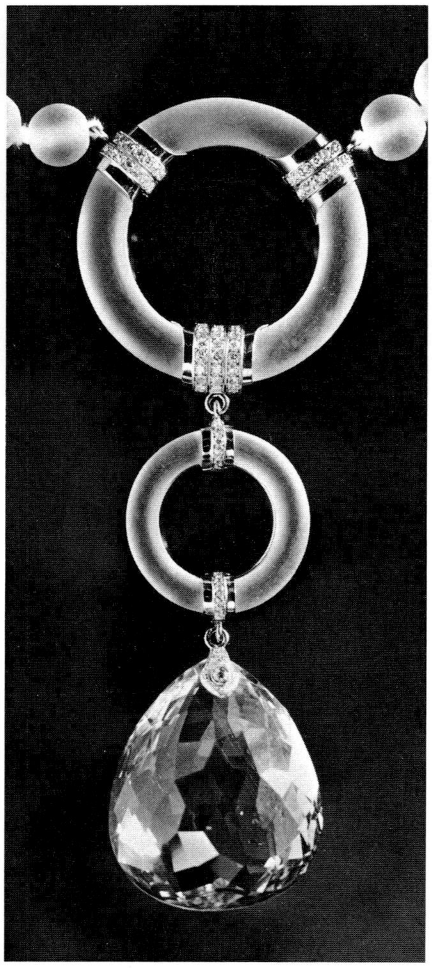

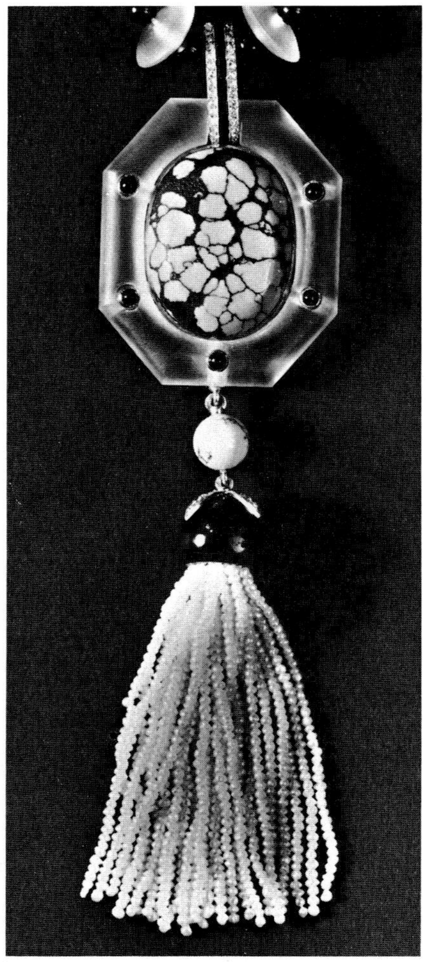

Georges Fouquet: pendant in turquoise, frosted rock crystal, diamonds, and black onyx with a pearl tassel. A. Lesieutre Collection. Photo: L. Sully-Jaulmes.

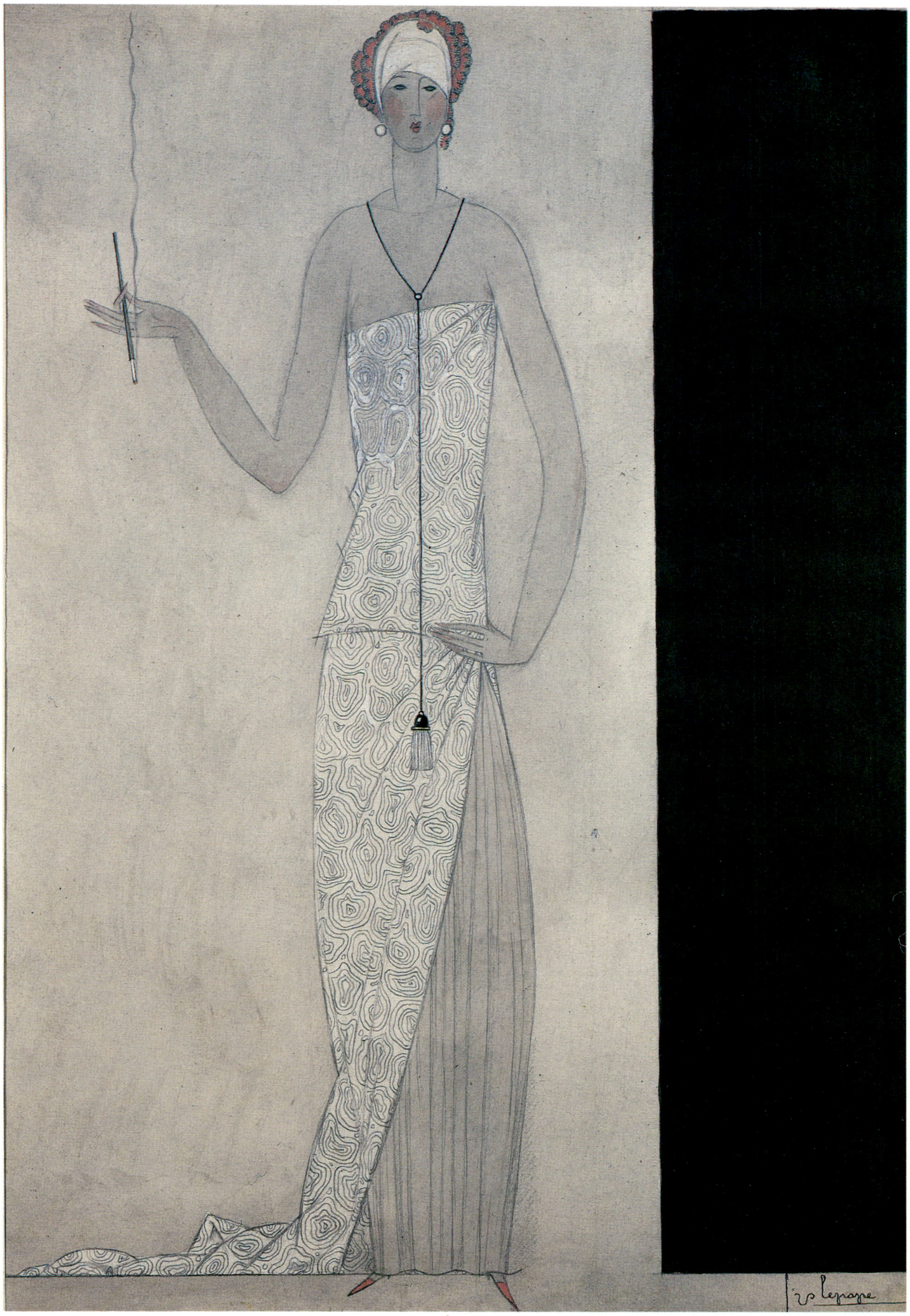

Illustration by Georges Lepape. Photo: L. Sully-Jaulmes

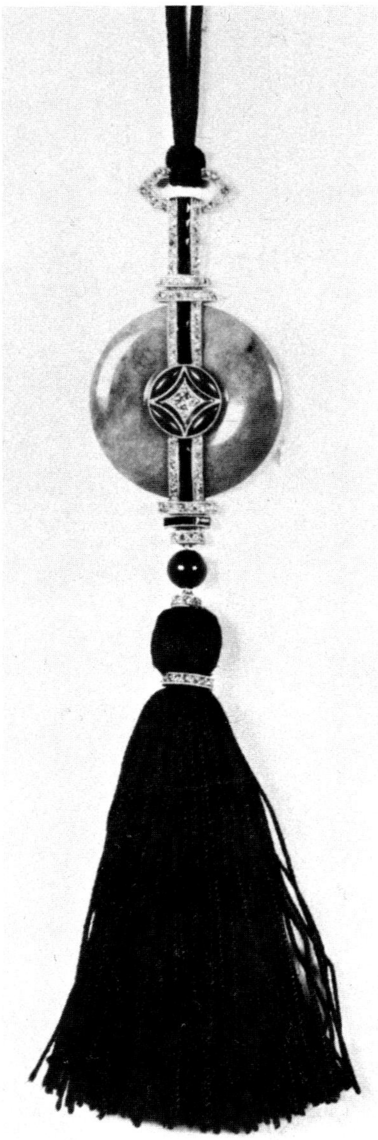

Boucheron: pendant consisting of a disc of jade, onyx and diamonds with a silk tassel, c. 1925. Boucheron Archives.

Boucheron: pendant in jade, onyx and diamonds with a silk tassel, c. 1925. Boucheron Archives.

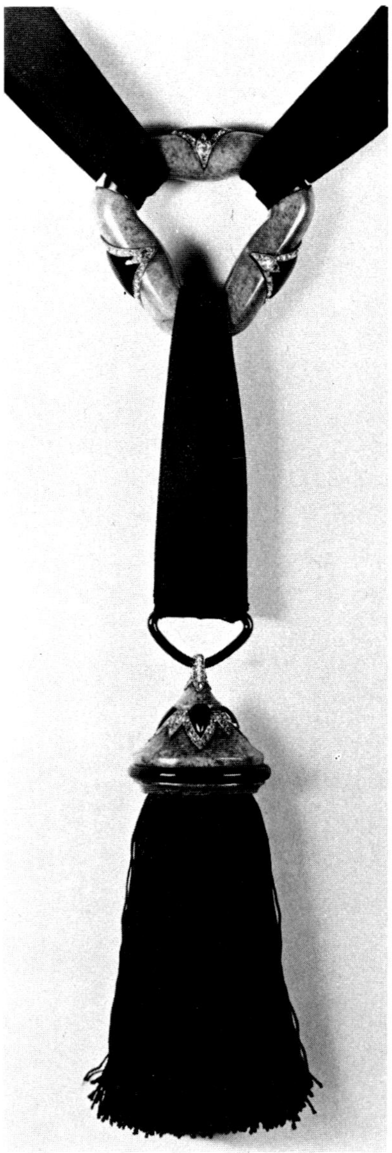

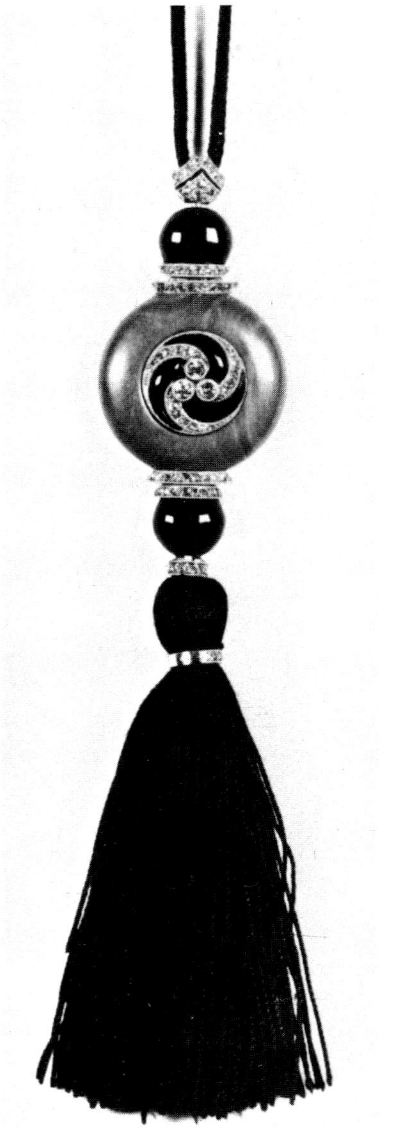

Boucheron: pendant consisting of a jade disc with a design in onyx and diamonds and a silk tassel, c. 1925. Boucheron Archives.

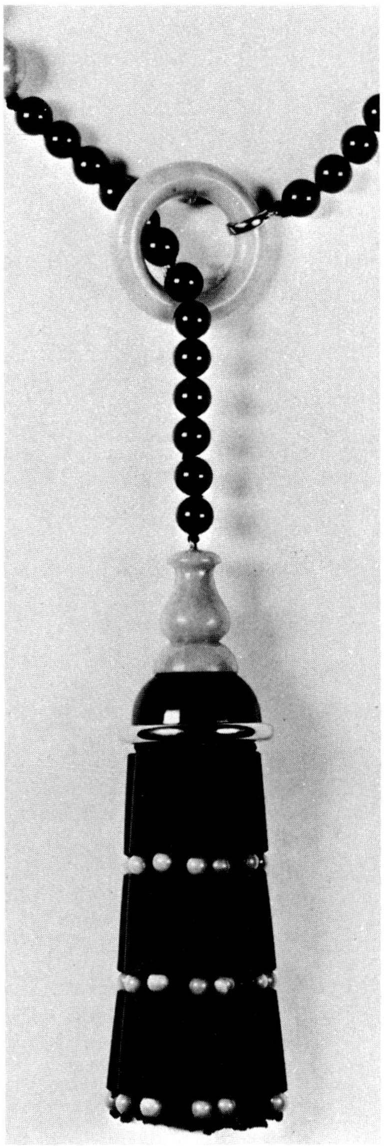

Boucheron: sautoir *in onyx beads and pendant consisting of a jade, onyx and black silk tassel decorated with pearls,* c. *1925.*

Georges Fouquet: sautoir *and tassel in crystal, black onyx, red enamel and white gold,* c. *1925.*

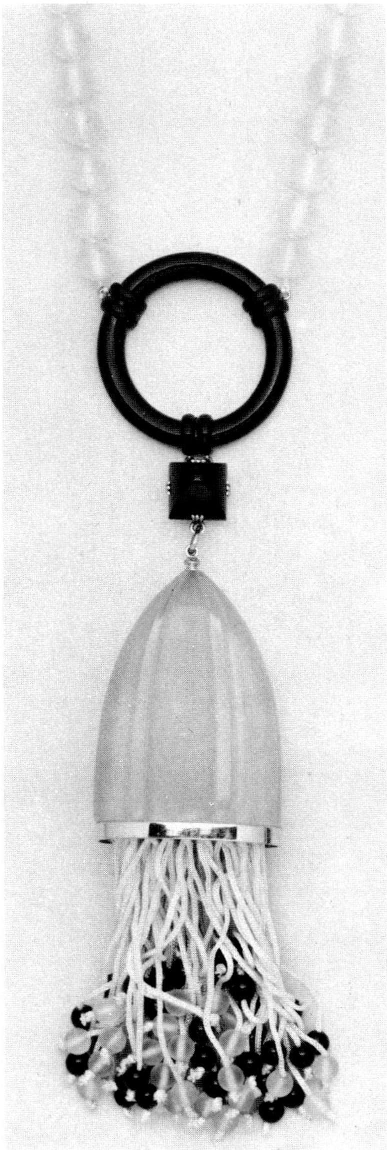

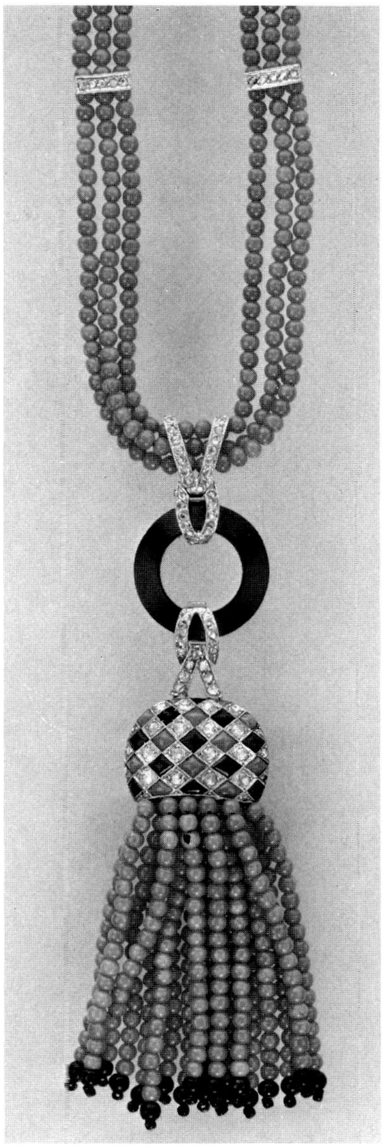

Anonymous: sautoir *consisting of three rows of coral beads with a pendant in the form of a tassel in diamonds, black onyx and coral beads. Christie's.*

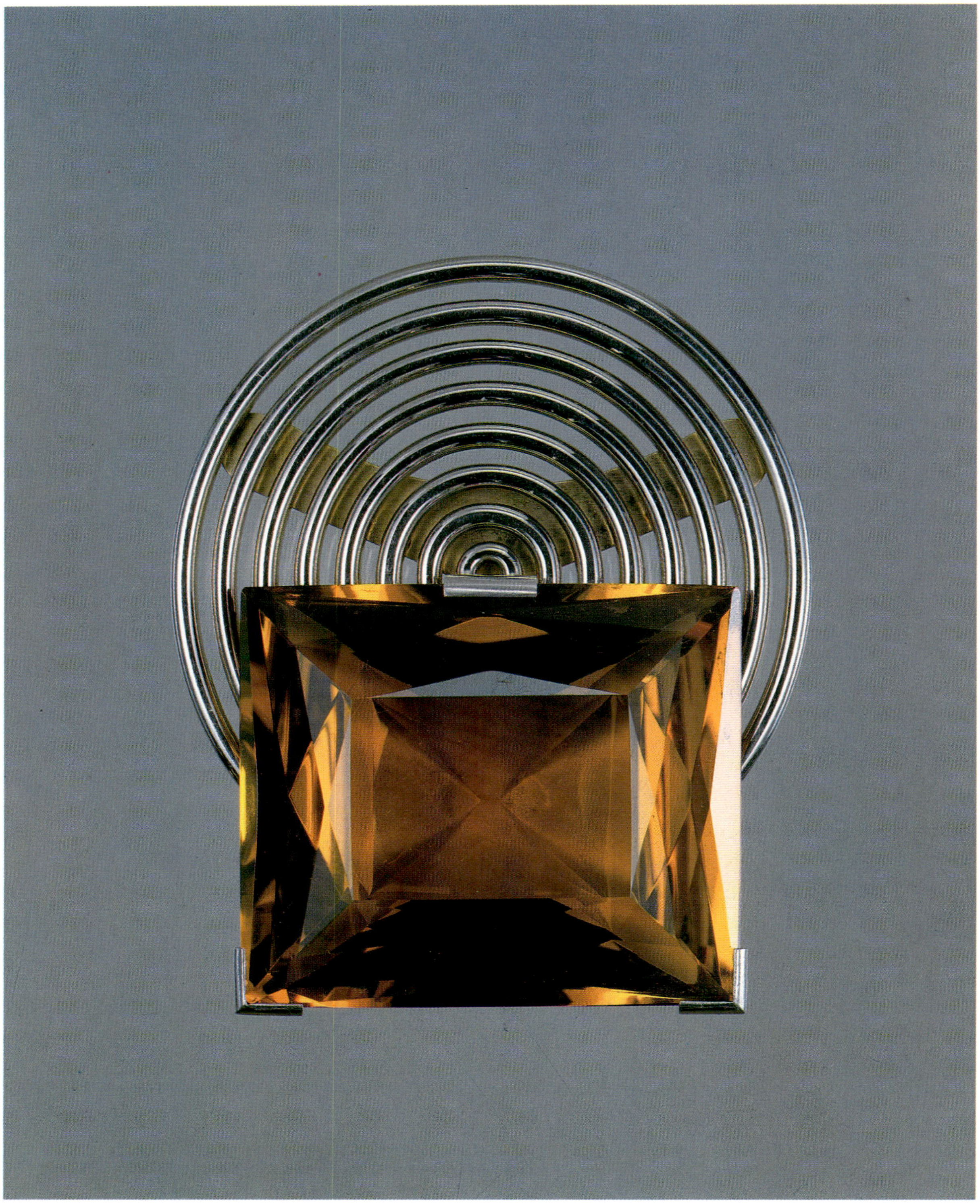

Jean Fouquet: pendant in citrine and grey gold; on the back a barrette fastening in gold. Originally the upper part was decorated with a platinum fillet set with diamonds which was removed by Jean Fouquet. A gold chain replaces the original silk cord. H. 8 cm, W. 7 cm. Private Collection. Photo: Musée des Arts Décoratifs, Paris.

Facing page: Georges Fouquet: pendant in frosted rock crystal, jade, lapis lazuli, brilliant-cut diamonds and calibré emeralds, mounted on platinum, 1923–24. Private Collection: Photo: Musée des Arts Décoratifs, Paris.

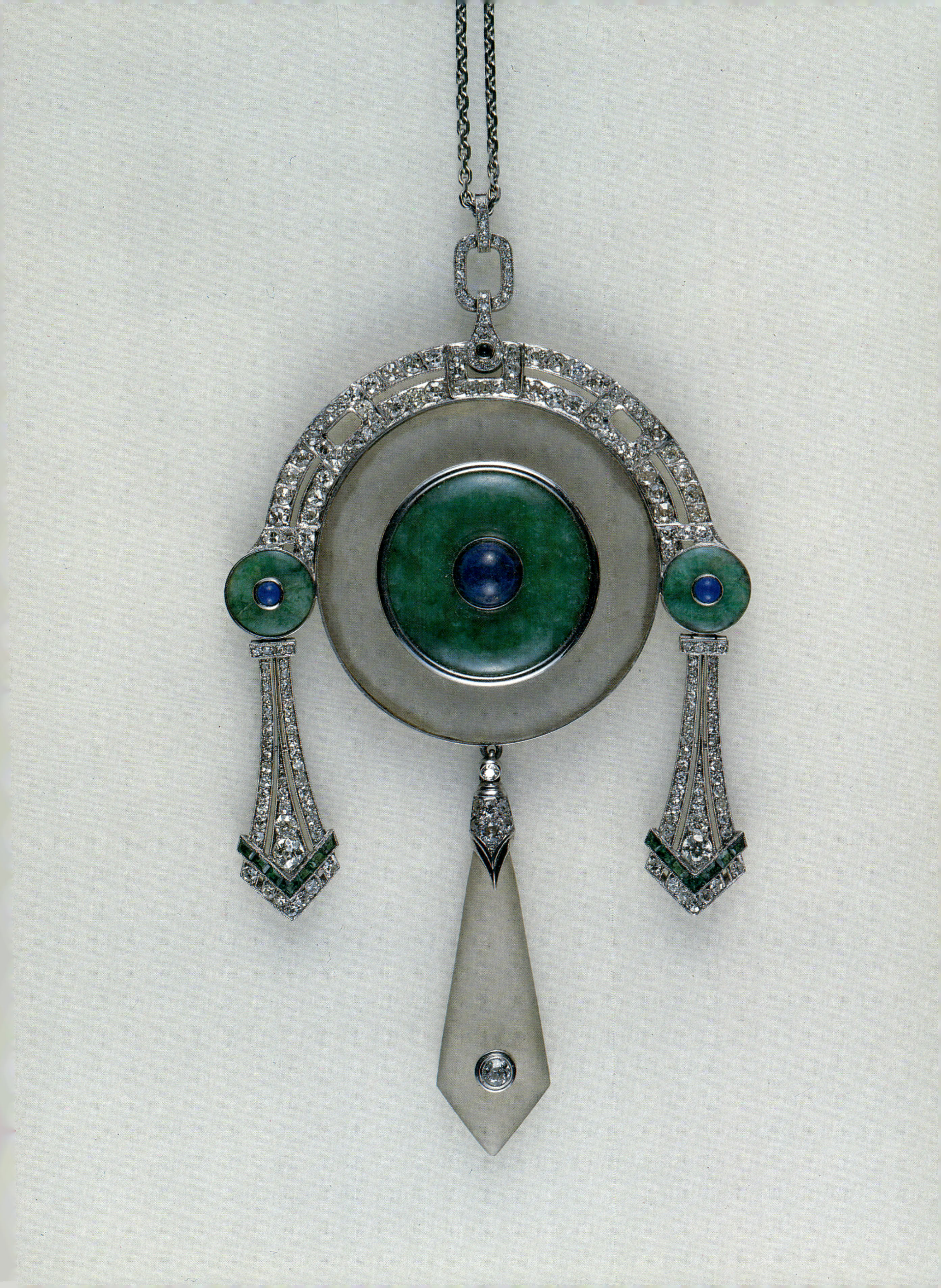

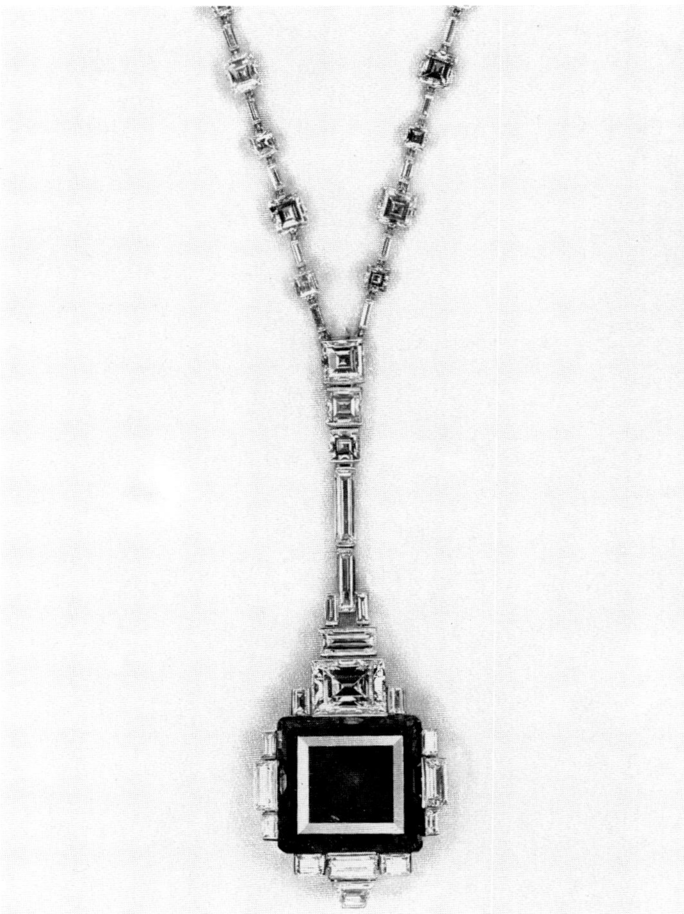

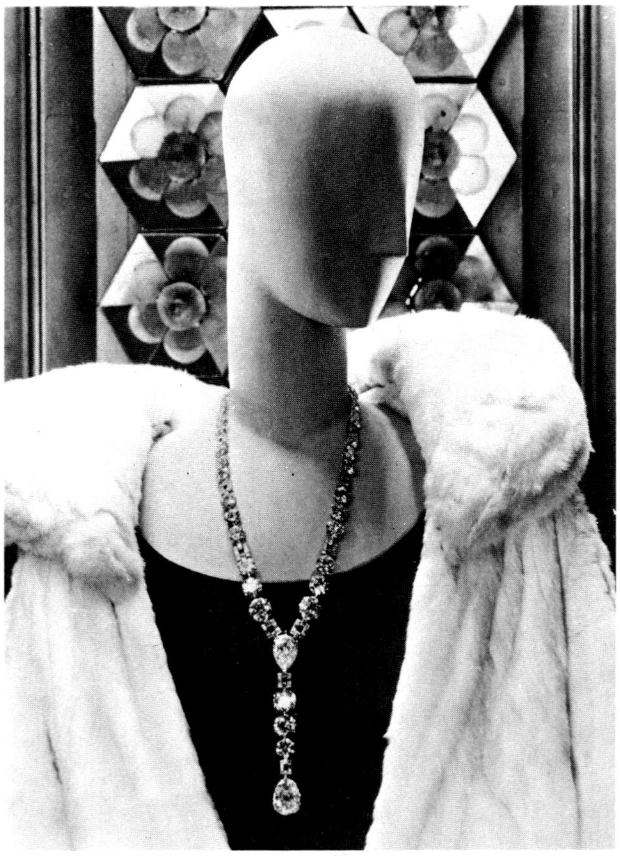

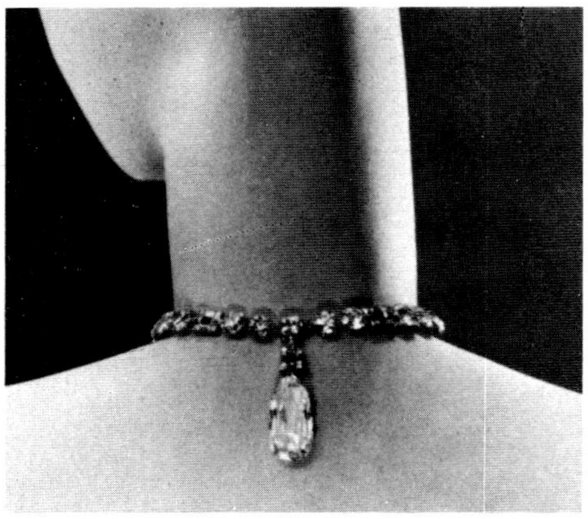

Mauboussin: sautoir-chain in square and baguette diamonds with a pendant bearing a very large square emerald surrounded by baguette diamonds, 1930.

Cartier: detail of the clasp with a pear-shaped diamond (see top right). Cartier Archives.

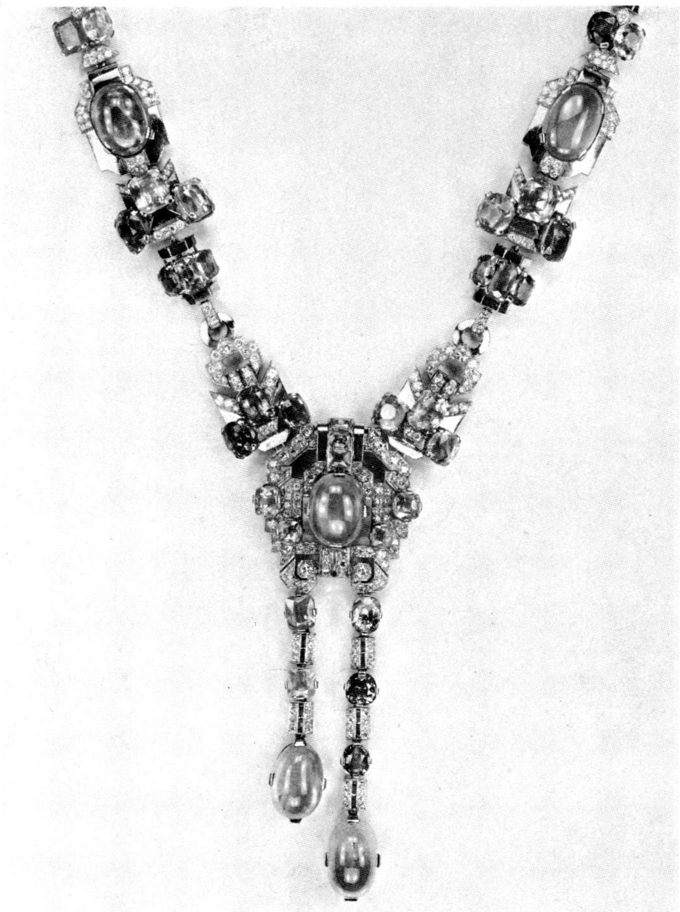

Cartier: necklace of graduated round diamond drops linked by other diamonds; pendant and clasp composed of round diamonds and three pear-shaped diamonds of 35, 38 and 40 carats, 1928. Cartier Archives.

Mauboussin: necklace-pendant in platinum, diamonds and cabochons of coloured stones, c. 1930.

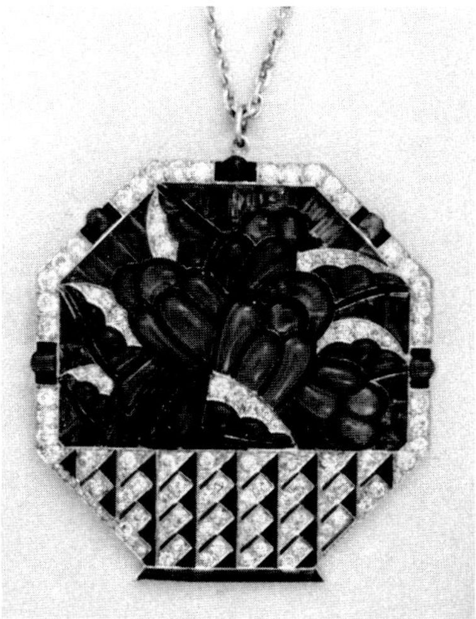

Mauboussin: pendant in platinum, diamonds, black onyx, baguette-cut sapphires and cabochons of coloured stones, c. 1925.

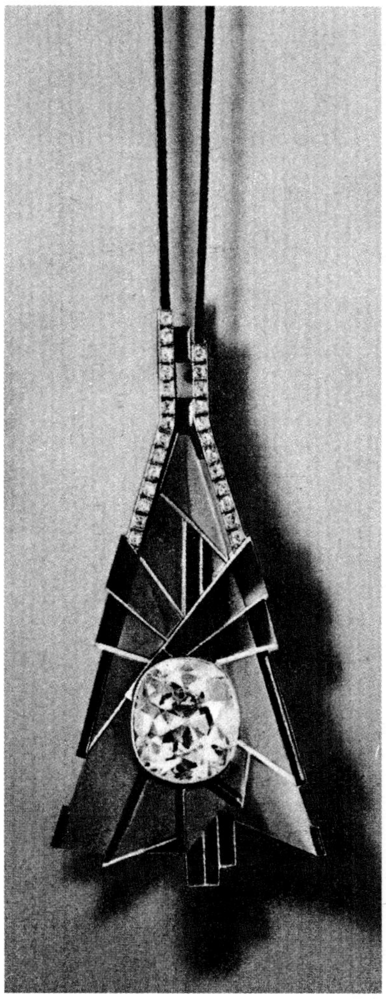

Dusausoy: pendant in platinum, diamonds, coral, brown and rust jasper and black onyx decorated with a 36 carat diamond, c. 1925.

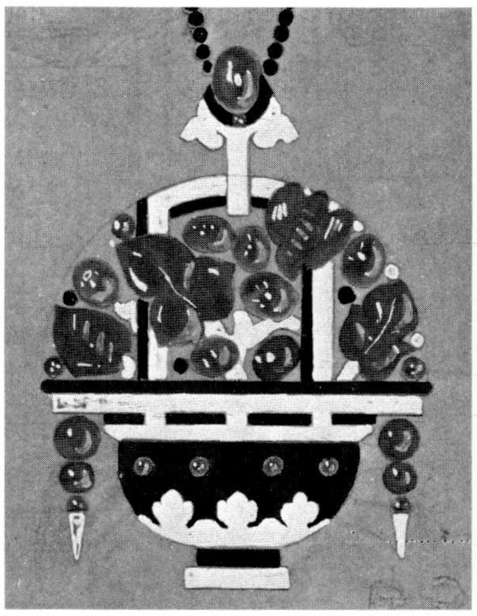

Cartier: gouache study for a pendant in onyx and diamonds decorated with ruby leaves and engraved emeralds, suspended from an onyx and emerald sautoir, *1923.*

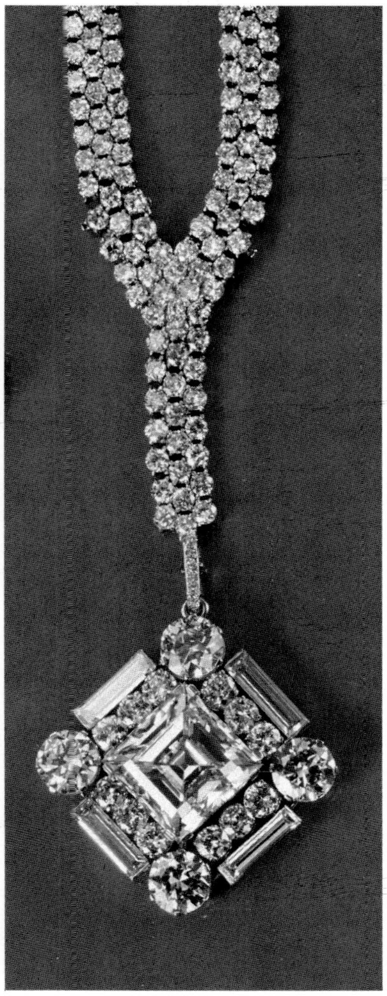

Anonymous: sautoir *consisting of three rows of small diamonds and a pendant decorated with a large square diamond surrounded by baguette-cut and rose-cut diamonds.*

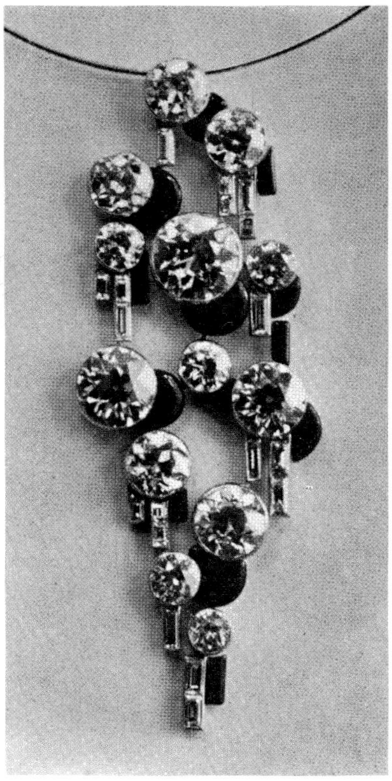

Dusausoy: pendant consisting of a cascade of baguette-cut and rose-cut diamonds and black onyx, presented at the Musée Galliéra Exposition in 1929, reproduced in Art et Décoration.

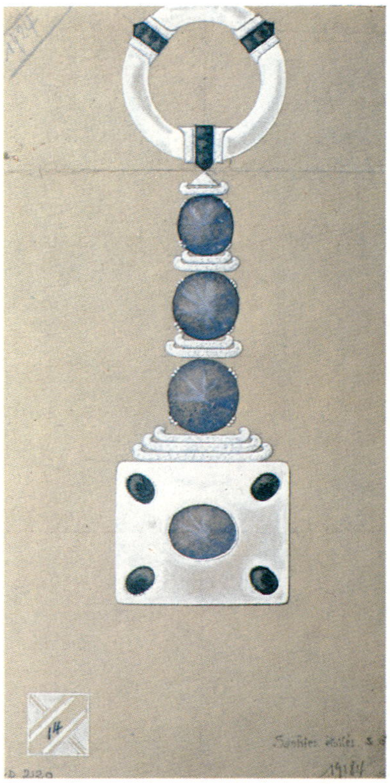

Georges Fouquet: study for a pendant in frosted rock crystal. The centre of the plaque is decorated with a sapphire cabochon and in each corner there is an emerald cabochon, 1924. Photo: Musée des Arts Décoratifs, Paris.

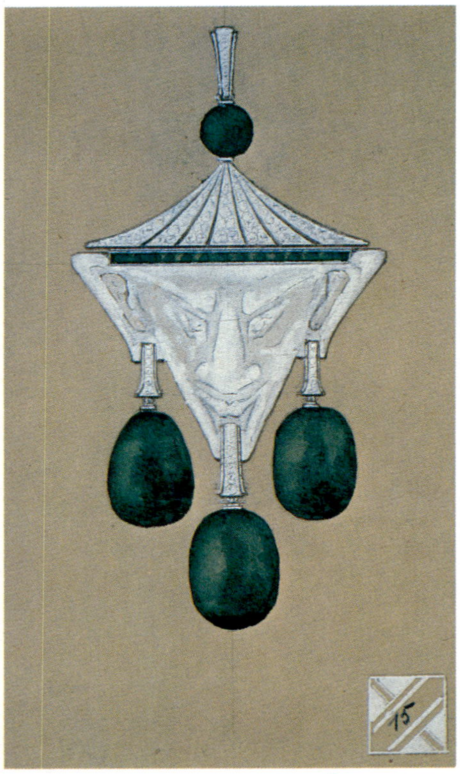

Georges Fouquet: study for a pendant depicting a Chinese mask in frosted rock crystal with emeralds and brilliant-cut diamonds, 1924. Photo: Musée des Arts Décoratifs, Paris.

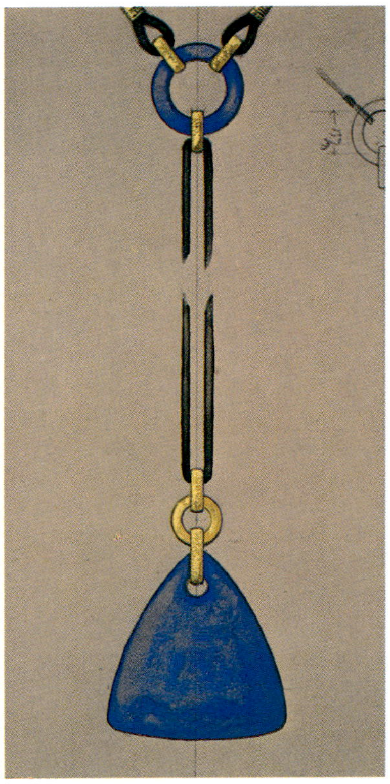

Georges Fouquet: study for a pendant, c. 1925. Photo: Musée des Arts Décoratifs, Paris.

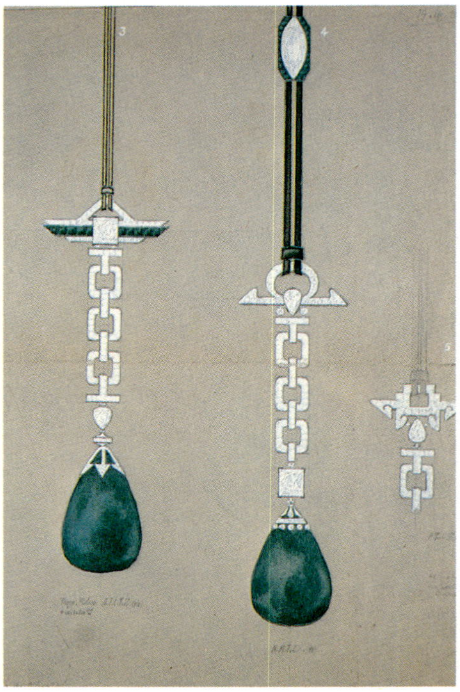

Georges Fouquet: studies for a pendant composed of links of platinum and brilliant-cut diamonds, from which hangs a pear-shaped emerald, 1927. Photo: Musée des Arts Décoratifs, Paris.

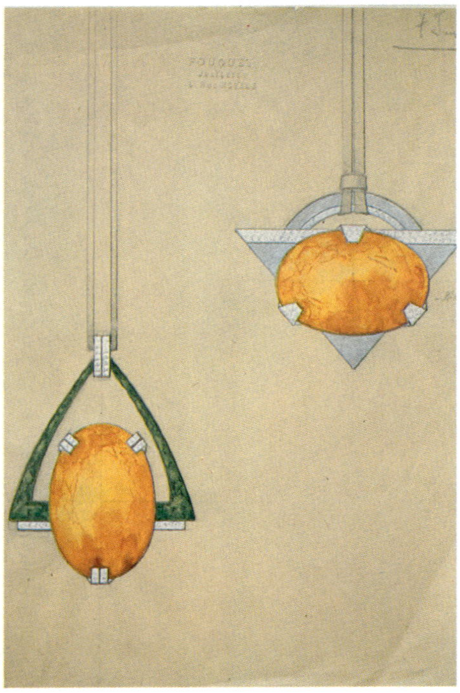

Jean Fouquet: studies for a pendant in grey gold and amber, 1928. Photo: Musée des Arts Décoratifs, Paris.

Cartier: brooch consisting of rubies, diamonds, pearl, onyx and tourmaline. Christie's.

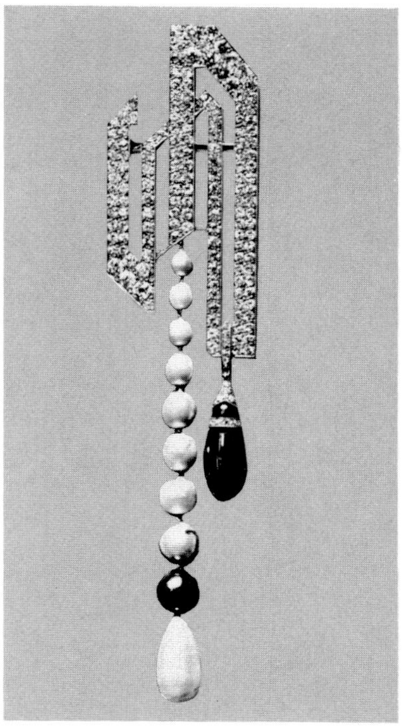

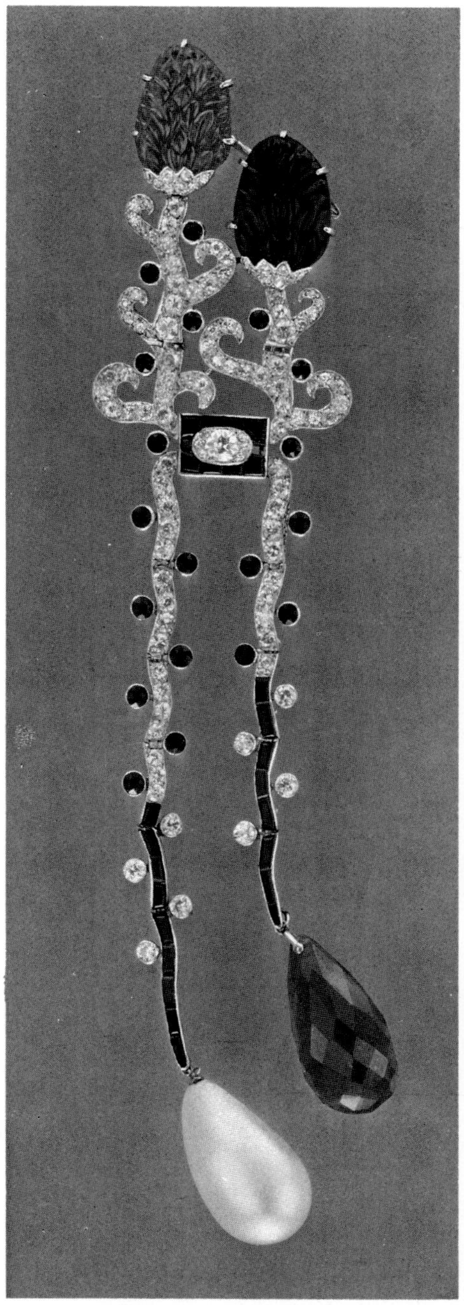

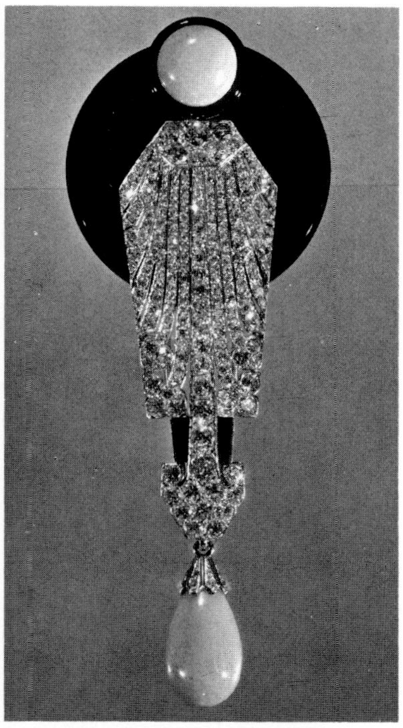

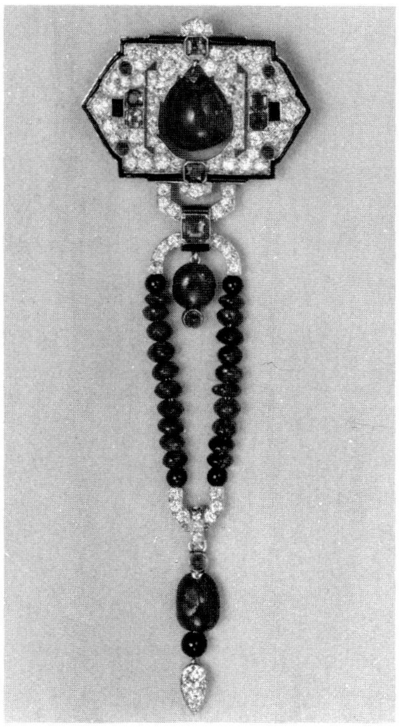

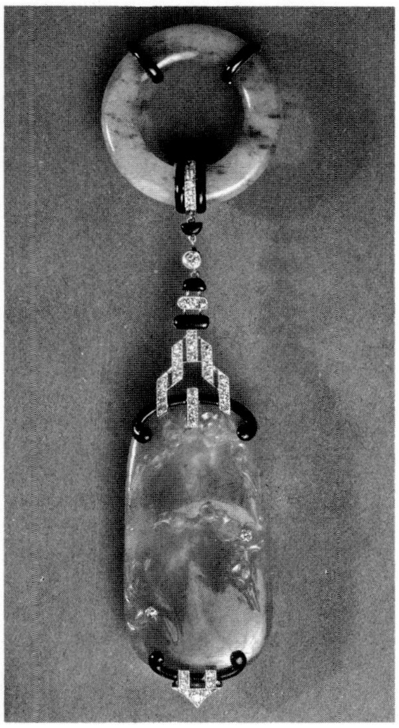

Dusausoy: brooch consisting of diamonds, emeralds and a strand of graduated pearls.

Anonymous: emerald and diamond brooch. Sotheby's, Geneva.

Georges Fouquet: brooch with disc in black onyx, coral cabochon and drop and brilliant-cut diamonds, mounted on platinum, 1924, signed. Private Collection. Photo: T. Heuer.

Georges Fouquet: brooch in engraved jade, brilliant-cut diamonds, platinum, black enamel, 1924, signed. Private Collection. Photo: L. Sully-Jaulmes.

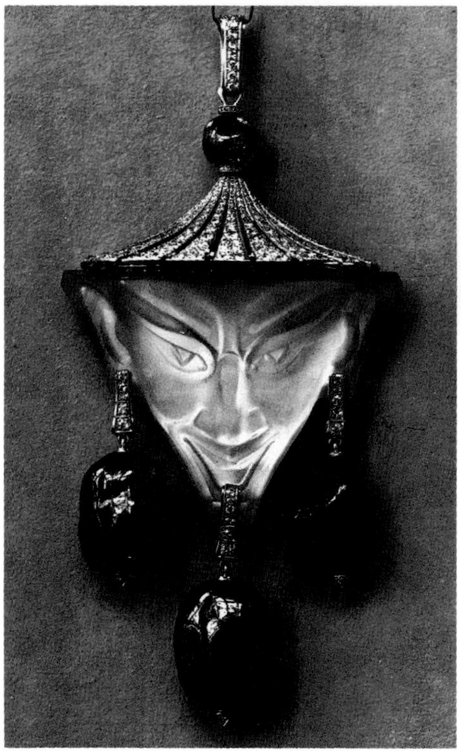

Georges Fouquet: Chinese mask pendant in frosted rock crystal, emeralds and brilliant-cut diamonds, 1924–25. Photo: Musée des Arts Décoratifs, Paris.

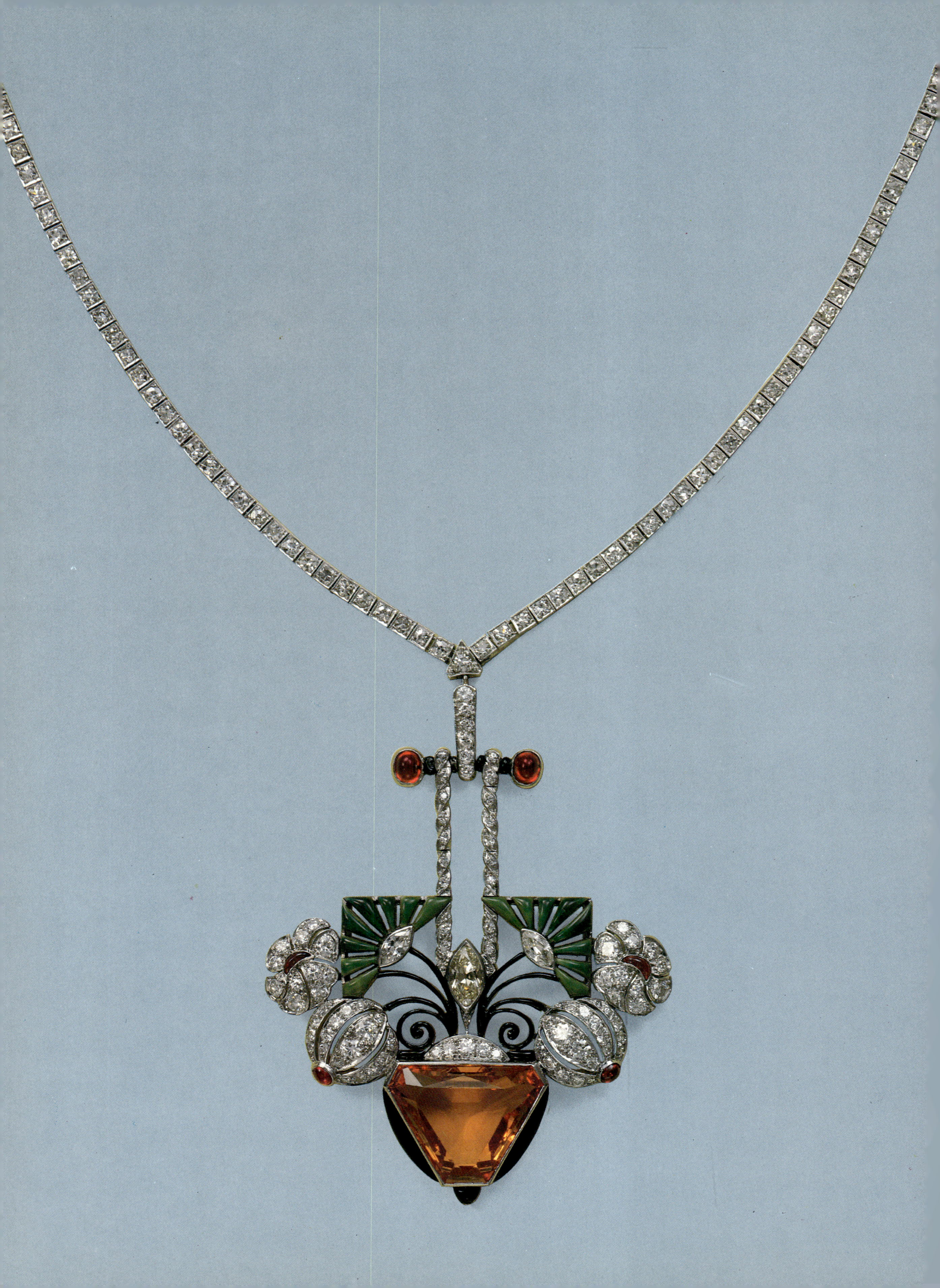

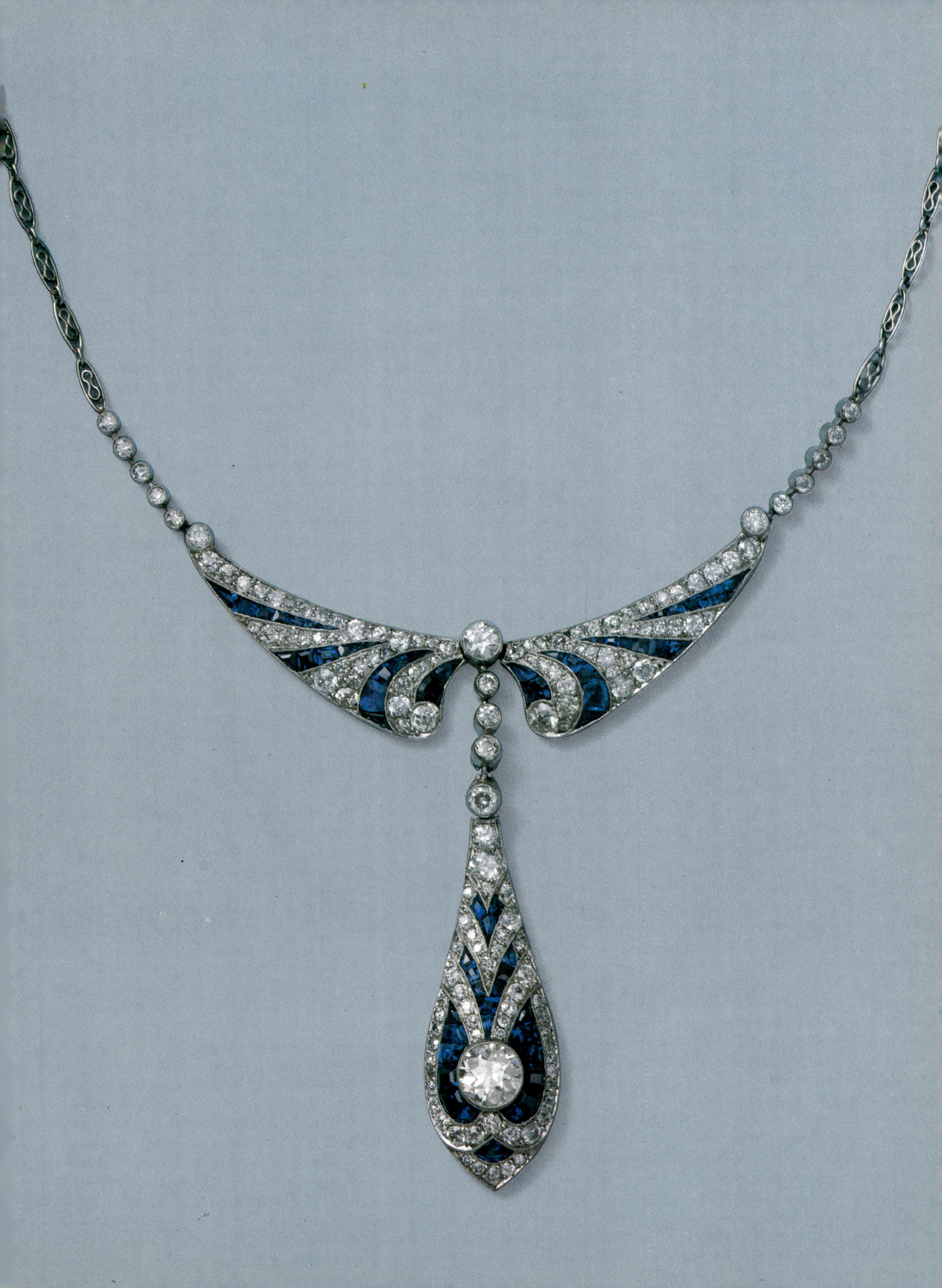

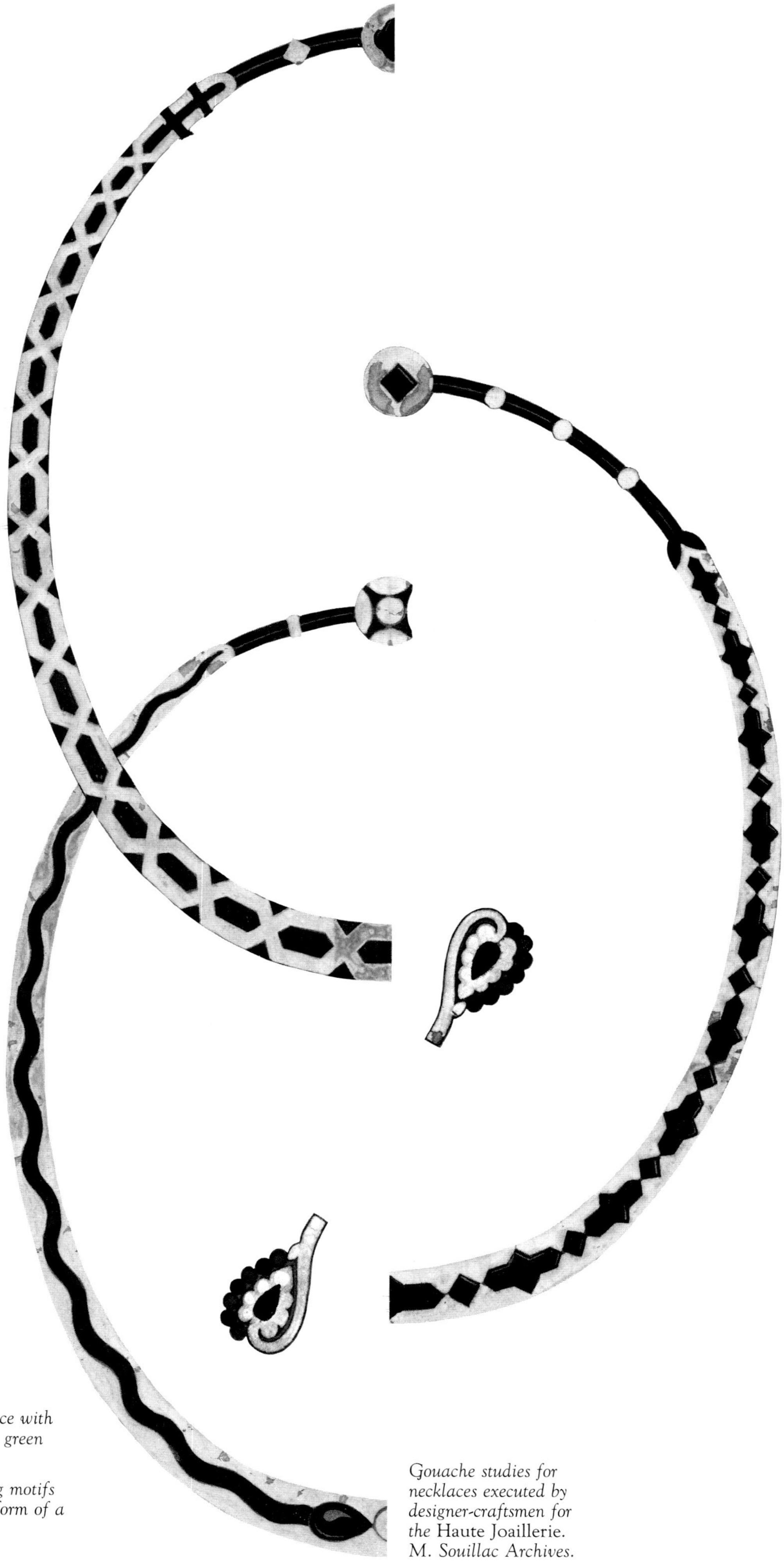

Preceding pages: Anonymous: necklace with pendant, in diamonds, rubies, topaz, green and black enamel. Christie's.

Van C.J. Begger: necklace with wing motifs from which hangs a pendant in the form of a drop in round diamonds and calibré *sapphires, Holland. Sotheby's.*

Gouache studies for necklaces executed by designer-craftsmen for the Haute Joaillerie. *M. Souillac Archives.*

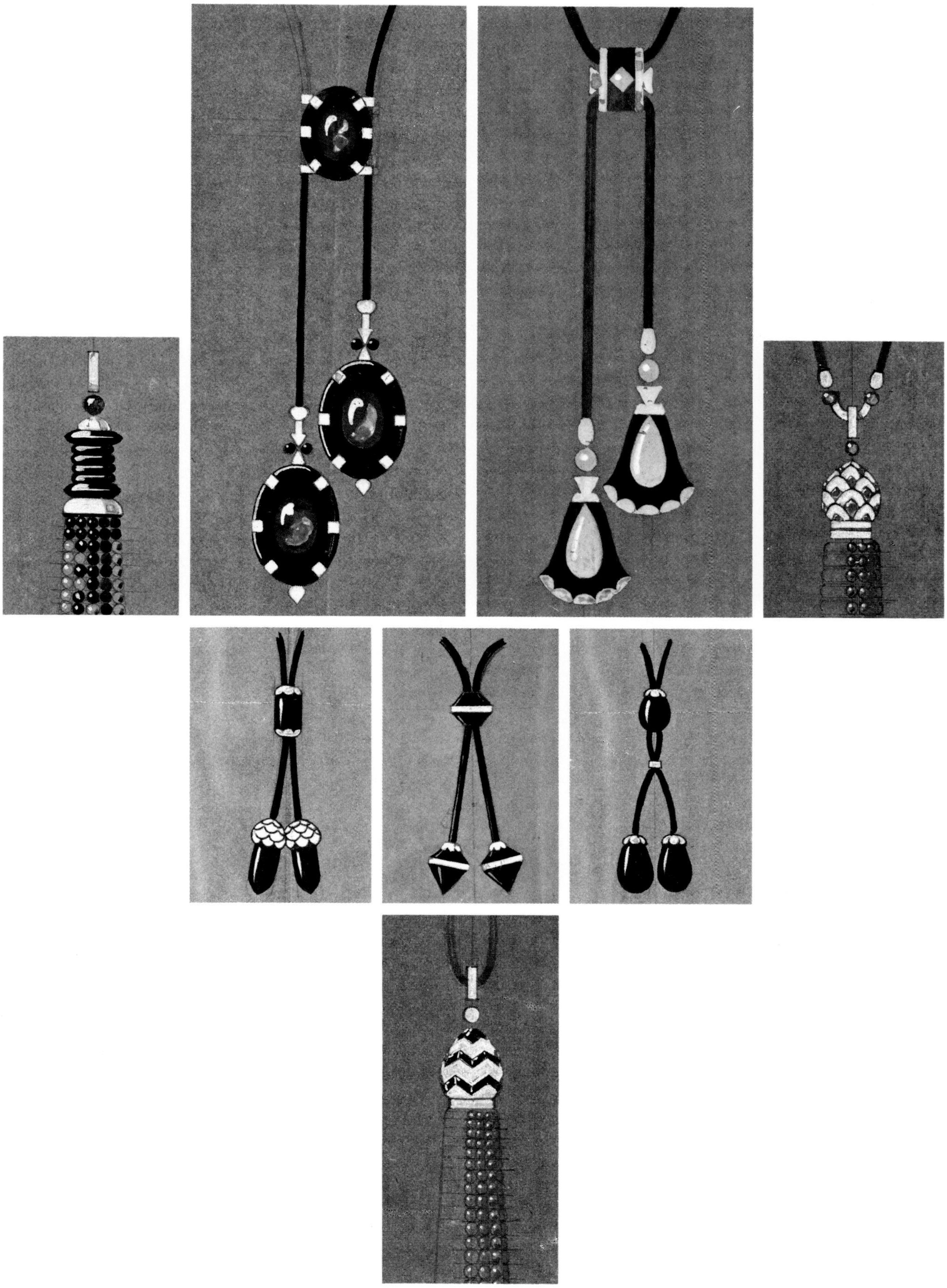

Gouache studies for pendants in the form of tassels executed by designer-craftsmen for the Haute Joaillerie.

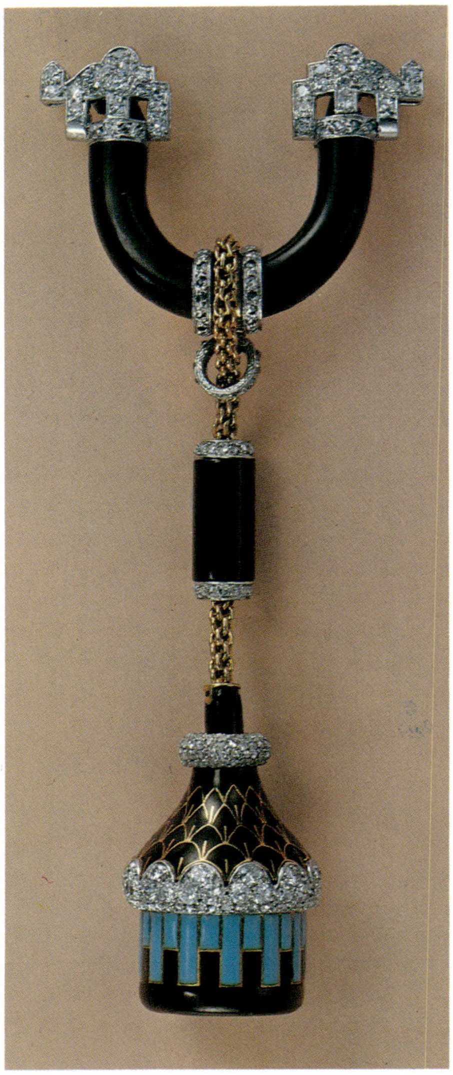

Cartier: pendant-watch in onyx, round diamonds, turquoise and black enamel. Christie's, Geneva.

Yard: pendant-watch in diamonds and onyx; watchcase in round diamonds and onyx; winder decorated with a sapphire cabochon, signed.

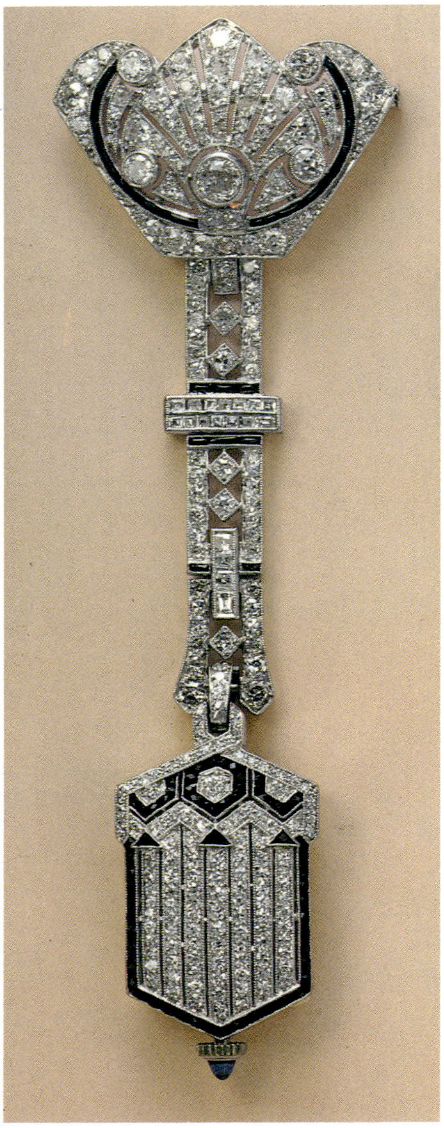

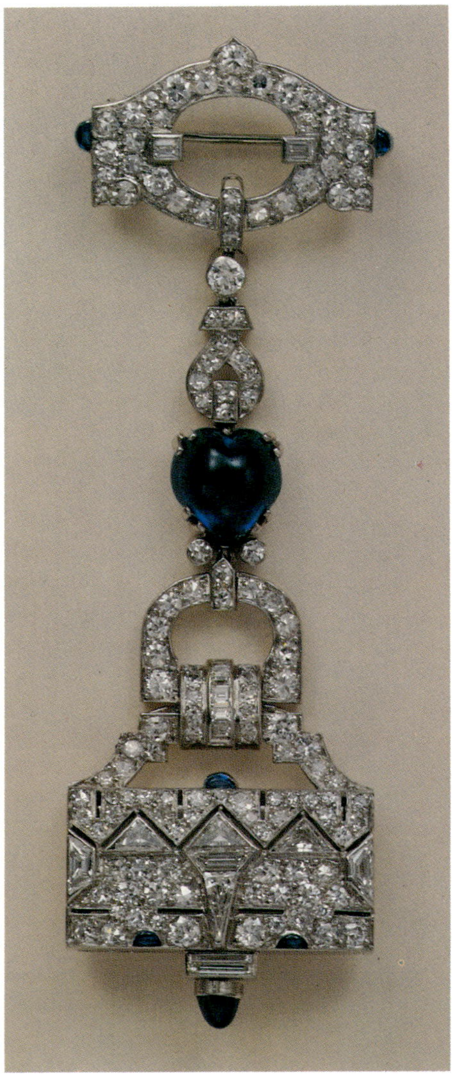

Anonymous: pendant-watch consisting of a watchcase decorated with round and fantaisie-cut diamonds attached to a ring, which serves as a fastening, by a flexible diamond chain decorated with a heart-shaped sapphire cabochon.

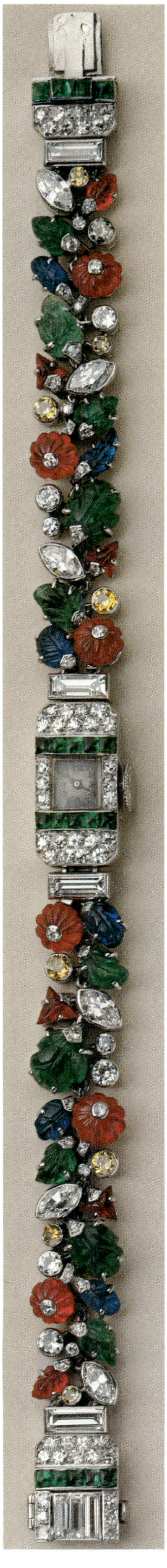

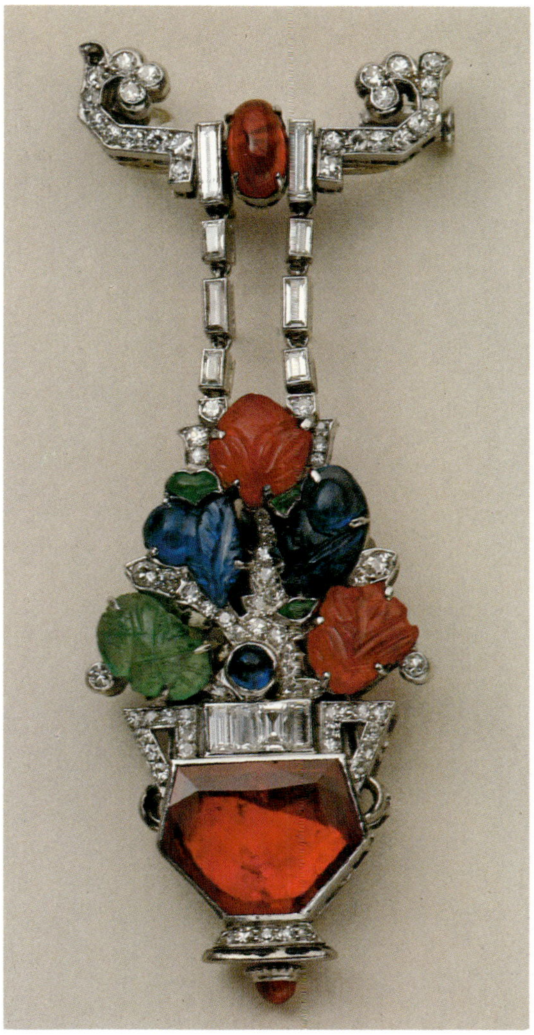

Ostertag: watch-bracelet in engraved rubies, sapphires and emeralds, and diamonds, mounted on platinum, c. 1930.

Mauboussin: pendant-watch in the form of a vase of flowers, with engraved rubies, sapphires and emeralds, round and baguette diamonds, c. 1930.

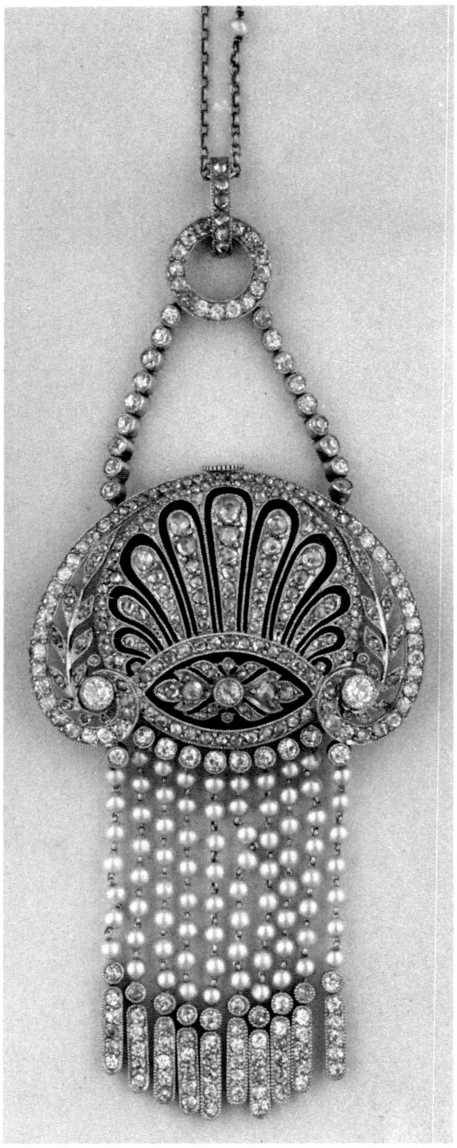

Chaumet: pendant-watch in rose-cut diamonds and blue enamel; fringe of cultured pearls and diamonds, c. 1920. Sotheby's, Geneva.

Cartier: seal-watch mounted in the French Regency (1715–23) style in jade, black enamel, diamonds, onyx, rubies and emerald cabochons; attachment consisting of a pear-shaped diamond on a cushion set with rose-cut diamonds and calibré *rubies, 1924. Cartier Archives.*

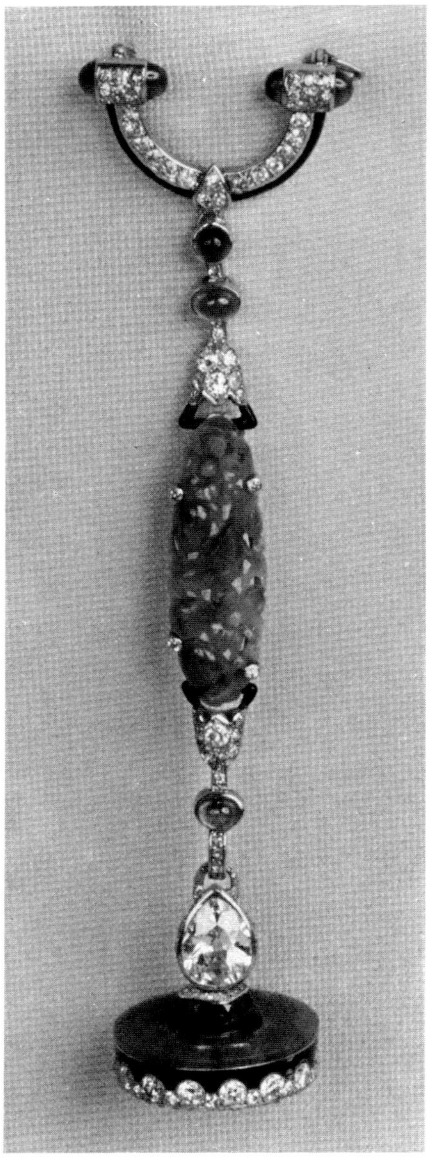

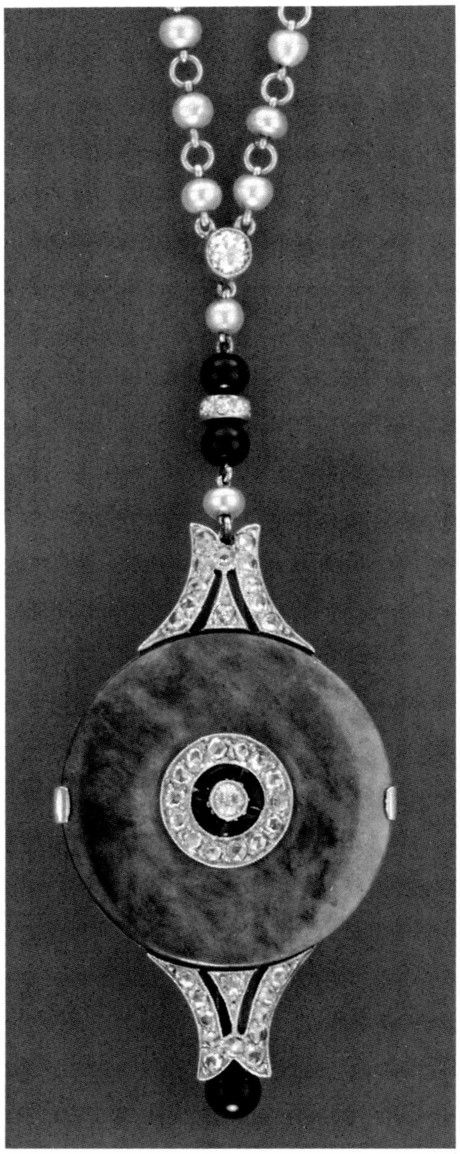

Tiffany: pendant-watch consisting of a jade disc decorated at the centre with onyx and round, rose-cut diamonds, suspended from a chain of pearls, onyx beads and diamond rondelles; winder in the form of an onyx bead. Christie's, New York.

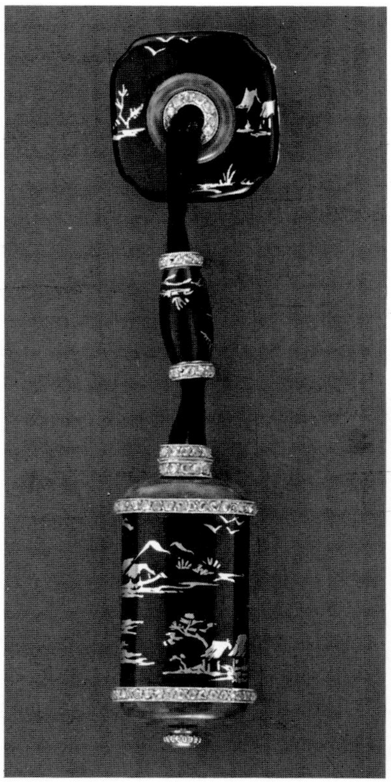

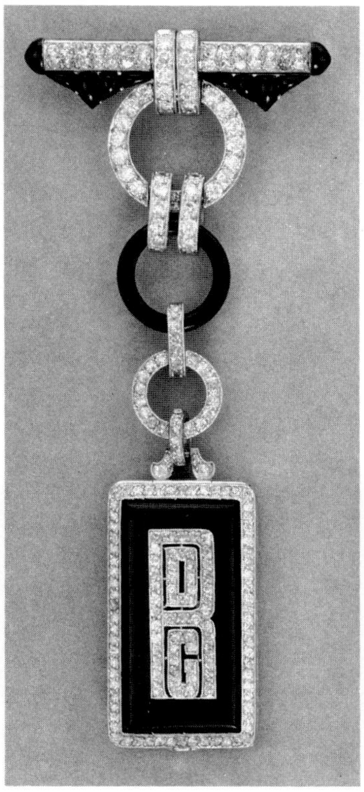

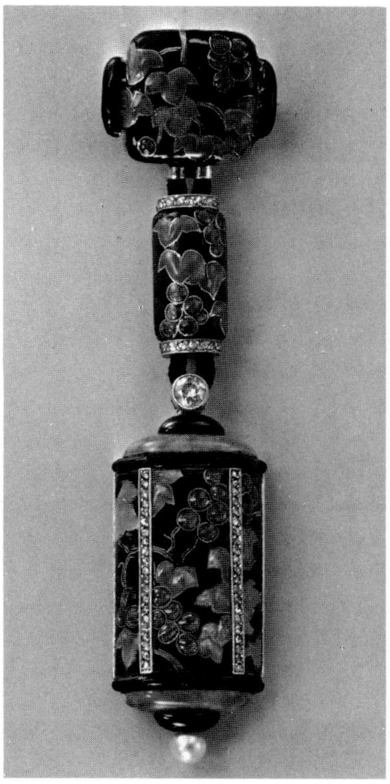

Anonymous: brooch-pendant in diamonds and black onyx, with the monogram DGR, mounted on platinum. Christie's, New York.

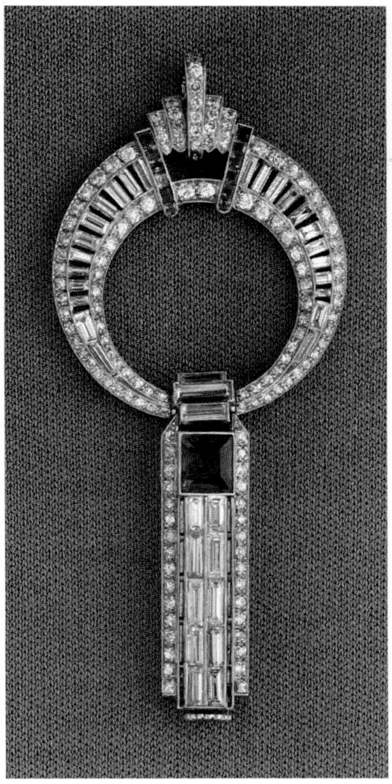

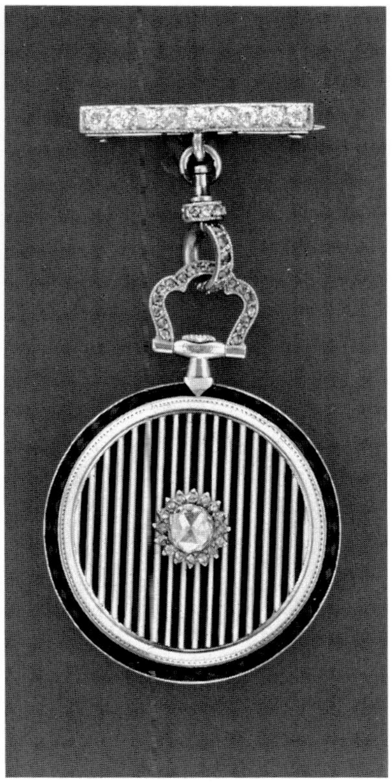

Verger: pendant-watch (back view), cylindrical, oval watchcase decorated with a Chinese-style landscape in black and yellow enamel, ornamental border of diamonds and green enamel imitating jade; movement by Vacheron.

Anonymous: pendant-watch in emeralds and round and baguette diamonds. Sotheby's.

Lacloche: pendant-watch in black enamel with leaf motifs in green enamel, berries in blue enamel, diamonds and a pearl winder signed. Christie's, Geneva.

Cartier: pendant-watch with a circular watchcase, striped with white and black enamel and with a black onyx border and a rose-cut diamond at the centre. Christie's.

Tavanne: slide-action pocket watch in red and black enamel. M. Souillac Collection. Photo: J.B. Rouault.

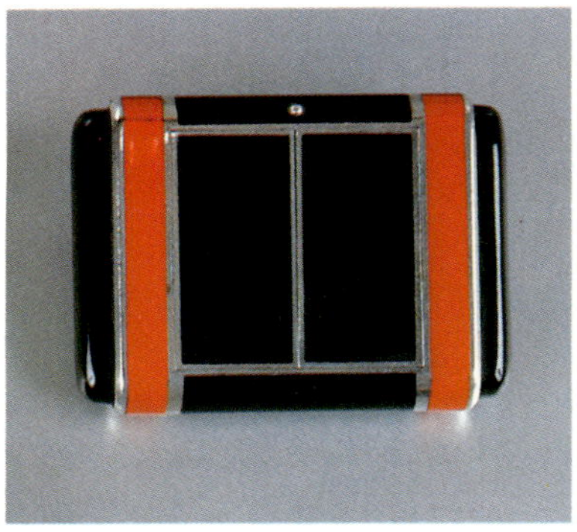

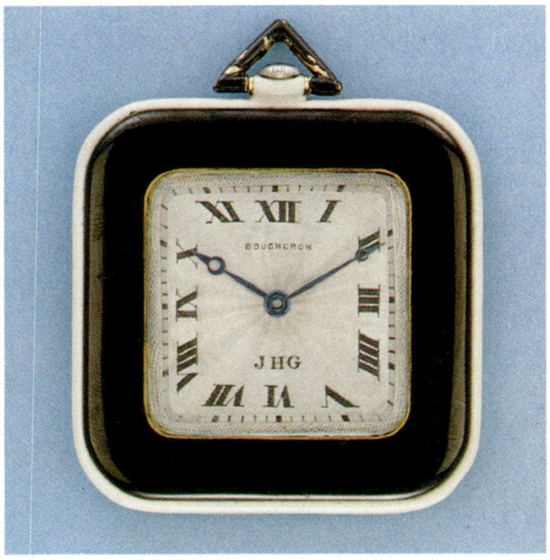

Tonnel: slide-action pocket watch in red and black enamel. M. Souillac Collection. Photo: J.B. Rouault.

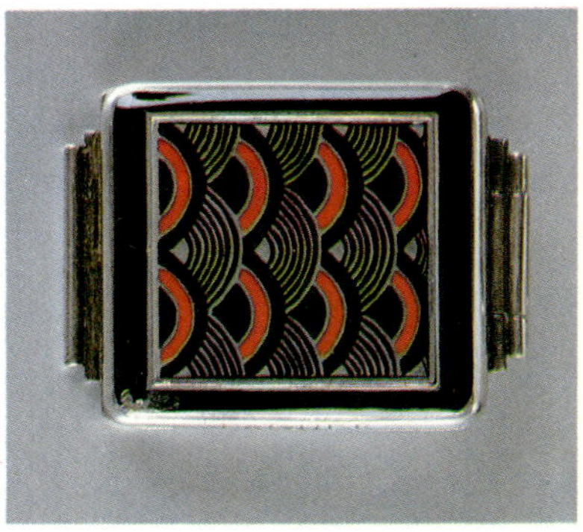

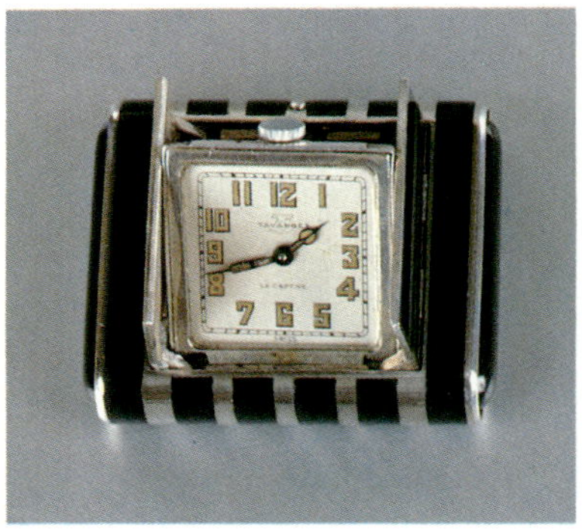

Tavanne: slide-action pocket watch in silver and black enamel. M. Souillac Collection. Photo: J.B. Rouault.

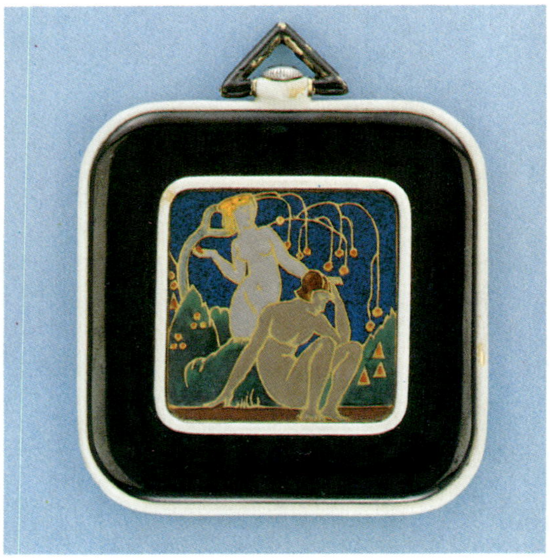

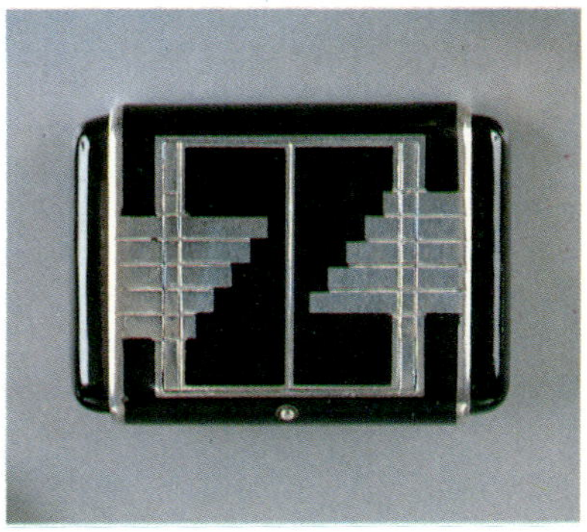

Tavanne: slide-action pocket watch in silver and black enamel. M. Souillac Collection. Photo: J.B. Rouault.

Boucheron: pocket watch (face and back) in black and white enamel and coloured cloisonné *enamel representing Adam and Eve in the Garden of Eden, signed. Christie's, New York.*

Facing page: Anonymous: pendant-watch in gold and blue and white enamel. H.12 cm. M. Souillac Collection. Photo: J.B. Rouault.

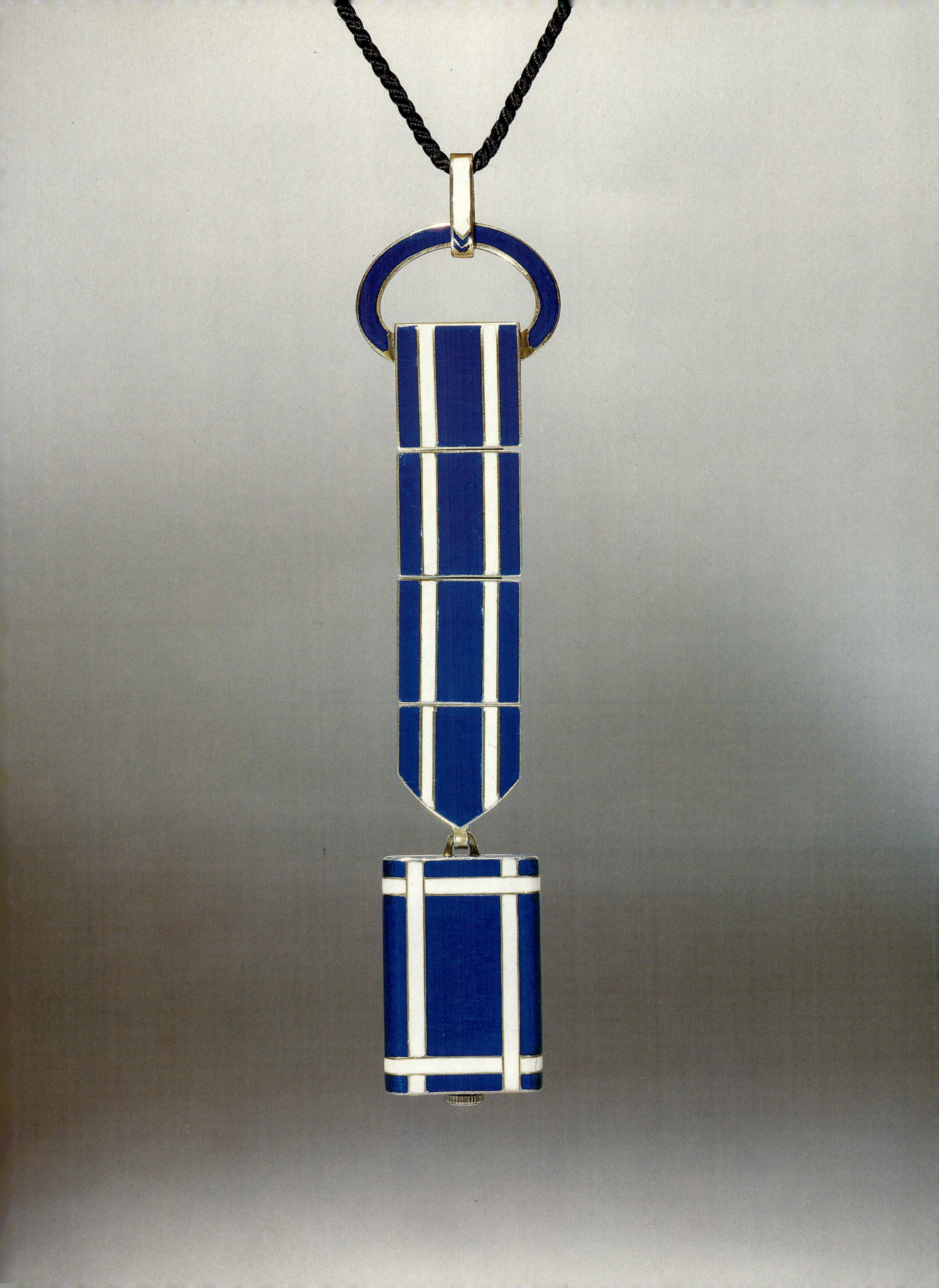

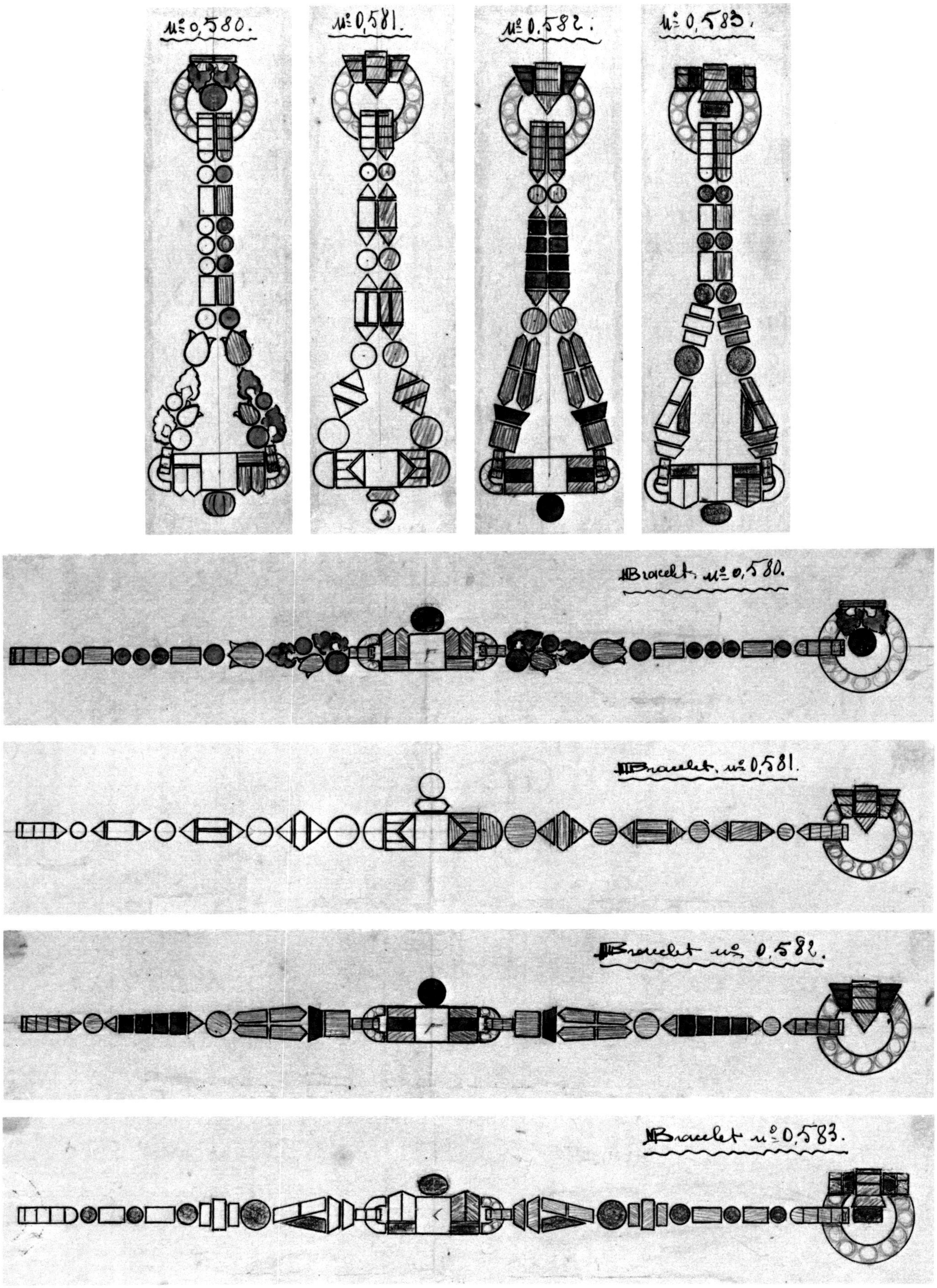

Gouache studies for watch-bracelets designed to be worn also as pendant-watches, executed by designer-craftsmen for the Haute Joaillerie. *Danenberg Collection.*

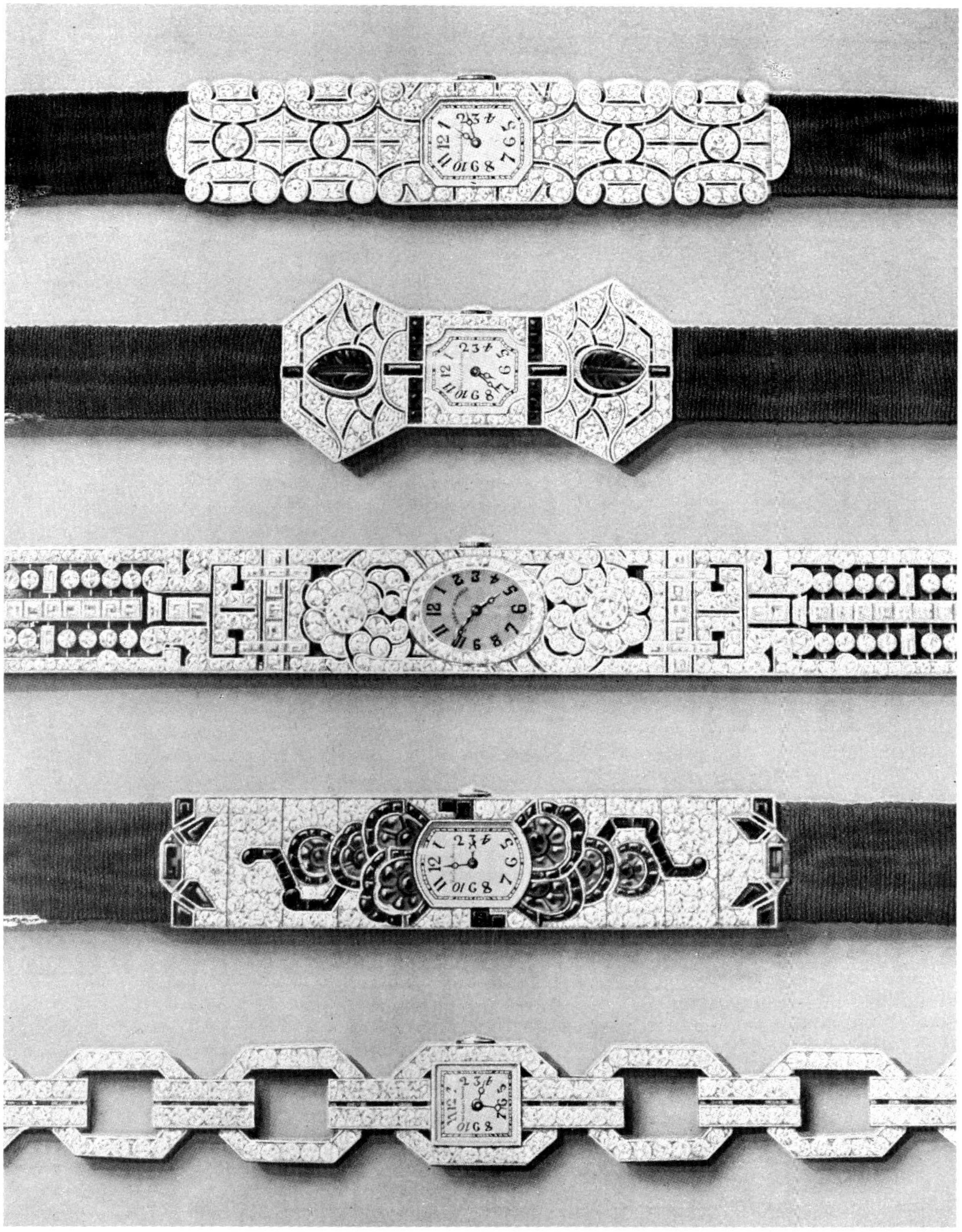

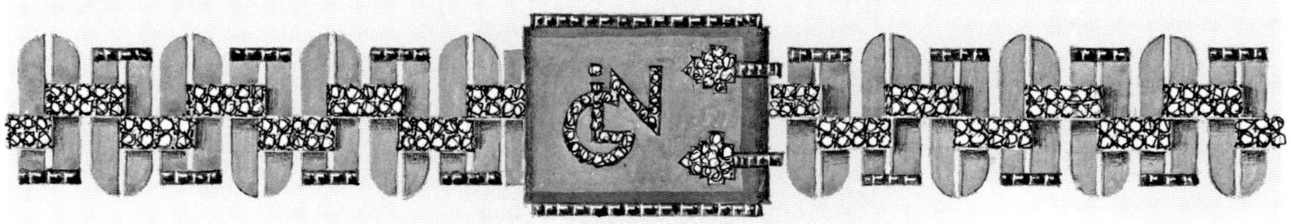

Van Cleef & Arpels: page from a watch-bracelet catalogue, watchcases decorated with diamonds and coloured stones, the straps made of diamonds or moiré silk, c. 1925. *Van Cleef & Arpels Archives.*

Mauboussin: gouache study for a watch-bracelet in platinum, diamonds and rubies, the watchcase hidden; bears a monogram. Mauboussin Archives.

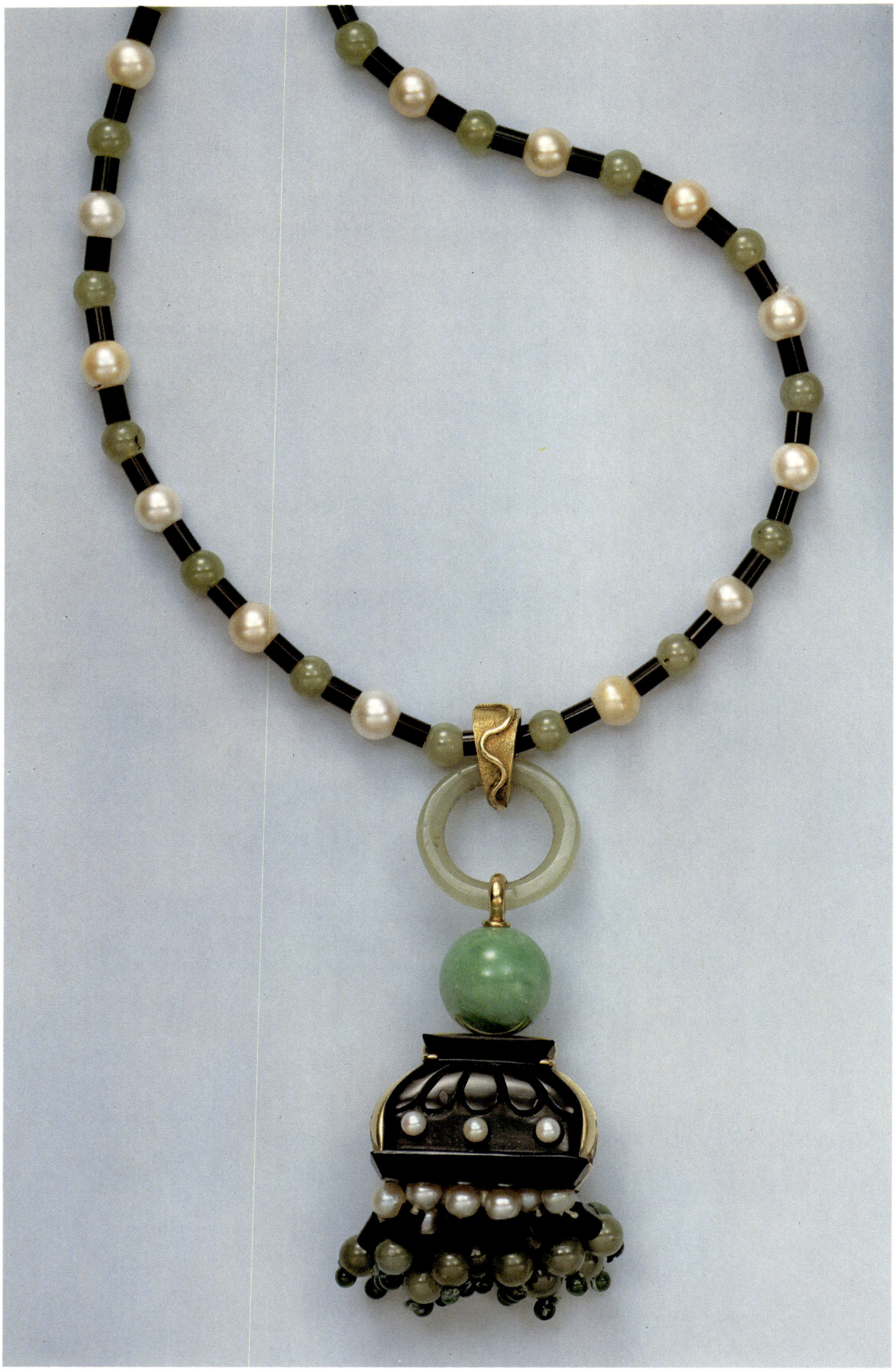

Cartier: sautoir and tassel pendant in jade, pearls and black onyx, signed. Christie's, Geneva.

Facing page: Lalique: necklace in glass and gold. Scarabs composed of moulded blue glass plaques alternate with plaques bearing a design of branches, mounted in gold, c. 1925. Sotheby's, Monte Carlo.

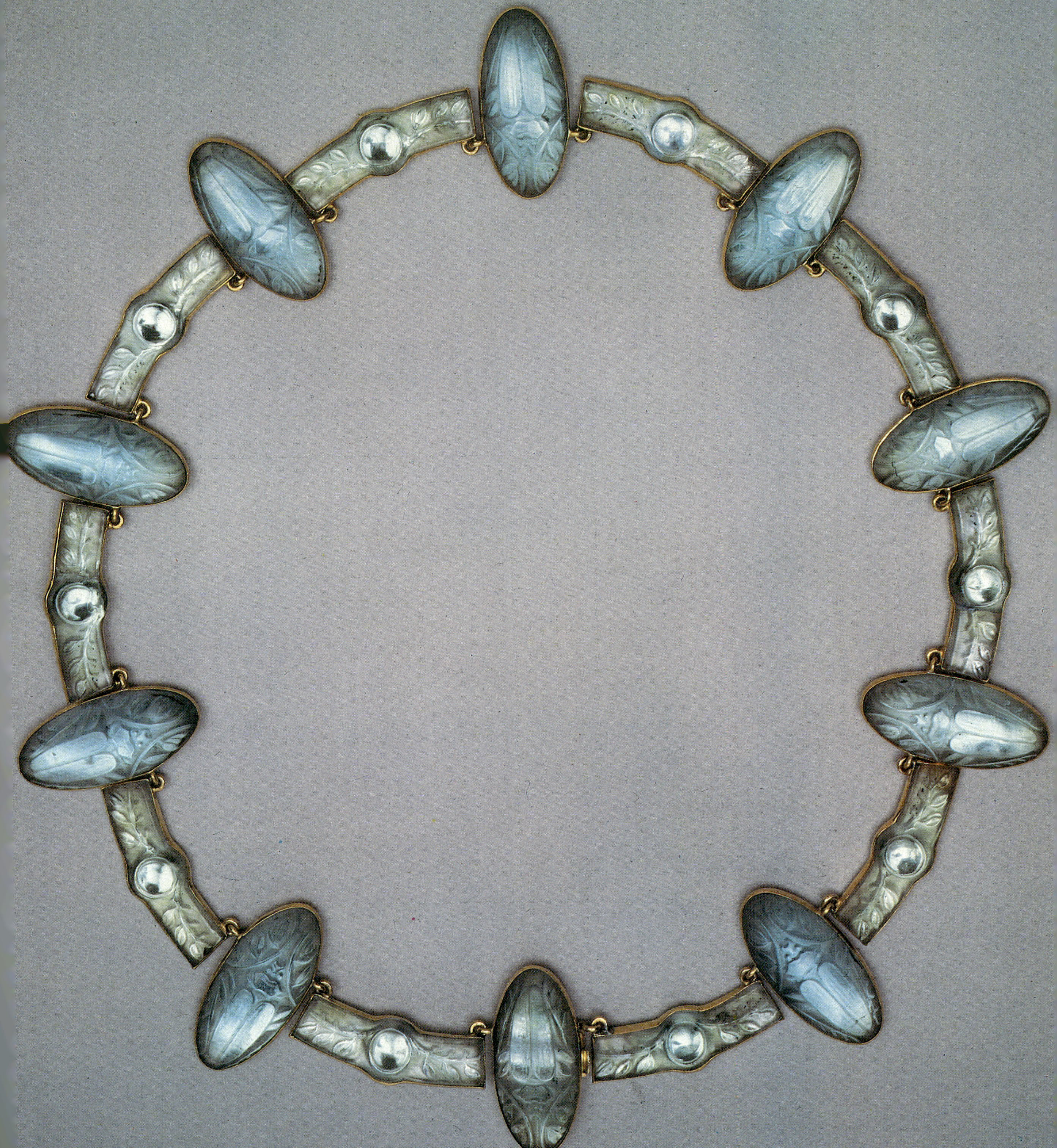

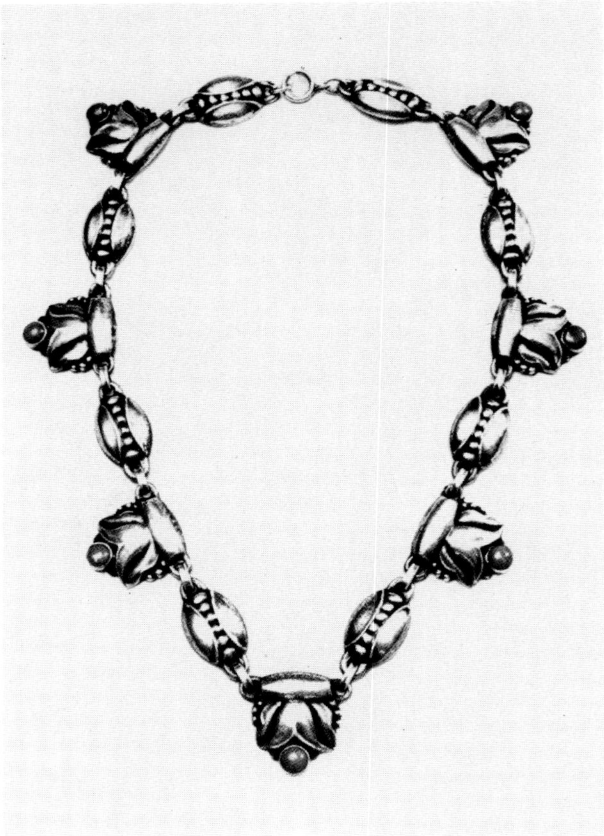

Georg Jensen: silver necklace, c. 1930.

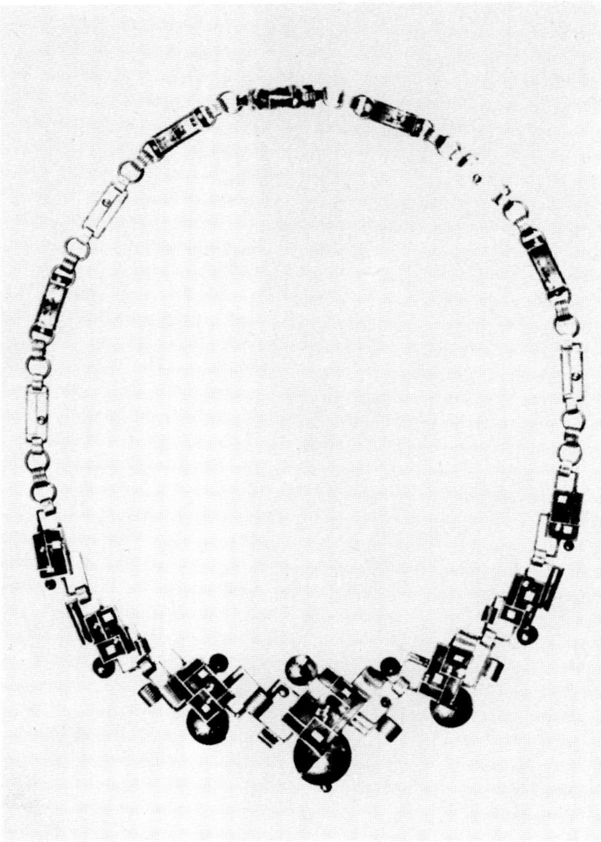

Theo Ortmann: silver necklace, c. 1930. Stedelijk Museum, Amsterdam.

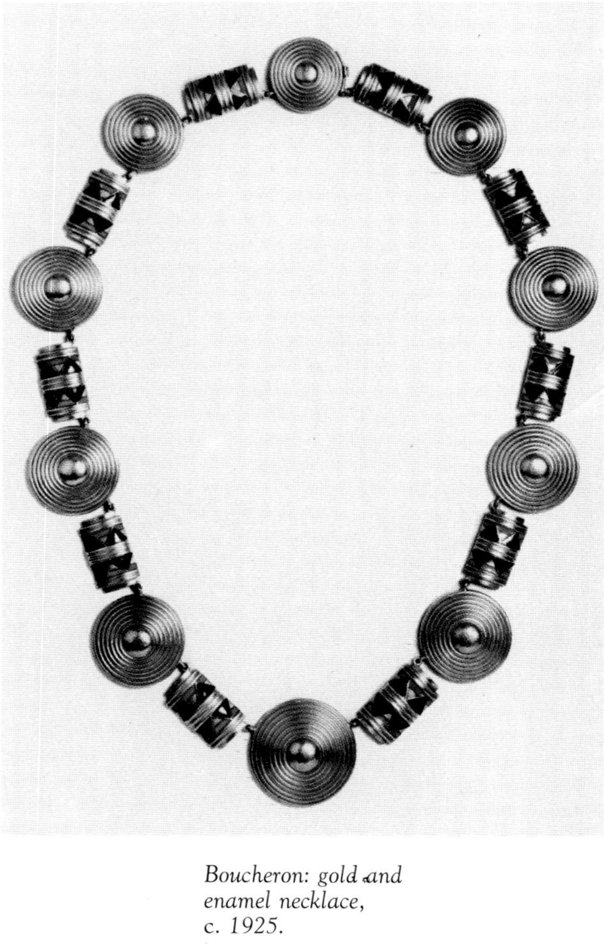

Boucheron: gold and enamel necklace, c. 1925.

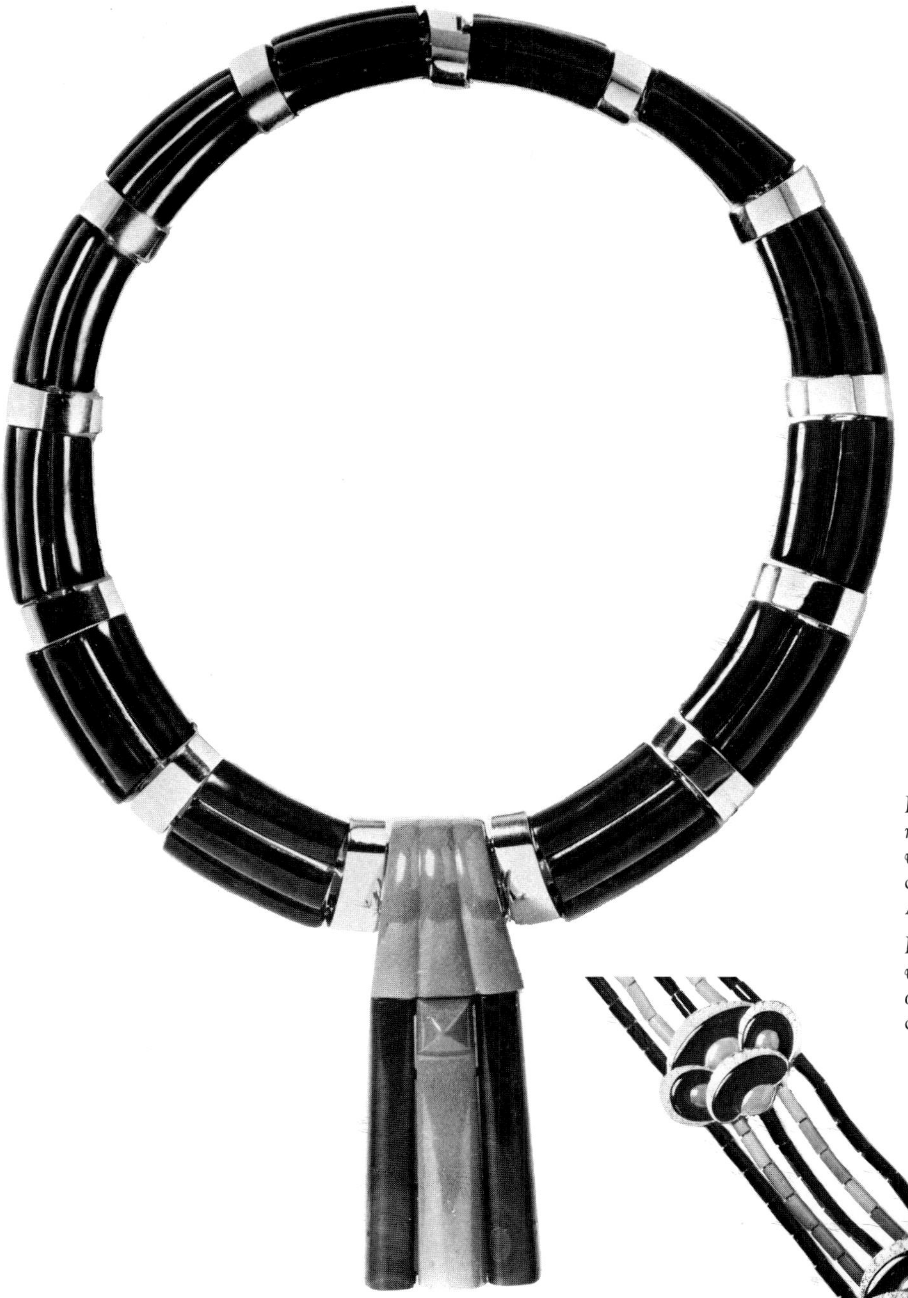

Boucheron: coral and malachite necklace with gold links, c. 1925. Boucheron Archives.

Boucheron: necklace with pendant in coral, onyx and diamonds, c. 1927.

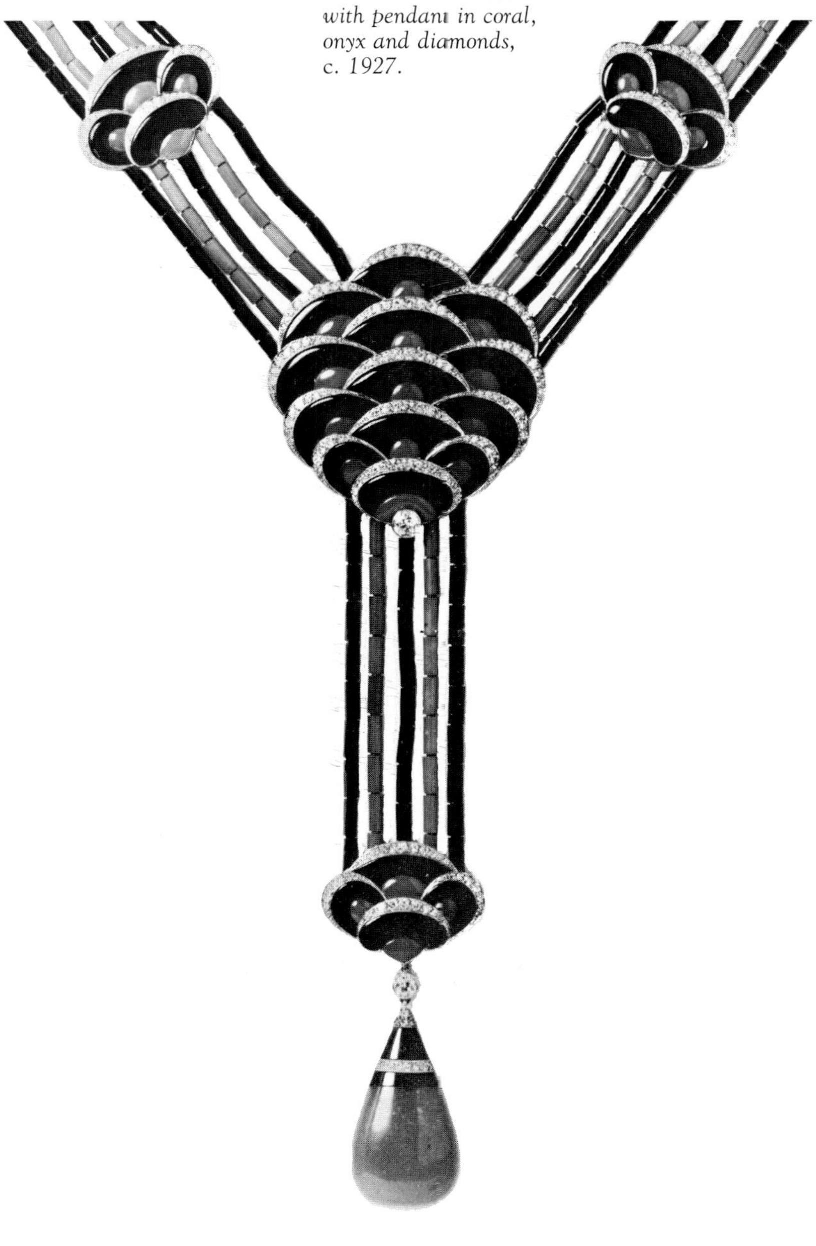

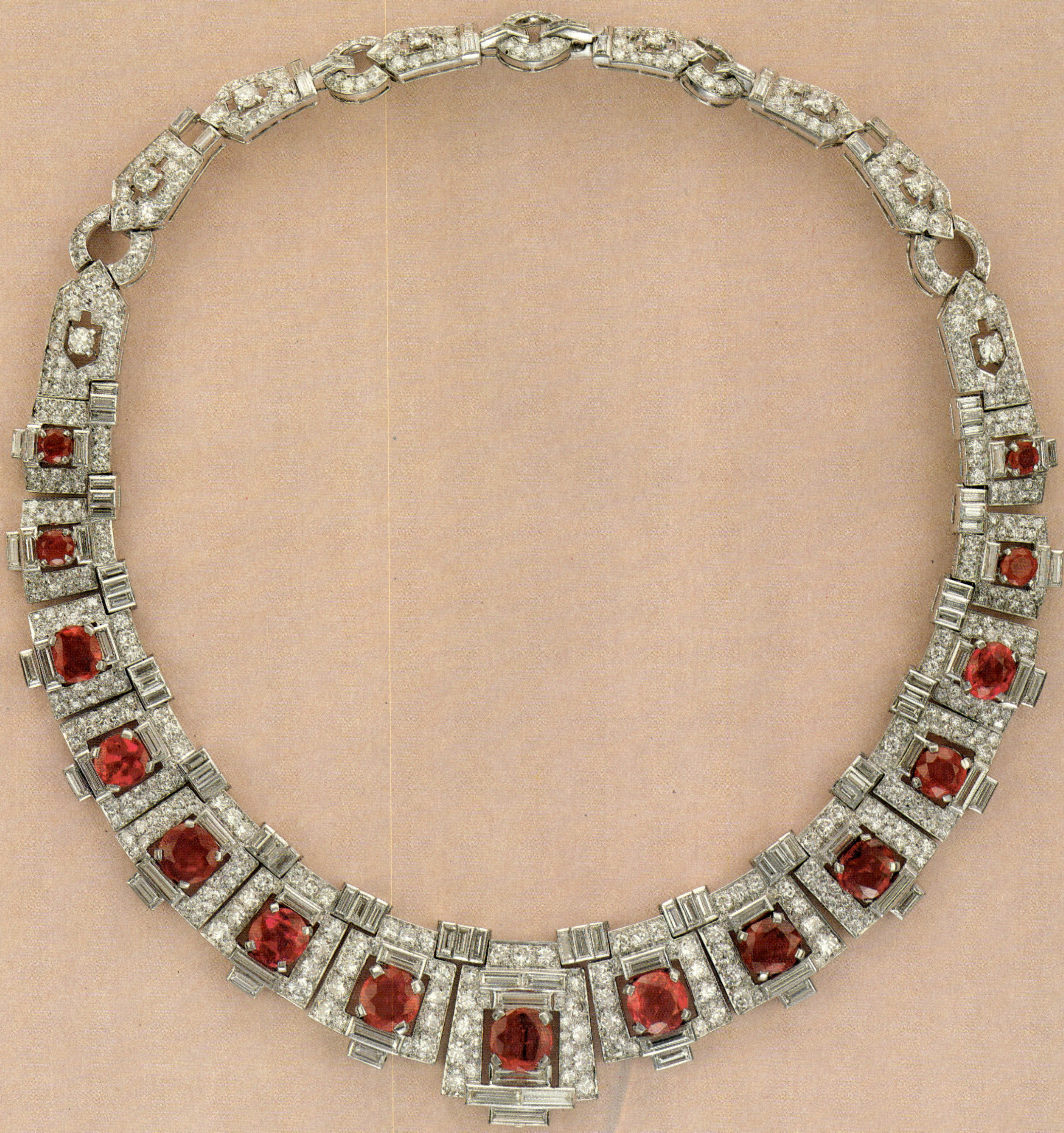

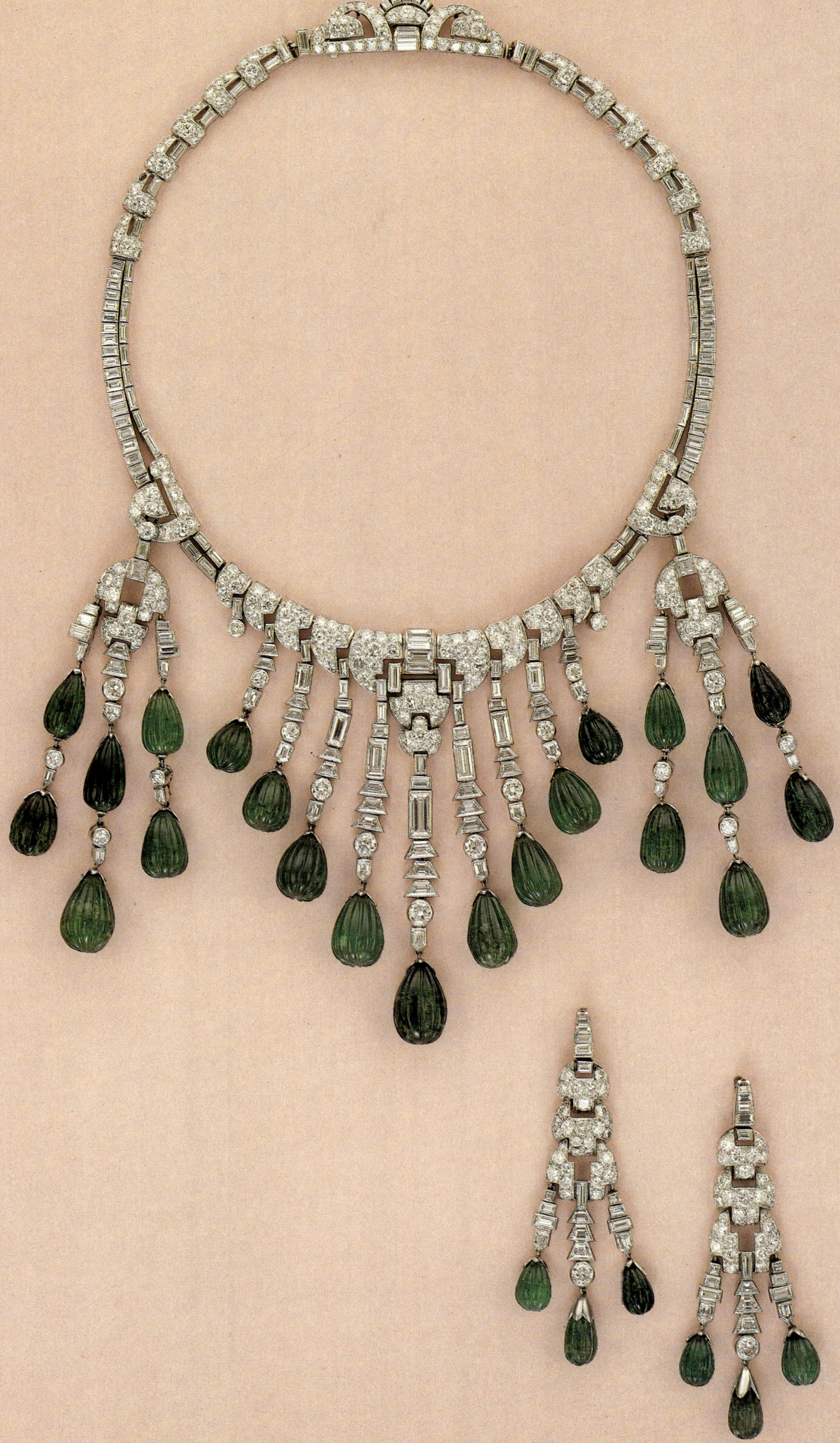

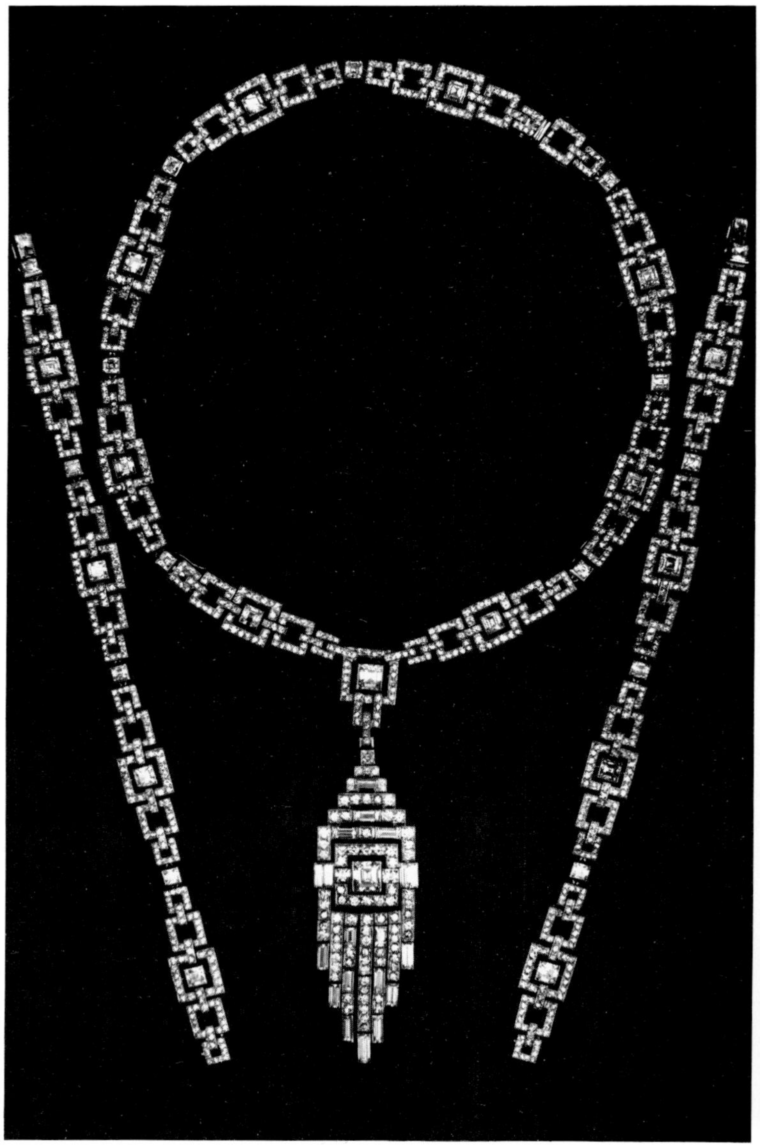

Anonymous: diamond chaîne d'huissier *(chain of office), which can be transformed into a necklace and a pair of bracelets.* M. *Souillac Collection.*

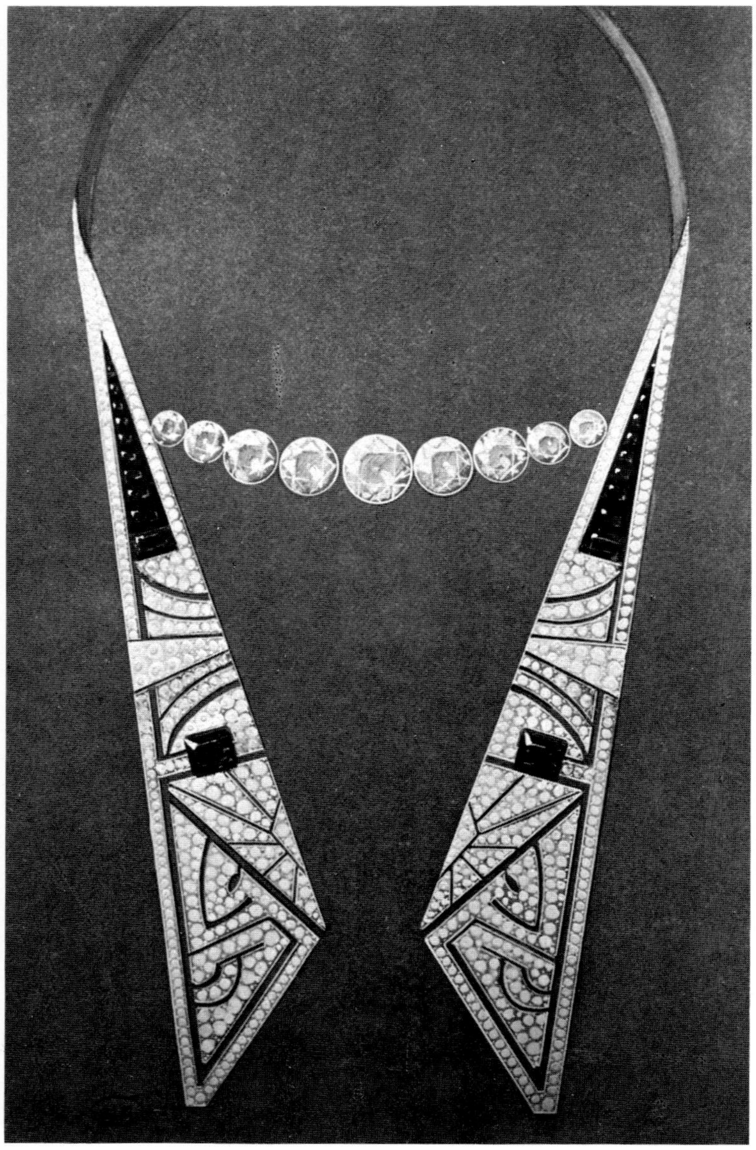

Dusausoy: study for a necklace in diamonds, emeralds and rubies, mounted on platinum.

Preceding pages: Cartier: diamond and ruby necklace, mounted on platinum, signed. Christie's, New York.

Ostertag: necklace and girandole *earrings in diamonds and engraved emeralds. The lateral 'chandelier' motifs of the necklace can be replaced by the pendant earrings, signed. Christie's, New York.*

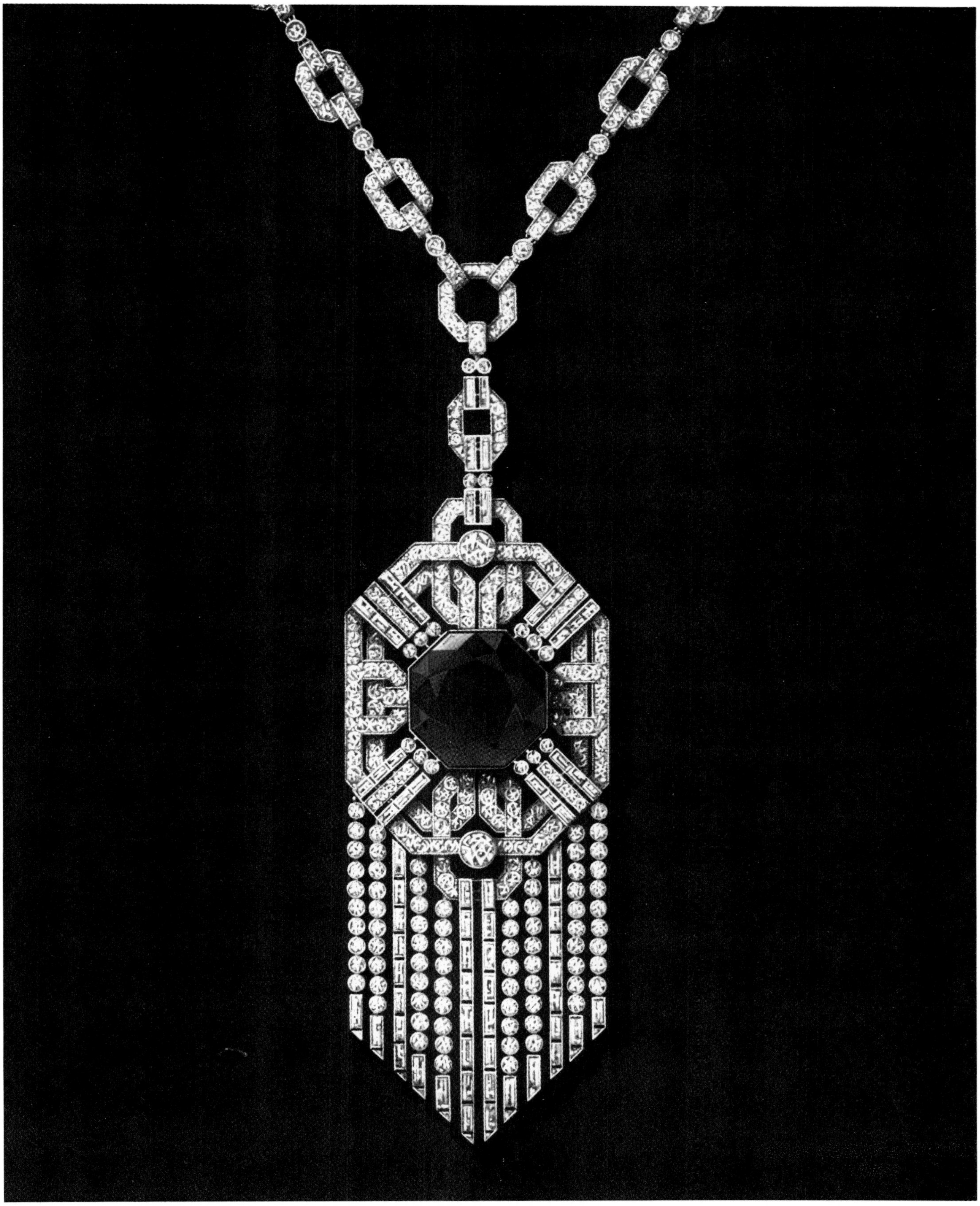

Van Cleef & Arpels: diamond chain and pendant with geometric motifs and fringes of round and baguette diamonds, decorated at the centre with an octagonal, faceted emerald, 1925. Van Cleef & Arpels Archives.

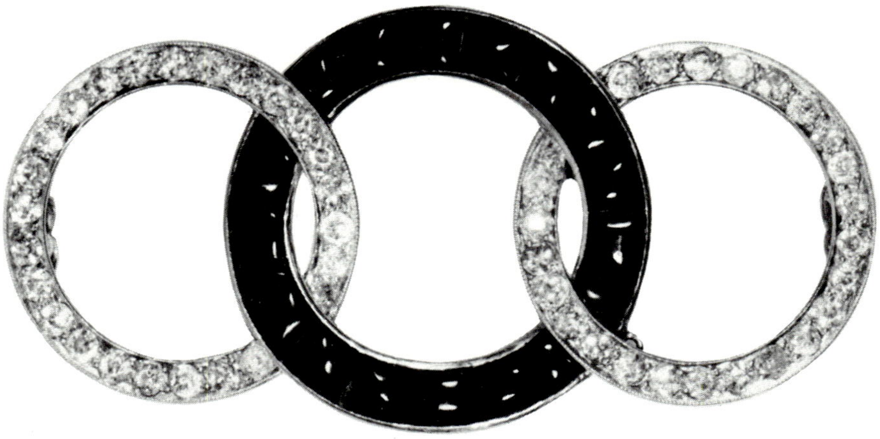

Jean Fouquet: platinum, diamond and jet brooch, c. 1930, signed. Sotheby's.

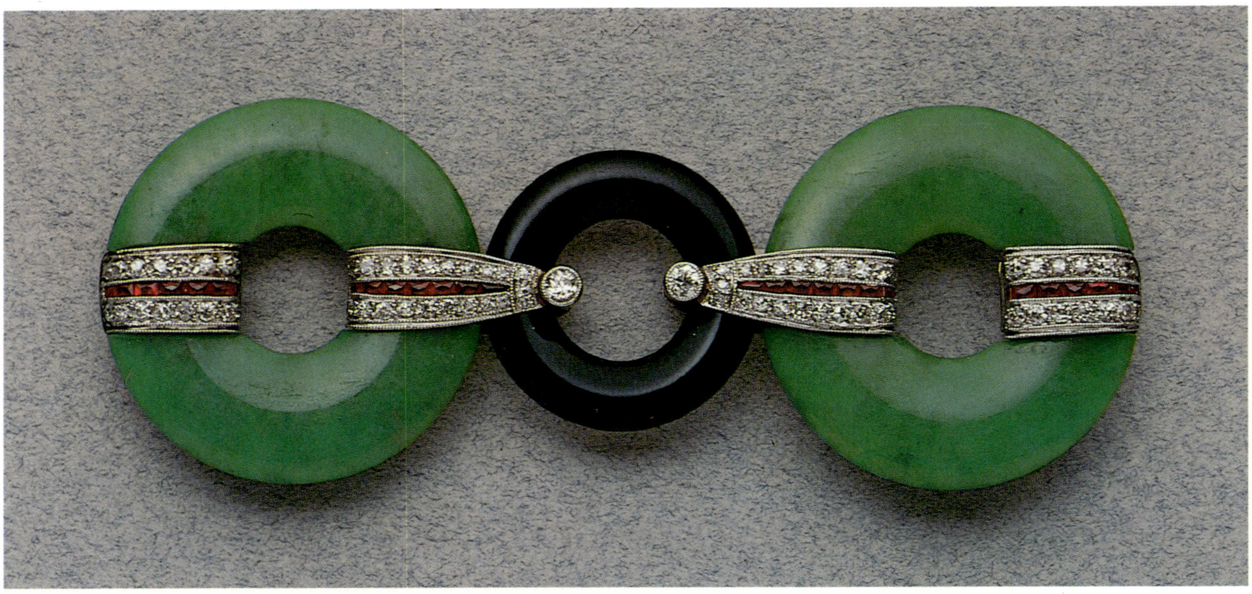

Anonymous: brooch consisting of jade and onyx discs, calibré *rubies, diamonds and platinum, c. 1925. USA.*

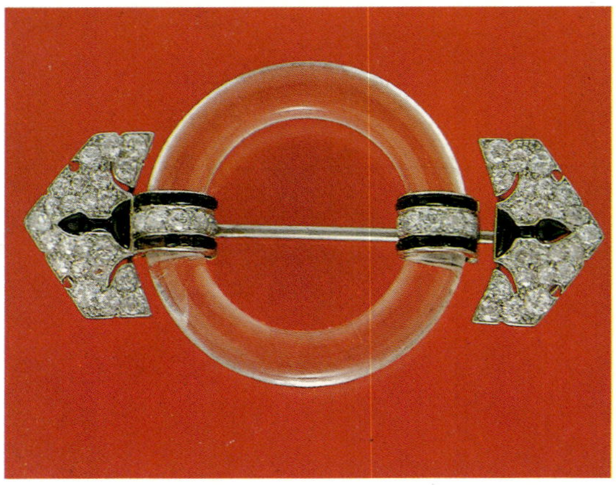

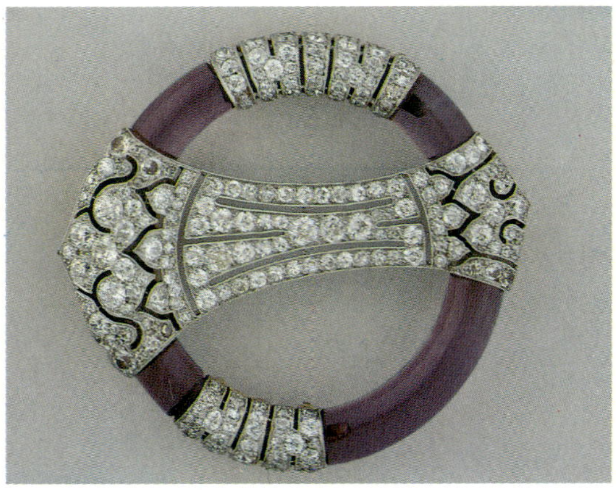

Anonymous: brooch consisting of a rock crystal ring, diamonds and baguettes of calibré onyx, mounted on platinum and white gold. Christie's, New York.

Chaumet: amethyst and diamond brooch.

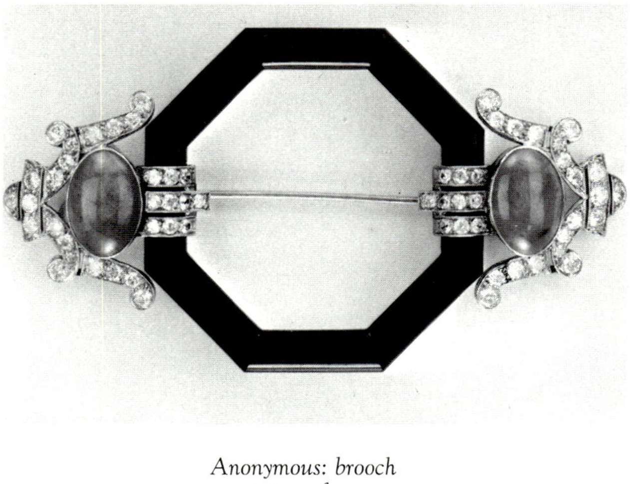

Anonymous: brooch consisting of an onyx ring decorated on both sides with a diamond and platinum motif surrounding an oval jade cabochon. Christie's.

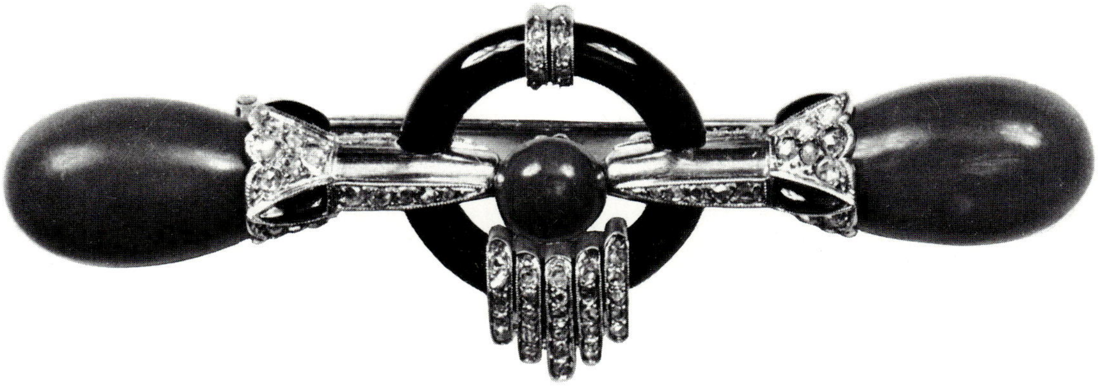

Anonymous: grey gold brooch with rose-cut diamonds, a central circular section in black onyx, and red coral beads. Etude Champin–Lombrail–Gautier.

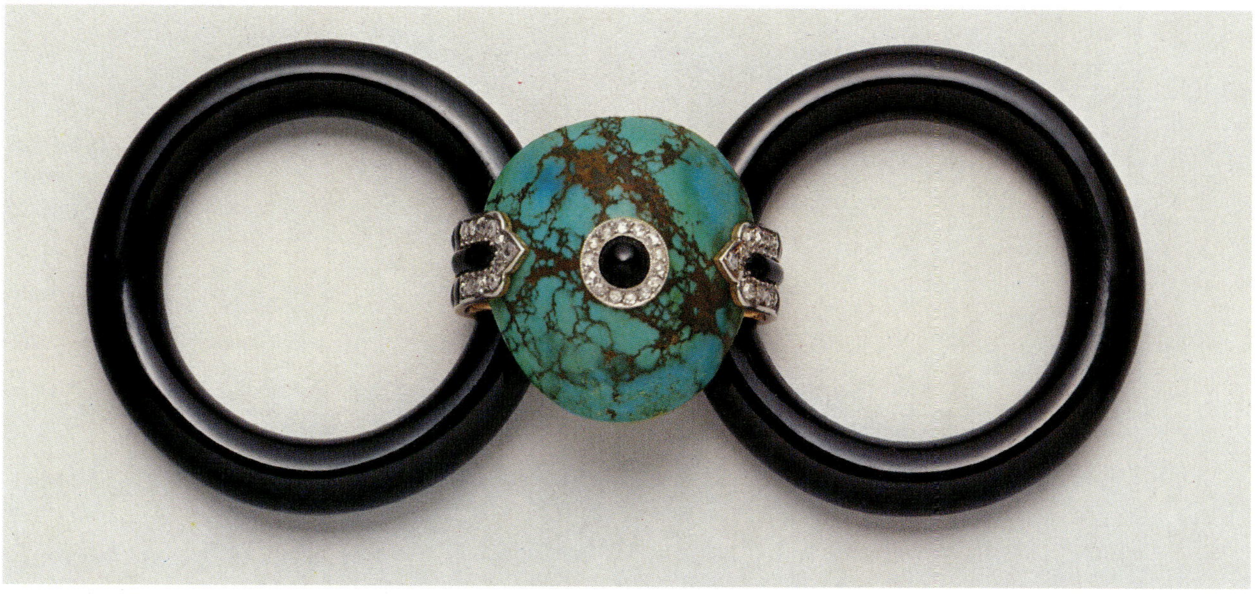

Cartier: buckle-brooch in turquoise, onyx, diamonds and platinum. Private Collection.

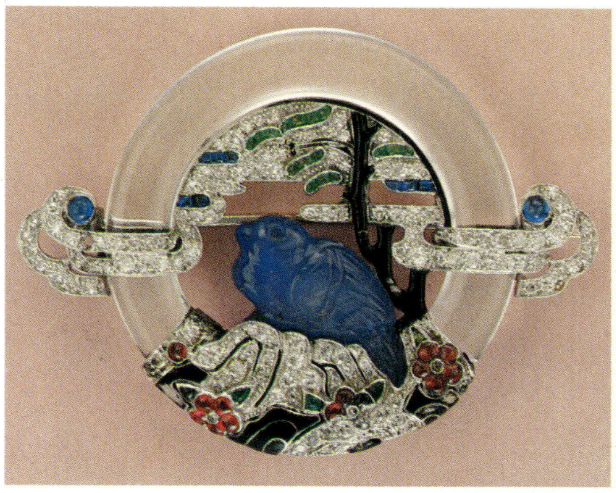

Anonymous: brooch in diamonds, rock crystal, rubies, sapphires, emeralds and black enamel. Christie's.

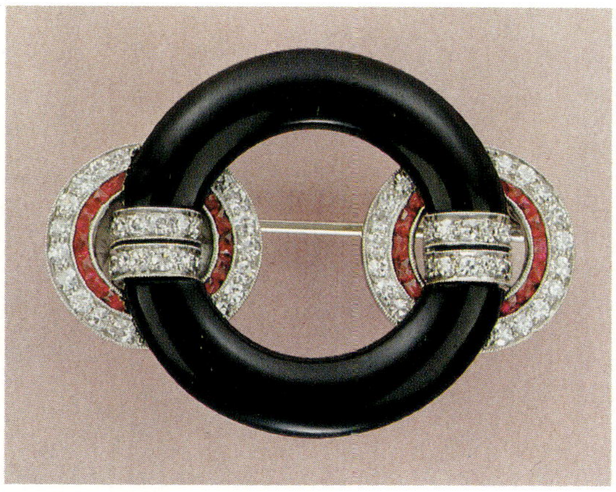

J.E. Caldwell: ruby, diamond and black onyx brooch, signed. Christie's, New York.

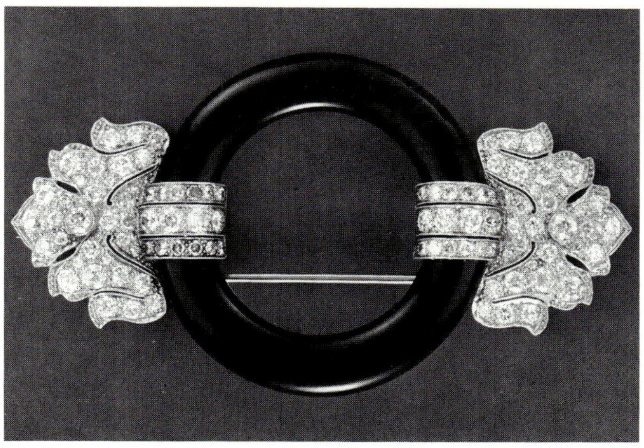

Anonymous: buckle-brooch in black onyx with side motifs in diamonds, mounted on platinum. Christie's.

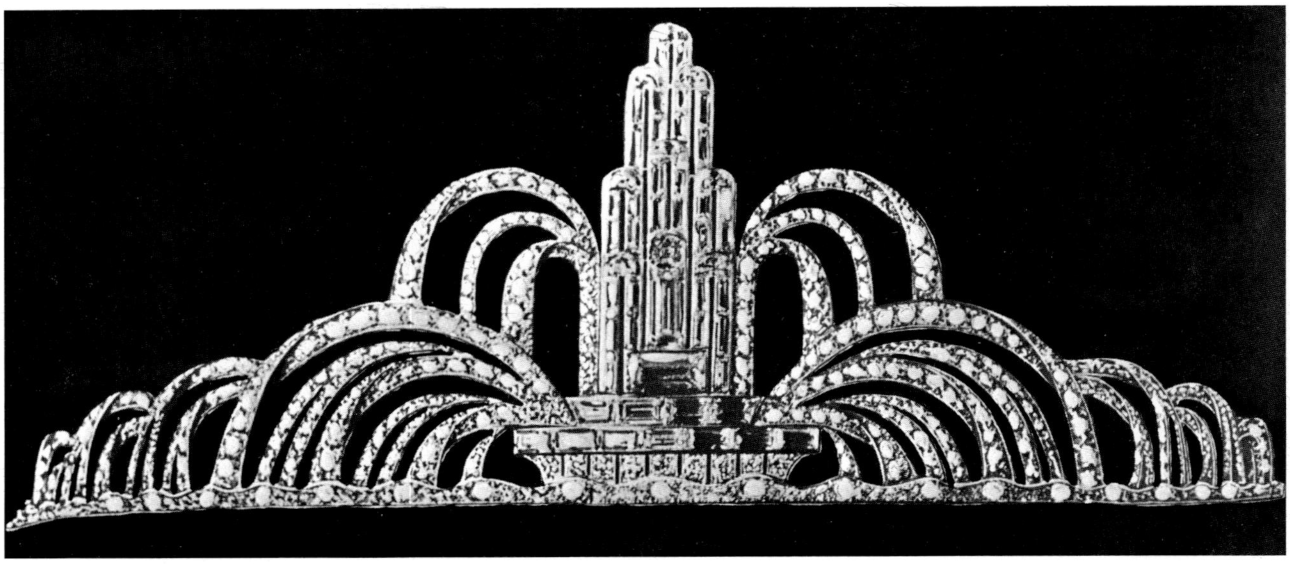

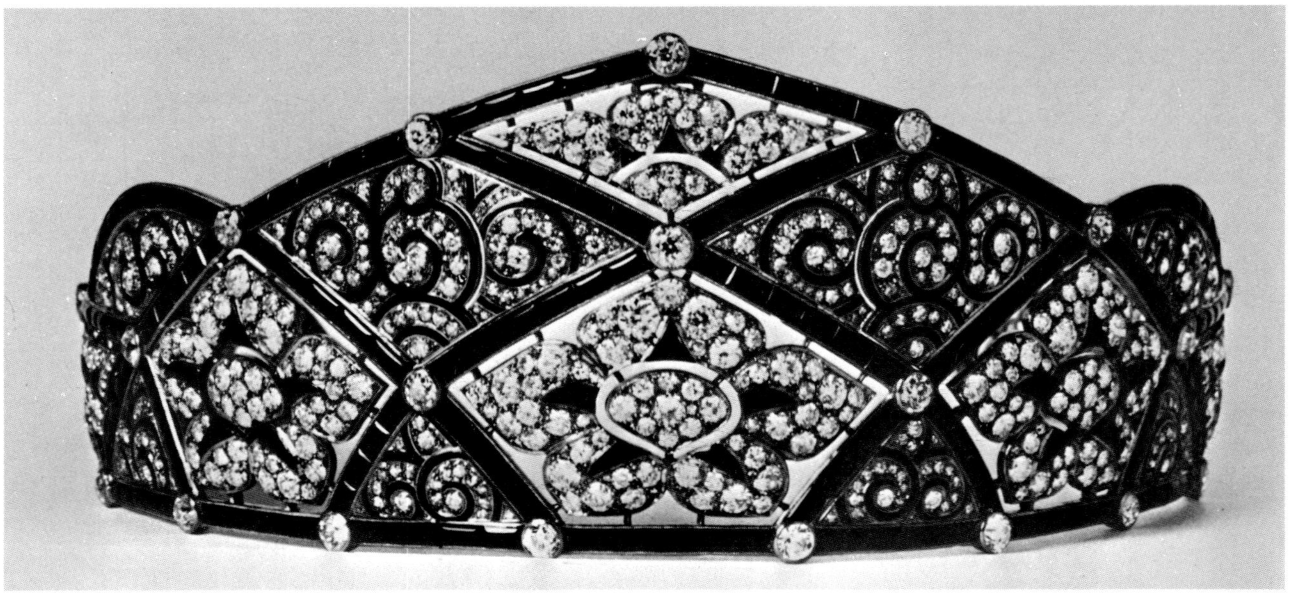

Mauboussin: tiara with fountain motifs in diamonds. Mauboussin Archives.

Boucheron: tiara with stylized flowers in diamonds and black onyx. Boucheron Archives.

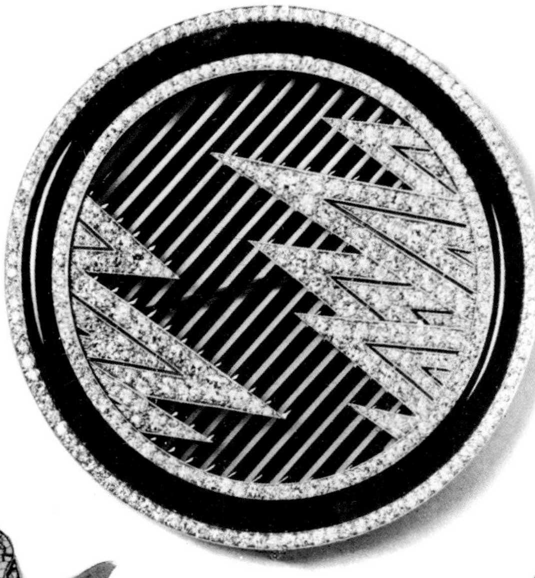

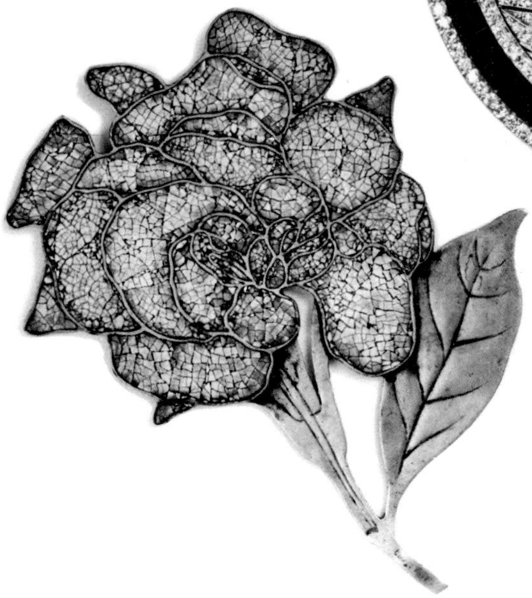

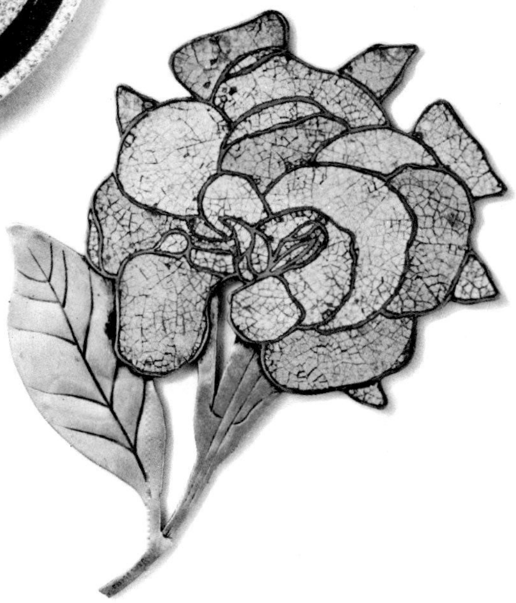

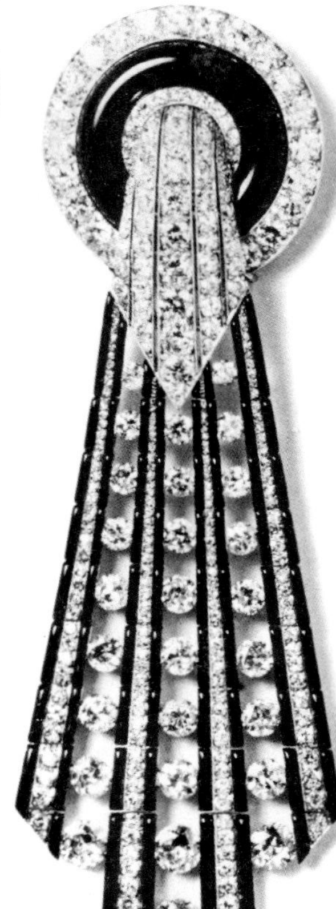

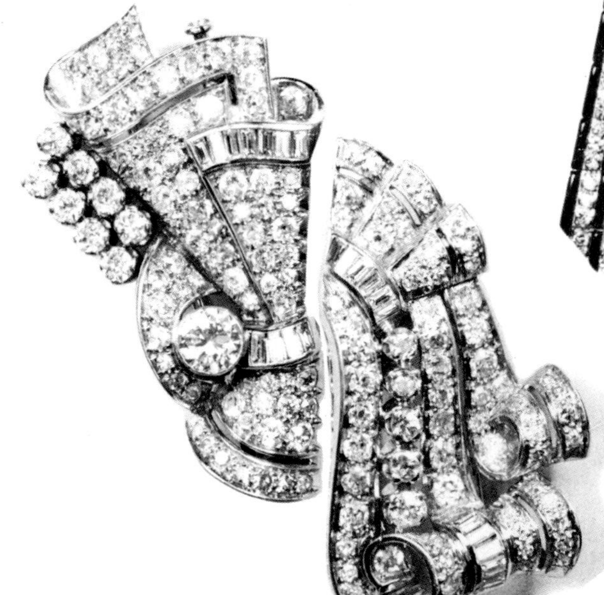

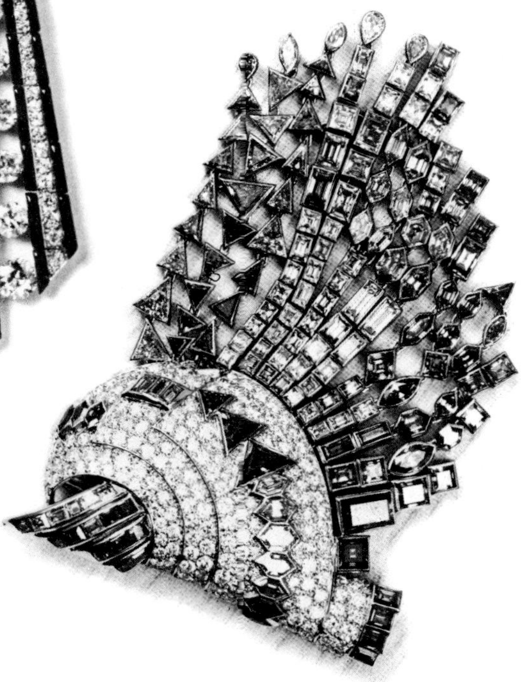

Jean Dunand: flower brooch in nickel silver enamelled with eggshell. Sotheby's.

Anonymous: two clips in platinum, set with brilliant-cut diamonds. Etude Champin–Lombrail–Gautier.

Boucheron: 'storm' brooch: the lightning composed of brilliants, the lines of rain of black enamel; mounted on platinum.

Boucheron: diamond, black enamel and black onyx brooch. Boucheron Archives.

Jean Dunand: flower brooch in nickel silver enamelled with eggshell. Sotheby's.

Anonymous: brooch in round, baguette, triangular and trapezoidal diamonds.

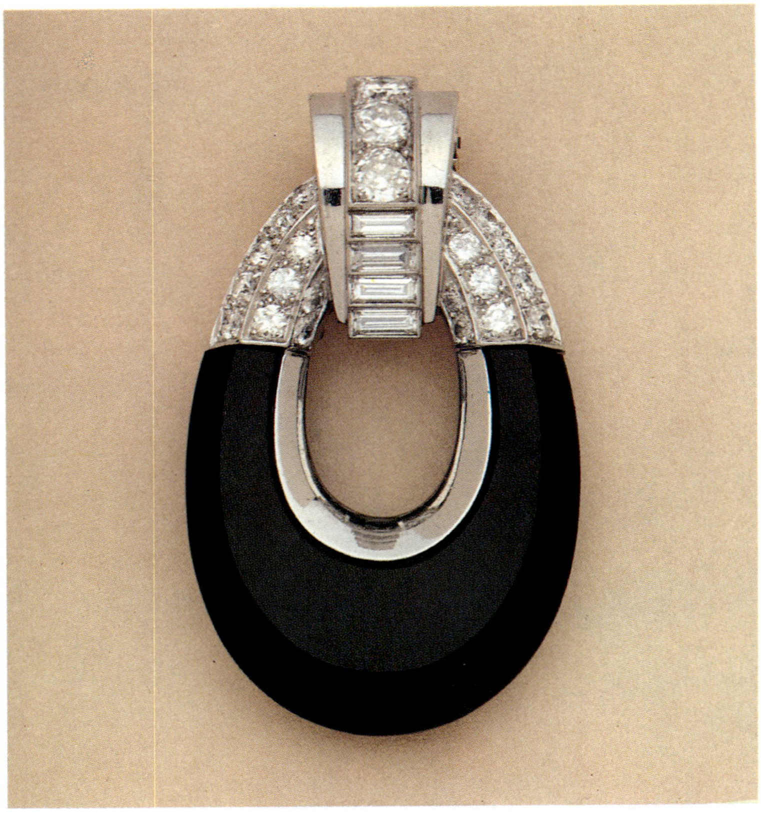

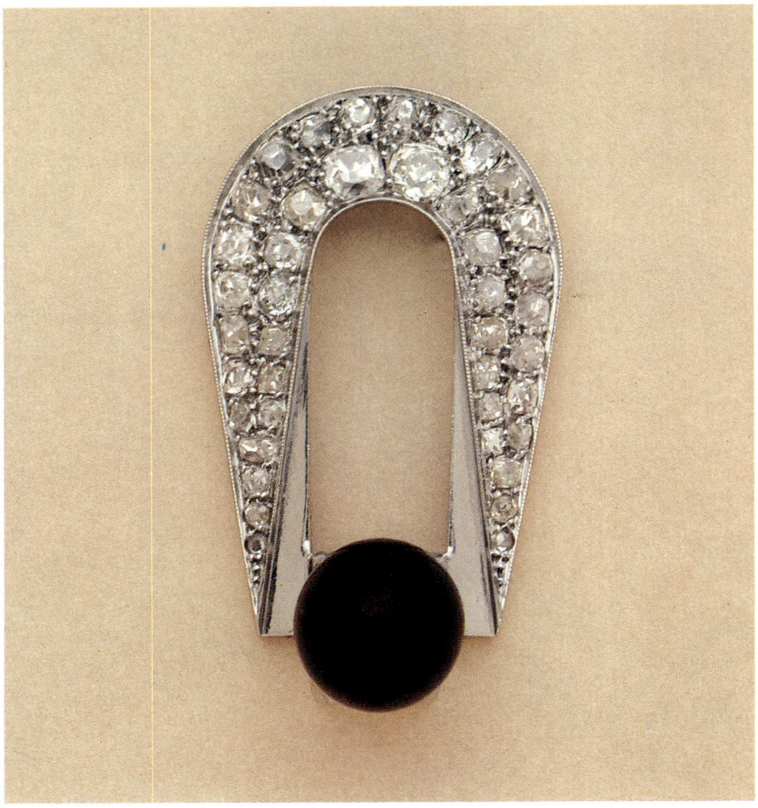

Mauboussin: brooch in diamonds and onyx, white gold and platinum, c. 1930, signed. Primavera Gallery, New York.

Raymond Templier: brooch in diamonds, platinum and black onyx, c. 1930, signed. Primavera Gallery, New York.

Facing page: Boucheron: brooch in sculpted lapis, jade, black enamel and engraved citrine, c. 1925, signed. Primavera Gallery, New York.

René Boivin: brooch in rock crystal, platinum, black enamel, diamonds and coloured sapphires, c. 1930, signed.

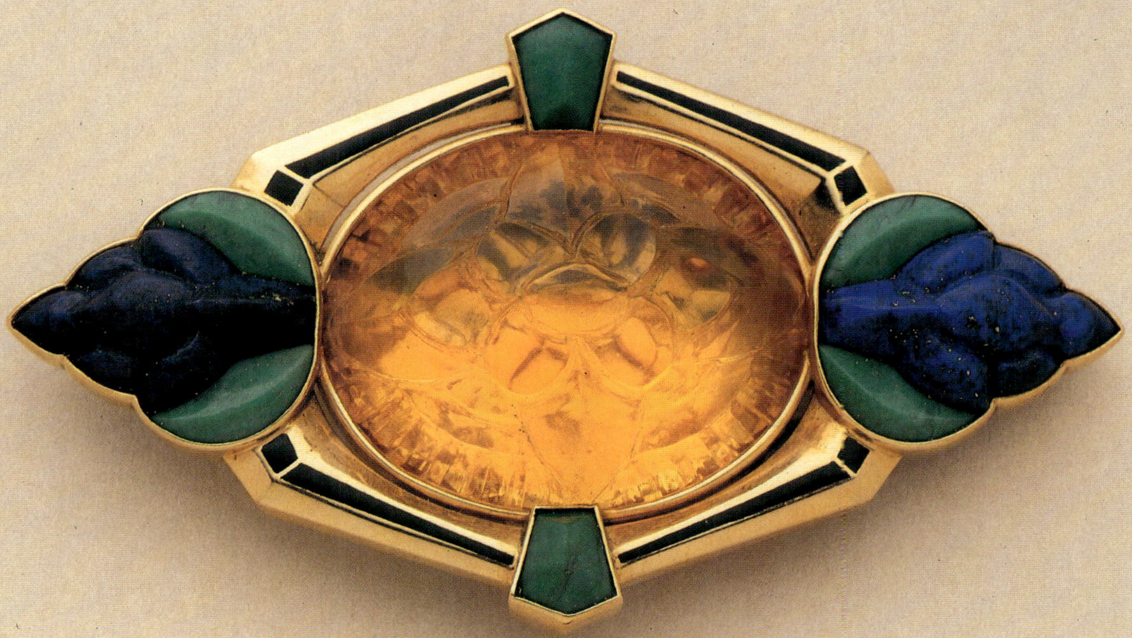

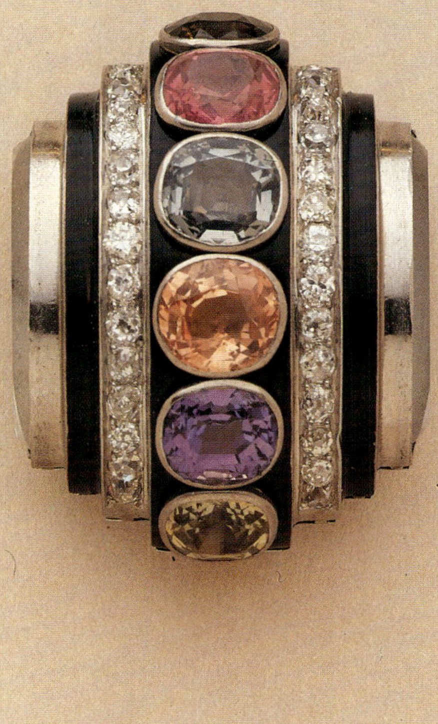

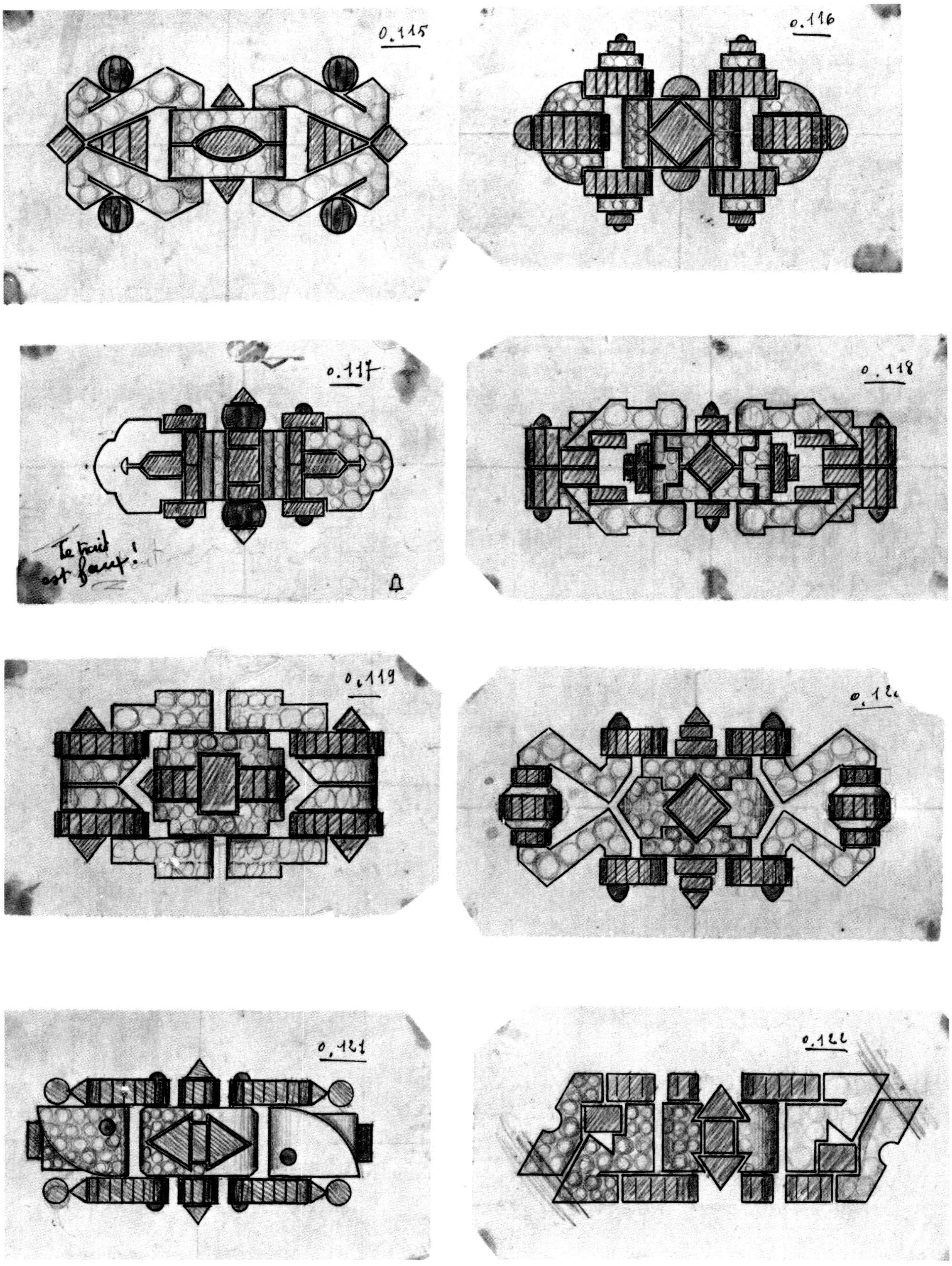

Gouache studies for watch-bracelets executed by designer-craftsmen for the Haute Joaillerie. *Danenberg Collection.*

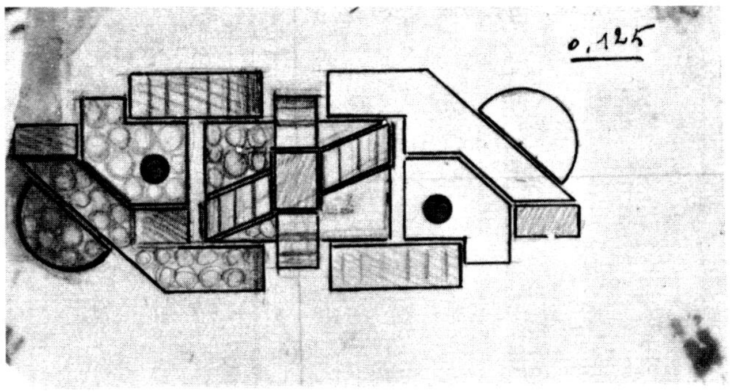

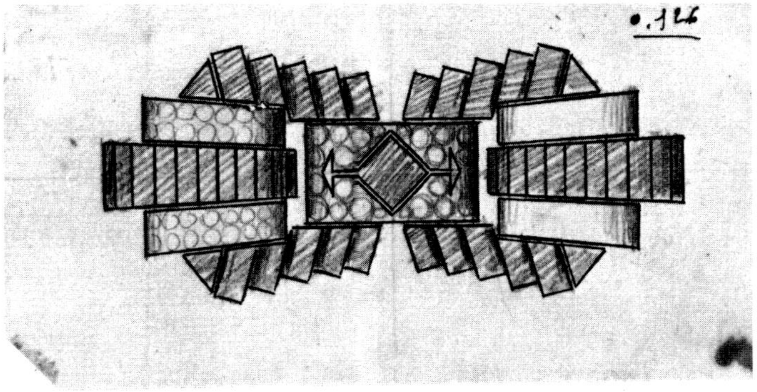

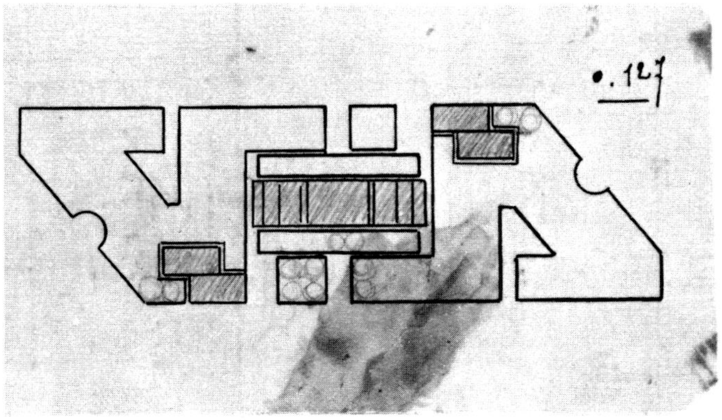

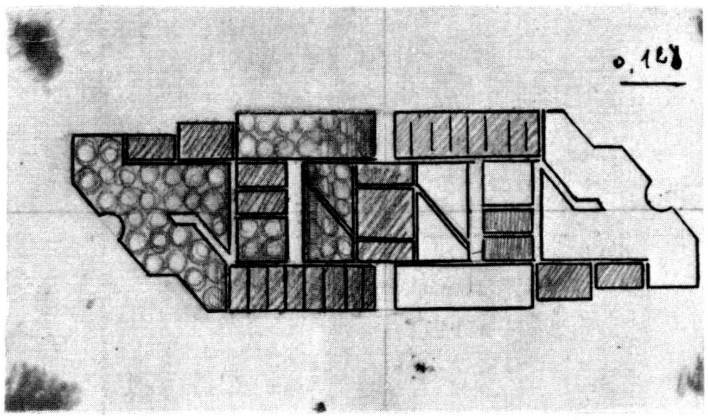

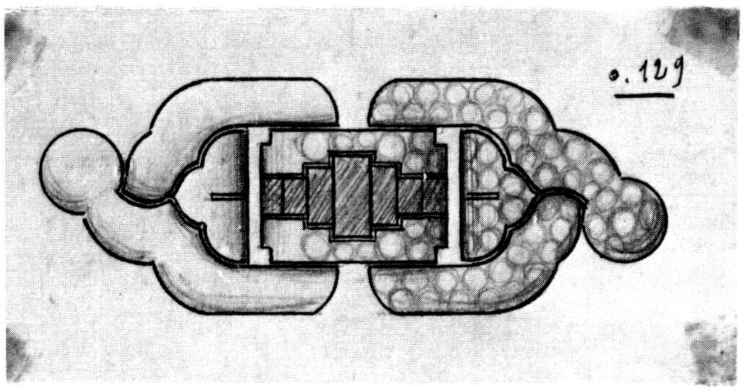

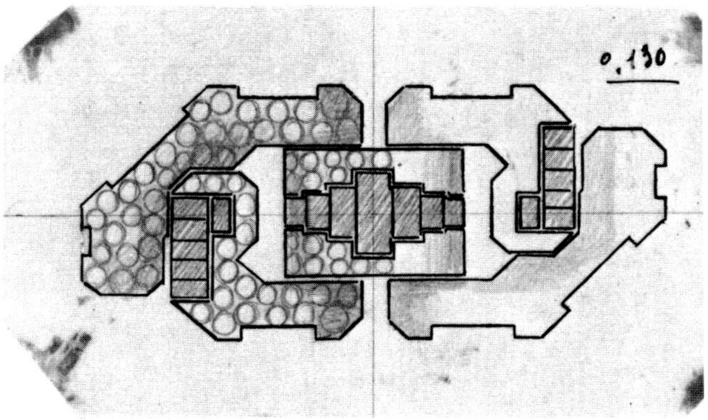

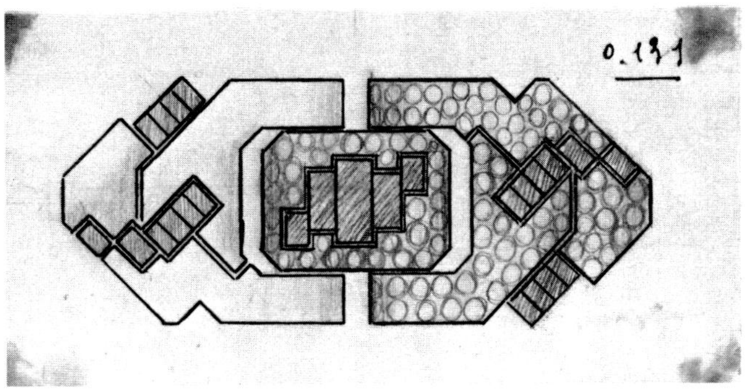

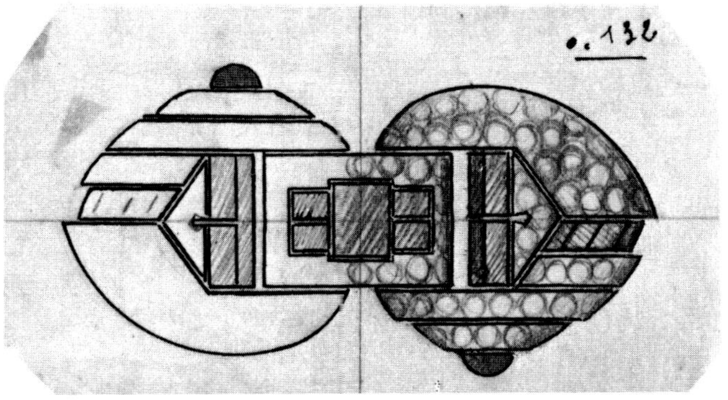

Gouache studies for watch-bracelets executed by designer-craftsmen for the Haute Joaillerie. *Danenberg Collection.*

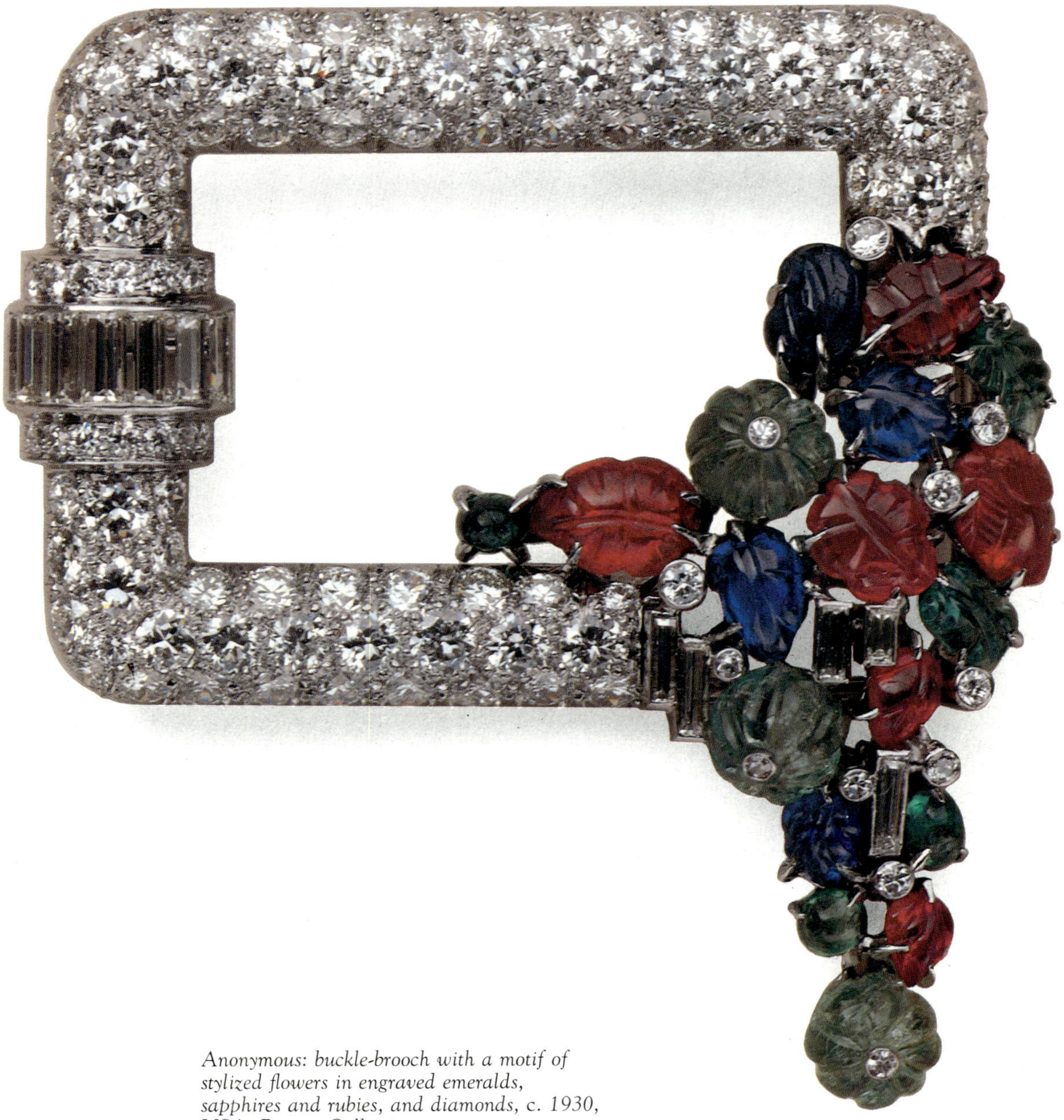

Anonymous: buckle-brooch with a motif of stylized flowers in engraved emeralds, sapphires and rubies, and diamonds, c. 1930, USA. Private Collection.

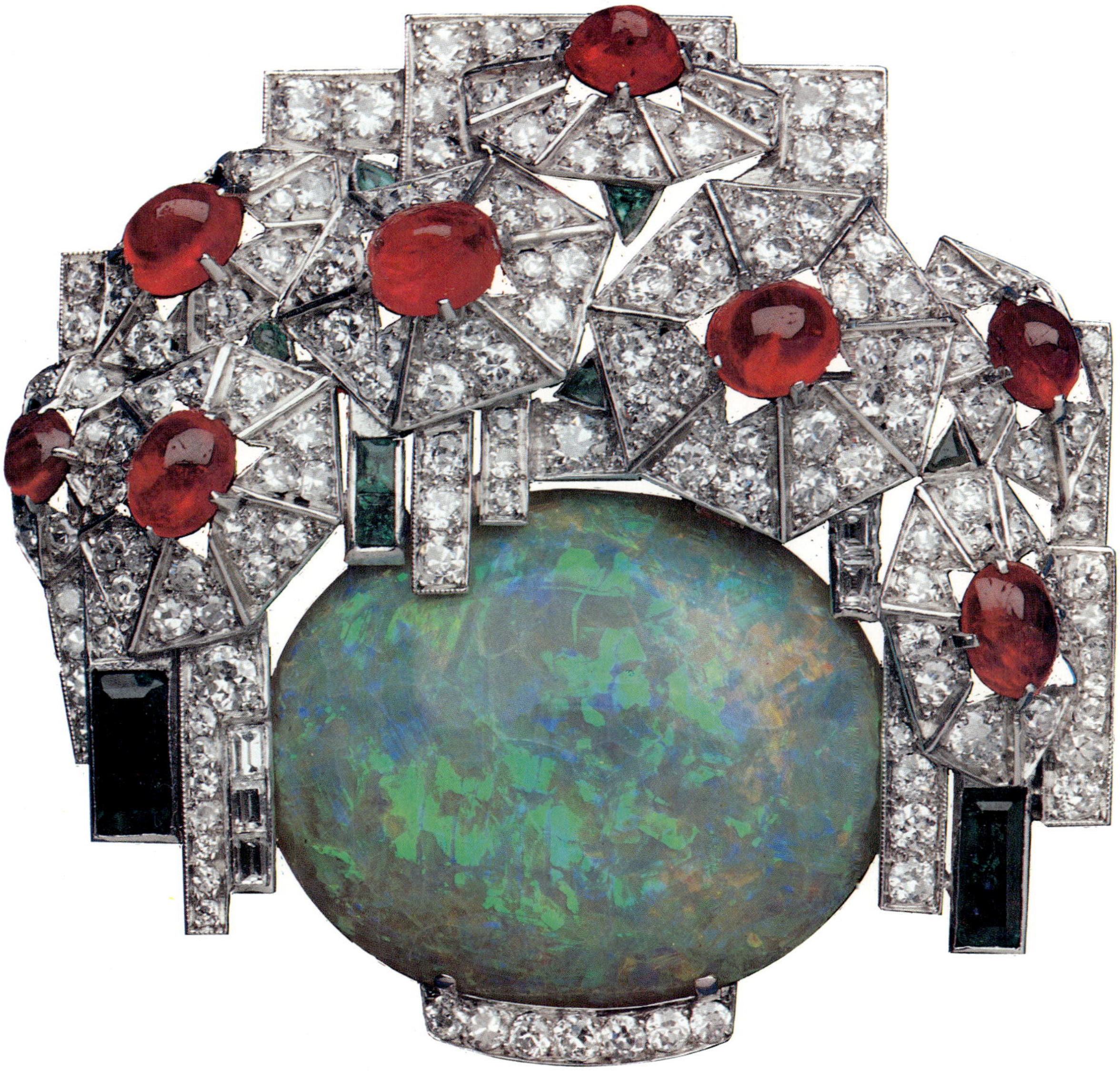

Dusausoy: brooch in diamonds, rubies, emeralds and opal mounted on platinum, executed for the 1925 Paris Exposition. H. 5.1 cm, W. 5.6 cm. Knut Günther Collection, Frankfurt, London, Paris. Photo: Günther Lotze.

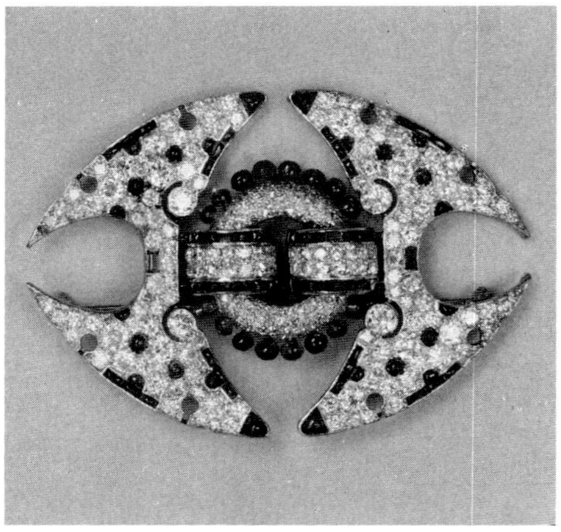

Cartier: brooch in diamonds, ruby and emerald cabochons, mounted on platinum. Sotheby's.

Anonymous: brooch in the form of a stylized bow in diamonds and onyx with an emerald at the centre, mounted on white gold. Christie's.

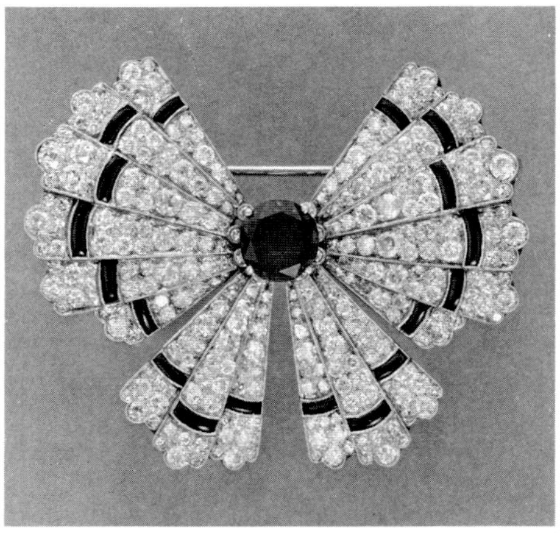

*Anonymous: emerald and diamond brooch dep cting the Aesop fabl*ᶓ*, 'The Sour Grapes'. Sotheby's.*

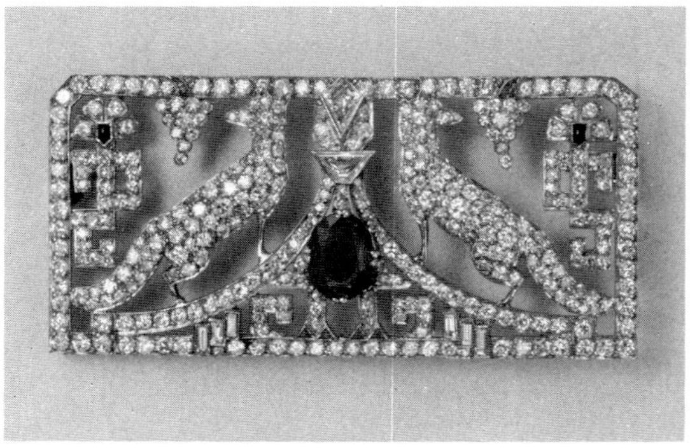

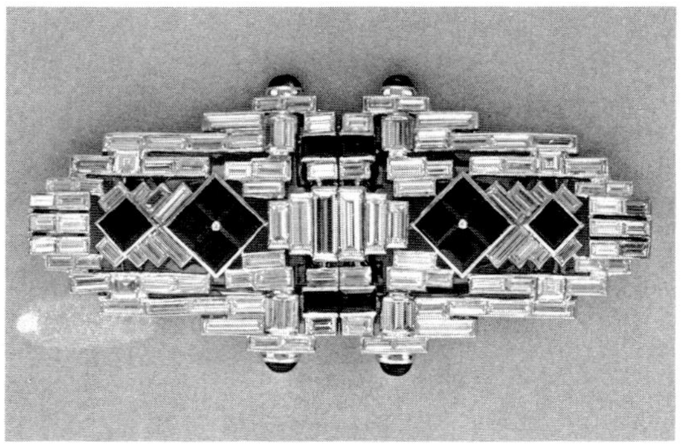

Anonymous: double-clip brooch in emeralds and baguette diamonds forming a geometric design, mounted on platinum and white gold. Sotheby's, Geneva.

Anonymous: ruby, emerald and diamond brooch. Sotheby's, Geneva.

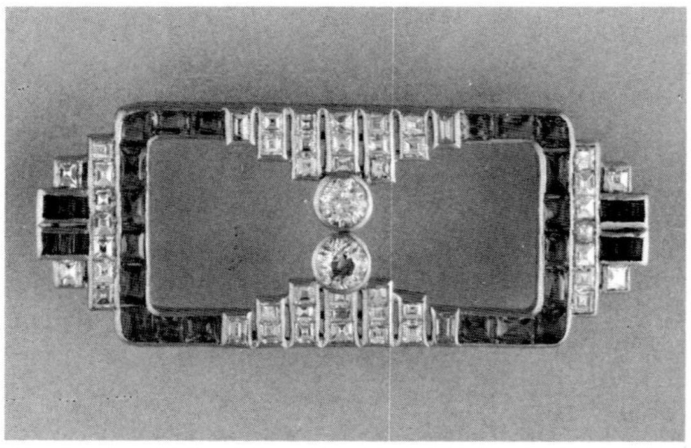

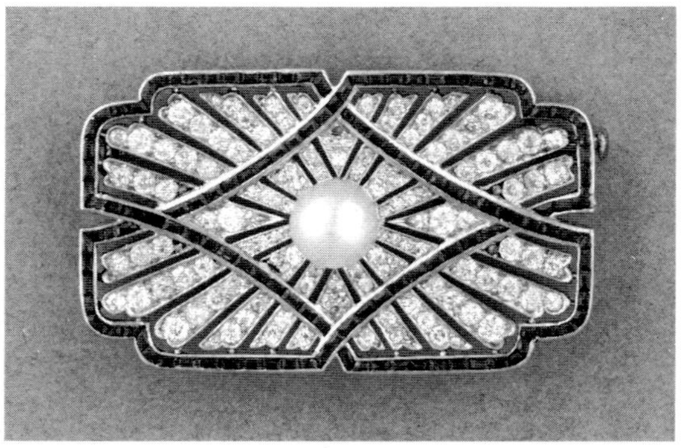

Anonymous: diamond and sapphire brooch with a cultured pearl at the centre. Sotheby's, Geneva.

Anonymous: brooch in round and baguette diamonds. Sotheby's.

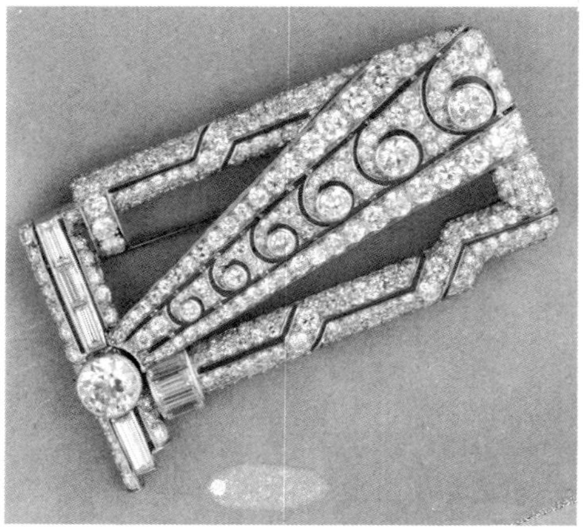

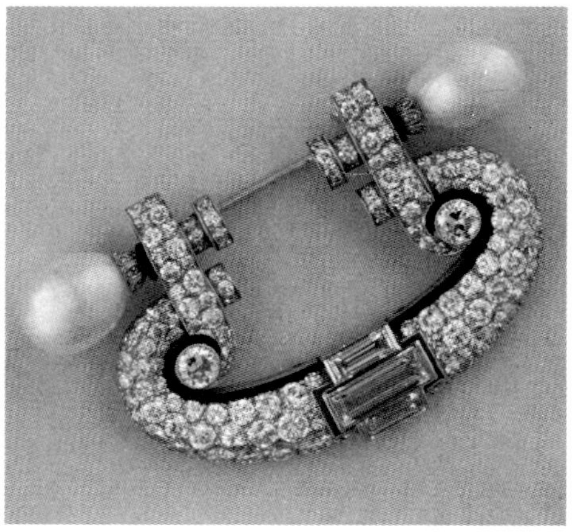

Cartier: brooch in round and baguette diamonds, with a pearl on each side. Sotheby's.

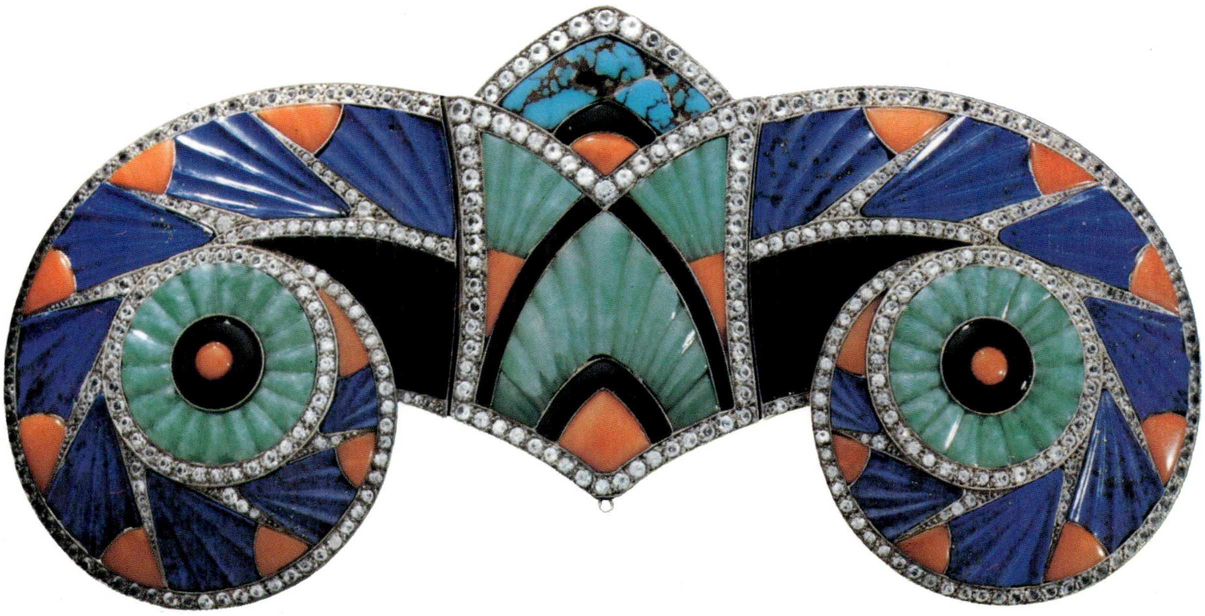

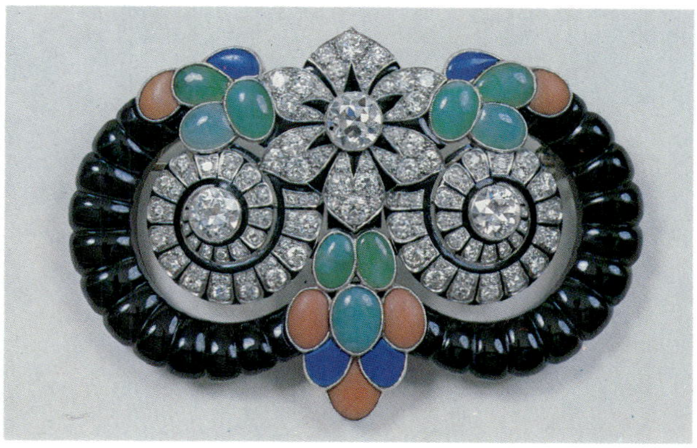

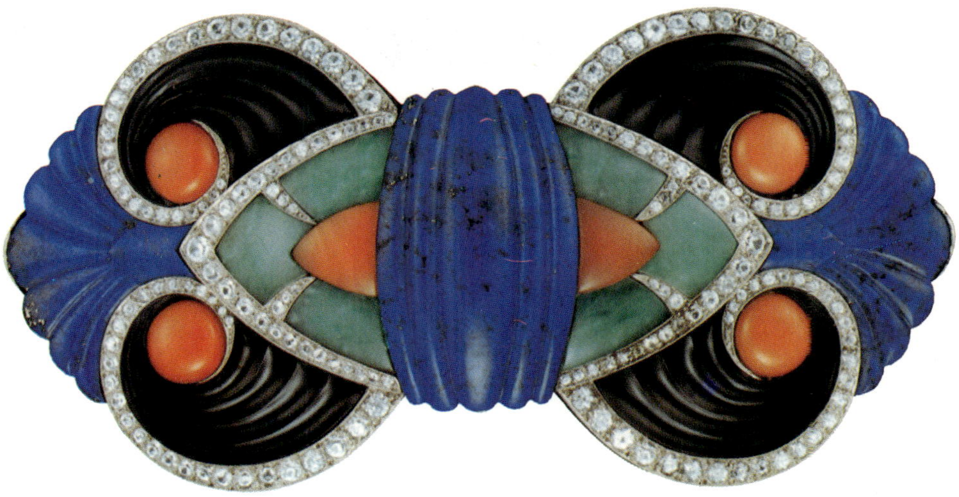

Boucheron: corsage ornament in lapis, coral, jade, onyx and diamonds on a gold mount. Executed for the 1925 Paris Exposition.

Boucheron: double-scroll brooch, in grey gold set with diamonds, jade, jadeite, coral, lapis and onyx. Etude Couturier–Nicolay.

Boucheron: corsage ornament in lapis, onyx, coral, jade and diamonds on a mount of palladium gold. Executed for the 1925 Paris Exposition. Boucheron Archives.

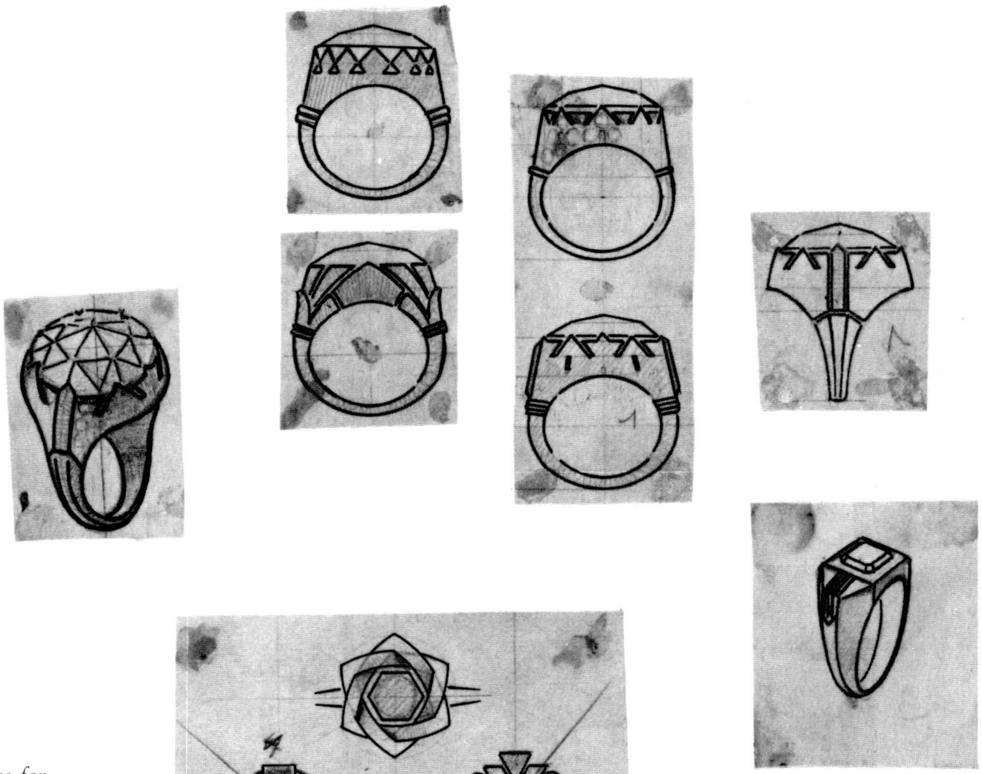

Gouache studies for rings executed by designer-craftsmen for the Haute Joaillerie. *Danenberg Collection.*

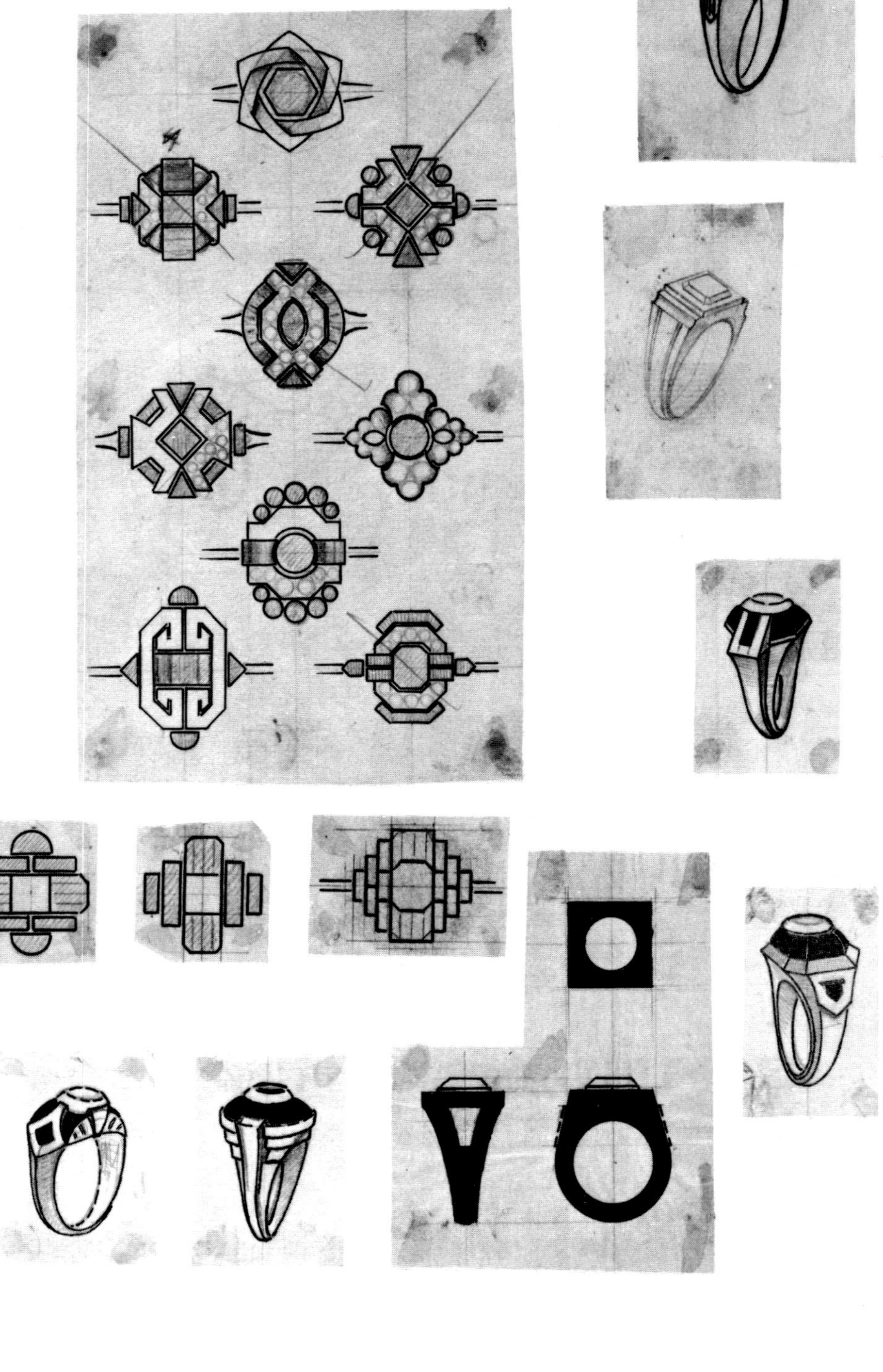

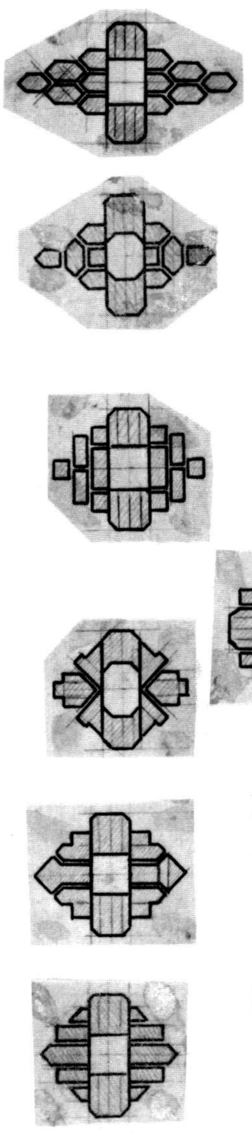

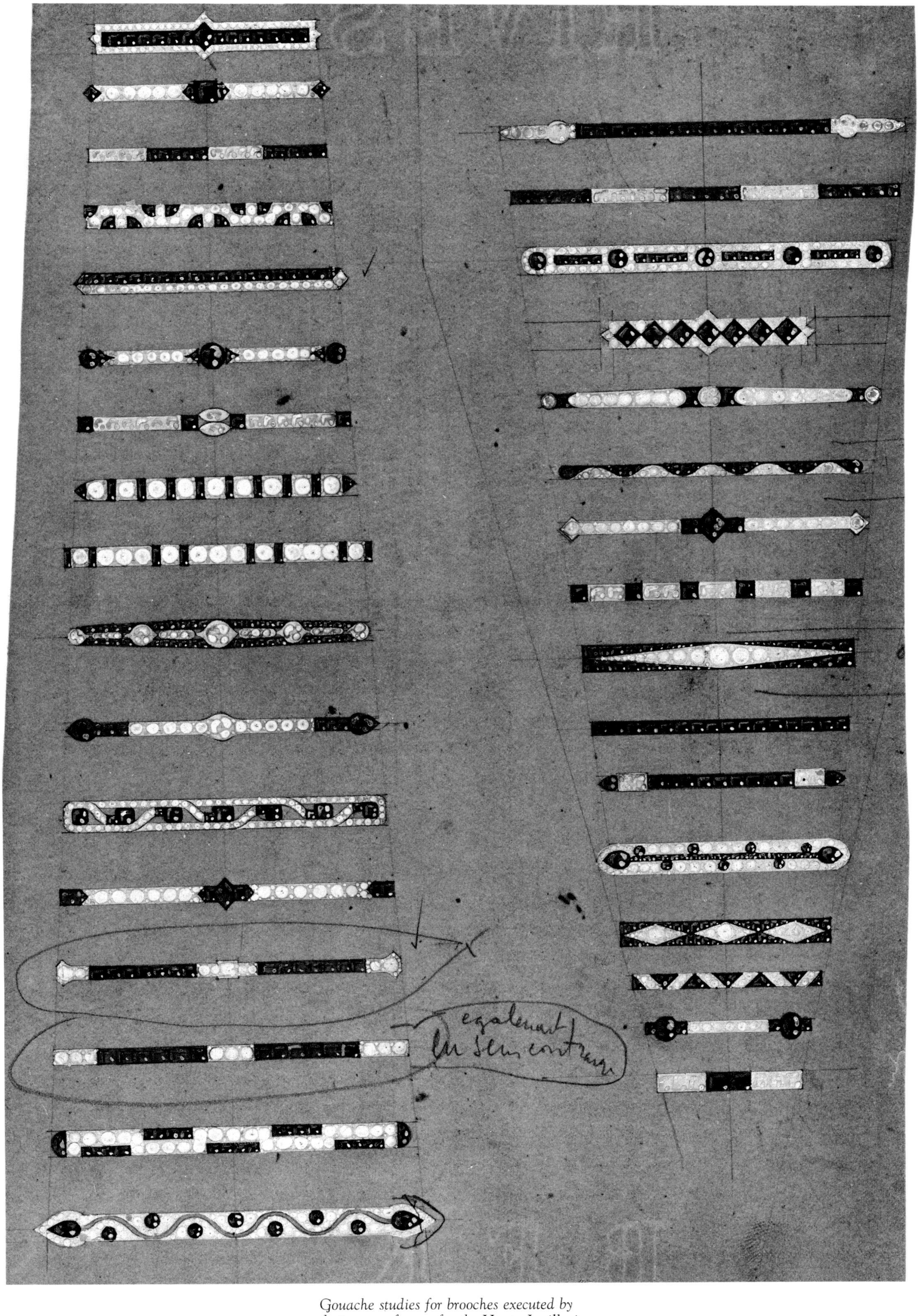

Gouache studies for brooches executed by designer-craftsmen for the Haute Joaillerie. *Danenberg Collection.*

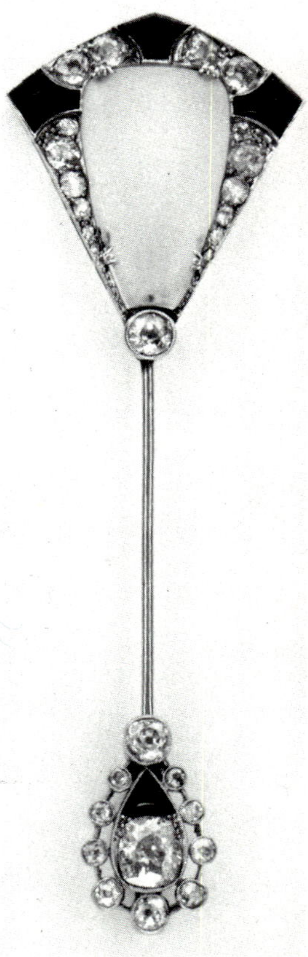

Anonymous: jabot pin comprising a plaque of frosted crystal surrounded by diamonds and onyx. The point of the pin is decorated with diamonds and a triangular onyx cabochon. Mount of platinum and white gold. Christie's, New York.

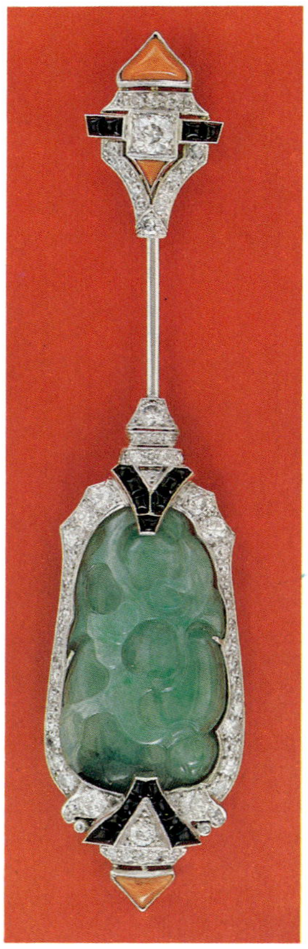

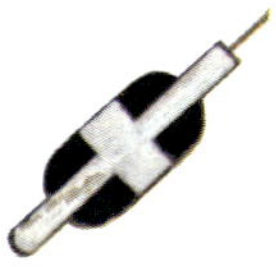

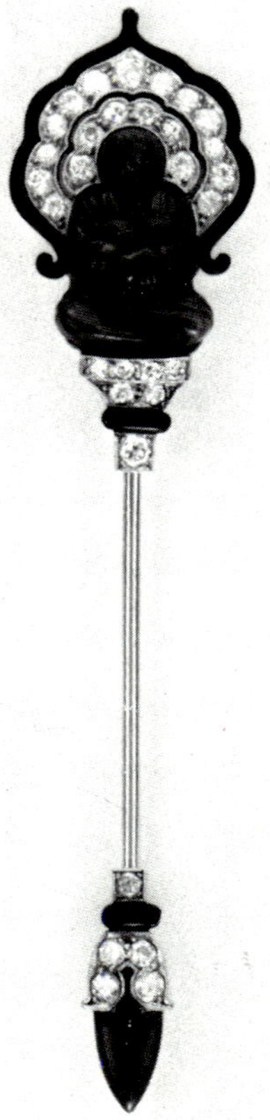

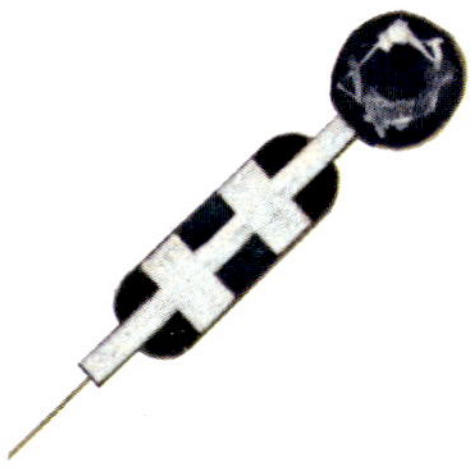

Cartier: jabot pin depicting a buddha in engraved coral surrounded by a mandorla in diamonds and black enamel. The point of the pin is decorated with a lotus flower in coral and diamonds. Platinum mount. Christie's, New York.

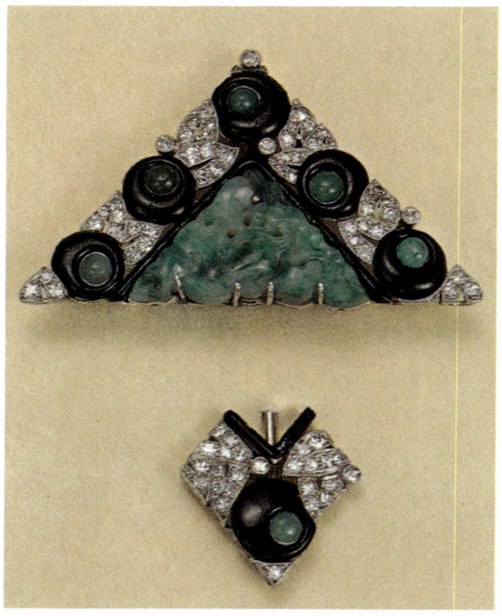

Anonymous: jabot pin in engraved jade, black enamel and diamonds. Sotheby's.

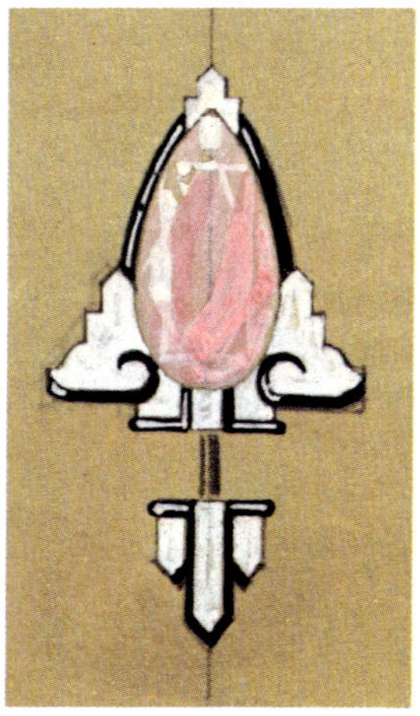

Top: Anonymous: jabot pin in engraved jade surrounded by round diamonds and onyx motifs. The point of the pin is decorated with diamonds, onyx and a coral cabochon. Christie's.

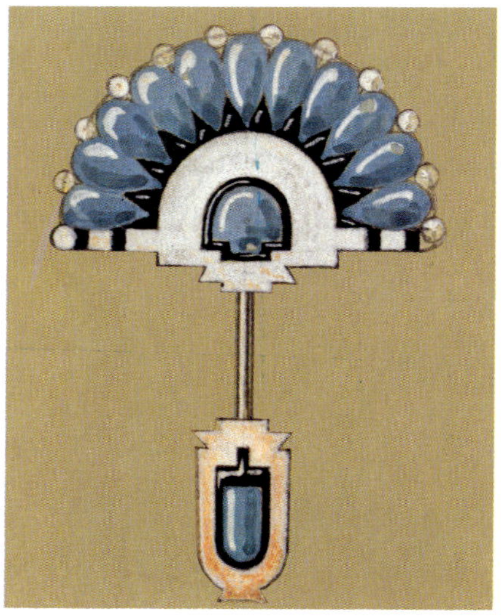

Three gouache studies for jabot pins executed by designer-craftsmen for the Haute Joaillerie. M. Souillac Archives.

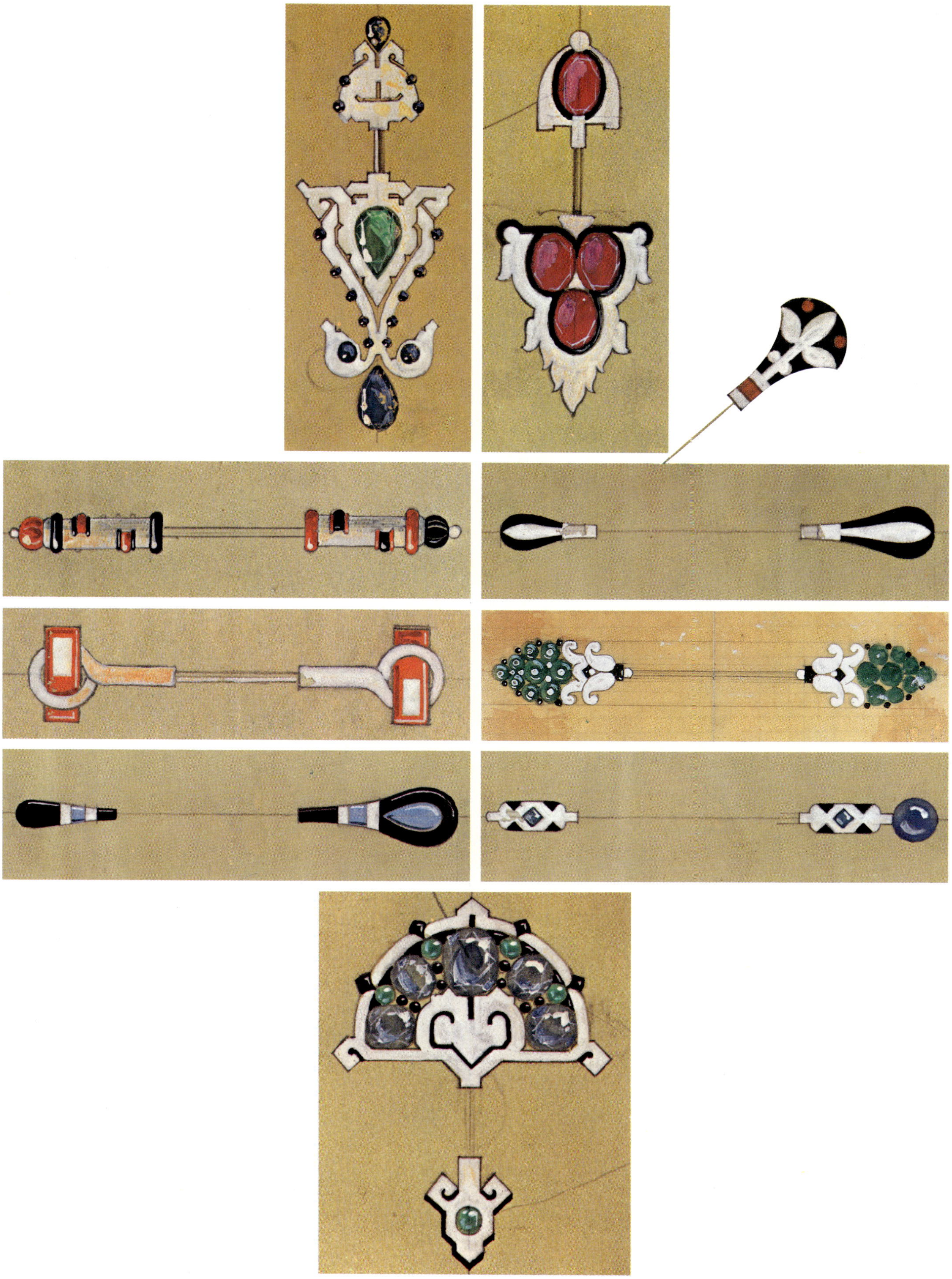

Gouache studies for jabot pins executed by designer-craftsmen for the Haute Joaillerie. *M. Souillac Archives.*

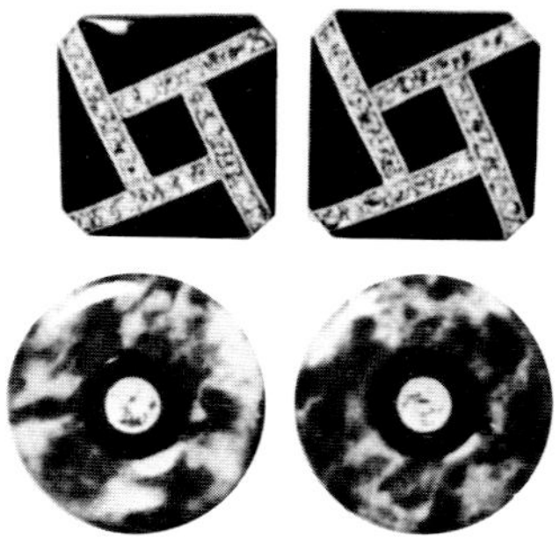

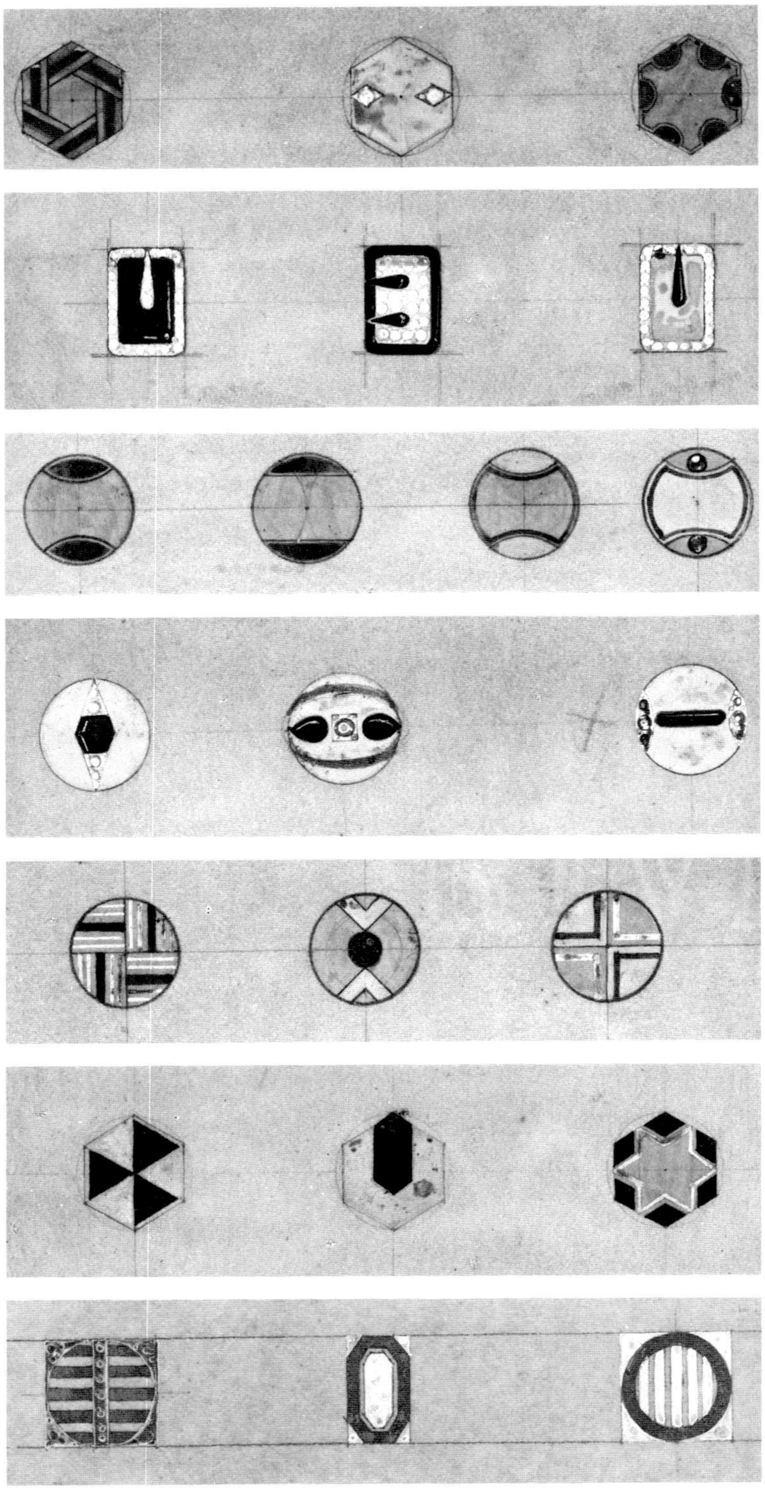

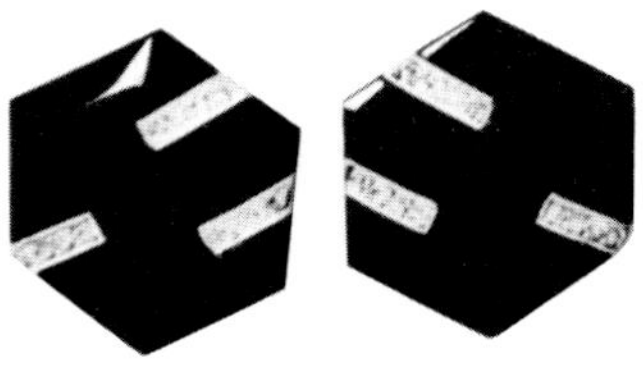

Left and right: Boucheron: cuff-links in hardstones and diamonds. Boucheron Archives.

Centre: preliminary designs in gouache for cuff-links executed by designer-craftsmen for the Haute Joaillerie. *M. Souillac Archives.*

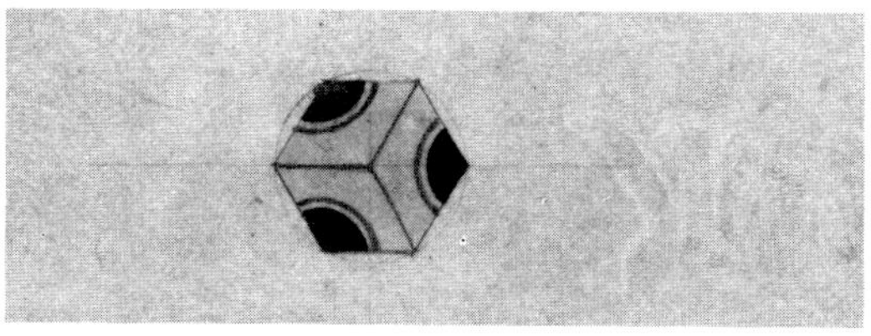
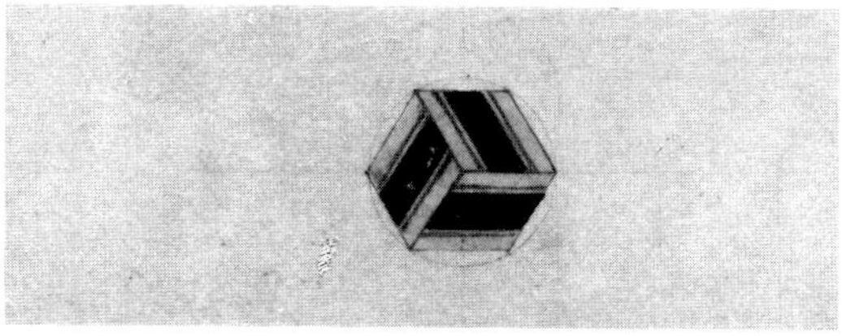
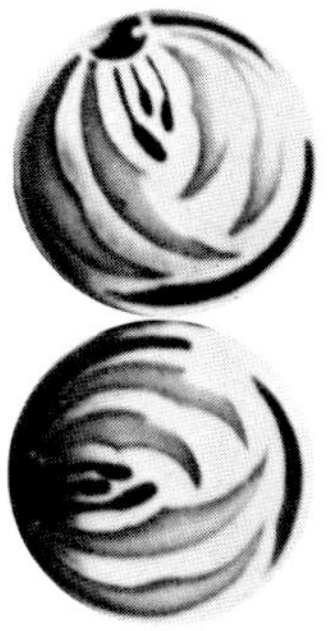
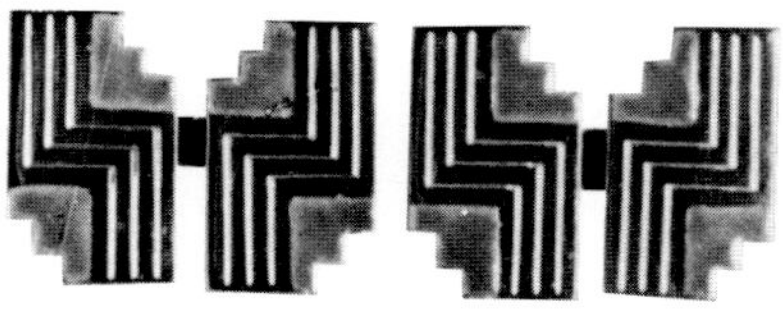
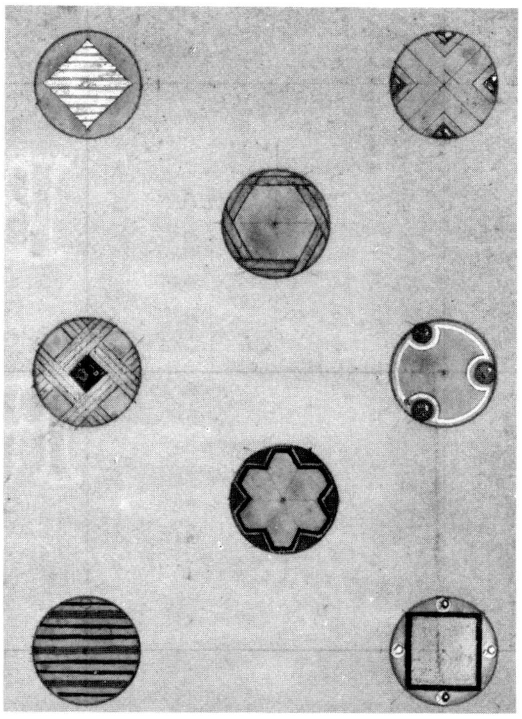
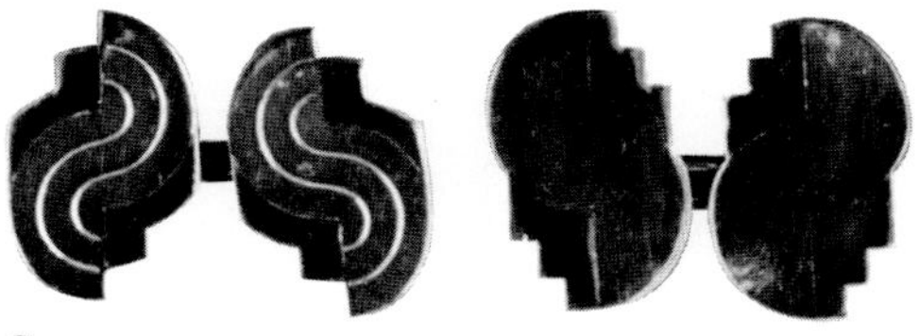
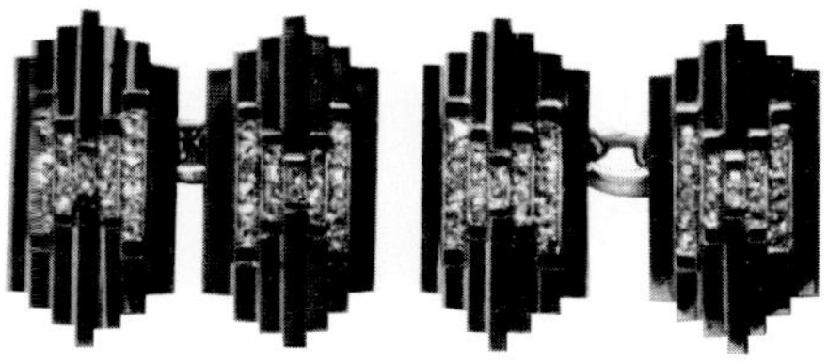
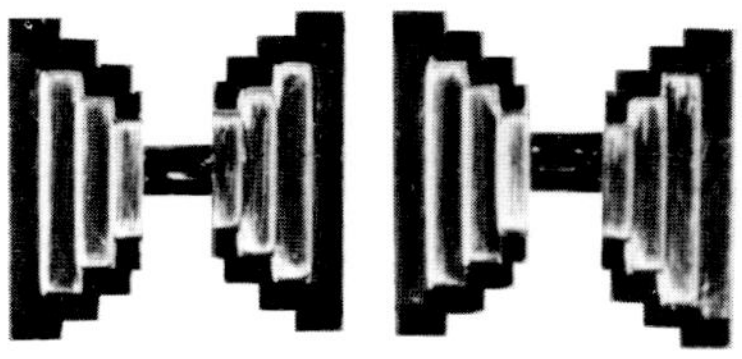
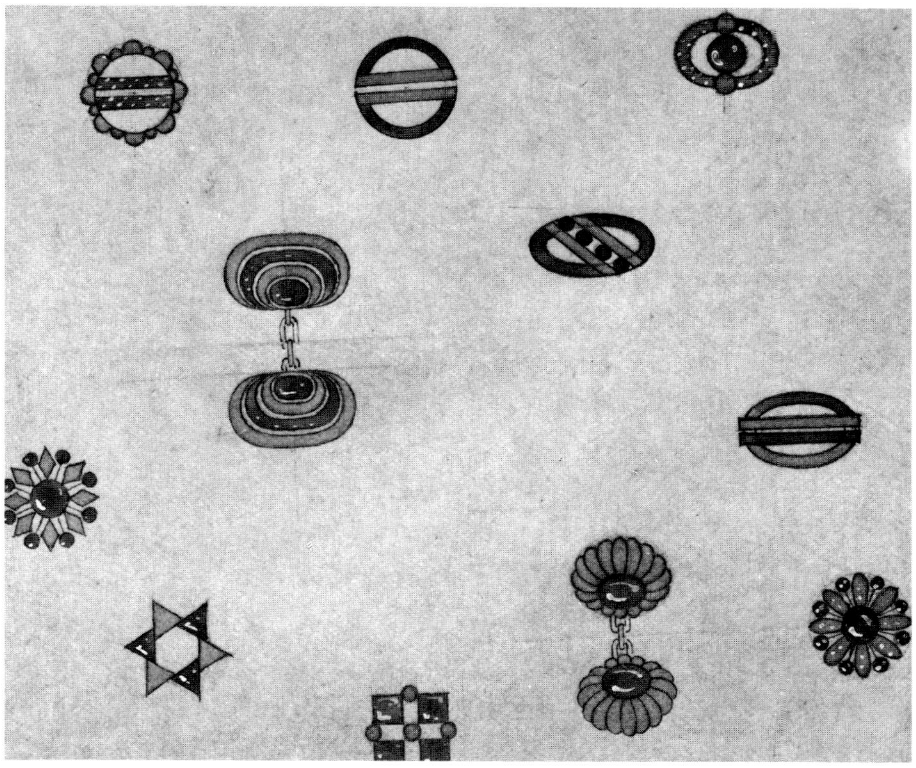

Left: Raymond Templier: cuff-links in precious metal and enamel. Courtesy of L. and B. Heuer.

Centre: preliminary designs in gouache for cuff-links executed by designer-craftsmen for the Haute Joaillerie. *M. Souillac Archives.*

Right, top to bottom: Boucheron: cuff-links. Boucheron Archives.

Raymond Templier: cuff-links in precious metal and enamel. Courtesy of L. and B. Heuer.

Raymond Templier: cuff-links in precious metal and diamonds. Courtesy of L. and B. Heuer.

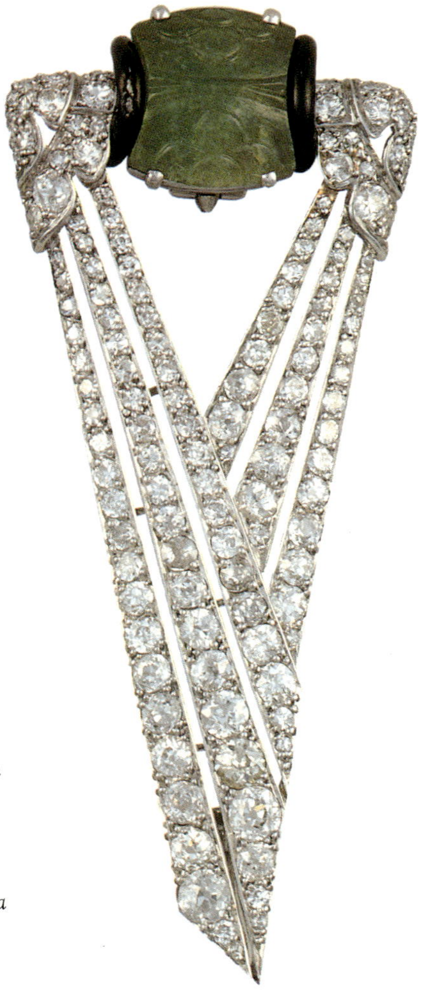

Anonymous: brooch comprising an engraved emerald with black enamel borders, and round diamonds. Sotheby's.

Anonymous: pendant-brooch in the form of a scarab, in diamonds, tiger's eye, brown and black cloisonné *enamel, France. Christie's.*

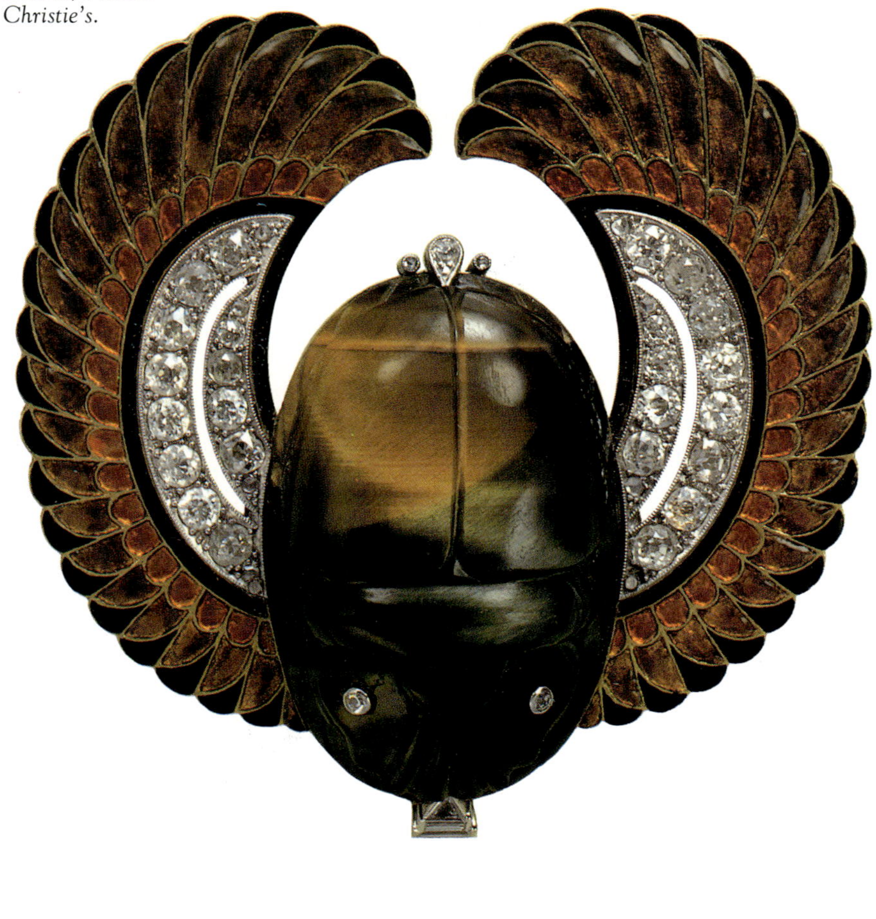

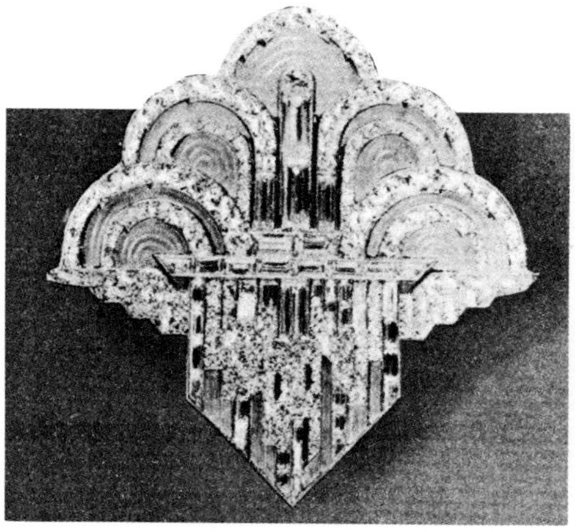
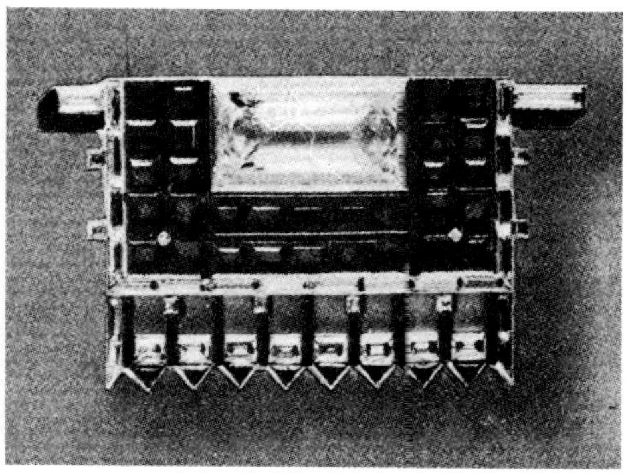
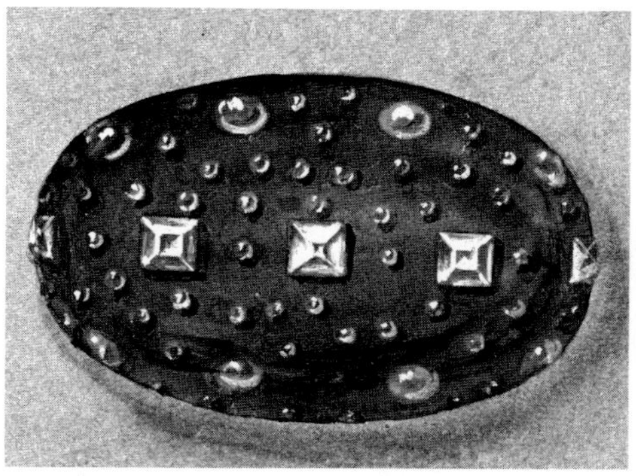
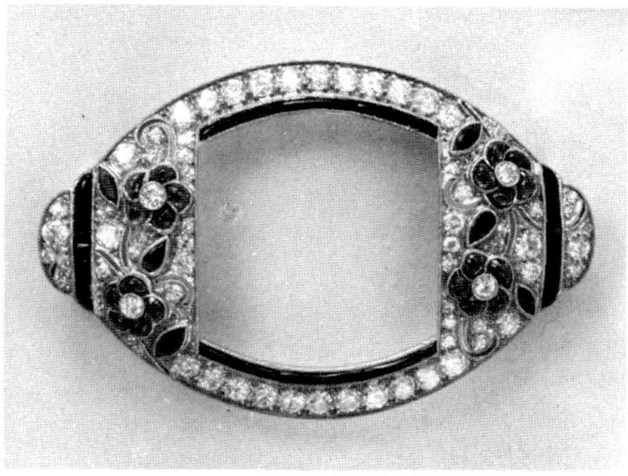
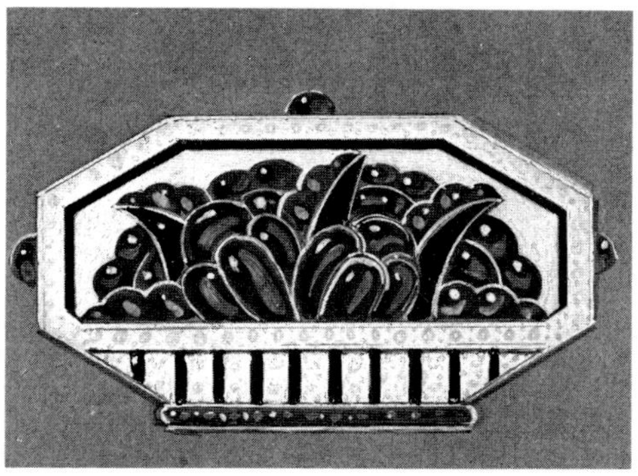
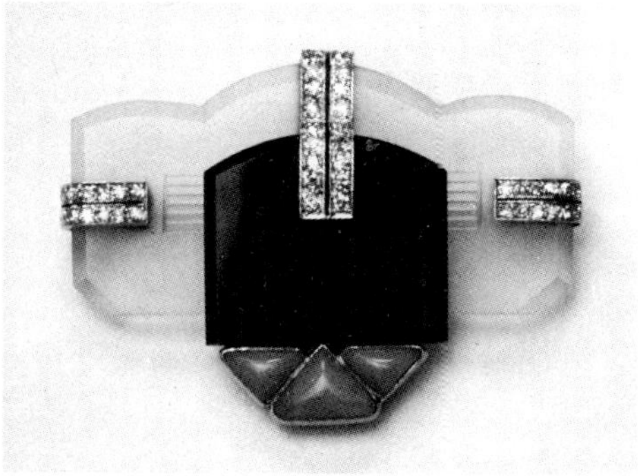
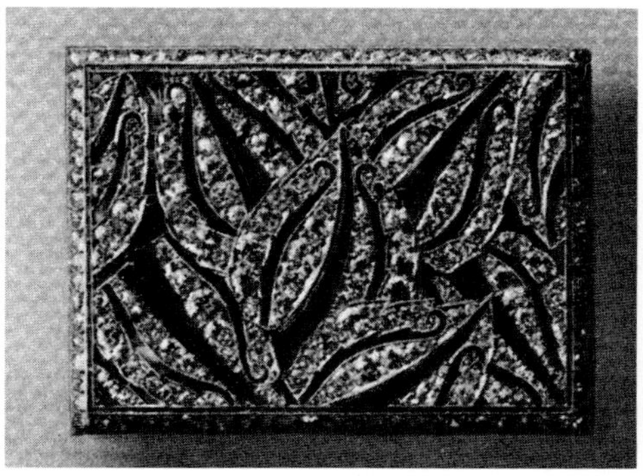
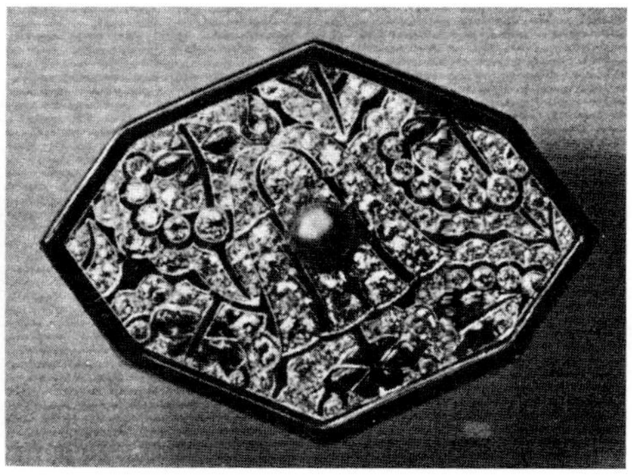

Mauboussin: 'fountain' brooch in engraved and frosted crystal, decorated with diamonds mounted on platinum. 1925 Exposition, Paris.

Boivin: sandalwood brooch, studded with gold, c. 1930. Boivin Archives.

Mauboussin: gouache study for a brooch in platinum, diamonds, onyx and cabochons of coloured stones, c. 1925.

Altenloh: brooch. 1925 Exposition, Paris.

Mauboussin: brooch with a large rectangular diamond surrounded by sapphires and small diamonds. 1925 Exposition, Paris.

Boucheron: brooch in sapphire cabochons, emeralds, diamonds and onyx. Sotheby's.

Anonymous: brooch in white gold, rock crystal, coral, onyx and diamonds, c. 1925. Jesse & Laski Gallery Collection, London.

Coosemans: brooch. 1925 Exposition, Paris.

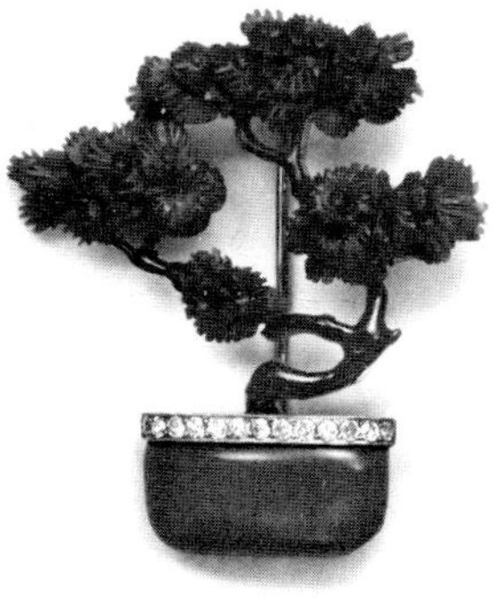

Anonymous: jade, diamond and enamel brooch in the form of a bonsai tree: branches in black enamel, leaves in engraved jade, pot in red enamel and diamonds. Christie's.

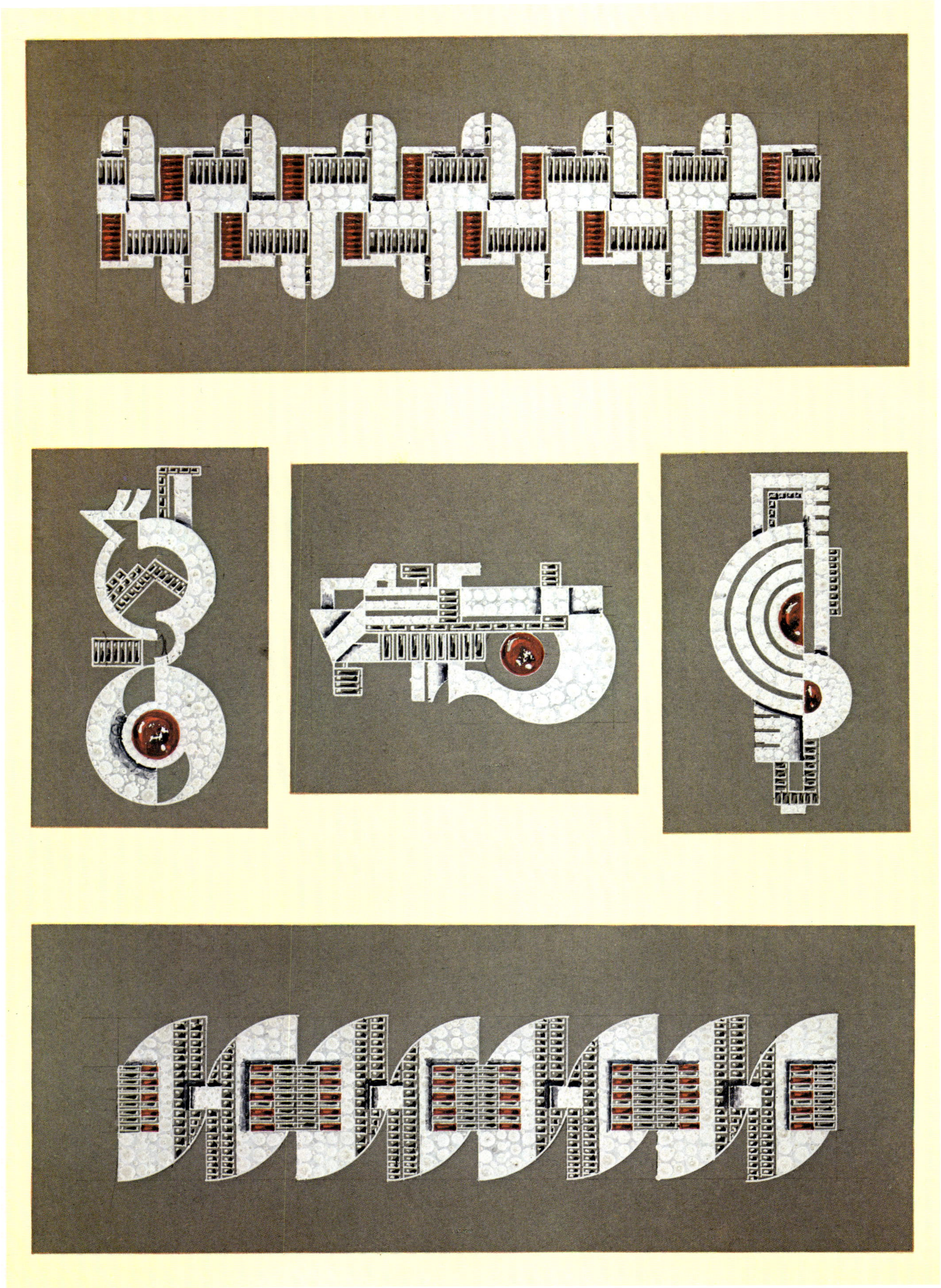

Mauboussin: gouache studies for brooches and bracelets in platinum, rubies and diamonds.

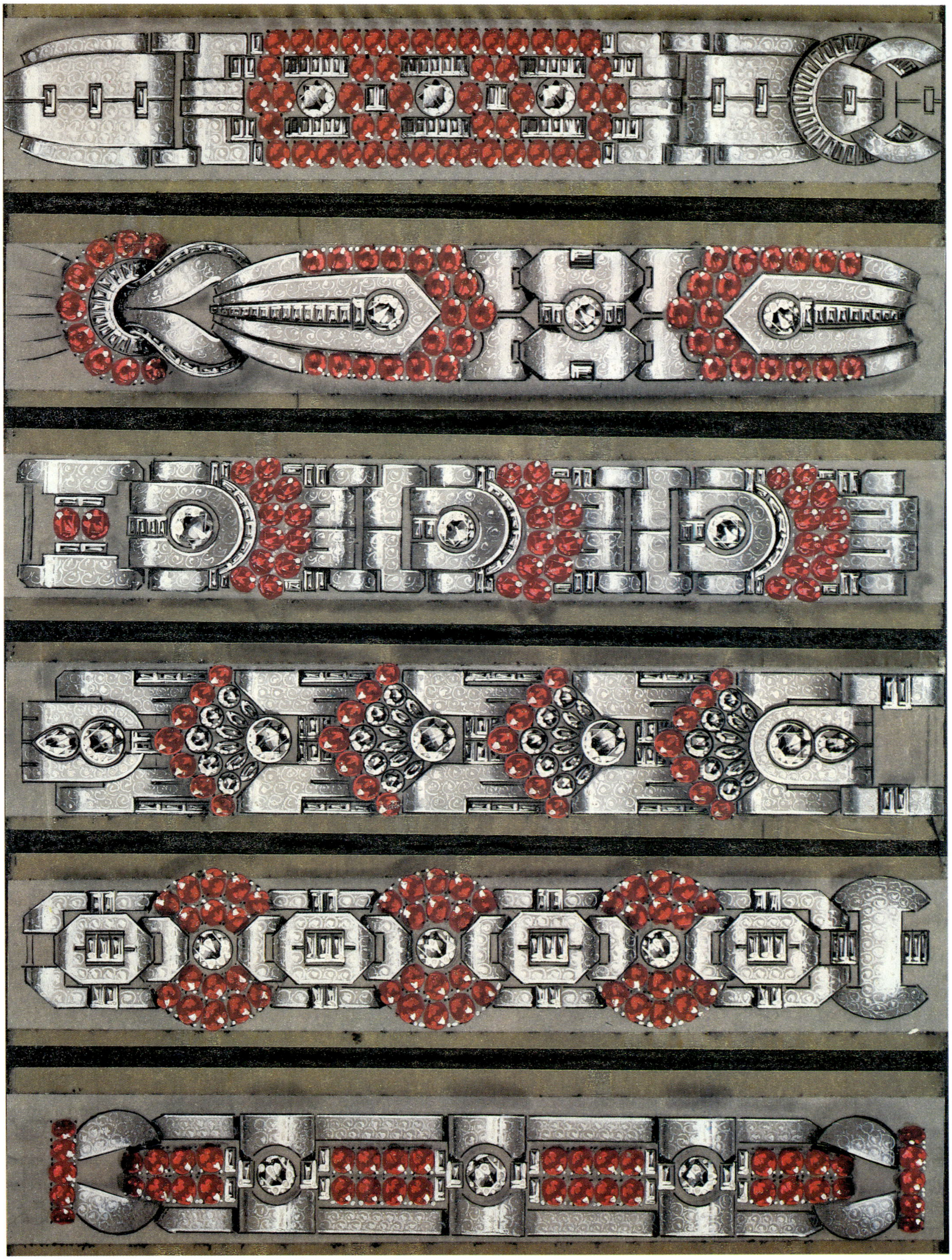

Van Cleef & Arpels: gouache studies for bracelets in platinum, faceted rubies, round diamonds and baguette diamonds. Work executed between 1926 and 1930. Van Cleef & Arpels Archives.

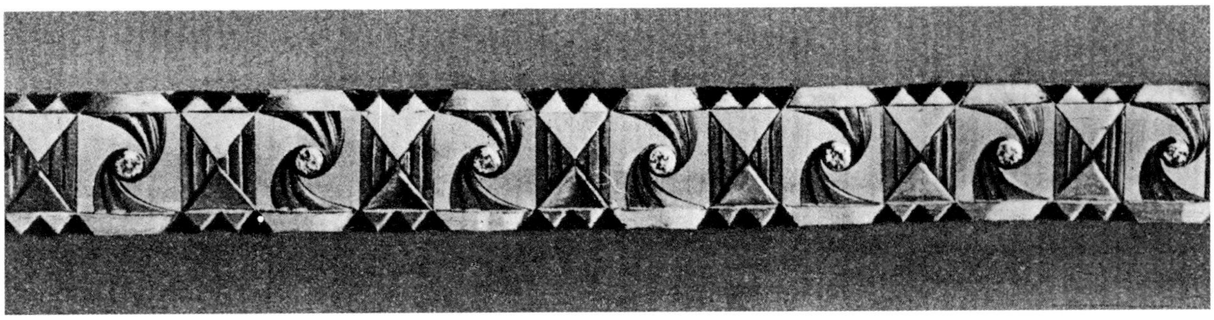
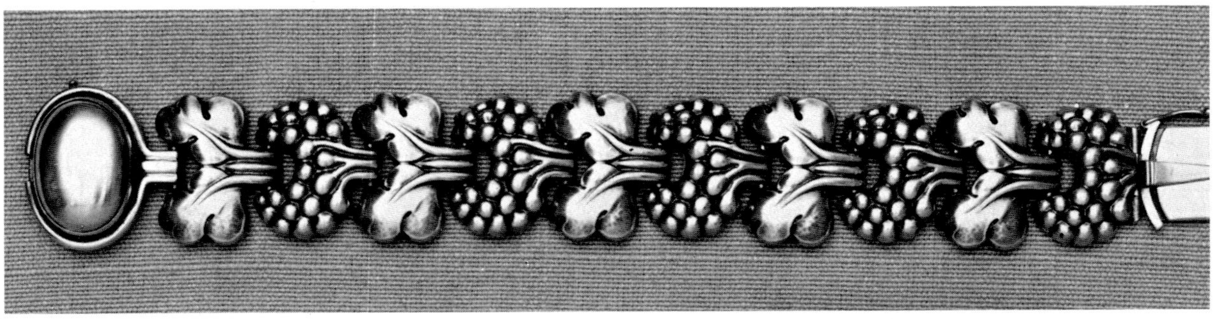
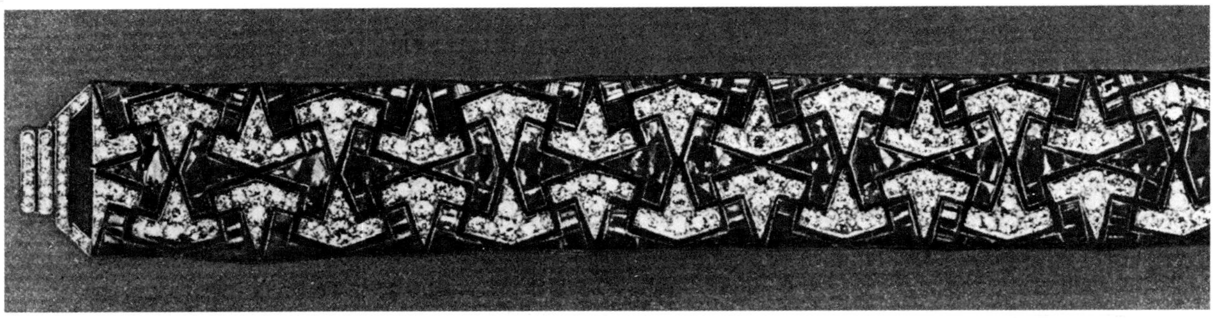
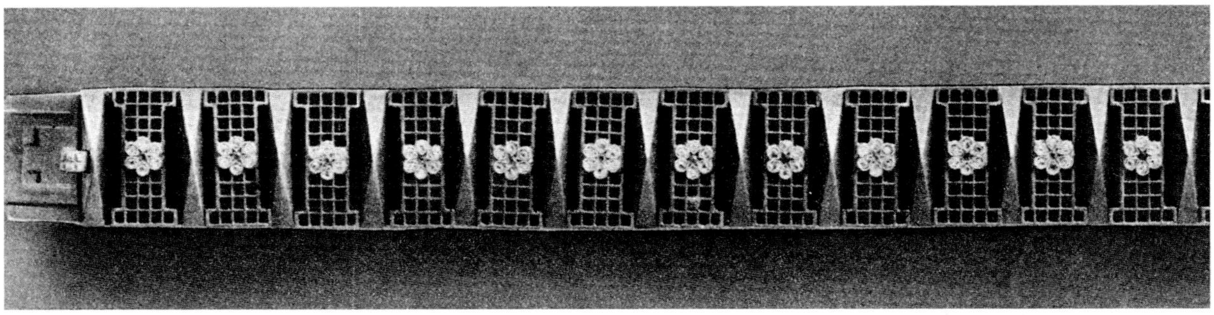
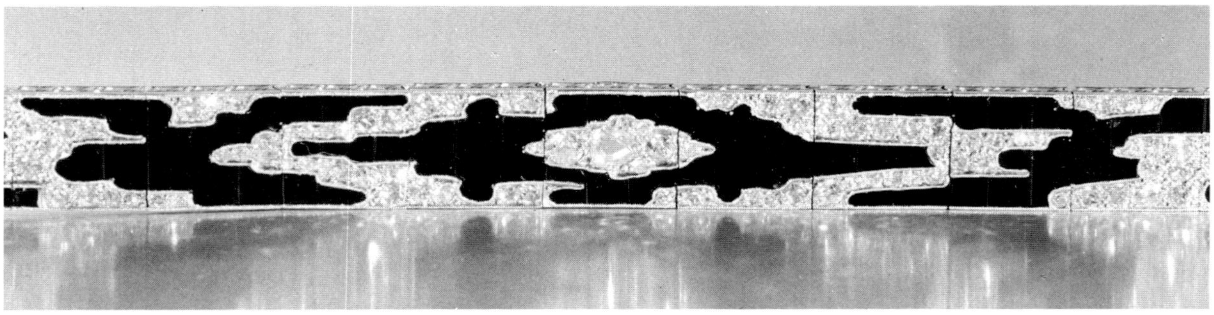

H. Dubret: gold, black enamel and diamond bracelet. 1925 Exposition, Paris, French section.

Georg Jensen: silver bracelet, 1924, Copenhagen.

Giacomo Ravasco: bracelet. 1925 Exposition, Paris, Italian section.

Masriera y Carreras: bracelet. 1925 Exposition, Paris, Spanish section.

Anonymous: diamond and black onyx bracelet. M. Souillac Collection. Photo: J.B. Rouault.

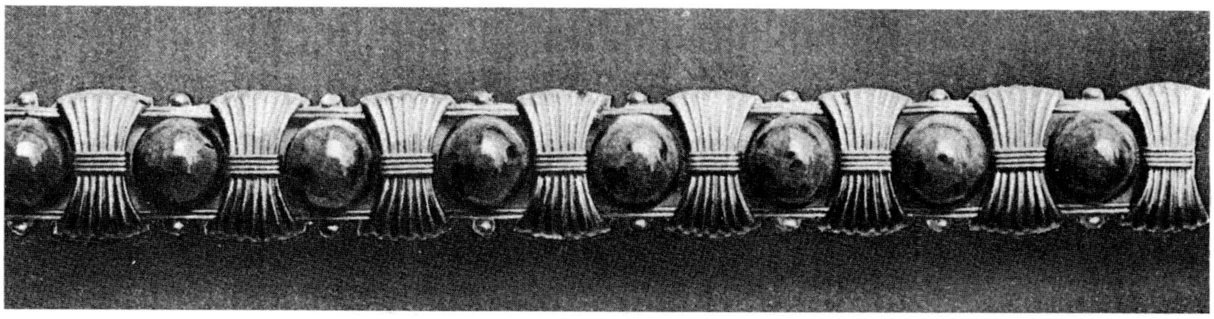

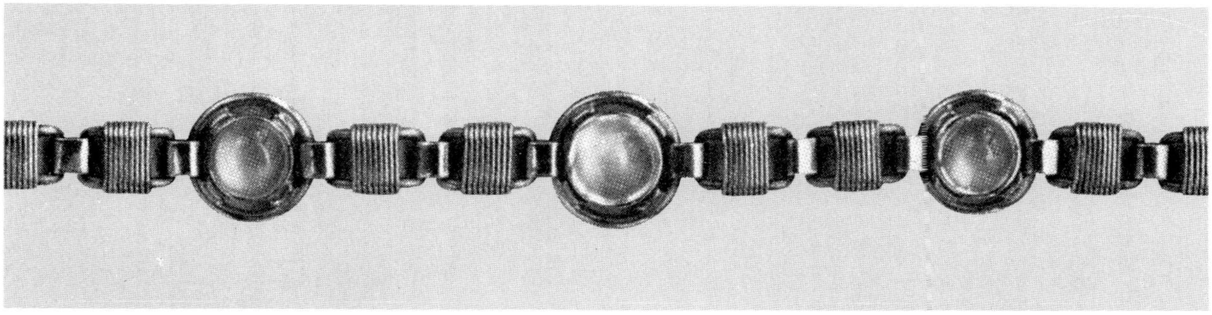

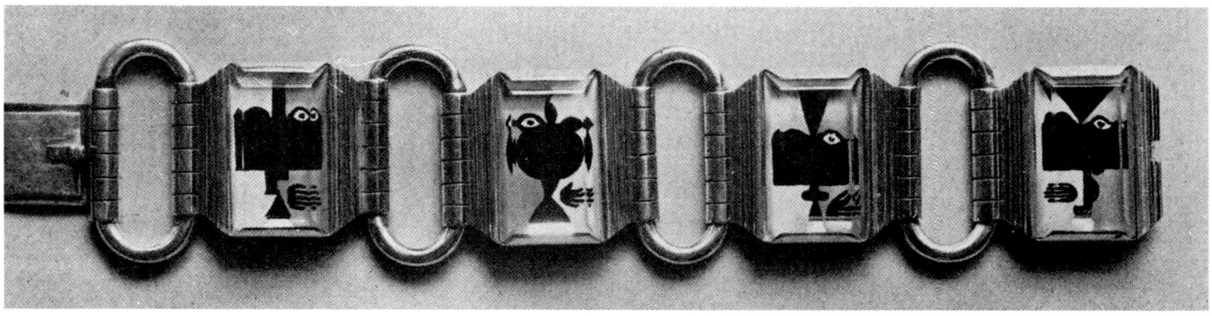

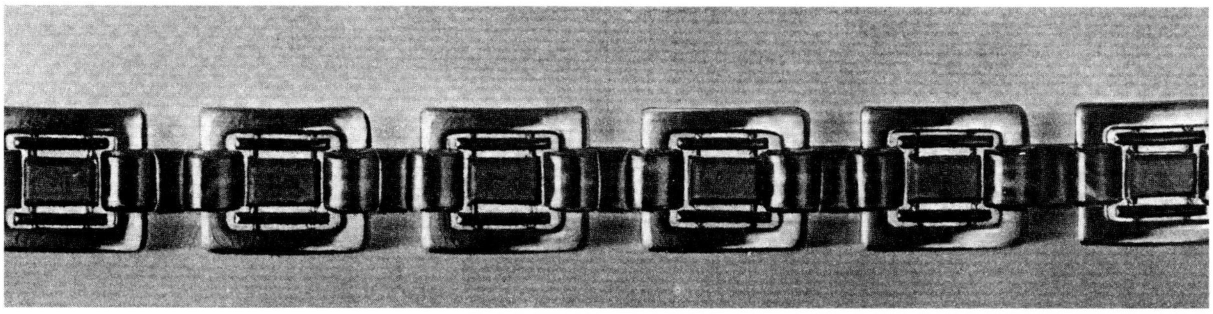

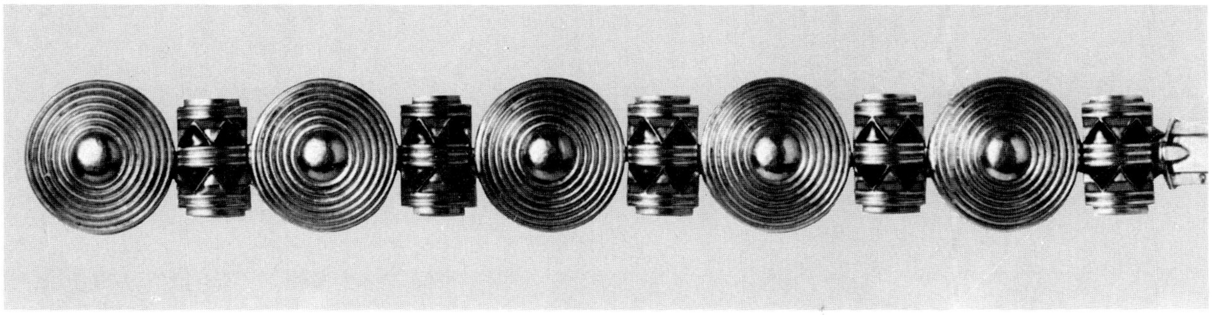

H. Dubret: gold bracelet with jade cabochons. 1925 Exposition, Paris, French section.

Siegfried Boès: gold bracelet with moonstones.

Jean Desprès, Etienne Cournault: bracelet in silver and engraved glass. Reproduced in Art et Décoration.

Paul Brandt: bracelet. 1925 Exposition, Paris.

Boucheron: bracelet in precious metal and enamel. Boucheron Archives.

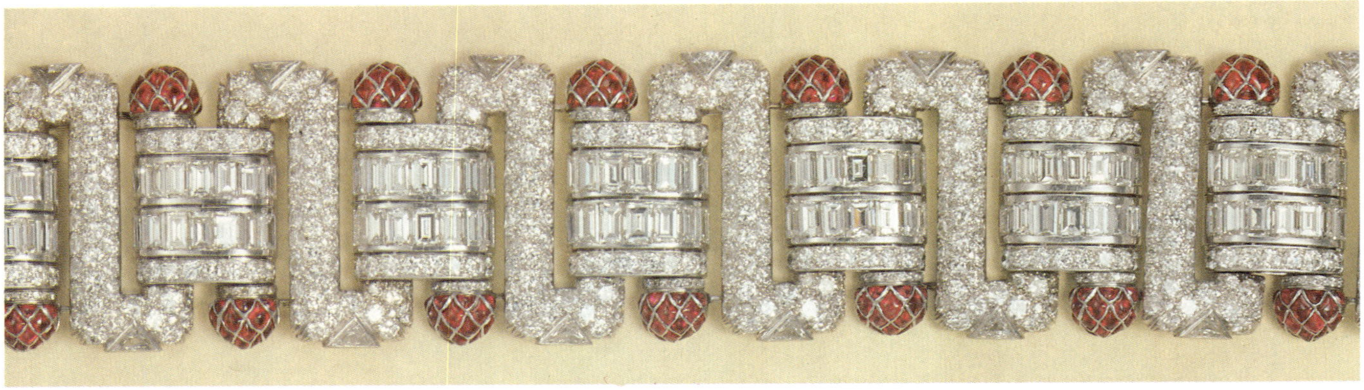

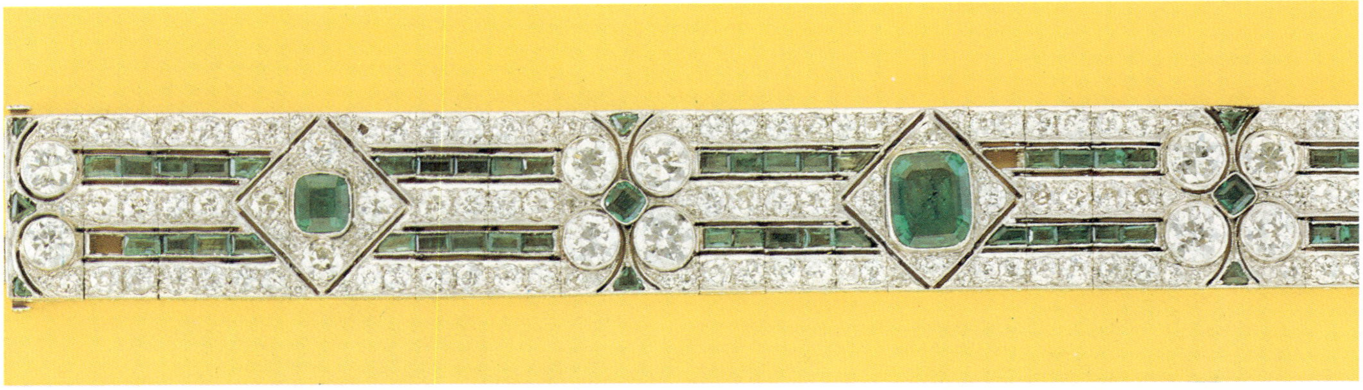

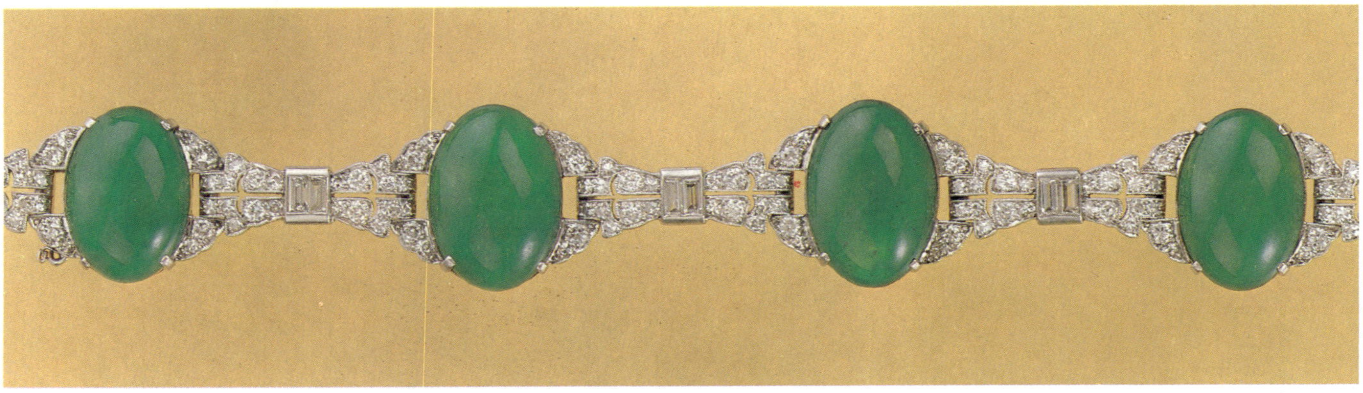

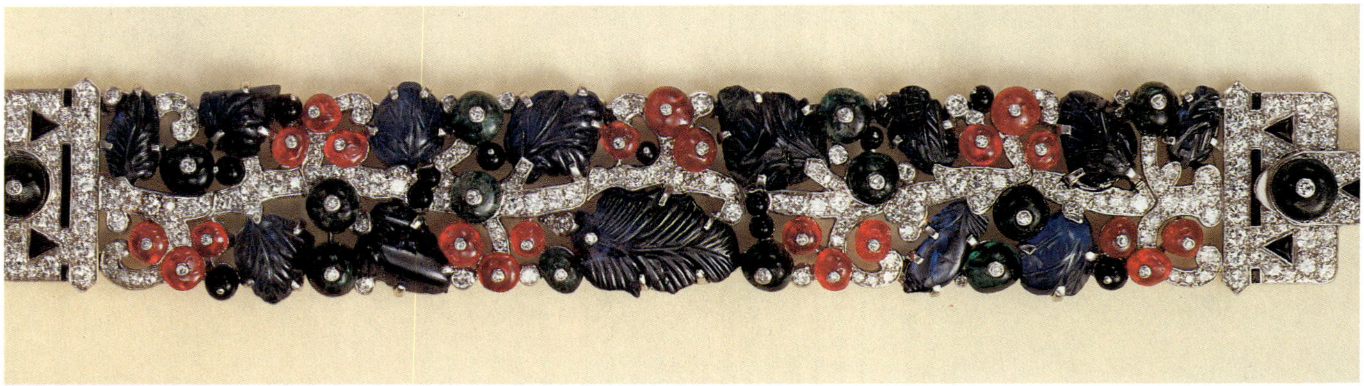

Anonymous: diamond bracelet with ruby cabochons, mounted on platinum. Sotheby's, Geneva.

Anonymous: bracelet comprising rows of round diamonds and baguette-cut emeralds, decorated with cushion-shaped emeralds. Christie's.

Anonymous: bracelet comprising oval jade cabochons linked by motifs in round and baguette diamonds, mounted on platinum. Christie's.

Cartier: diamond bracelet with engraved sapphire leaves, emerald, ruby and black onyx berries, signed. Christie's, Geneva.

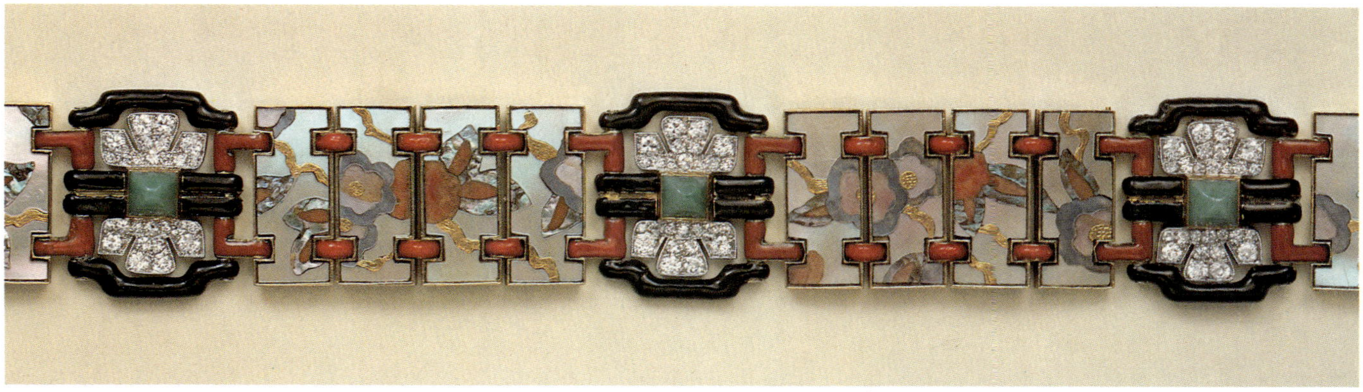

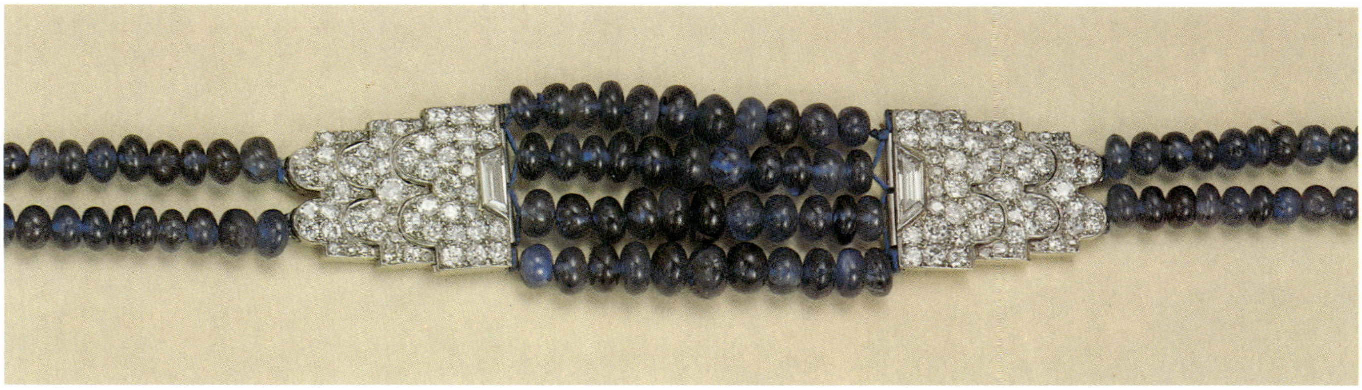

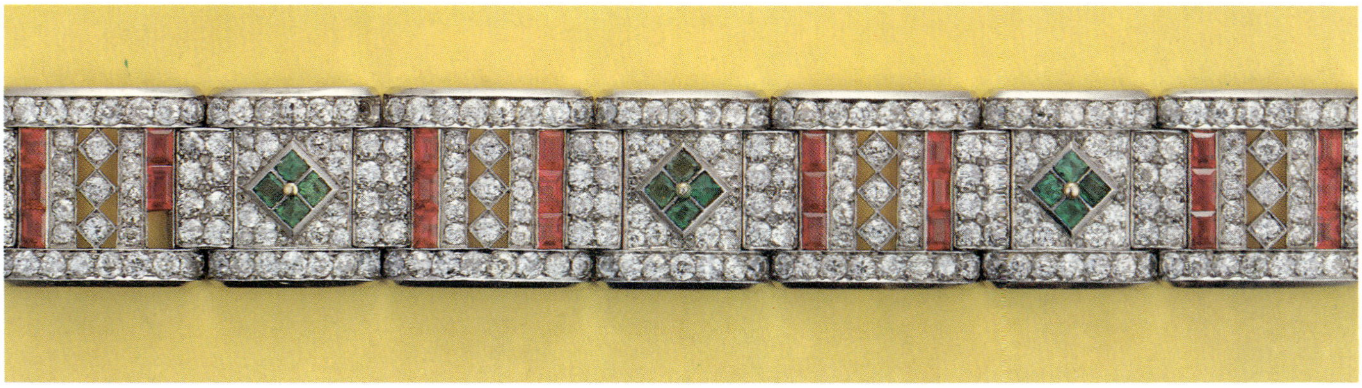

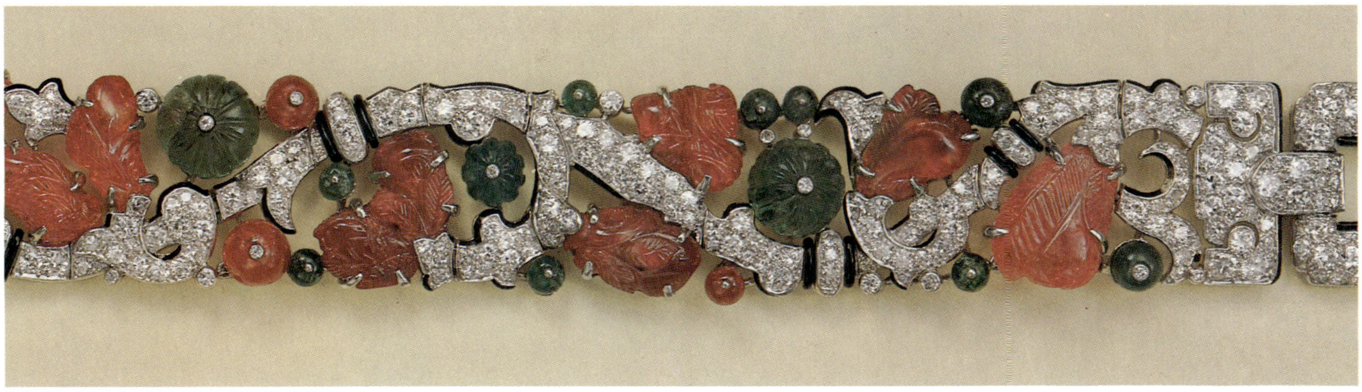

Anonymous: bracelet in the oriental style composed of rectangles of mother-of-pearl bearing a floral design, alternating with geometric motifs in diamonds, jade and black enamel, joined to the former by red enamel links. Christie's, Geneva.

Anonymous: bracelet comprising diamonds and rows of sapphire beads, mounted on platinum. Sotheby's, Geneva.

Anonymous: diamond bracelet with lines of calibré rubies and motifs of square-cut emeralds. Christie's, New York.

Cartier: bracelet composed of stylized branches in diamonds and black enamel, engraved ruby leaves, and berries consisting of ribbed emerald cabochons, small ruby cabochons and emerald beads. Christie's.

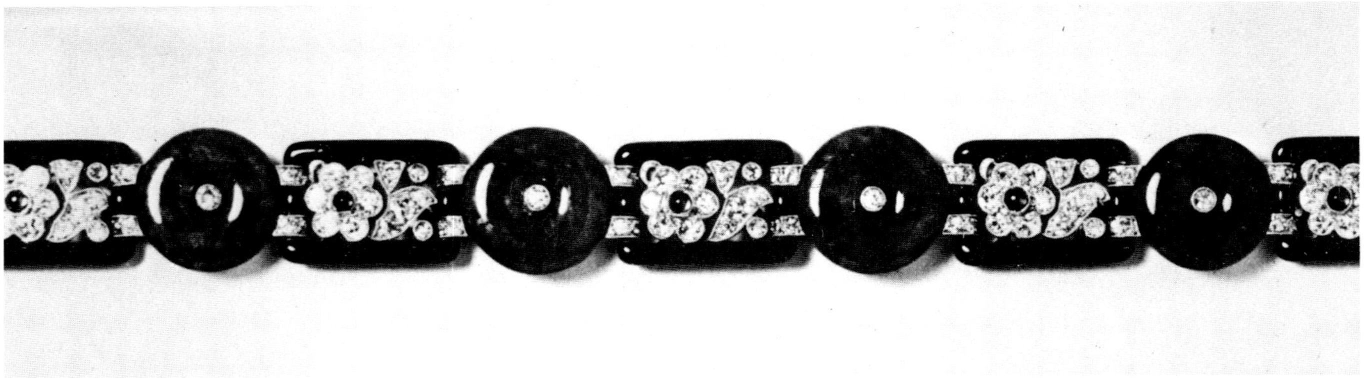

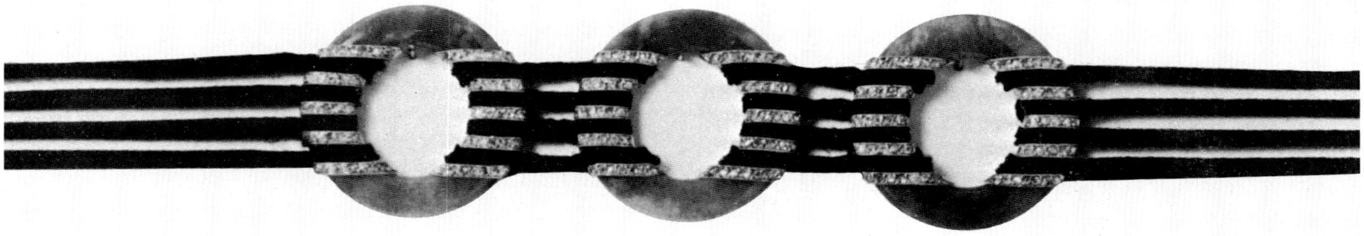

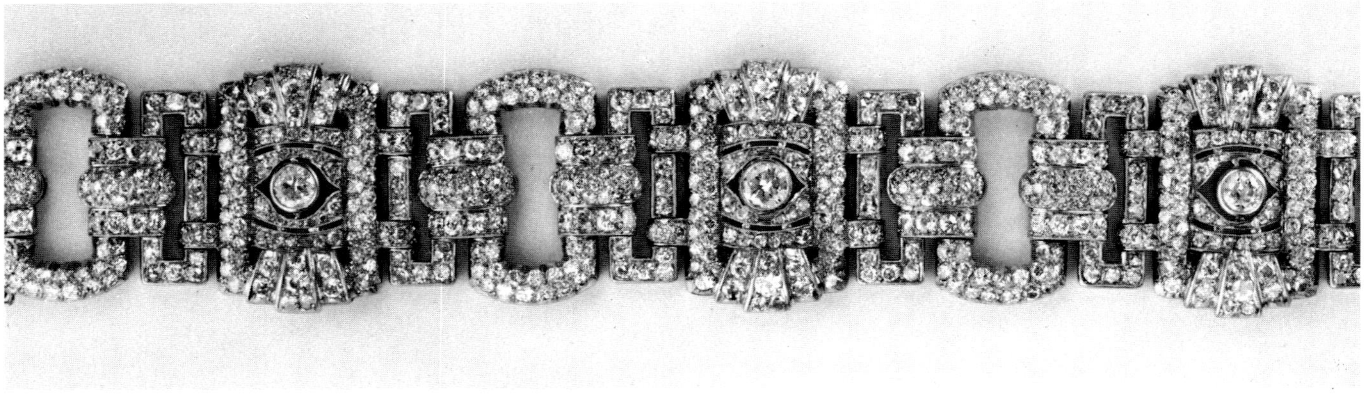

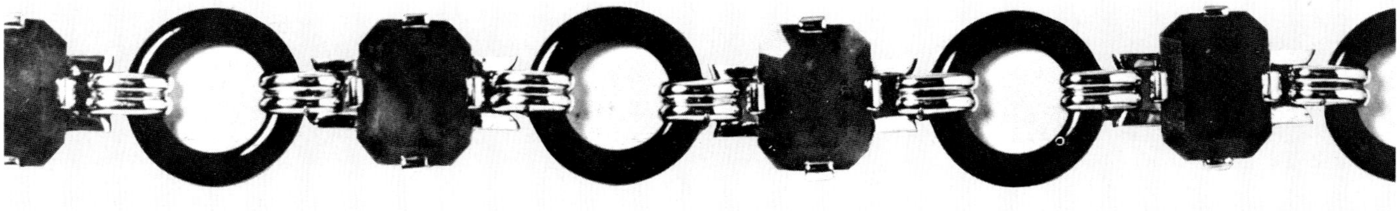

Boucheron: bracelet composed of jade discs, each set with a diamond, linked by onyx plaques with floral diamond motifs, c. 1925.

Boucheron: bracelet composed of three jade rings set with diamonds and linked by black silk cords, c. 1925. *Boucheron Archives.*

Anonymous: bracelet composed of three diamond motifs, with geometric diamond links, mounted on platinum. Christie's, New York.

Boucheron: bracelet composed of onyx rings and hardstones, attached by gold links, c. 1925.

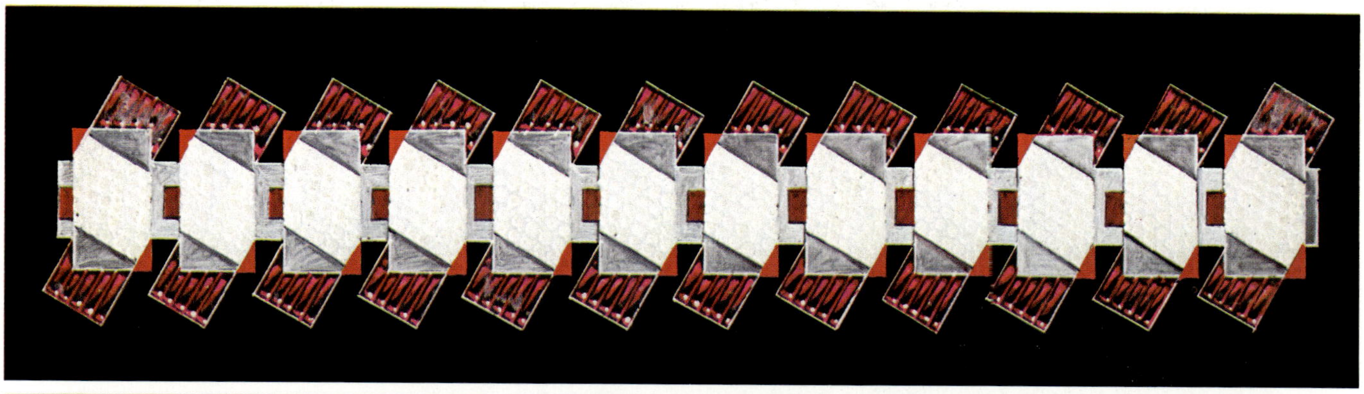

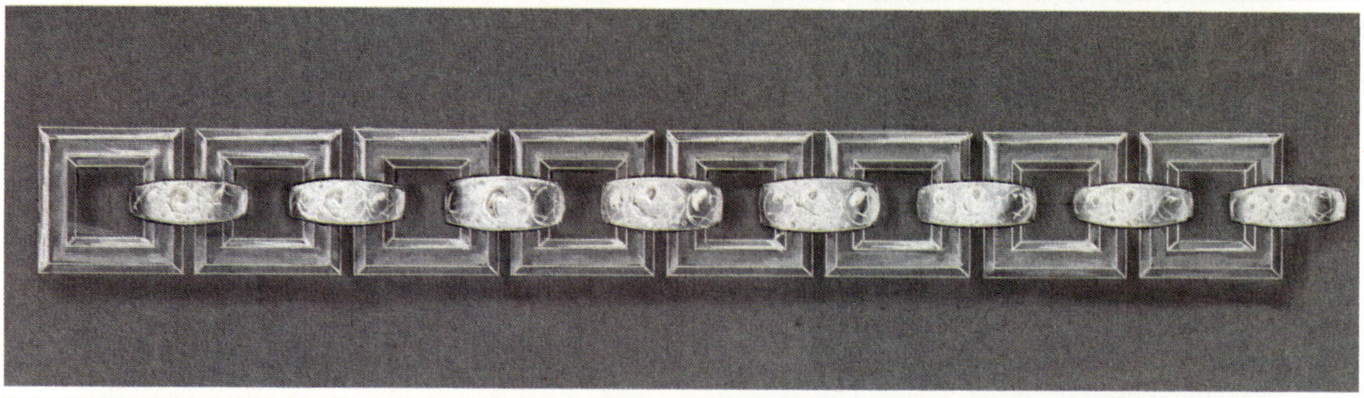

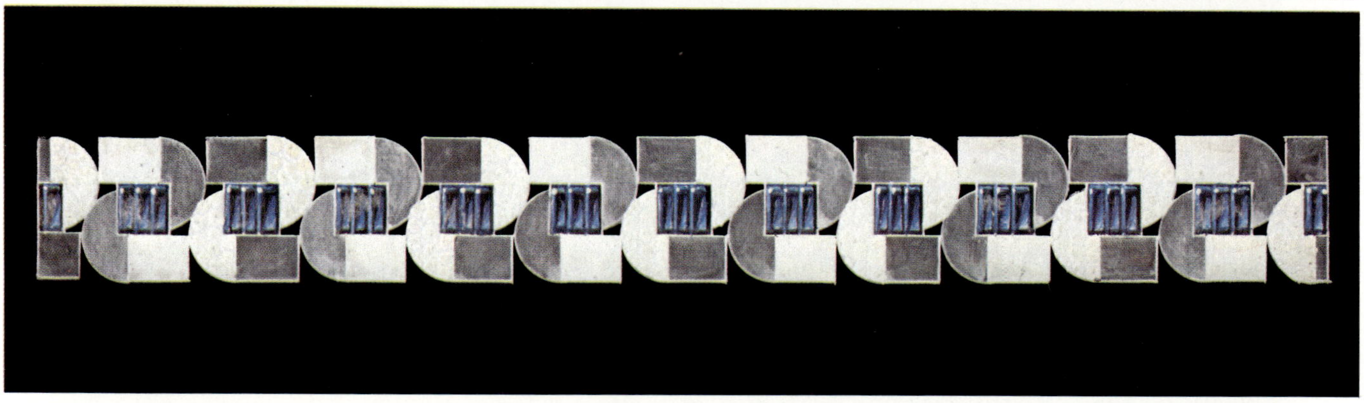

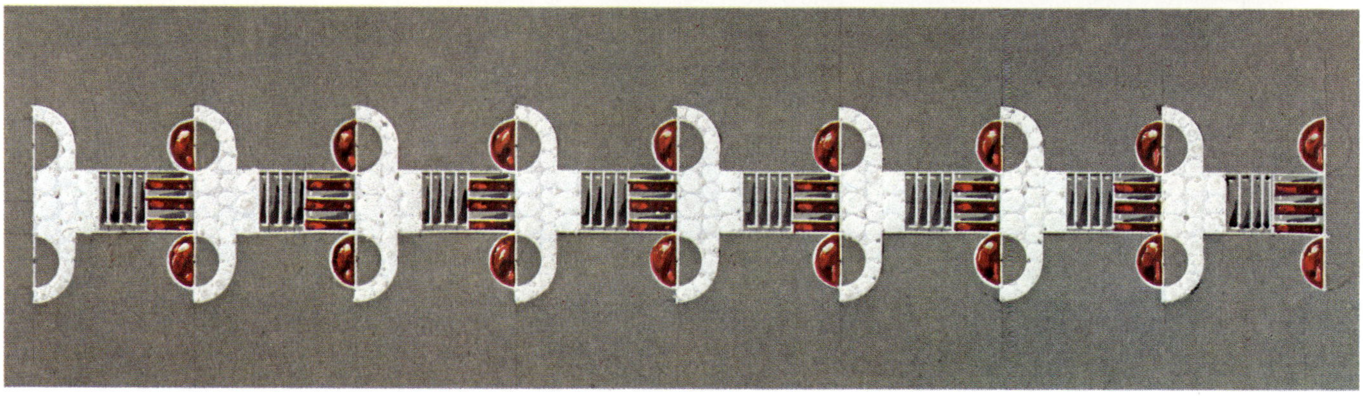

Mauboussin: gouache study for a bracelet in platinum, diamonds and rubies. Mauboussin Archives.

Boivin: gouache study for a bracelet in rock crystal and diamonds. Boivin Archives.

Mauboussin: gouache study for a bracelet in platinum and sapphires. Mauboussin Archives.

Mauboussin: gouache study for a bracelet in platinum, diamonds and rubies. Mauboussin Archives.

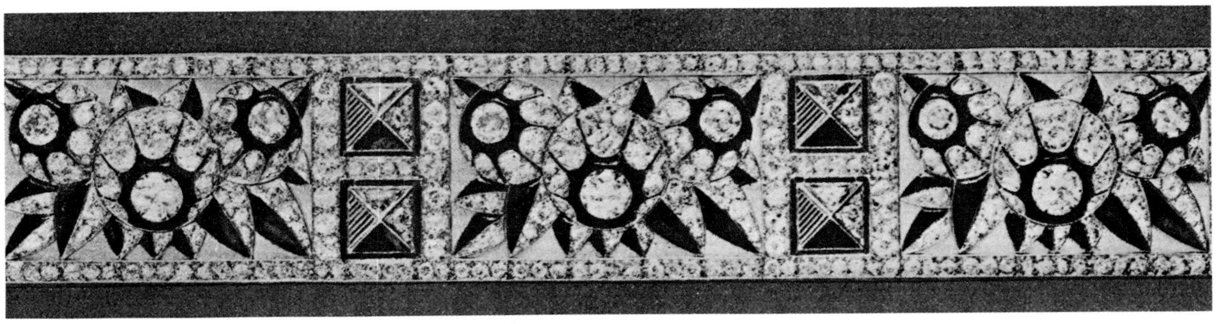

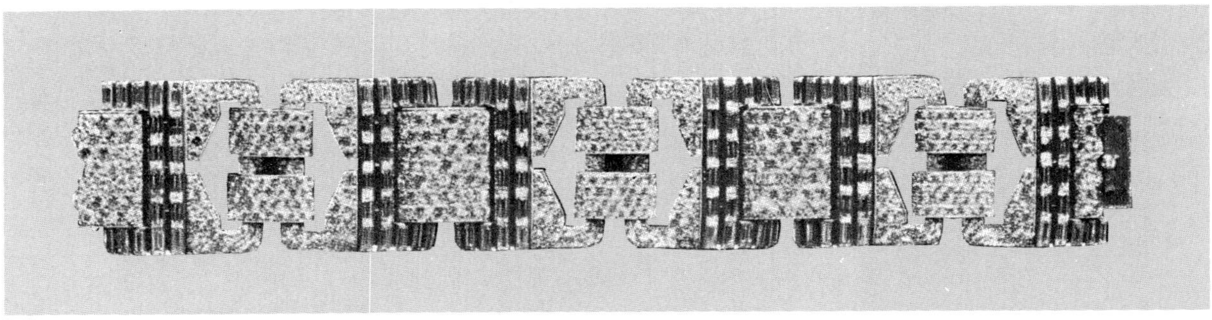

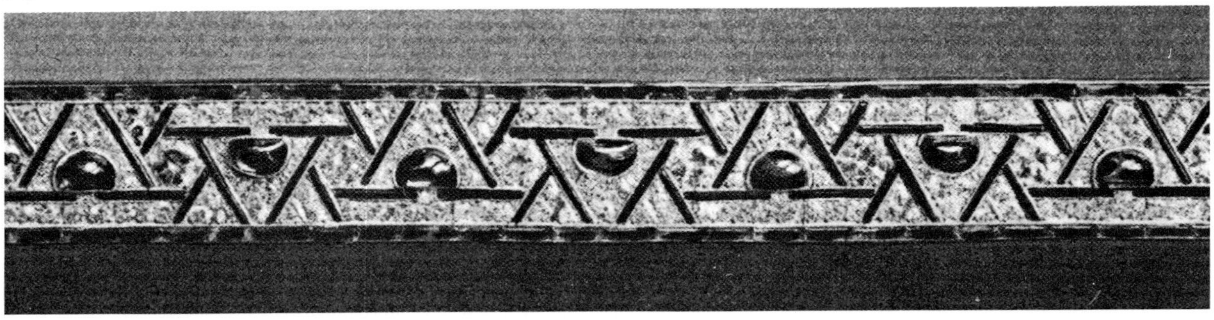

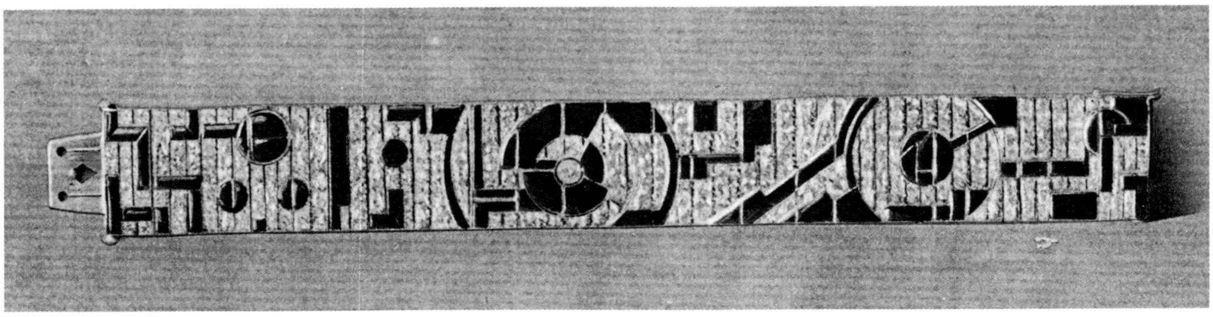

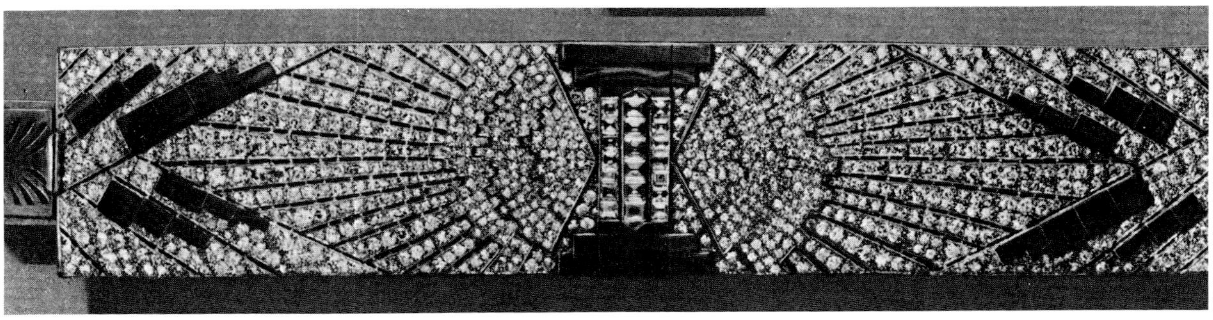

Mauboussin: bracelet in diamonds and black enamel on mother-of-pearl, mounted on platinum, shown at the 1925 Exposition in Paris.

Chaumet: diamond bracelet reproduced in Art et Décoration, *August 1929.*

Wolfers: bracelet shown in the Belgian section at the 1925 Exposition in Paris.

Gérard Sandoz: bracelet in diamonds, onyx and coral, shown at the 1925 Exposition in Paris.

Raymond Templier: bracelet in platinum, diamonds and malachite, shown at the 1925 Exposition in Paris.

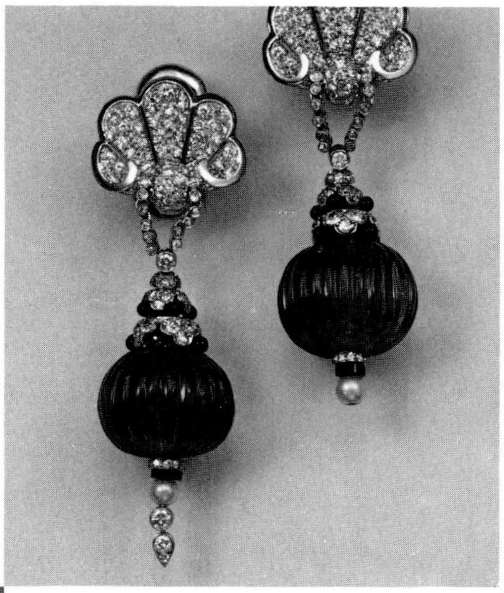

Right: *Verdura: pendant earrings composed of ribbed emerald cabochons decorated with onyx, diamonds and a pearl, attached to a stylized shell motif in diamonds. Christie's, Geneva.*

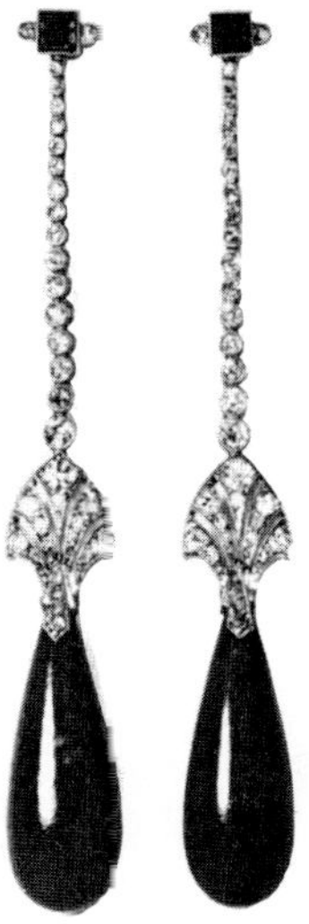

Boucheron: *pendant earrings composed of onyx drops and diamonds, c. 1925. Boucheron Archives.*

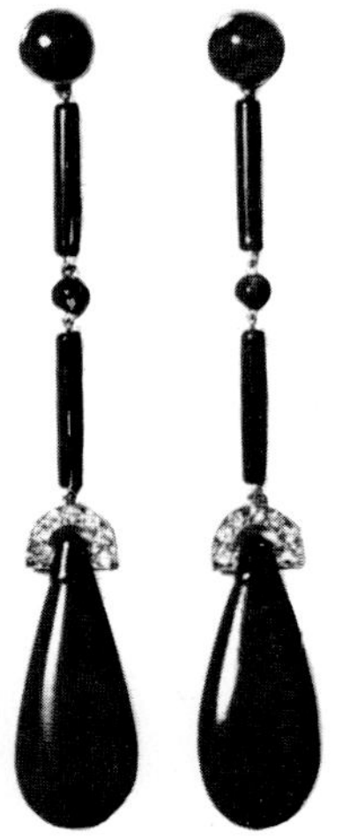

Boucheron: *pendant earrings in onyx and diamonds, c. 1925. Boucheron Archives.*

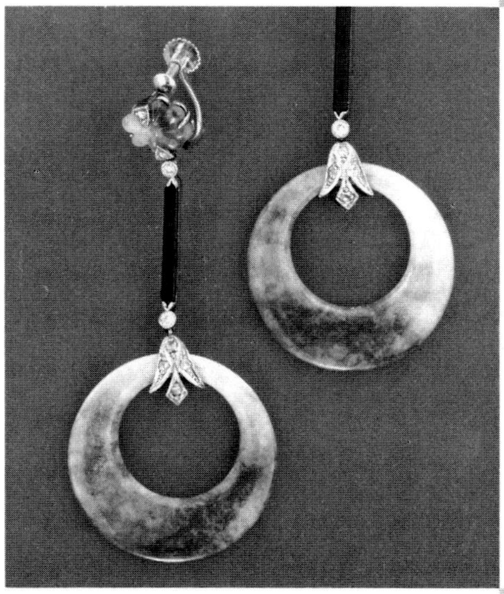

Below: *Anonymous: pendant earrings composed of a jade ring with a stylized diamond flower, attached by an onyx link to an engraved jade motif. Christie's.*

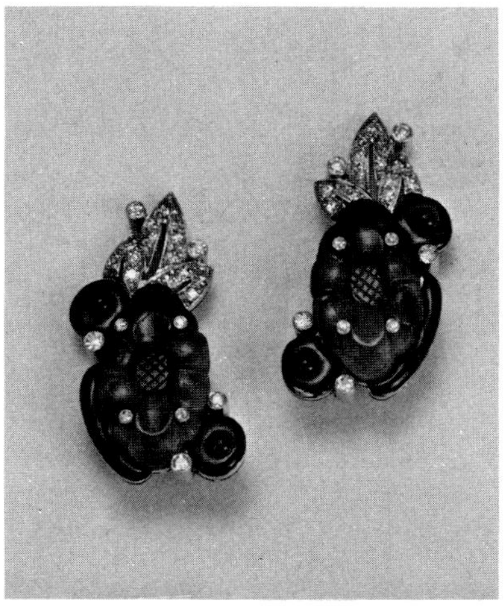

Centre: *Anonymous: ear clips in engraved jade, black enamel and diamonds. Sotheby's, Geneva.*

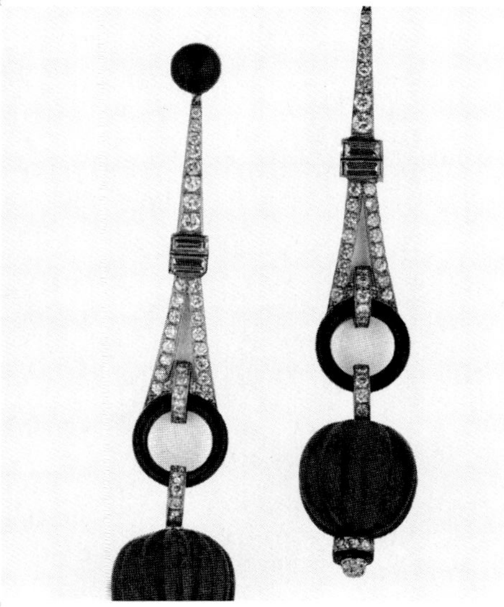

Above: *Anonymous: pendant earrings composed of a ribbed emerald cabochon decorated with onyx and diamonds. Sotheby's, Geneva.*

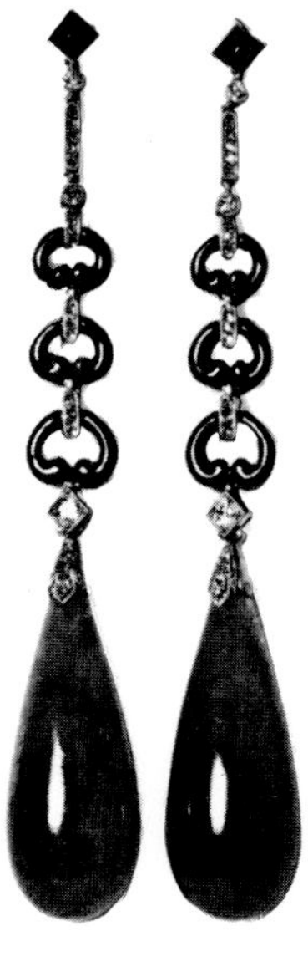

Boucheron: *pendant earrings composed of jade drops suspended from onyx rings linked with diamonds, c. 1925. Boucheron Archives.*

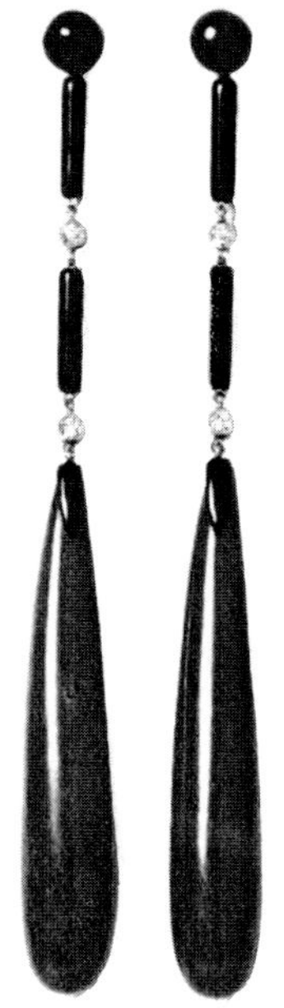

Boucheron: *pendant earrings composed of cornelian drops suspended from onyx rods linked with diamonds, c. 1925.*

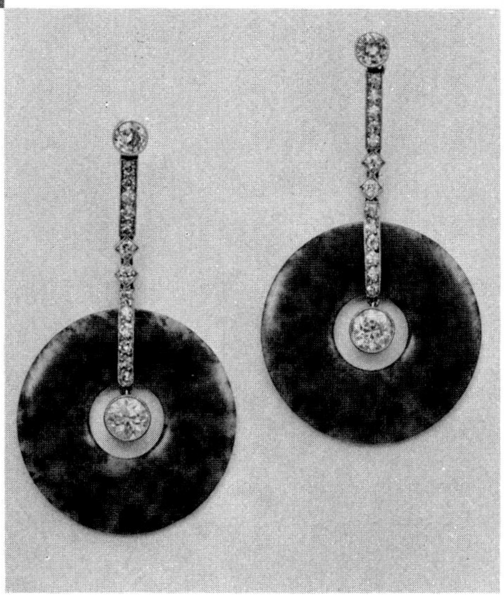

Lacloche: *pendant earrings composed of a jade ring with a free-hanging diamond at its centre, suspended from a line of calibré diamonds. Christie's.*

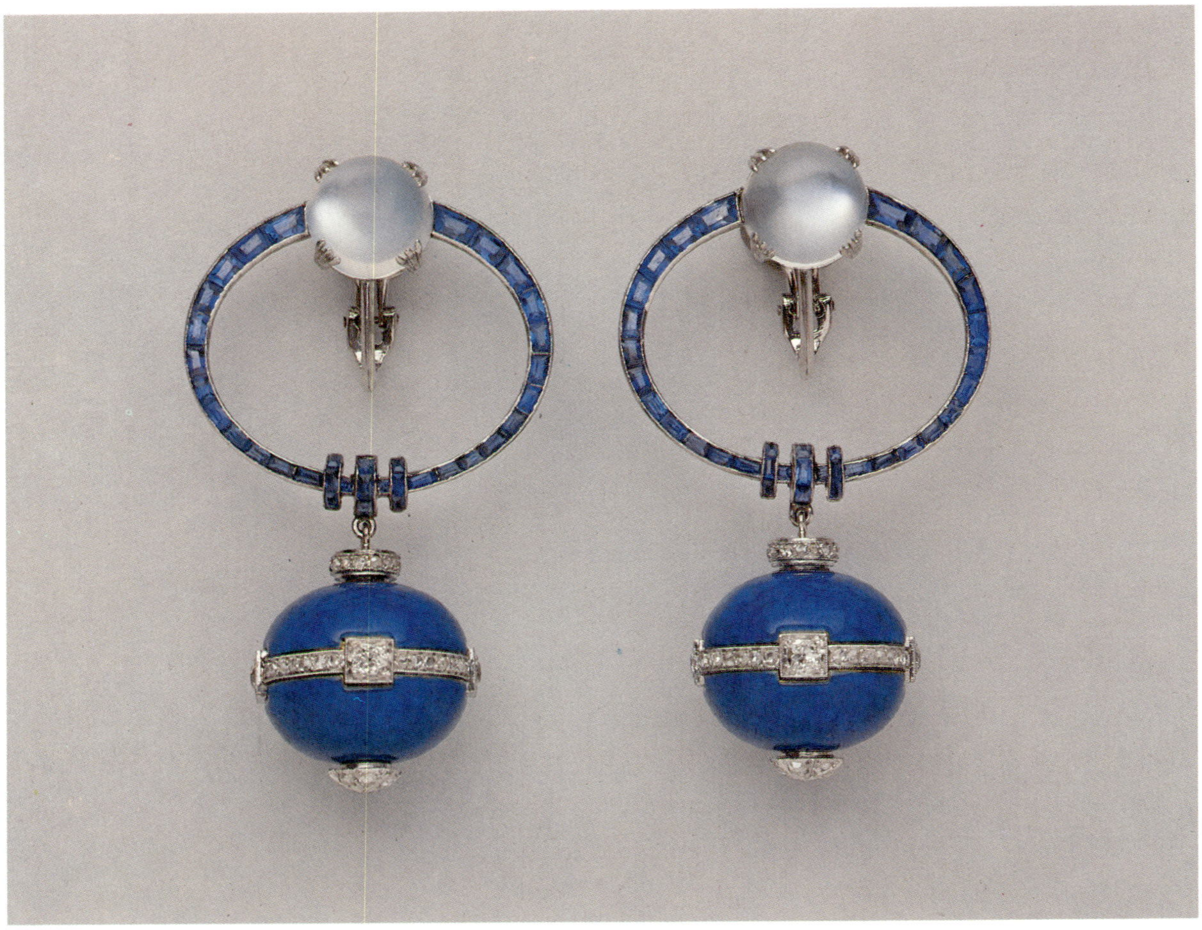

Georges Fouquet: pendant earrings in moonstones, sapphires, diamonds and blue enamel, c. 1925. Private Collection.

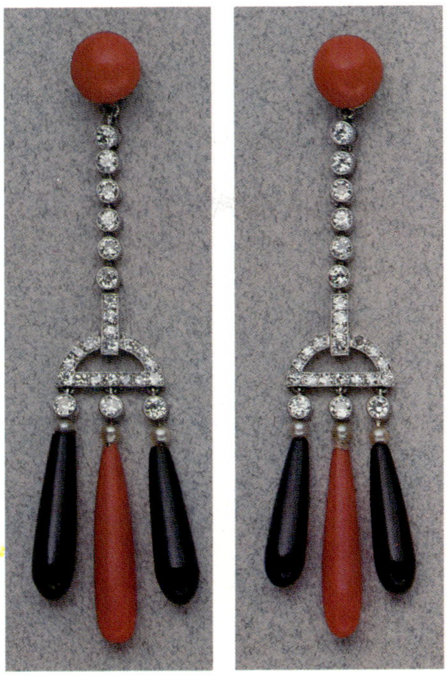

Van Cleef & Arpels: pendant earrings in coral, diamonds and black onyx. Private Collection.

Anonymous: ring set with a sapphire and with round and baguette diamonds.

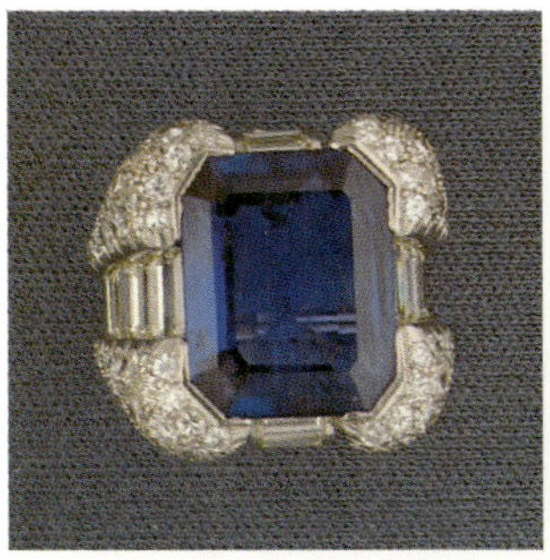

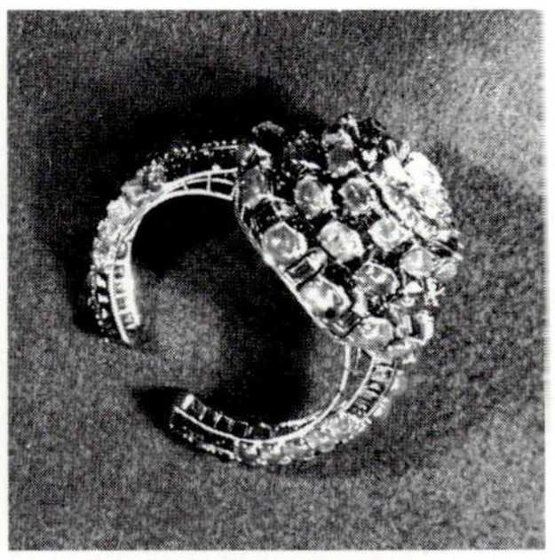

Mellerio: bracelet decorated with ruby and emerald cabochons, round and baguette diamonds, mounted on platinum.

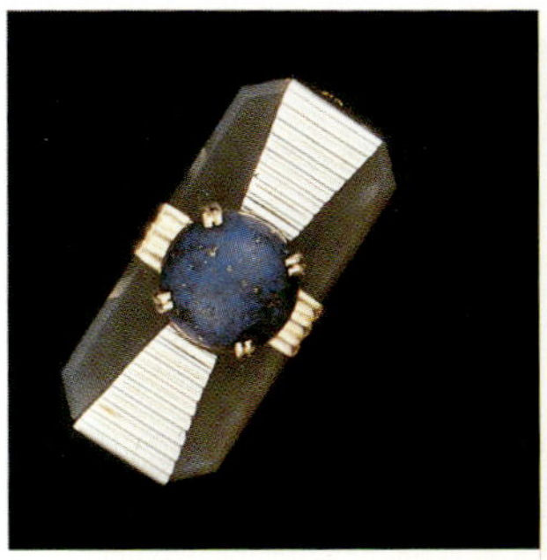

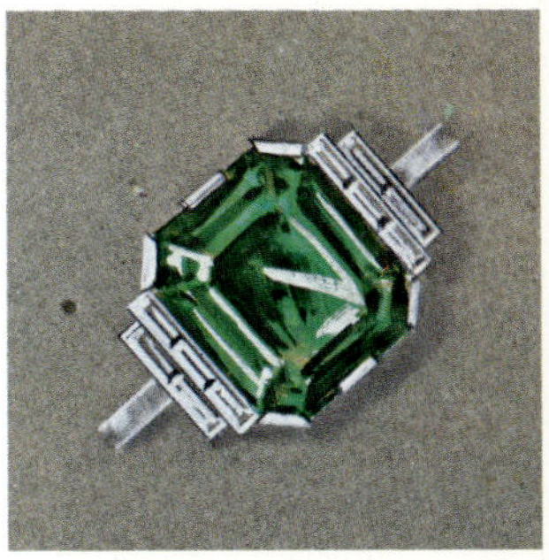

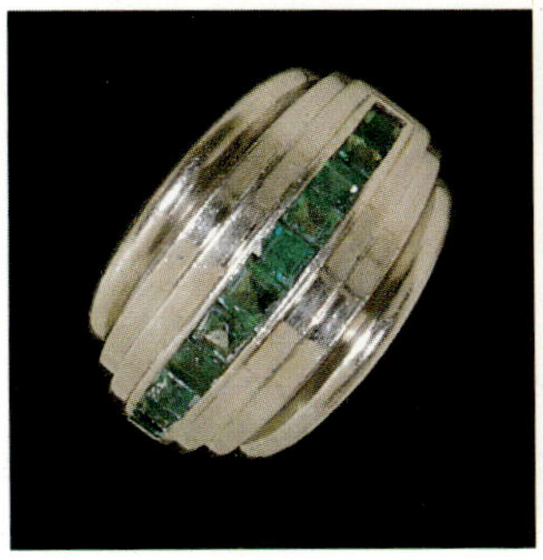

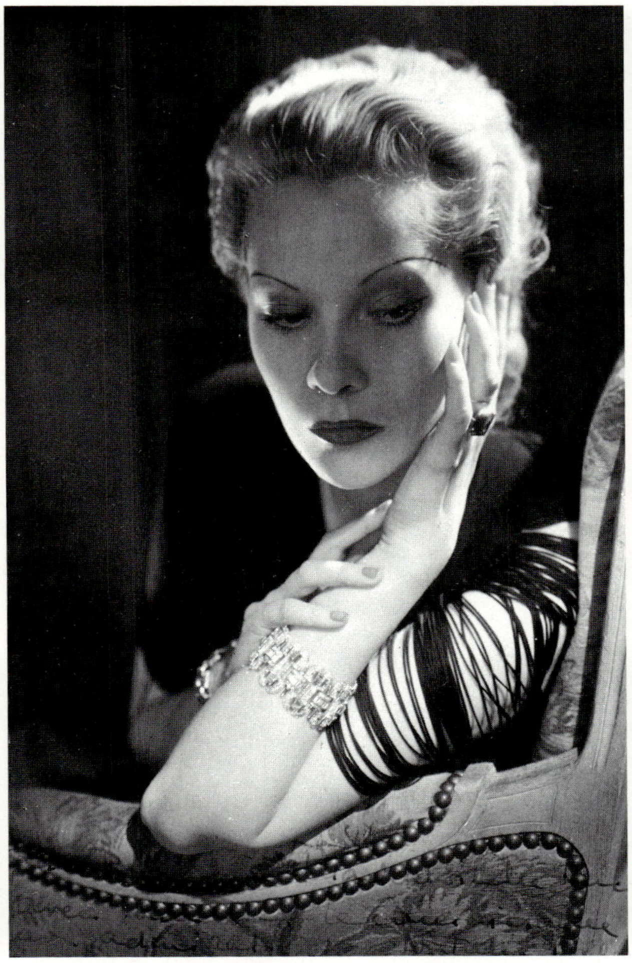

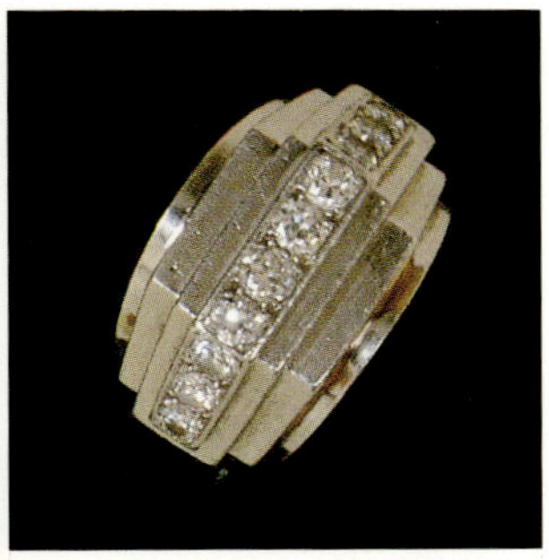

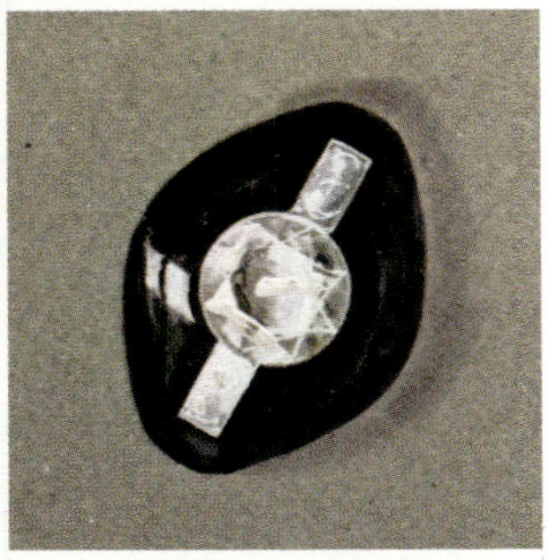

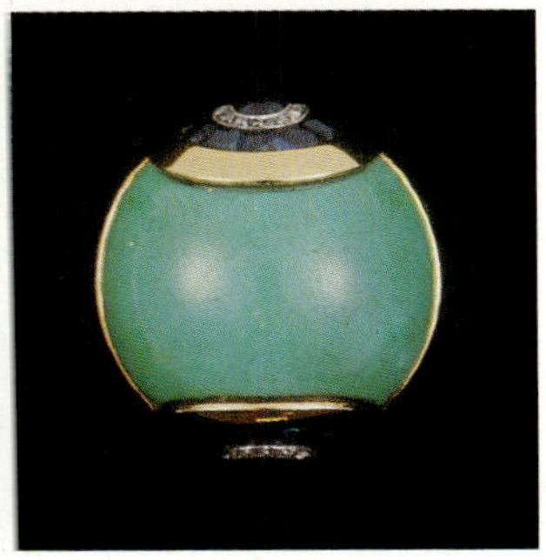

Boucheron: brooch in gold, silver, lapis and quartz, c. 1925. Sotheby's.

Boivin: gouache study for a ring in platinum, emerald and baguette diamonds.

Boucheron: platinum and emerald ring, c. 1925–30. Sotheby's.

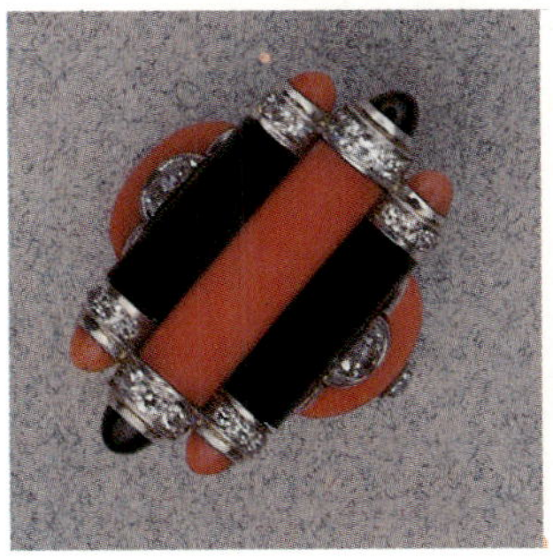

Cartier: onyx, coral and diamond ring, 1933. Private Collection.

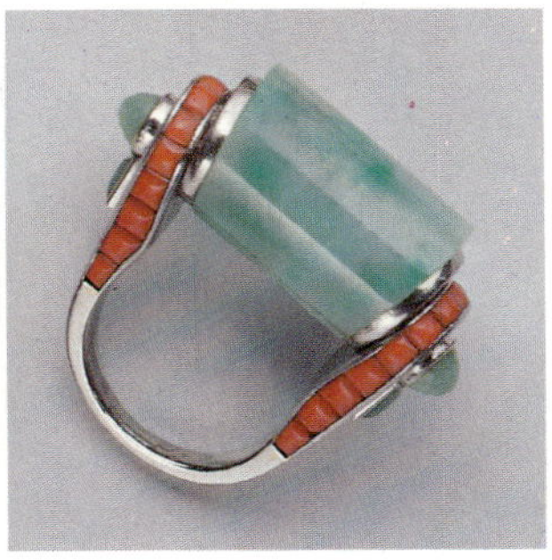

Anonymous: ring in jade, coral, white gold and platinum, c. 1930, France.

Boucheron (attr.): platinum and diamond ring, c. 1925–30.

Boivin: gouache study for an onyx and diamond ring.

Anonymous: ring in gold, sapphires, diamonds and green hardstone, c. 1925.

Boivin: gouache study for a rock crystal ring decorated with an emerald.

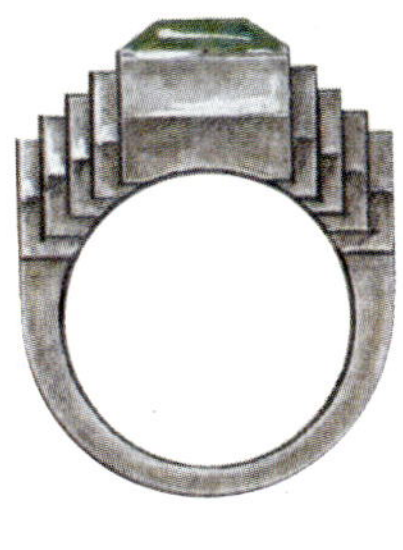

Centre: photograph of Princess Nathalie Paley. Musée de la Mode Archives, Paris.

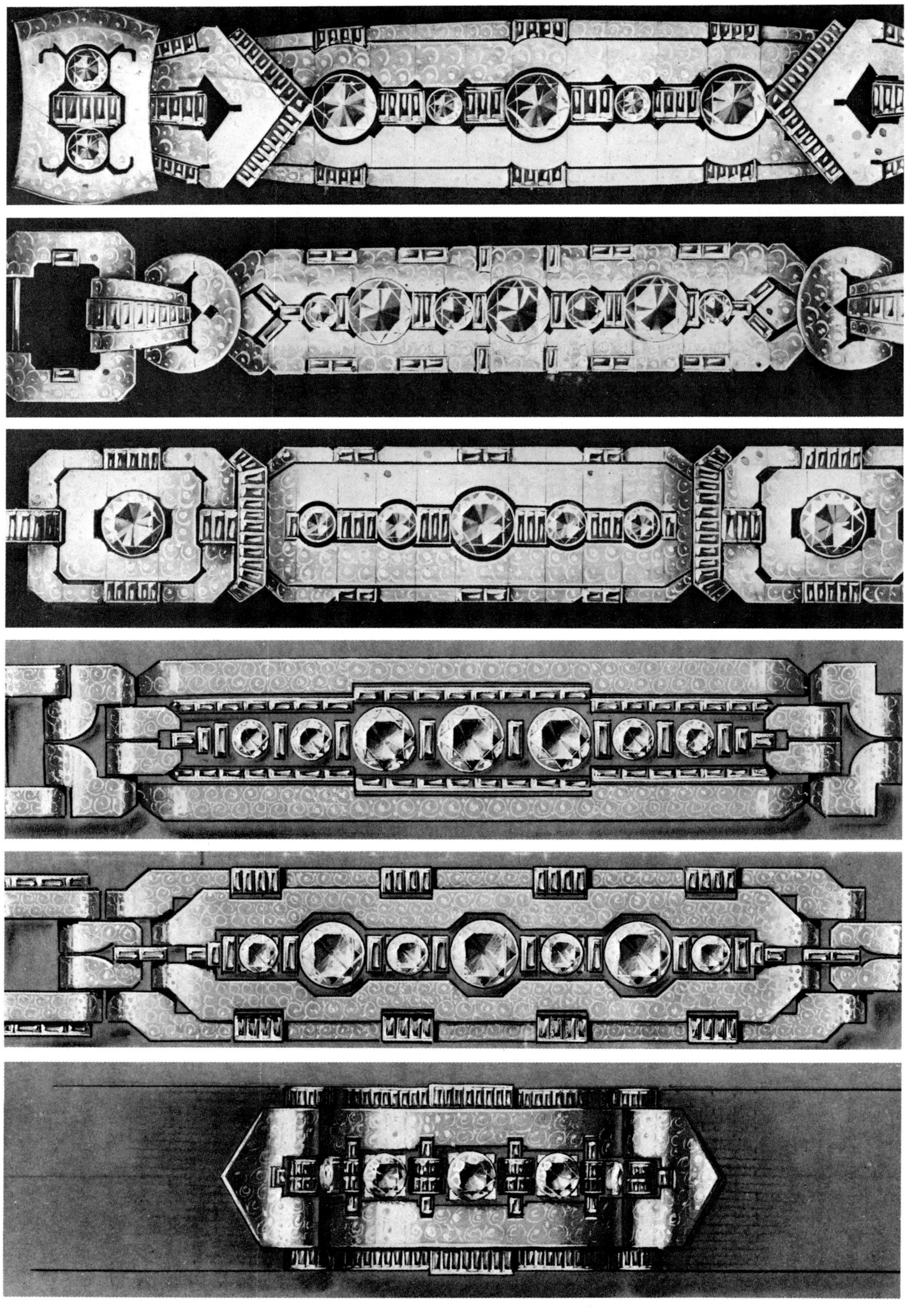

Van Cleef & Arpels: gouache studies for bracelets in platinum, round and baguette diamonds. Work executed between 1926 and 1930.

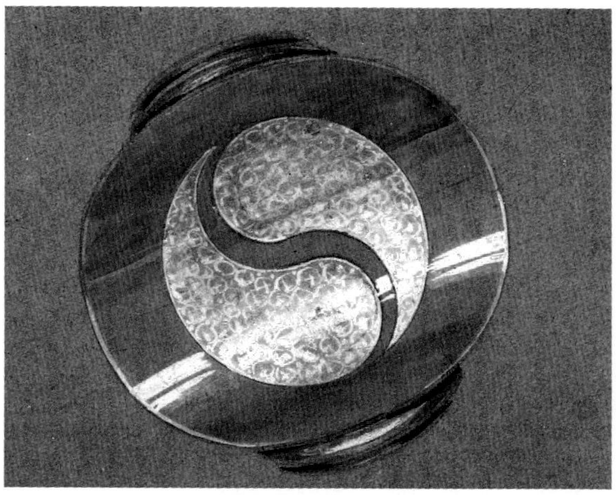

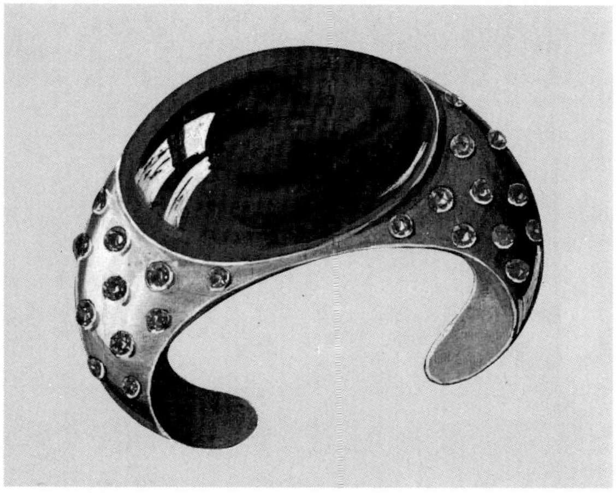

Boivin: 'saddle' bracelet in gold and diamonds. Boivin Archives.

Boivin: platinum bracelet decorated with a coral cabochon and studded with round sapphires.

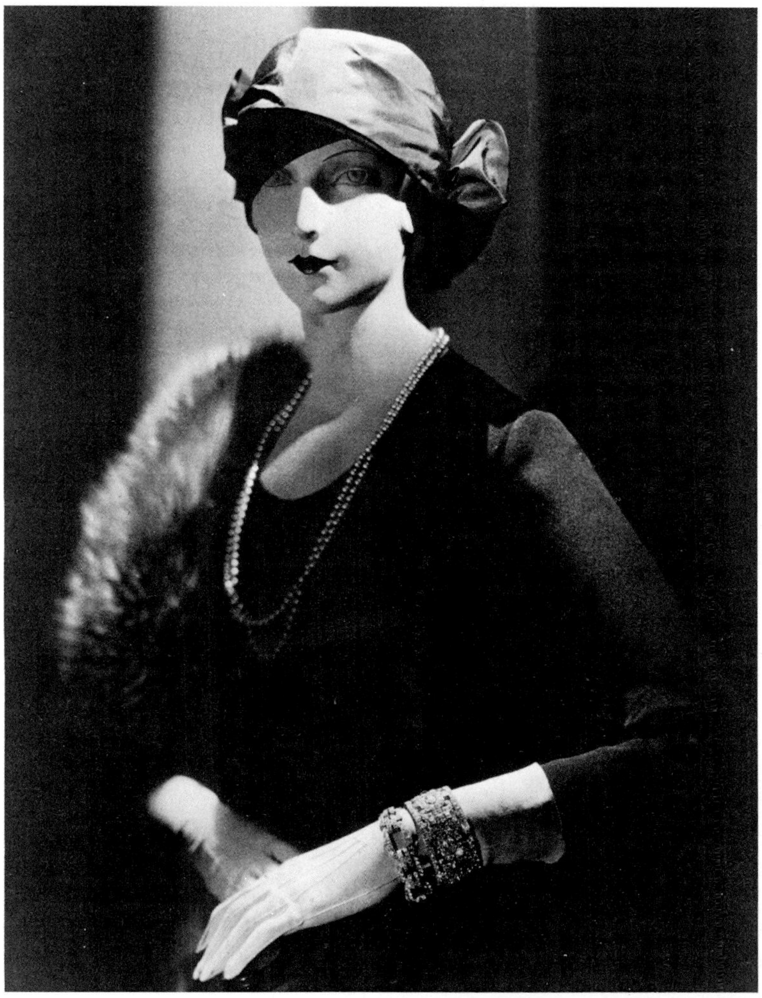

Siegel mannequin wearing jewelry by Mauboussin, dress and fox fur by Yteb. Photo: Hoyningen-Huene.

Boucheron: bracelet in faceted rock crystal with diamonds and coloured stones, c. 1925. Boucheron Archives.

Boivin: bracelet in platinum, diamonds and calibré sapphires.

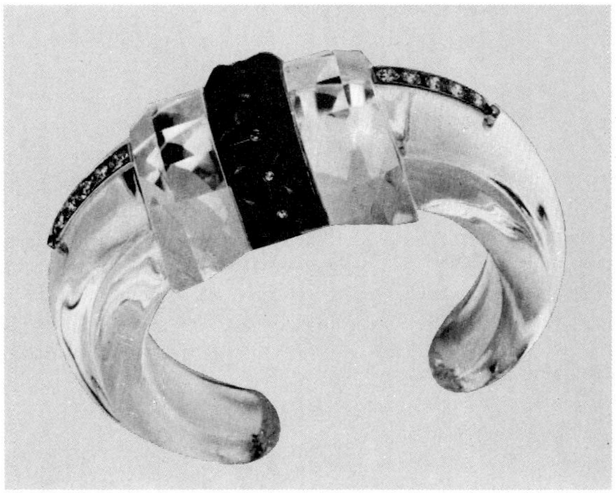

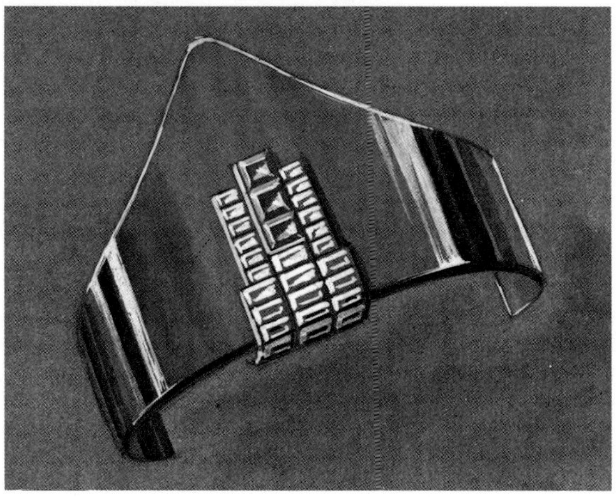

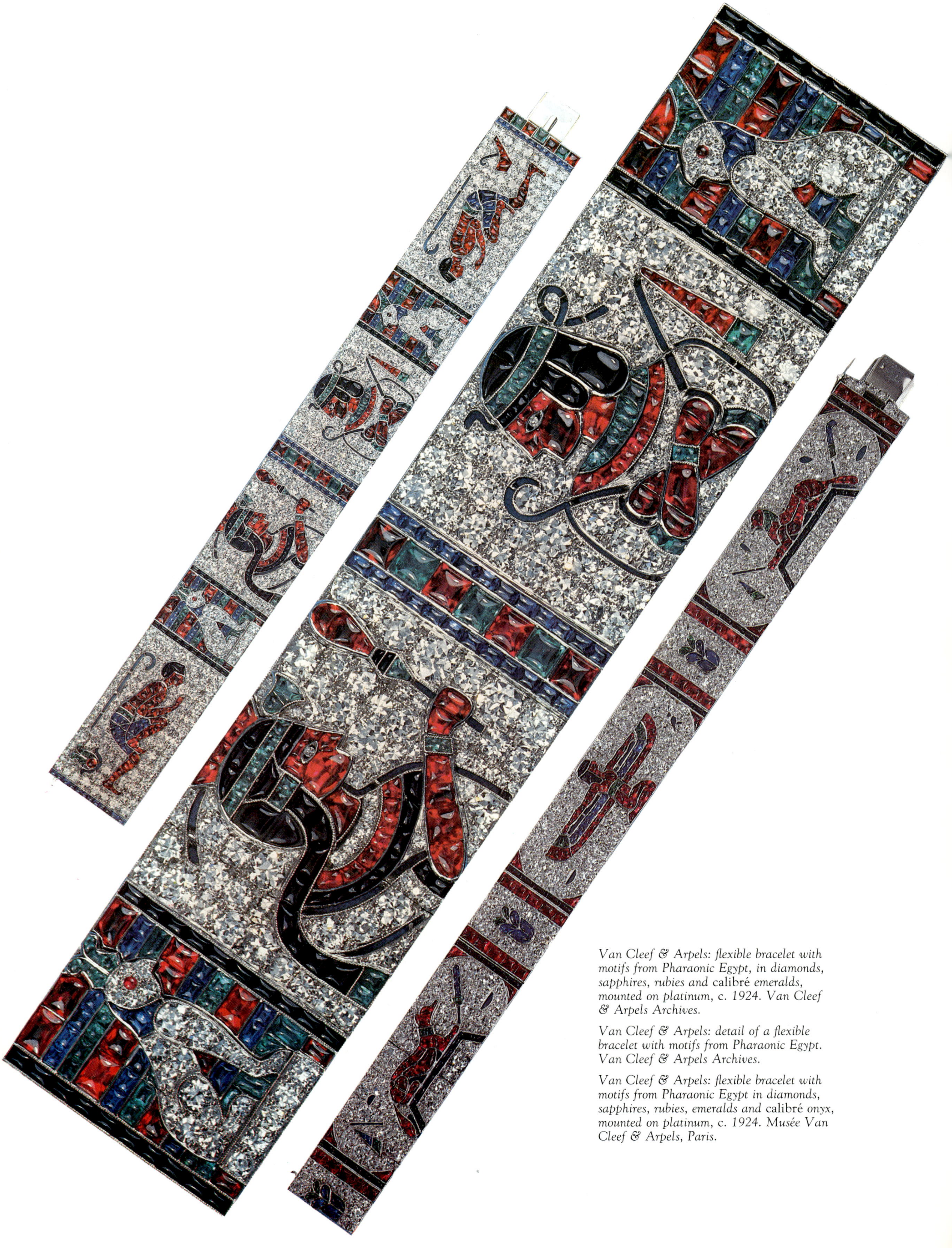

Van Cleef & Arpels: flexible bracelet with motifs from Pharaonic Egypt, in diamonds, sapphires, rubies and calibré *emeralds, mounted on platinum, c. 1924. Van Cleef & Arpels Archives.*

Van Cleef & Arpels: detail of a flexible bracelet with motifs from Pharaonic Egypt. Van Cleef & Arpels Archives.

Van Cleef & Arpels: flexible bracelet with motifs from Pharaonic Egypt in diamonds, sapphires, rubies, emeralds and calibré *onyx, mounted on platinum, c. 1924. Musée Van Cleef & Arpels, Paris.*

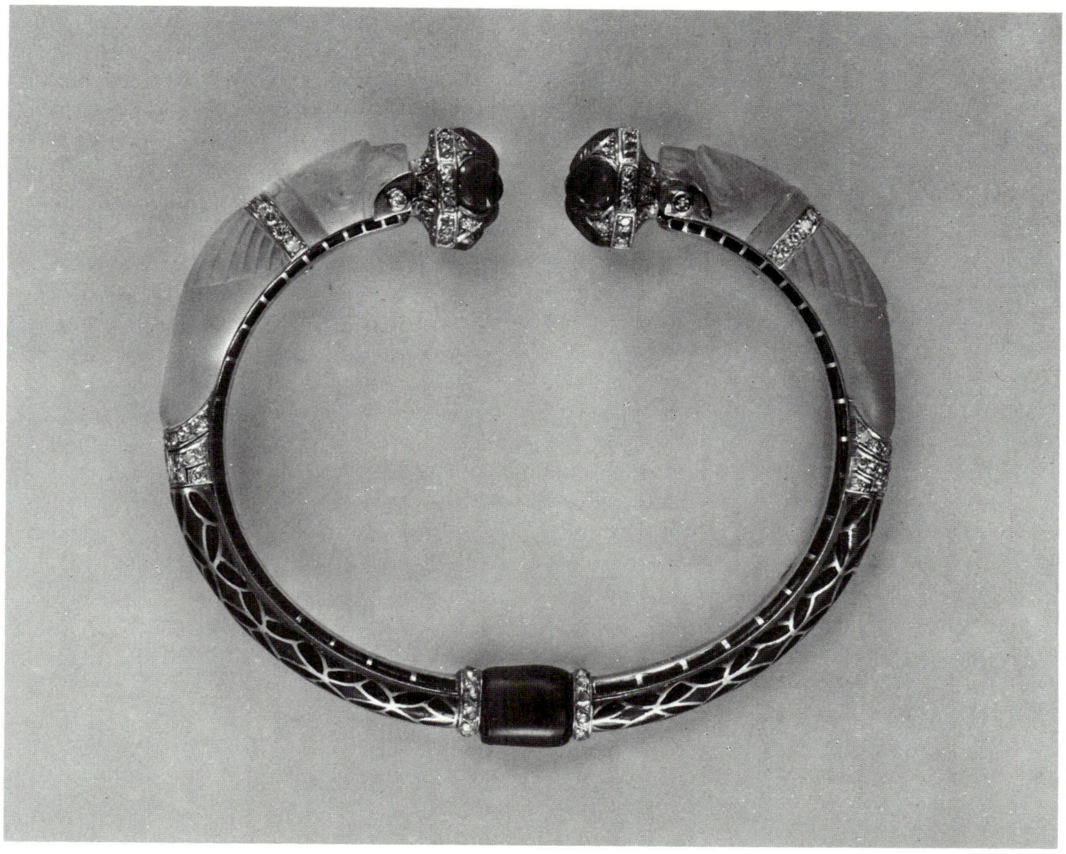

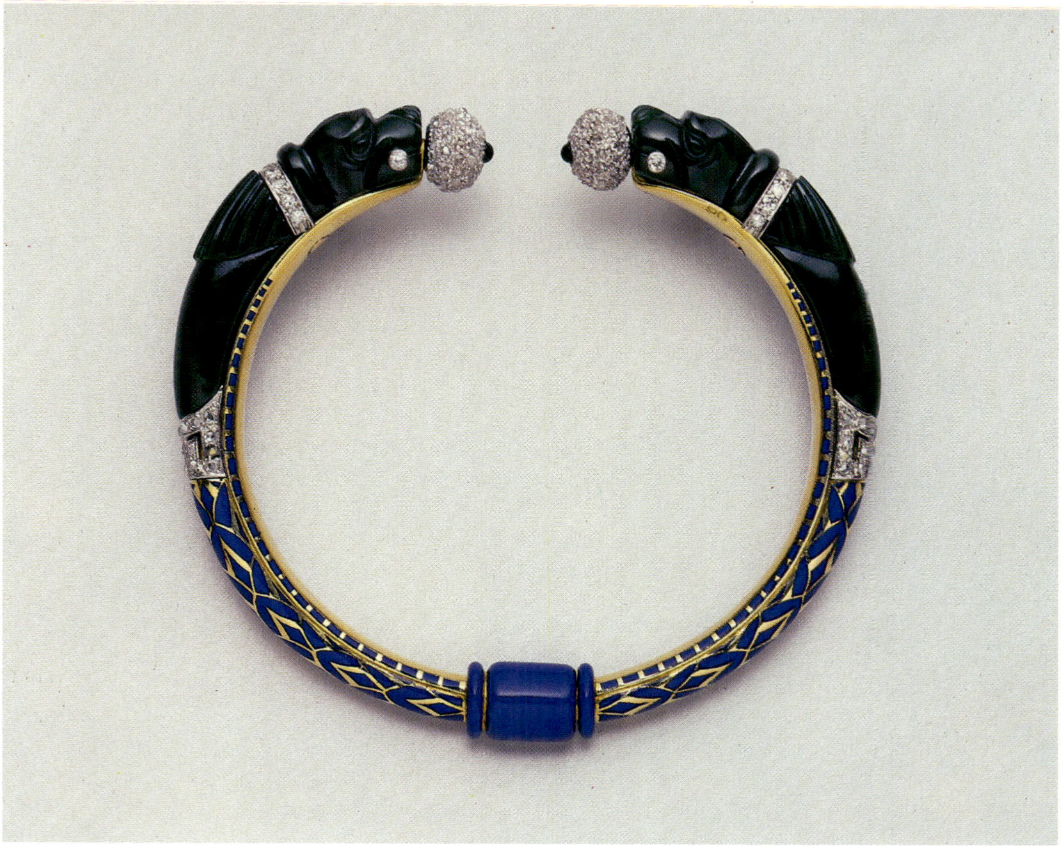

Lacloche: bracelet in rock crystal, ruby cabochons, diamonds and green and black enamel. Christie's, Geneva.

Anonymous: bracelet in engraved nephrite, blue enamel, diamonds and gold, France, c. 1928. Private Collection.

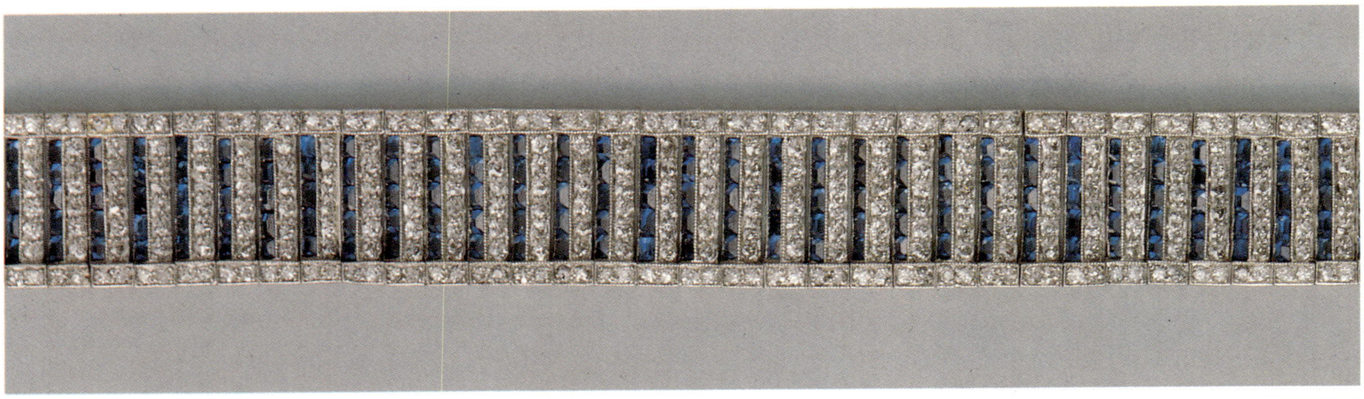

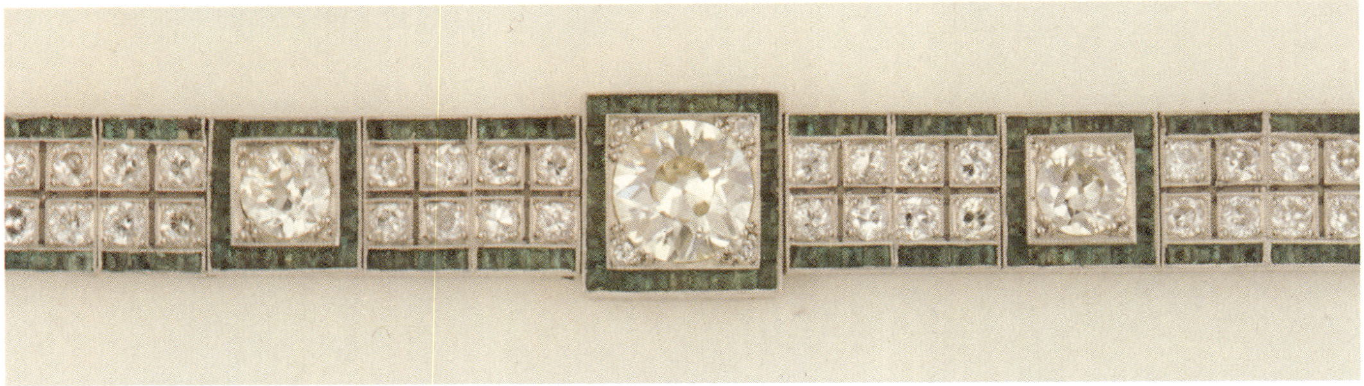

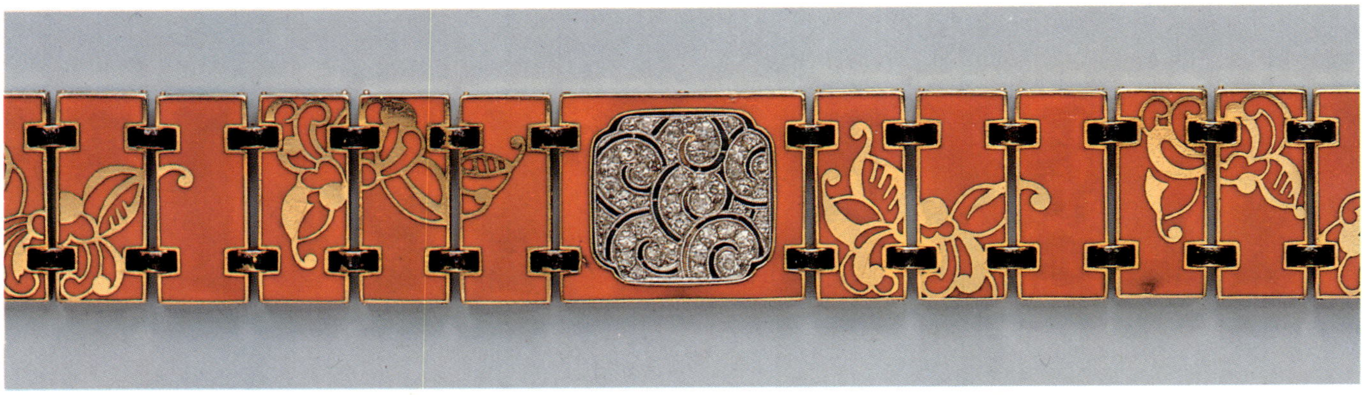

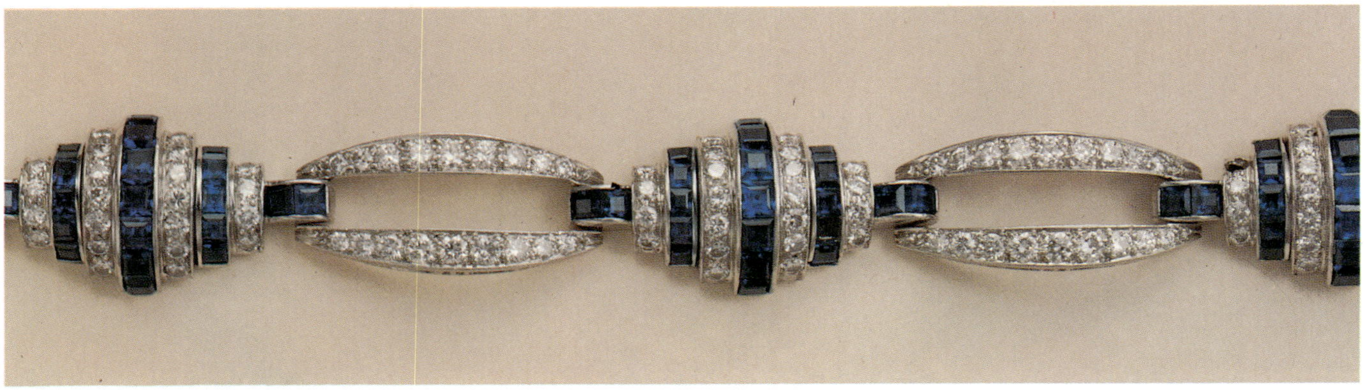

Anonymous: bracelet composed of alternate rows of calibré *sapphires and round diamonds, bordered with a row of diamonds. Sotheby's, Geneva.*

Anonymous: bracelet composed of square motifs bearing round diamonds bordered with baguette emeralds, alternating with motifs of smaller round diamonds bordered with baguette emeralds. Sotheby's, Geneva.

Marchak: bracelet in the oriental style composed of rectangles of red enamel with floral motifs in gold and a central plaque of diamonds; the rectangles attached with black enamel links, signed.

Anonymous: bracelet composed of motifs in calibré *sapphires and diamonds, attached by oval diamond links. Christie's, Geneva.*

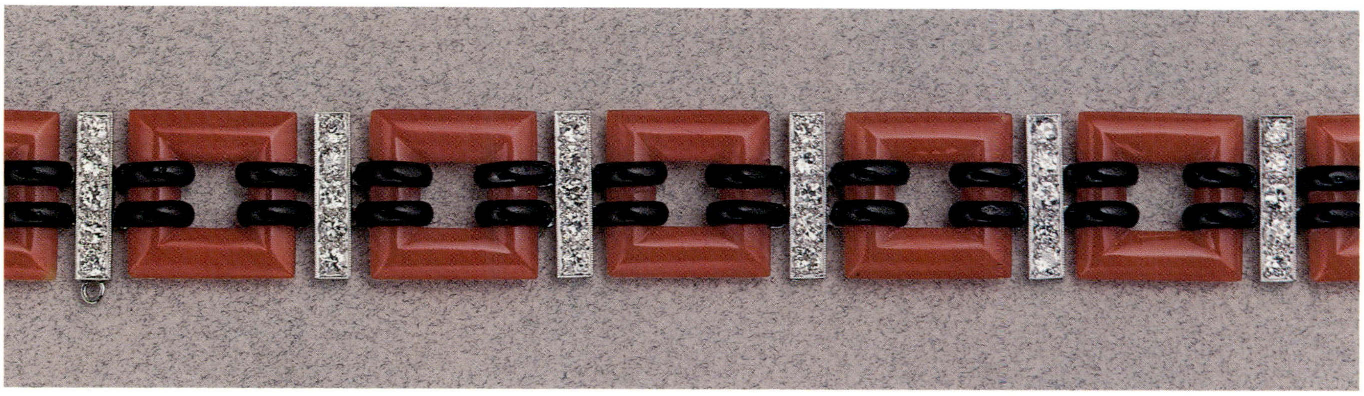

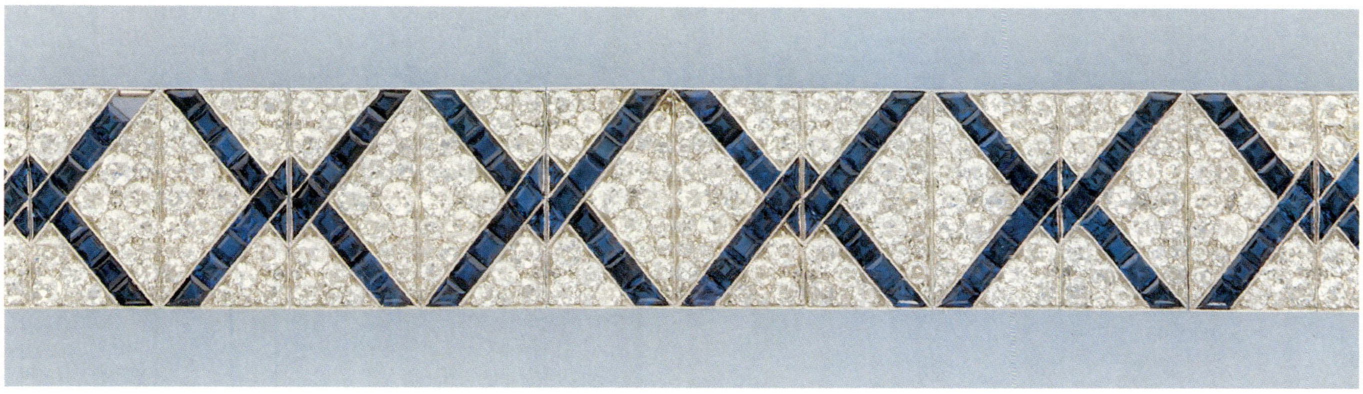

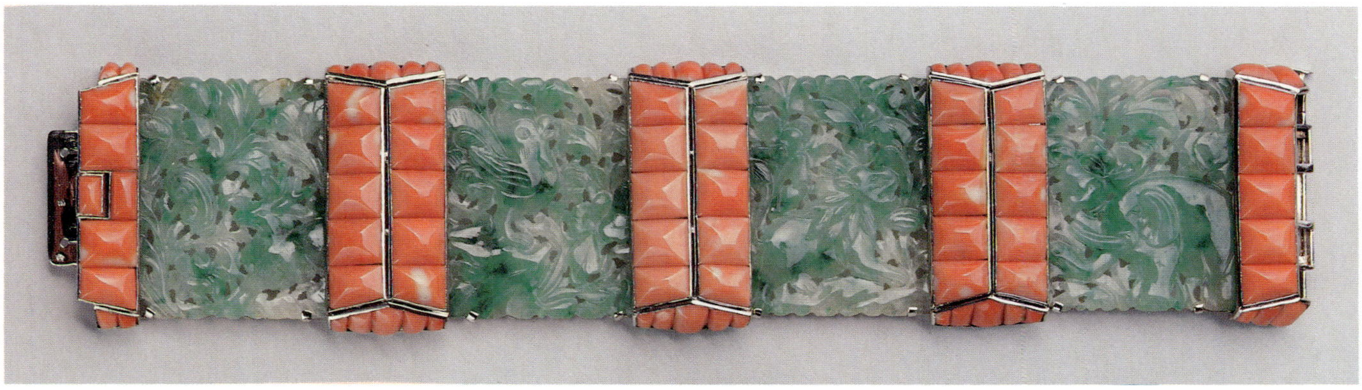

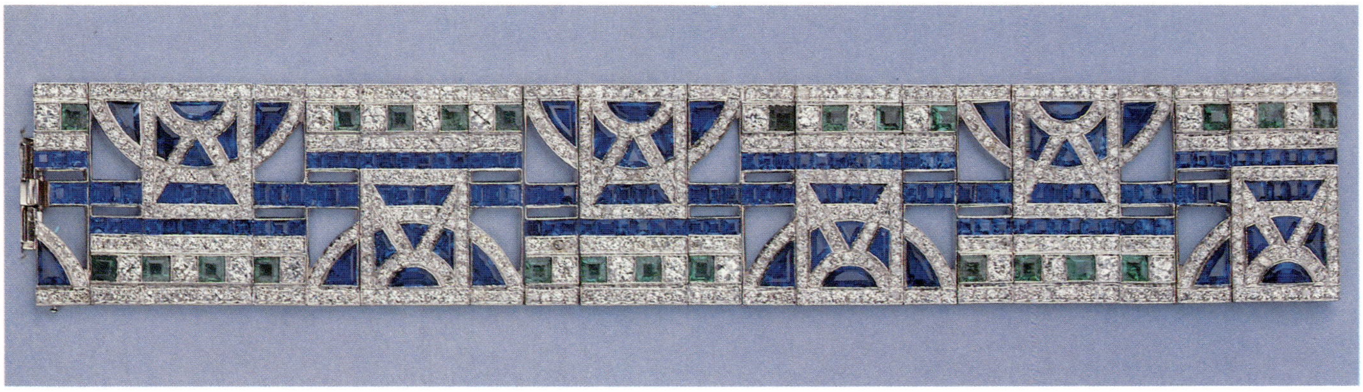

Van Cleef & Arpels: bracelet in coral, onyx and diamonds, 1923. Private Collection.

Anonymous: bracelet composed of calibré *sapphires forming a geometric pattern on a diamond ground, mounted on platinum.* Christie's, *New York.*

Anonymous: bracelet in engraved jade and coral, mounted on white gold, France, c. *1930. Private Collection.*

Georges Fouquet: bracelet in calibré *emeralds and sapphires, and diamonds, mounted on platinum,* c. *1925.*

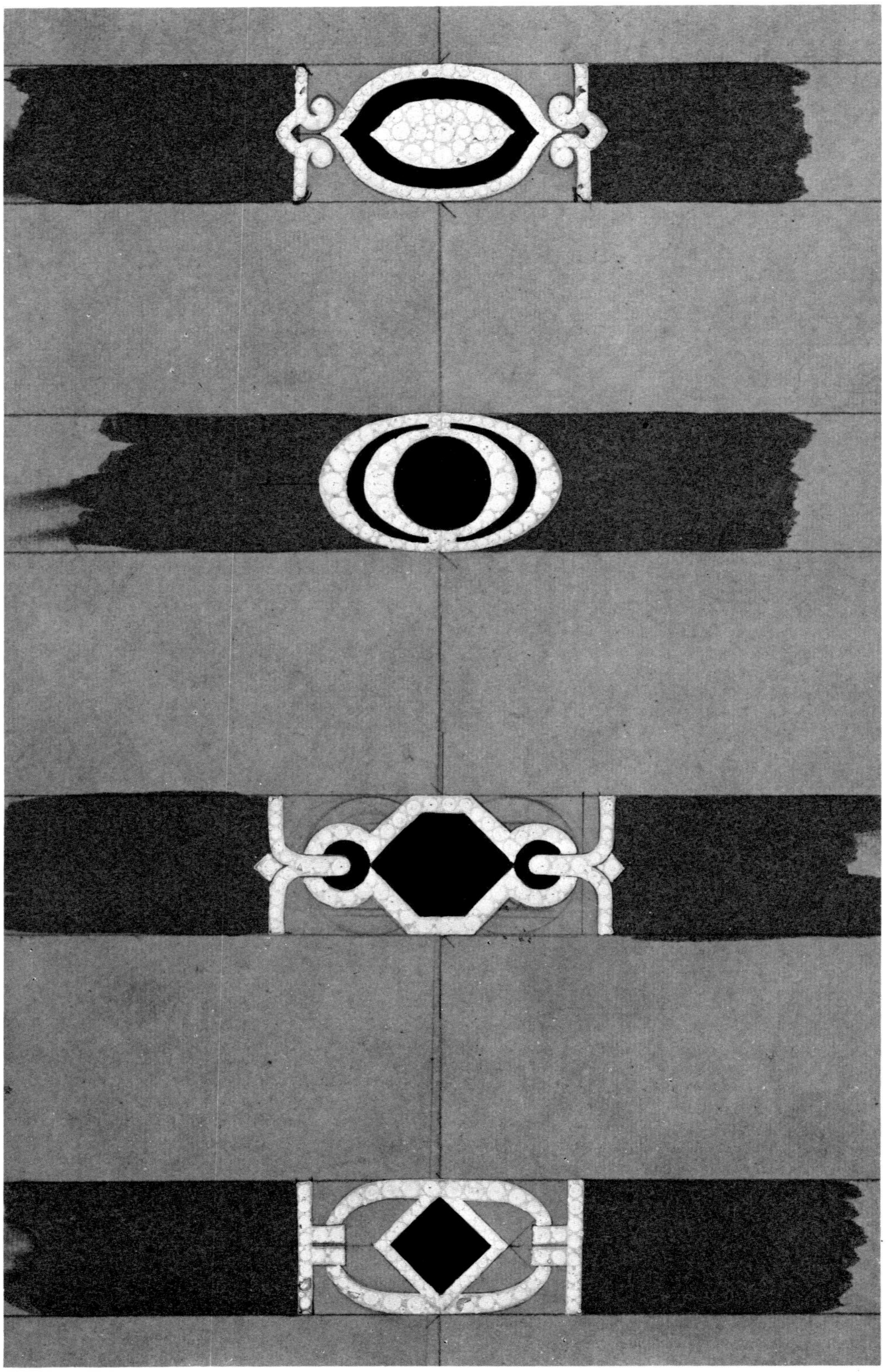

Gouache studies for belt-buckles executed by designer-craftsmen for the Haute Joaillerie. *Danenberg Collection.*

Facing page: Dusausoy: parure consisting of a pendant, bracelet and ring in diamonds, onyx and platinum, c. *1928, signed. Primavera Gallery, New York.*

Following pages: Jean Fouquet: bracelet in white gold, yellow gold and onyx pyramids, signed. Primavera Gallery, New York.

René Boivin: bracelet in onyx, diamonds and white gold, c. *1930. Primavera Gallery, New York.*

Gustave Miklos: brooch in yellow gold and white gold, executed in 1927 by Raymond Templier, signed. Private Collection. Photo: T. Heuer and J.B. Rouault.

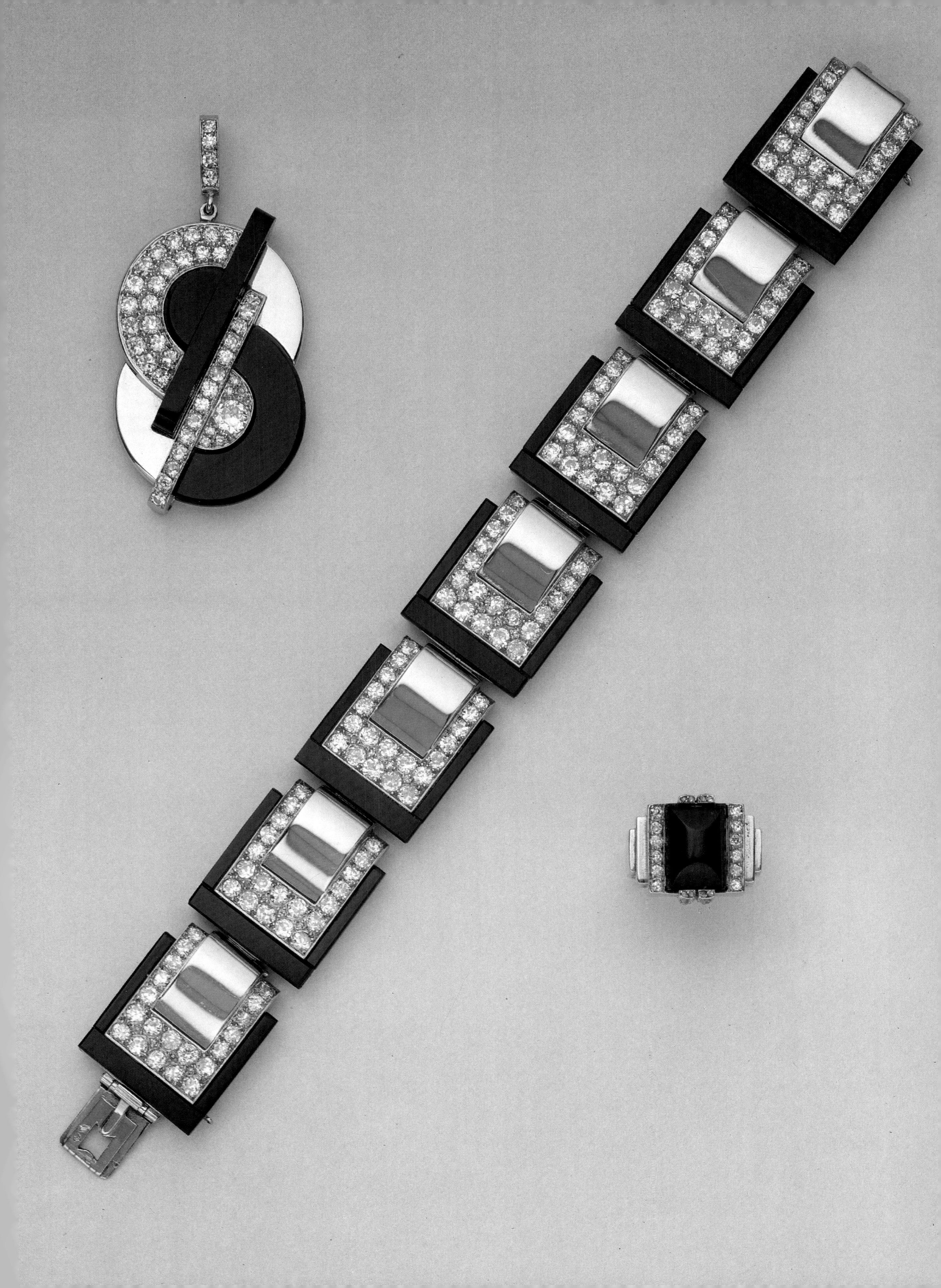

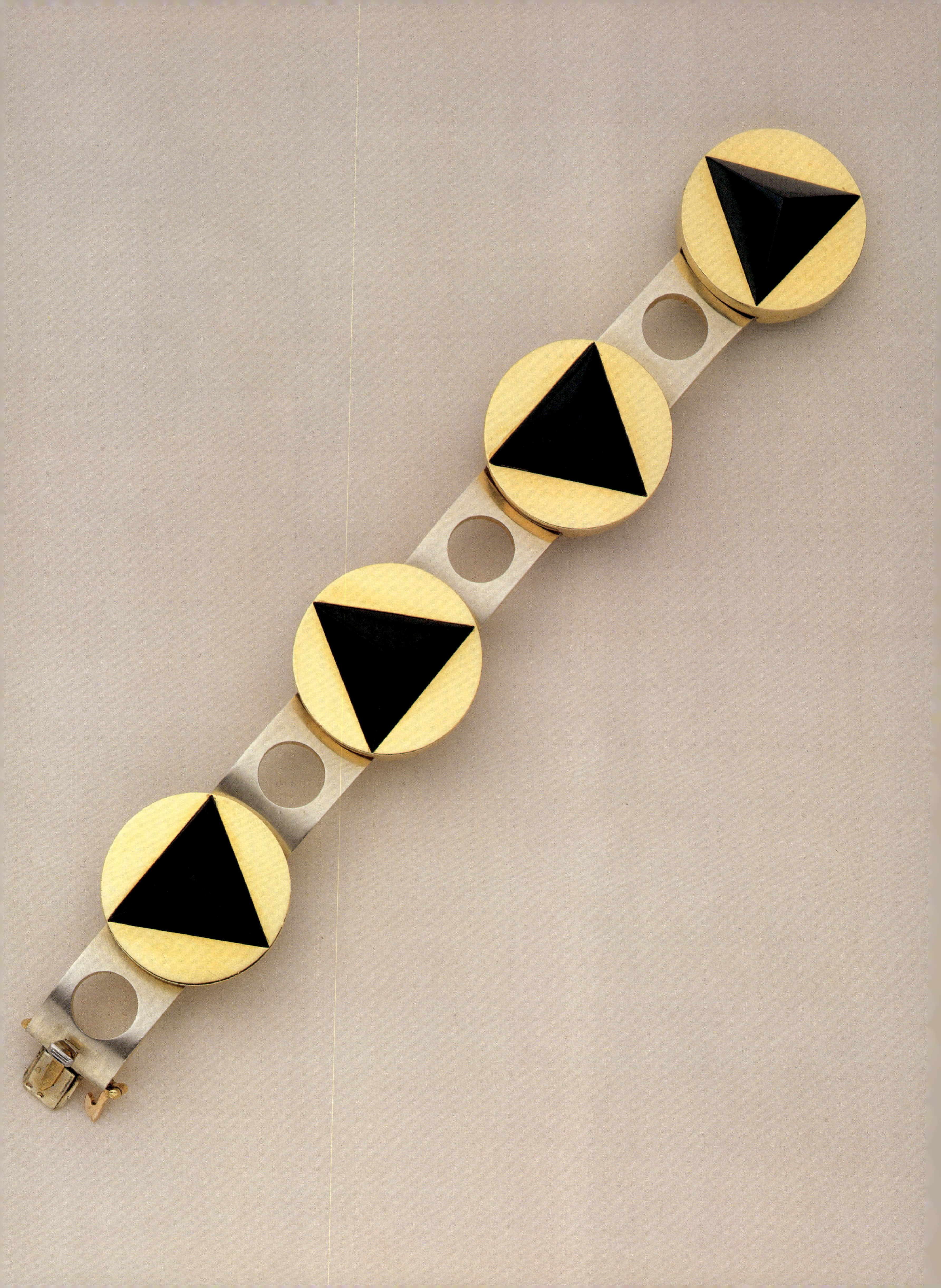

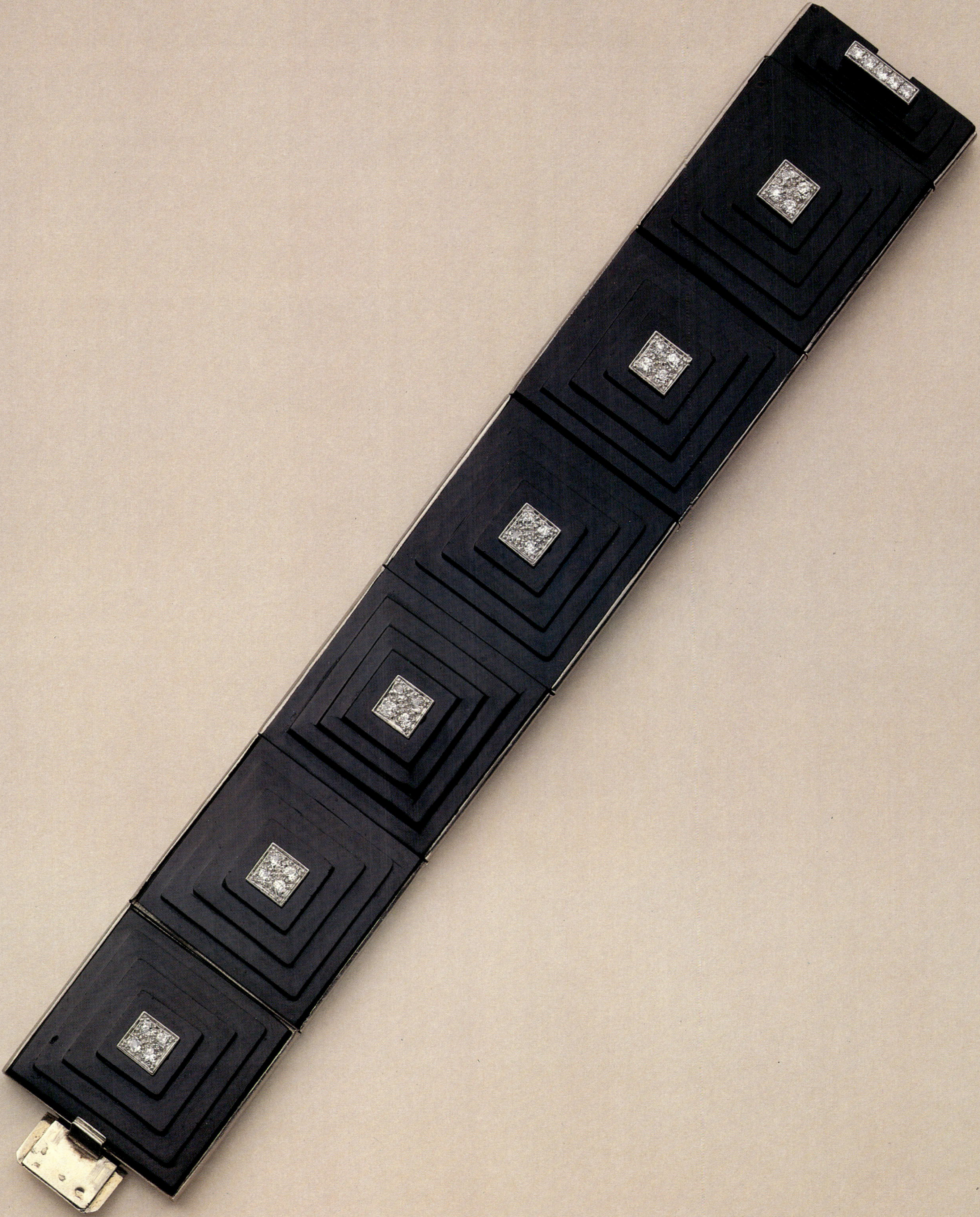

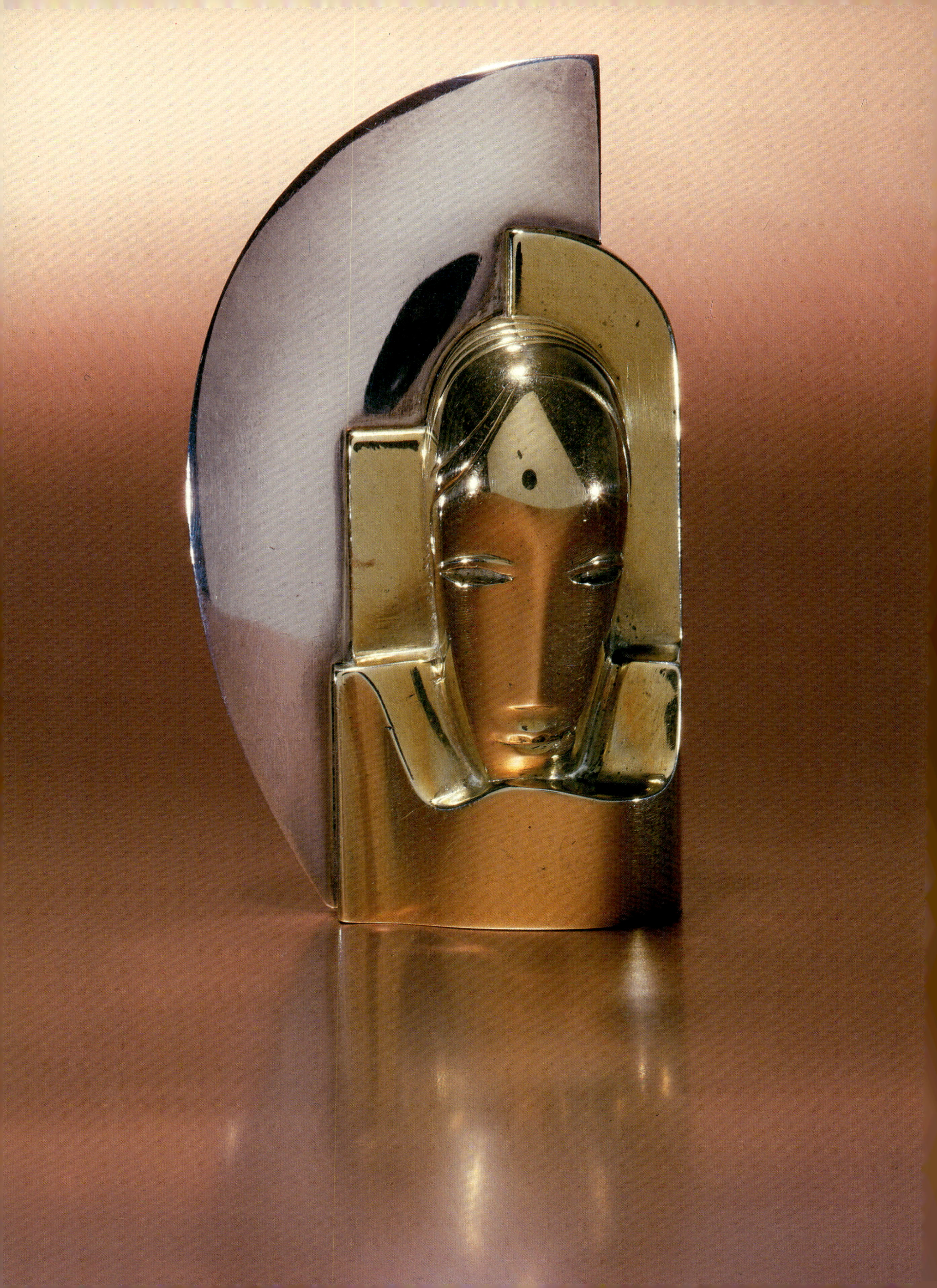

THE PIONEERS

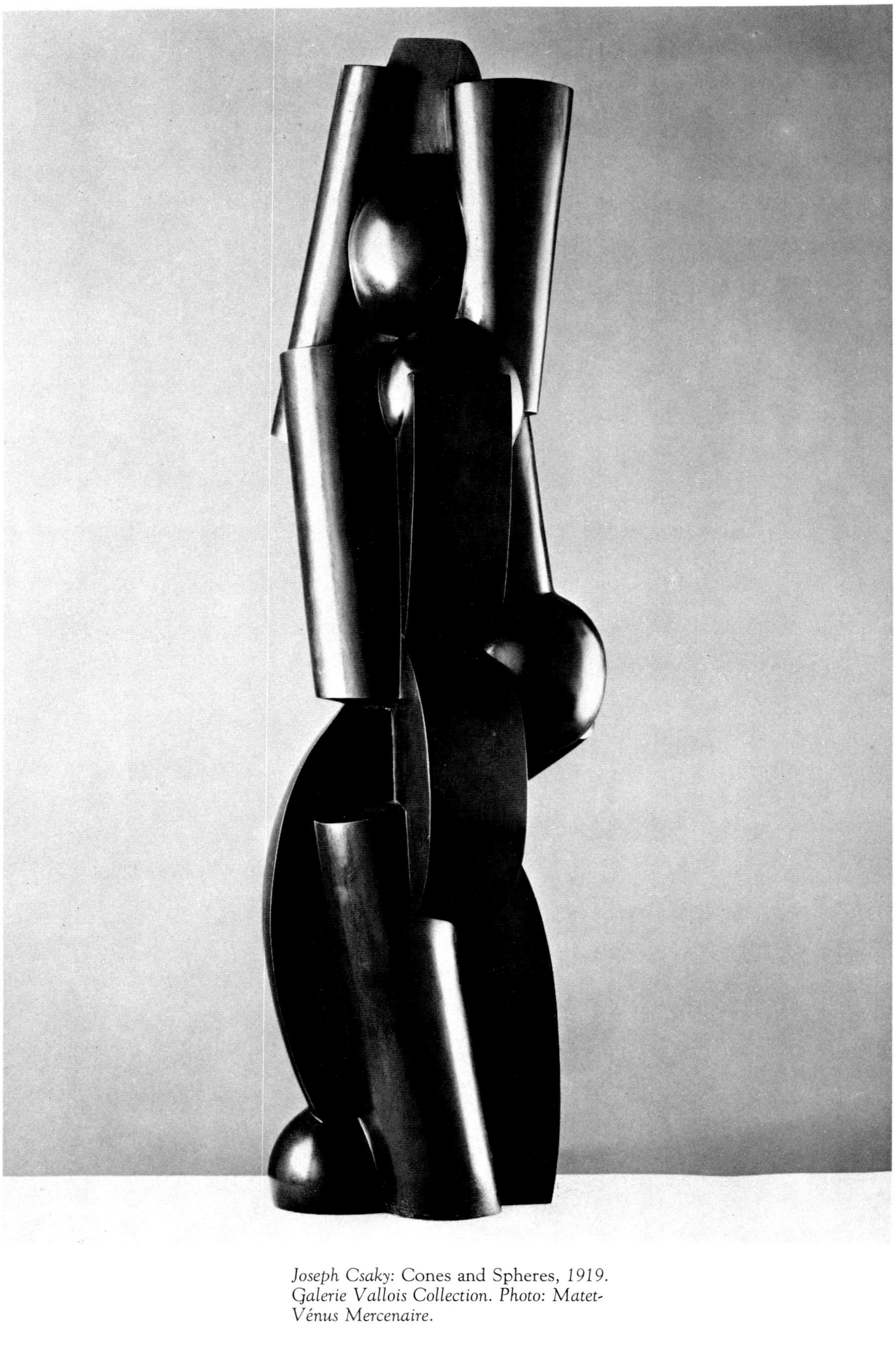

Joseph Csaky: Cones and Spheres, *1919. Galerie Vallois Collection. Photo: Matet-Vénus Mercenaire.*

THREE ARTISTS WHO ATTRACTED a great deal of attention at the time of the 'Exposition Internationale des Arts Décoratifs' in 1925 – Jean Fouquet, Gérard Sandoz and Raymond Templier – left the Société des Artistes Décorateurs in 1929 to join the Union des Artistes Modernes alongside architects such as Hélène Henry, René Herbst, Francis Jourdain, Robert Mallet-Stevens and Charlotte Perriand, all fierce defenders of Modern Art, which they believed should spring from contemporary life. Jean Després joined them at the Pavillon de Marsan exhibition in 1930.

This generation, roughly the same age as the century, challenged the generation that had gone before, cut itself off from the tradition of the *Haute Joaillerie* and played a principal part in the aesthetic revolution which flourished in the Twenties.

All four were under thirty when the war ended – Gérard Sandoz was born in 1902, Jean Fouquet in 1899, Raymond Templier in 1891 and Jean Després in 1889 – and all were fostered by the *Haute Joaillerie*. Raymond Templier's grandfather, Charles, founded the Maison in 1849; Jean Fouquet's grandfather, Alphonse, entered into partnership with Eugène Deshayes in 1860 and set up shop at 176 rue du Temple, and Gérard Sandoz' grandfather, Gustave, a clockmaker, founded his Maison in the Palais Royal in 1861. Jean Després' parents ran a shop which sold works of art and jewelry in Avallon in the Yonne.

Their families, confident of their talent, encouraged them in their artistic endeavours. Raymond Templier studied at the Ecole Nationale des Arts Décoratifs from 1909 to 1912 and exhibited as early as 1911 – at the age of twenty – at the Salon des Artistes Décorateurs. Gérard Sandoz, on the completion of his studies, was initiated into modern decorative art by his uncle, Paul Follot, and was very soon collaborating in the creations of the Maison Sandoz. Drawn to a writing career, Jean Fouquet received a classical education. Aware of his gifts as a designer, however, his father Georges persuaded him to work in the family Maison and, at twenty, he made his début in the rue Royale. All these young men were helped by the presence of a father who, far from wanting to see them constrained by tradition, encouraged them to give free rein to their talents. Jean Desprès, wishing to extend his apprenticeship in the family and enlarge his training, worked in the rue des Gravilliers for a friend of his father's, and at the same time studied design. During the war, an activity that he had not foreseen determined the aesthetic direction of his future creations: obliged to design aeroplane engines in a military workshop, he became fascinated by the mechanical world. The shape of a connecting rod, the outline of a crankshaft, the contour of a cam, the oblong of a fuselage impressed him with the pure, spare brilliance of metal, the cold precision of form and the perfect equilibrium from which harmony sprang. These men were artists but they were also theoreticians, and in their writings they set down and developed their ideas and their faith in modernity, trying with rigorous reasoning to win over the support of the undecided. Their numerous articles are the most precious accounts of the history of jewelry in the Twenties. In August 1929, Gérard Sandoz made a statement of primary importance. 'Bijoux d'Aujourd'hui', which appeared in the *Renaissance de l'Art Français et des Industries de Luxe*, summed up the objectives of the avant-garde: 'Today, a piece of jewelry, inspired directly by our contemporary aesthetic, must be simple, severe and constructed without superfluous ornament. Provided its technique and manufacture are beyond reproach, a well-designed piece of jewelry costing two hundred francs is as beautiful as an equally well-designed one costing two millions. There are very fine pieces of jewelry made simply of gold, and horrors that are smothered in diamonds. Similarly, there are exquisite pieces in which brilliants are cleverly distributed, and rubbish that looks like gold vermicelli. Let us have no preconceptions as to materials. Personally, I consider that before everything else one must think of the line and the general volume of the piece of jewelry to be created.' Militant in the cause of severity and the rigour of design and construction, which only colour and materials could modify, these avant-gardists glorified an aesthetic of plainness. The UAM's manifesto, published in 1934, enlightens us on their aims. It took up the text of Fénelon's letter to the Académie, in which a parallel was drawn between the eloquence of Demosthenes and that of Saint Augustine: 'A work only has true unity when one can take nothing away without drastic damage. It only has true order when one cannot displace a single part of it without weakening, without obscuring, without disturbing the whole. All ornament that is just ornament is excessive: get rid of it.' The same concern was expressed time and time again in their articles: 'How often do we see around us simple objects which could be so fine, deformed under the pretext of "decorative" art at any price. . . . We should put everything in its rightful place . . . and not assume that Art has to be either everywhere or nowhere, but that it is often present very simply and naturally without automatically needing "décor" adding to it . . .' (G. Sandoz, 'L'Art International d'Aujourd'hui', *Objets Usuels*, no 14).

In the Twenties, Paris witnessed an exuberant atmosphere of creative exchange. Craftsmen, painters, sculptors, musicians, poets and architects remade the world every night in Montparnasse cafés, exchanging ideas and nourishing mutual inspirations. Jean Després became friendly with Braque, Miró, the animal painter Paul Jouve, the sculptor Pompon and the ceramist Mayodon. In the rue Hallé, in Jean Dunand's studio, Paul Jouve, the engraver-illustrator François-Louis Schmied and the sculptors Miklos and Jean Lambert-Rucki formed an artistic community, forever drawing new resources from one another's creative powers. Jean Fouquet threw himself at an early age into the political and artistic fray. A friend of Louis Aragon and Paul Eluard – who, with André Breton and Philippe Soupault, under the banner of subversion, were to create Surrealism in 1924 – he was unreservedly loyal to the *esprit nouveau* (new spirit) as Le Corbusier conceived it: 'There is a new spirit; it is a spirit of construction and synthesis informed by a clear conception . . . there is one reigning faith, a total impartiality, a passion for conquest, a superb impulse which is propelling this age forward in search of victories. . . .' The foundation of the UAM, in which he actively participated, was to bring Fouquet closer still to avant-garde architecture.

Gone was the time when everyone was fighting for the so-called minor arts to be recognized and when their admission to the Salons Annuels was celebrated like a victory over the past. The recent interest taken by artists of all disciplines in the minor arts was vitally important, for a number of their creations enriched the output of the Twenties. Some of them, like Eric Bagge, collaborated with the Maison Fouquet. Bagge, architect, interior designer, furniture designer, wallpaper and fabric designer, who was to become Director of the Ecole Pratique de Dessin of the Chambre Syndicale de la Bijouterie-Joaillerie-Orfèvrerie, produced designs for pendants: among them, an onyx circle striated with diamonds; and a rectangular block of frosted rock crystal, worked in chevrons encrusted with onyx, bordered at the sides with onyx baguettes and diamonds, and decorated, at the top, with red enamel. The painter André Léveillé produced plaques of frosted rock crystal set with angular stones, brilliant aquamarine, topaz, amethysts, diamonds, sapphires, emeralds; and rigid bangles where gold was combined with black enamel, set with cabochon-cut stones and diamond diagonals, or with triangles, lozenges and circles of enamel in vivid colours – veritable paintings on a gold ground. Adolphe Mouron, a talented poster designer, better known by the name of Cassandre, also produced jewelry: bracelets and clasps and, in homage to the Cubists, the guitar pendant. Jean Lambert-Rucki, sculptor, mosaicist and fresco-painter, created bracelets, rings and clip earrings in beaten gold and silver, playing on primitive motifs, and masks which seemed to derive directly from African art. Miklos, who also worked in other artistic fields including *orfèvrerie*, stained glass and carpets, designed just one piece of jewelry – resembling sculpture and combining yellow and white gold – which was executed by Raymond Templier in 1927. The architect Charlotte Perriand, made herself a necklace out of ball-bearings, quite literally borrowed from the world of the machine, like the bracelet of ball-bearings in chromed steel made by Jean Fouquet in 1931. Another famous architect, Robert Mallet-Stevens, paid his tribute to the art of jewelry in 1930 when he created a pair of earrings and a number of cigarette cases covered in square mirrors. Georges Fouquet, in a letter addressed to the Musée des Arts Décoratifs in 1950, expressed his enthusiasm for exchanges of this kind which, over the years, continued to attract artists such as Arp, Braque, Calder, Cocteau, Dali, Man Ray and Fontana: 'I have always recommended calling in artists foreign to the art of jewelry and abandoning the specialized designer, because the architect brings his own special knowledge of masses and lines, the sculptor his knowledge of relief, the painter his knowledge of colour and, finally, the poster designer his knowledge of street art.' Jean Dunand, after studying sculpture, plaster modelling and metal chasing, and serving an apprenticeship in Jean Dampt's studio in Paris, developed an enthusiasm for the technique of lacquerwork. In 1912, he began to study under the tutelage of Sugawara, who had broken with the time-honoured tradition of secrecy, and with whom Eileen Gray had been working since 1907. In 1919, while still carrying on the solitary occupation of a coppersmith, he set up lacquer workshops which were to employ a hundred people. While refining techniques of patina and decoration on his metal vases, he embarked on a large scale project and presented at the 1925 Exposition a complete interior – the smoking room 'of a French Embassy abroad' – and in 1928 the gaming-room for the Ile de France liner. He was to collaborate some years later in fitting out the Atlantique and Normandie liners. Meanwhile, he applied lacquer surfaces to furniture designed by Pierre Legrain, Jacques-Emile Ruhlmann, Eugène Printz and Jean Goulden. This sculptor, coppersmith, cabinet maker and lacquerer also dabbled in *orfèvrerie-joaillerie*, creating for friends and relatives, necklaces, bracelets, earrings and belt-buckles, electing the combination of silver and lacquer with his favourite colours, white, red and black. Discovering by chance that diluted lacquer could be painted on to fabric, he made models for Madeleine Vionnet, designed hats for the modiste Agnès, and painted designs on dresses and scarves. René Robert, born into a family of musicians, painters, plaster modellers and interior designers, was also attracted to jewelry making. He trained to become a jeweler at the Ecole Professionnelle de Bijouterie-Joaillerie-Orfèvrerie in the rue du Louvre and his work favoured the use of silver, ivory, enamel, ebony and Chinese coral.

Amongst the designers principally concerned with jewelry, some expressed themselves through design alone, while others were also craftsmen who made their own models or, going beyond this, mobilized their imagination for other forms of expression. Jean Fouquet and Raymond Templier devised pieces of jewelry which they set out on paper with a few telling strokes, sketching the lines and indicating the choice of materials and colours. The workshop then took over the preparation of detailed sketches on whose precision the craftsman would rely. In 1929, Marcel Percheron, a former student at the Ecole Nationale des Arts Décoratifs, became a designer for Raymond Templier and these two combined their talents in a partnership that was to last thirty-six years, Raymond Templier conceiving and devising the piece of jewelry, Marcel Percheron developing the project and building the maquette. The latter's meticulousness and desire for perfection impelled him to produce drawings or even gouache studies for up to eighty necklaces before arriving at the final version. His demands sometimes reached the limit of technical possibility, making it formidably difficult for the craftsman to shape the material to match his conception. The craftsman Jean Després executed his jewelry designs himself and also made candlesticks, dinner services, boxes, cutlery and drinking cups. Gérard Sandoz was engaged in several activities at once: he designed jewelry and pieces of *orfèvrerie* which were executed under his supervision in a workshop with a staff of five or six craftsmen; for the professor and geographer Jean Brunhes, he made an academician's sword entirely of gold, lacquer, crushed eggshell and cornelian, with a shagreen scabbard; a painter and poster designer, he was also drawn to other means of artistic expression, in order to pursue which he shut down his Maison in the rue Royale in 1931 and devoted himself to the cinema and painting.

Ardent believers in modernity, the pioneers lived in perfect accord with their age, seeking inspiration in their environment, translating their ideas into pieces of jewelry with bold forms which had broken away from traditional ornamental design. Their aesthetic sensibility was influenced by the structure of the machine, the dynamics engendered by speed and new architectural forms; and they brought to their pieces of jewelry the skills of painters, sculptors and architects. If they sometimes transposed images from reality quite literally – as in Jean Fouquet's bracelet of chromed steel ball-bearings or Jean Desprès' 'crankshaft' brooch – their aim was to transcend appearance, to extract the essence from a form, to translate its strength and dynamic. In a world in love with speed, a piece of jewelry had to be read rapidly, caught in flight like a telegraphic image – a theme taken up by Jean Fouquet in the introduction to his book *Bijoux et Orfèvrerie*: 'a piece of jewelry may have the function of attaching or fastening on to some element of dress, but as a jewel it must, above all, adorn the costume. To fulfil this function, I will say it again and again, the piece of jewelry must be composed of elements which can be read at a distance. The miniature is detestable.' In the applied arts, the beauty of the functional object is of paramount importance and a piece of jewelry which lives up to its ultimate purpose cannot escape from this: it must complete an ensemble and mark the personality of the woman who is wearing it. These creations were not the most costly pieces of jewelry, destined to lie in a safe; their artistic quality alone was important. If jewelers like those of the *Haute Joaillerie* often used the most precious gemstones – rubies, emeralds and sapphires – the pioneers had a preference for aquamarine, topaz, citrine, coral, onyx, turquoise and jade or even less well-known stones such as malachite, labradorite and hematite. To avoid the dispersion of light, a large stone, surrounded by bare metal and adorned with simple lines of small *calibré* stones – diamonds or topazes – became the centre of the composition. The richness of coloured stone cabochons was allied to the spareness of sharp-angled metal planes, arranged harmoniously on pendants, brooches or bracelets. We have, for example, the silver brooch by Jean Desprès, surmounted by a large citrine, or Jean Fouquet's pendant in which the bluish transparency of aquamarine seems to make the flat, striated platinum disc behind it vibrate. The severity of these conceptions was softened by coloured lacquer or enamel, favoured by the pioneers, as in Raymond Templier's rectangular or trapezoidal pendants combining green or grey enamel with diamond covered areas, a pendant by Jean Fouquet combining silver and green and black enamel and Gérard Sandoz' plaque-brooch assembling small diamonds and black and green enamelled figures. Unlike the *joailliers*, the pioneers considered that a piece of jewelry ought to be within everyone's means, and they explored the multiple possibilities of metal, in turn matt, burnished, tinted, *sablé* and beaten. In his bracelets, Raymond Templier alternated links of grey gold and red gold, or grey gold and platinum. Jean Fouquet, in a bangle, combined three colours of gold set with fine lines of diamonds and rubies. Gold and silver were juxtaposed on many models by Jean Després who created a brooch combining yellow gold, white gold, silver and lapis, in which the smooth polished metal vied with the luminous brilliance of pearly, beaten metal. More modestly, Raymond Templier used stainless steel and Jean Fouquet designed a necklace combining chromed metal with gold and ebony. Yet another of Després' innovations was the juxtaposition of silver and glass or the painted and engraved glass of the painter Etienne Cournault, where the contrasted elements achieve a perfect harmony. Artist-craftsmen such as Georges Bastard and André Rivaud democratized jewelry by using the cheapest materials. The pioneers, however, defended the unique piece, and especially the model created for a particular woman, to complement the oval of a face or the line of a hand.

Some of their pieces left the traditional concept of a parure far behind and were directed at a new kind of woman. Thus Després defined his position: 'I am not a *joaillier*, I don't deal in delicacy but in strength. My pieces of jewelry are large pendants, big rings. . . . It's not little girls' work.' He made a brooch using the motif of a crank arm; the bezel of a ring took on the appearance of a cam; the image of a crankshaft framed against a beaten metal plaque became a brooch; and gears were used to decorate pendants. While the *joailliers* made discreet use of linear, geometric compositions, softened by curves, the pioneers used combinations of broken lines and syncopated planes. Certain models of pendants and brooches abandoned harmonious equilibrium, throwing themselves out of alignment and producing jagged angles. Going beyond geometry, these compositions were informed with a dynamic quality: Raymond Templier's brooches and earrings seem caught in suspended motion; a brooch, fixed to the lapel of a tailor-made, resembles a comet, frozen in flight. If the *Haute Joaillerie* found its major source of inspiration in the East, the pioneers contented themselves with the modern European environment, thus provoking their detractors into accusing them of valuing the bolt above the rose.

'. . . As for jewelry, one should repeat that only those pieces count for posterity which recall an age whose imprint they have received and retained.' Emile Sedeyn's judicious remark on the intrinsic quality of jewelry takes on its full meaning for us today. Possessing a timeless and rare modernity, these pieces symbolize, half a century after their creation, the quintessence of Art Deco.

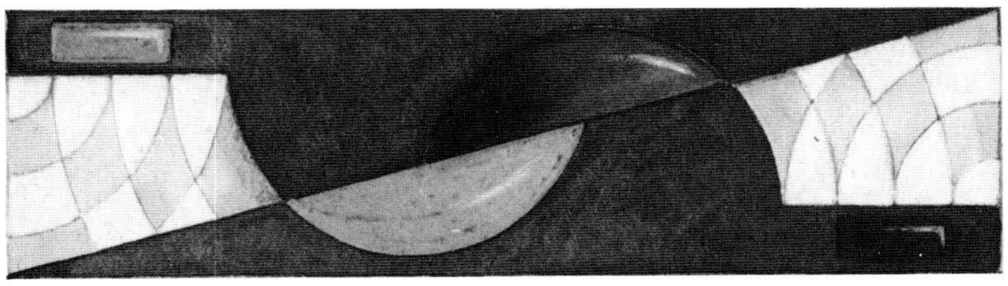

Gouache study for a clasp executed by Cassandre for Georges Fouquet.

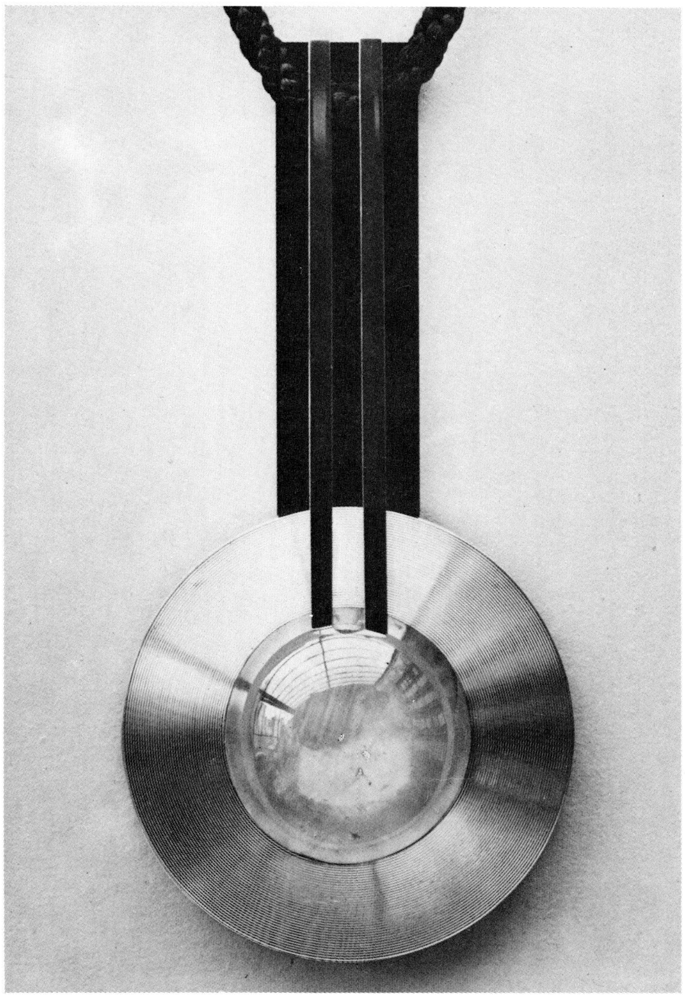

Jean Fouquet: pendant comprising a sapphire cabochon on a disc of white gold engraved with circles; on the upper part, a plaque of onyx with bands of polished grey gold, 1929.

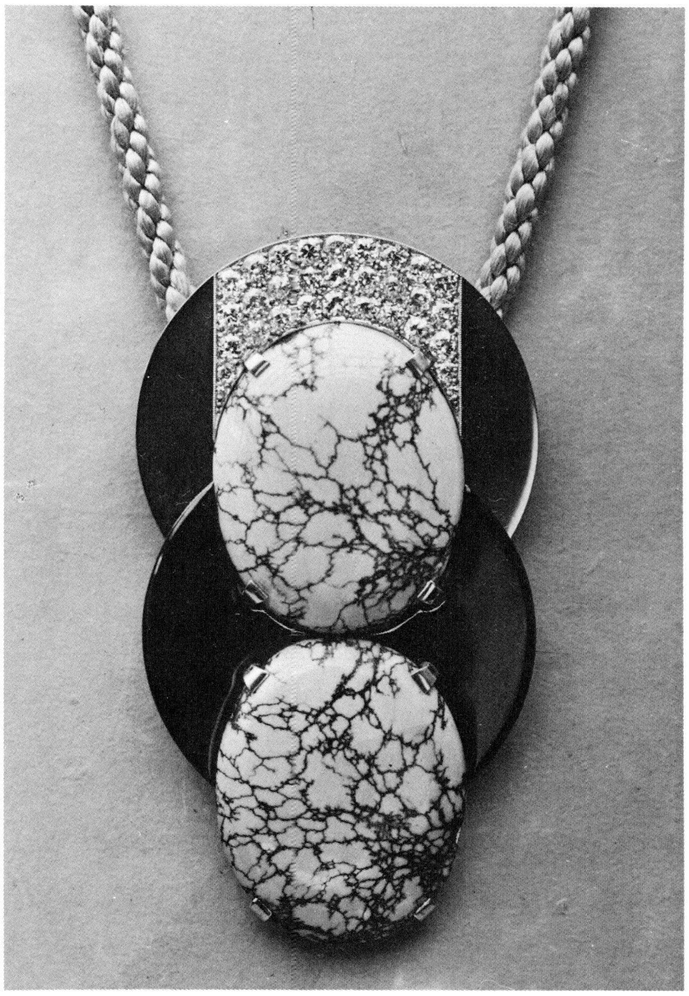

Jean Fouquet: pendant in turquoises, polished platinum, black enamel and brilliant-cut diamonds, 1930. Photo: Musée des Arts Décoratifs, Paris.

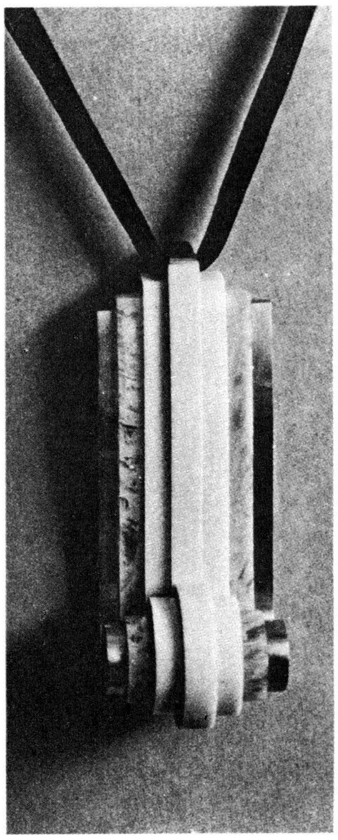

Raymond Templier: pendant in ivory, amber and red gold, reproduced in Art et Décoration, *July 1931.*

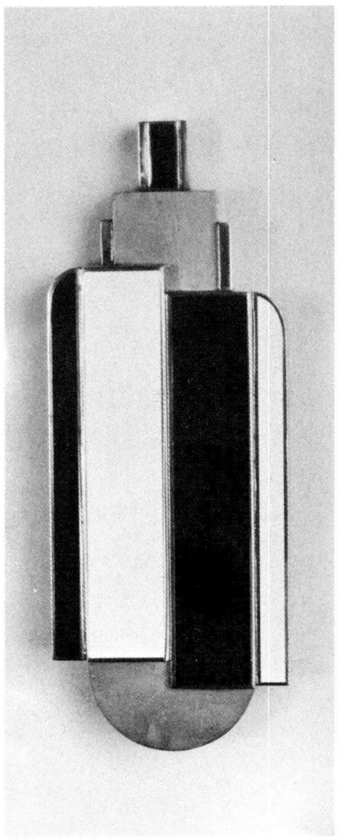

Gérard Sandoz: pendant in gold and white and black enamel, made for a member of his family, c. 1937, signed. Sotheby's, Monte Carlo.

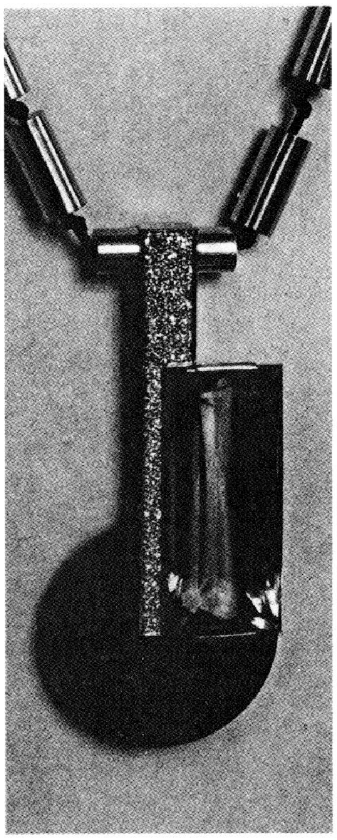

Jean Fouquet: pendant in white gold, lacquer, coloured stone and diamonds, reproduced in Art et Décoration, *July 1931.*

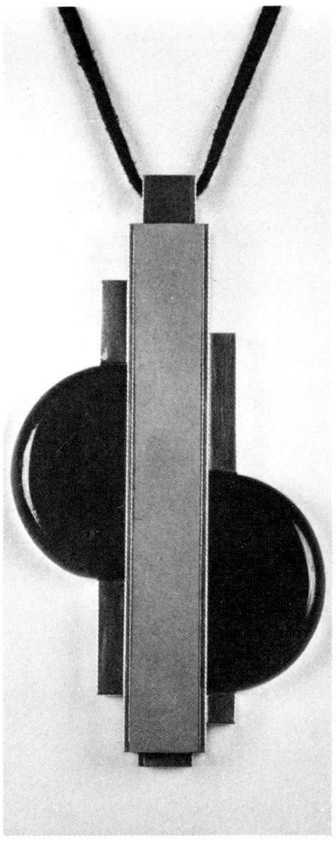

Gérard Sandoz: pendant in two colours of gold, aventurine and black onyx, c. 1928–30, signed. Sotheby's.

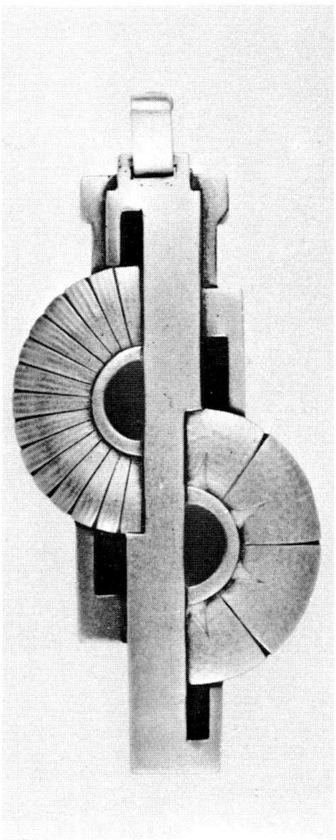

E. David: pendant in silver and black, green and yellow enamel, c. 1925. Sotheby's, Monte Carlo.

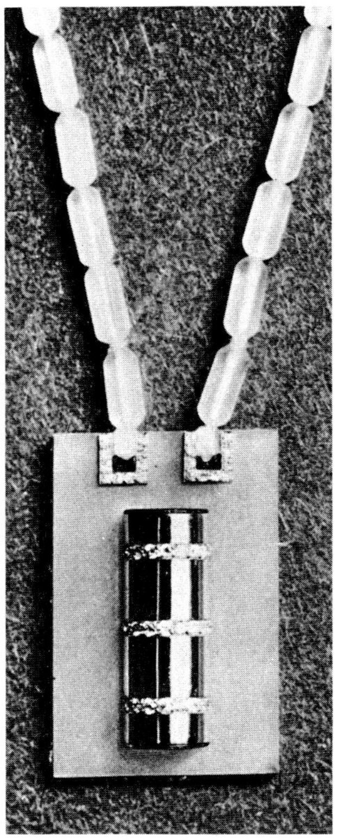

Jean Fouquet: pendant reproduced in his article 'Bijoux et Orfèvrerie' in Art International d'Aujourd'hui, *no 16, 1931.*

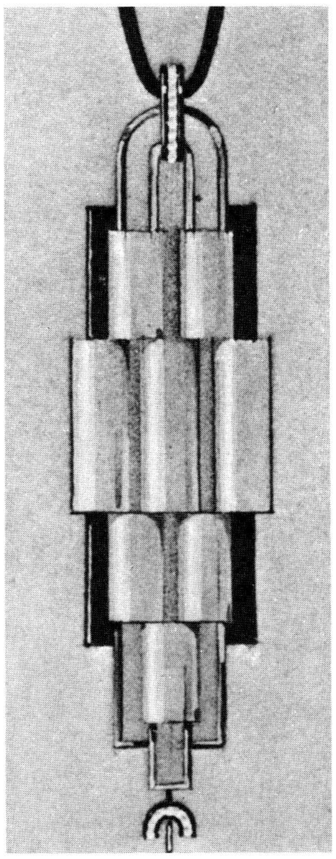

Henri Martin, Ecole Boulle: design for a pendant in matt crystal, black enamel, platinum and brilliants, reproduced in Jean Fouquet's 'Bijoux et Orfèvrerie' in Art International d'Aujourd'hui *no 16, 1931.*

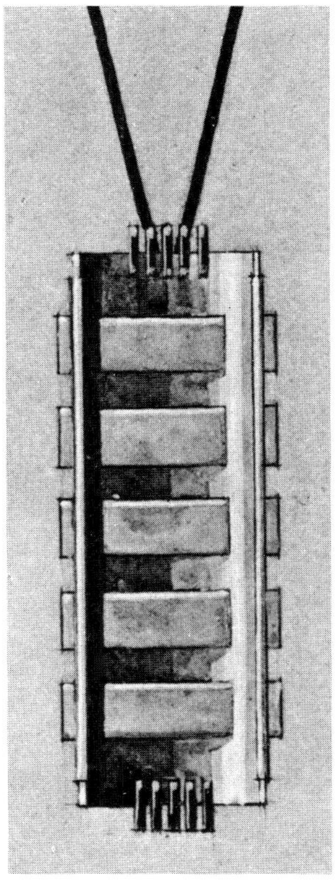

Henri Martin, Ecole Boulle: design for a pendant reproduced in Jean Fouquet's 'Bijoux et Orfèvrerie', ibid.

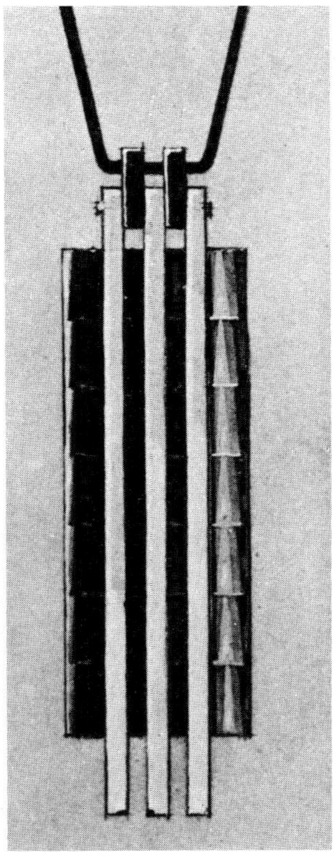

Henri Martin, Ecole Boulle: design for a pendant reproduced in Jean Fouquet's 'Bijoux et Orfèvrerie', ibid.

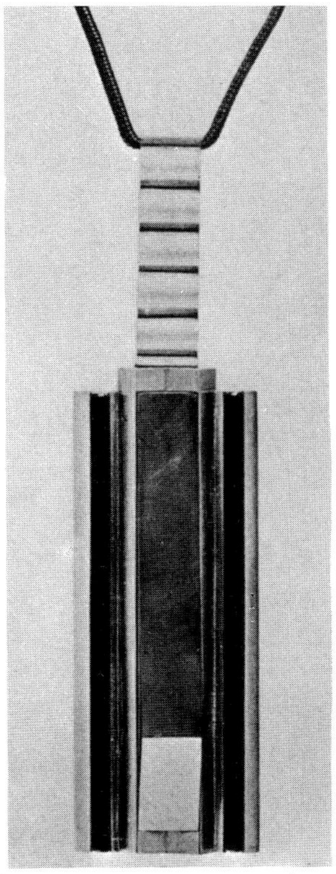

Gérard Sandoz: pendant reproduced in Jean Fouquet's 'Bijoux et Orfèvrerie', ibid.

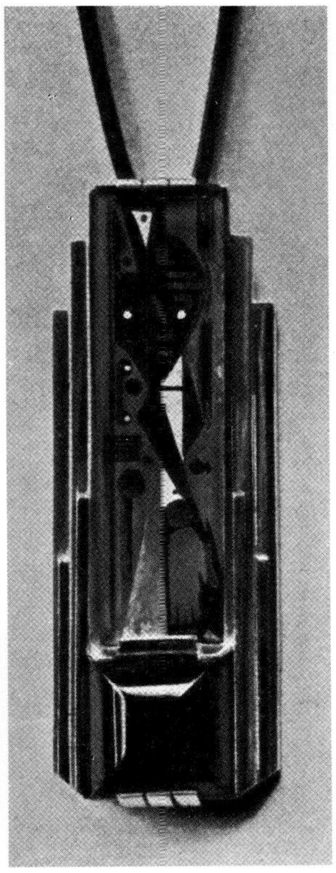

Jean Desprès: pendant in silver and glass engraved by Etienne Cournault reproduced in Art et Décoration, *April 1931.*

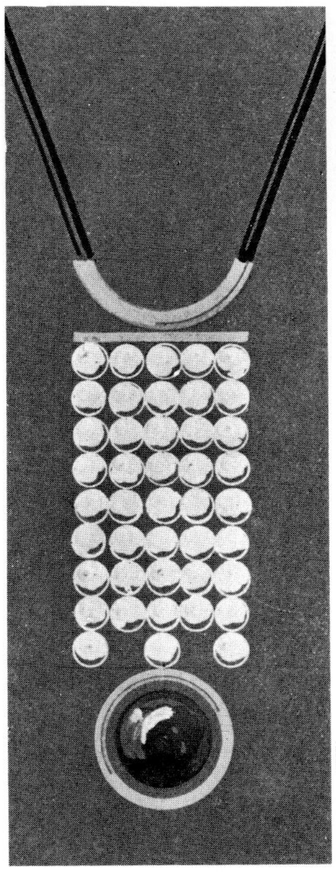

Pheulpin, Ecole Boulle: gold, pearl, and sapphire pendant reproduced in Art et Décoration, *March 1929.*

Following page: Gérard Sandoz: pendant in white gold, yellow gold, black onyx and rock crystal, c. 1927–28, signed. H. 14.2 cm, W. 8.4 cm. Private Collection. Photo: T. Heuer.

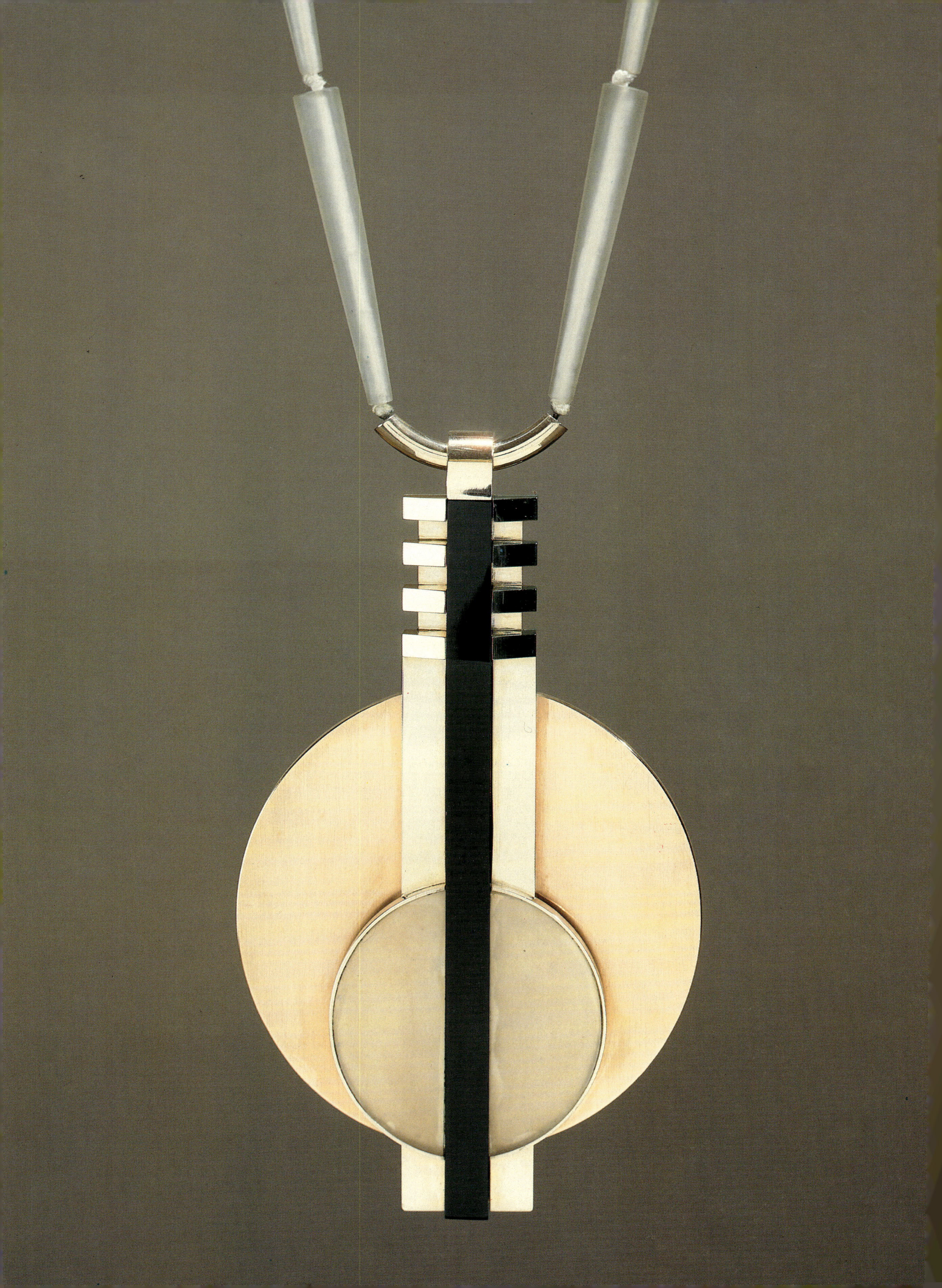

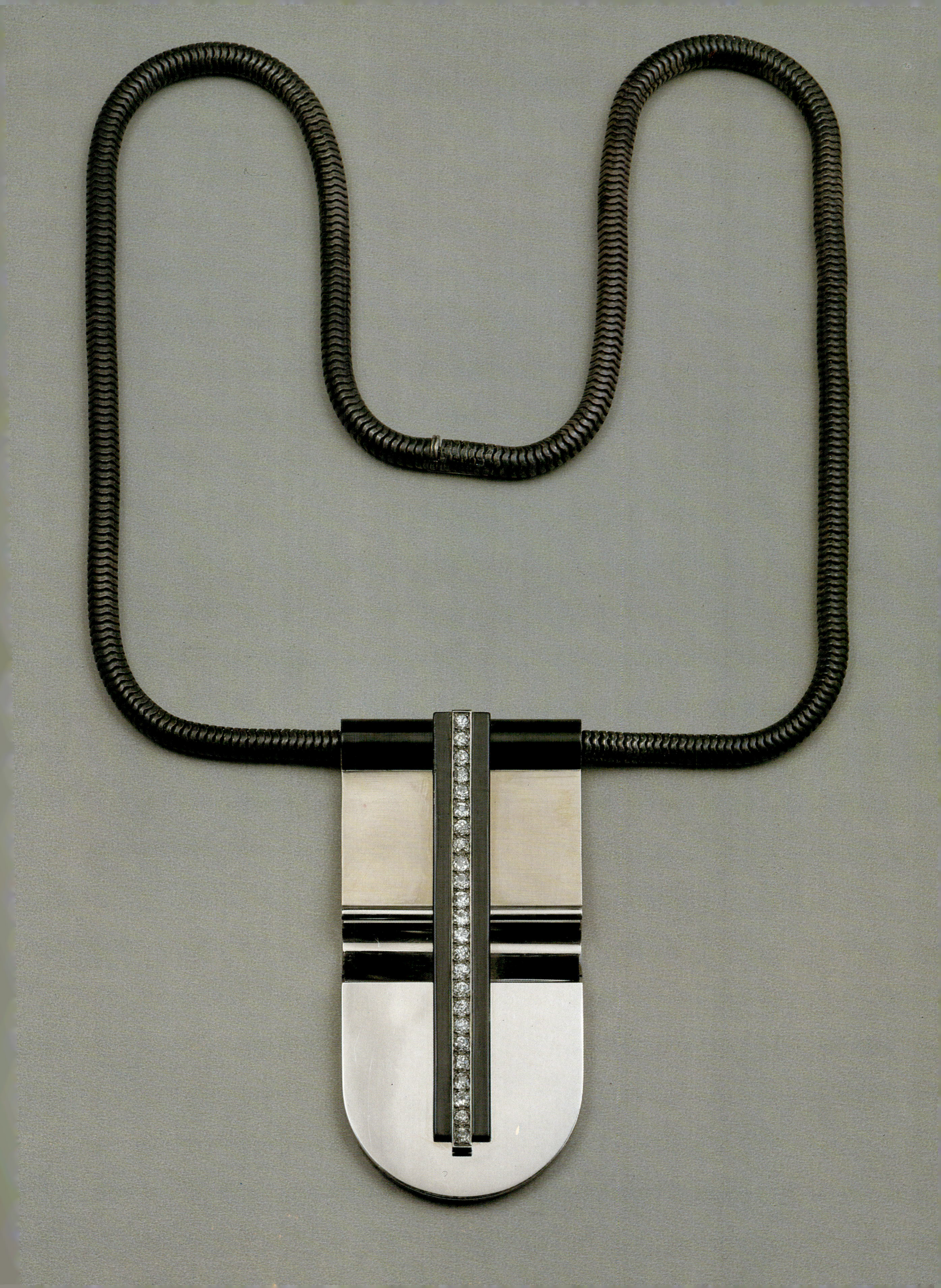

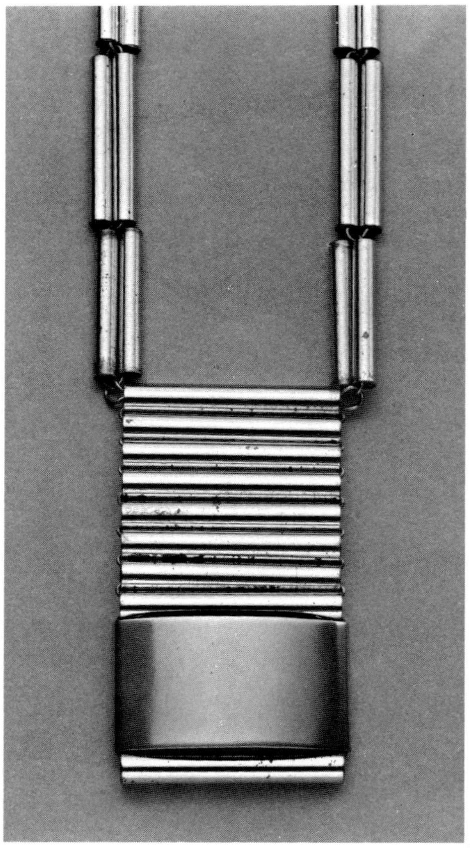

Cartier: clip brooch in white gold, aquamarine and diamonds, signed, c. 1925. Jesse & Laski Gallery Collection, London.

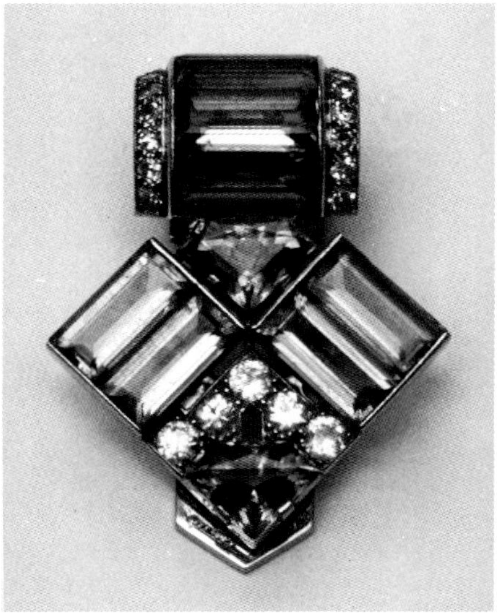

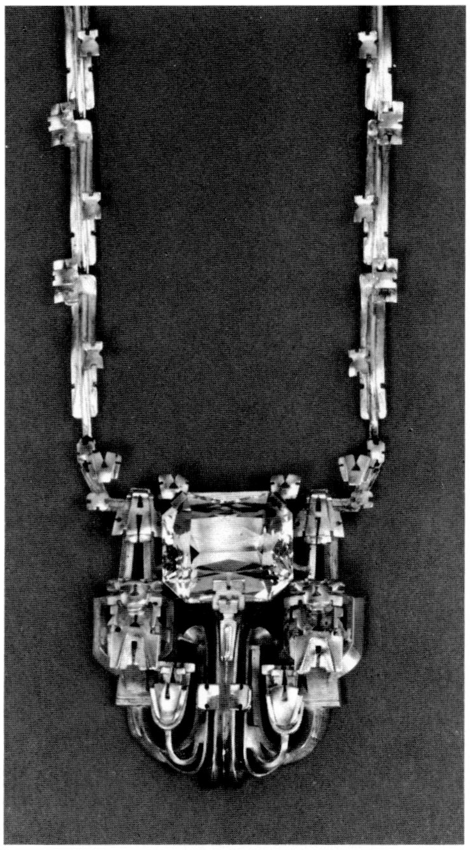

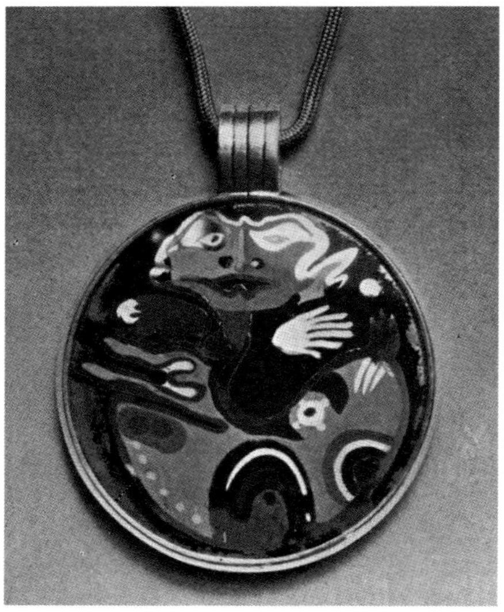

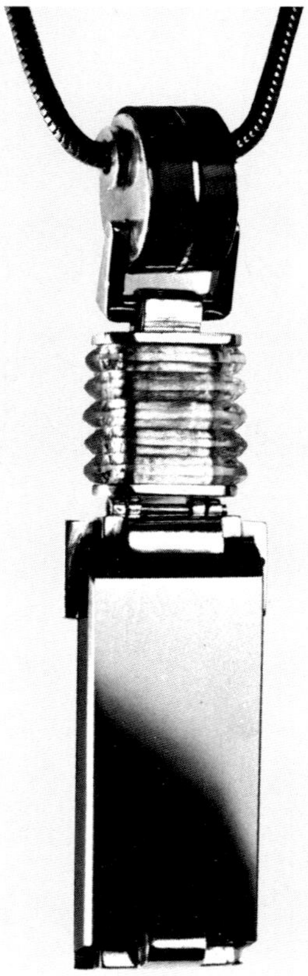

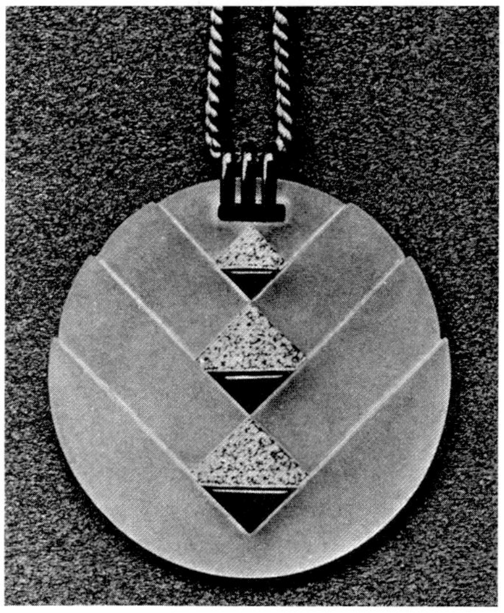

Naum Slutzky: pendant in base metal, 1930. Schmuckmuseum, Pforzheim.

Jean Desprès and Etienne Cournault: pendant in engraved glass, reproduced in Art et Décoration, August 1930.

Theodor Wende: pendant in gold and aquamarine, c. 1936. Schmuckmuseum, Pforzheim.

Georges Fouquet: circular pendant from a design by Eric Bagge, in frosted crystal, brilliants and onyx.

Gérard Sandoz: pendant in citrine, hematite, onyx and silver, 1928.

Preceding page: Jean Fouquet: pendant in grey gold, black lacquer and brilliant-cut diamonds; blackened silver cord, signed. H. 10 cm, W. 5 cm. N. Manoukian Collection. Photo: L. Sully-Jaulmes.

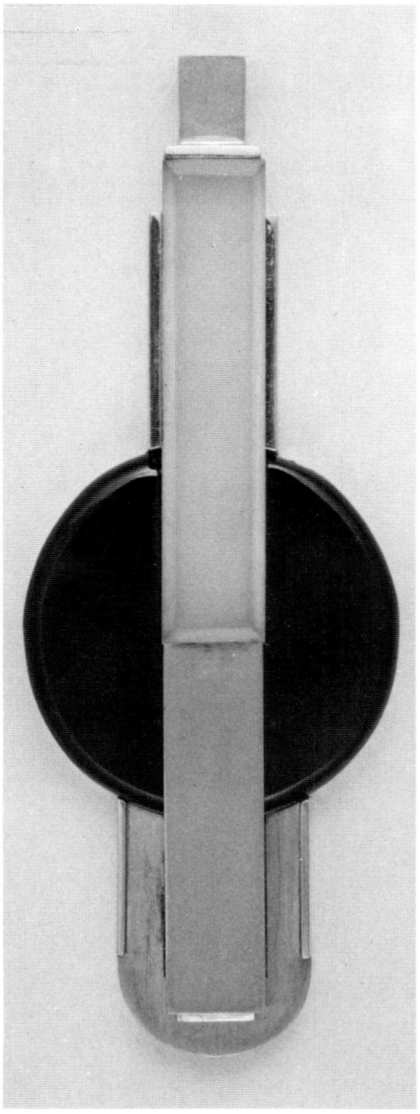

Gérard Sandoz: pendant in two colours of gold, frosted crystal and black onyx, c. 1928, signed. Sotheby's, Monte Carlo.

Raymond Templier: pendant, 1930. Courtesy of L. and B. Heuer.

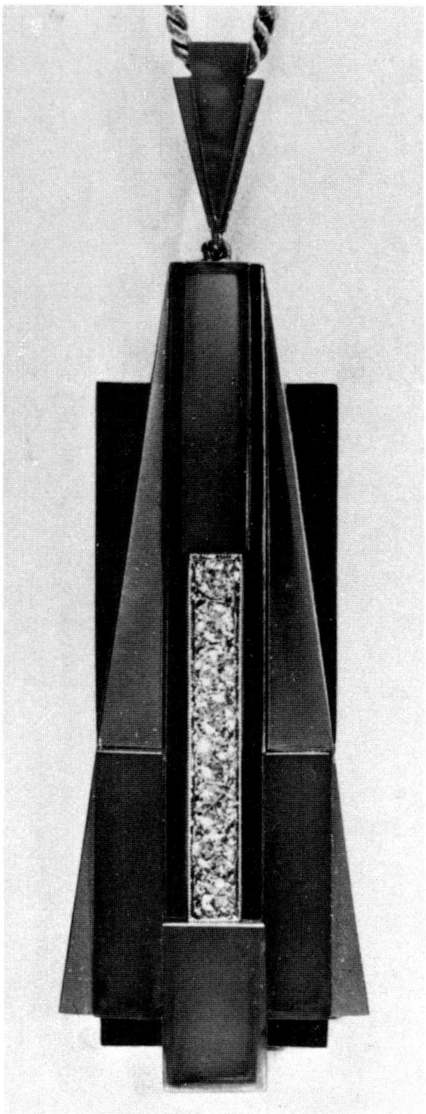

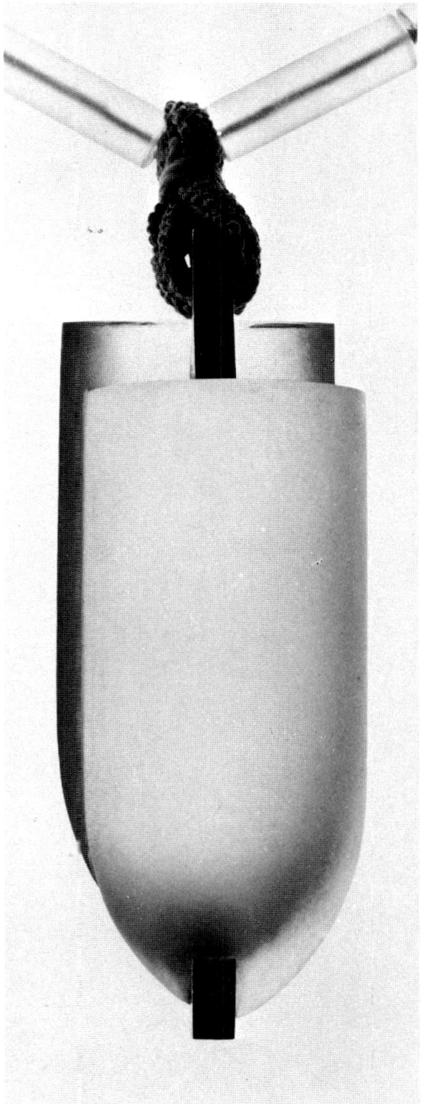

Jean Fouquet: 'artillery shell' pendant in polished platinum and crystal, c. 1927. Johanna Walker Collection. Photo: L. Sully-Jaulmes.

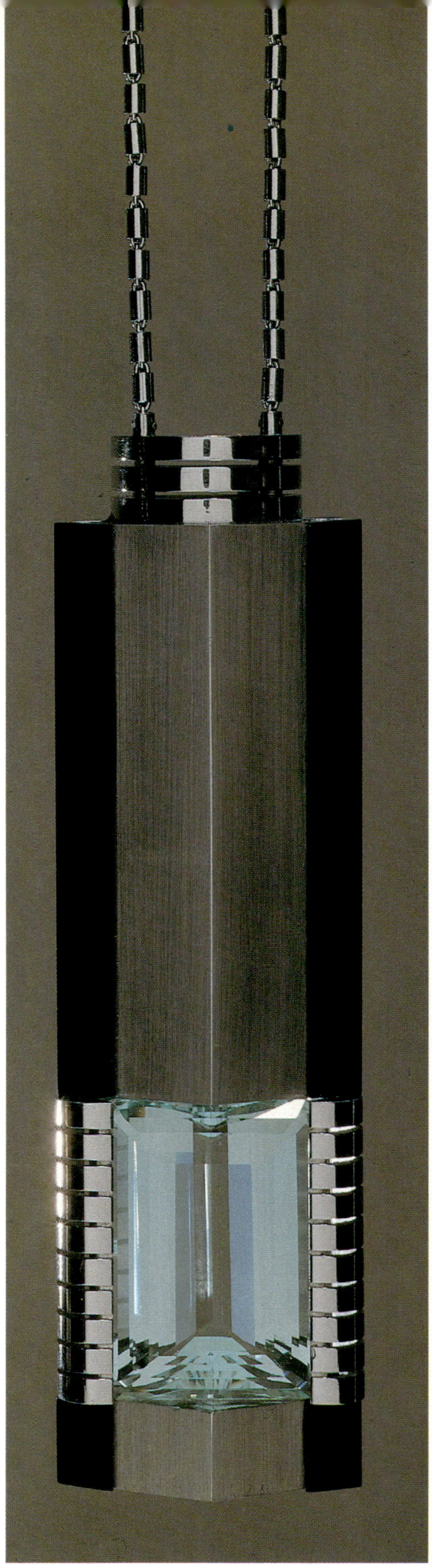

Gérard Sandoz: pendant in white gold, aquamarine and onyx, c. 1928, signed. H. 11.5 cm, W. 3.4 cm. Private Collection. Photo: T. Heuer and J.B. Rouault.

Gérard Sandoz: pendant in white gold, red gold and labradorite, c. 1928, signed. H. 10.4 cm, W. 3.6 cm. Private Collection. Photo: T. Heuer and J.B. Rouault.

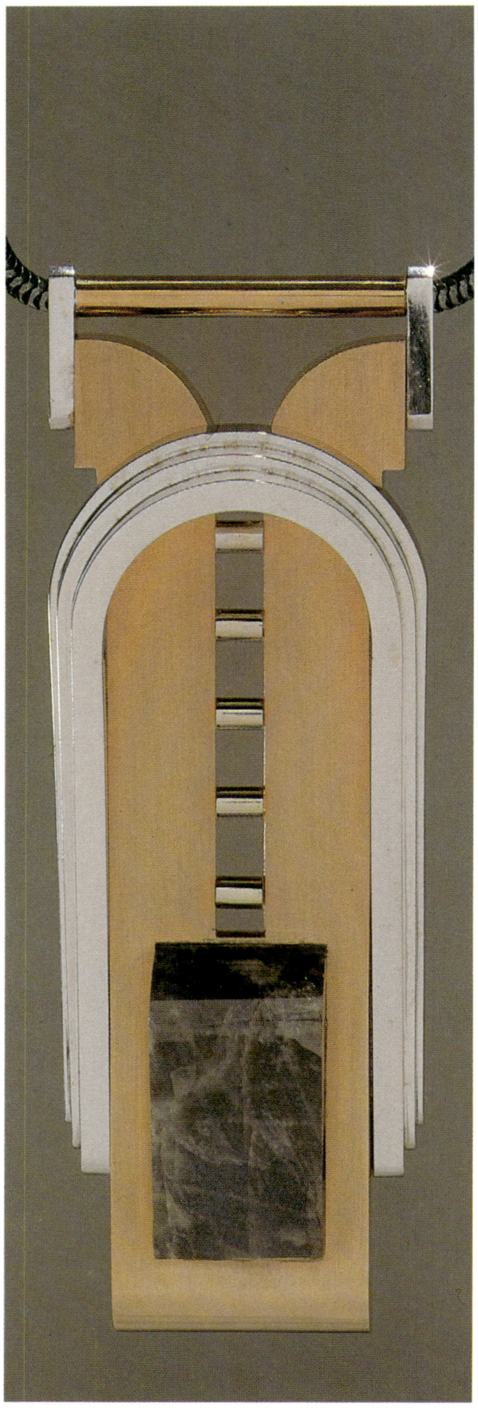

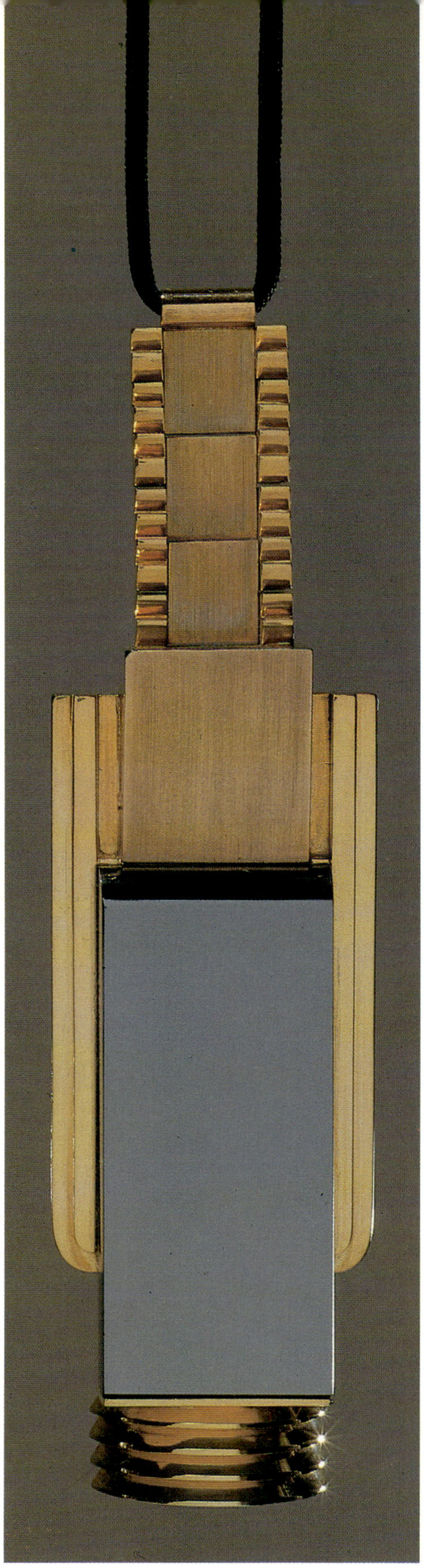

Gérard Sandoz: pendant in yellow gold, red gold and hematite, c. 1928, signed. H. 11.5 cm, W. 3.1 cm. Private Collection. Photo: T. Heuer and J.B. Rouault.

Facing page: Jean Fouquet: necklace in gold, platinum, silver, black lacquer and aquamarine, 1925–30, signed. H. 9 cm. Private Collection. Photo: T. Heuer.

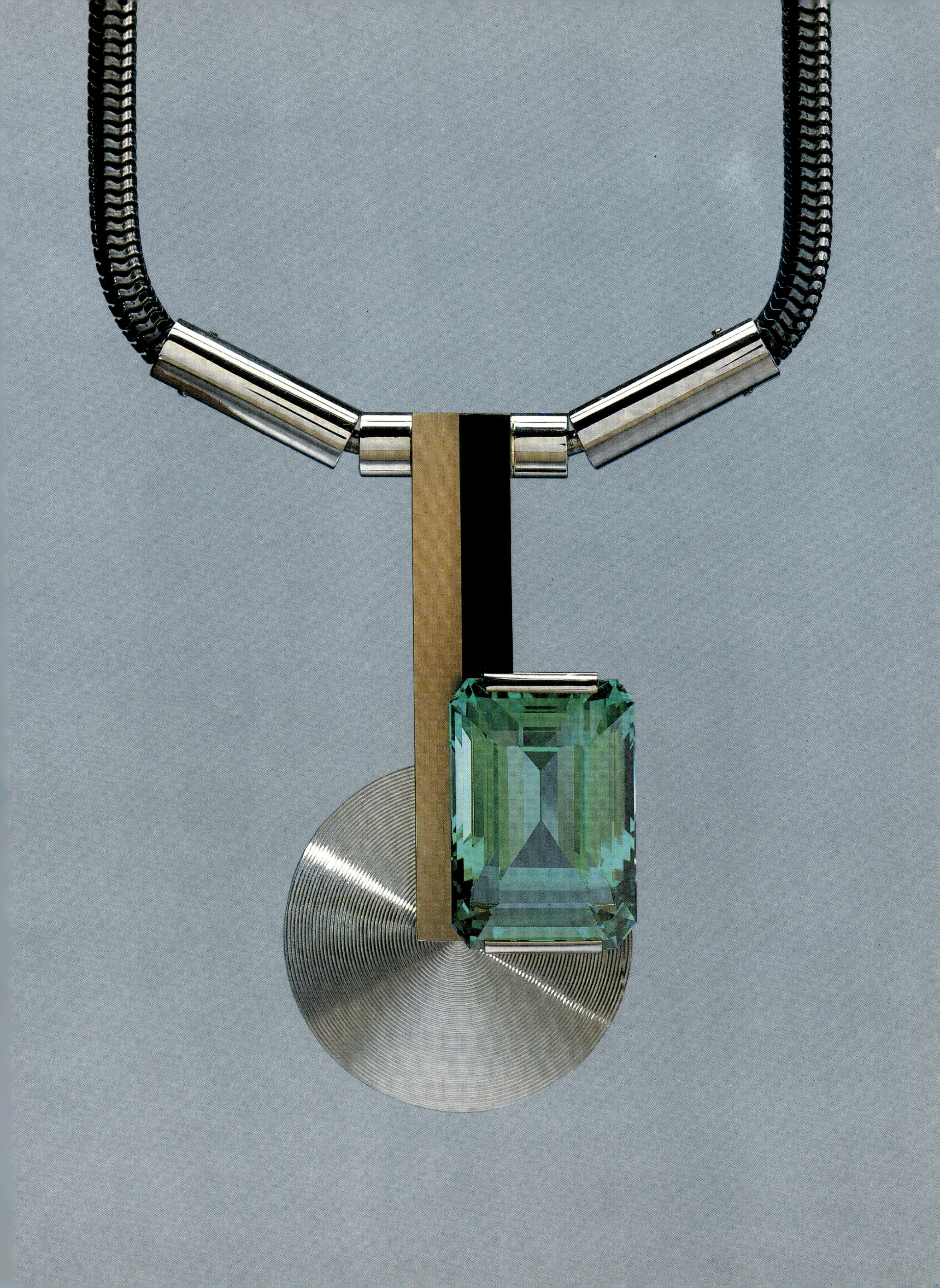

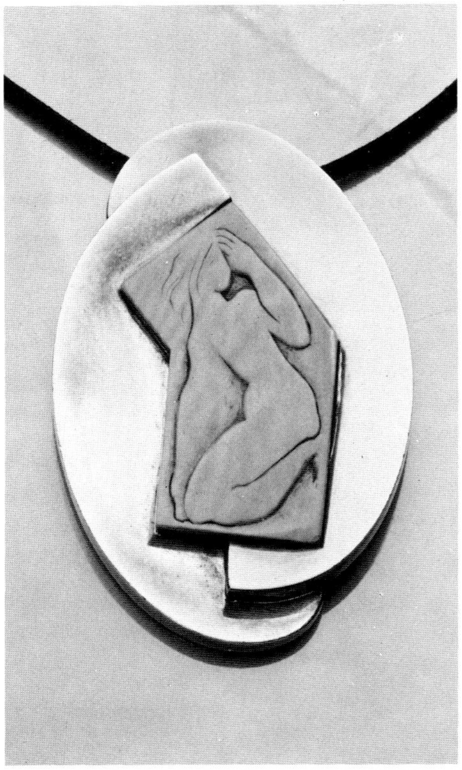

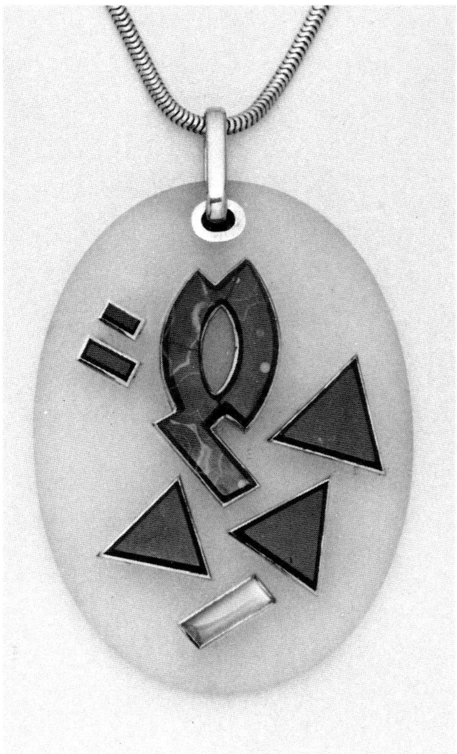

Csaky: gold pendant. Galerie Vallois, Paris. Photo: Vénus Mercenaire.

Georges Fouquet: pendant from a design by André Léveillé in frosted crystal set with onyx and calibré *coloured stones, 1925. Private Collection.*

Jean Fouquet: pendant in brilliant-cut diamonds set in platinum, with polished metal cabochon, white gold, and coral bead, 1929. A. Lesieutre Collection. Photo: L. Sully-Jaulmes.

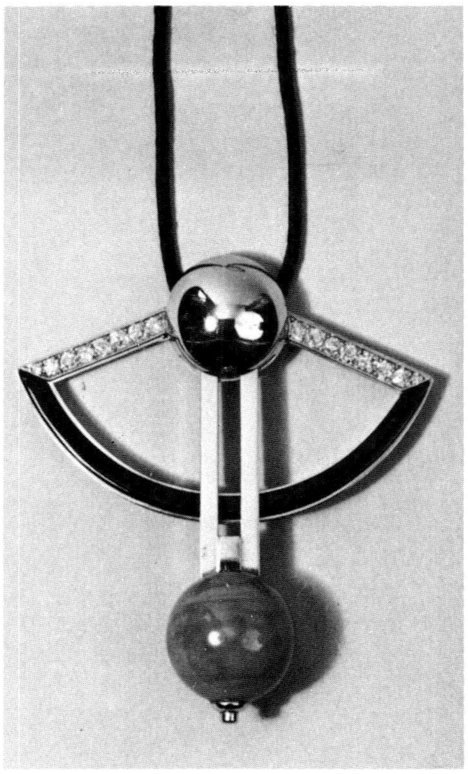

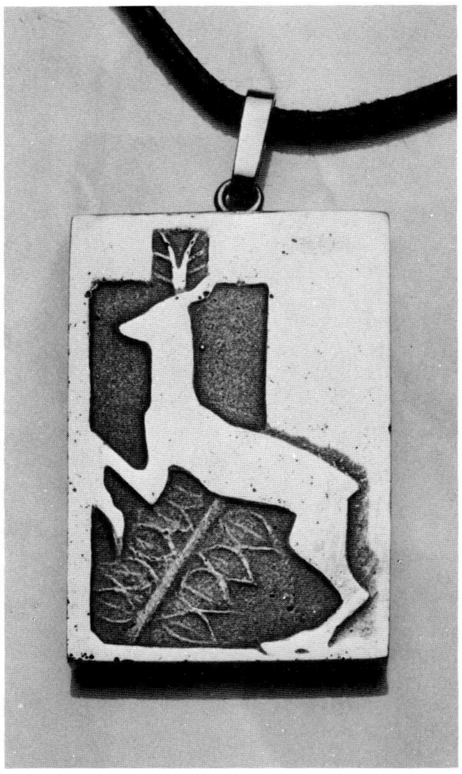

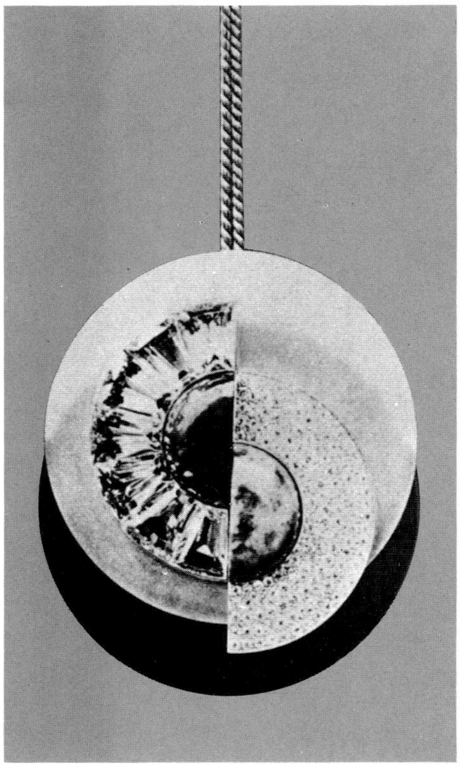

Raymond Templier and Csaky: silver, ivory and gold pendant. Galerie Vallois, Paris. Photo: Vénus Mercenaire.

Georges Fouquet: pendant from a design by Cassandre in frosted crystal, onyx, coloured stones and diamonds, 1925.

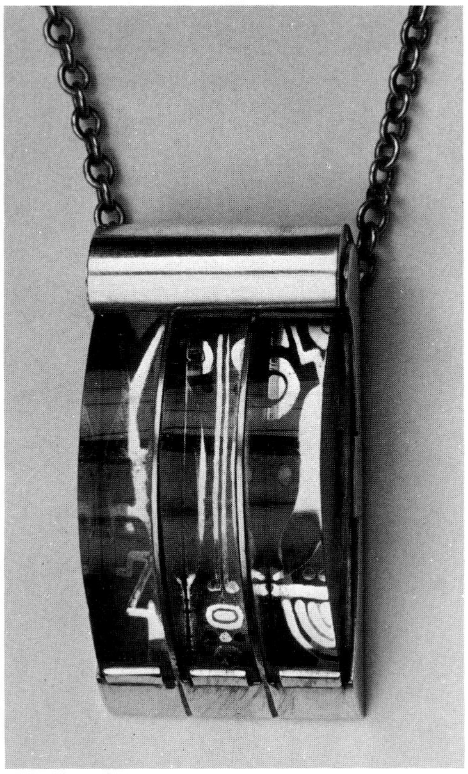

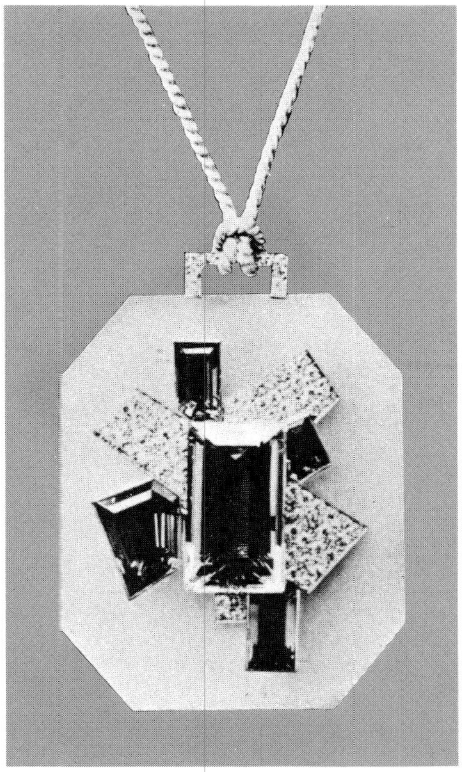

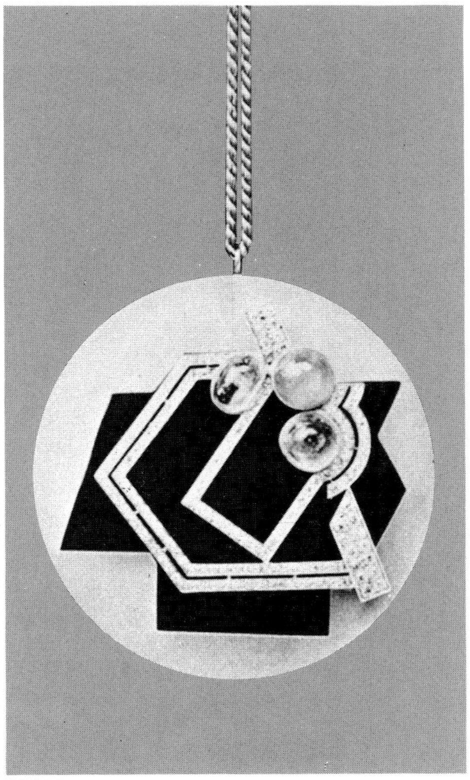

Jean Fouquet: pendant in silver and green and black lacquer. Félix Marcilhac Collection. Photo: L. Sully-Jaulmes.

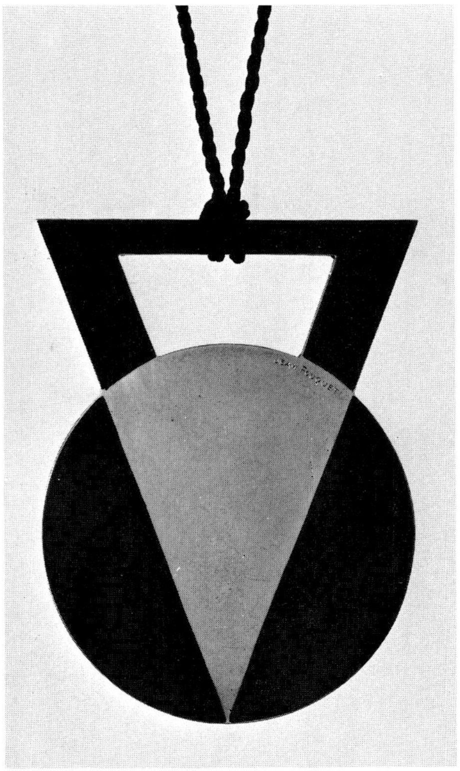

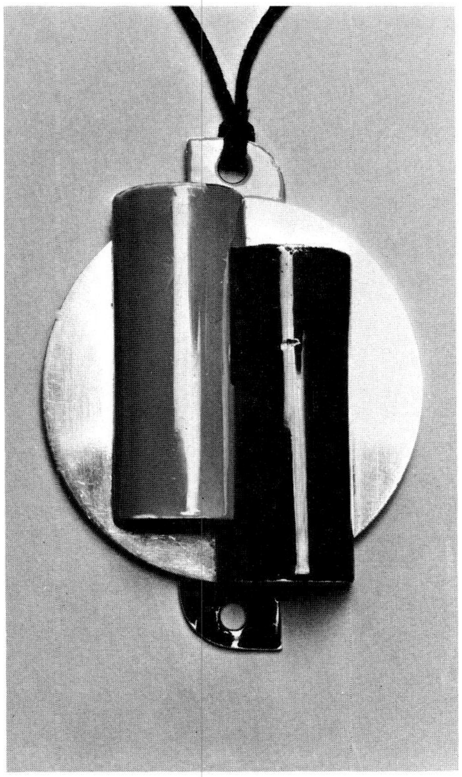

Jean Després: pendant in silver and glass engraved by Etienne Cournault, c. 1930. Musée des Arts Décoratifs, Paris. Photo: L. Sully-Jaulmes.

Georges Fouquet: pendant from a design by André Léveillé in frosted crystal and coloured stones, probably aquamarine, topaz, amethysts and diamonds, 1925.

Georges Fouquet: pendant from a design by André Léveillé in frosted crystal, onyx, sapphires and emeralds, with diamond cabochons, 1925.

Jean Fouquet: pendant in silver and black, red and pale-blue lacquer, 1928.

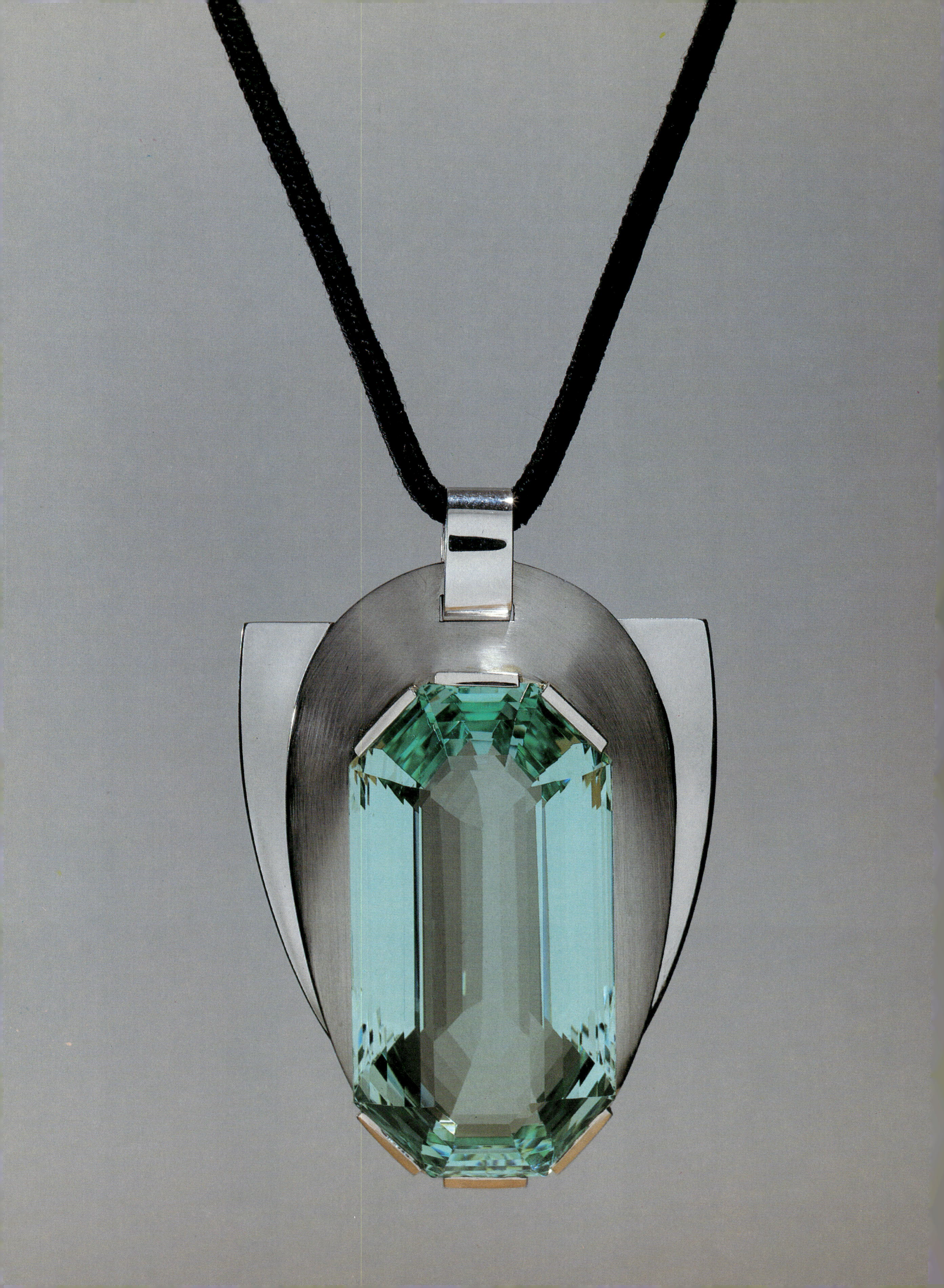

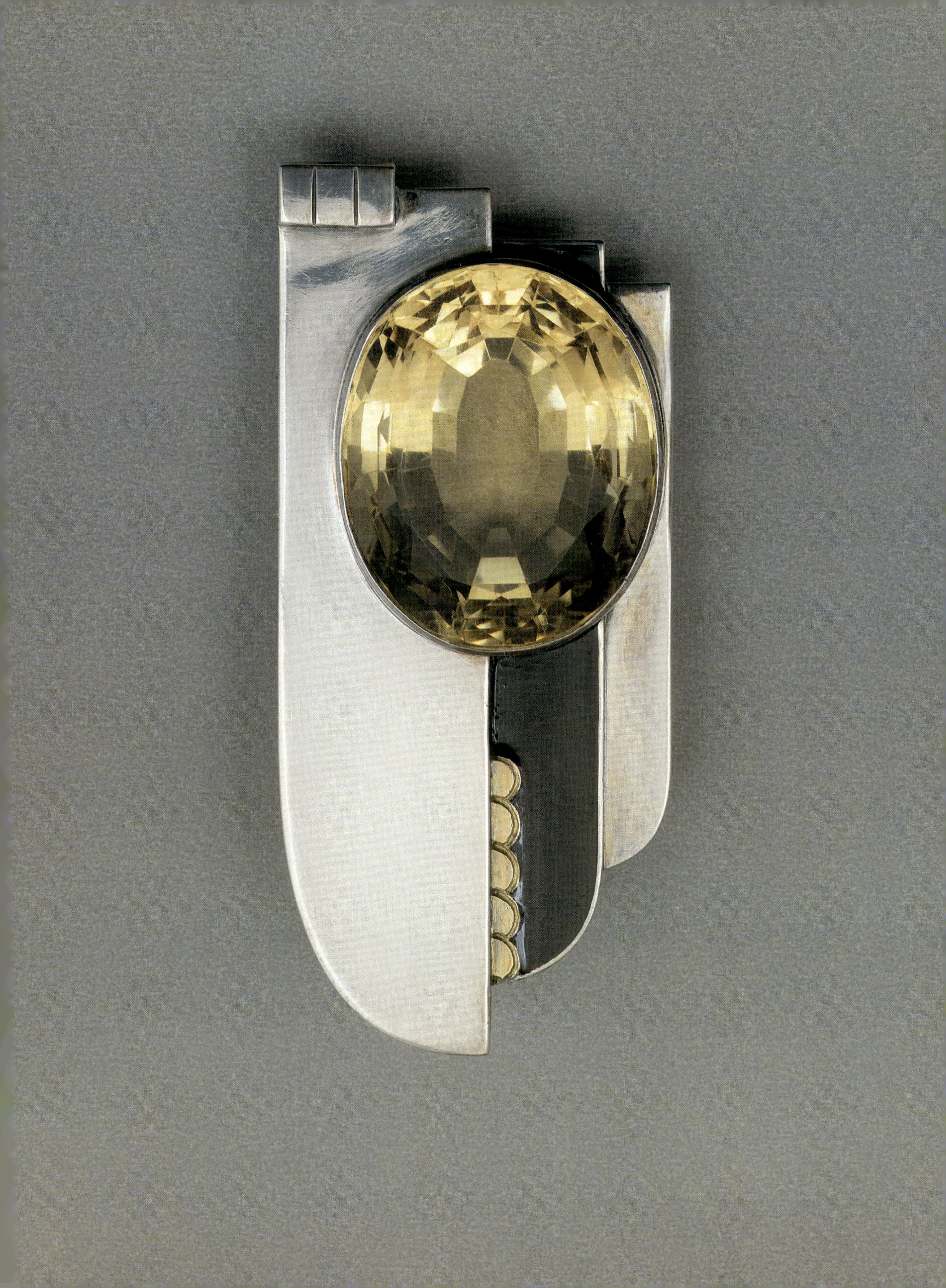

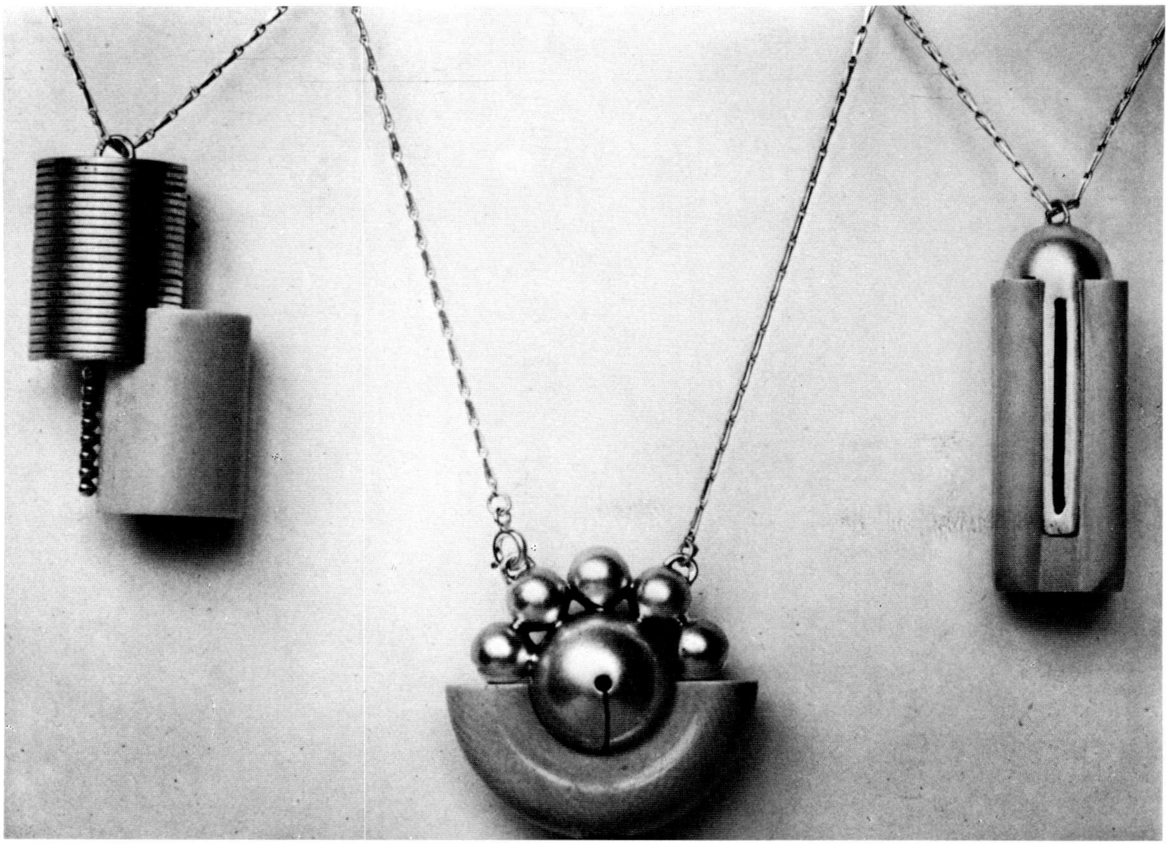

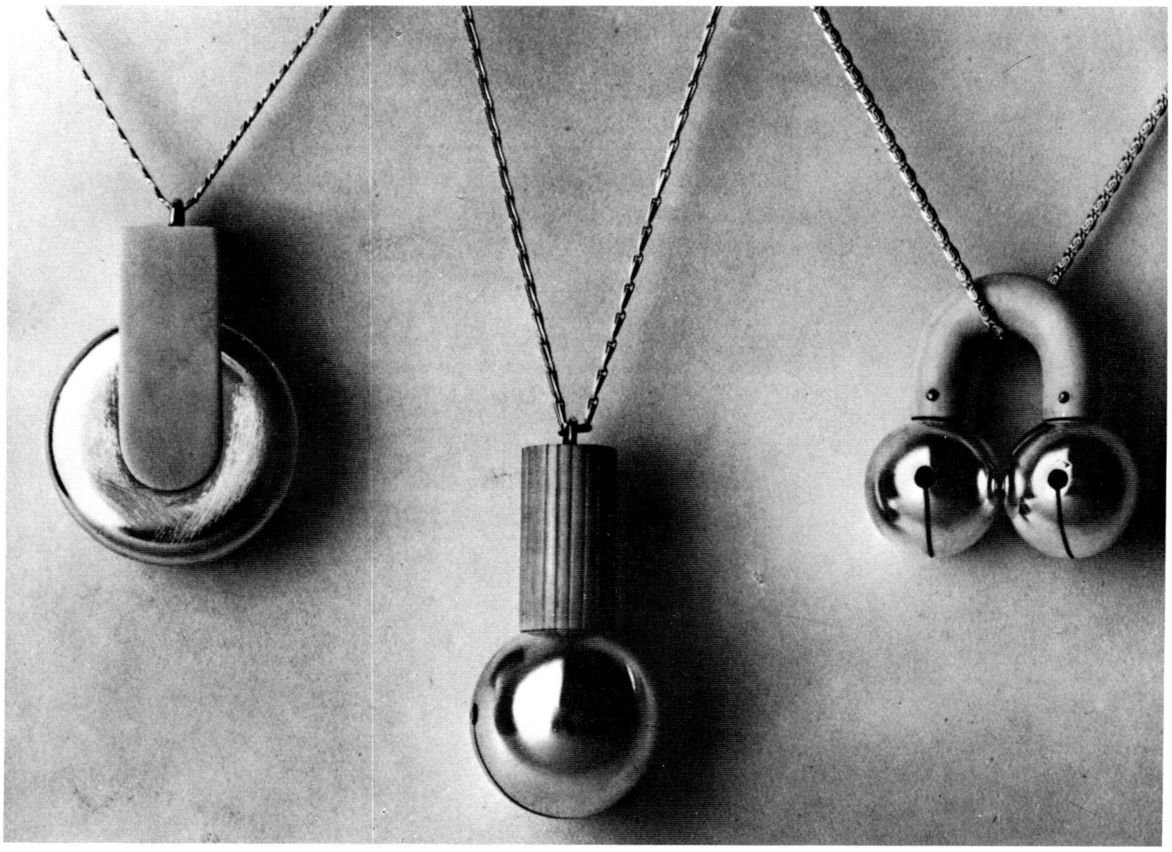

Puiforcat: ivory and silver pendants, c. 1925. Puiforcat Archives.

Facing page: Jean Desprès: silver necklace, c. 1925, signed. Primavera Gallery, New York.

Preceding pages: Raymond Templier: platinum and aquamarine pendant, 1928, signed. H. 6.5 cm, W. 4.5 cm. Photo: T. Heuer and J.B. Rouault.

Jean Desprès: pendant in silver, citrine and black enamel, signed. H. 8 cm, W. 3.5 cm. N. Manoukian Collection. Photo: L. Sully-Jaulmes.

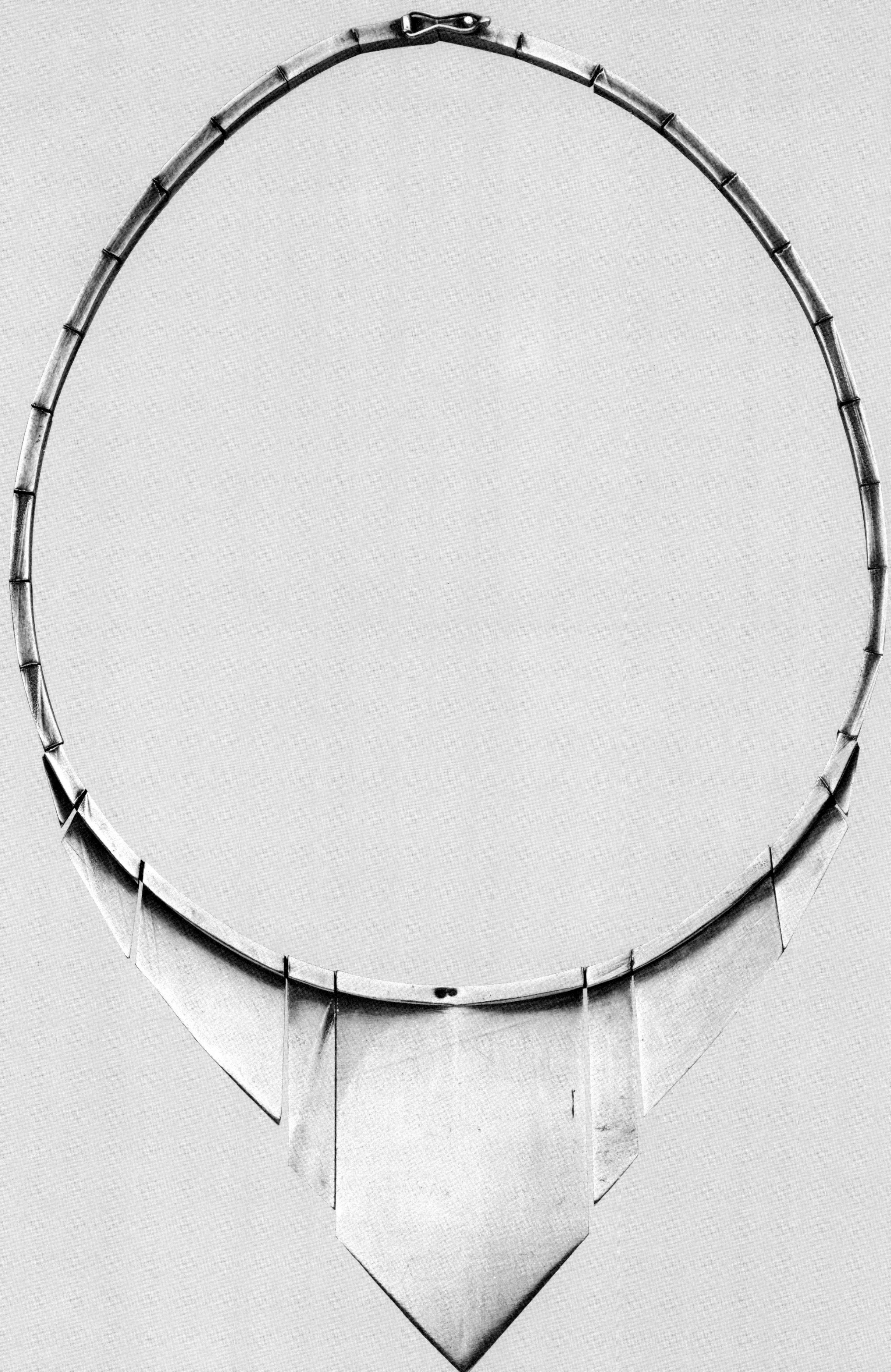

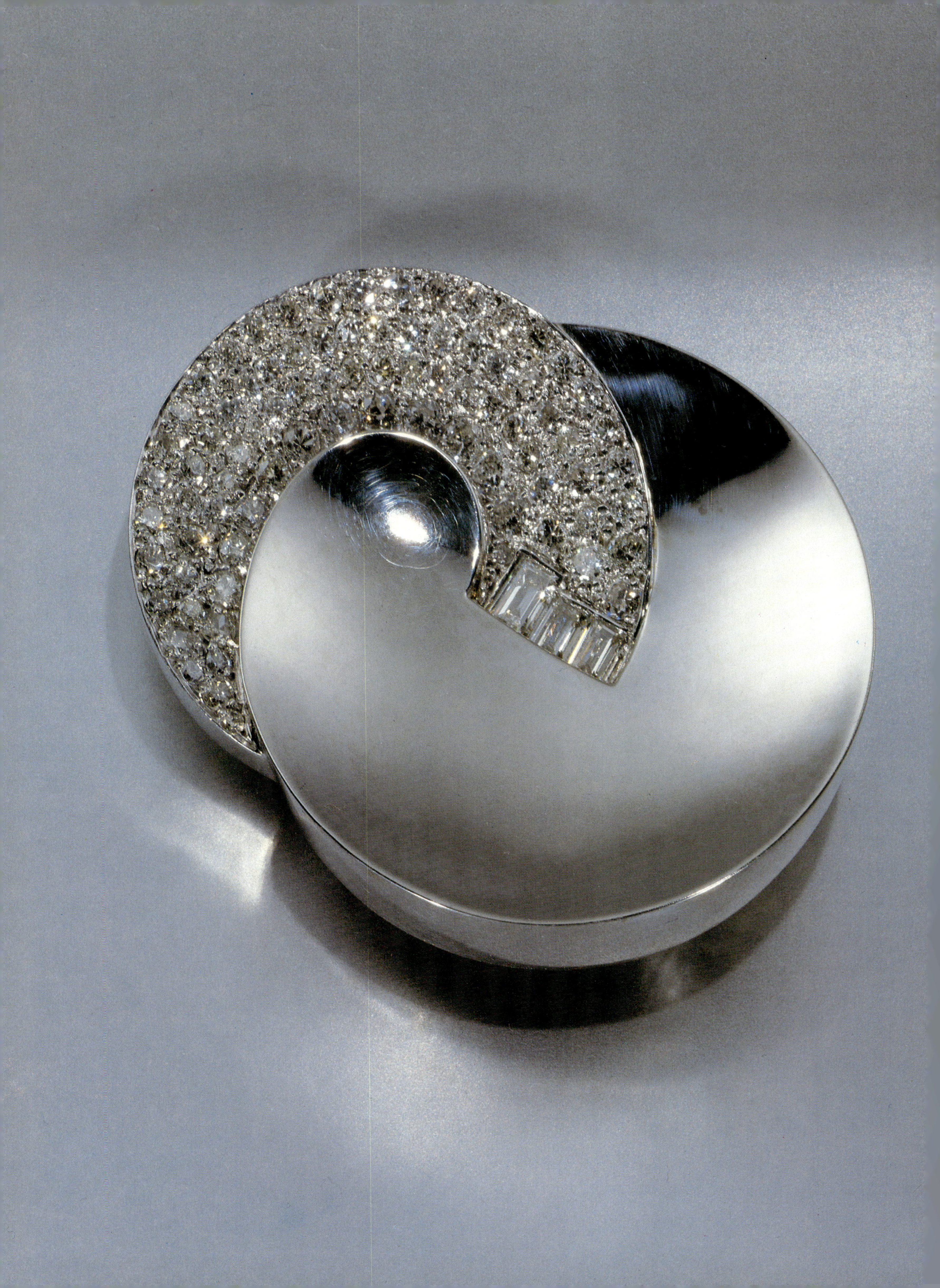

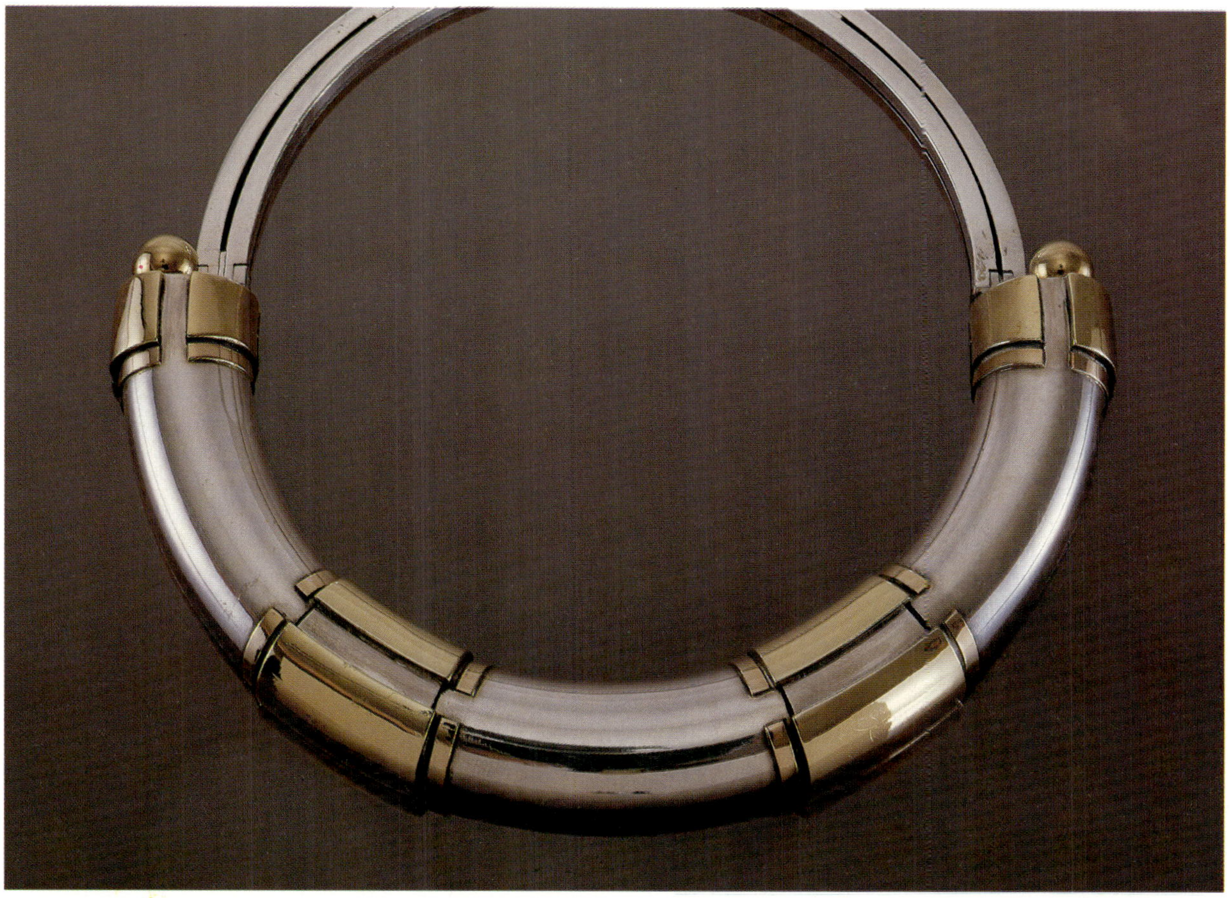

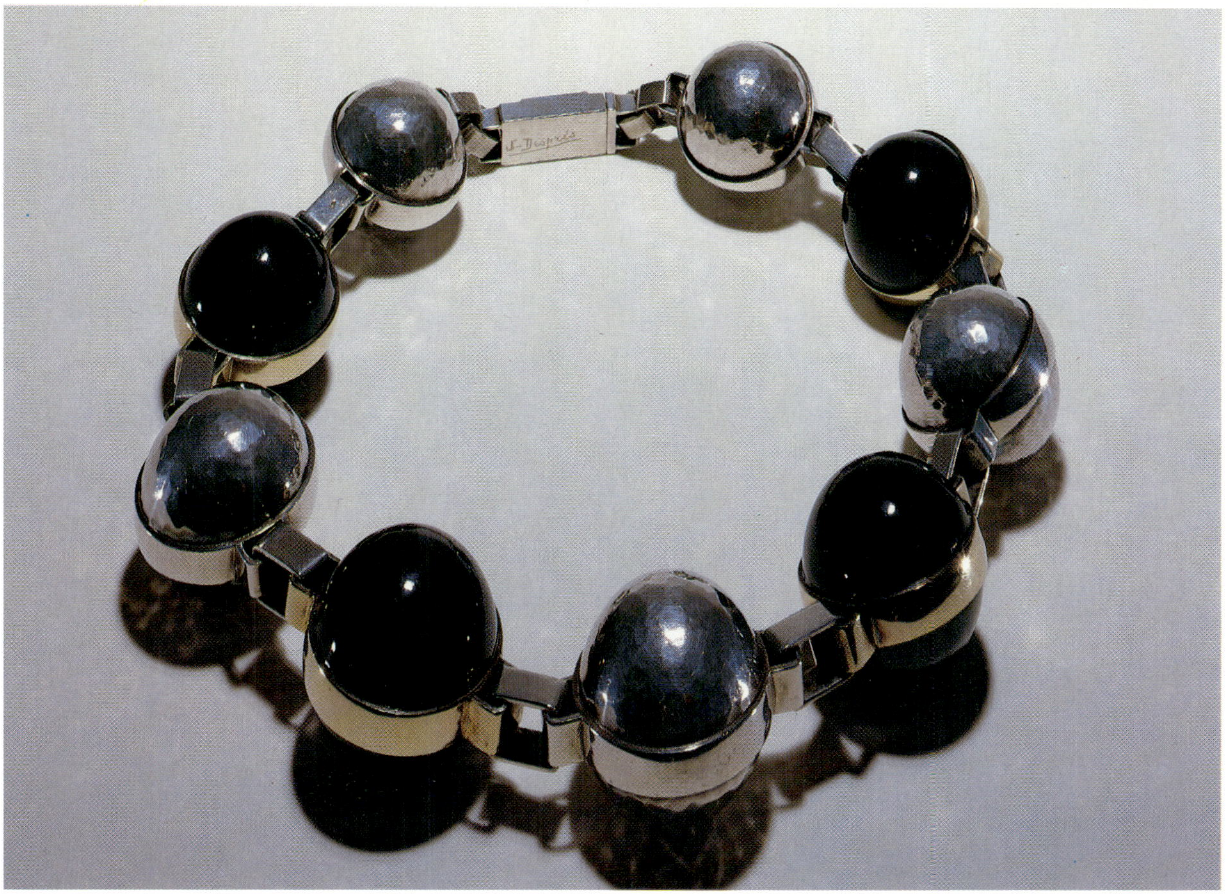

Jean Desprès: necklace in silver and gold, first model executed in 1912, signed. Private Collection. Photo: T. Heuer and J.B. Rouault.

Jean Desprès: necklace in silver, gold and black lacquer, signed. Photo: T. Heuer and J.B. Rouault.

Facing page: Raymond Templier: platinum and diamond brooch, 1930, signed. L. 4.6 cm, W. 3.7 cm. Private Collection. Photo: T. Heuer and J.B. Rouault.

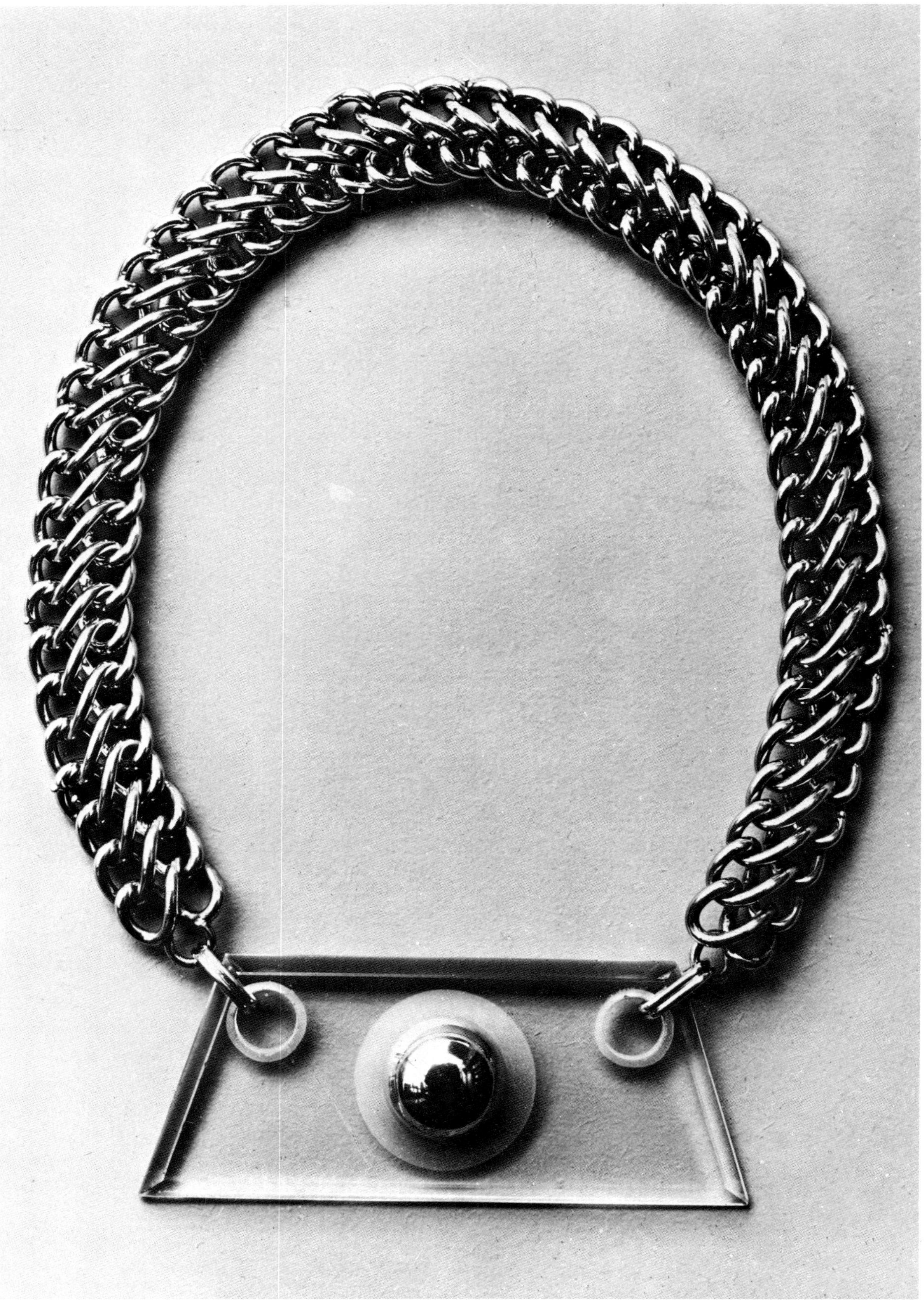

Jean Fouquet: necklace in chromed metal and glass, 1931–32. Photo: Musée des Arts Décoratifs, Paris.

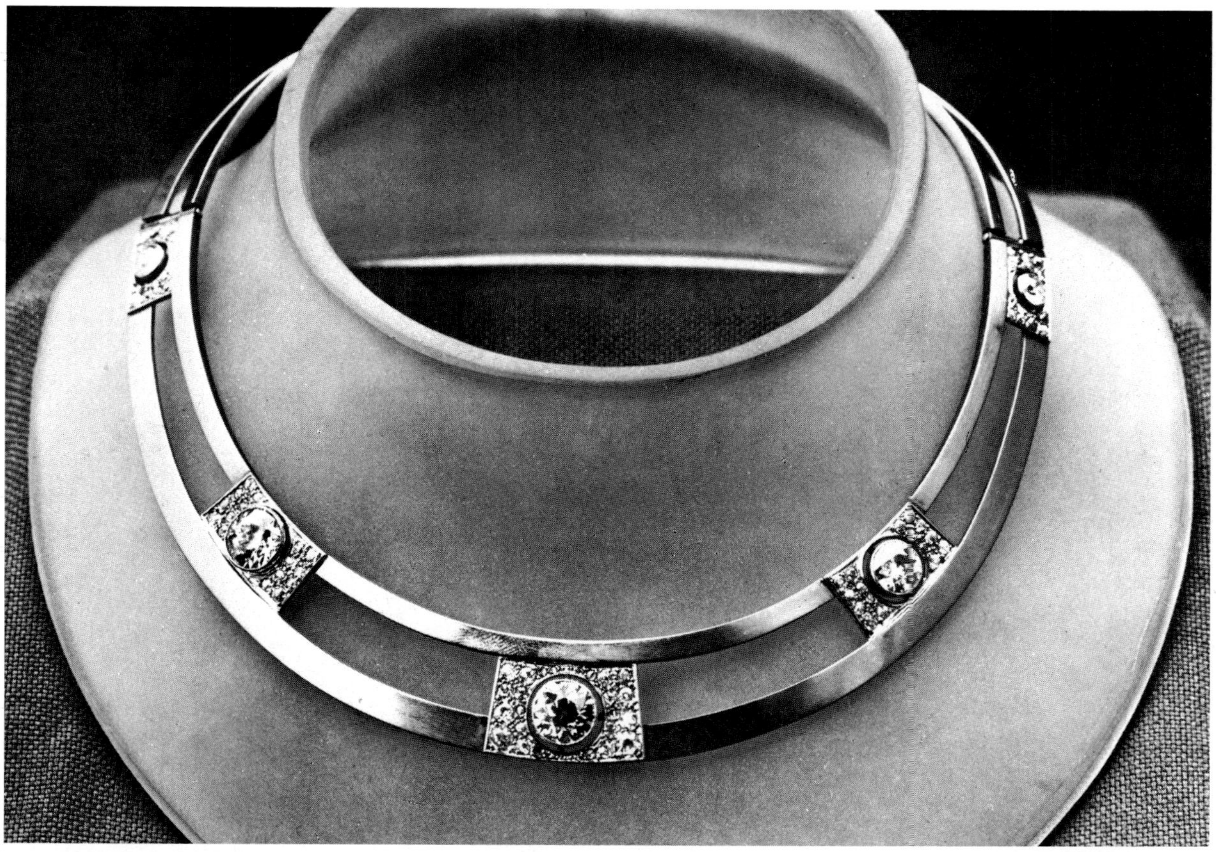

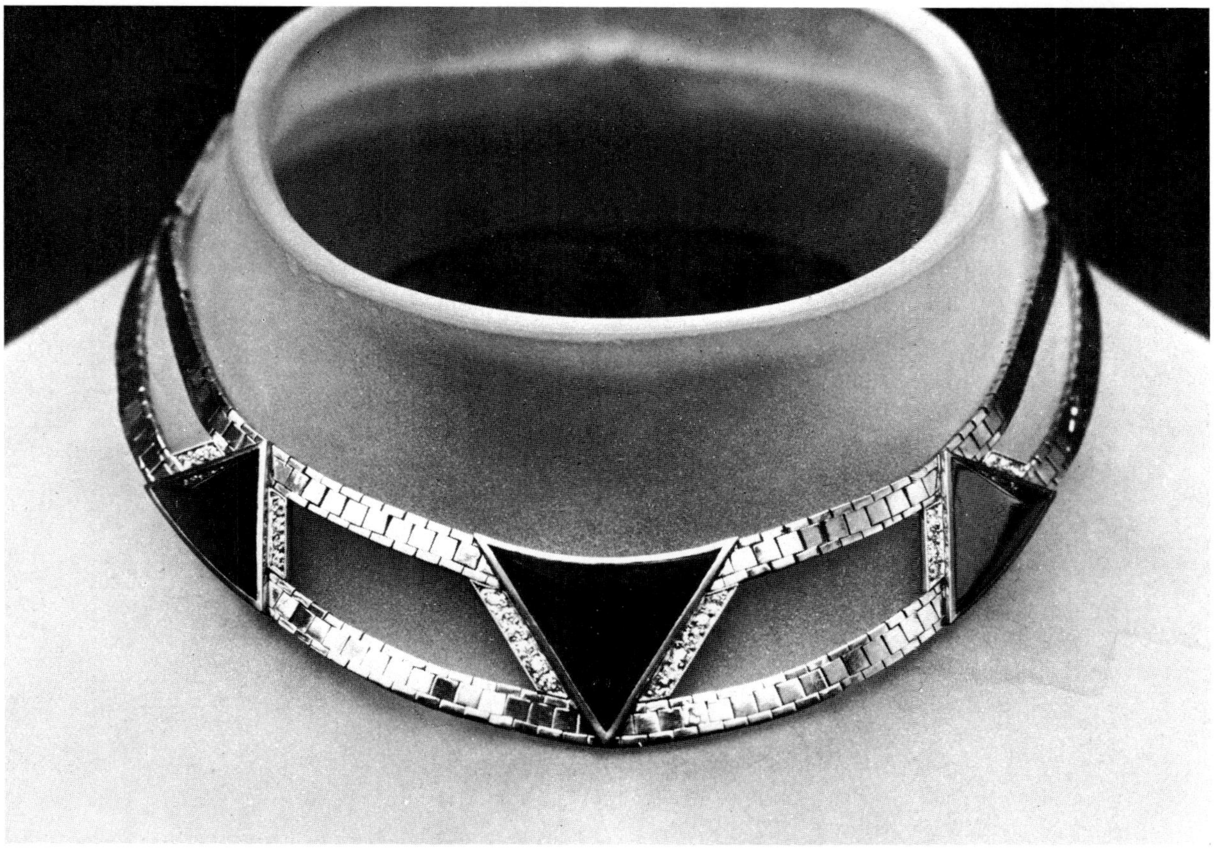

Jean Fouquet: necklace in white gold and diamonds, 1932–33. Photo: Musée des Arts Décoratifs, Paris.

Jean Fouquet: necklace in grey gold, onyx (?) and diamonds, c. 1930. Photo: Musée des Arts Décoratifs, Paris.

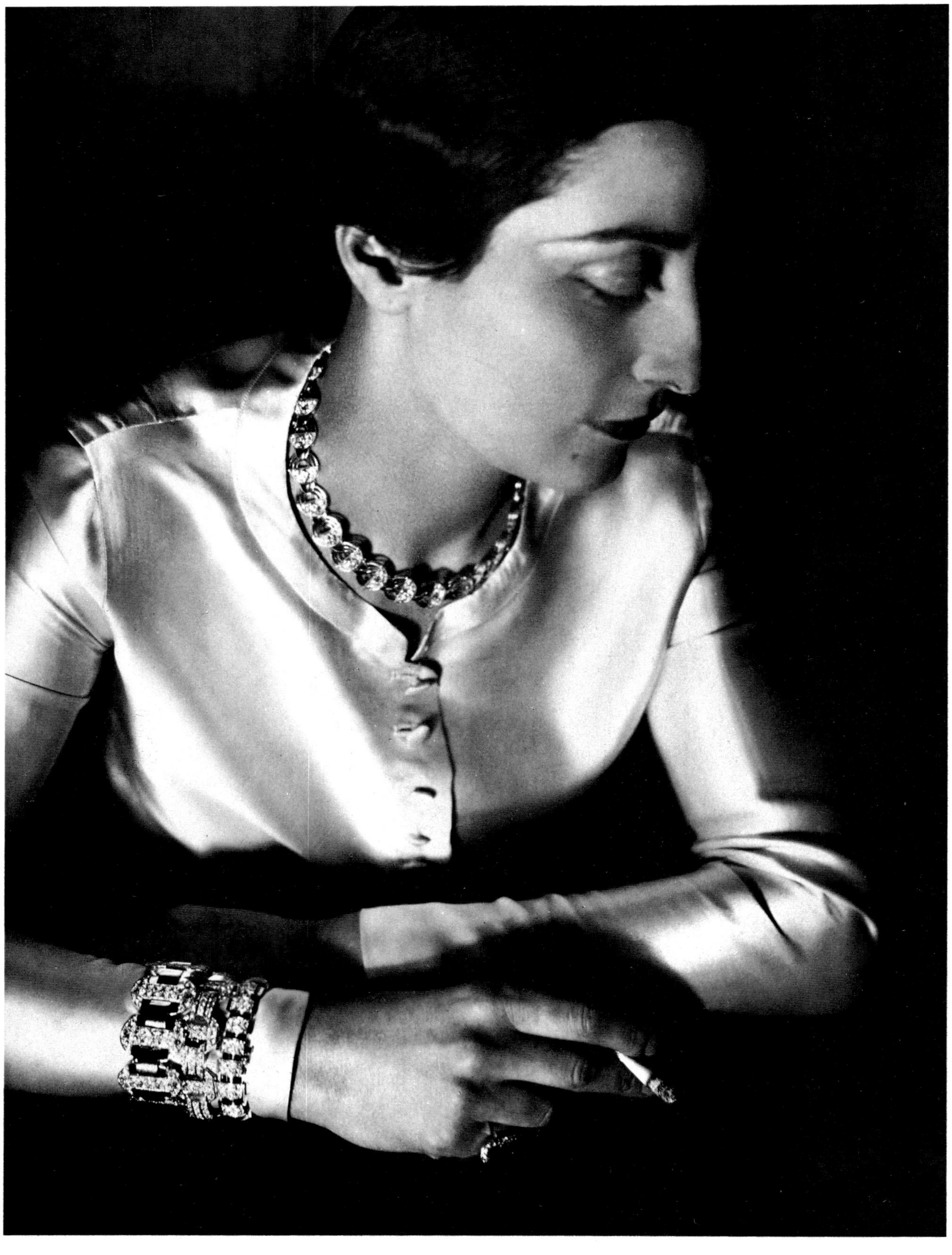

Young woman wearing jewelry by Raymond Templier. Photo: Germaine Krull.

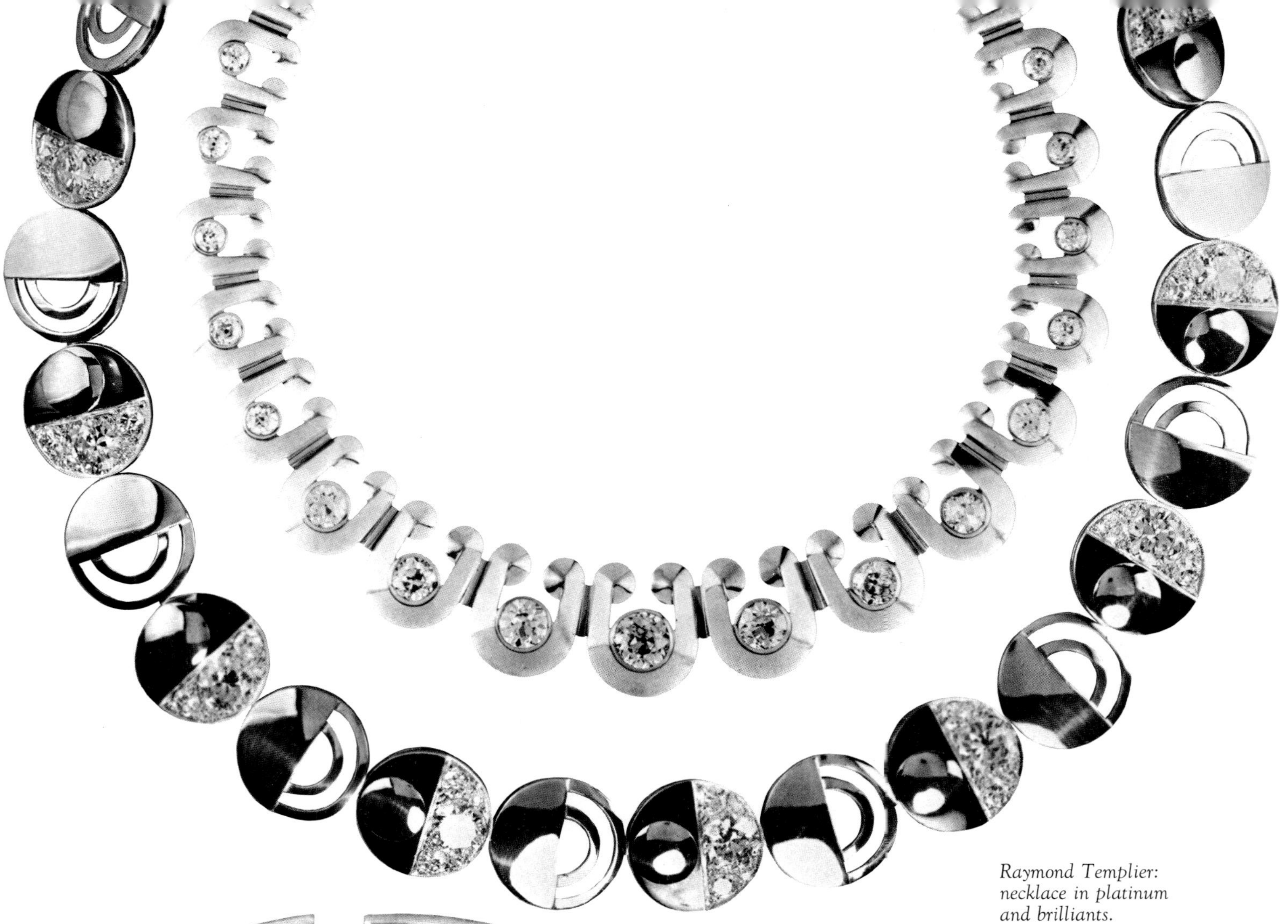

Raymond Templier: necklace in platinum and brilliants. Courtesy of L. and B. Heuer.

Raymond Templier: necklace in platinum, brilliants and black lacquer, c. 1930. Courtesy of L. and B. Heuer.

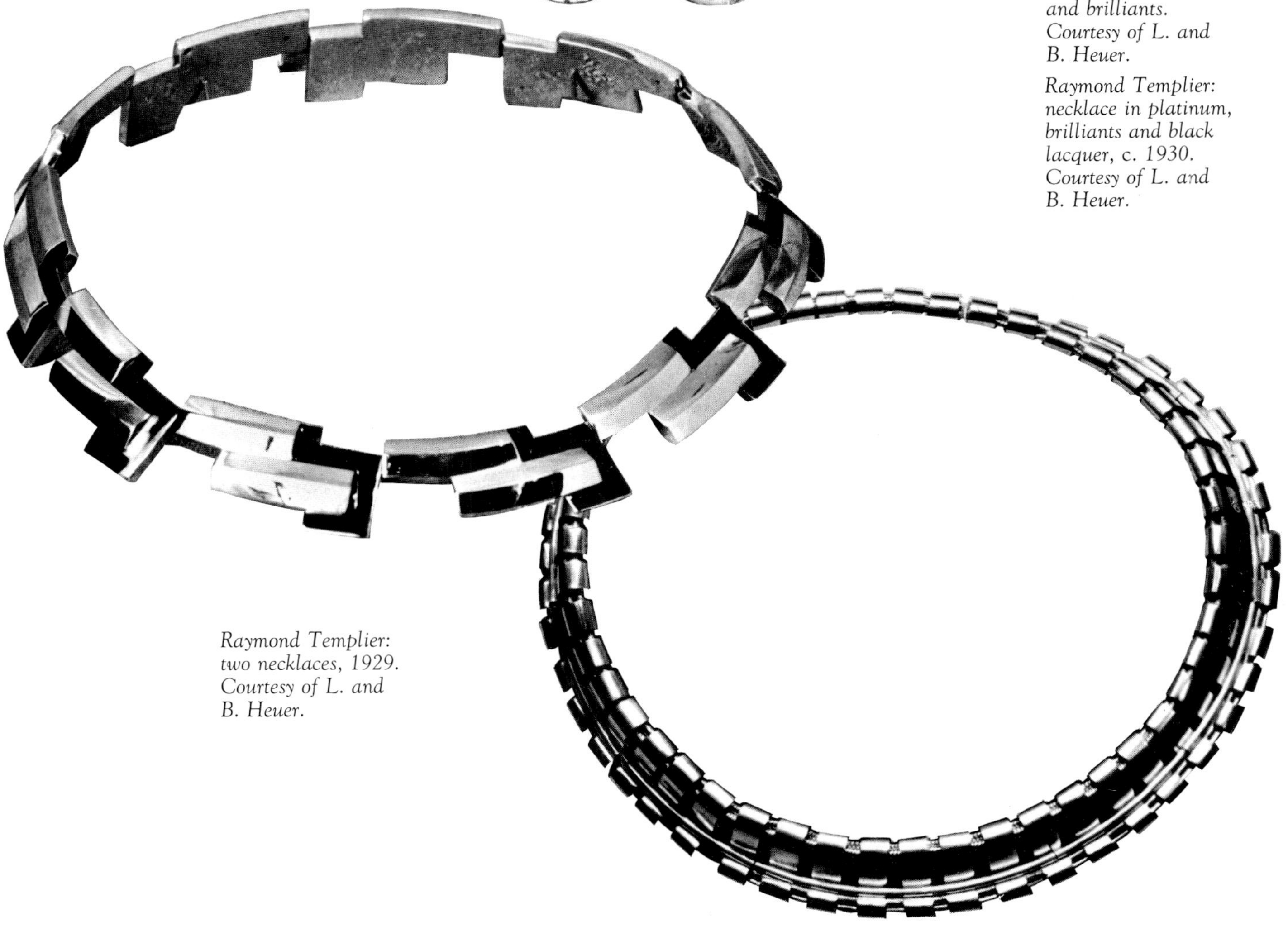

Raymond Templier: two necklaces, 1929. Courtesy of L. and B. Heuer.

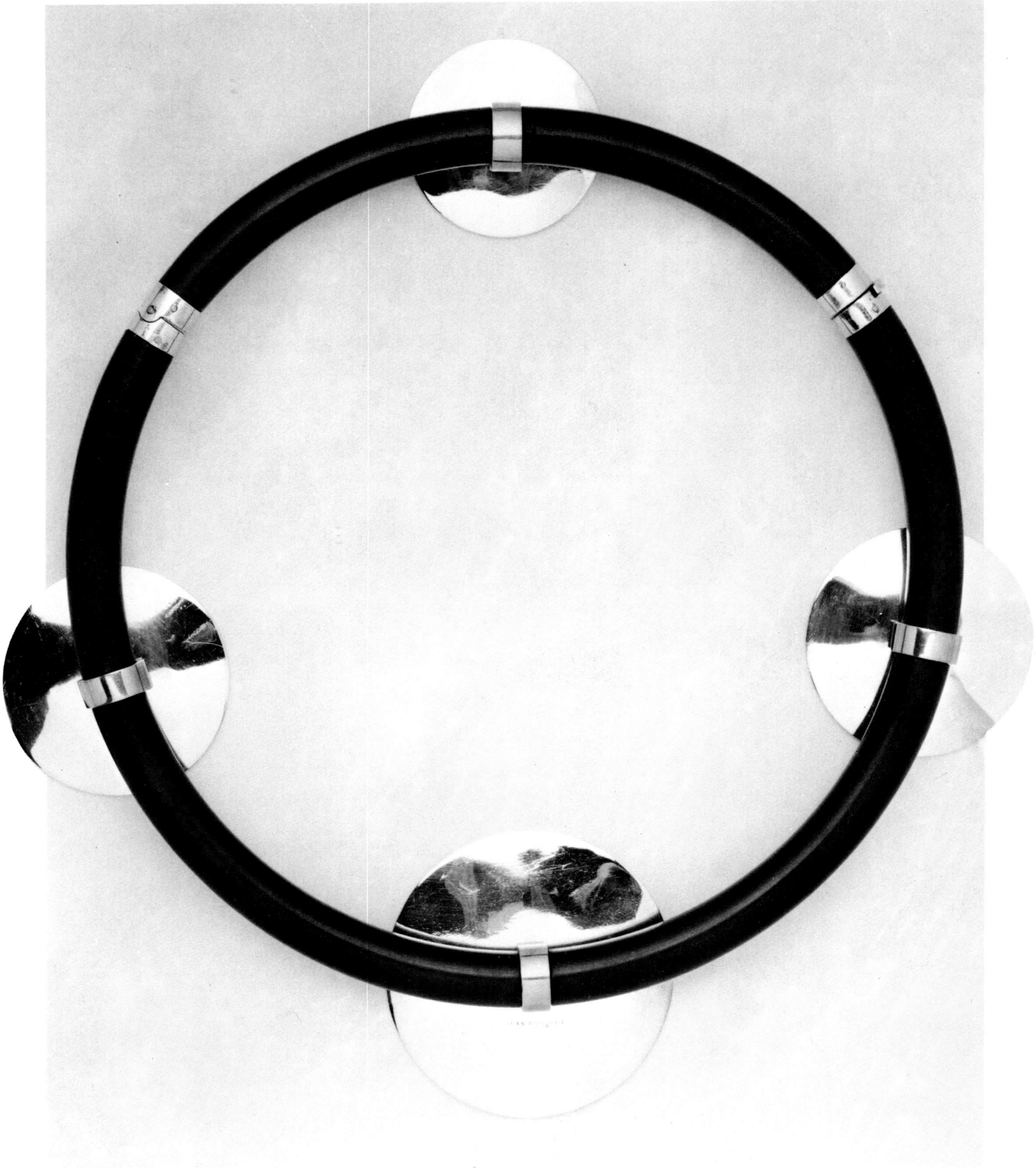

Jean Fouquet: necklace in ebony, chromed metal and gold, 1931, signed. Private Collection.

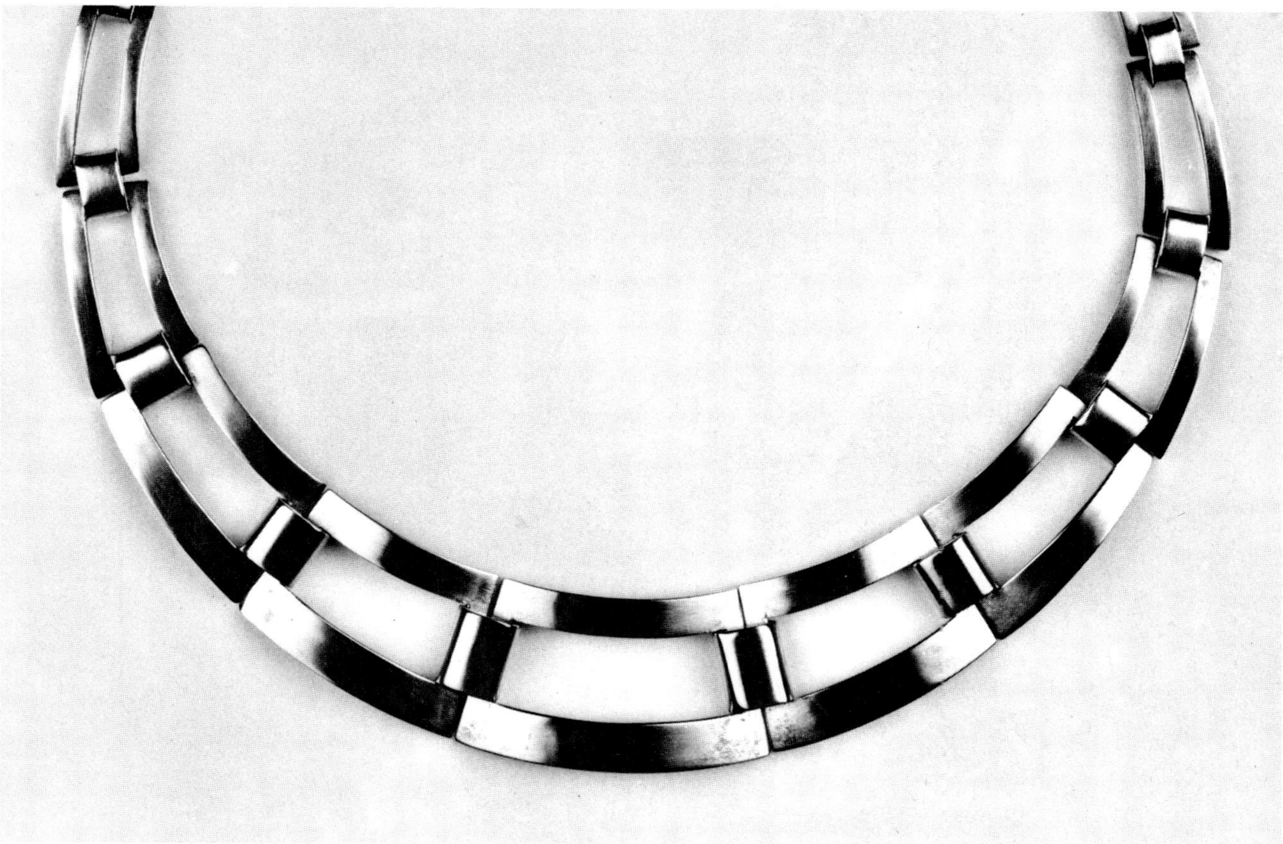

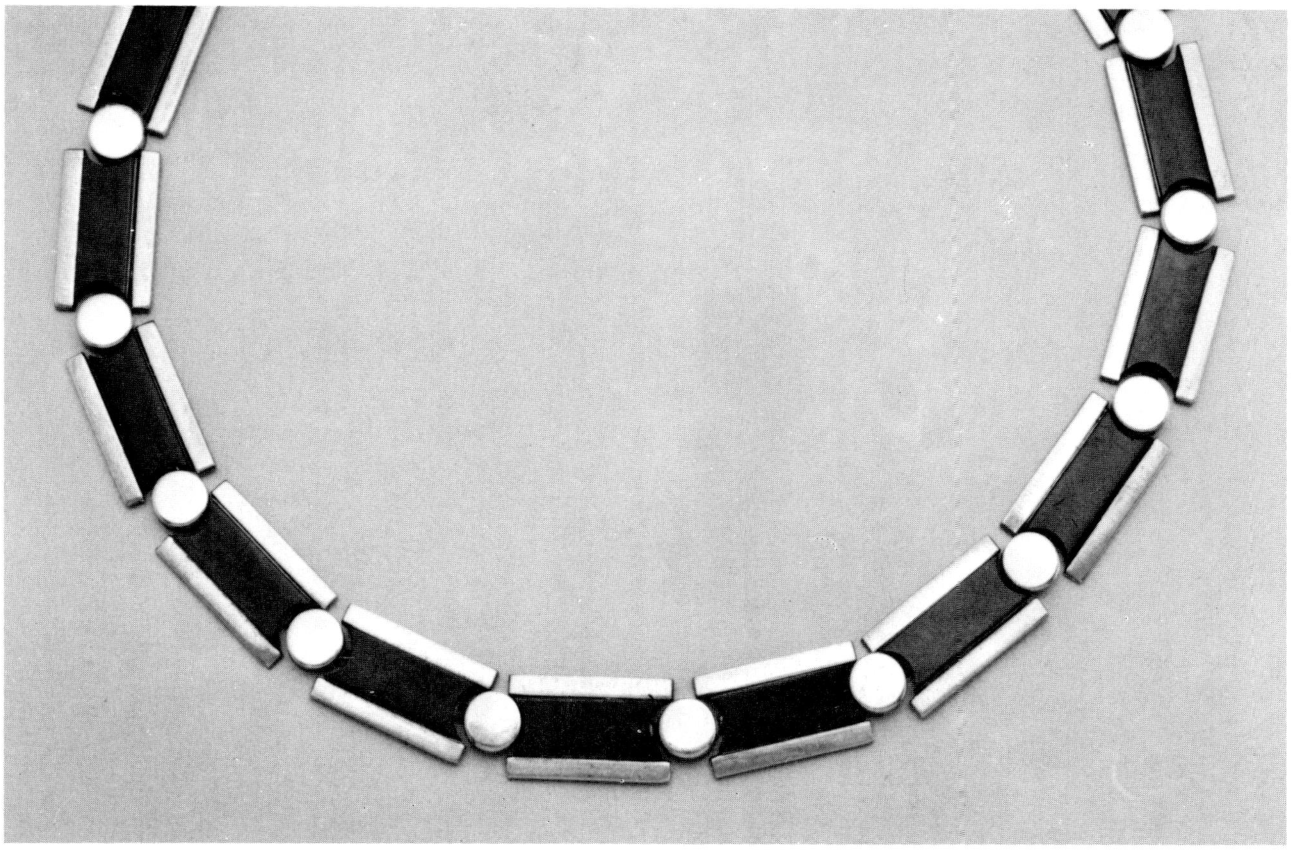

Jean Desprès: necklace in vermeil, c. 1934. Musée des Arts Décoratifs, Paris. Photo: L. Sully-Jaulmes.

Anonymous: necklace in silver and hardstones. Solange Morane Collection.

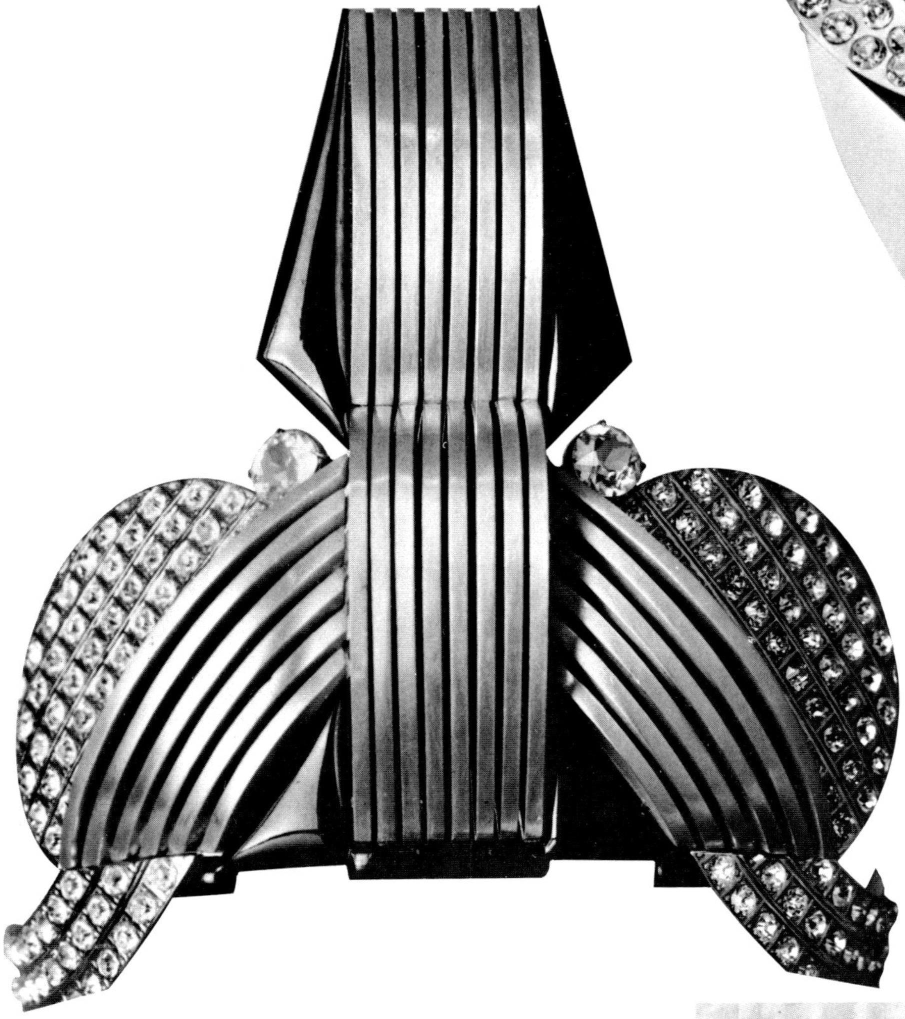

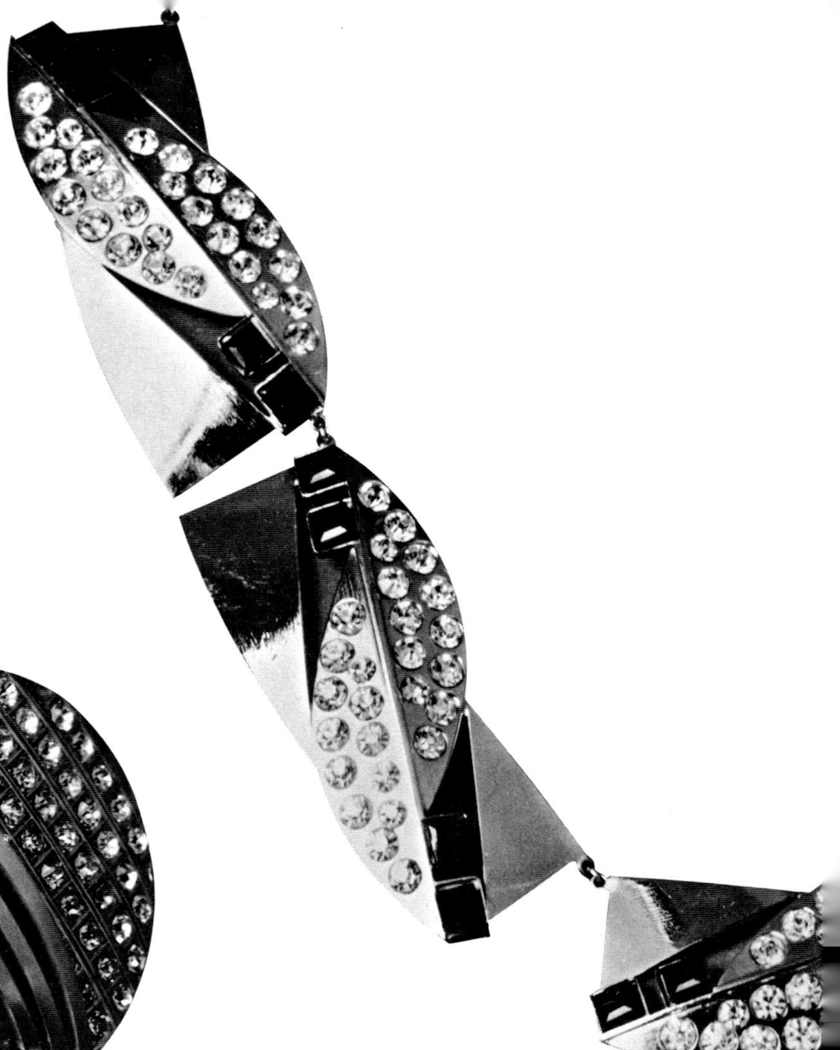

Jewelry by Raymond Templier, made for Brigitte Helm, the heroine of Marcel l'Herbier's film L'Argent, *1928. Courtesy of L. and B. Heuer.*

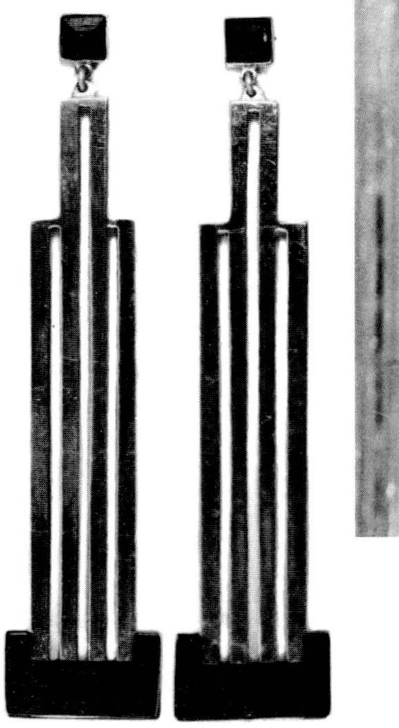

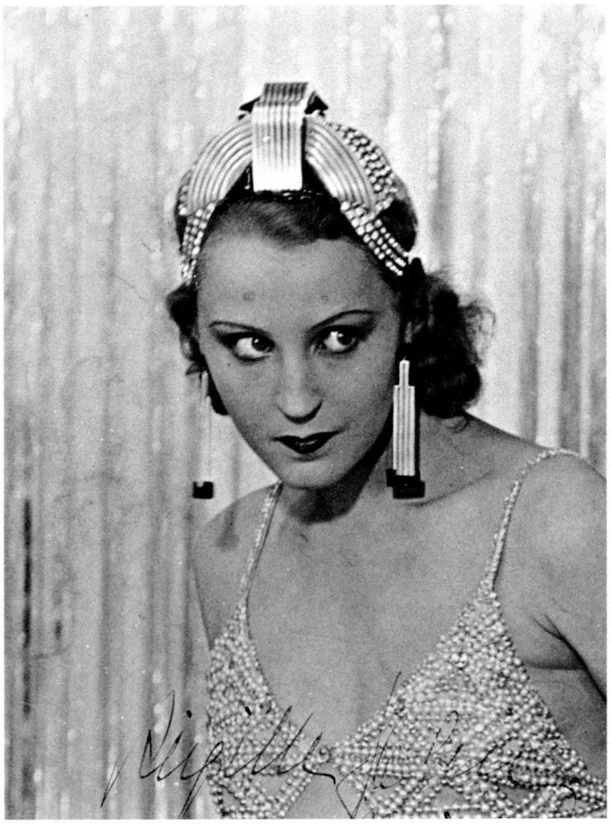

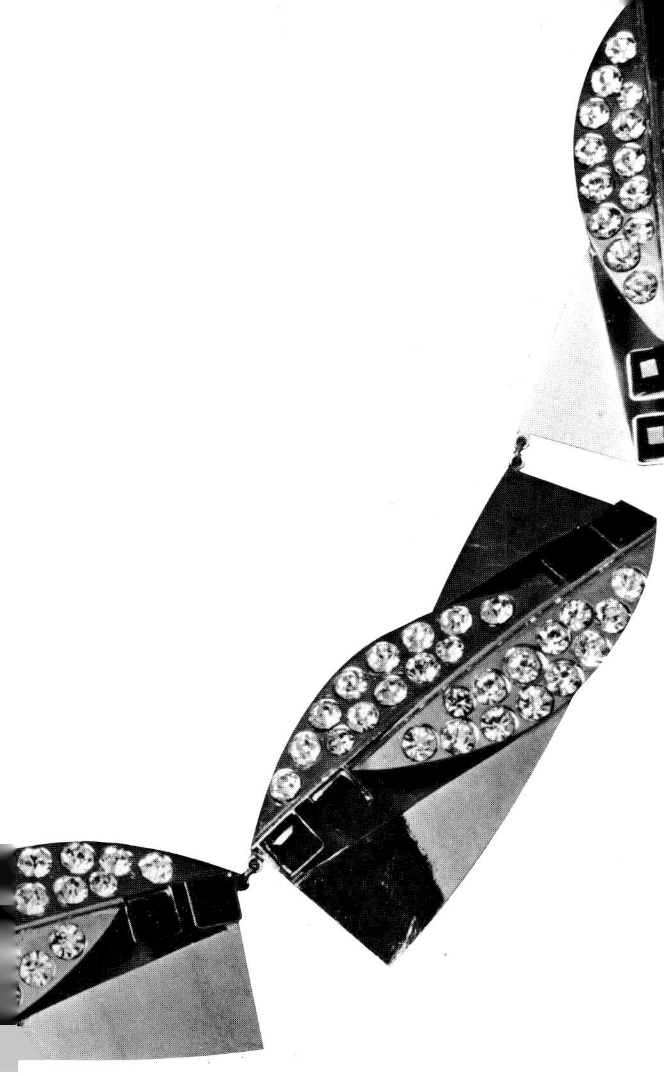

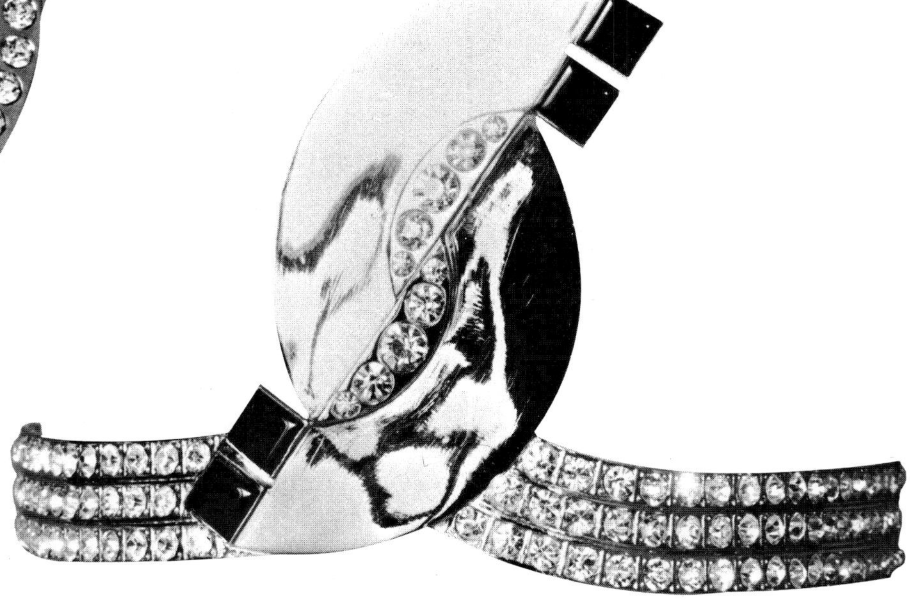

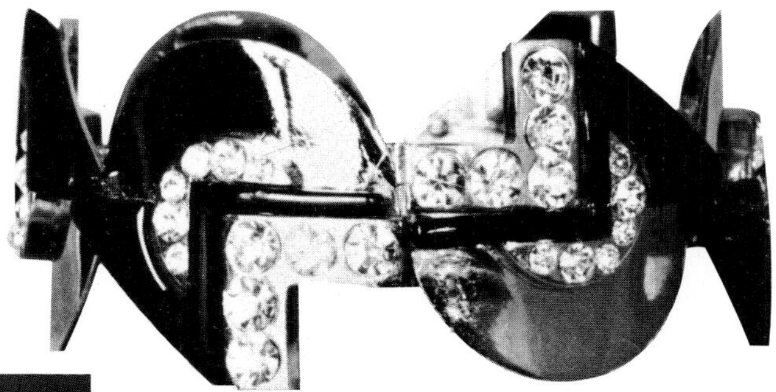

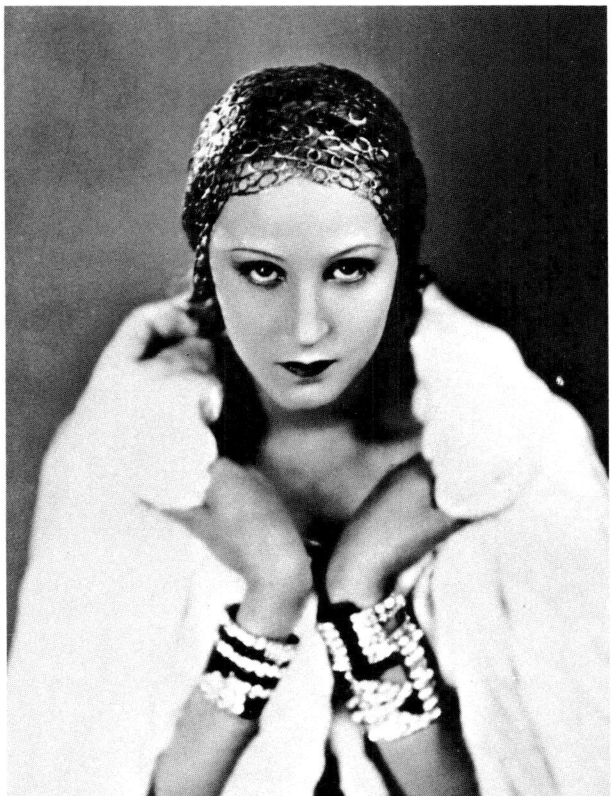

Jewelry by Raymond Templier, made for Brigitte Helm, the heroine of Marcel l'Herbier's film L'Argent, *1928. Courtesy of L. and B. Heuer.*

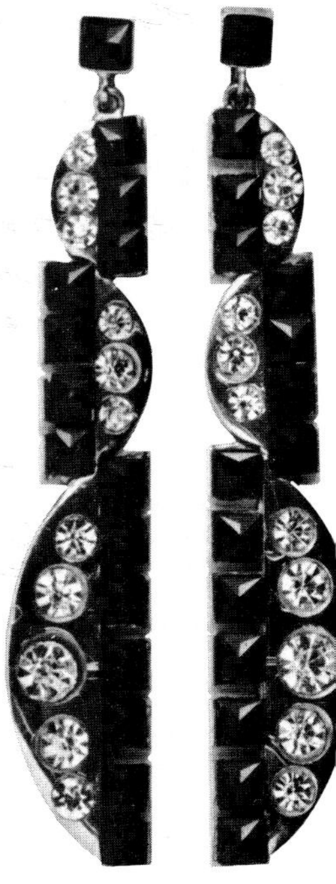

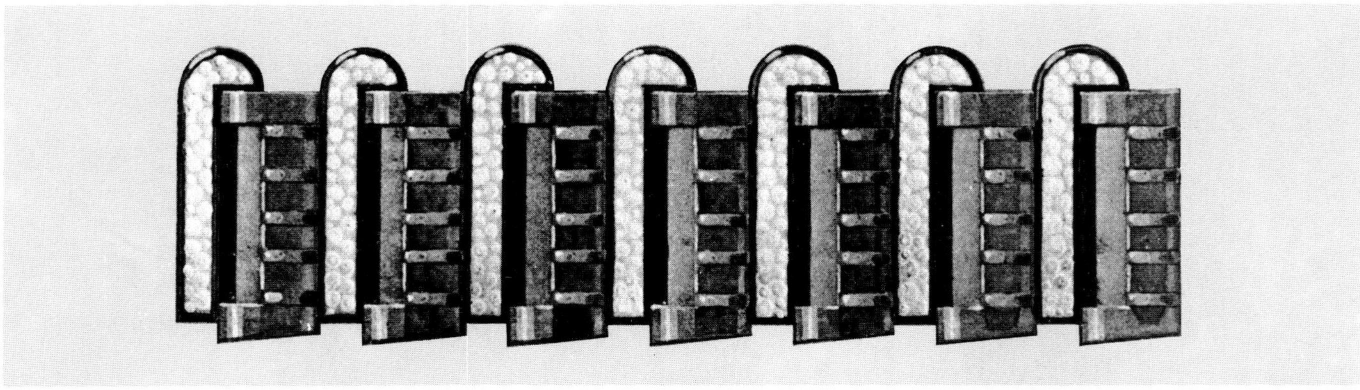

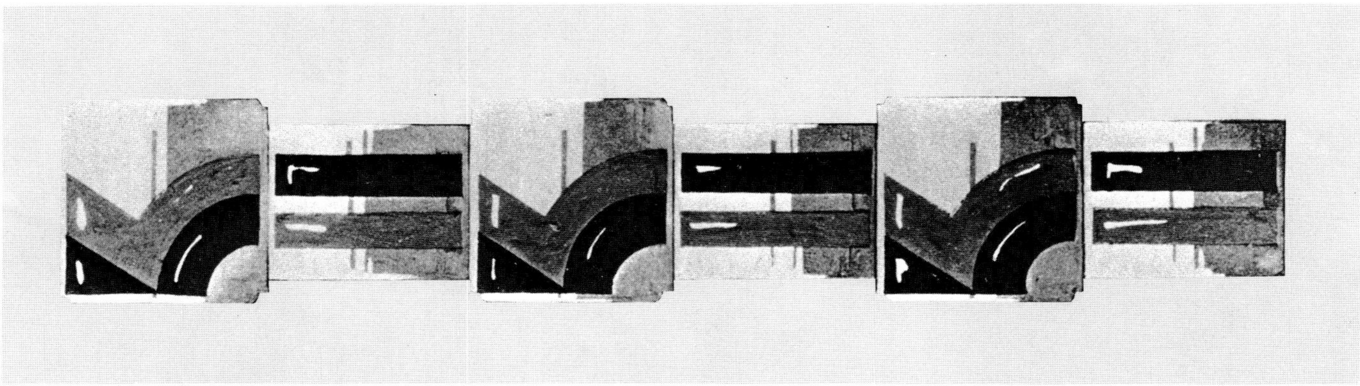

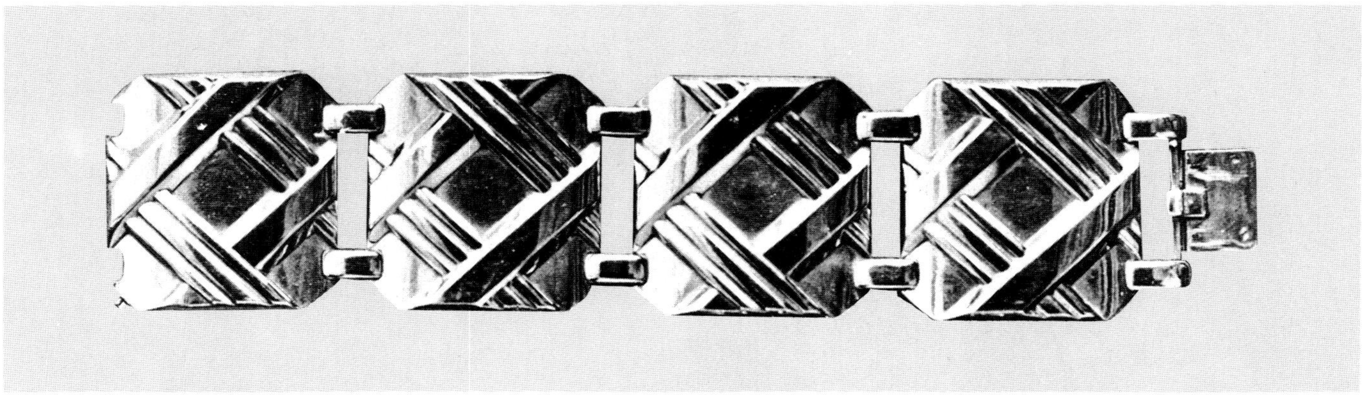

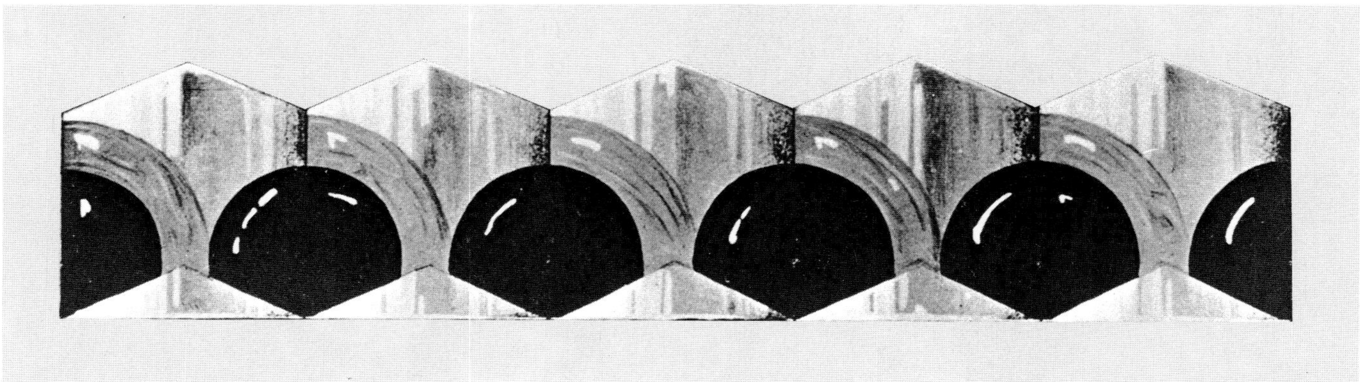

Henri Martin: study for a bracelet reproduced in Jean Fouquet's 'Bijoux et Orfèvrerie', 1931.

Paul Brandt: study for a bracelet reproduced in Jean Fouquet's 'Bijoux et Orfèvrerie', 1931.

Georges Fouquet: bracelet executed from a design by André Léveillé, reproduced in Jean Fouquet's 'Bijoux et Orfèvrerie', 1931.

Paul Brandt: study for a bracelet reproduced in Jean Fouquet's 'Bijoux et Orfèvrerie', 1931.

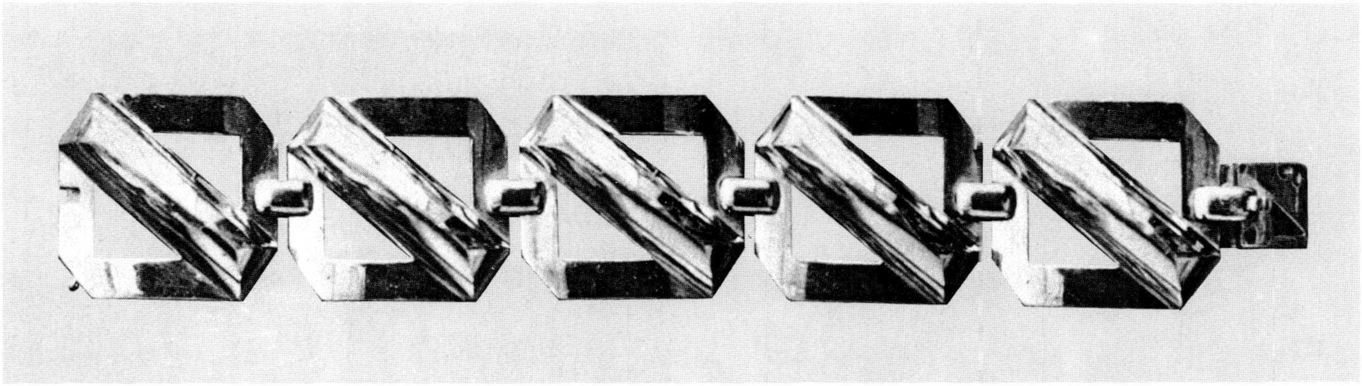

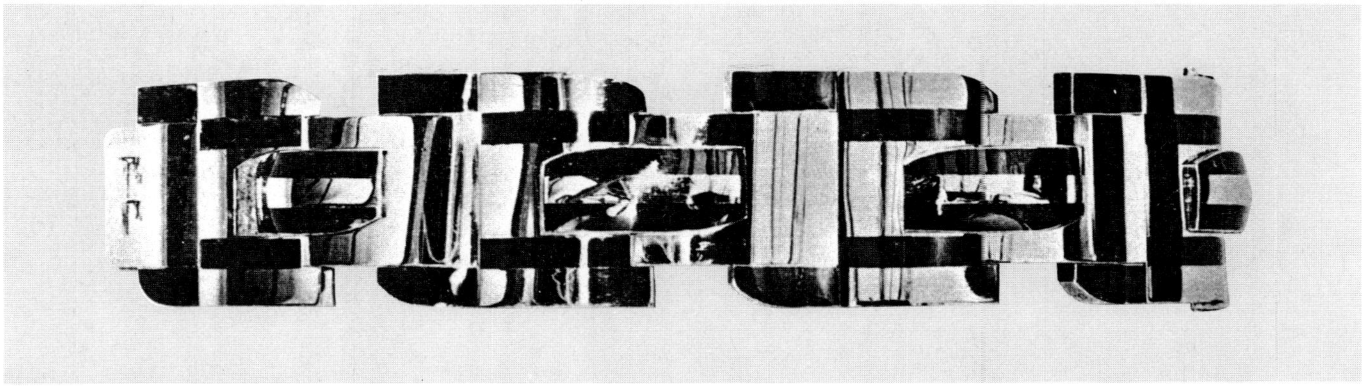

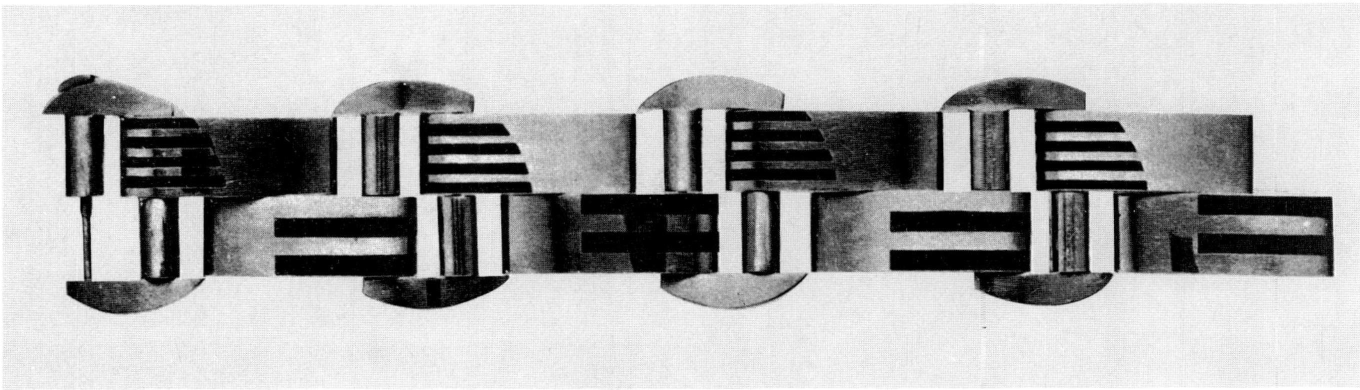

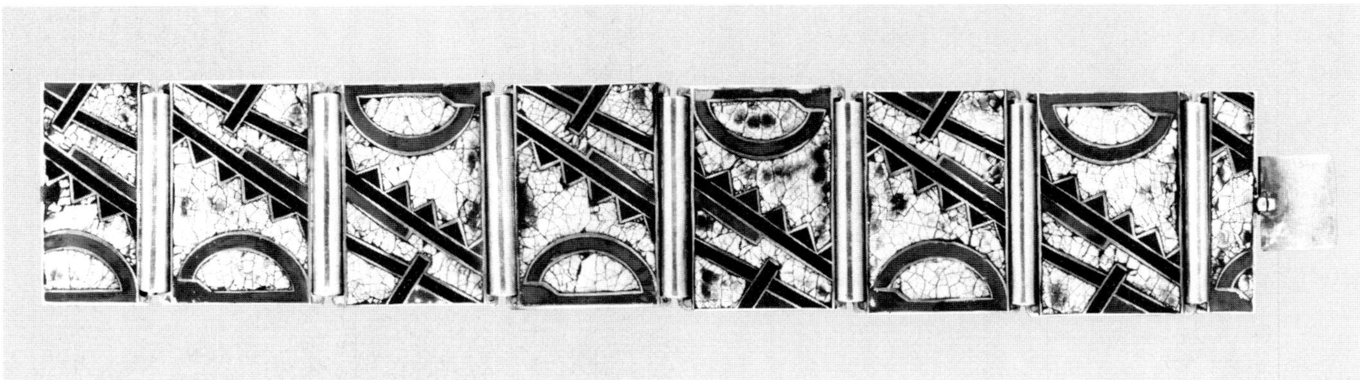

Georges Fouquet: bracelet executed from a design by André Léveillé, reproduced in Jean Fouquet's 'Bijoux et Orfèvrerie', 1931.

Gérard Sandoz: bracelet reproduced in Jean Fouquet's 'Bijoux et Orfèvrerie', 1931.

Gérard Sandoz: bracelet reproduced in Jean Fouquet's 'Bijoux et Orfèvrerie', 1931.

Paul Brandt (attr.): bracelet in silver and eggshell lacquer, composed of rectangular panels with a pattern of bands, chevrons and semicircles in black and green lacquer, c. 1925–30.

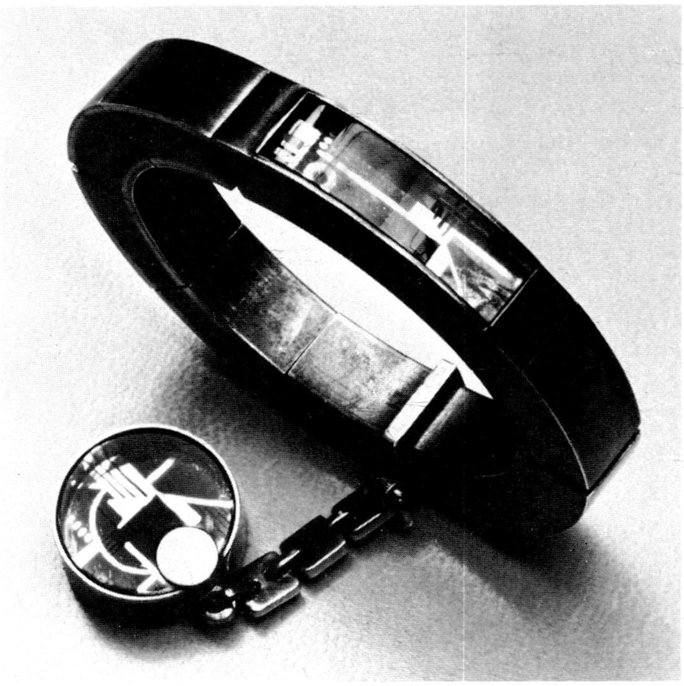

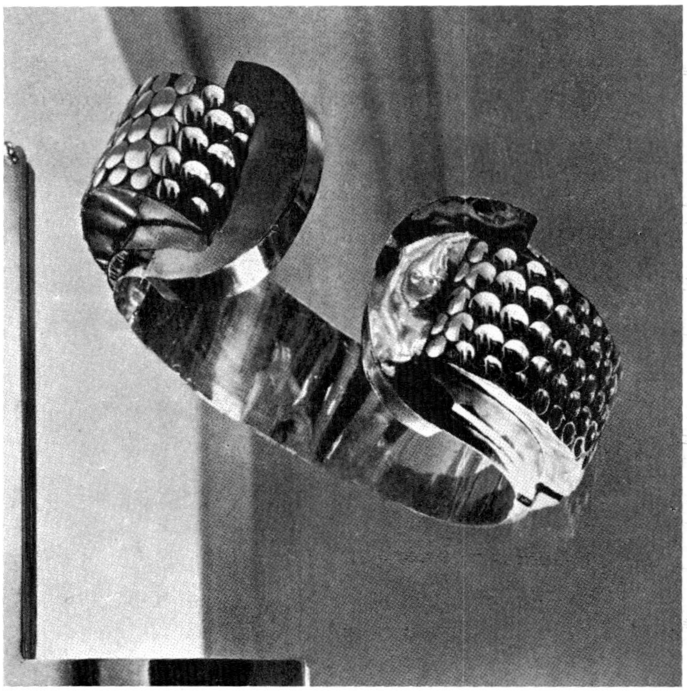

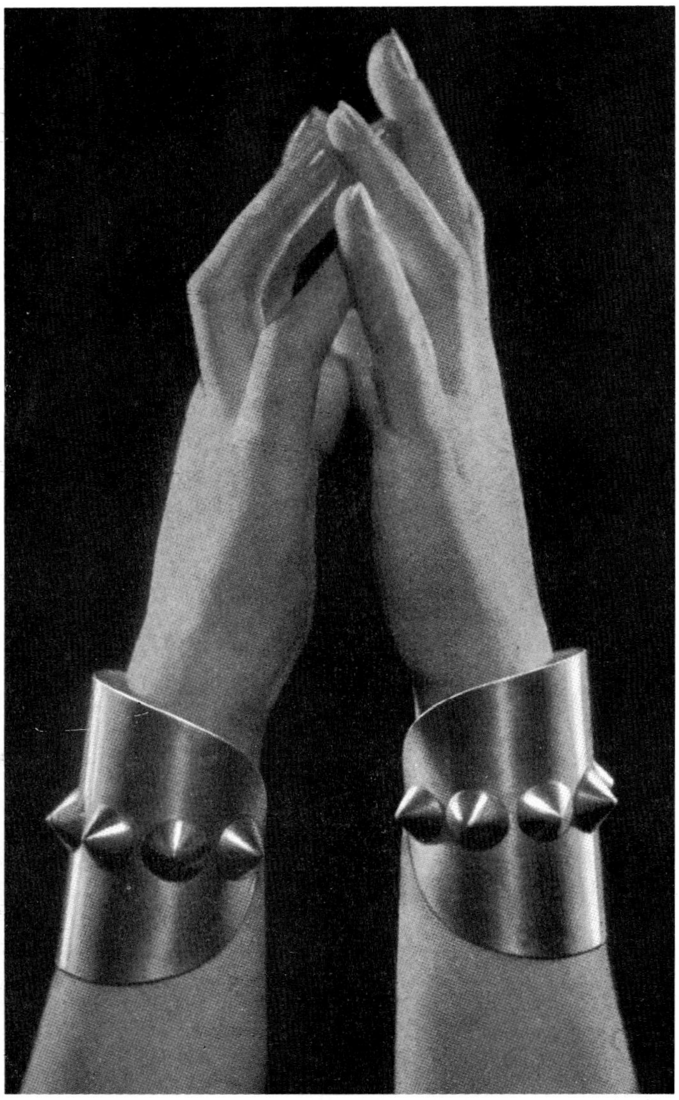

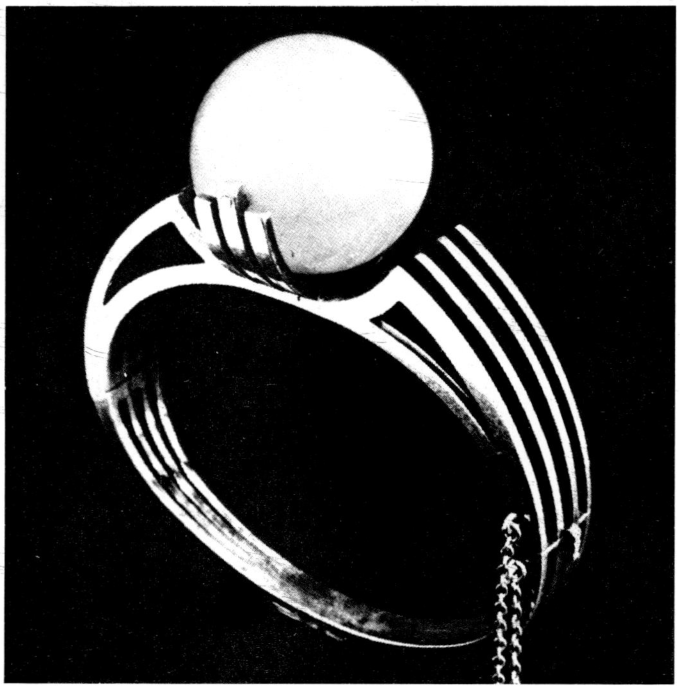

Jean Desprès: bangle with glass engraved by Etienne Cournault. Walker Collection. Photo: L. Sully-Jaulmes.

Raymond Templier and René Herbst: jeweler's shop sign.

René Robert: silver bangles reproduced in Art et Décoration, *September 1935.*

A. Jillander: bangle in silver with jade ball, Denmark. Jesse & Laski Gallery Collection, London.

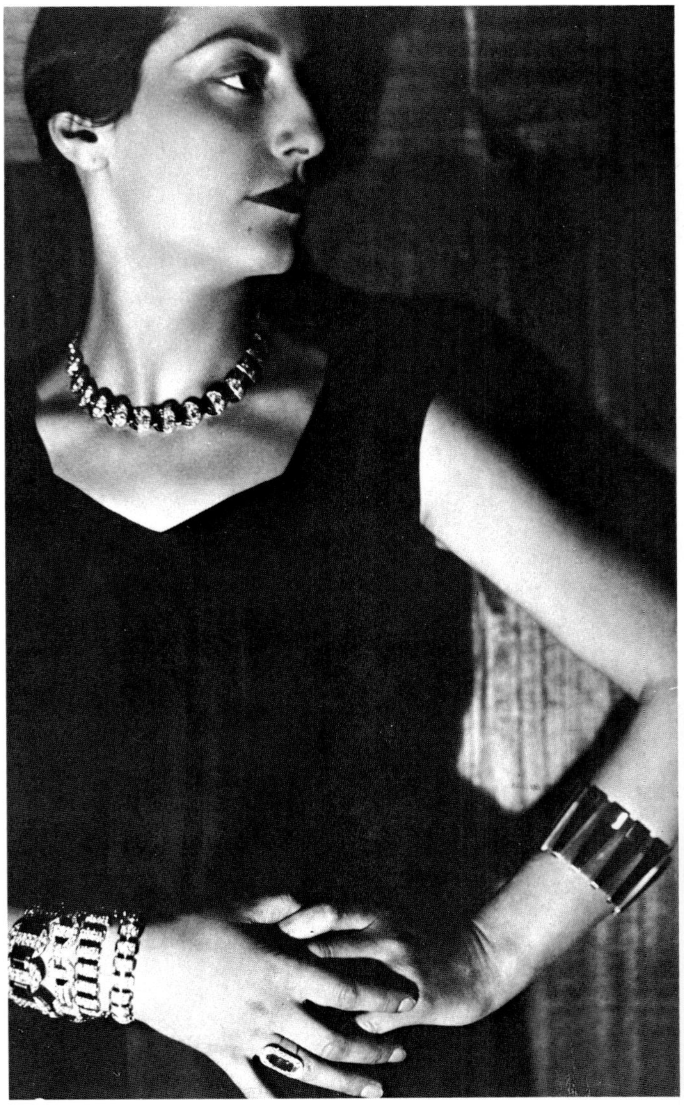

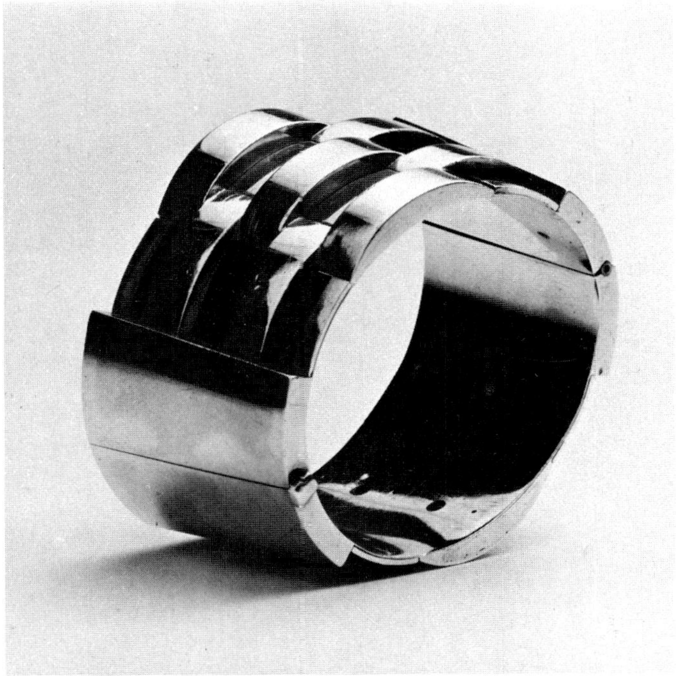

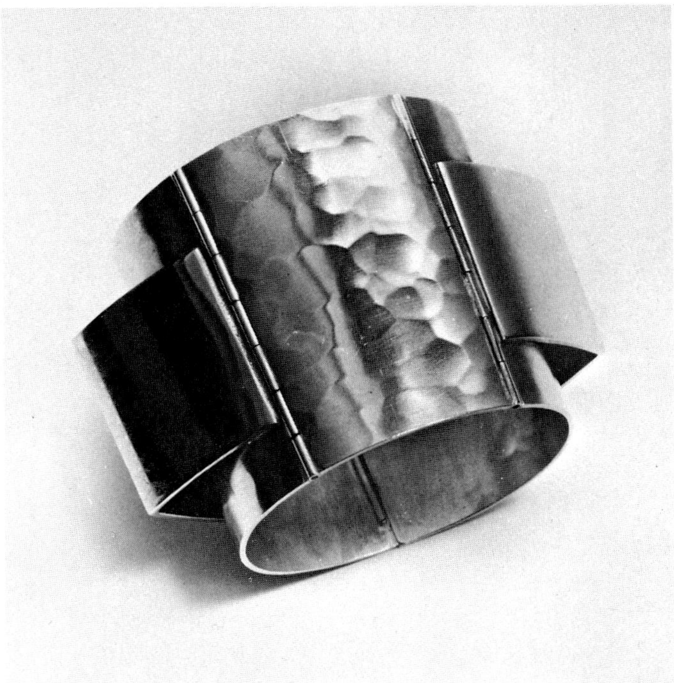

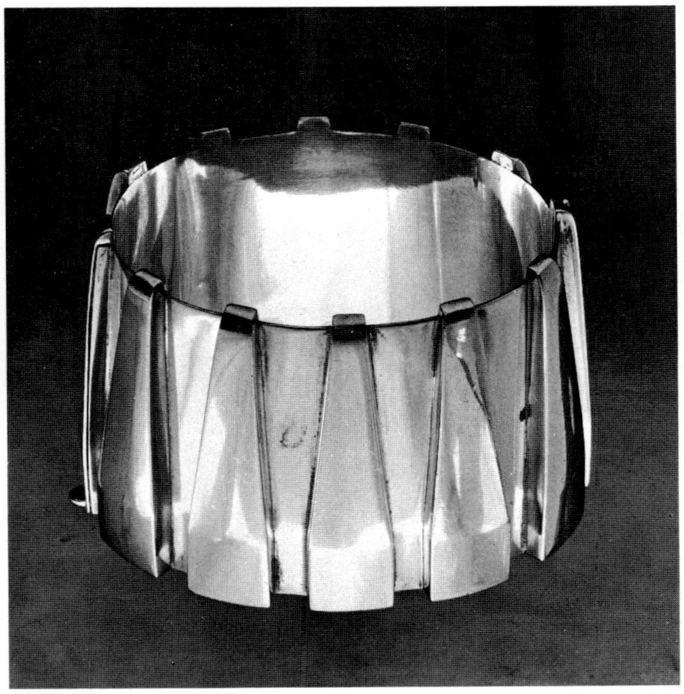

Raymond Templier: bangle in silver and black lacquer. Private Collection. Photo: L. Sully-Jaulmes.

Jean Desprès: silver bangle, signed. Private Collection. Photo: T. Heuer and J.B. Rouault.

Photograph of a young woman wearing Raymond Templier's jewelry. Photo: Germaine Krull.

Raymond Templier: silver bangle, 1930. Private Collection. Photo: T. Heuer and J.B. Rouault.

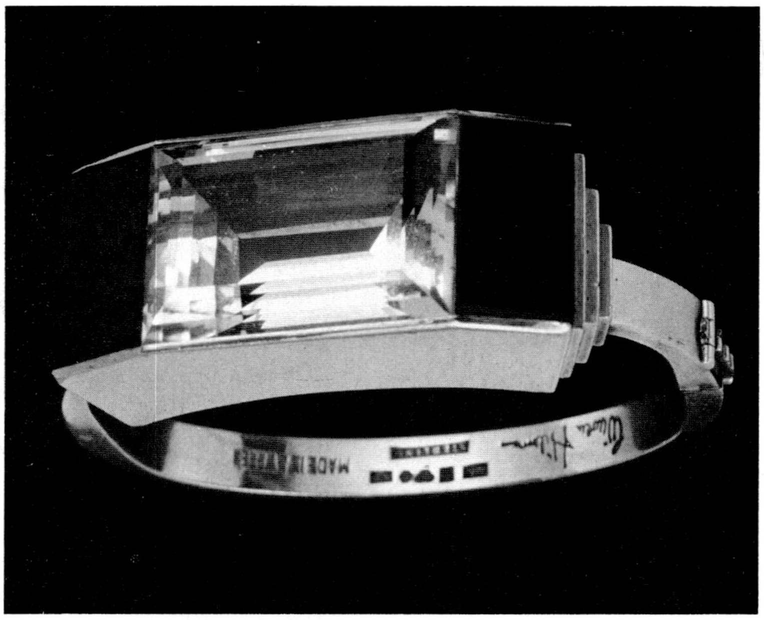

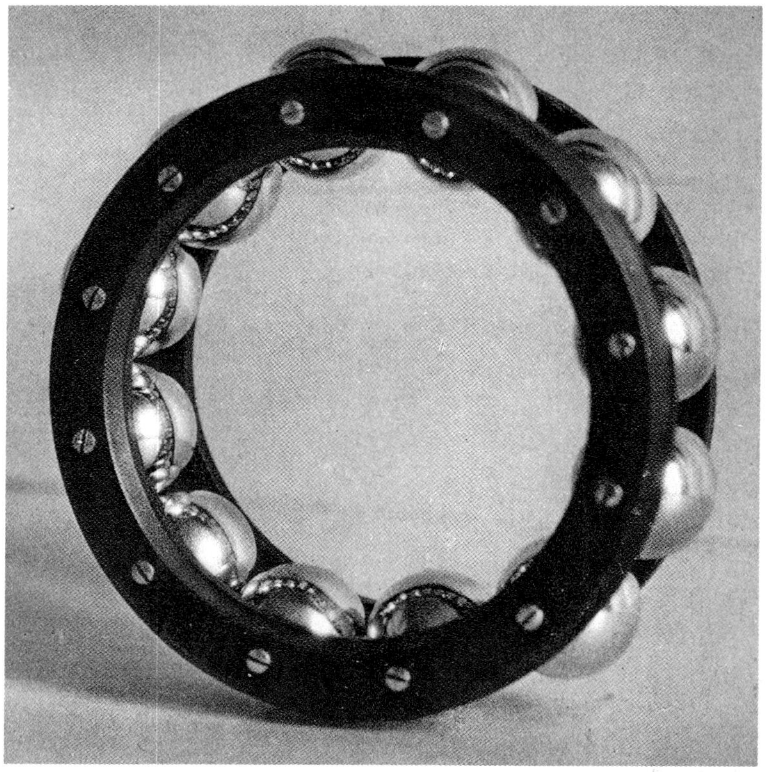

Wiwen Nilsson: silver and crystal bangle, 1936, Sweden. Jesse & Laski Gallery Collection, London.

Jean Fouquet: 'ball-bearing' bangle in ebonite and chromed metal, 1931, reproduced in Art et Décoration, *April 1932.*

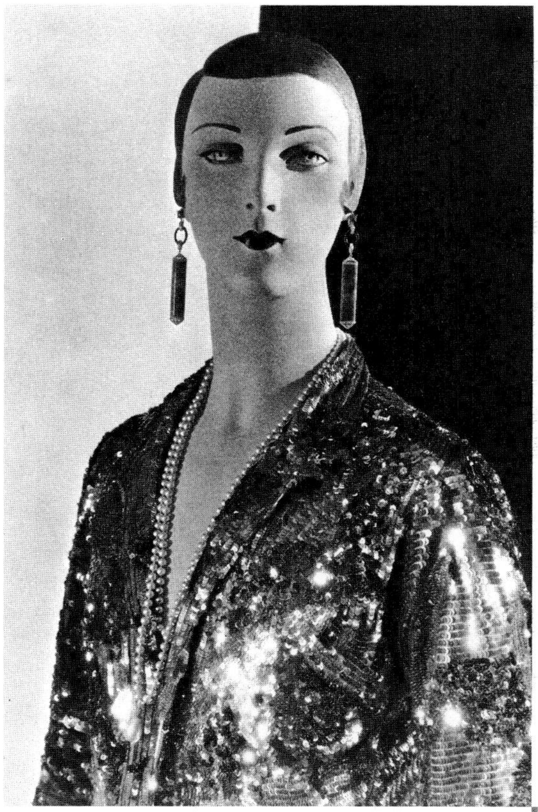

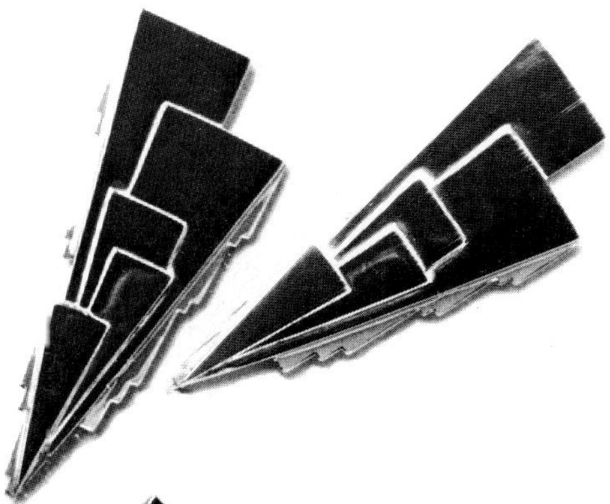

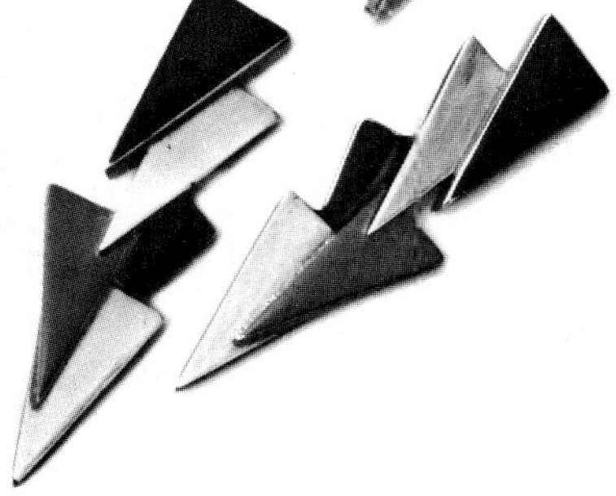

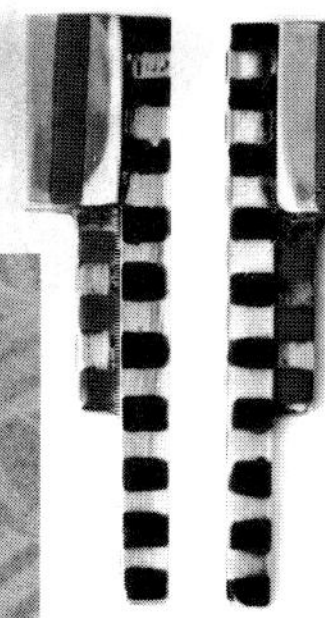

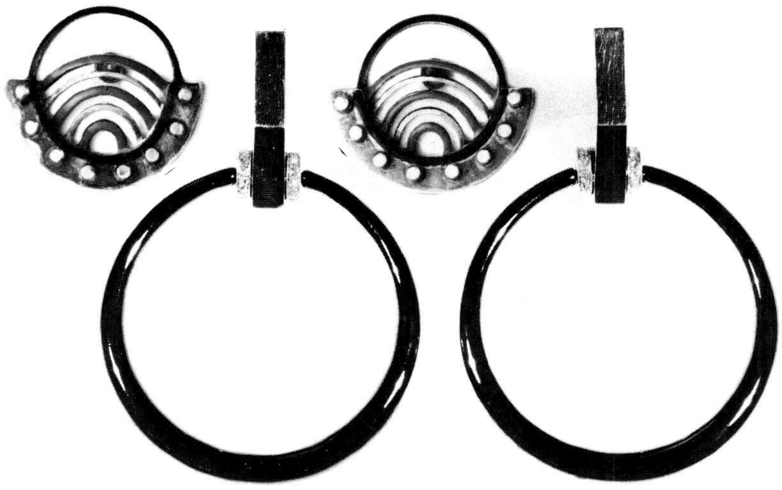

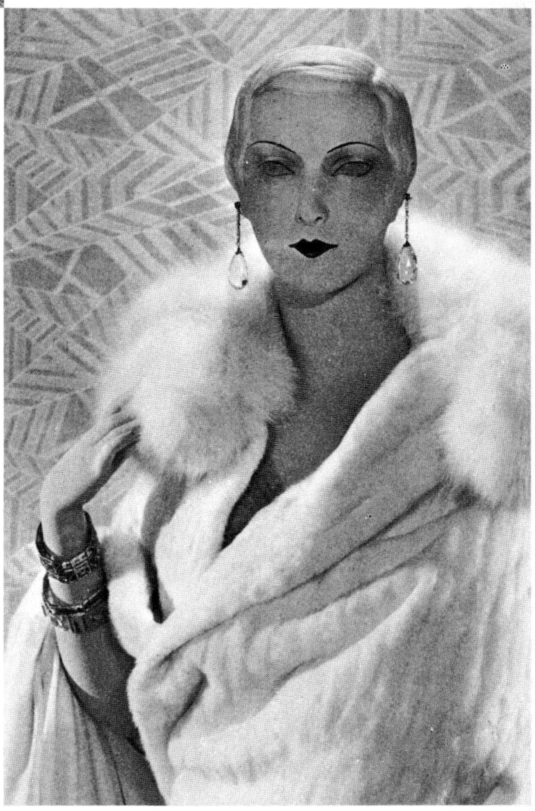

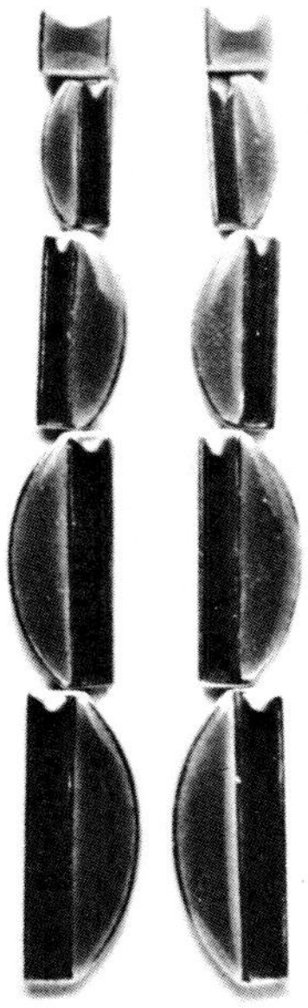

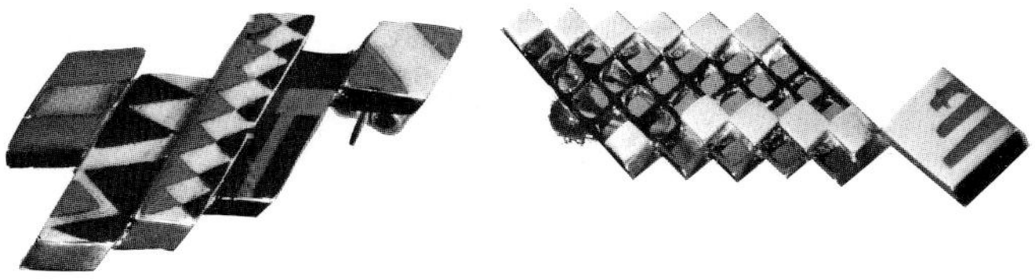

Clockwise from top left: Siegel mannequin wearing jewelry by Jean Fouquet, smoking jacket by Cheruit. Photo: Hoyningen-Huene.

Raymond Templier: ear clips, 1925. Courtesy of L. and B. Heuer.

Jean Dunand: ear clips in silver and red and black lacquer. c. 1925. Sotheby's, Monte Carlo.

Jean Dunand: ear clips in silver and red and black lacquer, c. 1925. Sotheby's, Monte Carlo.

Siegel mannequin wearing jewelry by Jean Fouquet, fur by Jean Patou. Photo: Hoyningen-Huene.

Jean Dunand: ear clips in silver and red and black lacquer, c. 1925. Sotheby's, Monte Carlo.

Raymond Templier: pendant earrings, c. 1929.

Anonymous: pendant earrings in white gold and black patinated steel, set at the sides with two rows of false brilliants, c. 1930. Sotheby's, Monte Carlo.

Jean Dunand: ear clips in silver and red and black lacquer, c. 1925. Sotheby's, Monte Carlo.

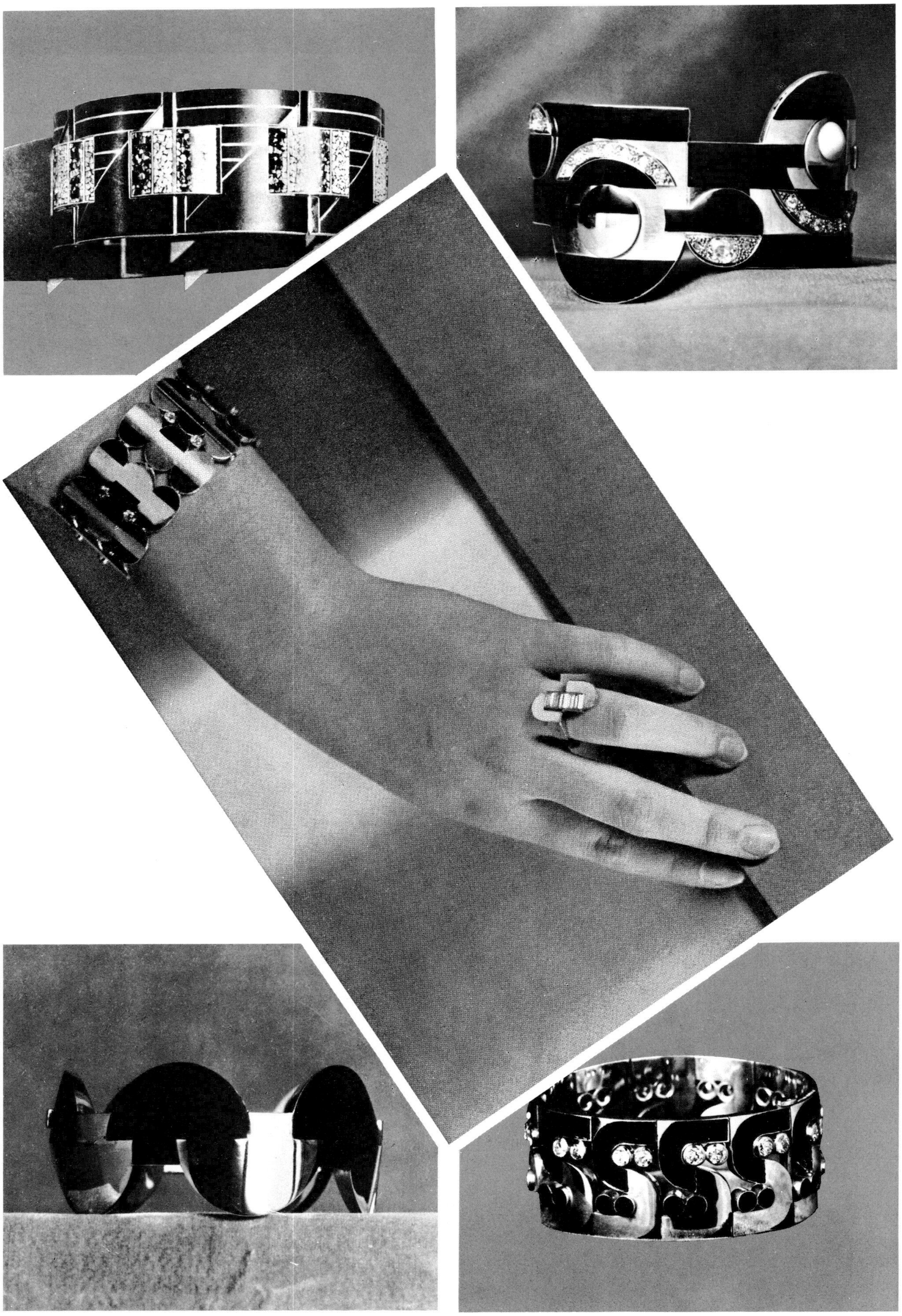

Top left: Gérard Sandoz: bangle reproduced in Jean Fouquet's 'Bijoux et Orfèvrerie', 1931.

Centre: Raymond Templier: platinum and diamond ring, bangle in silver, platinum, black lacquer and diamonds. Reproduced in Art et Décoration, *February 1930.*

Raymond Templier: three bangles, c. *1928.*

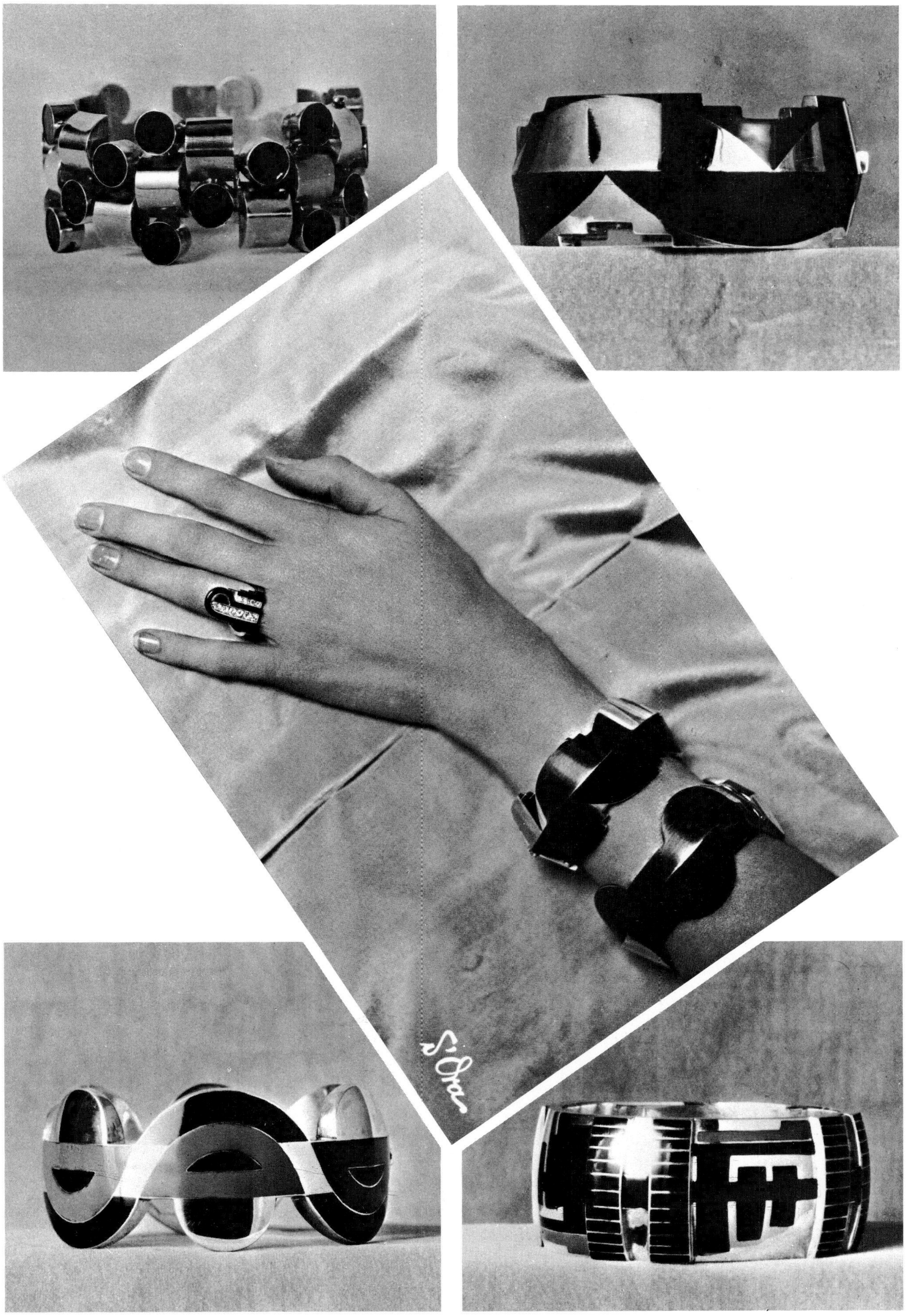

Raymond Templier: four bangles, c. 1928.
Centre: Raymond Templier: ring and bangles, 1927.

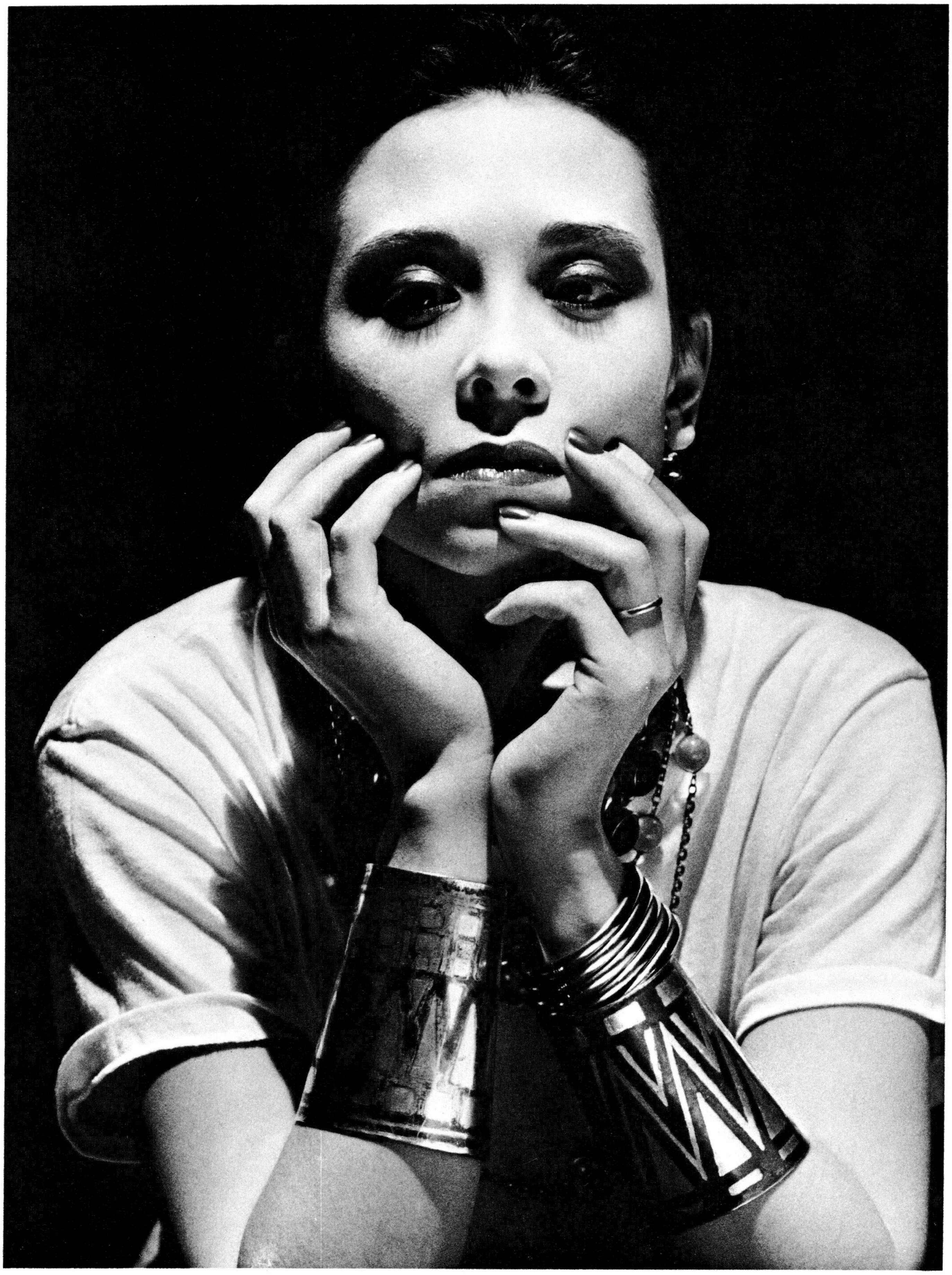

Tina Chow wearing bangles by Jean Dunand. Photo: Alice Springs.

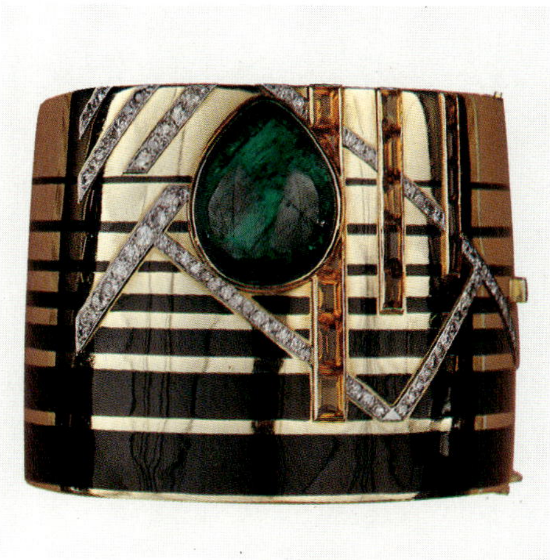

Georges Fouquet: bangle from a design by André Léveillé in gold, black enamel, baguettes of calibré topaz and brilliant-cut diamonds, with an emerald cabochon, 1925, signed. Private Collection. Photo: L. Sully-Jaulmes.

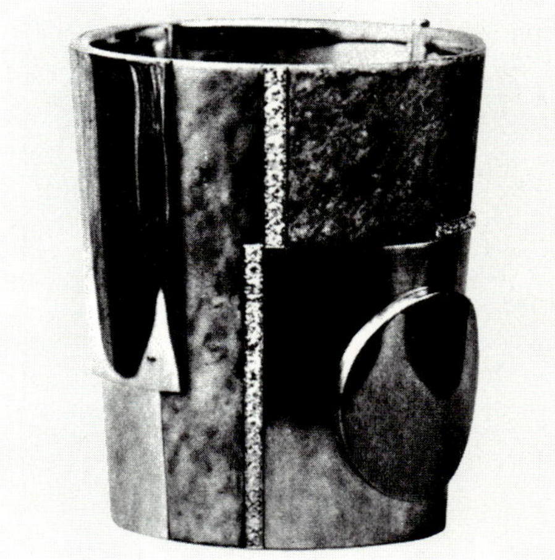

Jean Fouquet: bangle in gold, Osmior, enamel and diamonds, 1927.

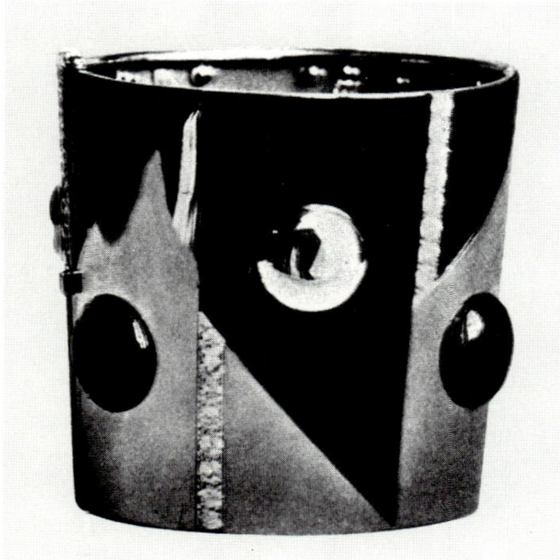

Jean Fouquet: bangle in polished platinum, black enamel, onyx and platinum cabochons and brilliant-cut diamonds, c. 1927.

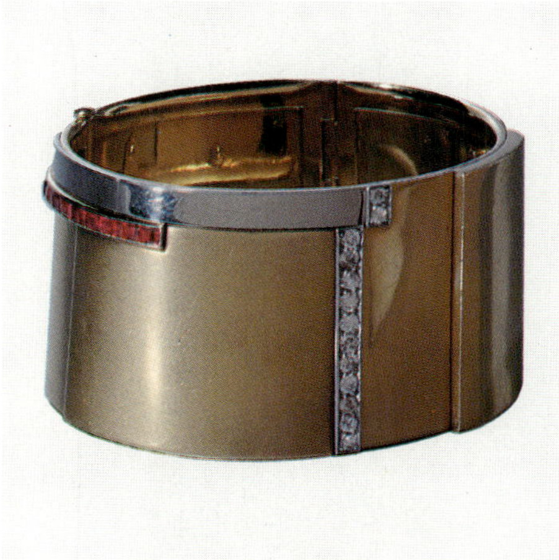

Jean Fouquet: bangle in three colours of gold, brilliants and rubies, c. 1925. M. Souillac Collection. Photo: J.B. Rouault.

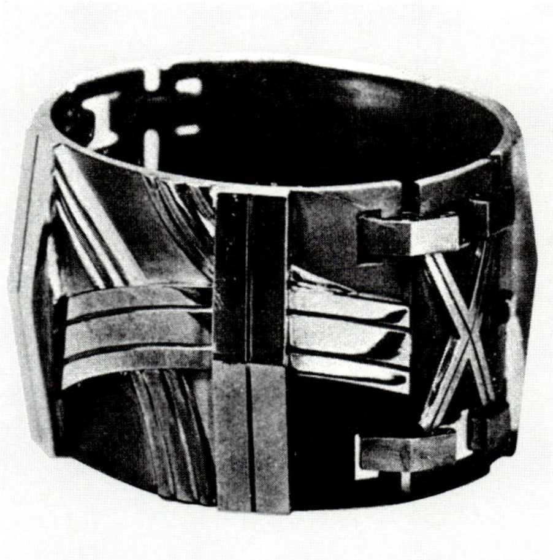

Jean Fouquet: bangle composed of four hinged plaques, gold or silver, 1925.

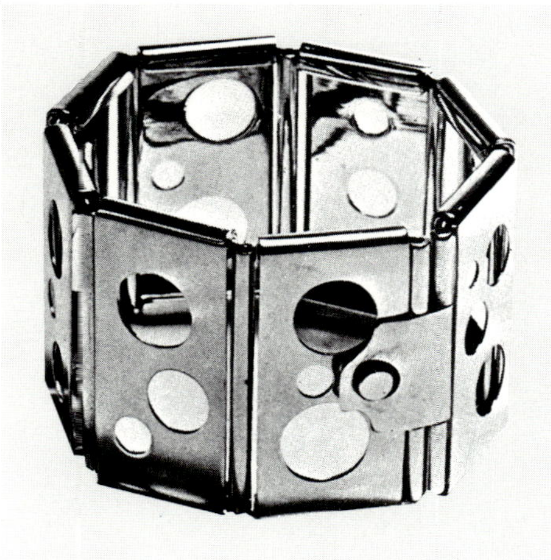

Naum Slutzky: silver bangle, c. 1930. Museum für Kunst und Gewerbe, Hamburg.

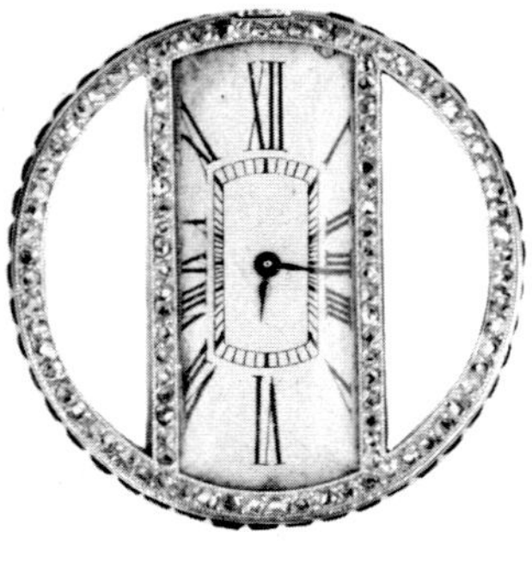

Cartier: pocket watch in rock crystal and diamonds with calibré *sapphires round the edge. M. Souillac Collection. Photo: J.B. Rouault.*

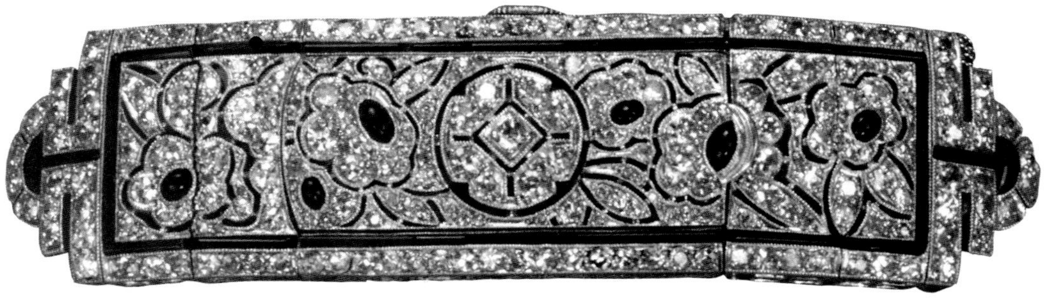

Anonymous: watch-bracelet in diamonds and onyx, dial hidden. Sotheby's.

Anonymous: brooch-watch in diamonds, emeralds and black onyx mounted on platinum. Christie's, New York.

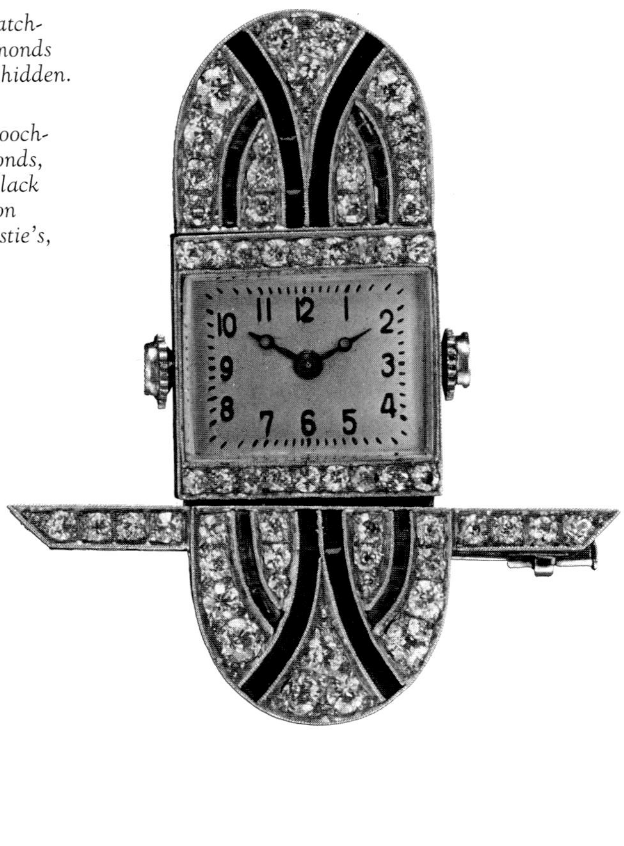

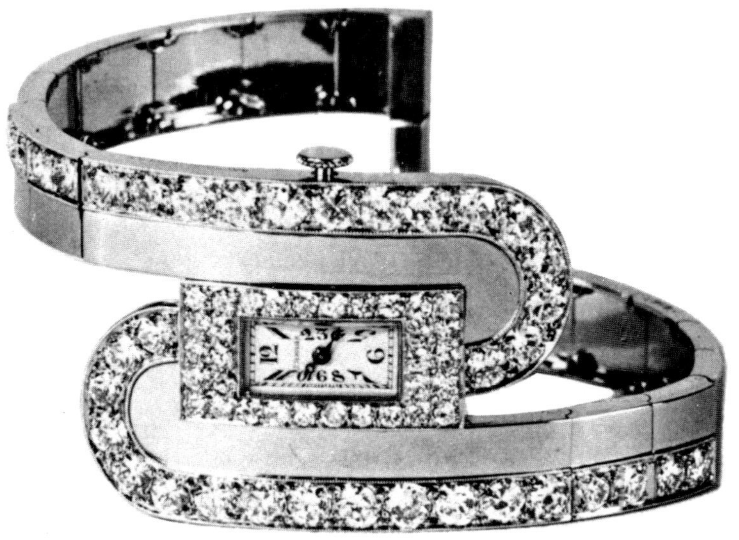

Raymond Templier: watch-bracelet in platinum and brilliants, 1930. Courtesy of L. and B. Heuer.

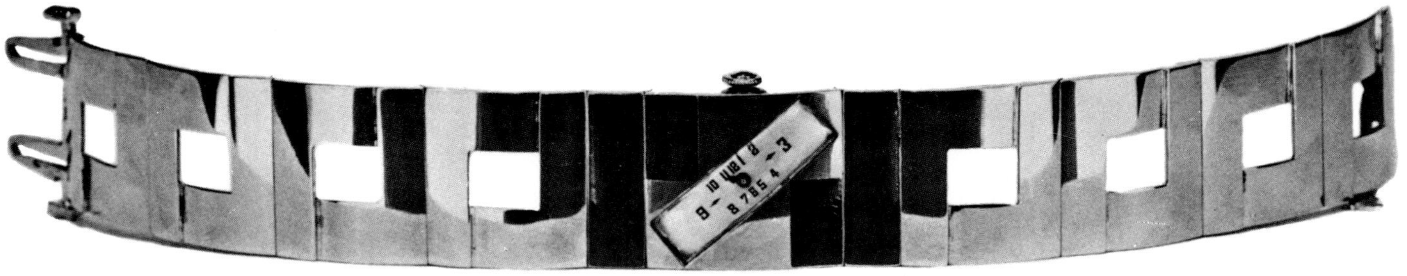

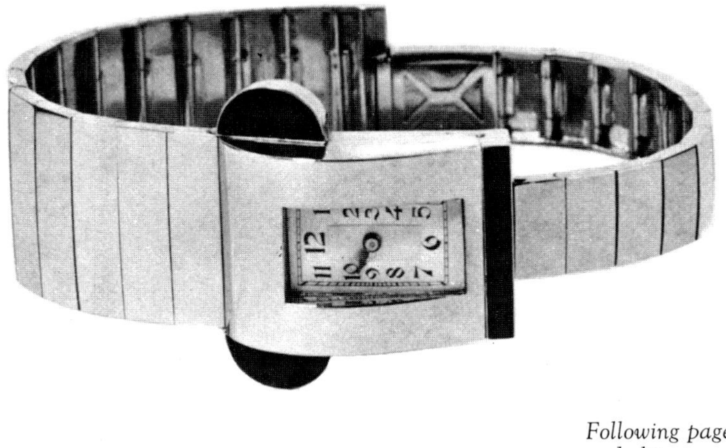

Raymond Templier: two watch-bracelets, c. 1929. Courtesy of L. and B. Heuer.

Following pages: Suzanne Belperron: bangle and clips in rock crystal and gold, c. 1935. Primavera Gallery, New York.

Anonymous: silver bangle, France, c. 1925. Primavera Gallery, New York.

Raymond Templier: bangle in silver and black enamel, c. 1925, signed. Primavera Gallery, New York.

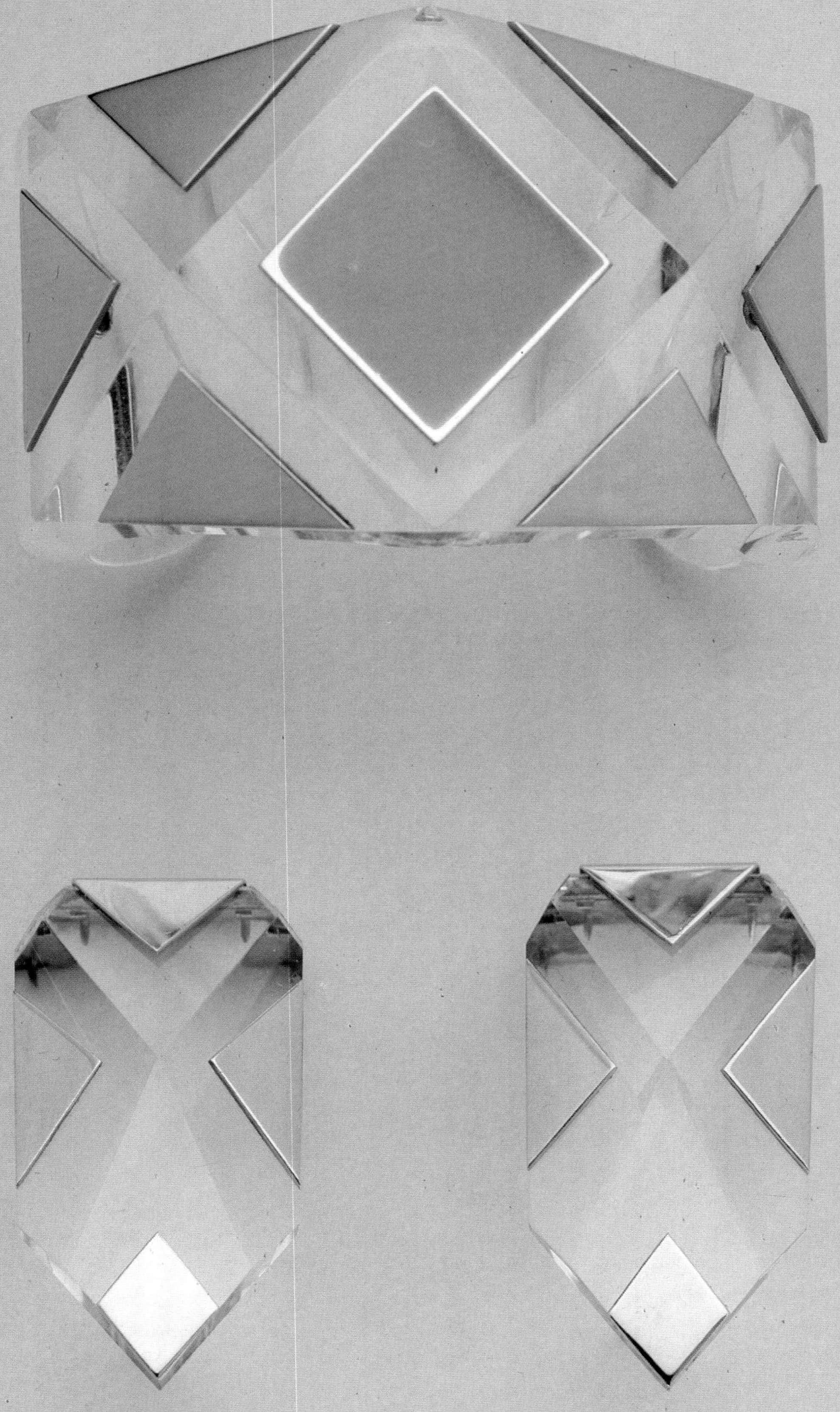

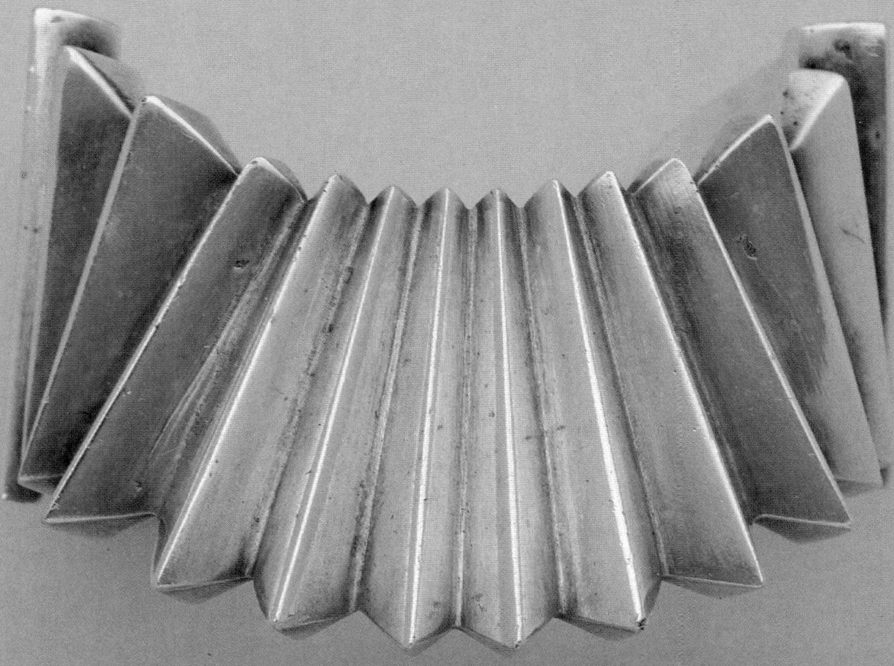

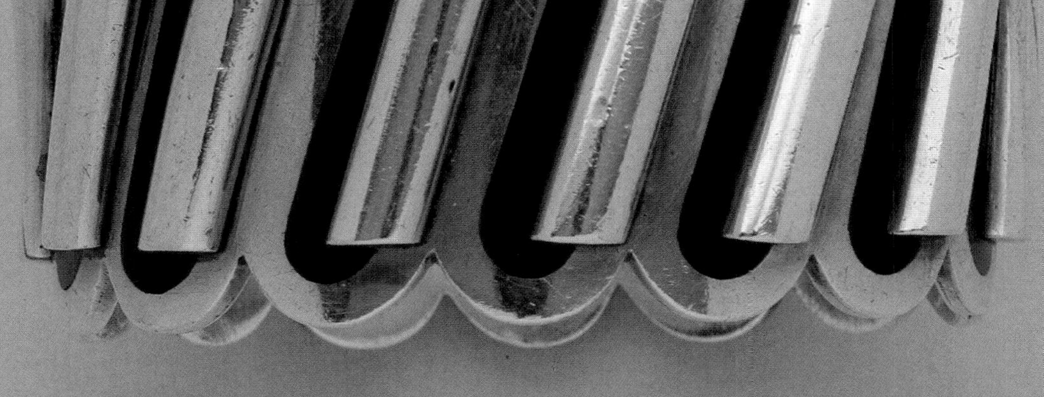

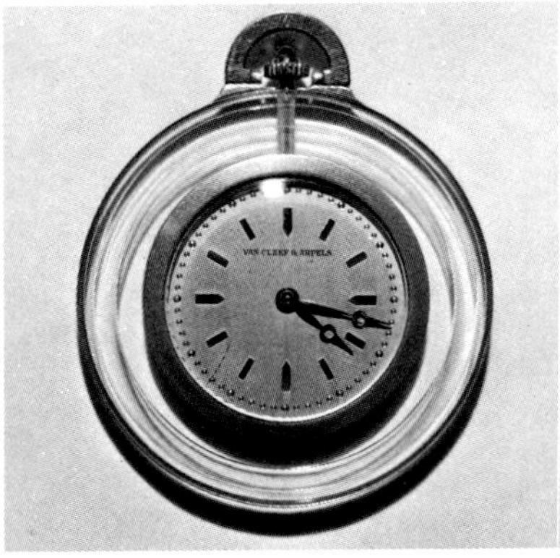

Van Cleef & Arpels: pocket watch in rock crystal, diamonds and platinum; winder with sapphire cabochon. Van Cleef & Arpels Archives.

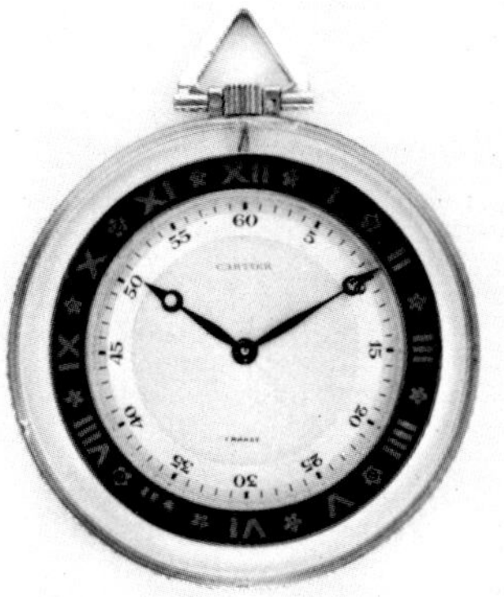

Cartier: pocket watch in rock crystal, diamonds, black enamel, the movement visible at the back of the watch, c. 1926, signed. Christie's.

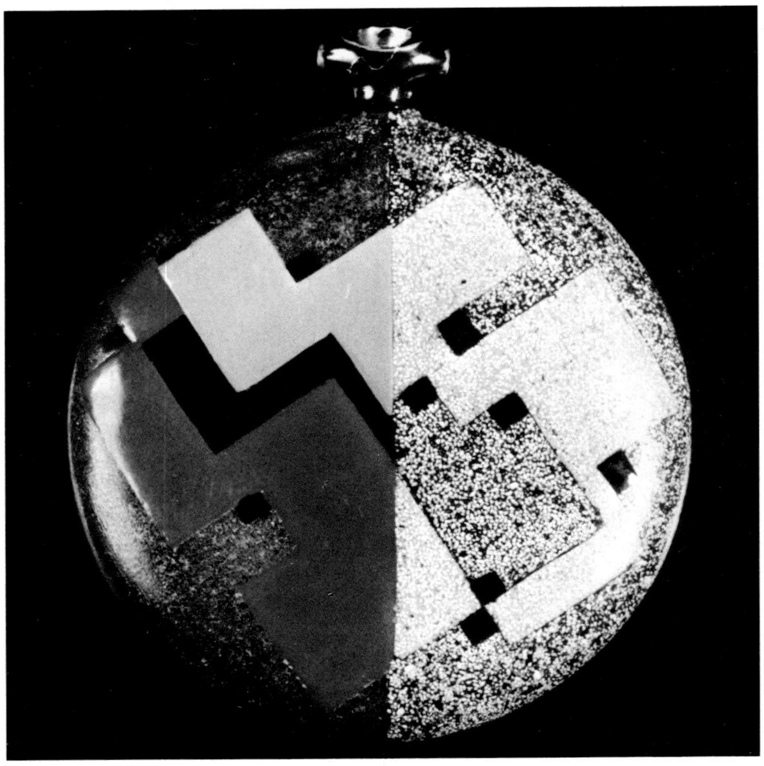

Jean Dunand: pocket watch in polychrome lacquer, eggshell and iron filings. Photo: L. Sully-Jaulmes.

Below: Lacloche: pocket watch (face and back) in platinum and engraved rock crystal, reproduced in Art et Décoration, *July 1921.*

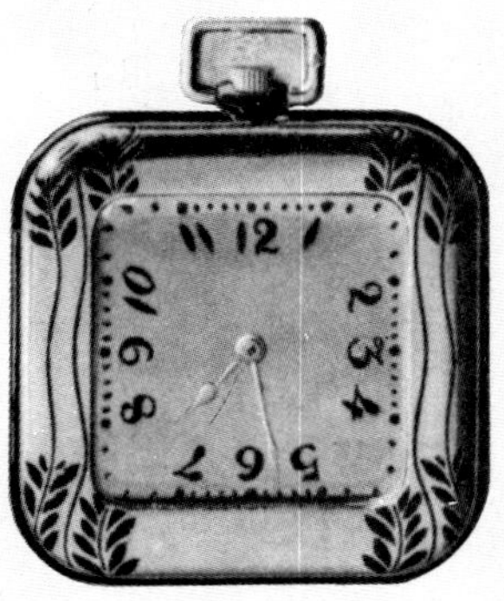

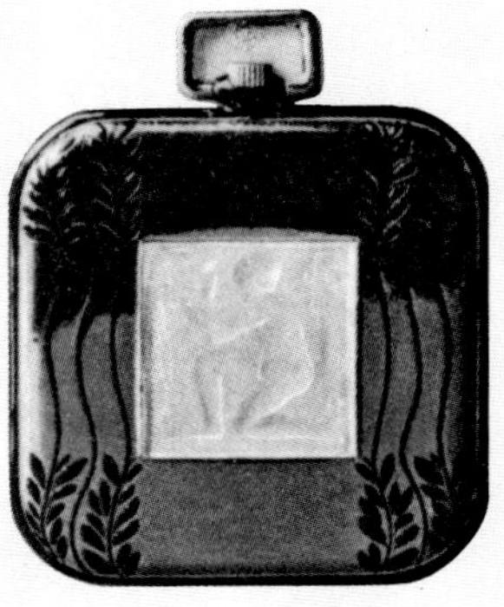

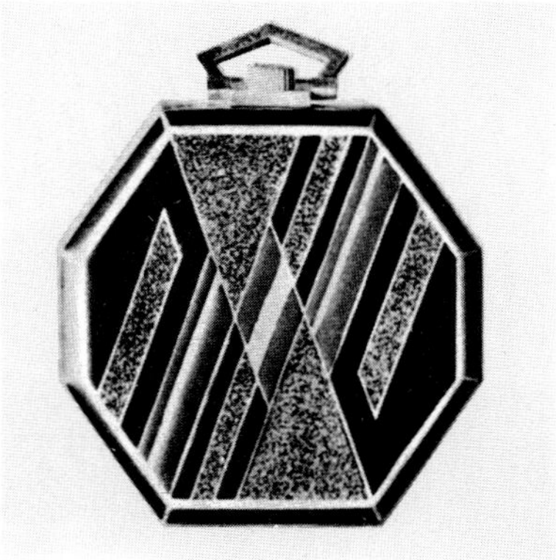

Gérard Sandoz: pocket watch reproduced in Jean Fouquet's 'Bijoux et Orfèvrerie', 1931.

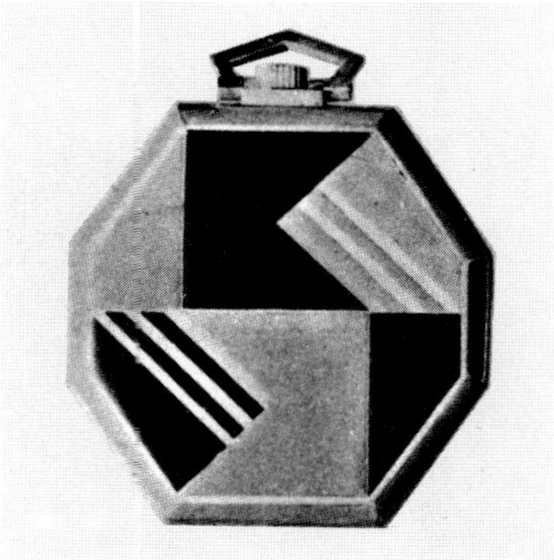

Gérard Sandoz: design for a pocket watch reproduced in Jean Fouquet's 'Bijoux et Orfèvrerie', 1931.

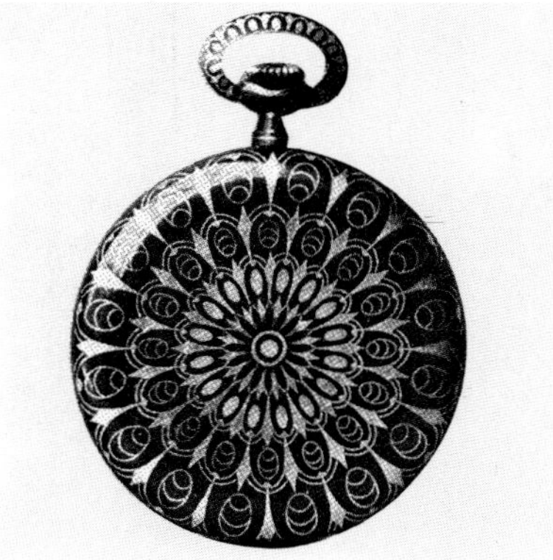

Jean Dunand: pocket watch reproduced in Art et Décoration, July 1921.

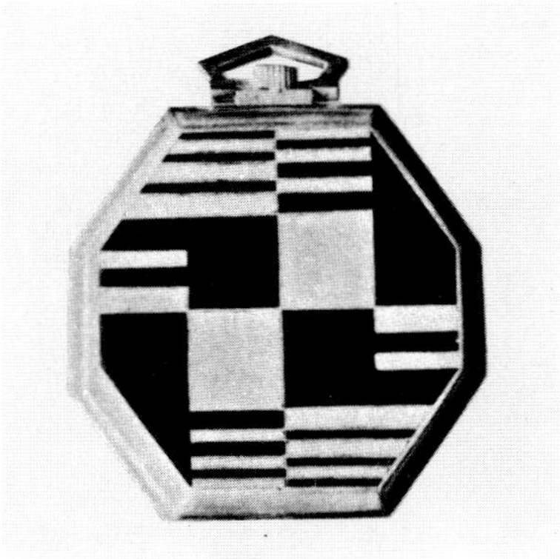

Gérard Sandoz: design for a pocket watch reproduced in Jean Fouquet's 'Bijoux et Orfèvrerie', 1931.

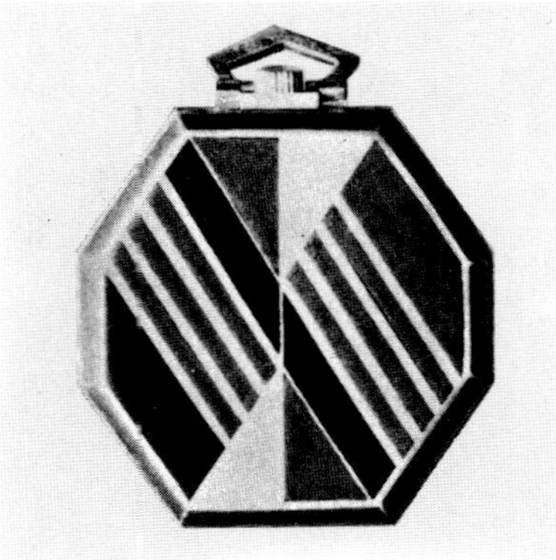

Gérard Sandoz: design for a pocket watch reproduced in Jean Fouquet's 'Bijoux et Orfèvrerie', 1931.

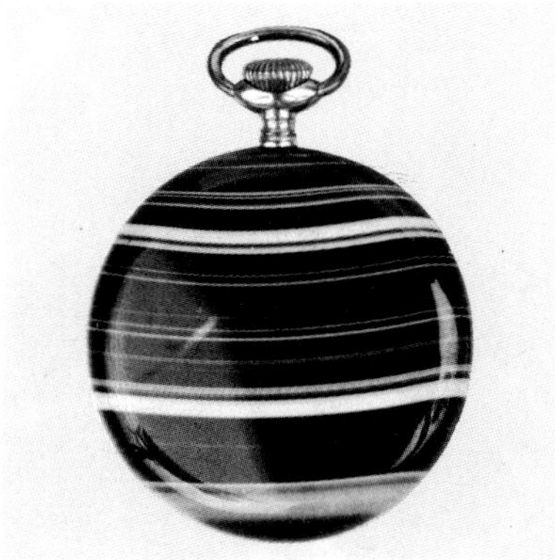

Anonymous: pocket watch in agate and vermeil. M. Souillac Collection.

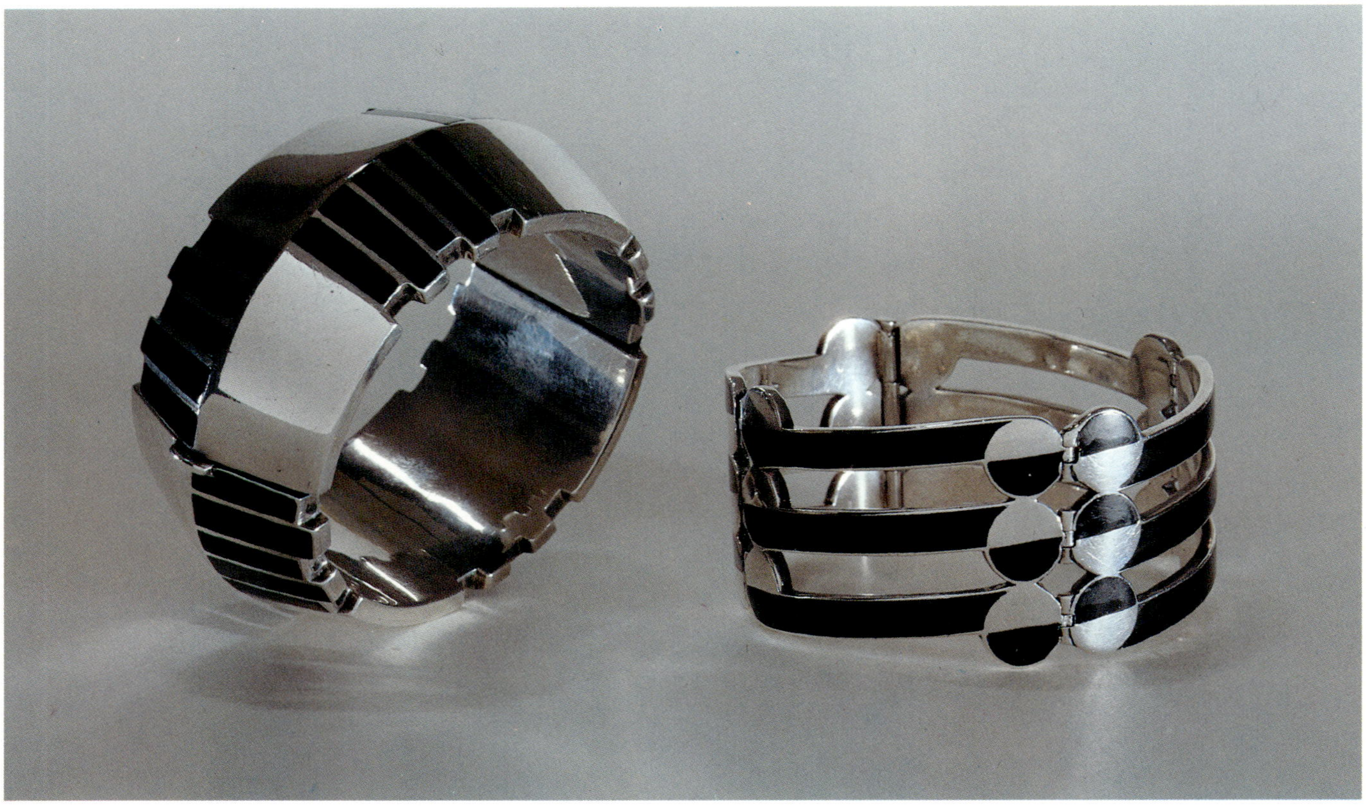

Above: Raymond Templier: bangles in silver and black lacquer (left, 1927). Private Collection. Photo: T. Heuer and J.B. Rouault.

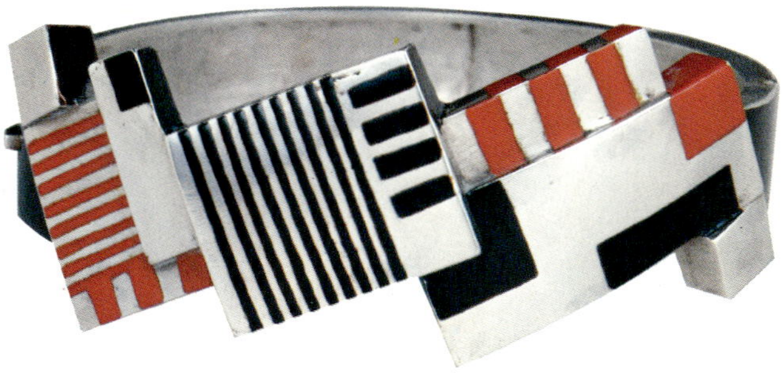

Left: Jean Dunand: bangle with geometric pattern in silver and red, orange and black lacquer, c. 1925. Galerie Vallois. Photo: Vénus Mercenaire.

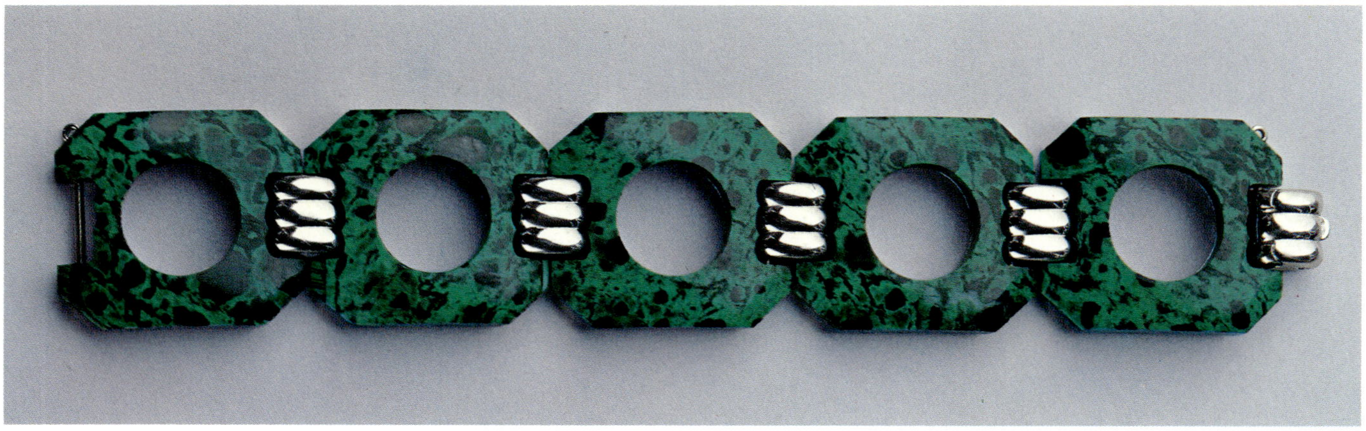

Jean Fouquet: bracelet in white gold and chloromelanite, c. 1927.

Jean Fouquet: bangle in Osmior, jade cabochons and black enamel, reproduced in Art et Décoration, August 1929.

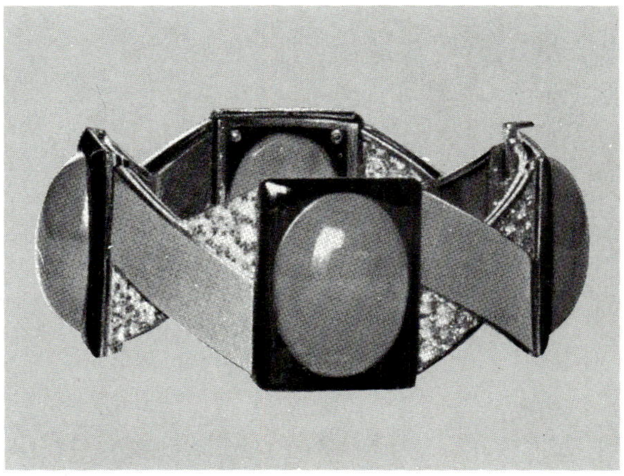

Georg Jensen: bracelet in silver and moonstones, 1927, Denmark. Georg Jensen Archives, Copenhagen.

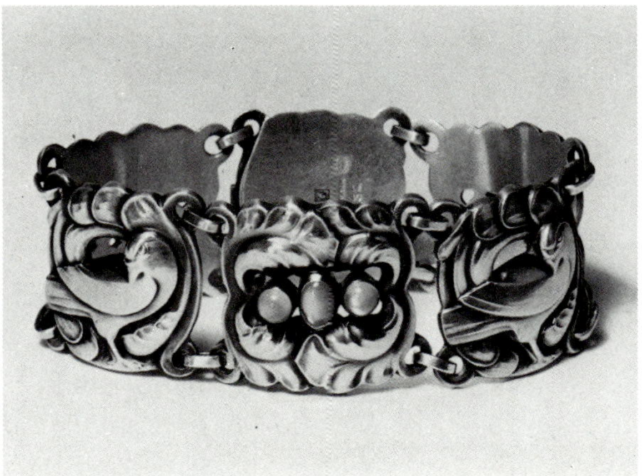

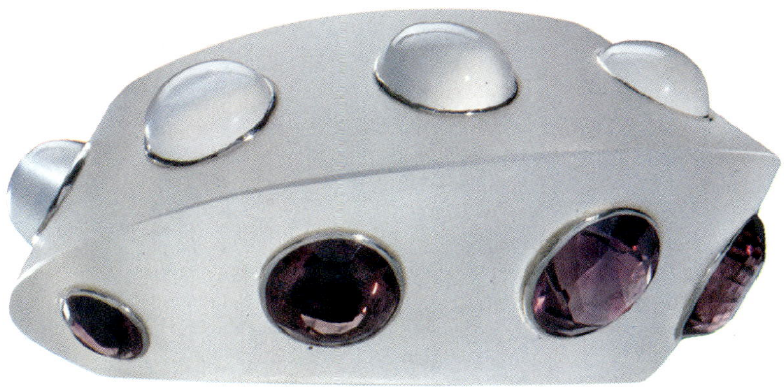

Jean Fouquet: bangle in rock crystal set with amethysts and moonstones in platinum, c. 1930. Private Collection. Photo: T. Heuer.

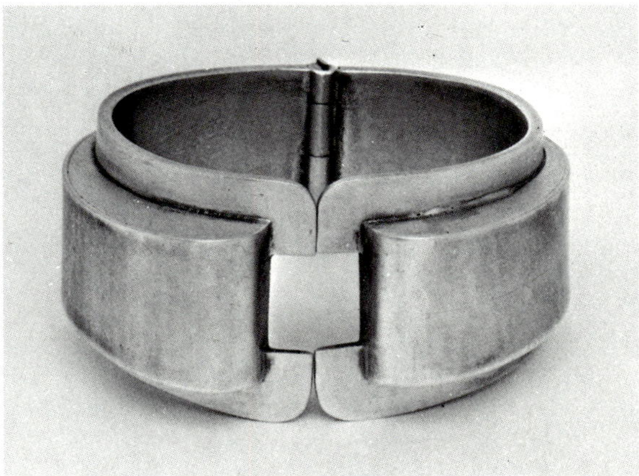

Raymond Templier: silver bangle composed of two hinged sections with band in relief on a flat, cut-away ground, c. 1930, signed. Sotheby's, Monte Carlo.

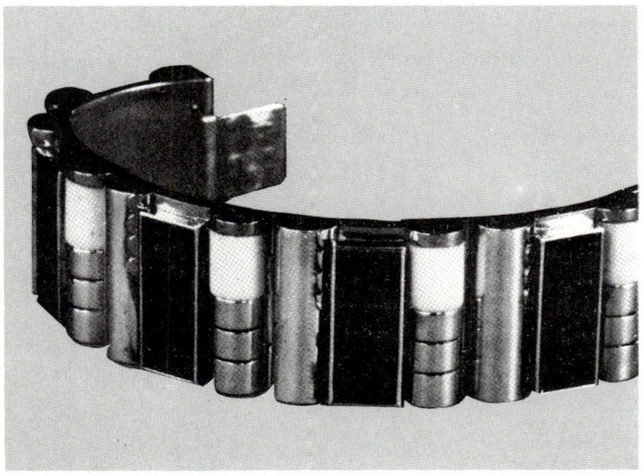

Jean Desprès: bracelet in jasper, ivory and gold, reproduced in Art et Décoration, September 1933.

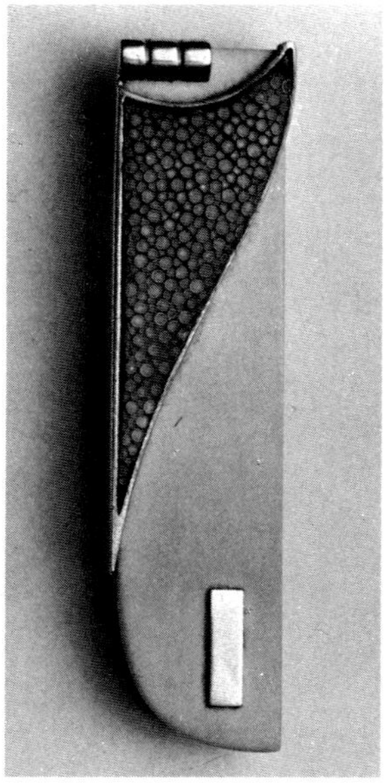

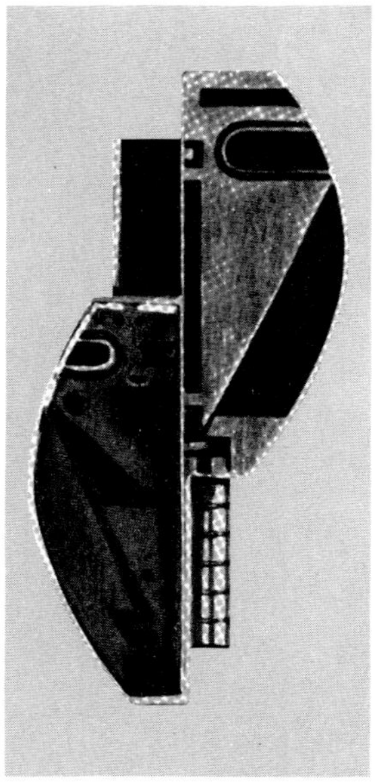

Jean Desprès: brooch in ivory, shagreen, silver and vermeil, c. 1930, signed. Musée des Arts Décoratifs, Paris. Photo: L. Sully-Jaulmes.

Jean Desprès: 'double mask' brooch in silver and glass engraved by Etienne Cournault, reproduced in Art et Décoration, *September 1933.*

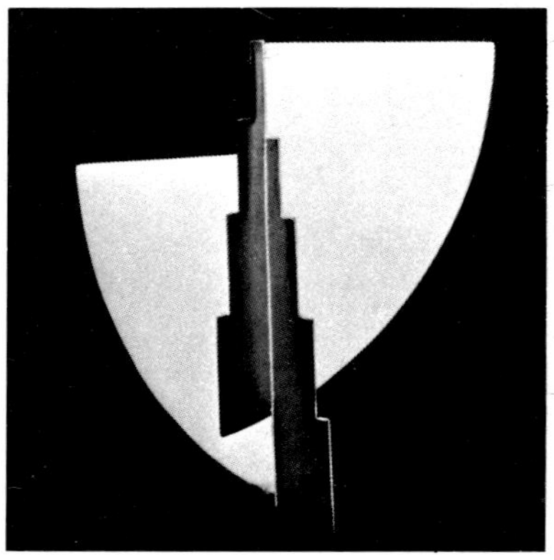

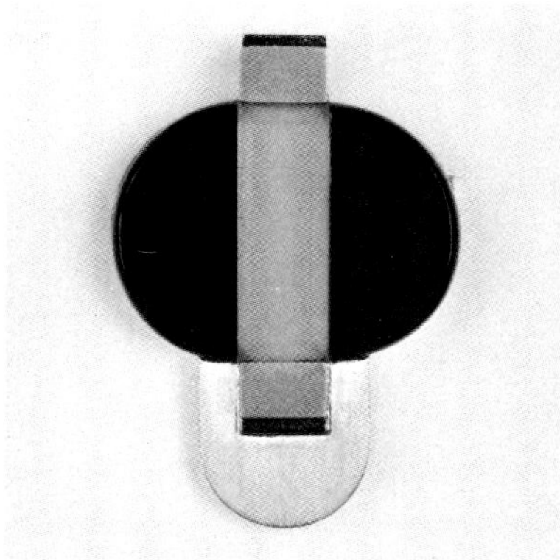

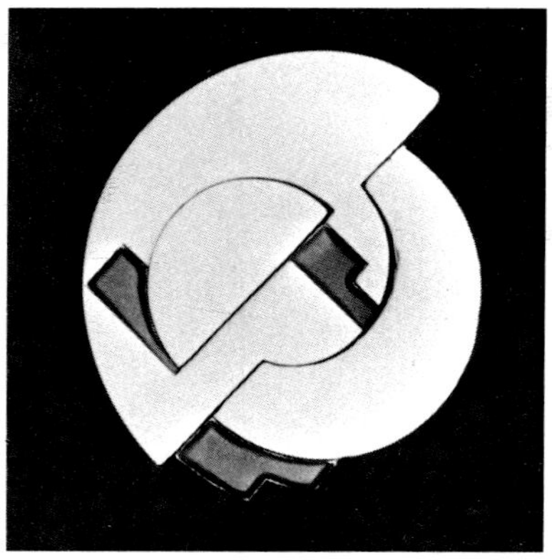

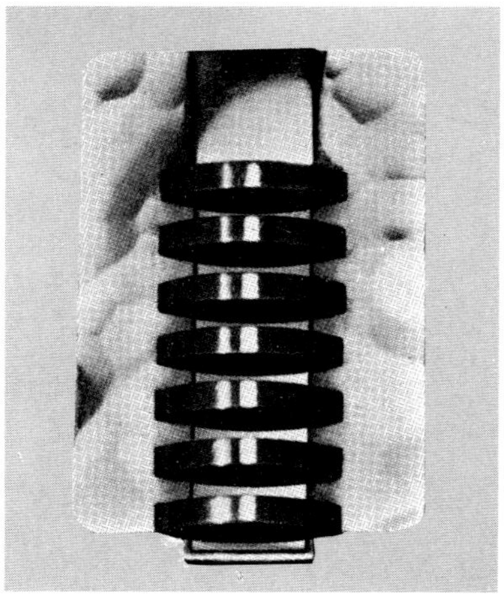

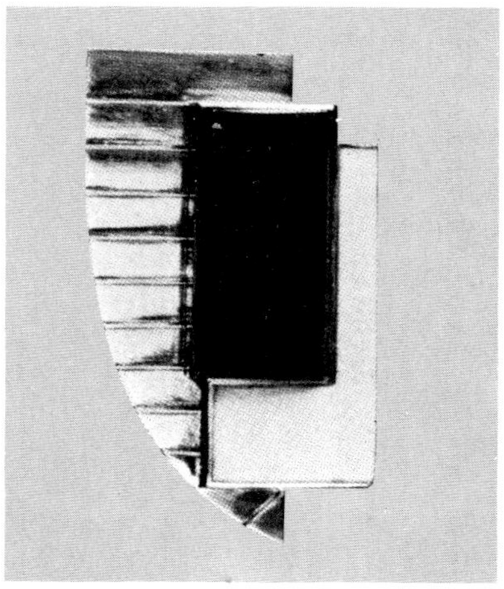

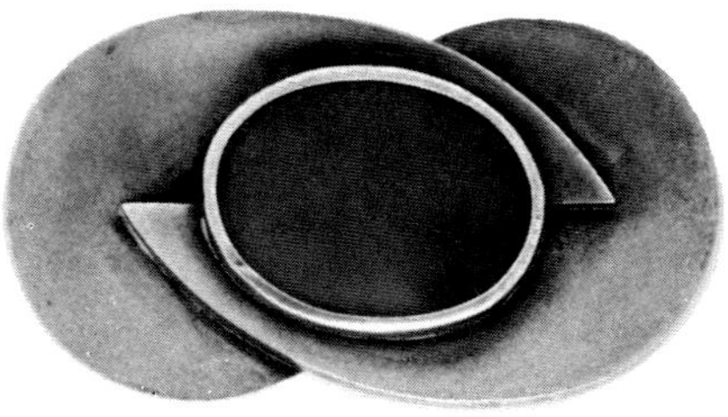

Centre, left to right: Raymond Templier: brooch, c. 1927. Courtesy of L. and B. Heuer.

Gérard Sandoz: brooch in two colours of gold, frosted crystal and black onyx, 1928, signed. Sotheby's, Monte Carlo.

Raymond Templier: brooch, c. 1927. Courtesy of L. and B. Heuer.

Third row: Jean Desprès: brooch reproduced in Art et Décoration, *December 1935.*

Jean Desprès: ivory, gold and jasper brooch reproduced in Art et Décoration, *September 1933.*

Bottom: Raymond Templier: brooch in gilded silver and amber-coloured agate, c. 1930. Sotheby's, Monte Carlo.

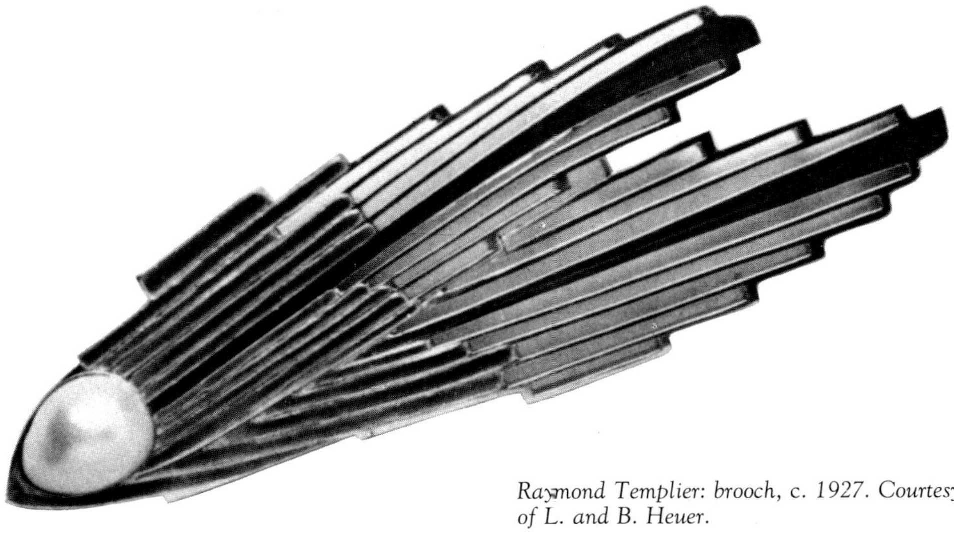

Raymond Templier: brooch, c. 1927. Courtesy of L. and B. Heuer.

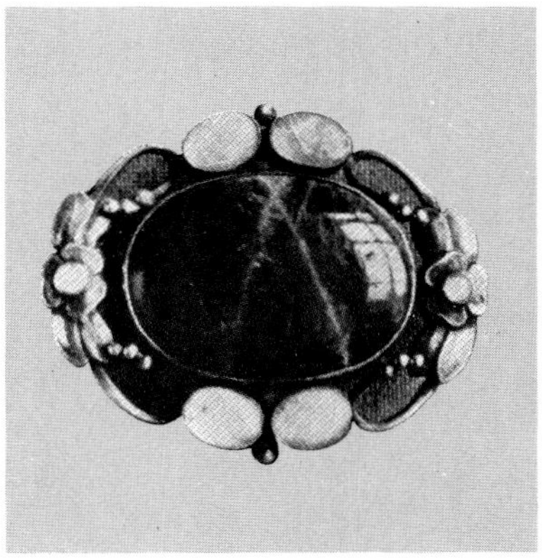
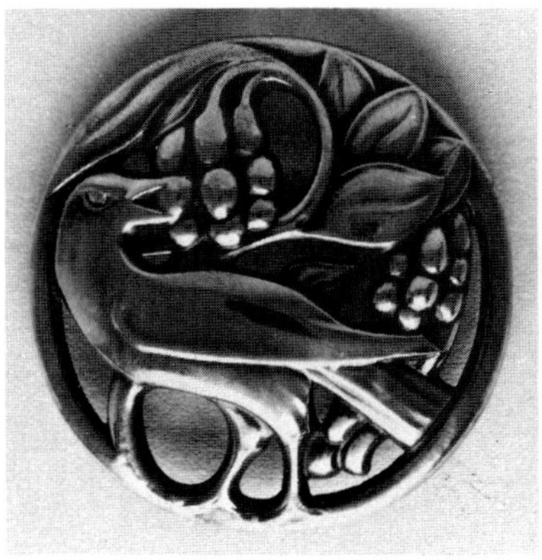
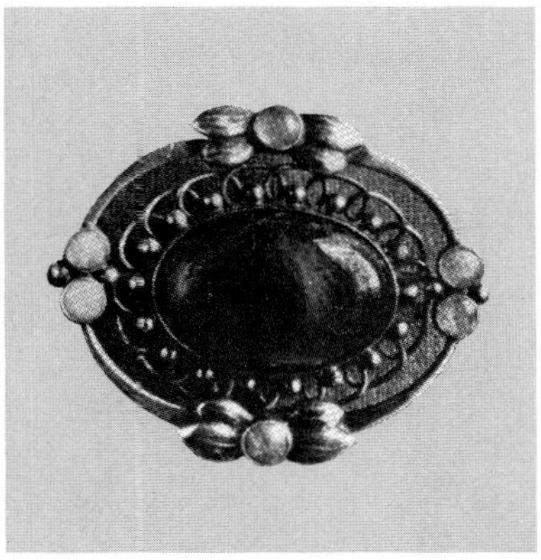
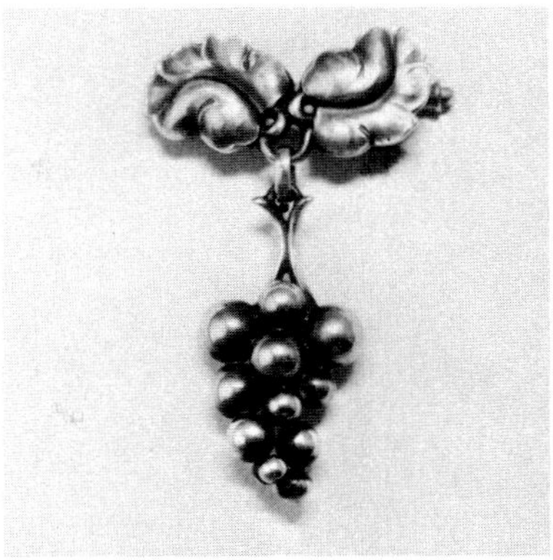
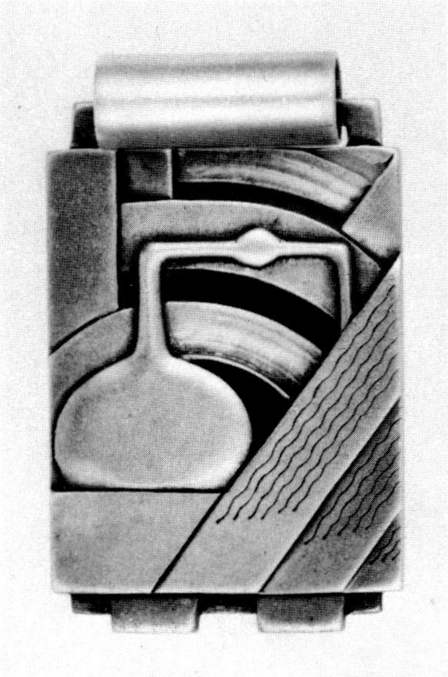
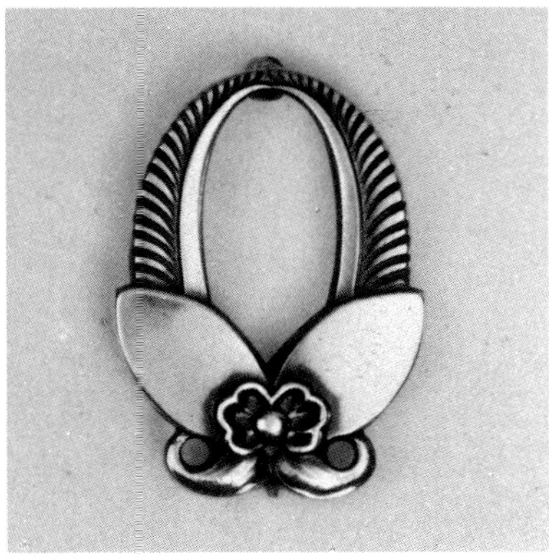

Centre, left to right: Georg Jensen: brooch in silver and stones, reproduced in Art et Décoration, *March 1922.*

Georg Jensen: silver brooch designed by Harald Nielsen, 1931. Georg Jensen Archives, Copenhagen.

Georg Jensen: brooch in silver and stones, reproduced in Art et Décoration, *March 1922.*

Bottom, left to right: Georg Jensen: silver brooch, 1919. Georg Jensen Archives, Copenhagen.

E. David: pendant in silver and black, blue and pale-green enamel, c. 1925. Sotheby's, Monte Carlo.

Georg Jensen: silver brooch designed by Gundorph Albertus, 1932. Georg Jensen Archives, Copenhagen.

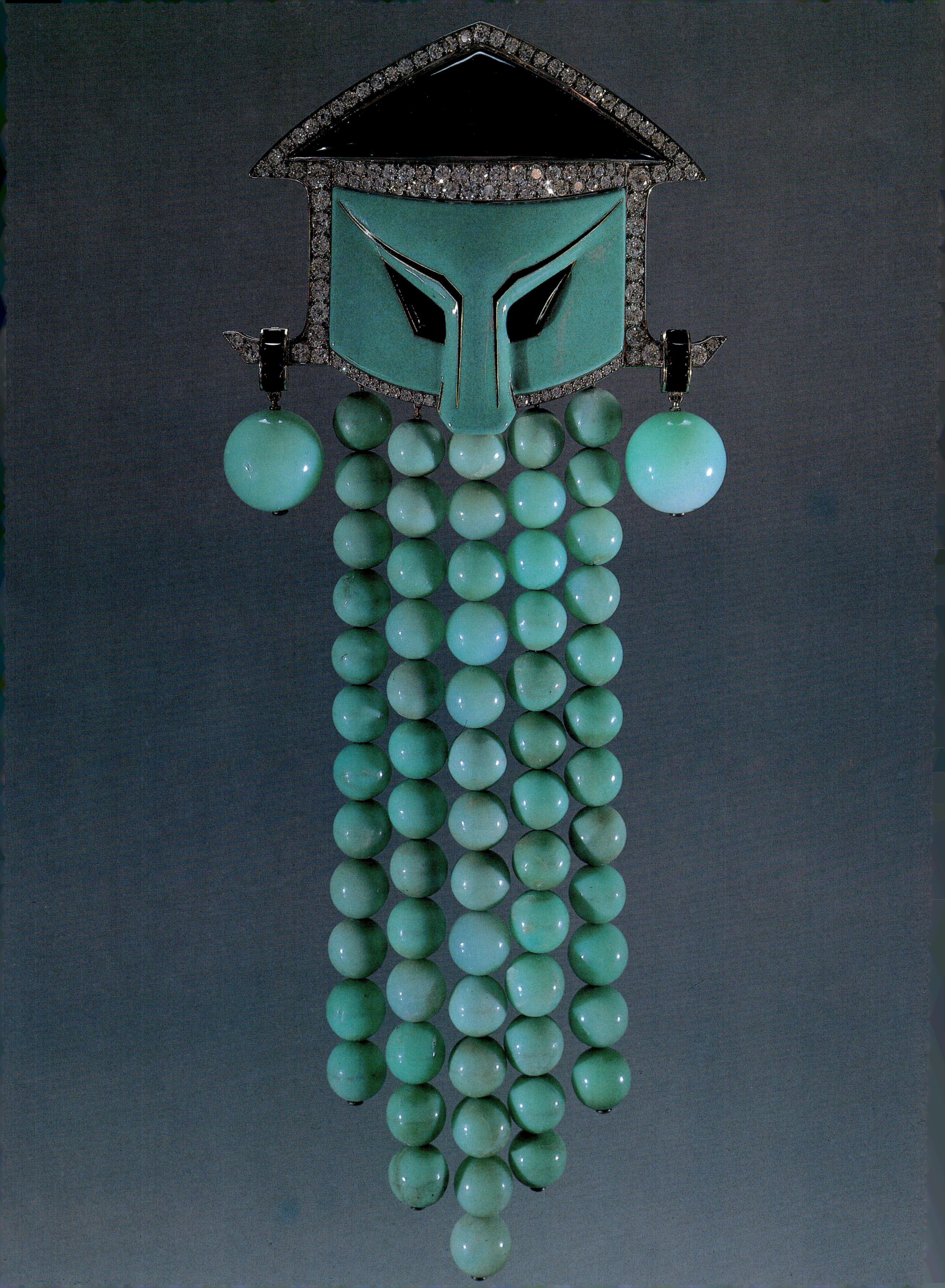

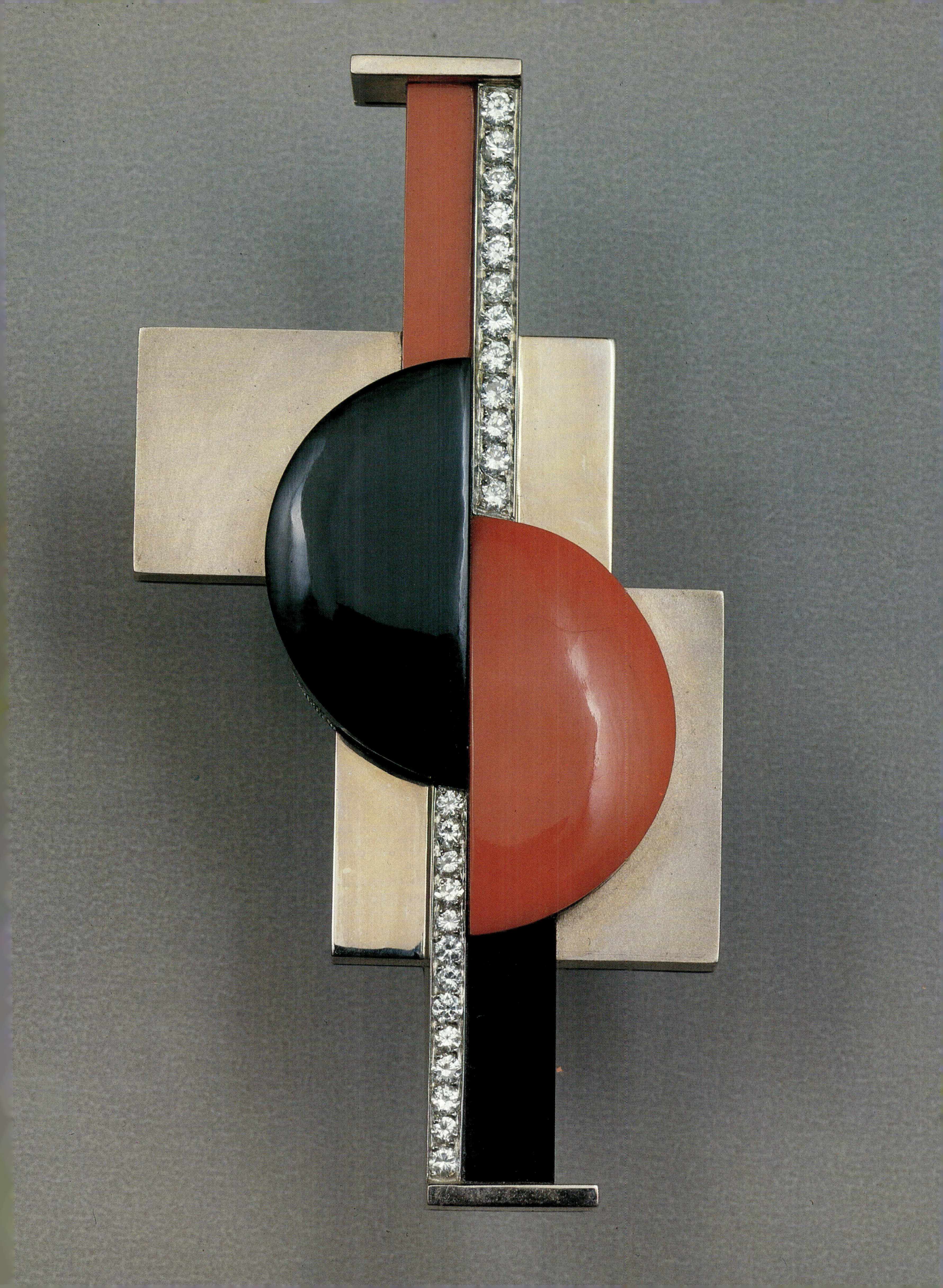

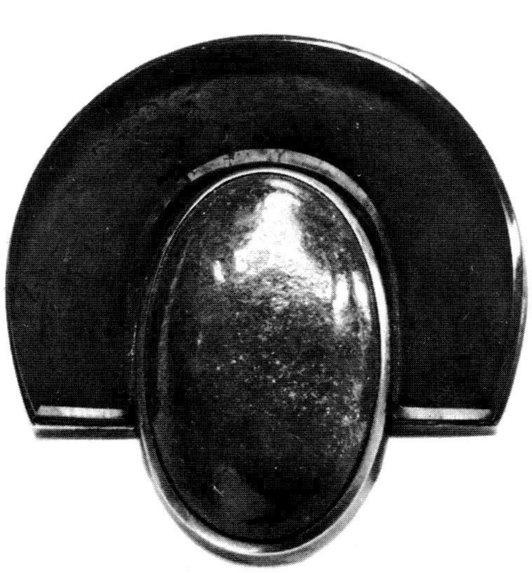

Raymond Templier: brooch in silver and lapis. A. Lesieutre Collection. Photo: L. Sully-Jaulmes.

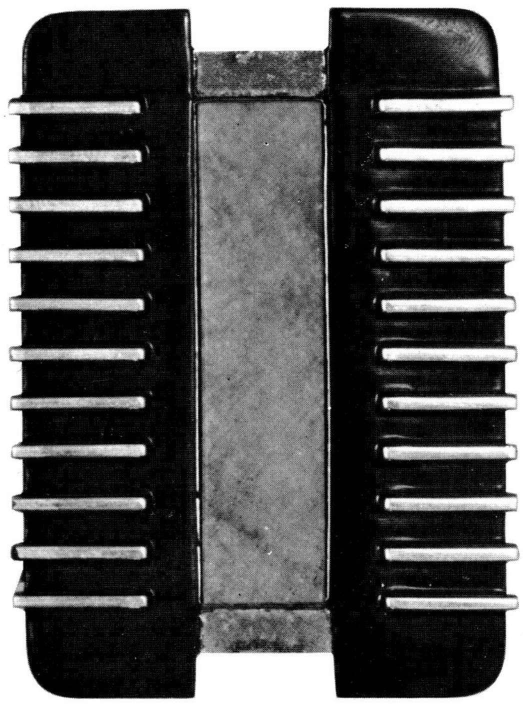

Jean Desprès: brooch in silver, gold and blue enamel, signed. A. Lesieutre Collection. Photo: L. Sully-Jaulmes.

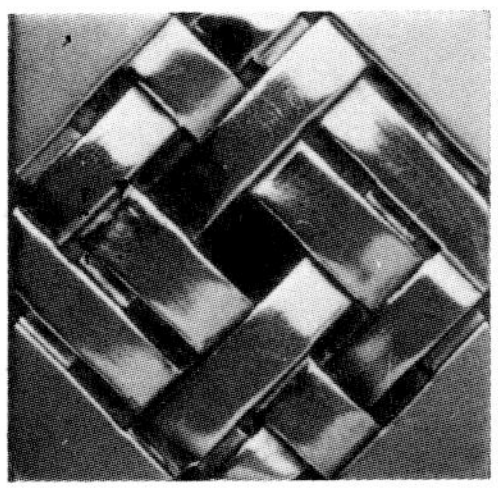

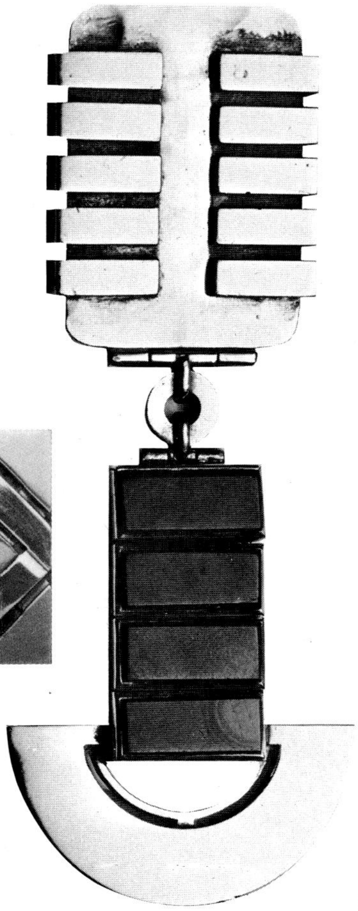

Jean Desprès: brooch in two colours of silver, signed. A. Lesieutre Collection. Photo: L. Sully-Jaulmes.

Jean Desprès: 'French Regency' brooch in silver, vermeil and malachite, c. 1930, signed. Musée des Arts Décoratifs, Paris. Photo: L. Sully-Jaulmes.

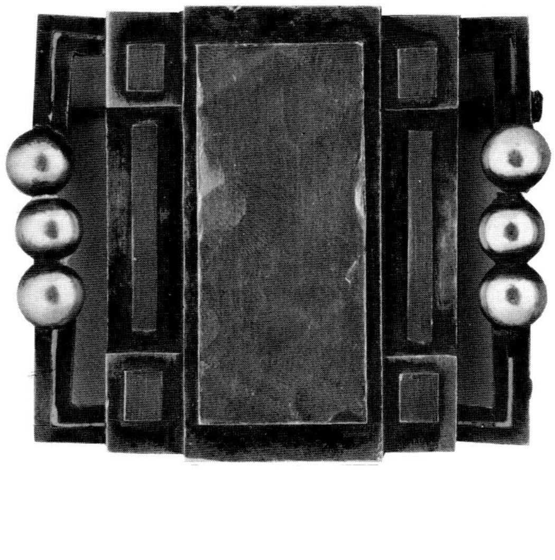

Jean Desprès: brooch in silver and gold, signed. A. Lesieutre Collection. Photo: L. Sully-Jaulmes.

Preceding pages: Georges Fouquet: corsage ornament depicting a Chinese mask, the face in enamel, eyes and hair in onyx, jade beads and brilliant-cut diamonds, c. 1920–25. H. 22.5 cm, W. 9.5 cm. Private Collection. Photo: T. Heuer.

Gérard Sandoz: 'semaphore' brooch in diamonds, white gold, coral and jet, signed. H. 9 cm W. 4.5 cm. N. Manoukian Collection. Photo: L. Sully-Jaulmes.

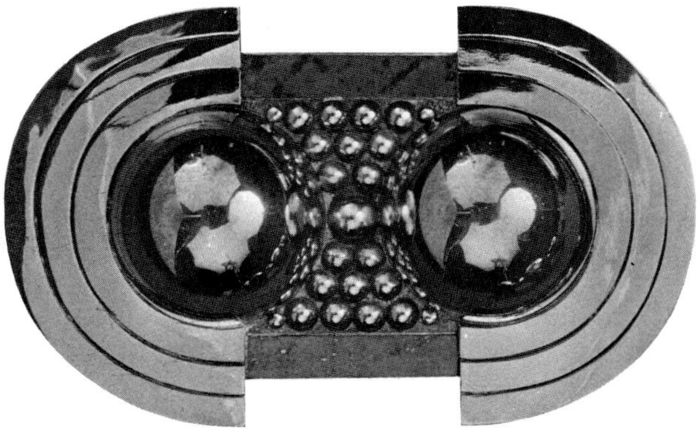

Jean Desprès: brooch in yellow gold and white gold, silver and lapis, comprising two semicircles joined by a panel with a bubbled surface. Private Collection. Photo: L. Sully-Jaulmes.

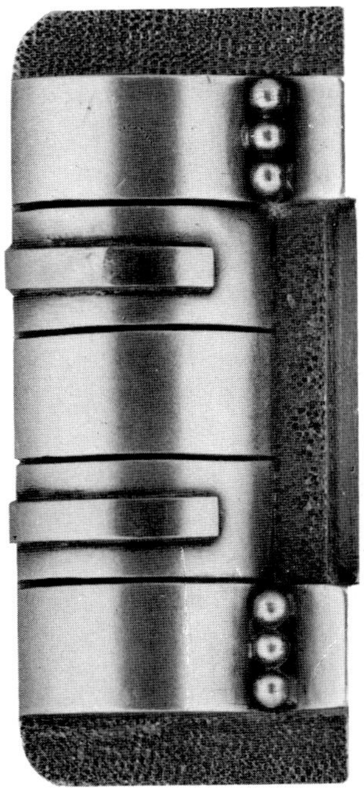

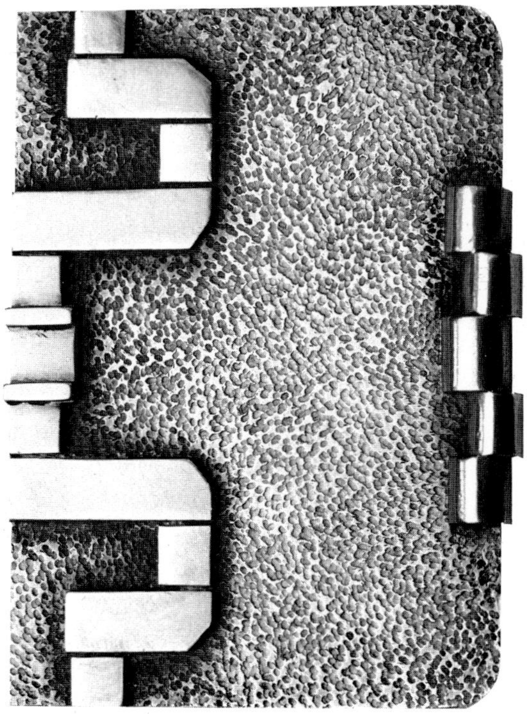

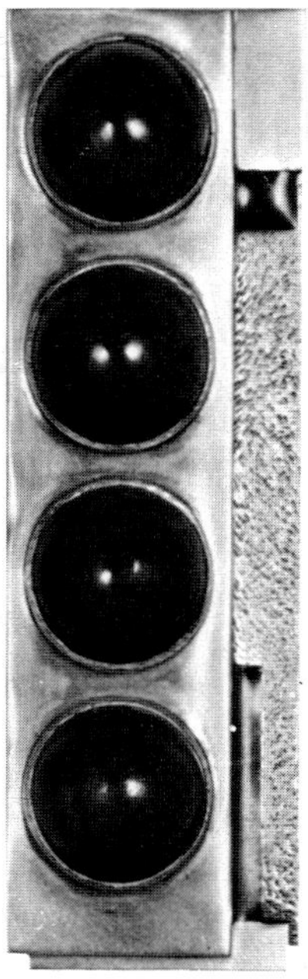

Centre, left to right: Jean Desprès: brooch in silver and three colours of gold, c. 1930, signed. Sotheby's, Monte Carlo.

Jean Desprès: 'crankshaft' brooch in polished and matt silver, c. 1930, signed. Musée des Arts Décoratifs, Paris. Photo: L. Sully-Jaulmes.

Jean Desprès: pendant in silver, gold, lacquer and lapis, c. 1928–30, signed. Sotheby's, Monte Carlo.

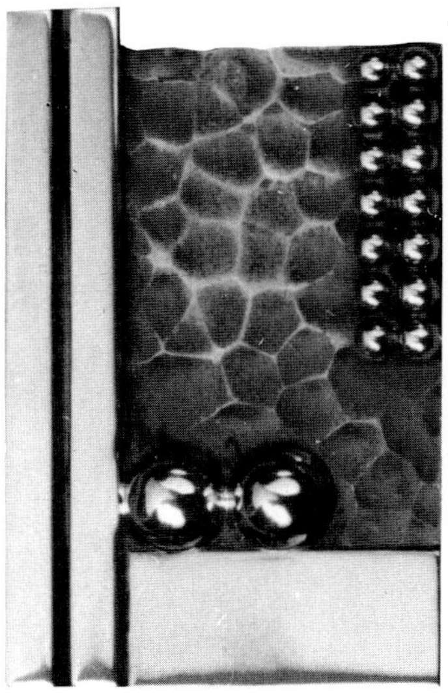

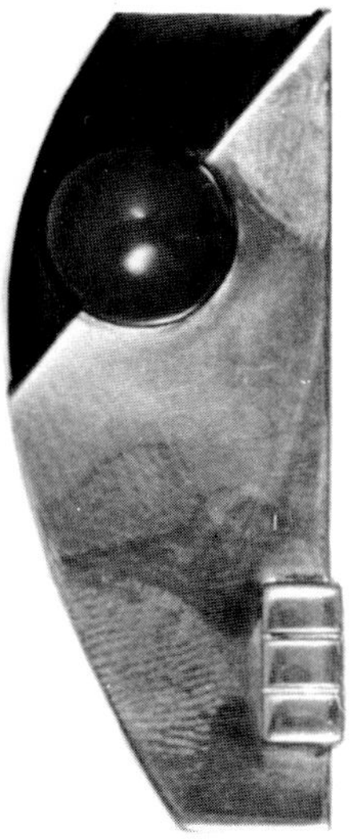

Bottom, left to right: Jean Desprès: brooch in silver, polished gold and sablé gold. A. Lesieutre Collection. Photo: L. Sully-Jaulmes.

Jean Desprès: brooch in gold and black enamel with silver clips and round coral inset, c. 1925, signed. A. Lesieutre Collection.

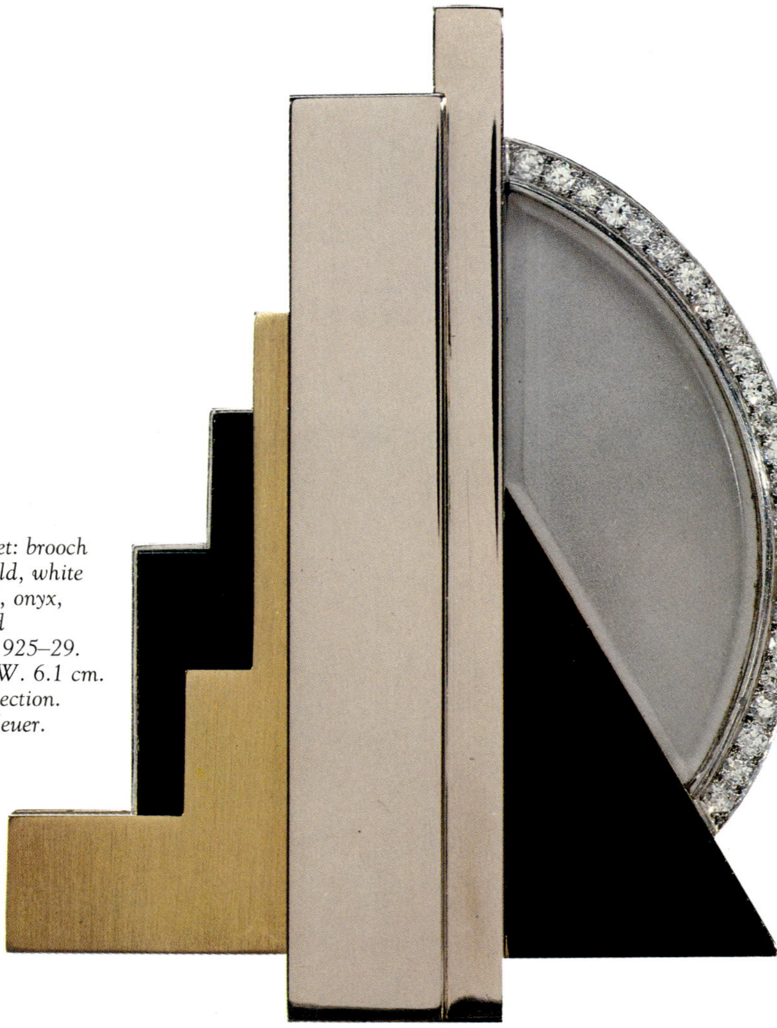

Jean Fouquet: brooch in yellow gold, white gold, crystal, onyx, lacquer, and diamonds, 1925–29. H. 7.8 cm, W. 6.1 cm. Private Collection. Photo: T. Heuer.

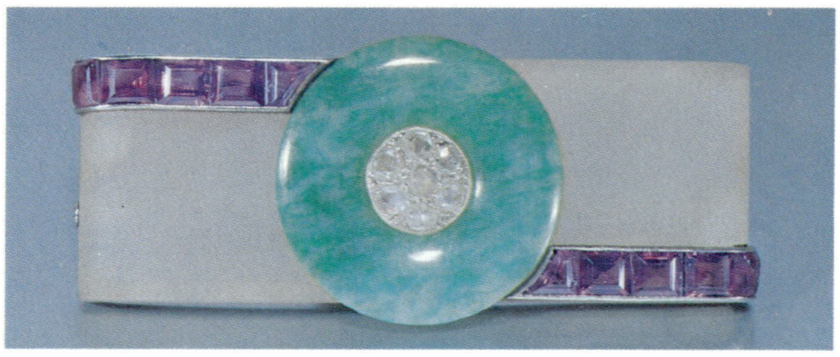

Maison Fouquet: brooch in frosted rock crystal, jade, diamonds and amethyst baguettes. M. Souillac Collection. Photo: J.B. Rouault.

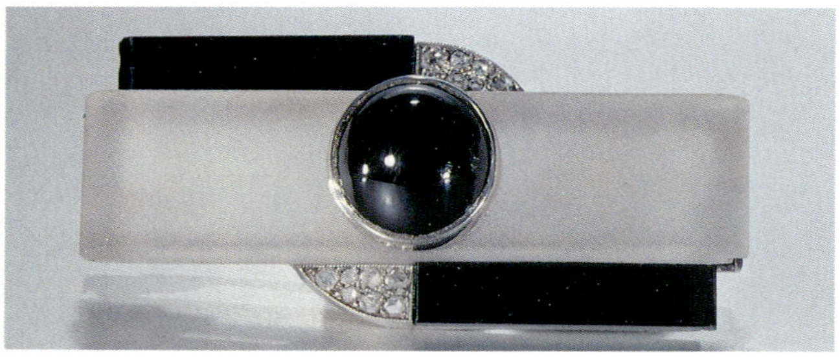

Maison Fouquet: brooch in frosted rock crystal, onyx cabochon and baguettes, and diamonds. M. Souillac Collection. Photo: J.B. Rouault.

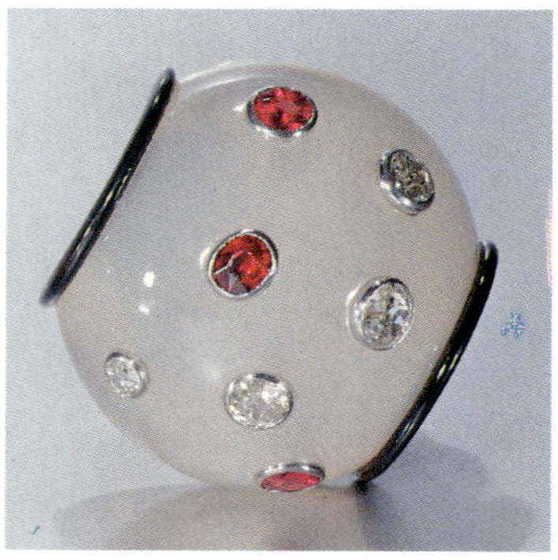

Jean Fouquet: white agate brooch, set with rubies and diamonds and bordered with black enamel. M.Souillac Collection. Photo: J.B. Rouault.

Jean Fouquet: brooch reproduced in his article 'Bijoux et Orfèvrerie', 1931.

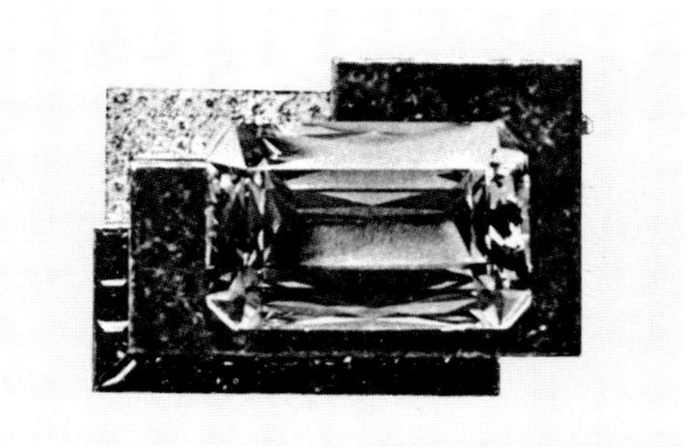

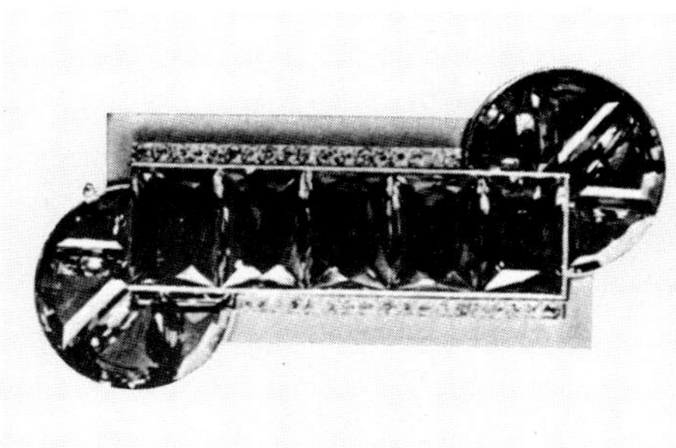

Jean Fouquet: brooch in amethysts, topazes, diamonds and blue enamel, c. 1927, reproduced in his article 'Bijoux et Orfèvrerie', 1931.

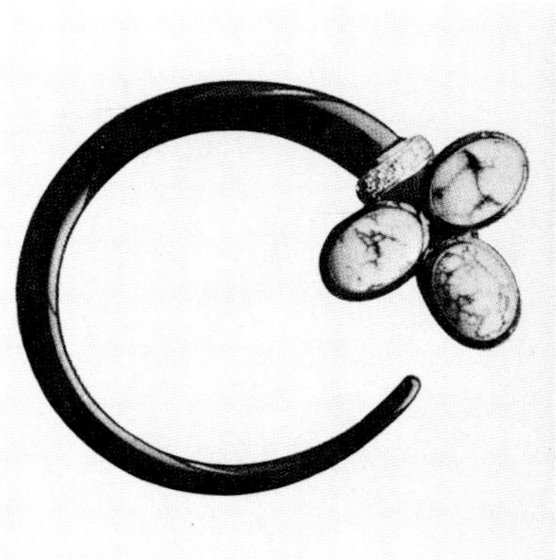

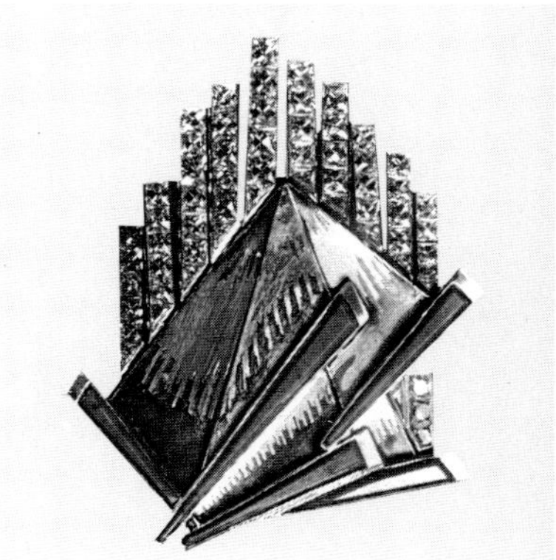

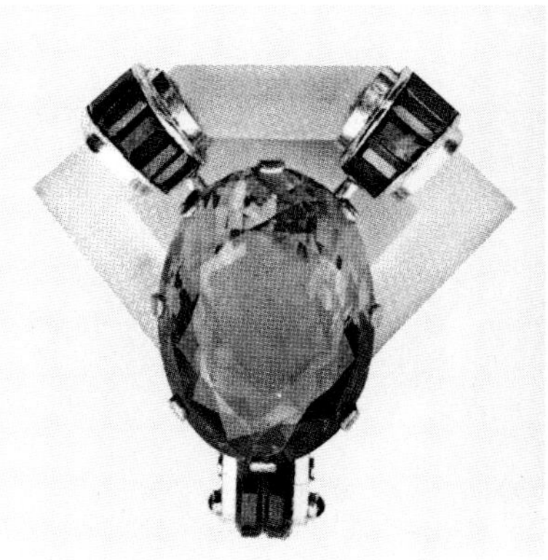

Georges Fouquet: brooch in onyx, turquoises and brilliant-cut diamonds, 1925–30. Photo: Musée des Arts Décoratifs, Paris.

Raymond Templier: brooch. Courtesy of L. and B. Heuer.

Georges Fouquet: crystal, amethyst and platinum brooch, 1925–30. Kunstgewerbemuseum, Berlin.

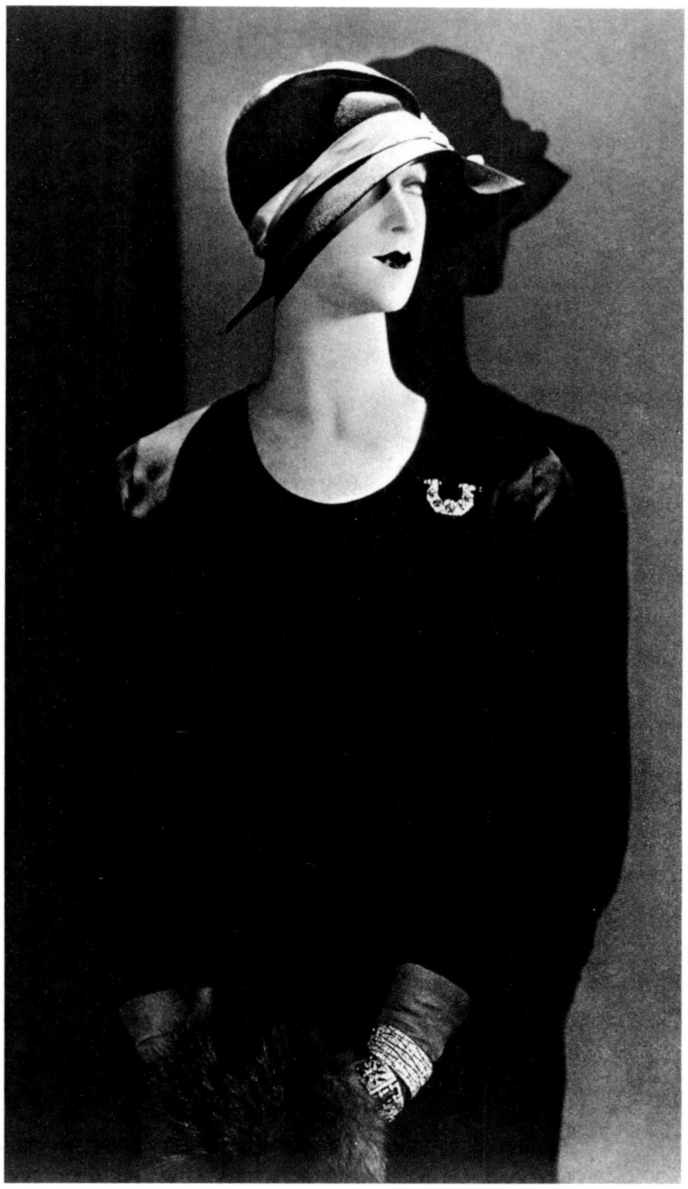

Siegel mannequin.

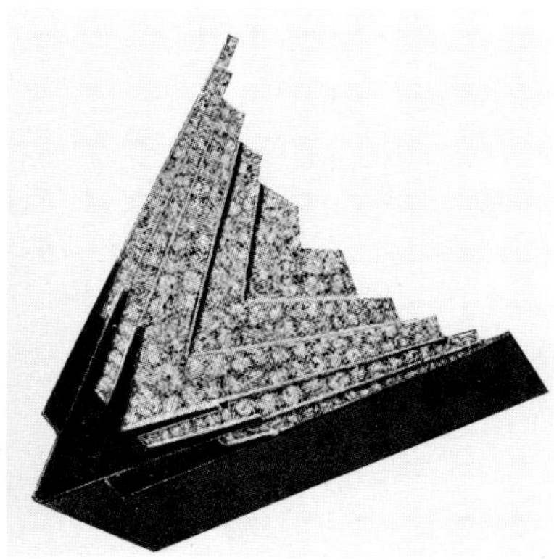

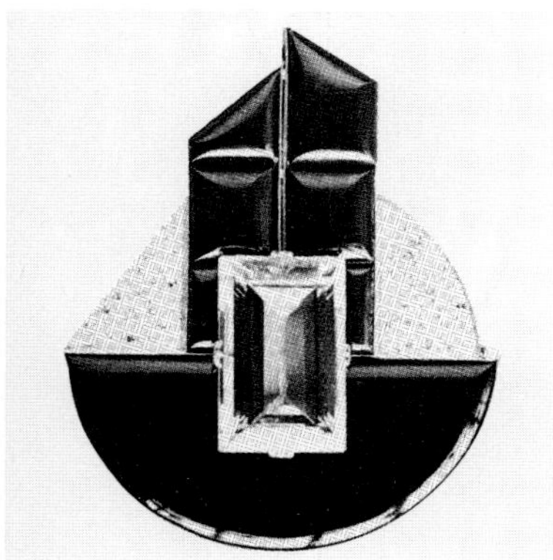

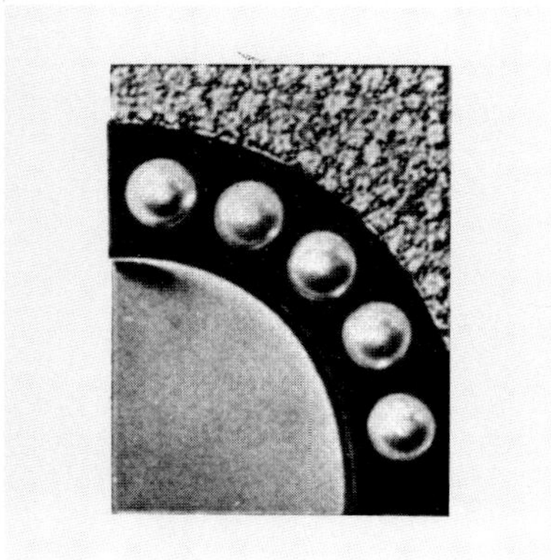

Raymond Templier: brooch in diamonds, platinum and green enamel, 1925 Paris Exposition.

Jean Fouquet: brooch in coloured stones and diamonds, 1925. Photo: Musée des Arts Décoratifs, Paris.

Paul Brandt: brooch in precious metal, diamonds, pearls and enamel, reproduced in Jean Fouquet's 'Bijoux et Orfèvrerie', 1931.

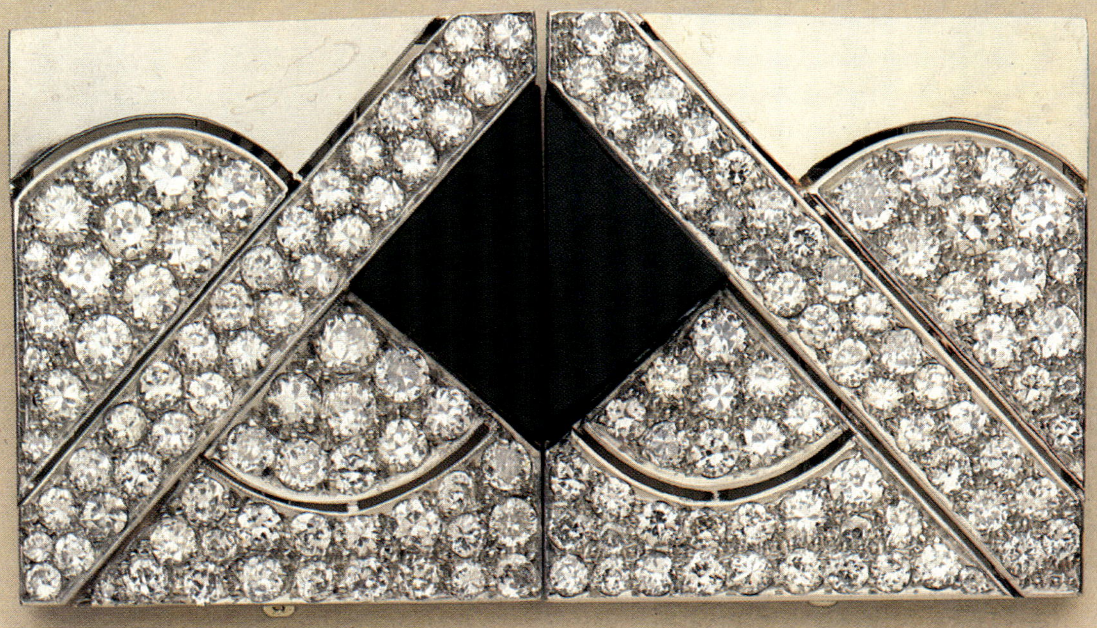

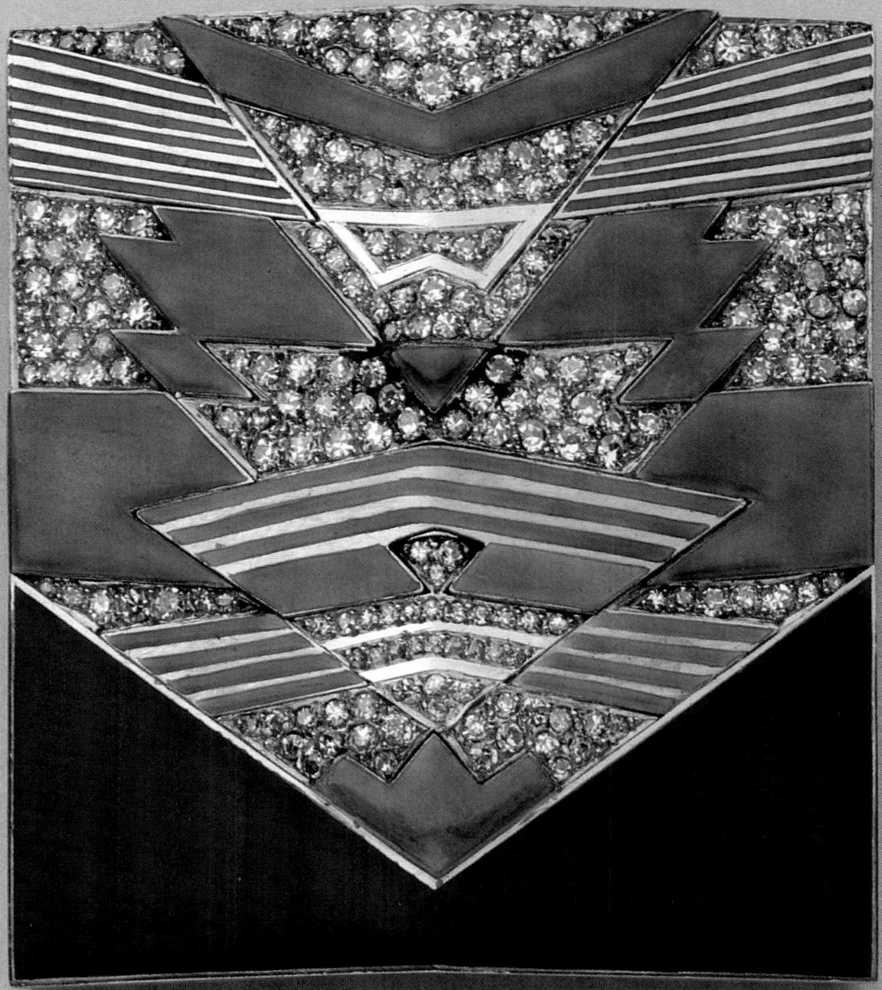

Raymond Templier: ring, 1930. Courtesy of L. and B. Heuer.

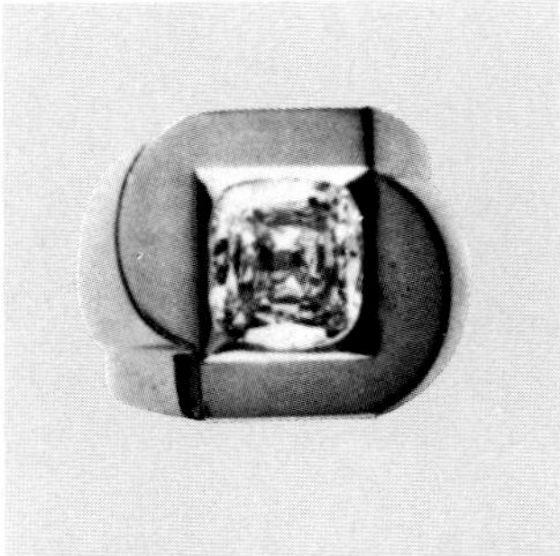

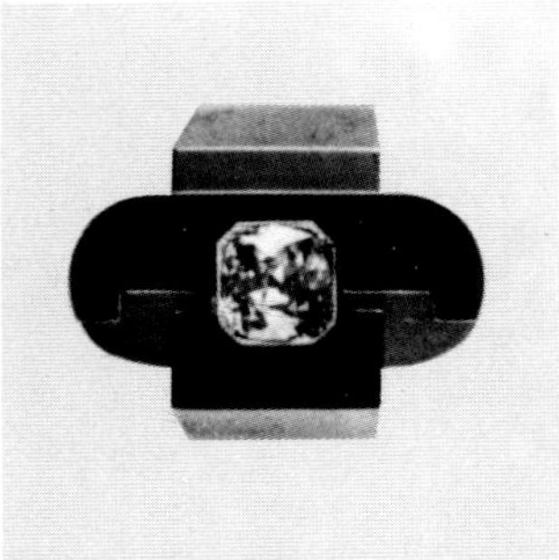

Raymond Templier: ring, 1930. Courtesy of L. and B. Heuer.

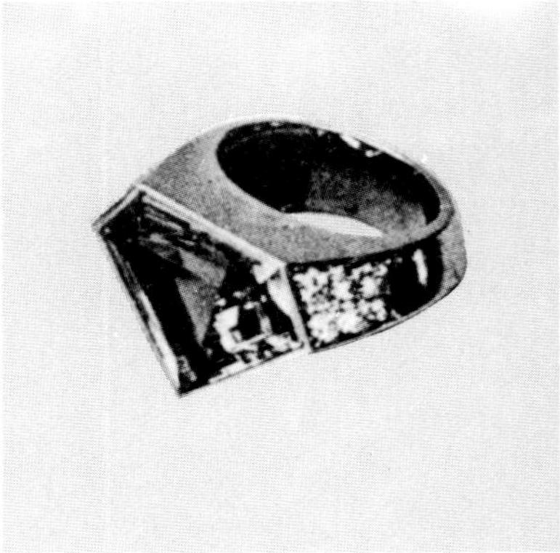

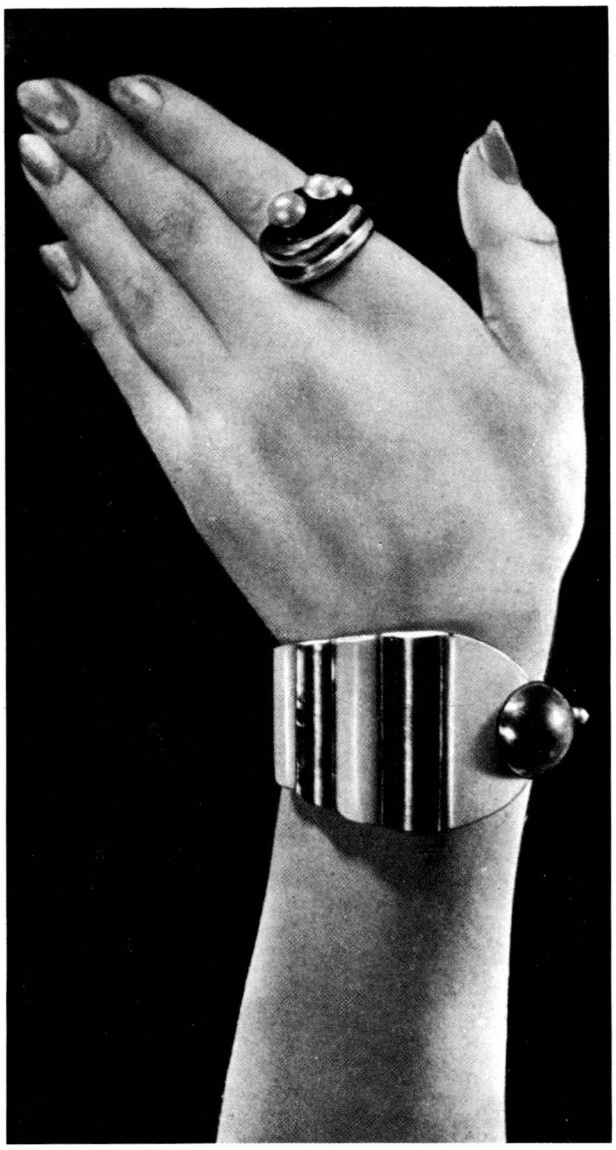

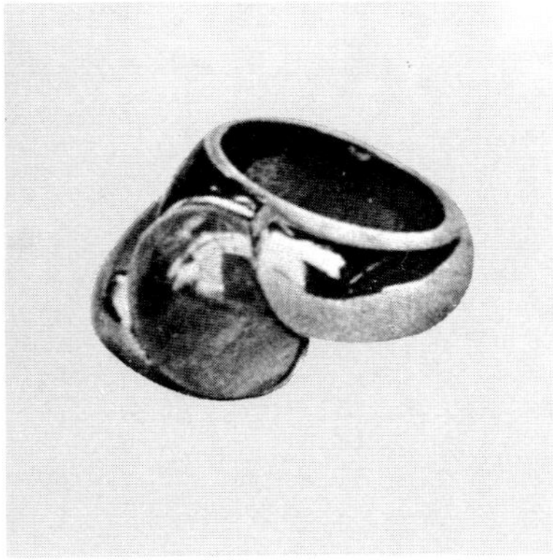

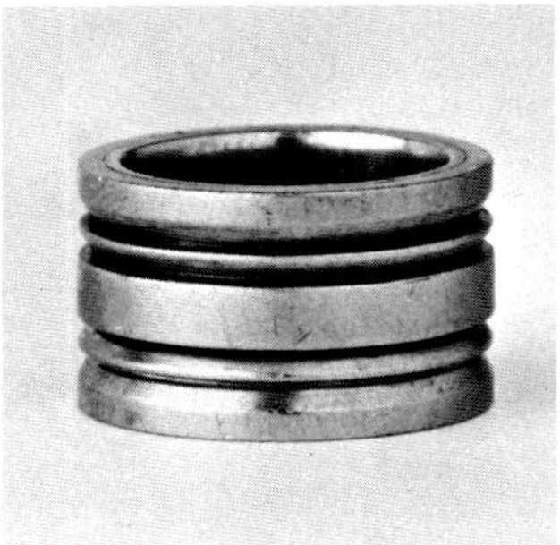

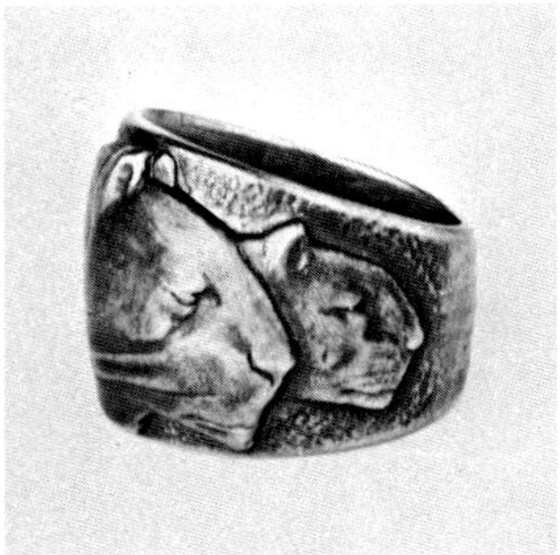

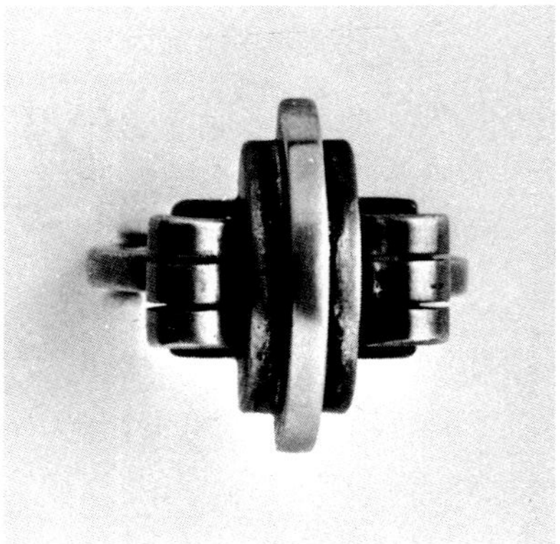

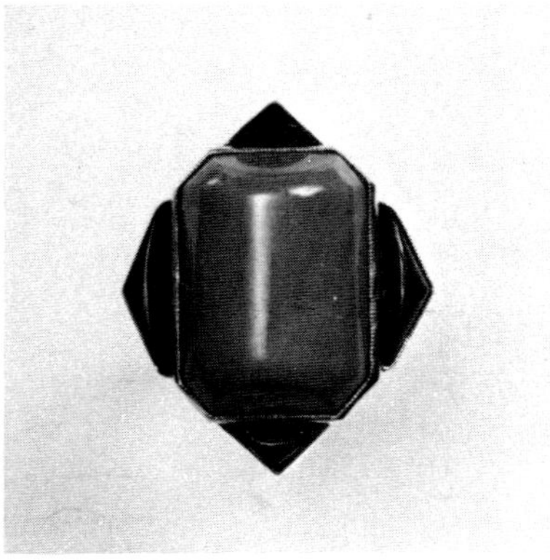

Jean Fouquet: ring in gold, platinum and hardstone, c. 1927, reproduced in his article 'Bijoux et Orfèvrerie', 1931.

Raymond Templier: steel ring, c. 1930, signed. Sotheby's.

Jean Desprès: silver and gold ring, c. 1930, signed. Sotheby's.

Centre: René Robert: bracelet in gold, silver and ivory; ring in silver, Chinese lacquer and pearls, reproduced in Art et Décoration.

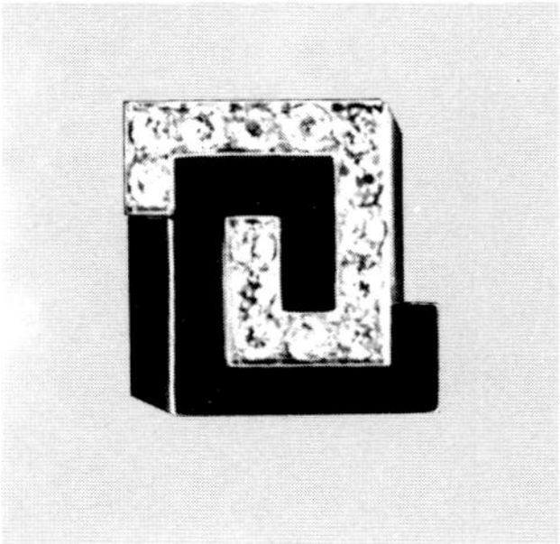

Raymond Templier: ring, 1929. Courtesy of L. and B. Heuer.

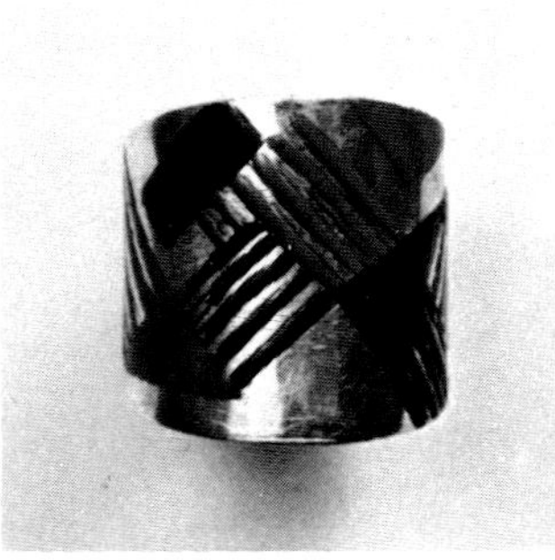

Jean Dunand: ring in silver, black, red and brown lacquer. M. Souillac Collection.

Jean Fouquet: ring in gold, platinum, hardstone and semi-precious stone, c. 1927, reproduced in his article 'Bijoux et Orfèvrerie', 1931.

Delon: bronze ring with two panthers sculpted in bas relief, c. 1930, signed. Sotheby's, Monte Carlo.

Cartier: ring with coral cabochon and onyx. M. Souillac Collection.

Preceding pages: Paul Brandt: pair of clips in diamonds, onyx, white gold and platinum, signed.

Raymond Templier: brooch in diamonds, white gold, green and dark-grey lacquer, signed, executed for the 1925 Paris Exposition. Primavera Gallery, New York.

Jean Desprès: silver ring, reproduced in Art et Décoration.

Jean Desprès: silver ring, reproduced in Art et Décoration, *September 1933.*

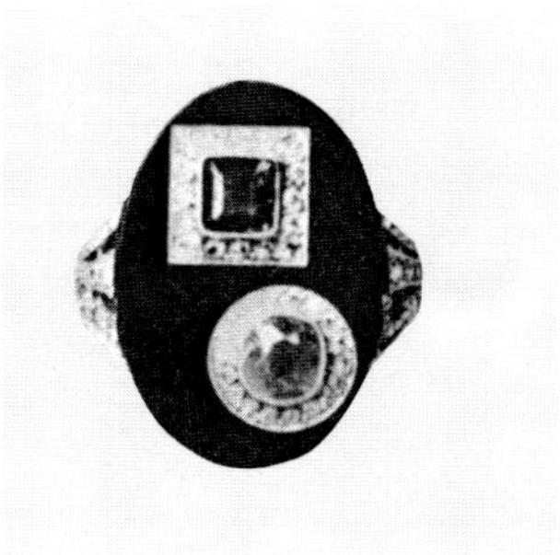

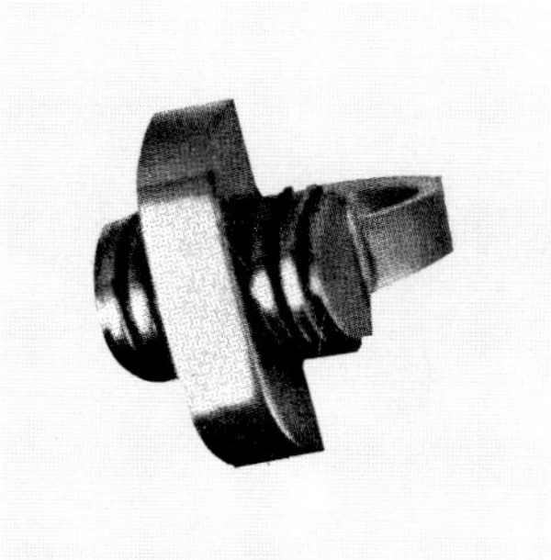

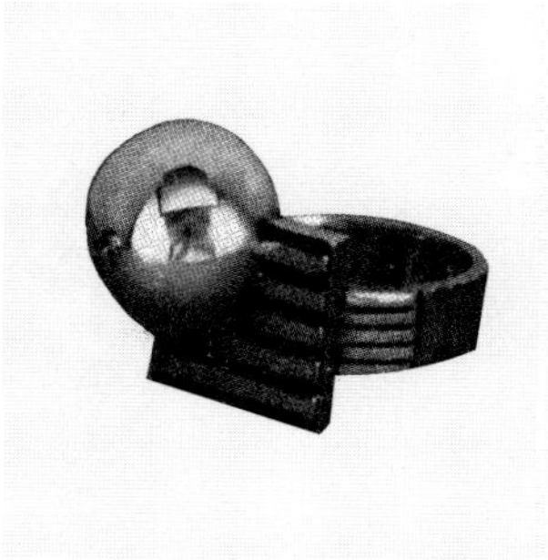

Centre: Elizabeth Treskow: ring in gold, pearls and precious stones, Cologne, 1928. Schmuckmuseum, Pforzheim.

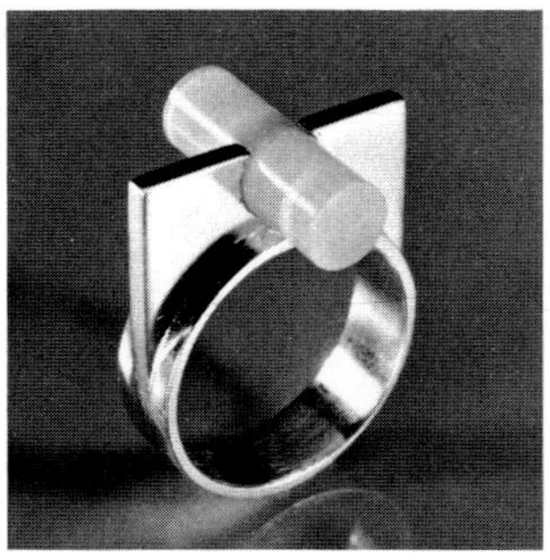

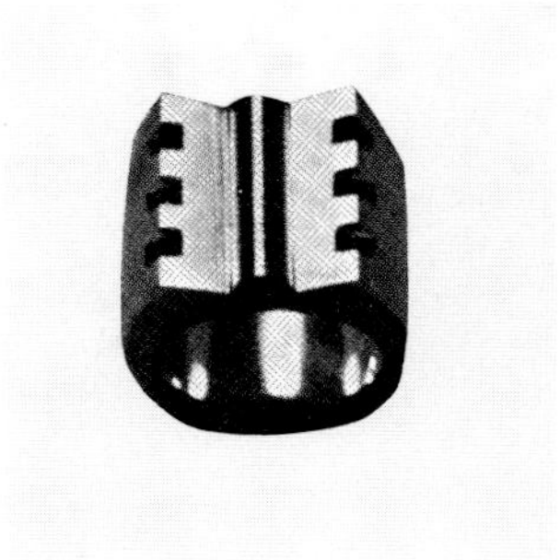

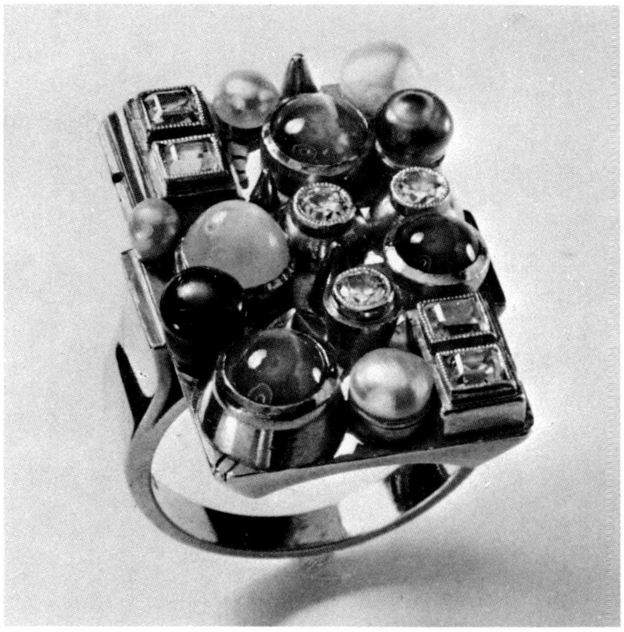

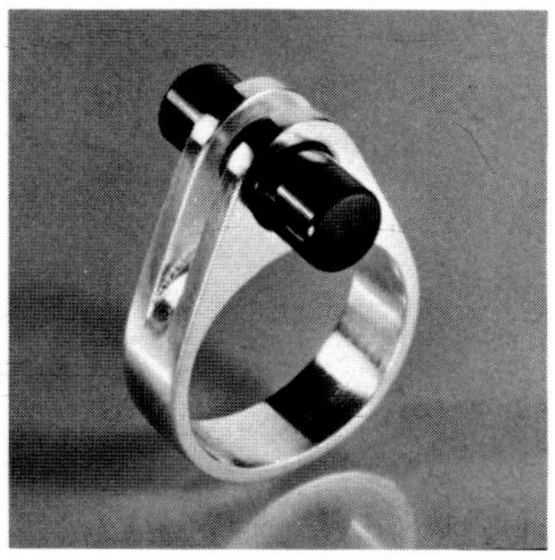

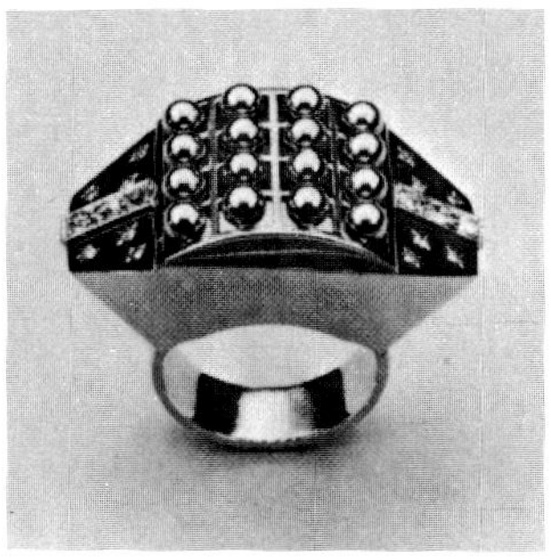

Georges Fouquet: ring in onyx set with coloured stones and diamonds, from a design by André Léveillé, 1925.

Fritz Schwerdt: silver and agate ring, 1930. Schmuckmuseum, Pforzheim.

Gérard Sandoz: man's ring, reproduced in Art et Décoration, *December 1929.*

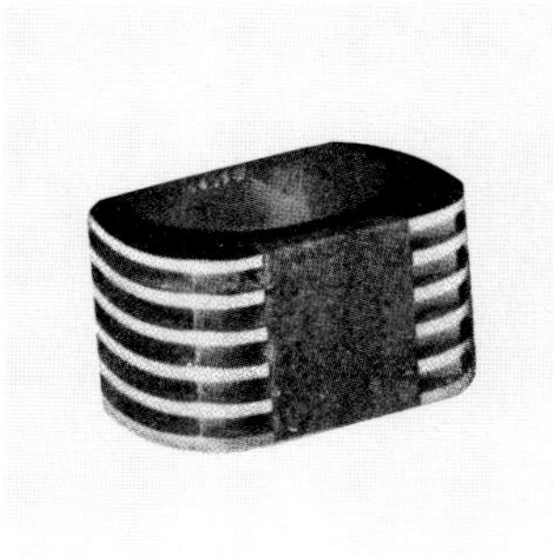

Jean Fouquet: ring in Osmior, white gold and lapis, reproduced in Art et Décoration, *August 1929.*

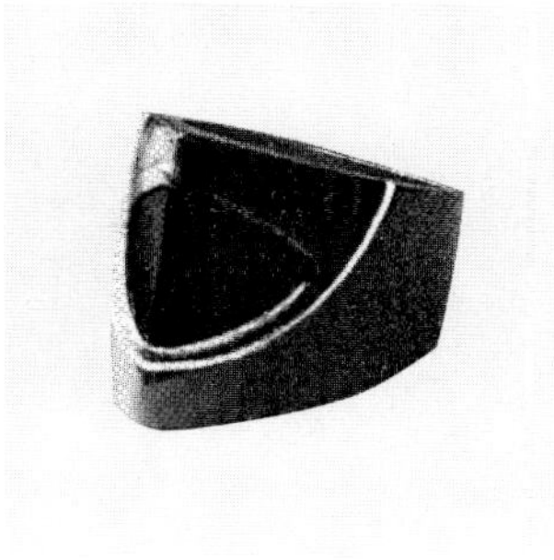

Jean Desprès: ring in silver and crude ore, reproduced in Art et Décoration, *September 1933.*

Fritz Schwerdt: silver and onyx ring, Germany, c. 1929. Schmuckmuseum, Pforzheim.

Jean Fouquet: ring in gold, platinum and brilliant-cut diamonds, c. 1936. Private Collection.

Below: Jean Fouquet: rock crystal ring set with amethysts and moonstones in platinum, c. 1930. Private Collection. Photo: T. Heuer.

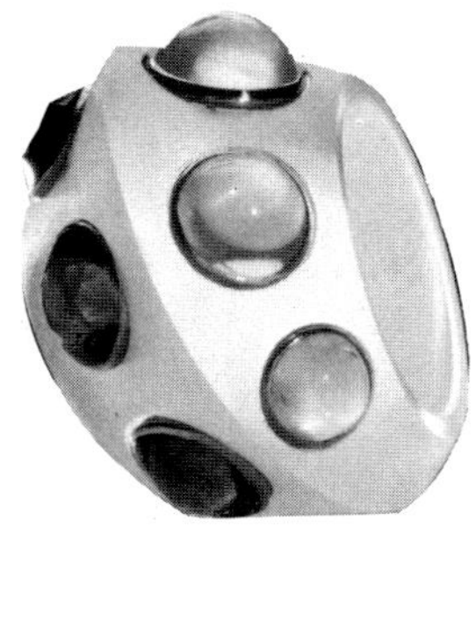

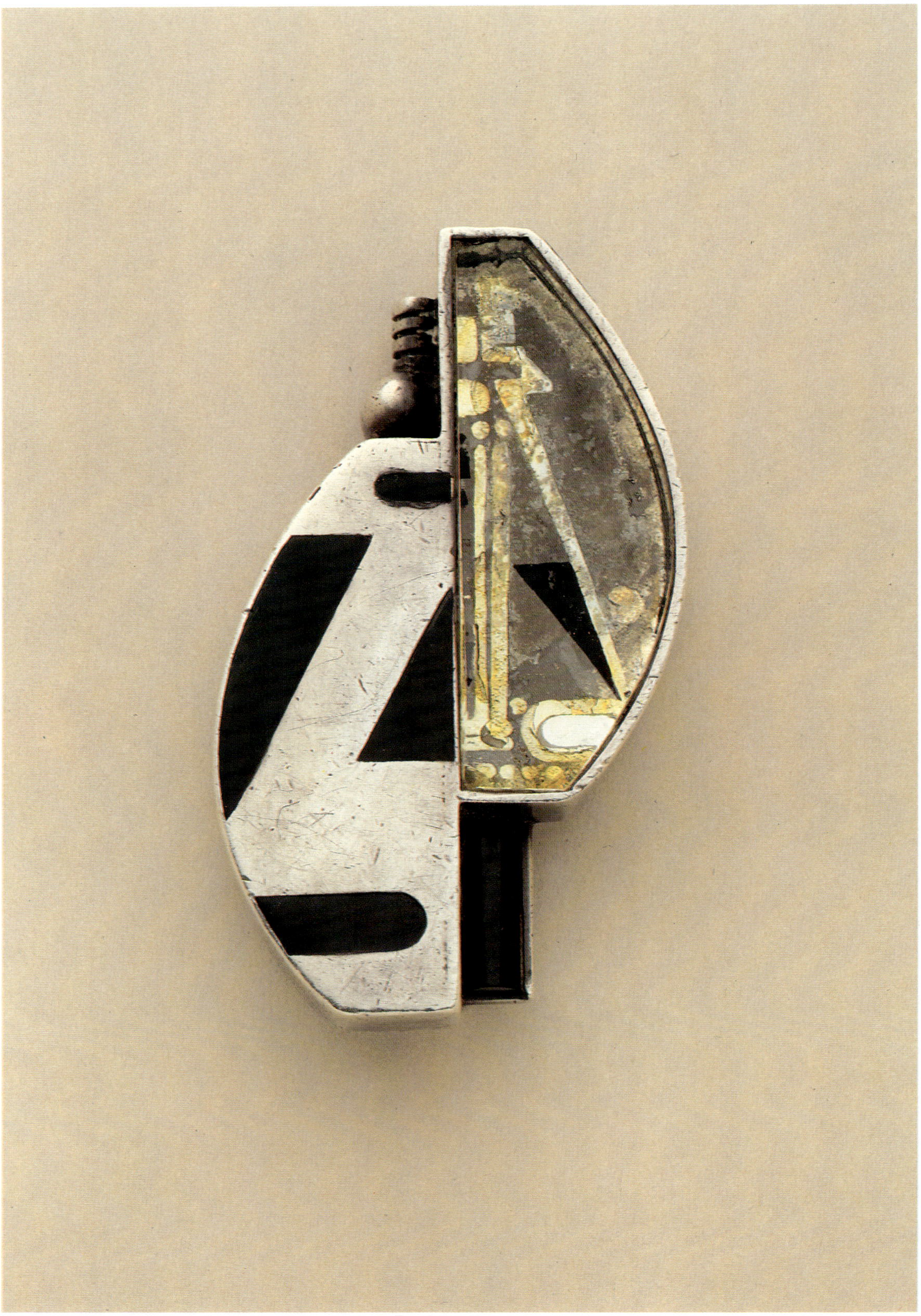

Jean Desprès: brooch in silver, black enamel and glass painted by Etienne Cournault, signed. Primavera Gallery, New York.

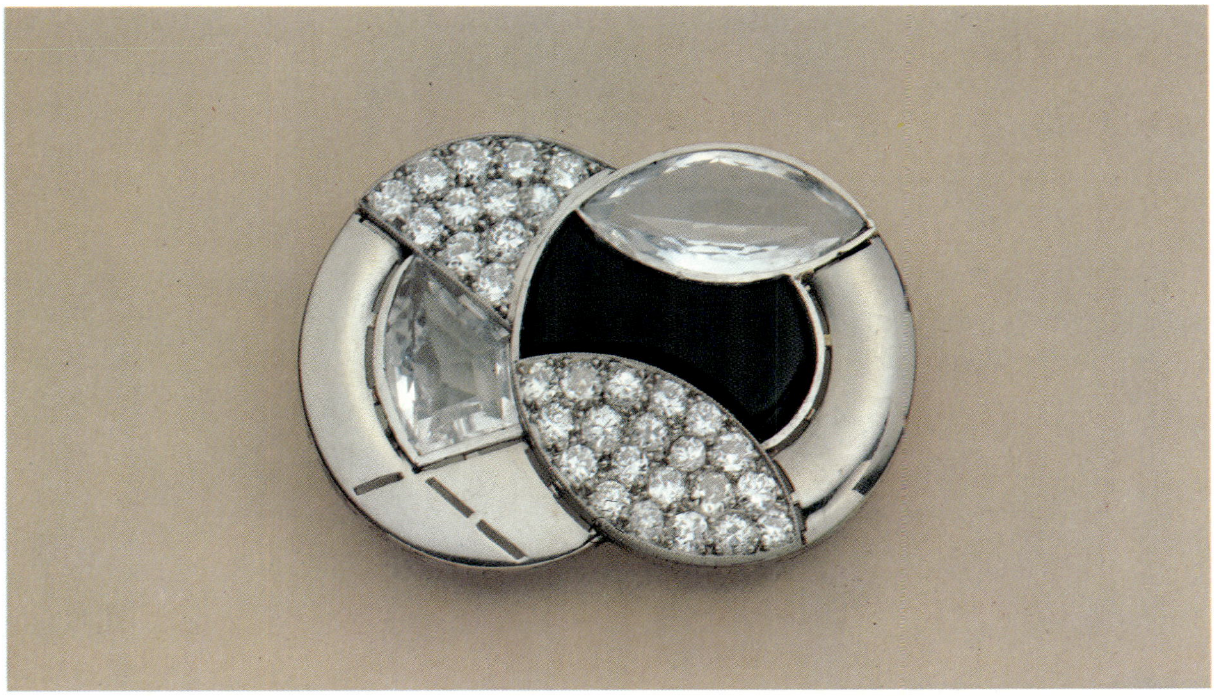

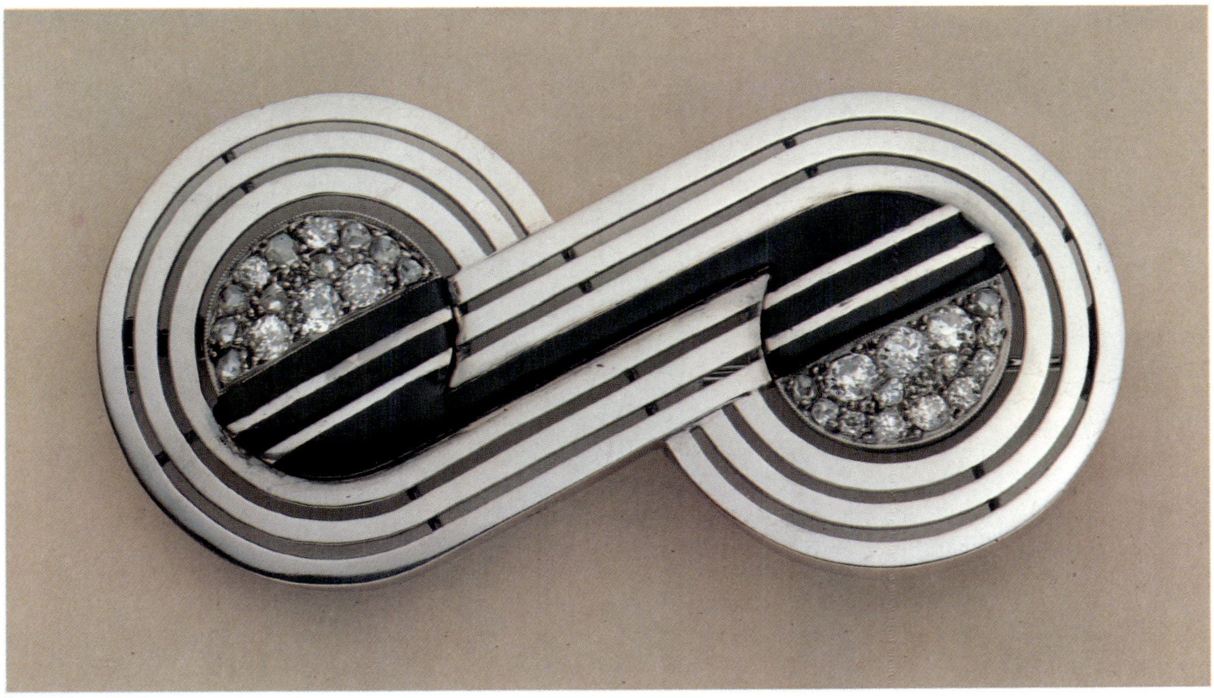

Paul Brandt: brooch in faceted rock crystal, onyx and white gold, c. 1930, signed. Primavera Gallery, New York.

Raymond Templier: brooch in diamonds, white gold and black lacquer, c. 1925, signed. Primavera Gallery, New York.

Paul Brandt: five designs for rings reproduced in Jean Fouquet's 'Bijoux et Orfèvrerie', 1931.

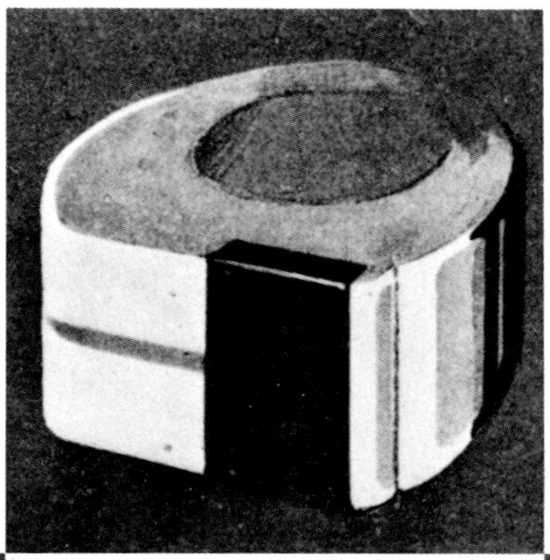

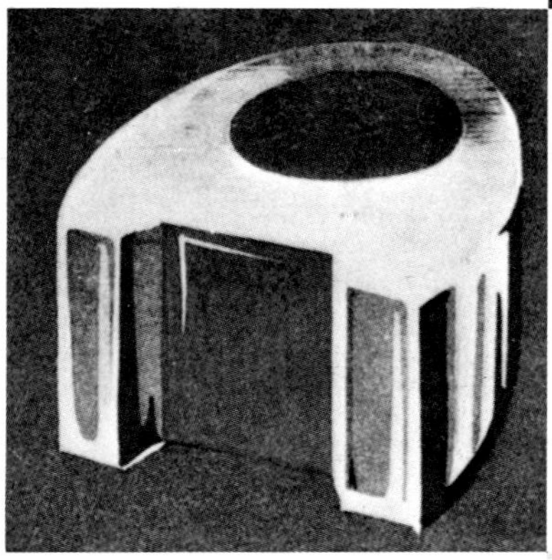

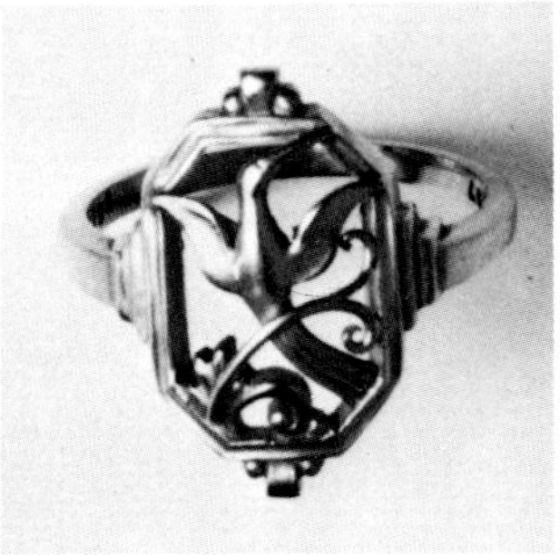

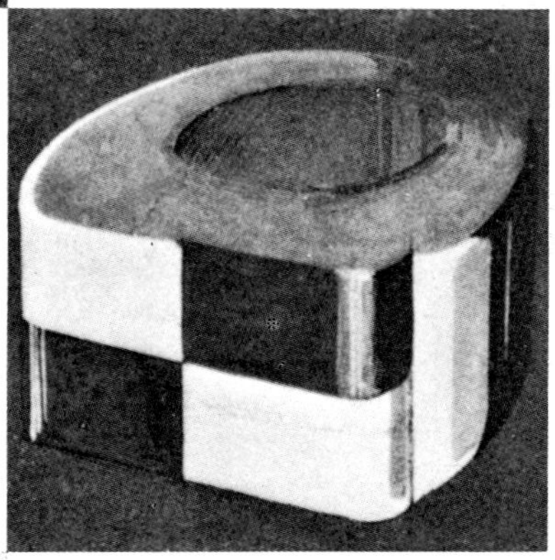

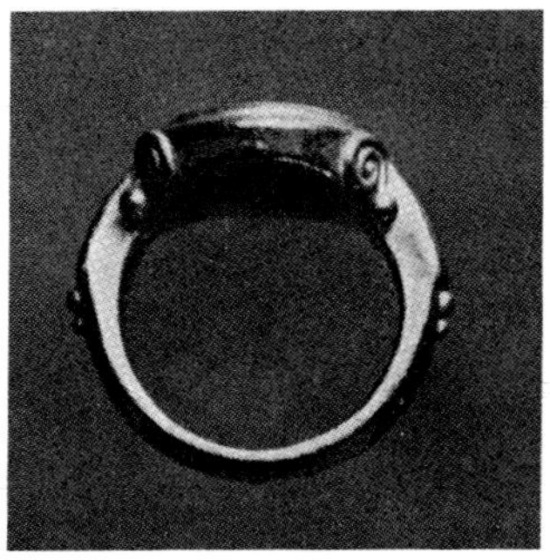

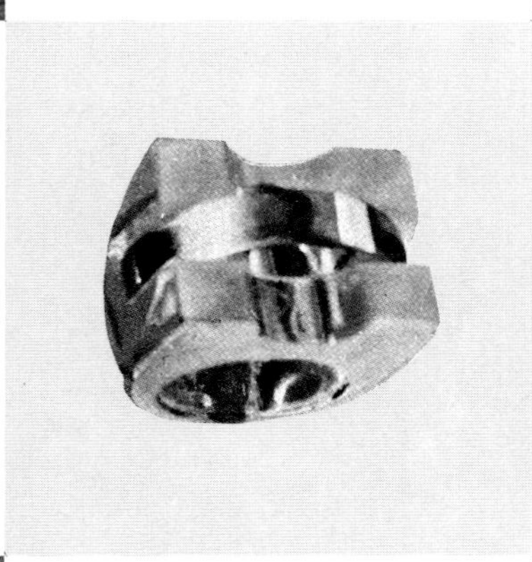

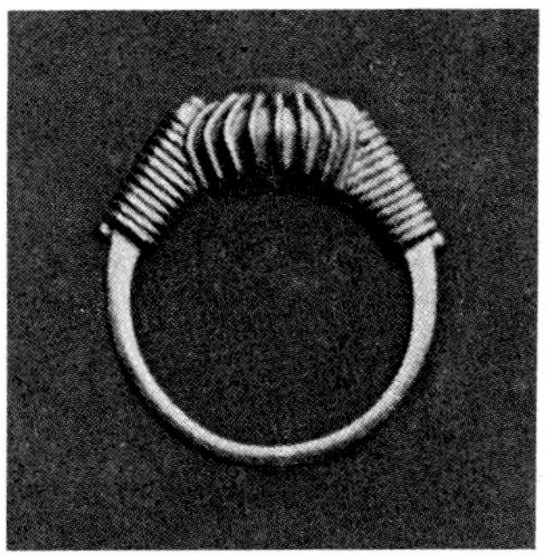

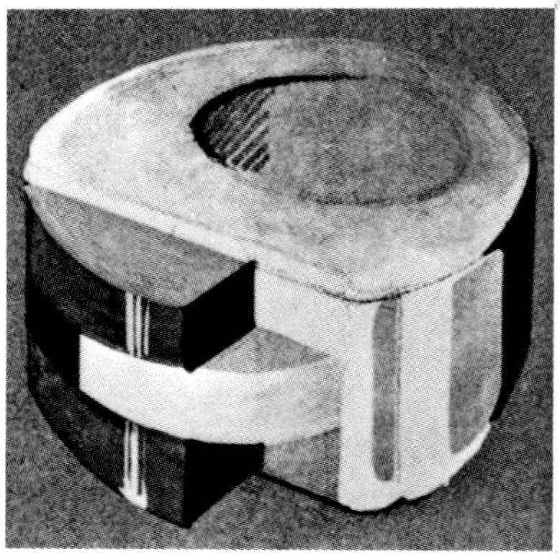

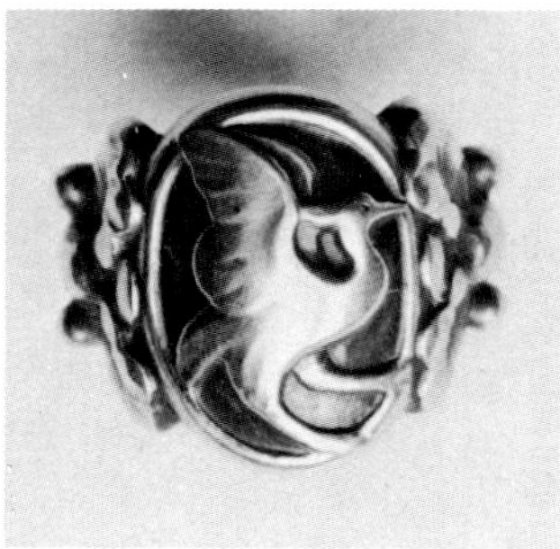

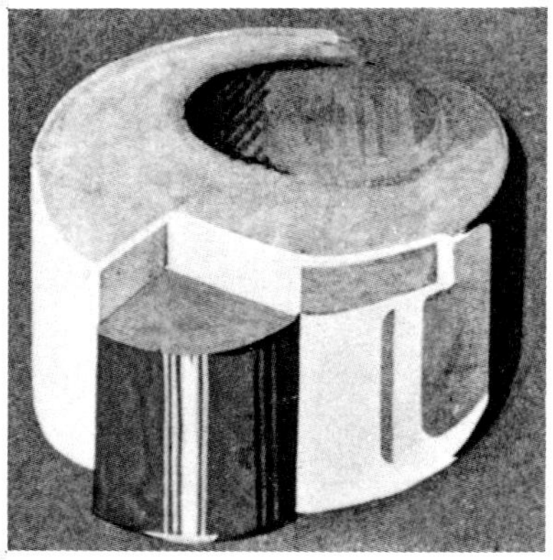

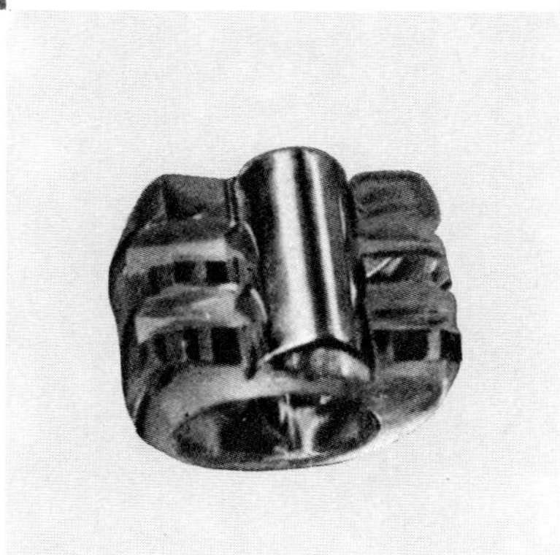

Centre column, second from top to bottom: Georg Jensen: silver ring designed by Gundorph Albertus, 1927. Georg Jensen Archives, Copenhagen.

Paul Brandt: ring in platinum and rock crystal, reproduced in Art et Décoration, *July 1931.*

Georg Jensen: silver ring, c. 1918. Georg Jensen Archives, Copenhagen.

Paul Brandt: platinum and rock crystal ring, reproduced in Art et Décoration, *July 1931.*

Left and right of centre: Charles Rivaud: two rings reproduced in Art et Décoration, *January 1924.*

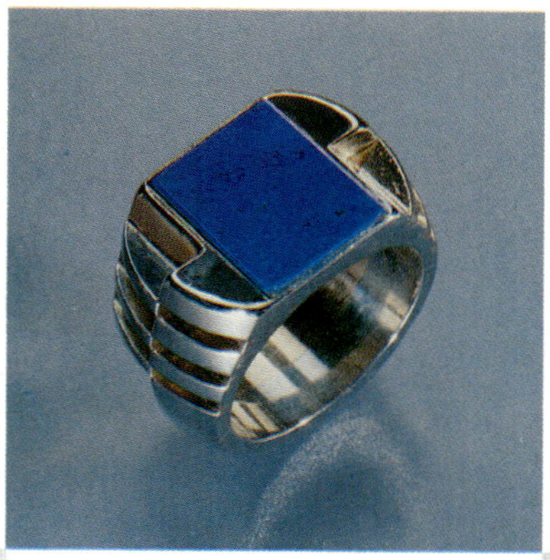

Jean Fouquet: ring in white gold, red gold and lapis, 1928. Private Collection.

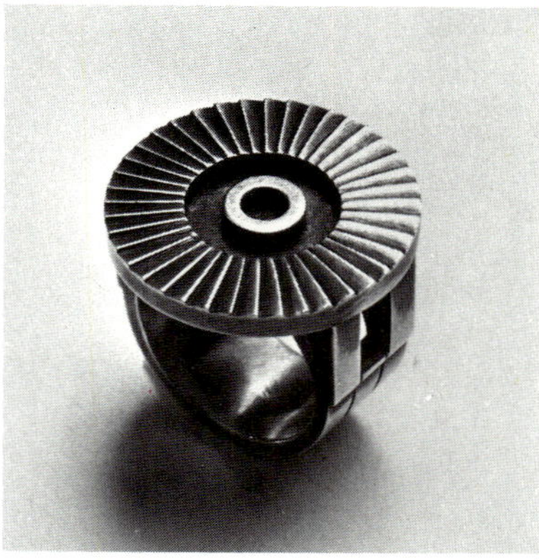

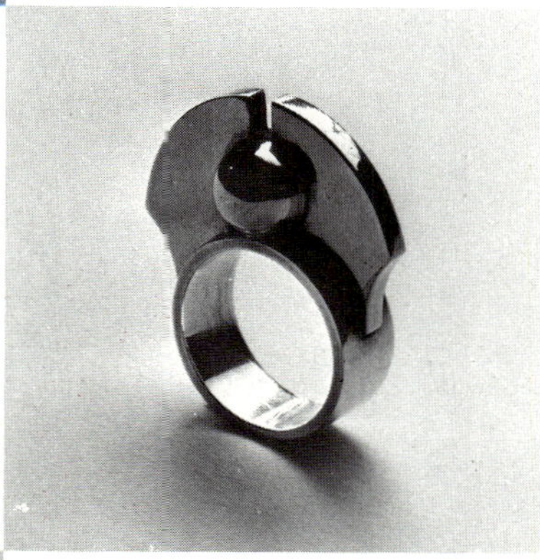

Jean Desprès: ring in silver, gold and lacquer, 1925, signed. Private Collection.

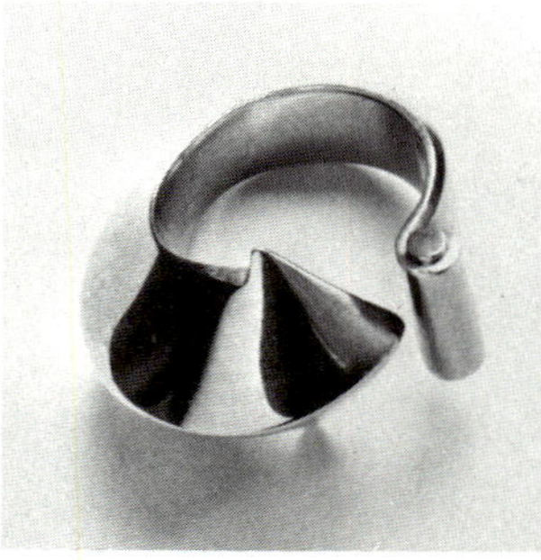

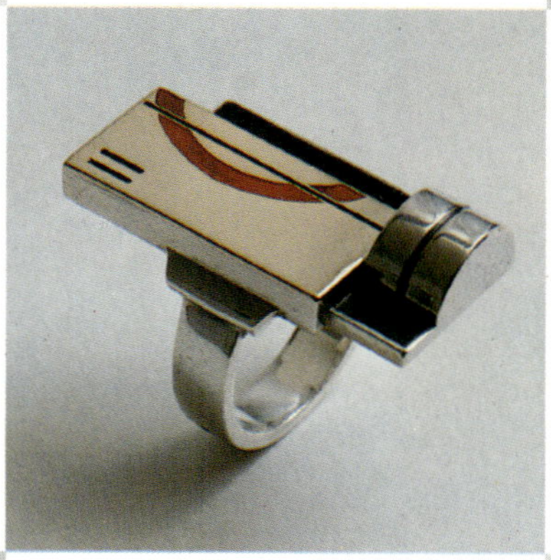

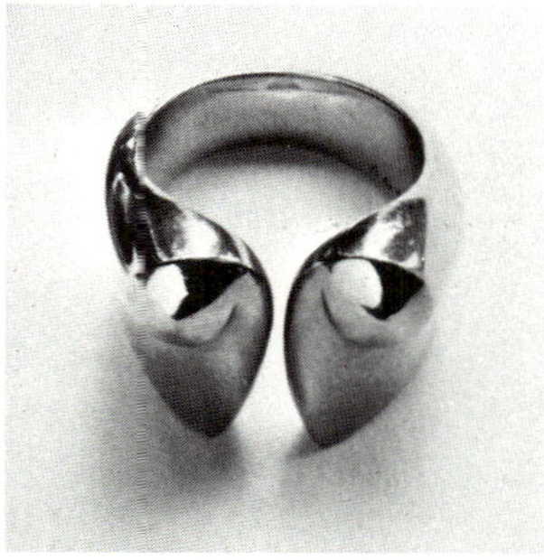

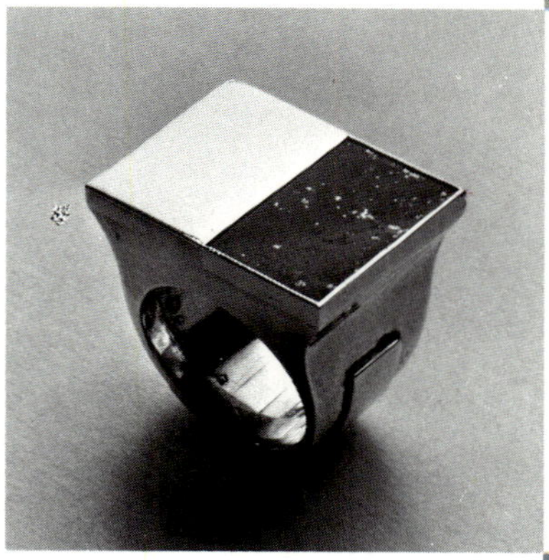

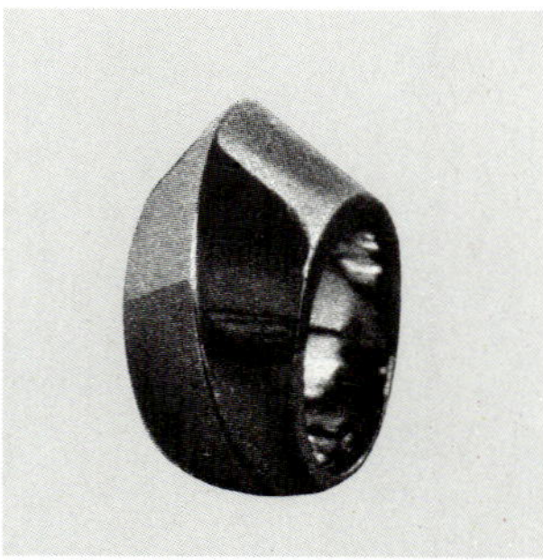

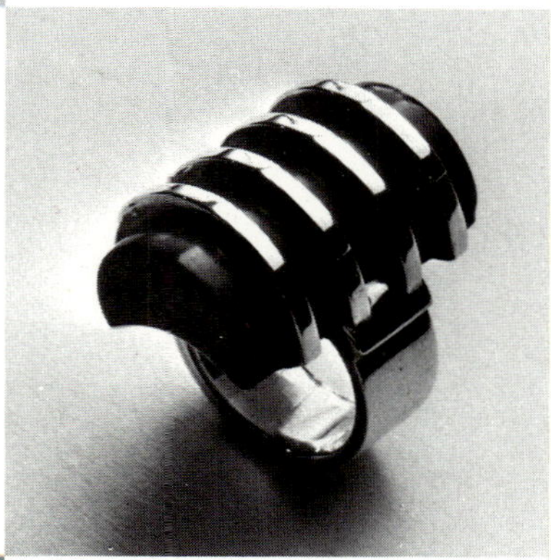

Jean Desprès: silver ring, reproduced in Art et Décoration, *September 1933.*

Raymond Templier: gold ring. A. Lesieutre Collection. Photo: L. Sully-Jaulmes.

Jean Desprès: ring in silver, vermeil *and lapis, signed. Musée des Arts Décoratifs, Paris. Photo: L. Sully-Jaulmes.*

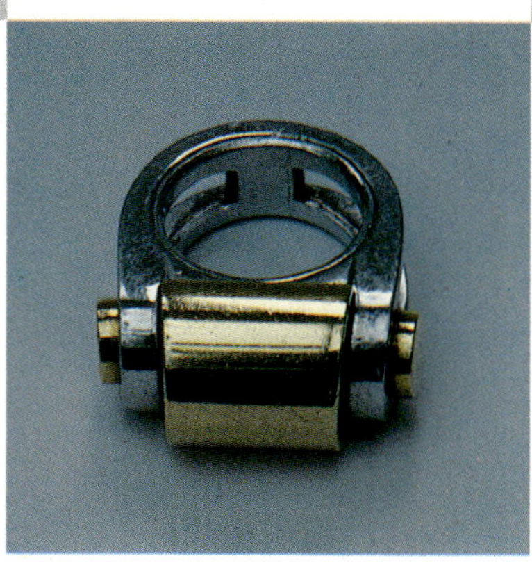

Jean Desprès: ring in silver and vermeil, *signed. Musée des Arts Décoratifs, Paris. Photo: L. Sully-Jaulmes.*

Anonymous: 'modernist' ring in steel and gold, Paris, c. 1925. Jesse & Laski Gallery Collection, London.

Jean Desprès: silver ring c. 1930, signed. Musée des Arts Décoratifs, Paris. Photo: L. Sully-Jaulmes.

Raymond Templier: gold ring. A. Lesieutre Collection. Photo: L. Sully-Jaulmes.

Jean Desprès: ring in silver, vermeil *and blue lacquer, 1934, signed. Musée des Arts Décoratifs, Paris. Photo: L. Sully-Jaulmes.*

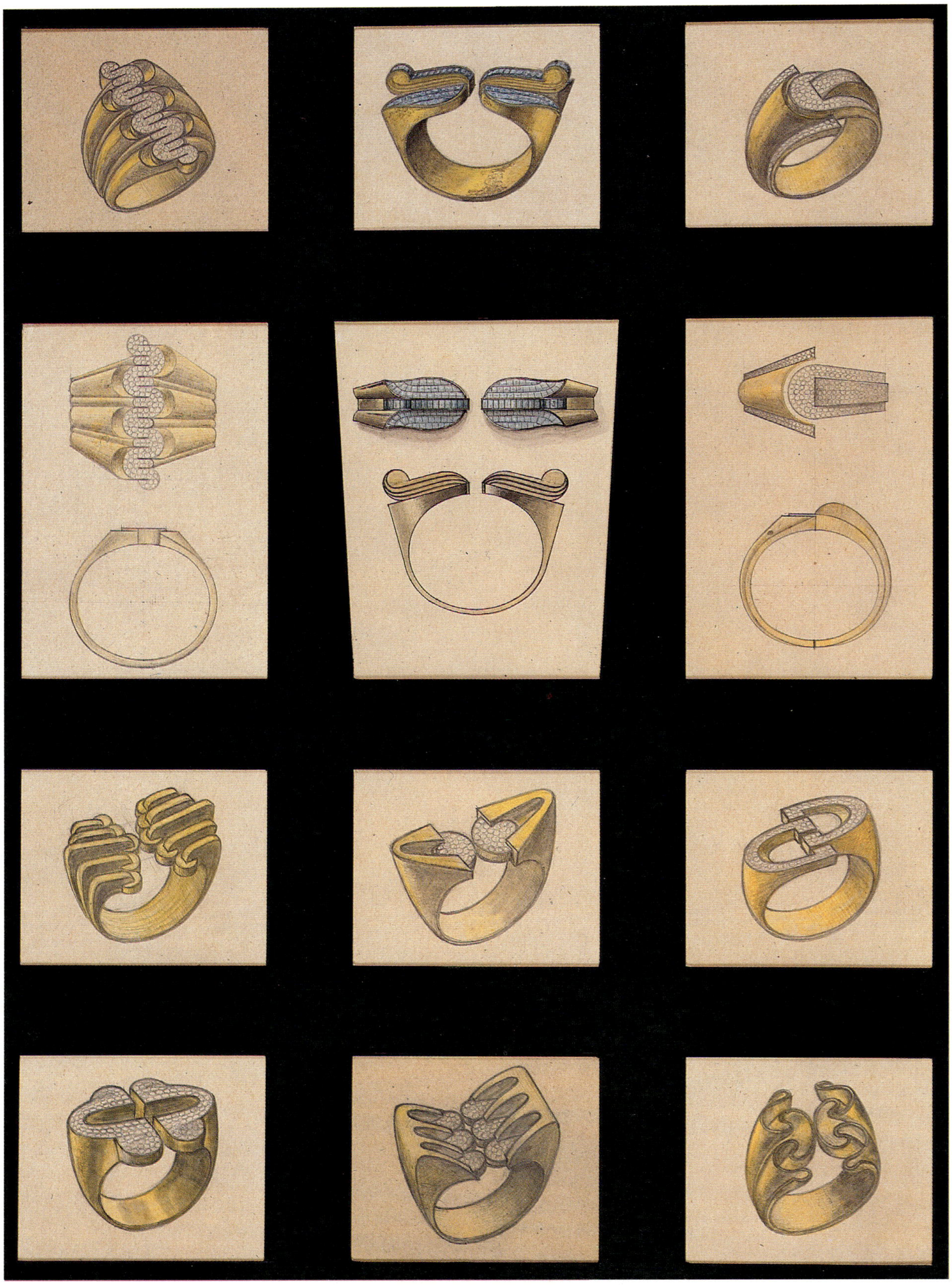

Raymond Templier: plate of designs for rings.
Courtesy of L. and B. Heuer.

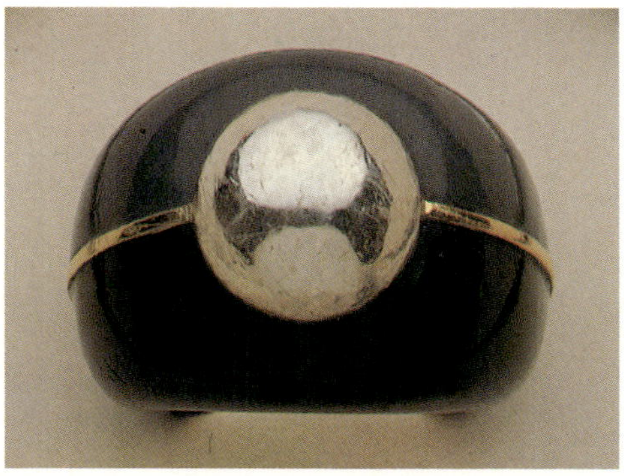

Jean Desprès: ring in gold, black enamel and silver, c. 1925, signed. Primavera Gallery, New York.

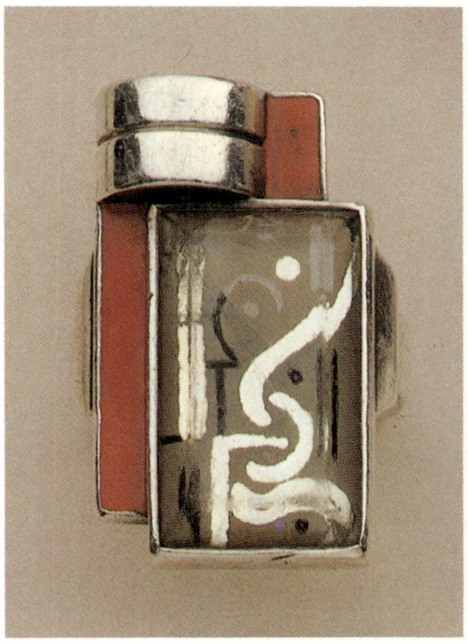

Jean Desprès: ring in red enamel and glass engraved by Etienne Cournault, mounted on silver, c. 1925, signed.

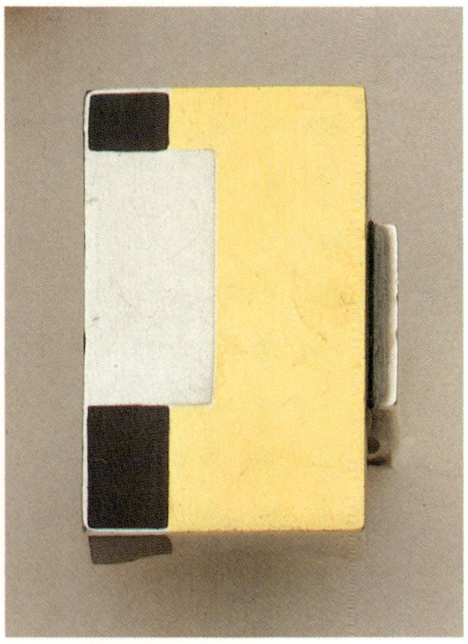

Jean Desprès: ring in grey and black enamel and gold, mounted on silver, c. 1925, signed. Primavera Gallery, New York.

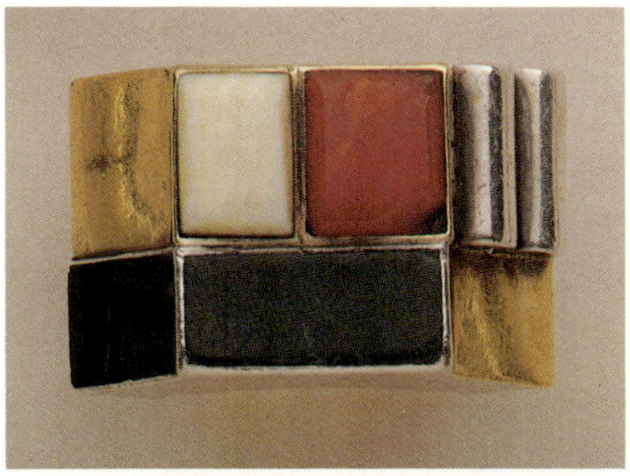

Jean Desprès: ring in coral, ivory, lapis and gold, mounted on silver, c. 1925, signed. Primavera Gallery, New York.

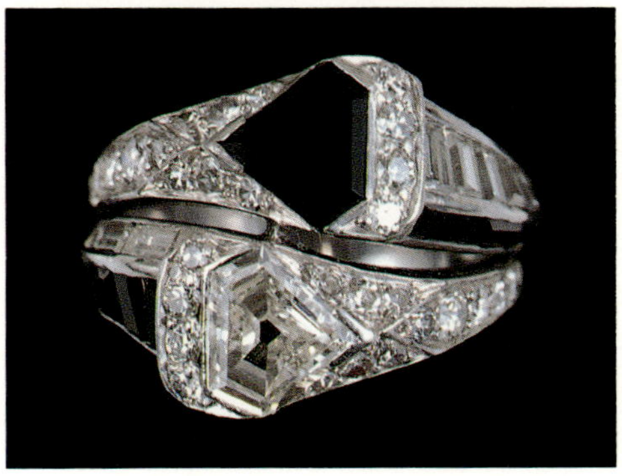

Anonymous: ring in white gold, baguette diamonds and black onyx, c. 1925. Jesse & Laski Gallery Collection.

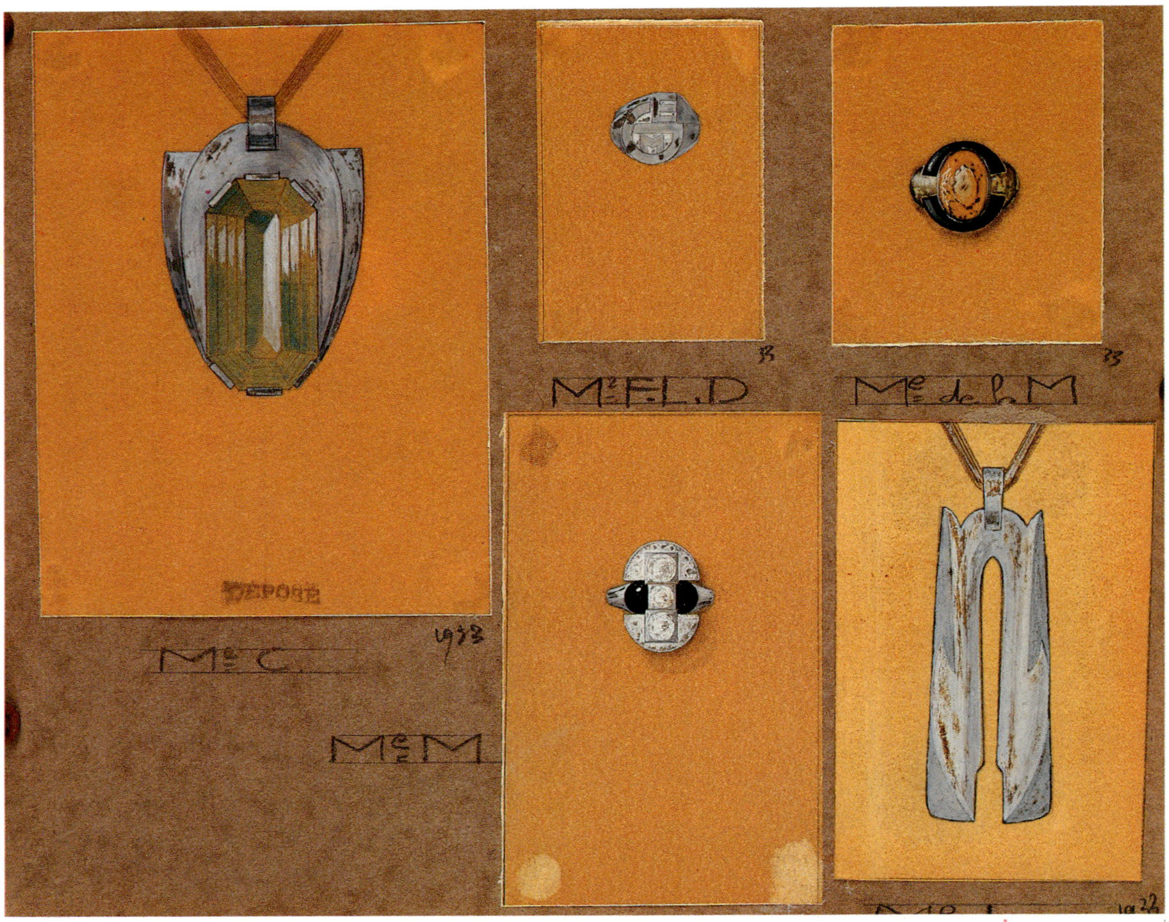

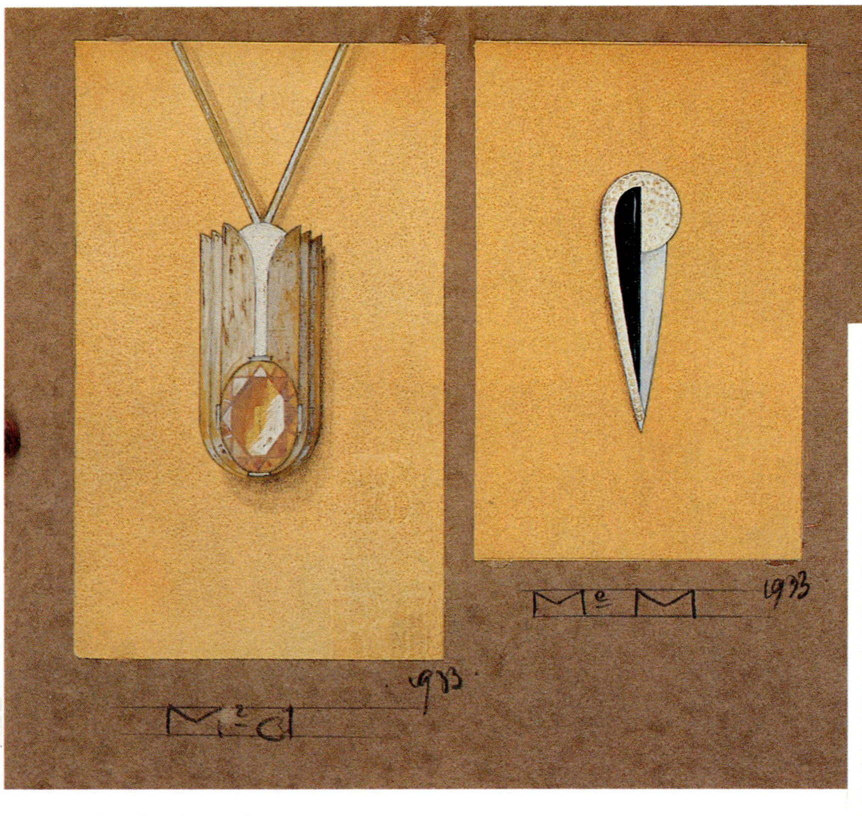

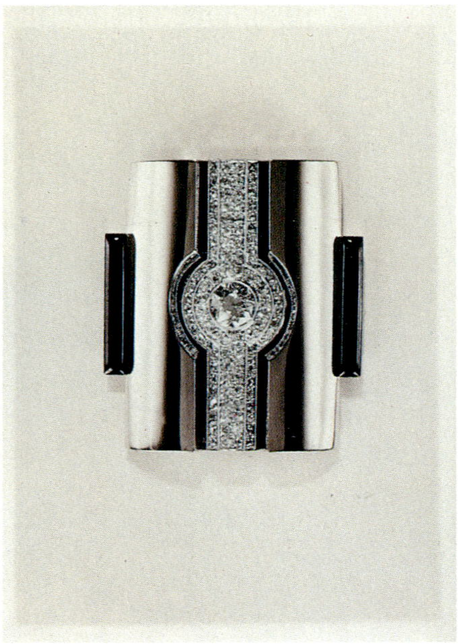

Jewelry designs by Raymond Templier. Courtesy of L. and B. Heuer.

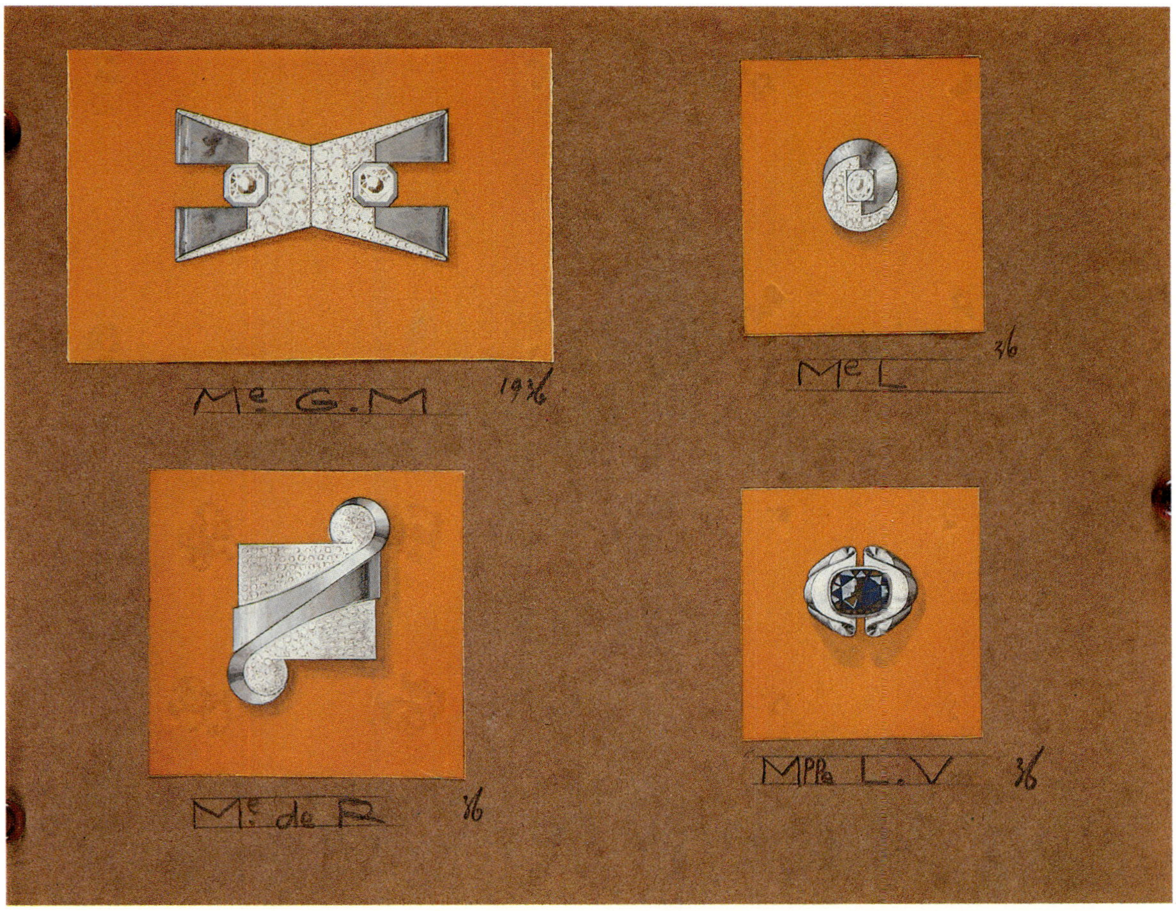

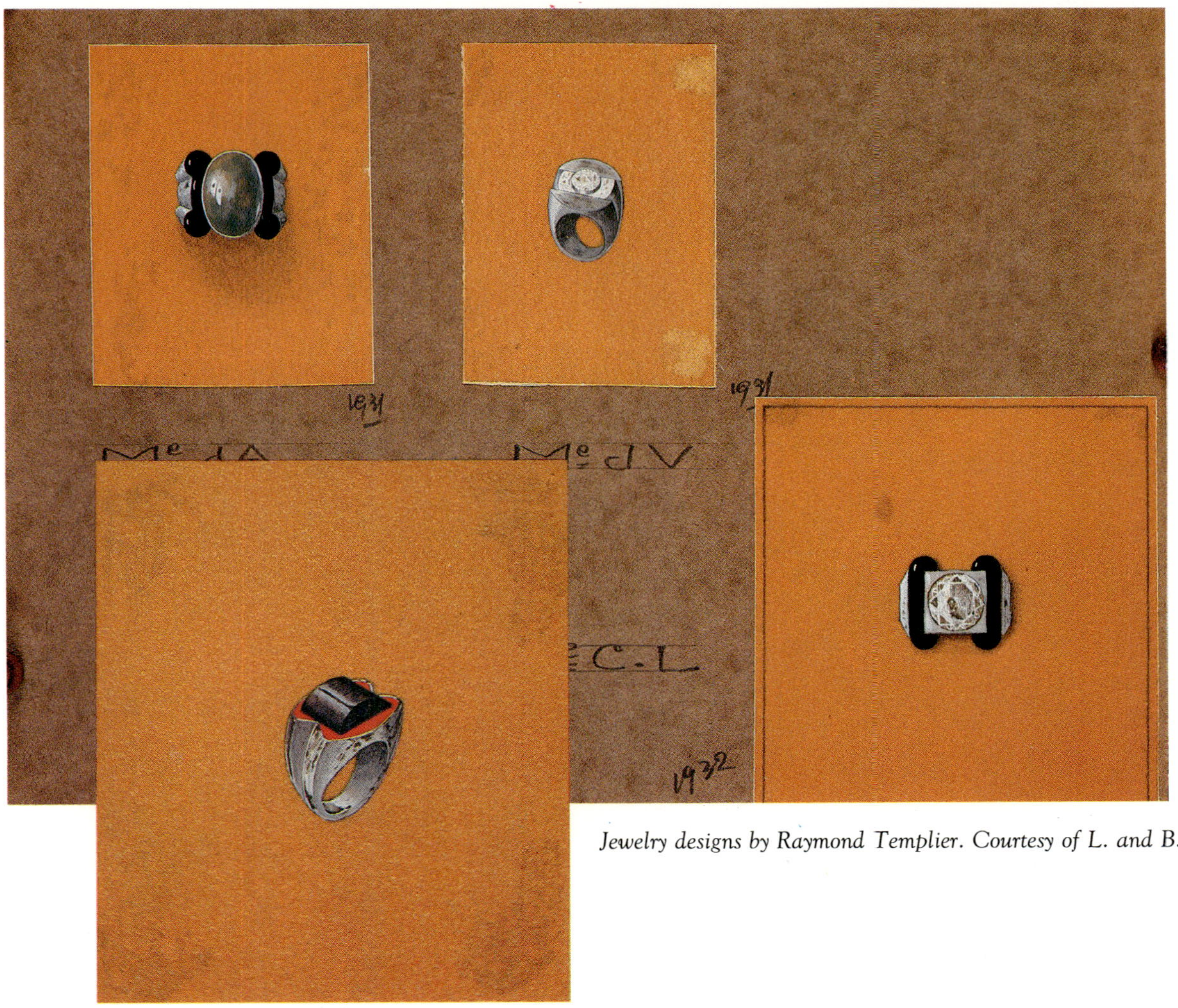

Jewelry designs by Raymond Templier. Courtesy of L. and B. Heuer.

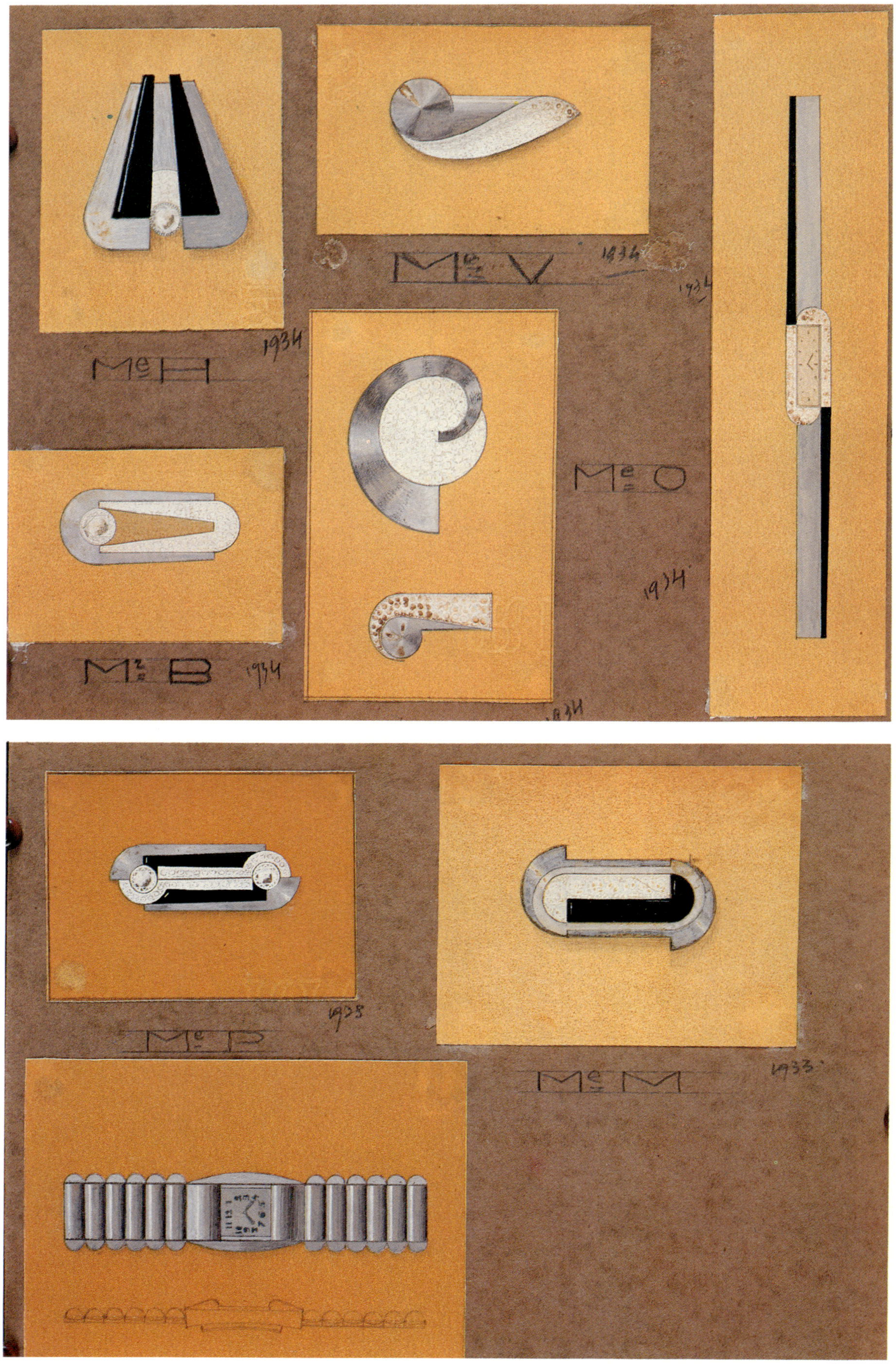

Jewelry designs by Raymond Templier. Courtesy of L. and B. Heuer.

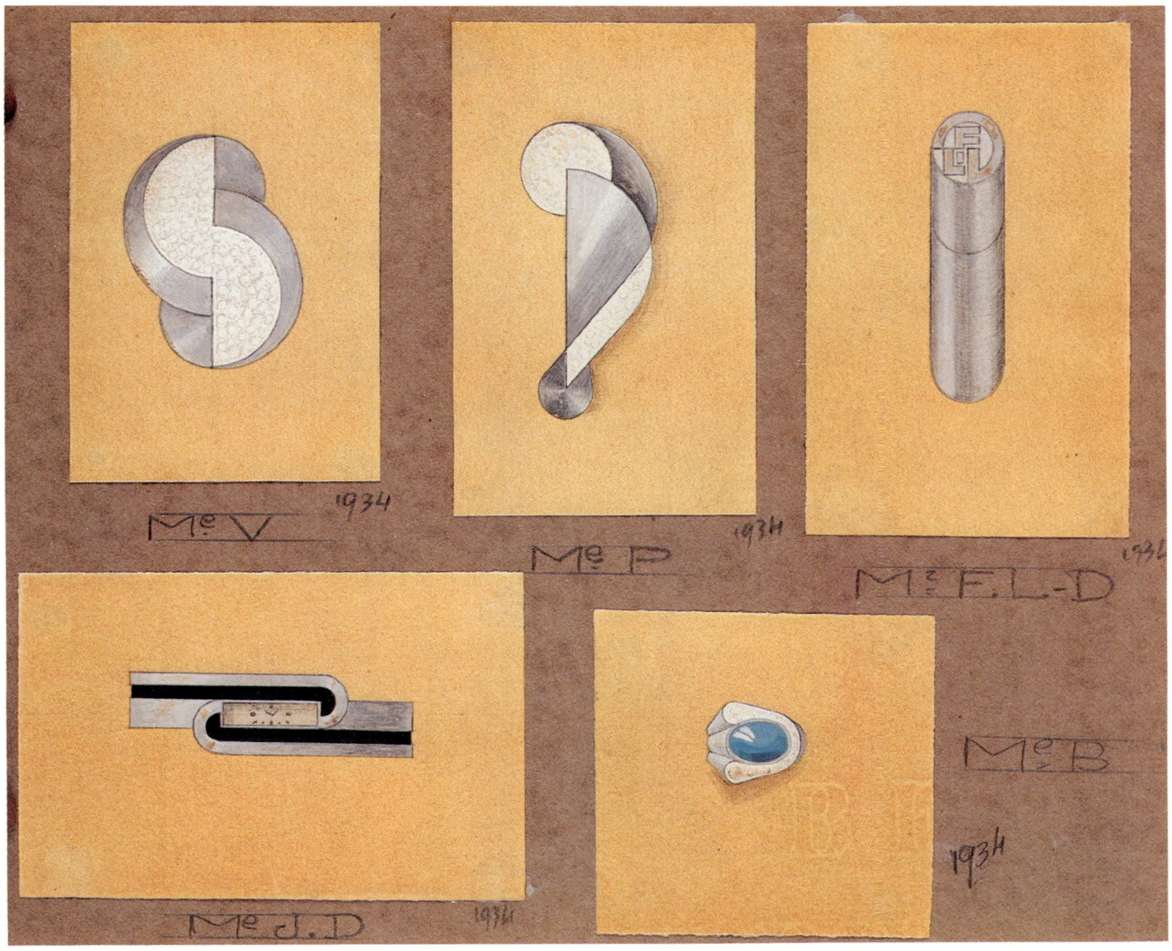

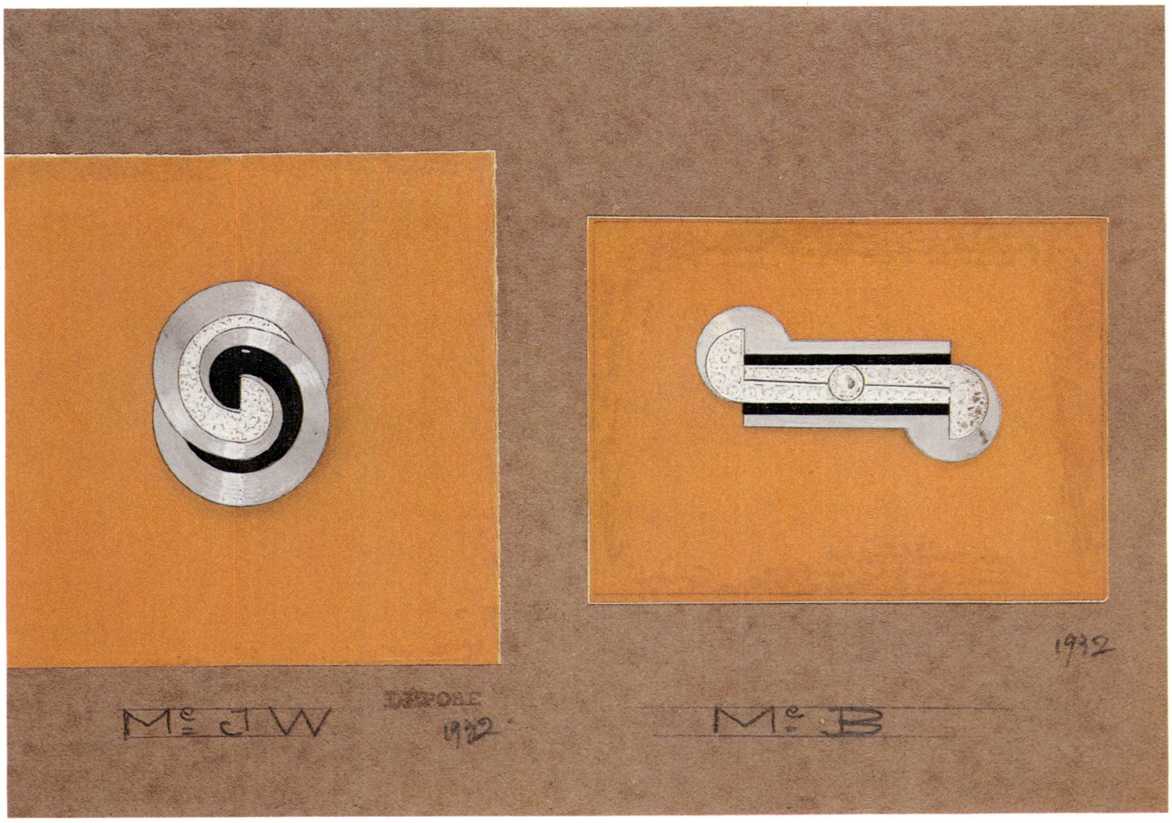

Jewelry designs by Raymond Templier. Courtesy of L. and B. Heuer.

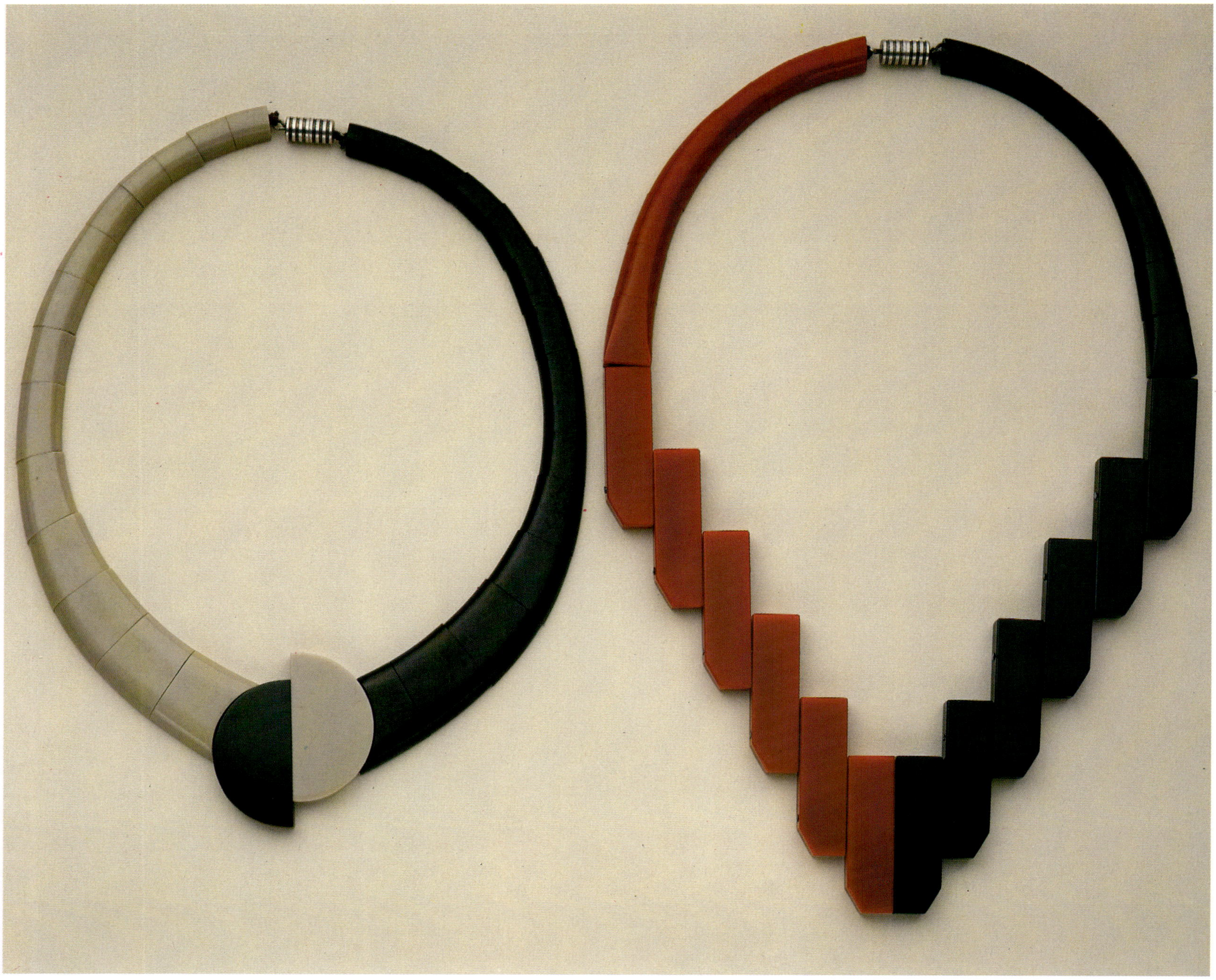

Auguste Bonaz: Galalith necklaces, signed.

COSTUME JEWELRY

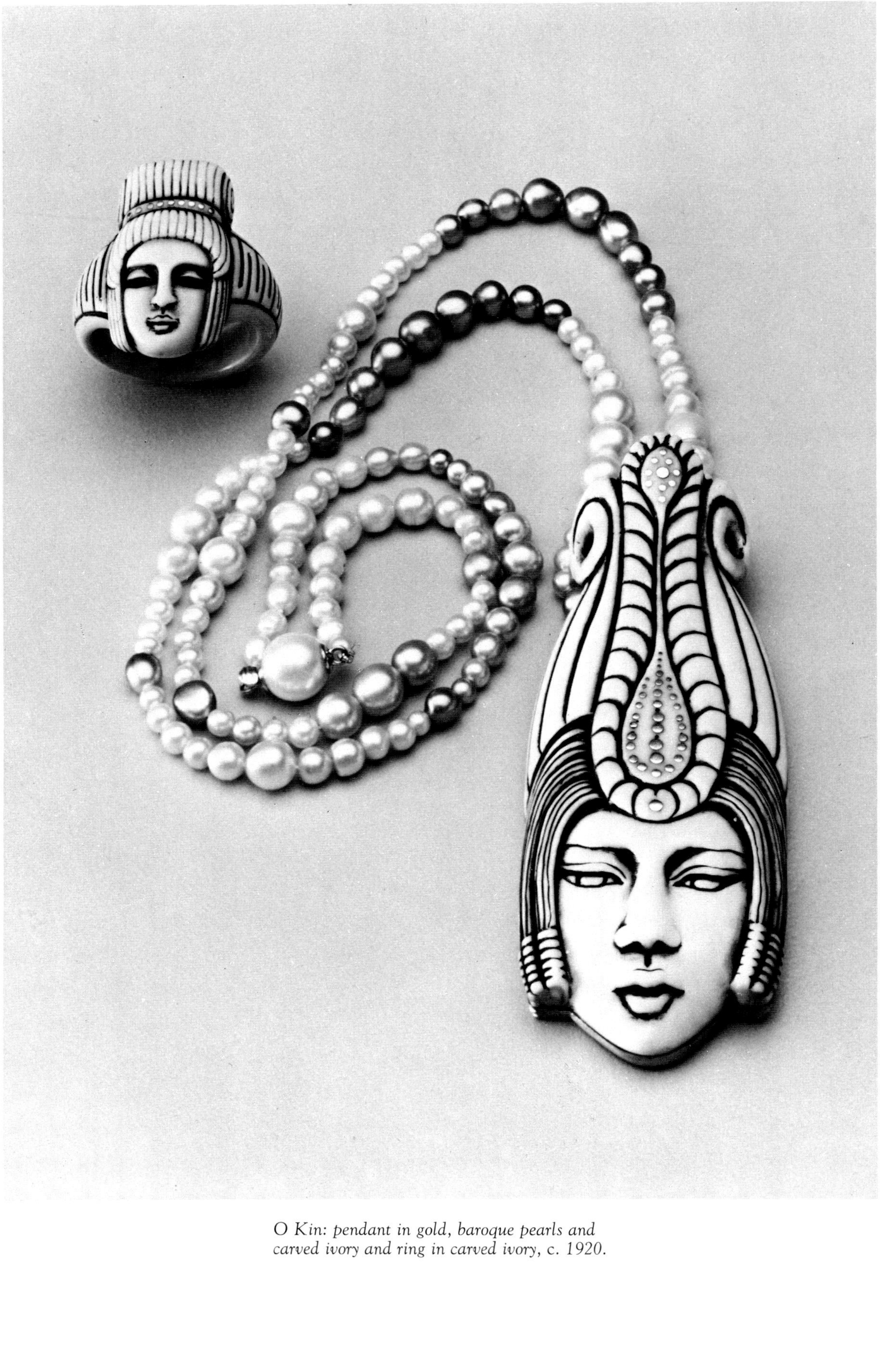

O Kin: pendant in gold, baroque pearls and carved ivory and ring in carved ivory, c. 1920.

IF BIJOUTERIE-JOAILLERIE WENT THROUGH a prosperous period of intense creativity in the Twenties, costume jewelry, too, enjoyed years of great success which time has only served to confirm. In the art of *parure*, costume jewelry constitutes a branch distinct from both *bijouterie* and *joaillerie*.

While practitioners of the latter had the privilege of working in expensive and precious, often rare, materials, costume jewelry was in no way limited with regard to materials. For a long time designated 'imitation jewelry', its role was reduced to that of copying precious pieces of jewelry or simulating jewels. After the war, costume jewelers broke away from this type of work and produced original pieces quite independently, using materials which adapted well to decorative compositions and which were at the same time well within reach of even the most modest purse.

Costume jewelry formed a counterpoint to the *Haute Joaillerie* – which created unique pieces – by reproducing works in large numbers and keeping prices reasonable. Costume jewelry was facilitated by those economic circumstances which had developed mass-production: while unique pieces of jewelry were made to order, after study and discussion with the client, mass-produced pieces spread amongst the public with considerable success. Subject to the caprices of fashion, costume jewelry must seize popular fads as they come if items are to be launched successfully and if every fashion-conscious woman on a limited budget is to be tempted.

Couturiers and modistes swept their clientele along, proposing 'a piece of jewelry for every dress, a piece of jewelry for every hat', and promoted the increasingly popular 'couture jewelry', as it came to be called. Gabrielle Chanel played a pioneering role in this. Bored with the jewelry of the *joailliers*, she decided to have clips, brooches and sets of jewelry designed to her own taste. For her, jewelry had to be ornamental and amusing; she told how 'she willingly covers herself in pieces of jewelry because, on her, they always look false and she likes to put them on just as she would put on a scarf or a pair of stockings.' Jewelry was no longer reserved for gorgeous fabrics, for formal parties and balls; it went well with jerseys, tweeds and pullovers too. In London, Chanel never failed to surprise. She accompanied her day outfits with jewelry in a way that no woman in good society would have dared unless she was wearing a long dress: over a man's waistcoat she wore a cascade of pearls; on a sailor's beret she pinned *pavé*-set gems.

As far as Chanel was concerned, there were no longer places where the wearing of jewelry would be in bad taste; elegant women wore jewelry on the beach and in the sea. Following her example, all the couture houses profited from this vulgarization of jewelry and established a 'couture jewelry' department which was renewed seasonally along with the collections and which opened up new channels for the manufacturers. In November 1932, in her salons in the avenue Gabriel, Chanel and Paul Iribe organized an exhibition of diamond jewelry displayed on old wax mannequins:

tiaras, bracelets and necklaces, a shooting star which wound round the neck and sparkling butterfly bows. In the exhibition brochure Chanel explained her change of tack which had taken both the press and the public by surprise: 'the reason which led me initially to devise costume jewelry was that I found it free from arrogance in an age when ostentation was all too easy. But this consideration disappears in a period of financial crisis when an instinctive desire emerges again for authenticity in everything, thus restoring an amusing piece of paste jewelry to its true level.' But this exhibition was a luxurious interlude and the name of Gabrielle Chanel was always to remain linked with costume jewelry and trinkets.

The International Exposition of 1925 marked an important stage in the conquest of an ever-widening clientele. The manufacturers were so numerous that it was not possible to group all of them round the *Haute Joaillerie* and the visitor to the exhibition came across them in the temples of elegance, in the 'Clothing Accessories' section, in 'Fashion' or amongst the *Matières Plastiques* (plastic materials). It is impossible to list them all but the names of some appeared regularly in the press reviews and advertisements. Barboteaux exhibited *cloisonné* enamel jewelry; Miault jewelry in silver and beaten and enamelled copper; Truffier buckles and clasps for coats in silver or in *vermeil* with motifs of stylized flowers; Lespous et Parisien brooches in patinated silver set with imitation diamonds; Sasportas bracelets in enamelled gold set with engraved cornelian. Maréchal, Persianinoff, Galand, Chaumier, Schneider,

Fourrier and Le Moult should also be mentioned in passing.

At Piel's *Bijoux de fantaisie pour couture et mode* (costume jewelry for couture and fashion), models were created for the great couture houses in close collaboration with the fashion stylists: narrow belts composed of cabochons of engraved and patinated glass; clasps; buttons; necklaces of coloured pearls, amber or cornelian; buckles with motifs in *cloisonné* enamel for Patou, one of Piel's principal clients. A collection like the Greidenberg one displayed the most direct expression of the influence of Cubist art: here were buckles made in three colours of metal – silvered, gilded, oxydized – and composed of two structured sections from which emerged geometric designs in light relief. The more modest Bakelite jewelry of Auguste Bonaz was created according to the same criteria and played also on the contrast between simple, angular forms and the juxtaposition of clear colours: black/red and black/green. Bastard worked in ivory, marbled shell, mother-of-pearl, jade and coral and in 1922 Paul Bablet started producing multiples of jewelry in silver, gold, ivory and coral. It is worth noting that the materials used were not always of the cheapest kind and that the range within costume jewelry is very wide. The term refers primarily to the mass-production of a piece of jewelry which has been designed by an artist. Volumes would have to be written to list all the materials which the designers had at their disposal. In addition to natural materials such as amber, ivory, shell, mother-of-pearl, wood, coral, shagreen and jade, there were materials that had recently been discovered by chemists:

Rhodoid, Bakelite, synthetic stones, Galalith, imitation pearls, not to mention glass and crystal. The inexpensiveness of the material in no way excluded aesthetic value; as the UAM's manifesto put it: 'a beautiful material is not necessarily rare or precious. It is above all a material whose natural qualities or whose adaptability to industrial processes are pleasing to the eye and to the touch, and whose value derives from judicious use.'

In October 1930, the Chambre Syndicale inaugurated an 'Exposition de la Bijouterie de Fantaisie' in the salons of the Hôtel Moderne and every year, for a week at the beginning of Autumn, about sixty Maisons invited the public to judge their latest creations. The spread of costume jewelry to other countries was one of the most obvious signs of the vitality and quality of the French products. At

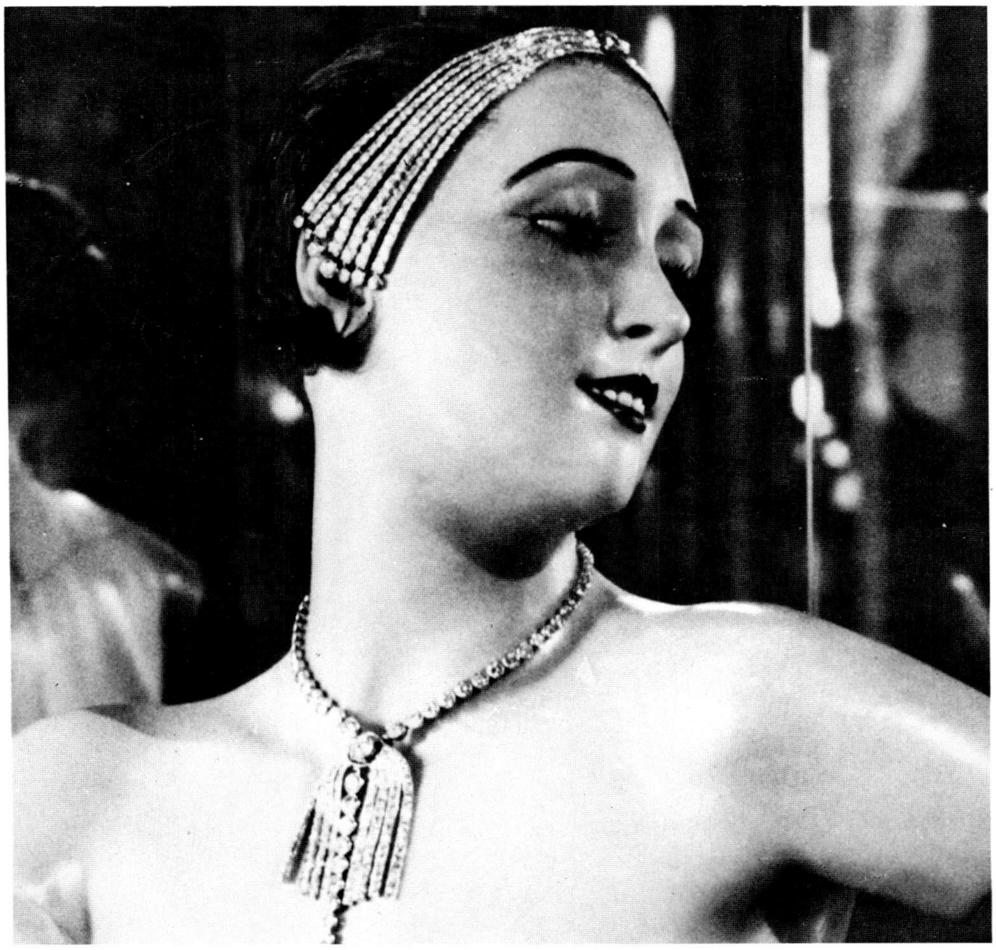

Mannequin wearing jewelry by Chanel from designs by Iribe, 1932. Photo: R. Viollet.

the time of the 'Exposition Coloniale' which was held in Paris in 1931, the decline in copies or imitations of the jewelry of the *Haute Joaillerie* confirmed the success and originality of costume jewelry. Artists and manufacturers, following the Exposition's theme, reproduced and adapted various forms of exotic jewelry, spiced with 'a hint of savagery', whose success was ensured by the fashionable women who wore them.

The economic difficulties and international stagnation into which the Thirties were plunged helped the development of costume jewelry: 'a woman always wants to make herself noticed through exterior signs and if she has to restrain expenditure on luxuries, she will seek out less expensive jewelry. This is, actually, in our opinion, the era of costume jewelry.' (Pierre Contreau, 1932).

These pieces of jewelry, by virtue of their artistic merit, exercised a real influence on public taste and consequently on the attitudes of manufacturers. The market for costume jewelry expanded to such an extent that craftsmen could no longer meet its needs and industry had to take over. If some saw in this the mediocrity of present times, the democratization of jewelry – for a long time the exclusive prerogative of the monied classes – fulfilled the aims of the UAM, who declared in their manifesto that: 'Modern art is a truly social art, a pure art which everyone can enjoy.'

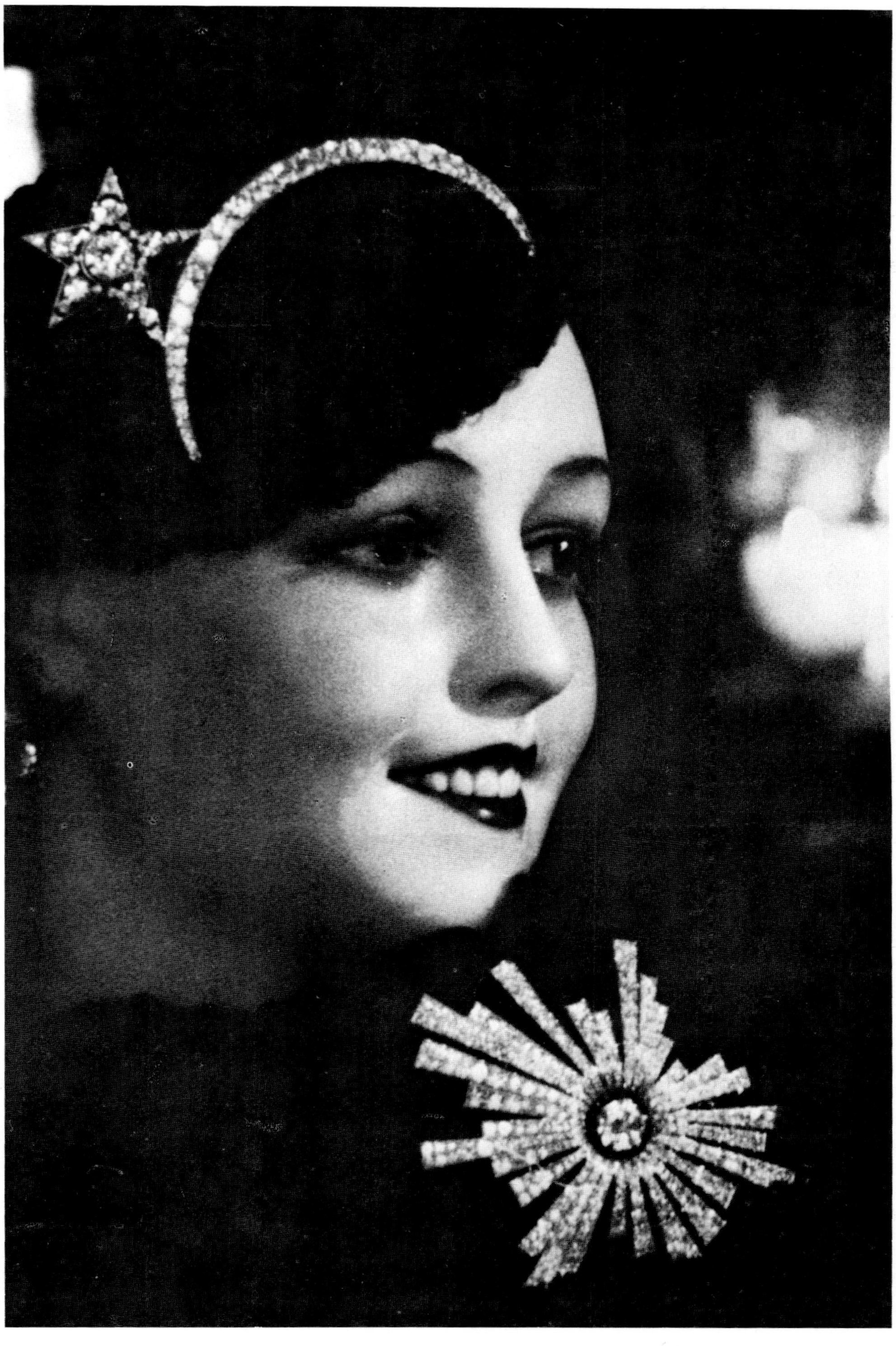

Mannequin wearing jewelry by Chanel from designs by Iribe, 1932. Photo: R. Viollet.

Following pages: Theodor Fahrner: necklace in citrine, marcasite and silver; bracelet and brooch in chalcedony, frosted rock crystal, amazonite and marcasite; rose quartz plaque at the centre of the brooch, signed.

Chanel: clips and ring in emeralds, rubies and gold, c. 1935, signed. Primavera Gallery, New York.

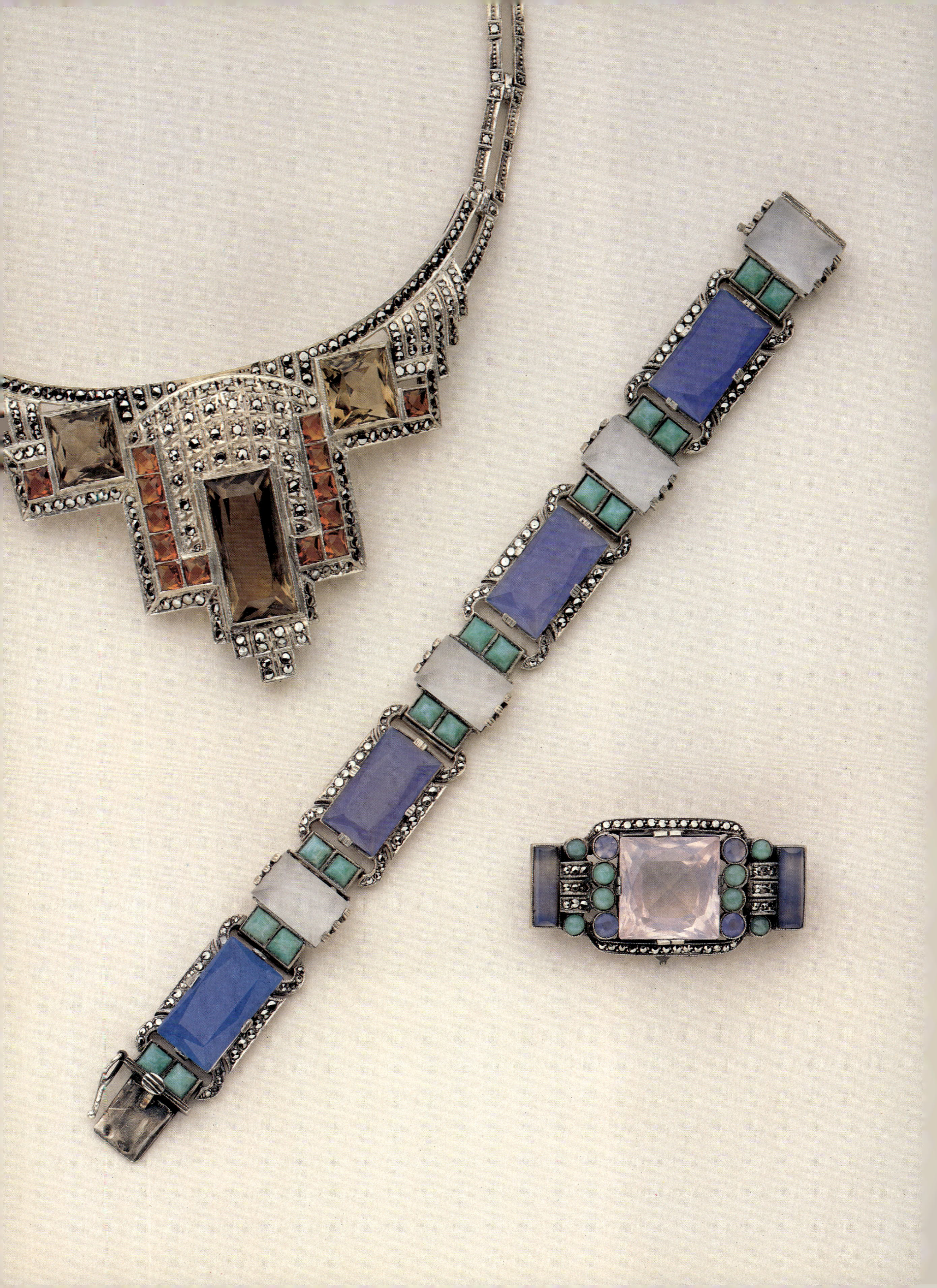

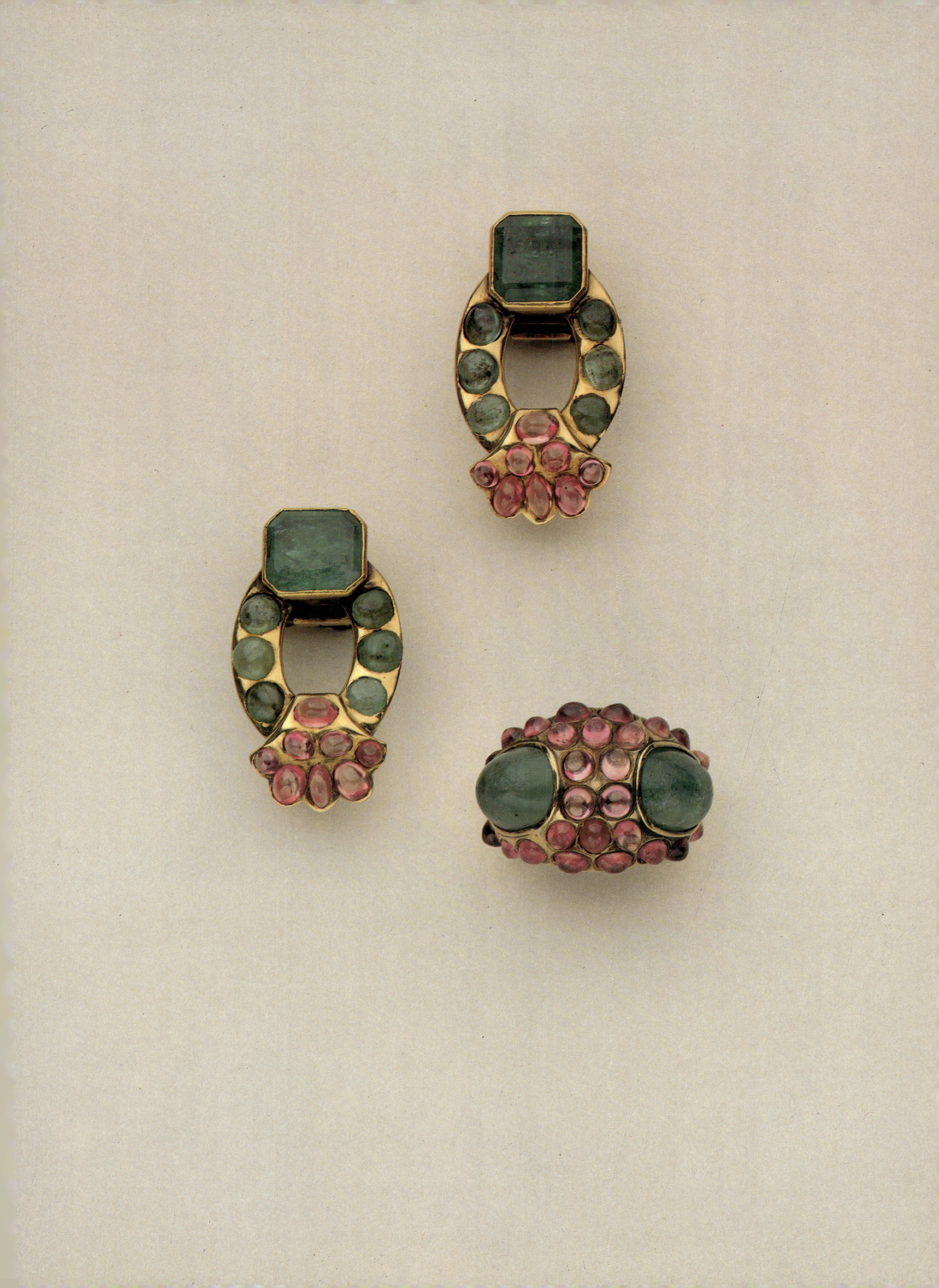

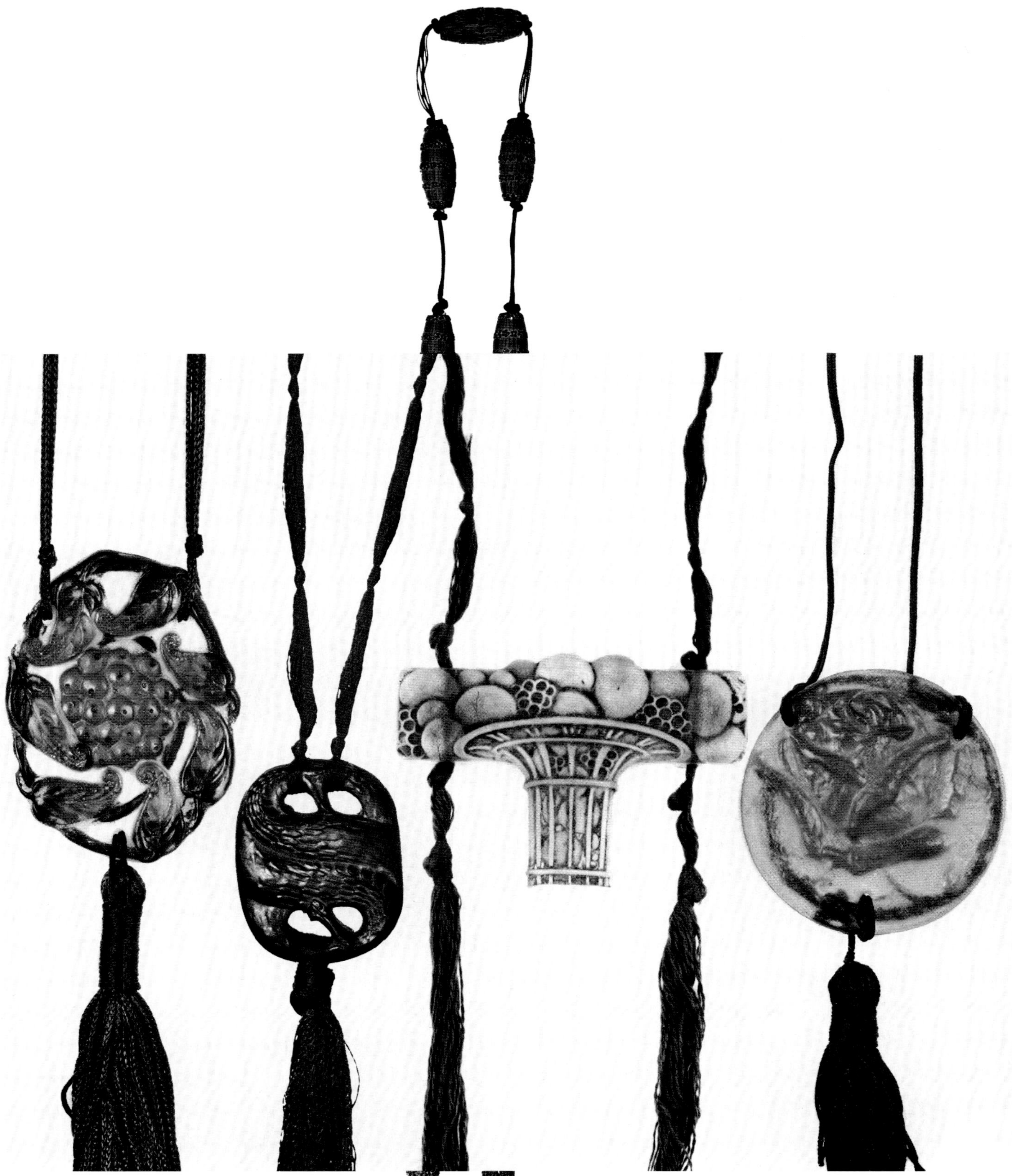
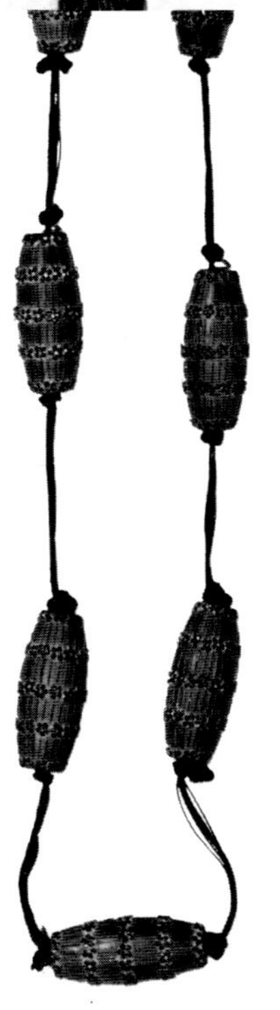

Left to right: Argy-Rousseau: white oval pâte de verre pendant with a design of red berries surrounded by green leaves and brown stems moulded in shallow relief, c. 1925, *monogrammed. Sotheby's,* Monte Carlo.

Lalique: pâte de verre sautoir *with a silk tassel,* c. 1925. *Lalique Archives.*

Lalique: glass pendant depicting a basket of fruit, with green silk cord, c. 1925, *signed. Sotheby's,* Monte Carlo.

Argy-Rousseau: circular pâte de verre pendant with a design of a dark-orange rose, moulded in shallow relief, on a colourless ground, monogrammed. Sotheby's.

Behind: Lalique: sautoir *of pâte de verre cylinders encrusted with floral motifs and attached together by a silk cord. Lalique Archives.*

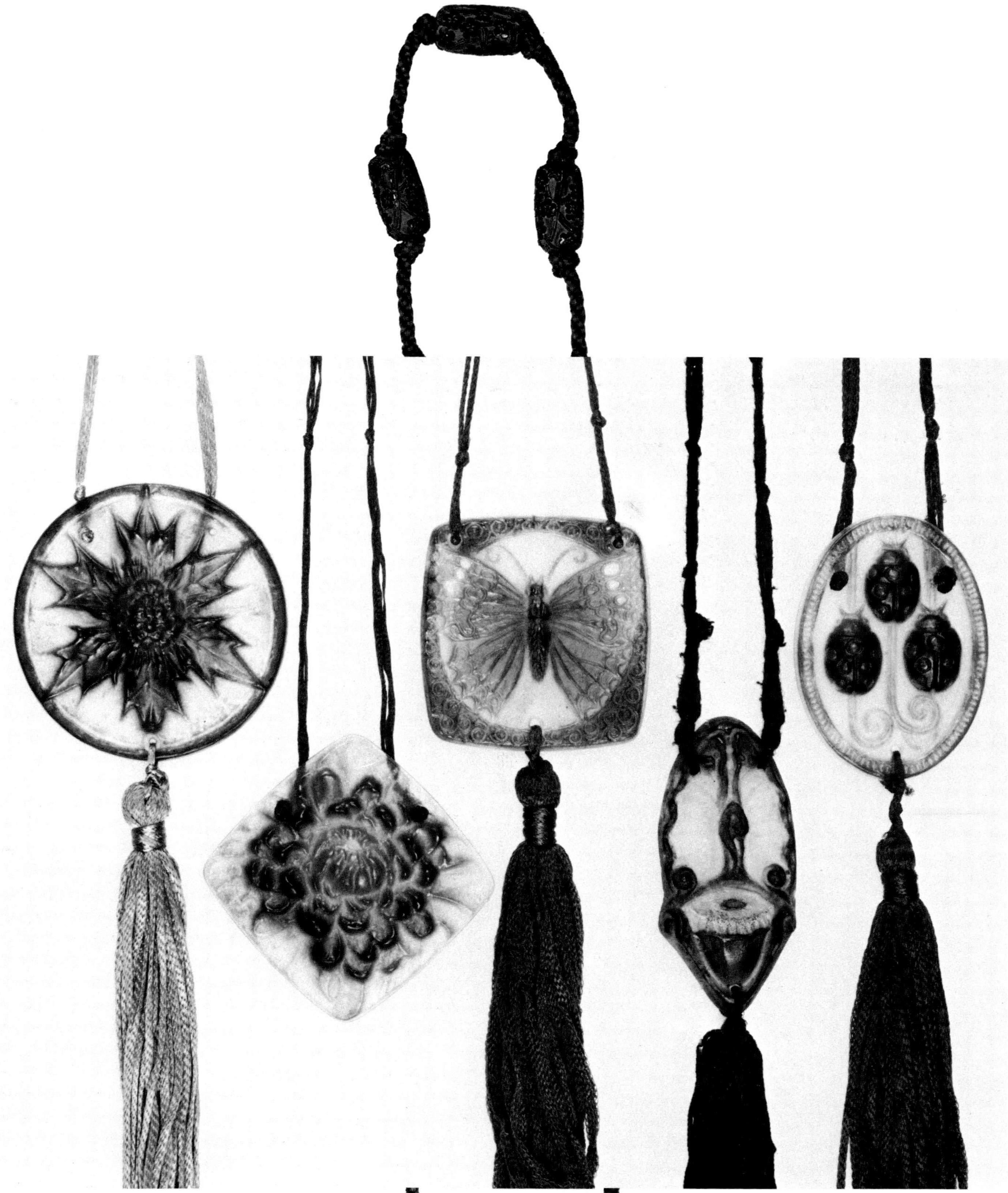

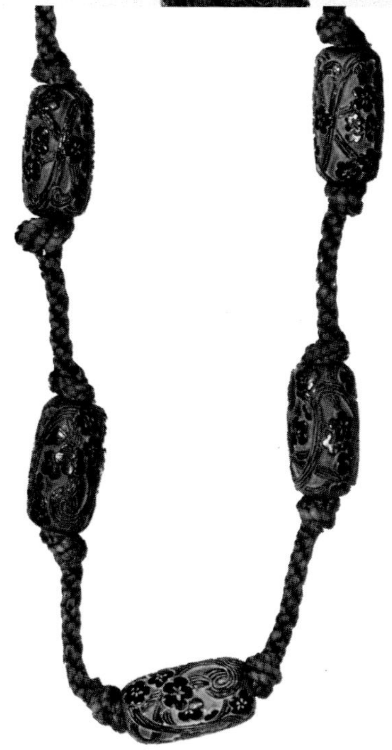

Left to right: Argy-Rousseau: *circular pendant in pâte de cristal with a thistle design in blue, red and green on a colourless ground, c. 1925. Sotheby's, Monte Carlo.*

Argy-Rousseau: pendant with a flower design in mauve and purple c. 1925. Sotheby's, Monte Carlo.

Argy-Rousseau: pendant in pâte de cristal with a design of a red and orange butterfly with white spots, black border, c. 1925. Sotheby's, Monte Carlo.

Anonymous: pâte de verre pendant with a design of flowers and stems, c. 1925. Sotheby's, Monte Carlo.

Argy-Rousseau: pendant in pâte de cristal depicting three black insects with green spots, c. 1925. Sotheby's, Monte Carlo.

Behind: Lalique: sautoir *composed of pâte de verre cylinders, encrusted with floral motifs, on a silk cord. Lalique Archives.*

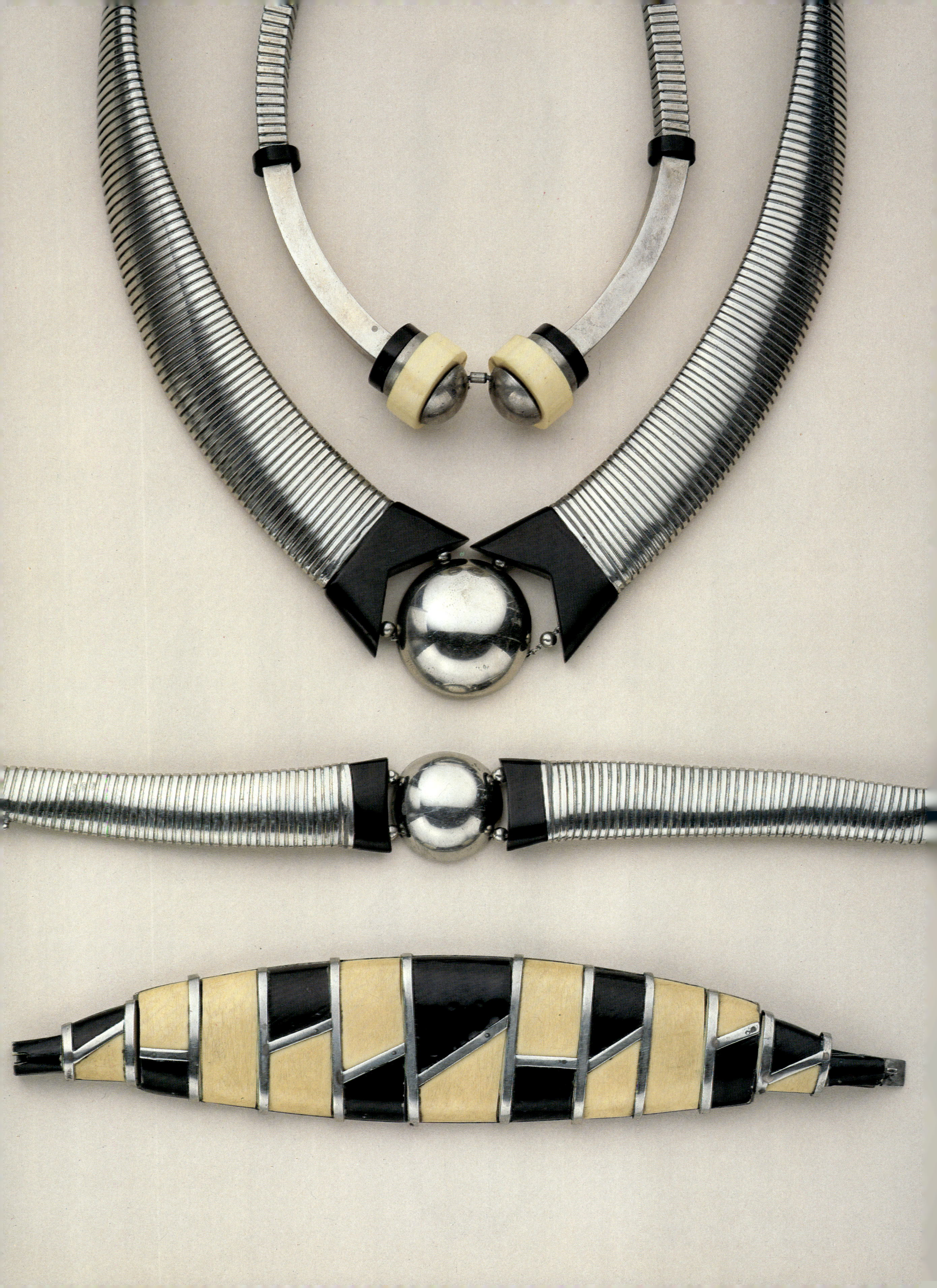

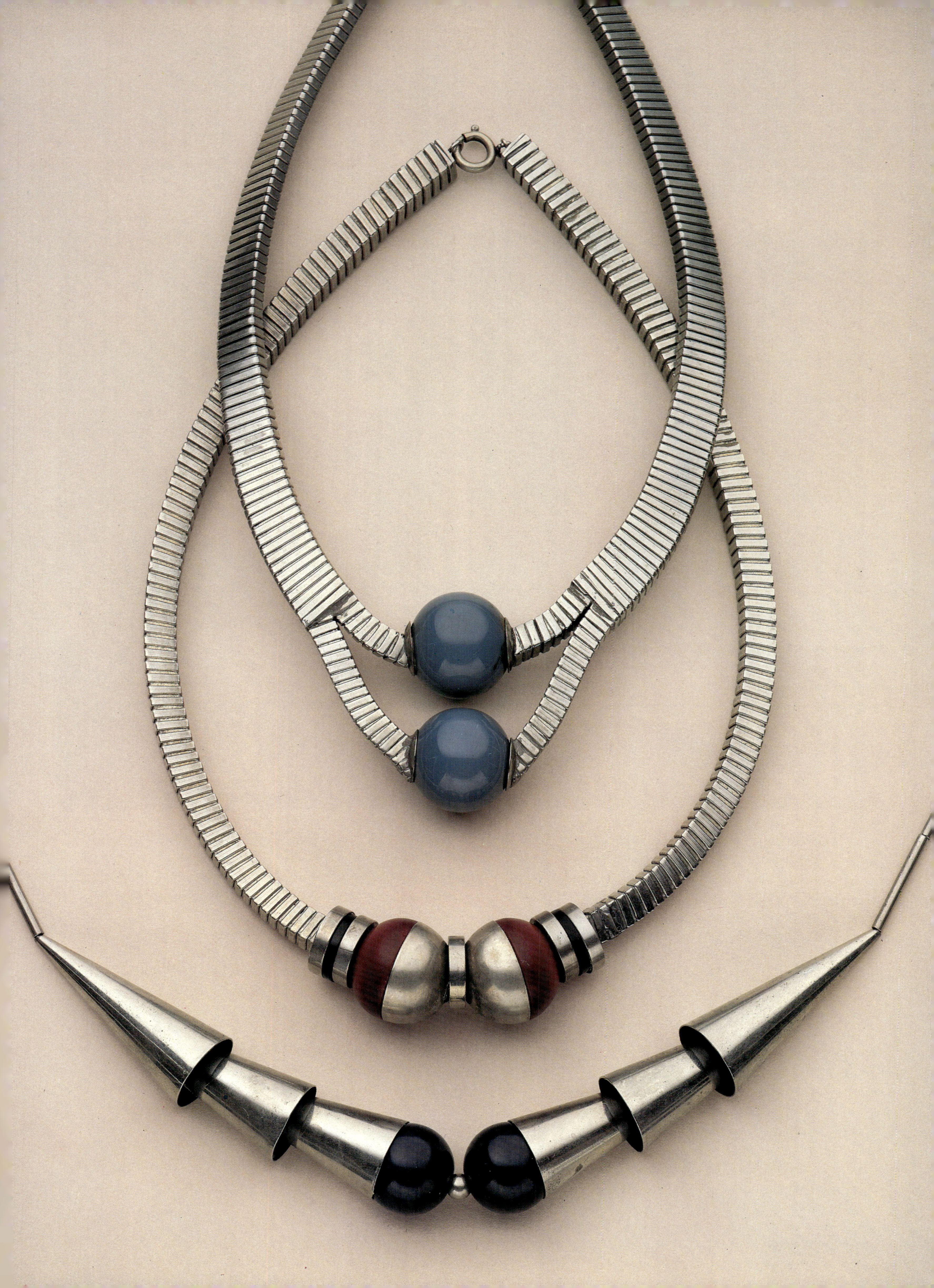

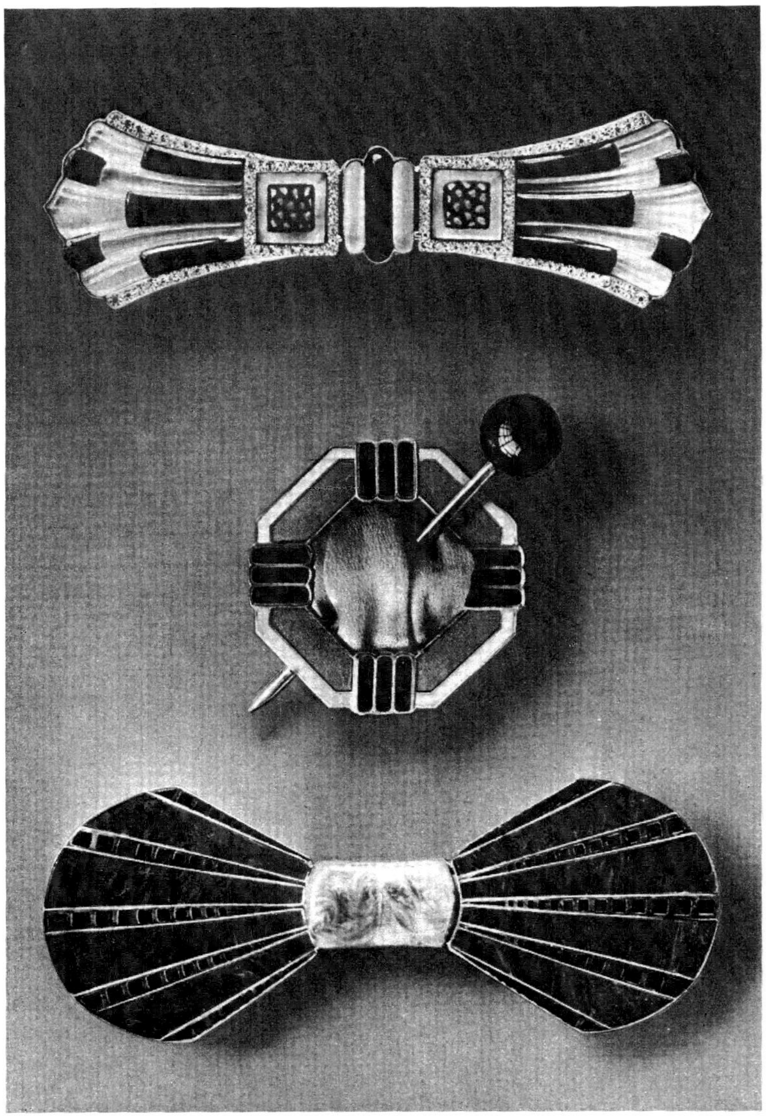

Paul Piel et Fils: clasp for a dress in silvered metal with rock crystal and black onyx cabochons, set with imitation diamonds, presented at the 1925 Paris Exposition.

Paul Piel et Fils: hat fastening in white metal enamelled blue and black, the pin decorated with a black onyx bead, presented at the 1925 Paris Exposition.

Paul Piel at Fils: clasp for a coat, enamelled black with raised lines of green nacrolacquer and decorated with a jade cabochon, presented at the 1925 Paris Exposition.

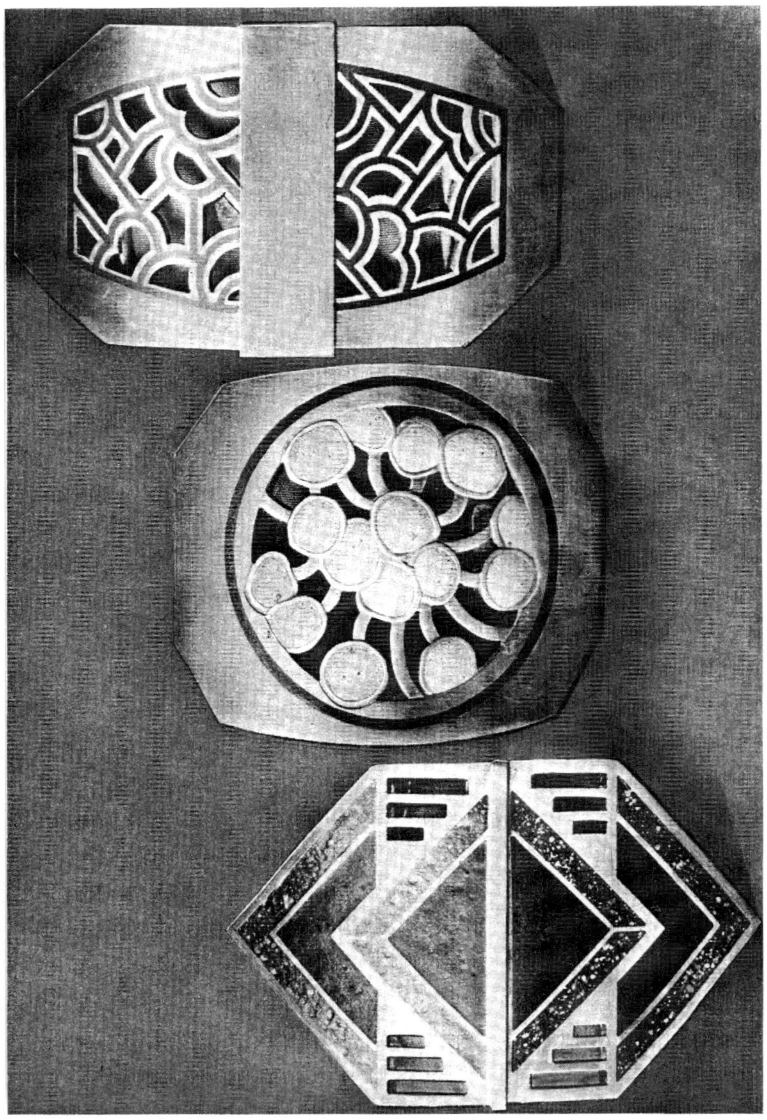

E. Maréchal: dress fastenings in silver and enamel presented at the 1925 Paris Exposition, French section.

Preceding pages: Anonymous: necklaces and bracelets in chrome and Bakelite. The bracelet at the foot of the left-hand page is signed 'Grundwald – made in France'. Primavera Gallery, New York.

Facing page: Anonymous: pendant in ivory, turquoise and gold with a silk tassel, France, c. 1925. Primavera Gallery, New York.

E. David: enamel and gold pendant, France, c. 1925, signed. Primavera Gallery, New York.

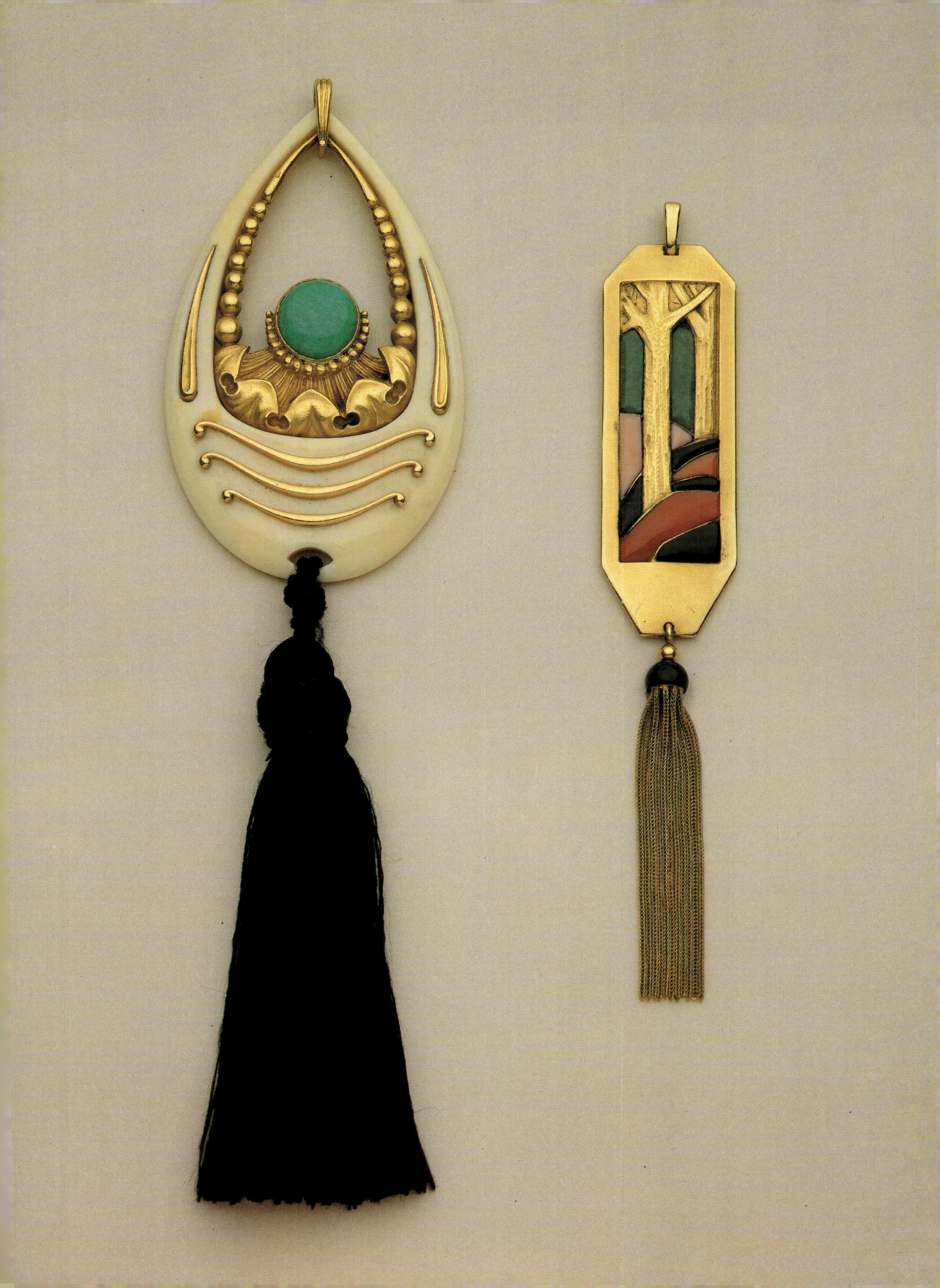

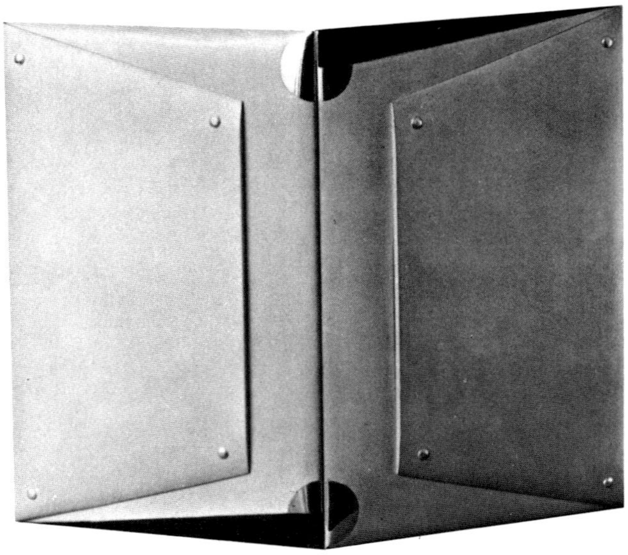

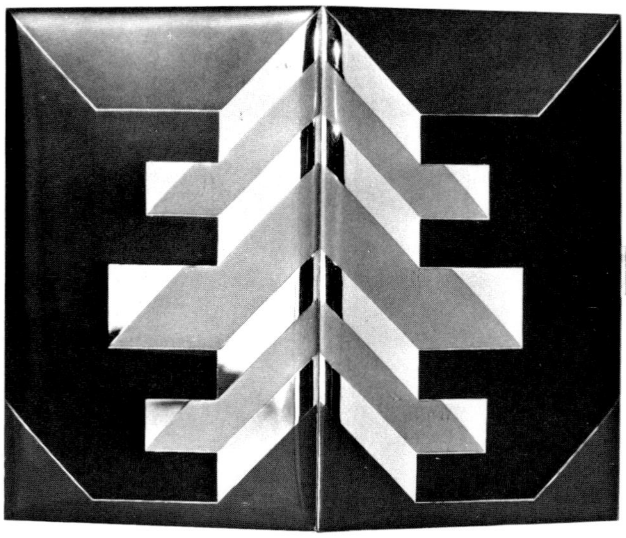

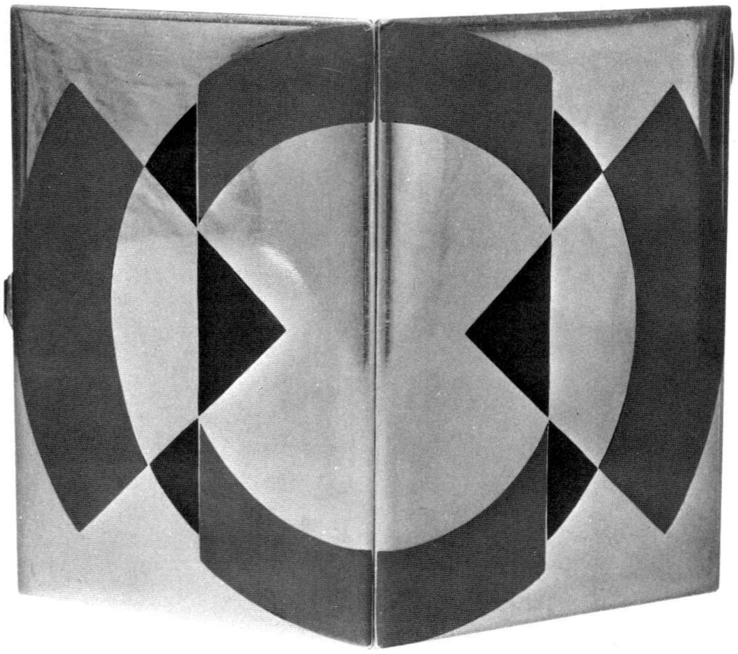

Raymond Templier: two cigarette cases in metal and lacquer, c. 1928. Courtesy of L. and B. Heuer.

Raymond Templier: cigarette case in silver and blue and black enamel. M. Souillac Collection. Photo: J.B. Rouault.

Raymond Templier: two cigarette cases, c. 1928. Courtesy of L. and B. Heuer.

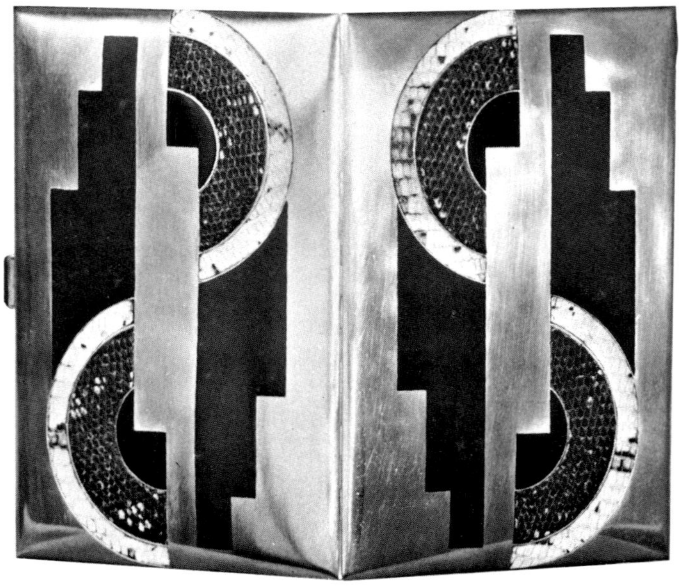

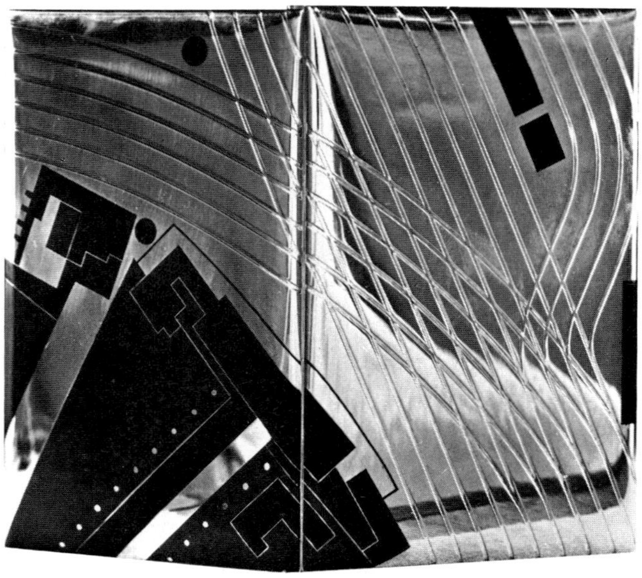

ACCESSORIES

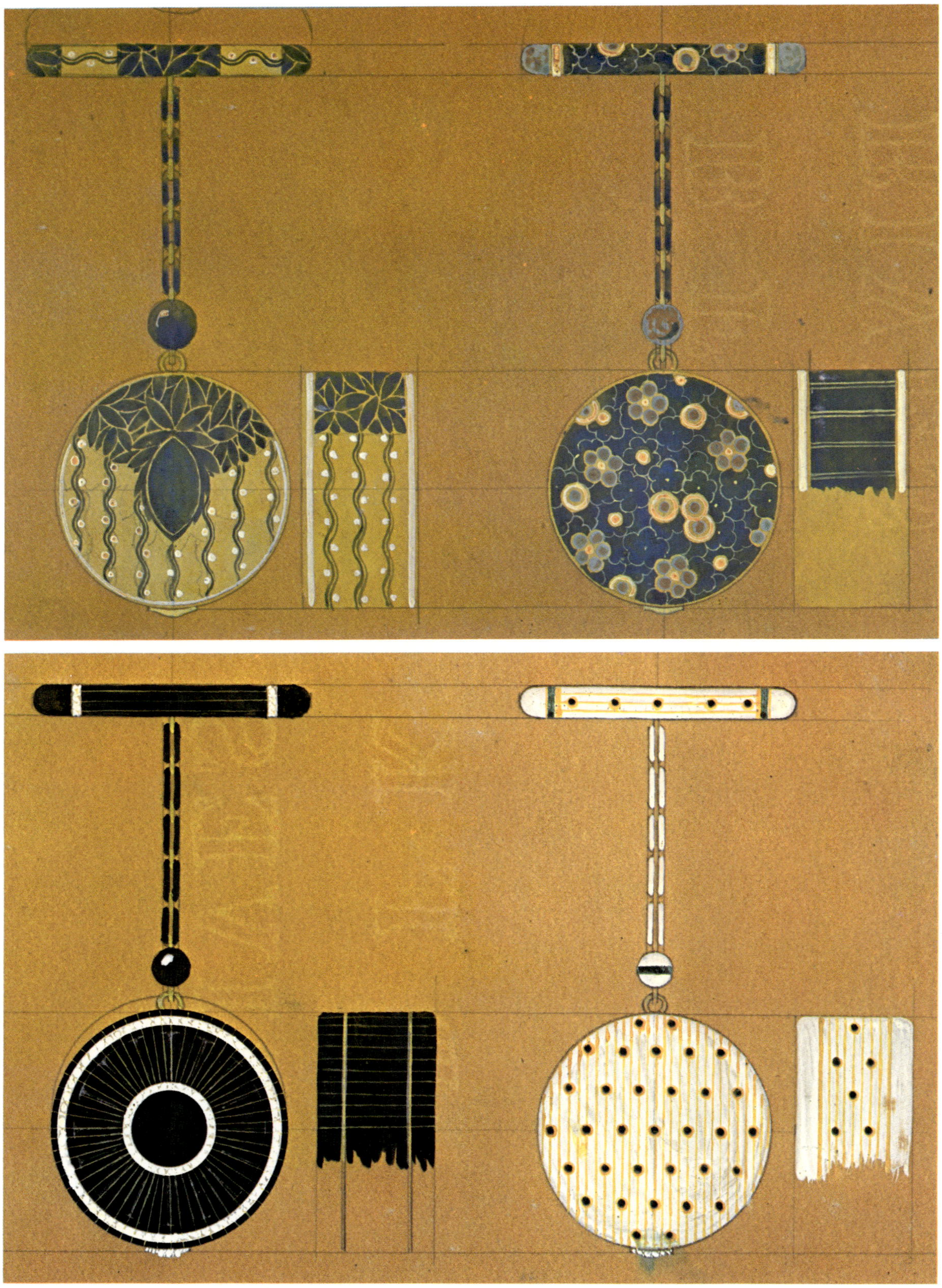

Gouache studies for vanity cases executed by designer-craftsmen for the Haute Joaillerie. *M. Souillac Archives.*

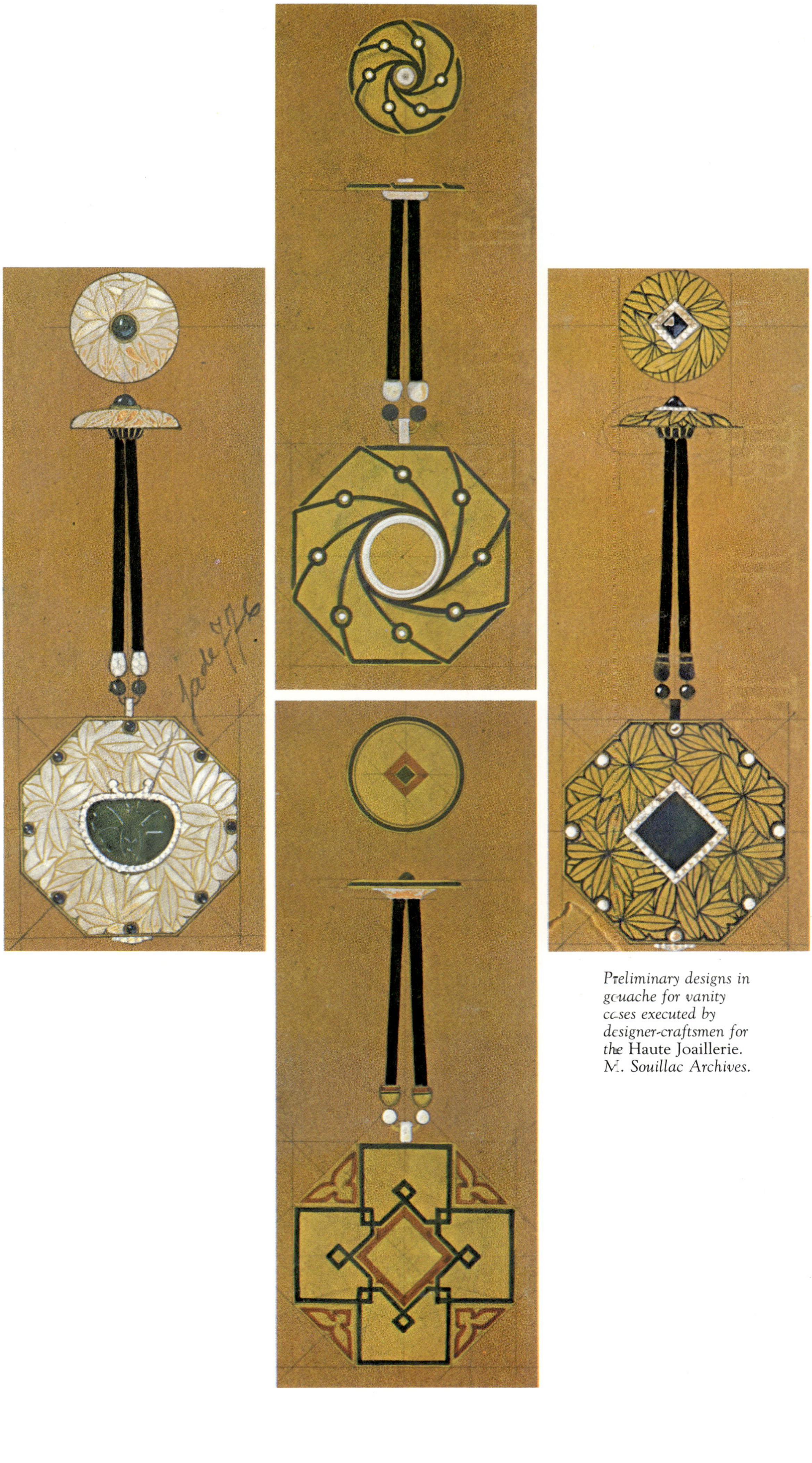

Preliminary designs in gouache for vanity cases executed by designer-craftsmen for the Haute Joaillerie. *M. Souillac Archives.*

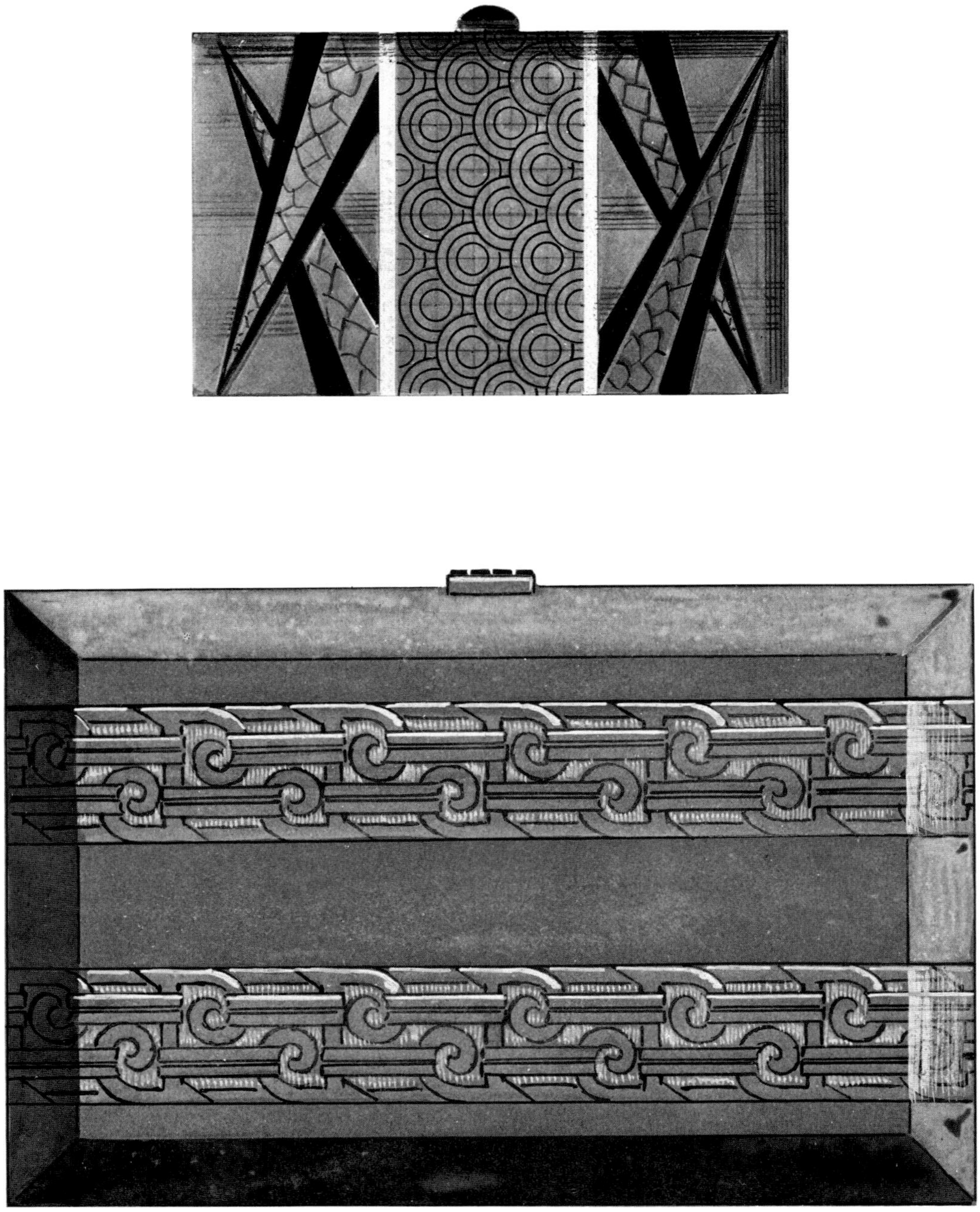

Chaumet: watercolour drawings of cigarette boxes, c. 1925. Chaumet Archives.

For the designers of the twenties, the most trivial item, a mere complement to elegance, offered a delightful pretext for combining the richest materials in the creation of a unique work of art – a work which could compete with the rarest pieces of the Renaissance and the eighteenth century. The new woman who emerged after the war required accessories consistent with her life style, and, to meet her needs, the designers created fashions of surpassing elegance and refinement. Madame de Pompadour's contemporaries wore ostentatious chatelaines, weighed down with the weapons of their coquetry; the women of the French Regency borrowed a taste for snuff from men; and the fashionable women of the *Années Folles*, in their turn, lit up oval cigarettes of the finest oriental tobacco and claimed the right to put on make-up in public. The utmost discretion in the use of make-up, authorized by women in good society, gave way after the war to an immoderate pleasure in its use – reserved until recently for actresses and *demi-mondaines* – and provoked an outcry in the traditional press. Whether she was travelling or in town, a woman's cosmetic treasures were indispensable to her, and jewelers devised ingenious little boxes which combined: a powder compact, a lipstick case, a shell comb, a mirror, some cigarettes, a lighter and sometimes even a miniaturized watch. In 1930, Louis Arpels called these beauty kits *minaudières* and registered a patent for the model in 1933. This term is often wrongly used since the Arpels Maison owned the exclusive right to the name. Louis Arpels derived the idea from a visit of one of his regular

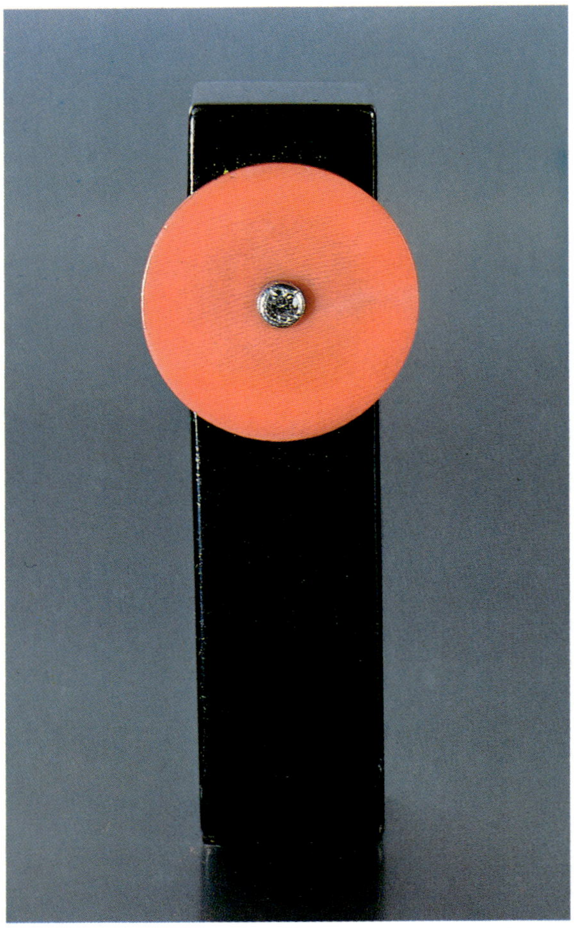

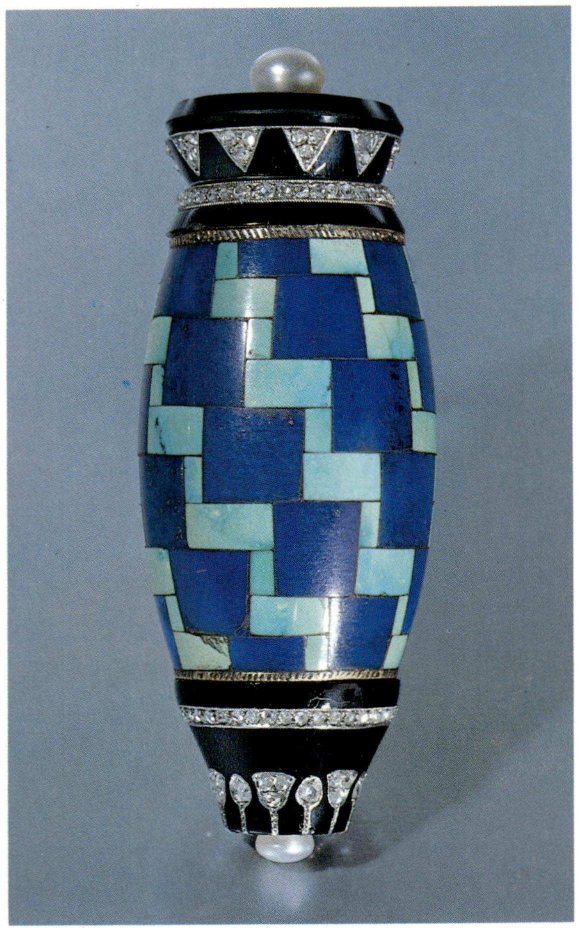

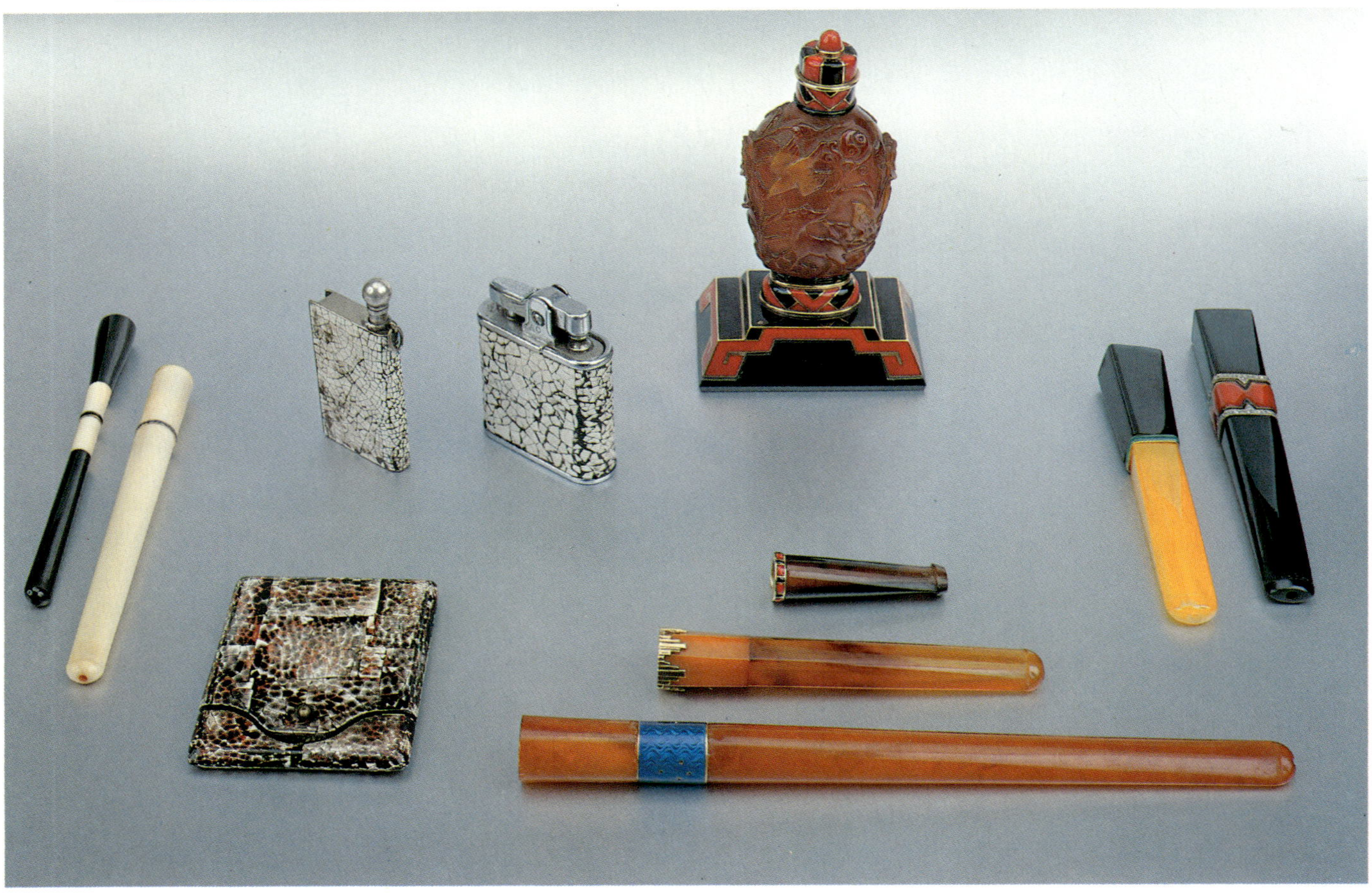

Cartier: lipstick case in black enamel on silver with a coral disc bearing a diamond at its centre. The tube appears when the disc is rotated. M. Souillac Collection.

Cartier: lipstick case in turquoise and lapis inlay set off with diamonds and onyx, decorated with a pearl at each end and mounted on gold and platinum. M. Souillac Collection. Photo: J.B. Rouault.

Smoking accessories: in the background, a Maison Maquet perfume bottle – converted into a lighter – in Peking glass mounted on gold, the base and stopper in onyx; to the left, two small lighters in silver covered with eggshell lacquer; in the foreground, a matchbox by Jean Dunand in lacquer and eggshell and cigarette holders in onyx, amber and ivory. M. Souillac Collection. Photo: J.B. Rouault.

clients, Florence Gould, the wife of an American railway magnate, who was carrying, instead of a handbag, one of those steel boxes containing fifty cigarettes. Arpels suggested that he should create, specially for her, an article that would suit her purpose and be more in keeping with a woman of fashion.

In America, the design of the *nécessaire*, or vanity case, was inspired largely by those curious little boxes with drawers, the *inro*, in which patent medicines were carried in China and Japan. The *nécessaire* won the approval of elegant women and provoked fierce competition among the great Maisons such as Cartier, Van Cleef, Lacloche and Janesich. Each article was unique, created to order for a client to whom several sketches and watercolour designs had been submitted. The profusion of these designs in the jewelers' archives illustrates the fertile imagination and ingenuity of the designer-creators, working either to commission or in the studios attached to the Maisons.

The Maisons of *Joaillerie* and the designer-craftsmen collaborated so closely that it is impossible to establish the origin of a piece and to separate out the sources of influence.

Boxes were designed or made, either on demand or by commission, in the workshops of Allard et Meyer (Place des Vosges), Kuppenheim (rue Volney), Chailloux (rue Turbigo), Louis Block (at Colombes), Strauss, Desmarès and Lavabre. These boxes had one common feature: the need to fit the largest possible number of elements in the minimum of space. Their forms and decoration were infinitely various. They were flat, oval or cylindrical; some

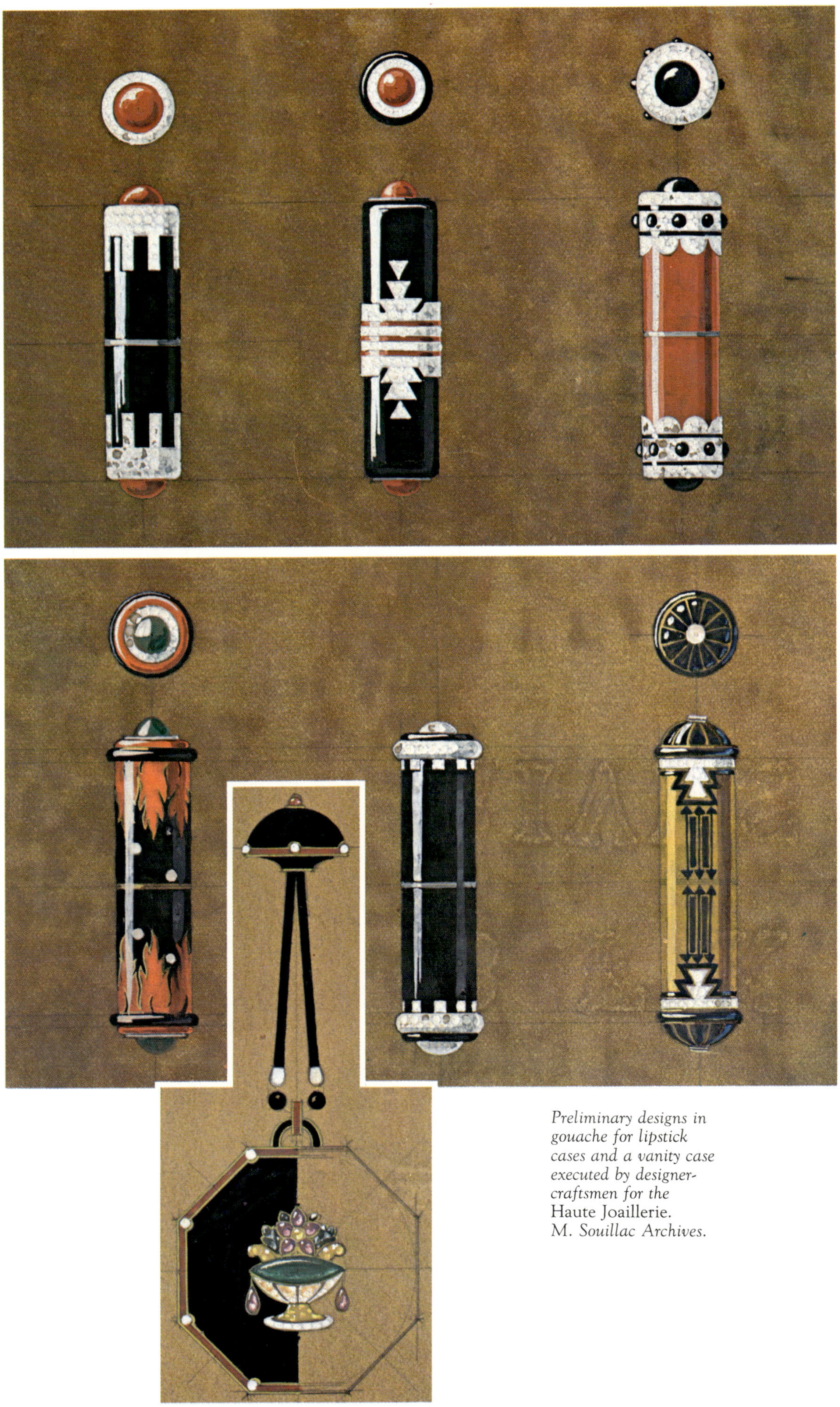

Preliminary designs in gouache for lipstick cases and a vanity case executed by designer-craftsmen for the Haute Joaillerie. M. Souillac Archives.

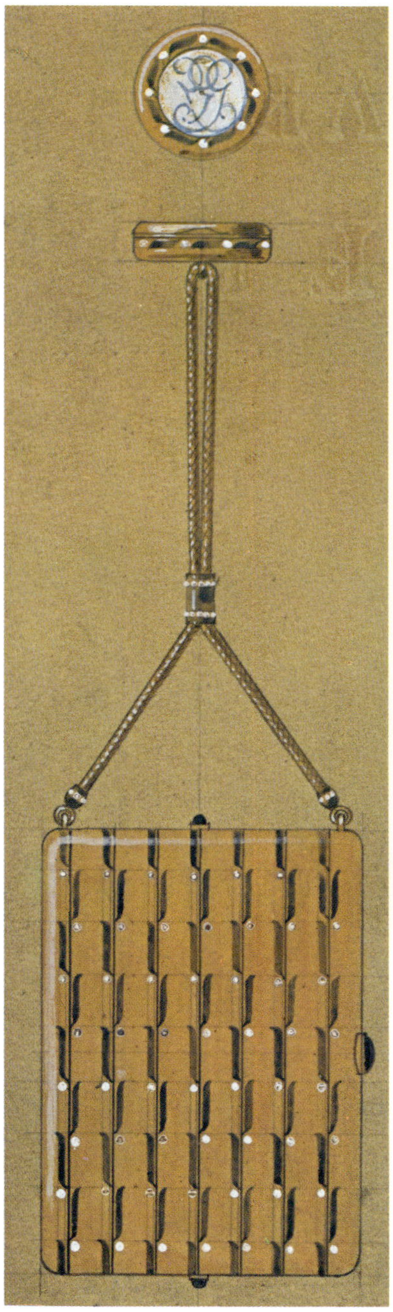

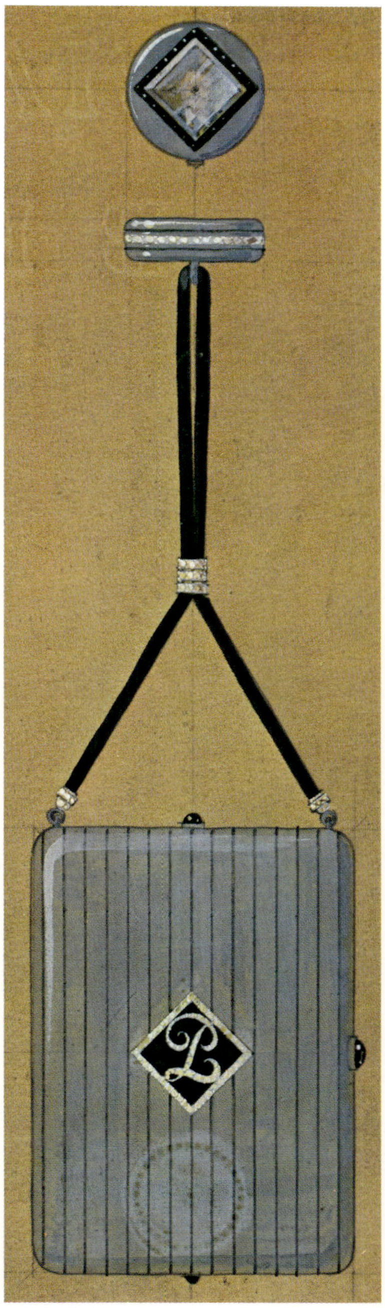

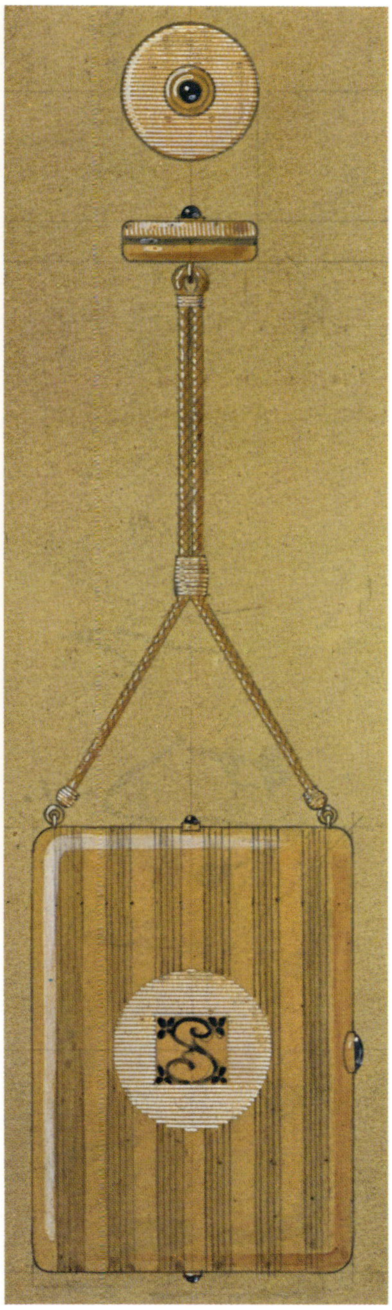

Preliminary designs in gouache for vanity cases executed by designer-craftsmen for the Haute Joaillerie. *M. Souillac Archives.*

were attached to a ring by a silk cord in the Japanese manner, others by an enamelled chain; sometimes the lipstick case took the place of the onyx ring. The decorative possibilities ranged from the use of the most discreet materials – as in Van Cleef's marvellous powder compacts embellished with combinations of curves and straight lines, where incandescent red jostled with black – to surfaces laden with figurative scenes, veritable paintings of precious stones and hardstones, assuming on the part of designer and craftsman a perfect mastery of technique. Persian hunting scenes, Chinese or Japanese landscapes, multicoloured birds of paradise and bouquets of flowers were depicted on these boxes. The most modest were decorated on one side, the more elaborate had decorative devices spilling from one side to the other. Fashionable women, enticed by the exotic, showed a partiality for scenes inspired by Persia, China, Japan and Egypt. When they chose simplicity, the designers relied on the harmony of the assembled stones and either stylized motifs or geometric lines providing a rhythm for the composition. Some *nécessaires* reconciled the two reigning tendencies of Art Deco and showed how they could be used to complement one another: figurative scenes with an oriental flavour were imposed on a geometric ground or decorated with a linear border. The jeweler combined golds, platinum and lacquer with jade, lapis, onyx, aventurine and amethyst. The most luxurious boxes were paved with brilliants set off with emeralds, rubies or sapphires. Lacquer and Chinese inlaid mother-of-pearl, modelled at times on ancient works of art, enlarged the range of materials at the artist's disposal, and these European mosaics of mother-of-pearl and precious stones undoubtedly held their own when compared with their Far Eastern models. The perfection of these objects makes one marvel at the length of time that specialized craftsmen must have devoted to them.

Some cigarette boxes were carved in a single piece from a block of jade, lapis, rock crystal or agate, and had as their only ornament a small stylized motif or the owner's monogram. The entire range of precious stones and hard-stones was not enough to satisfy artists who, like Jean Dunand, sought after unusual effects. Dunand discovered an unusual technique, later taken up by Gérard Sandoz, to make up for the absence of white in the colouring of lacquer: he simply placed a layer of crushed eggshell on a base of lacquer. Explaining how this was done, he said: 'A variety of effects can be obtained simply by applying eggshell to fresh lacquer in large crushed pieces, the inside of the shell uppermost, or, conversely, the outer side, or, again, in small juxtaposed pieces, or even sprinkled in fine particles.' On cigarette boxes Gérard Sandoz used the lacquer and eggshell combination together with metal, often silver, laid bare. Artists like Raymond Templier, Gérard Sandoz and Paul Brandt on the whole favoured geometric motifs in audacious combinations of bright colours, but they sometimes indulged their fancy and went in for figurative scenes. A series of cigarette boxes by Gérard Sandoz represented Paris and the winding roads of old Montmartre, the metro, a barge gliding under a bridge,

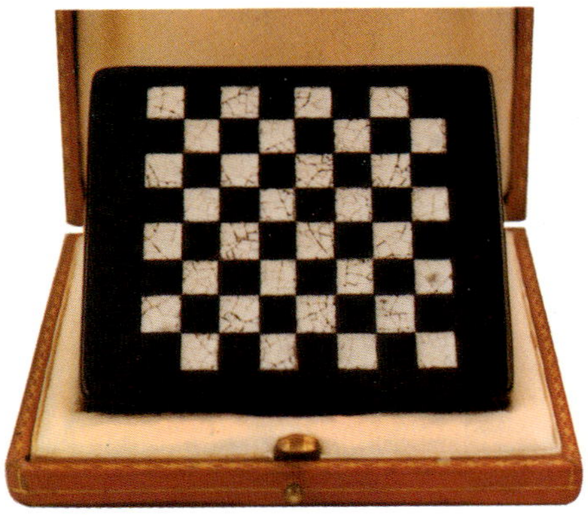

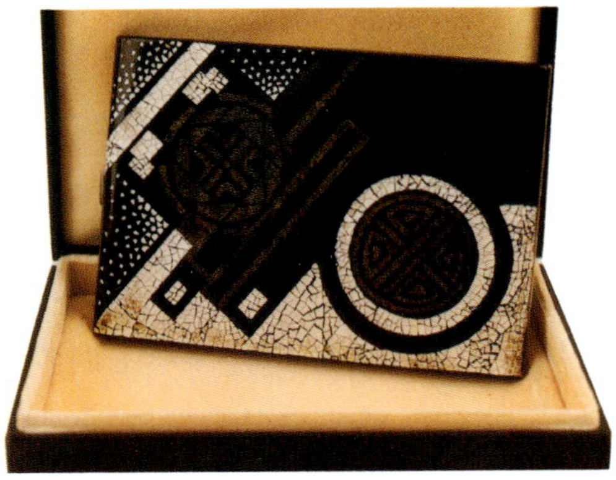

Jean Dunand: cigarette case in black lacquer and eggshell. M. Souillac Collection.

Gérard Sandoz: cigarette case in black lacquer and eggshell. M. Souillac Collection.

A Raymond Templier showcase and painting by Fernand Léger. Courtesy of L. and B. Heuer.

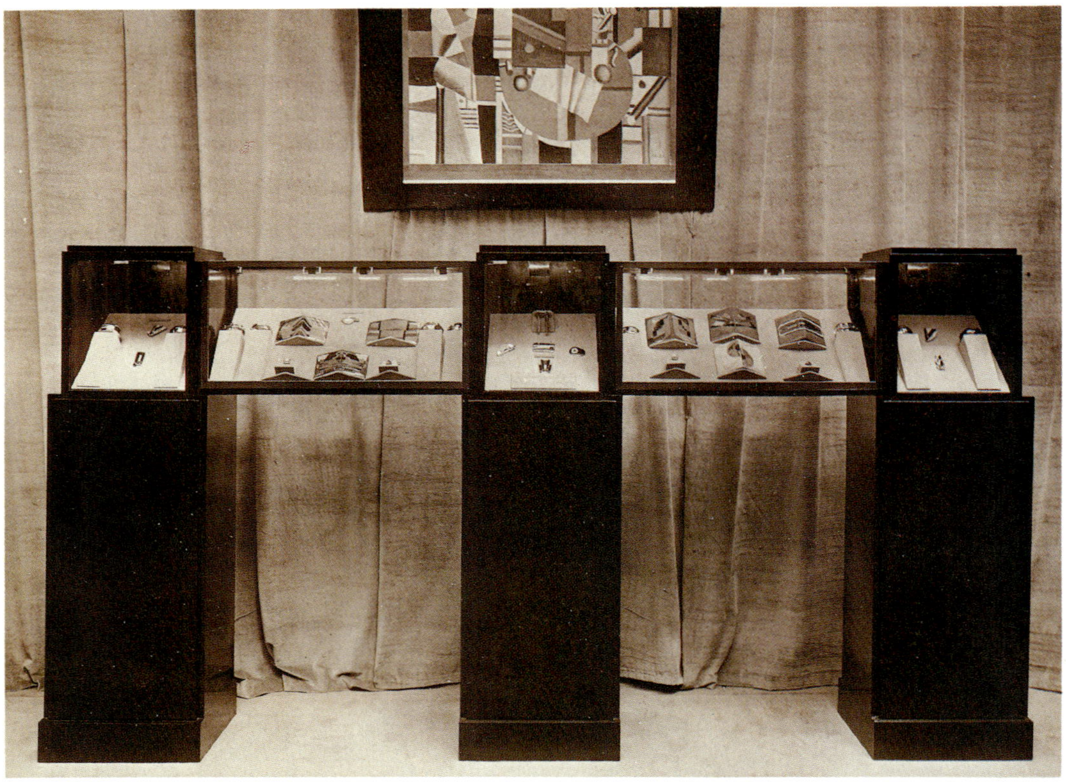

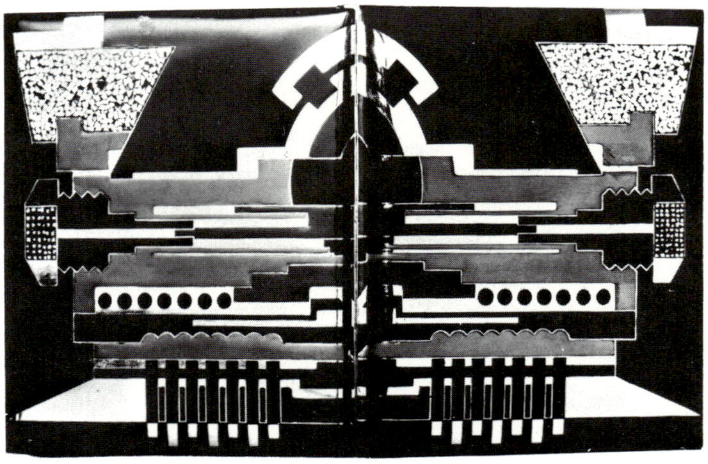

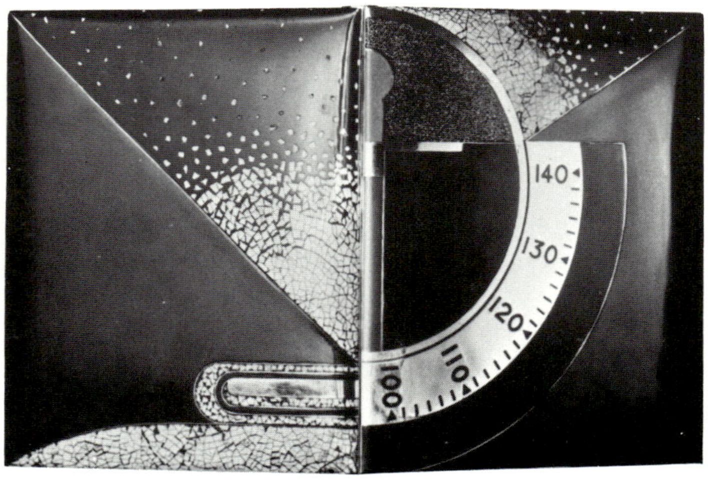

Raymond Templier: two cigarette cases in silver and lacquer. Courtesy of L. and B. Heuer.

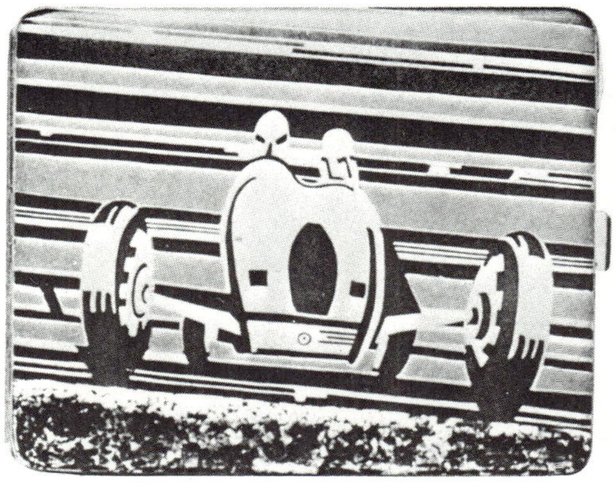
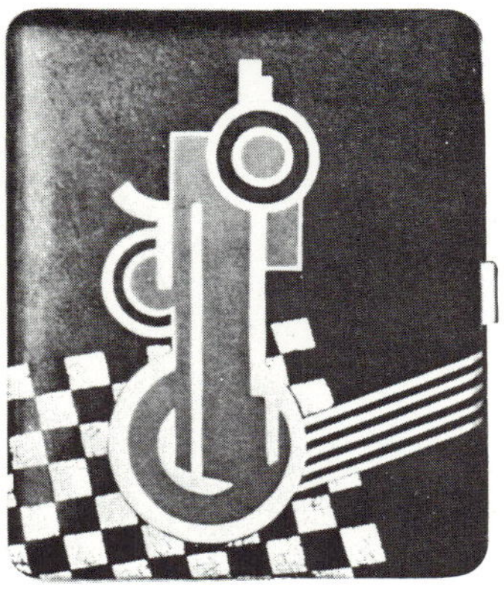

Gérard Sandoz: two cigarette cases reproduced in Jean Fouquet's 'Bijoux et Orfèvrerie', 1931.

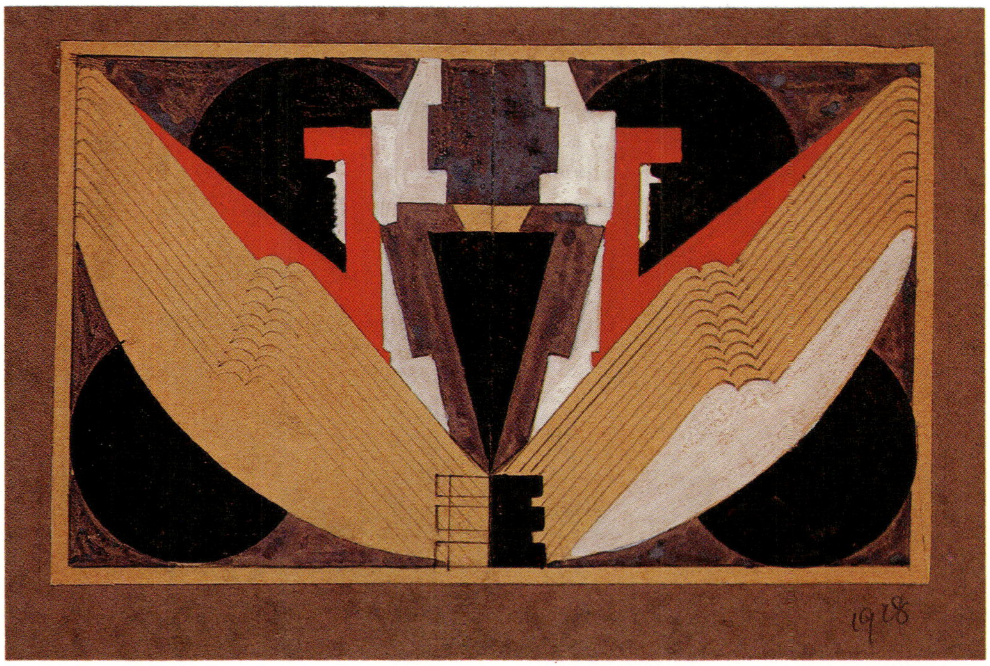

Raymond Templier: design for a cigarette case, 1928. Courtesy of L. and B. Heuer.

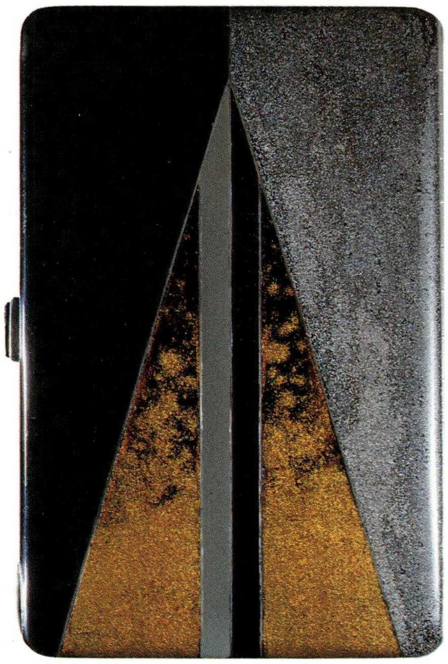

Gérard Sandoz: cigarette case in silver and multicoloured lacquers, c. 1928, signed. Private Collection. Photo: T. Heuer and J.B. Rouault.

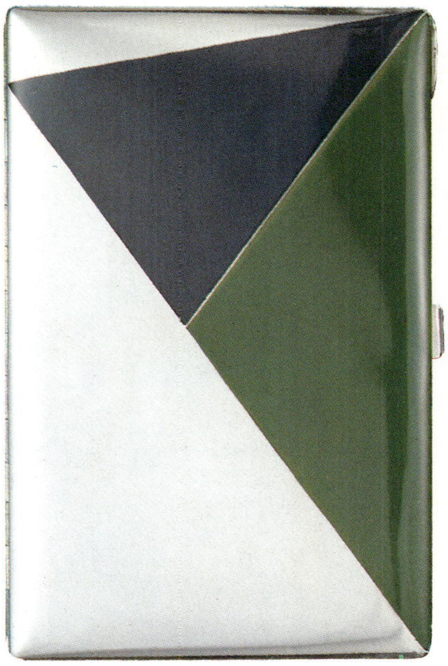

Raymond Templier: cigarette case in silver and blue and green lacquer, the catch set with a black hardstone, c. 1930, signed. Sotheby's.

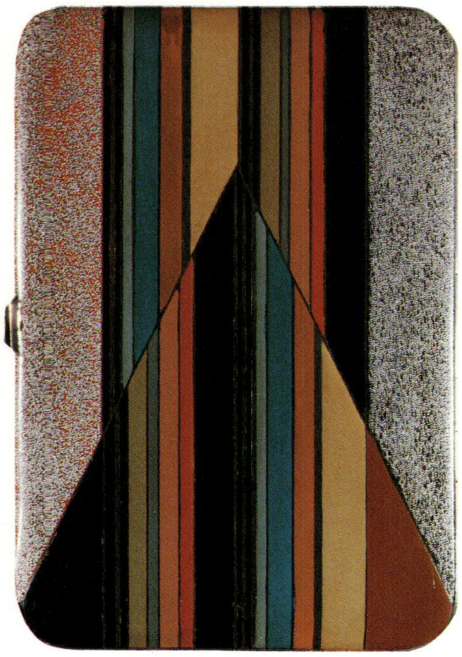

Gérard Sandoz: cigarette case in silver and multicoloured lacquers, c. 1928, signed. Private Collection. Photo: T. Heuer and J.B. Rouault.

and even the latest crazes: rugby, motor racing, boxing, the Charleston, baccarat, not to mention a sly reference to the mechanical world via images of factories and speedometers. Alongside the *nécessaires*, which were precious, fragile articles reserved for evening wear, jewelers produced a range of handbags for daywear, creating for the purpose rectangular clutch-bags in box calf or crocodile skin, decorated with the owner's monogram. The leather workers made exclusive models on commission for the jewelers (Hermès for Cartier, for example). These clutch-bags gave artists the opportunity to play with the colours of different leathers as the *joaillier* did with stones and metals. Fouquet, for example, juxtaposed white leather, red antelope and biscuit-coloured nappa. *Nécessaires* of metal and precious stones competed in lavishness and ingenuity with evening bags in oriental brocades, in ribbed taffeta and silk velvet, embroidered with pearls or gems and fastened with a jeweled clasp. Decorative motifs for these accessories were inexhaustible and became more ingenious from model to model, coloured geometric designs alternating with intertwined, stylized flowers in the Persian mode or with images of Egyptian origin.

Even objects least related to feminine adornment fired the designers' imaginations, and gold, platinum, hardstones and precious stones invaded everyday life, enriching every object whether useful or trivial: pen trays, paperweights, calendar hangers, cigarette holders, lighters, match-boxes, photograph frames, toilet requisites, penknives concealing propelling pencils. Jewelers deprived

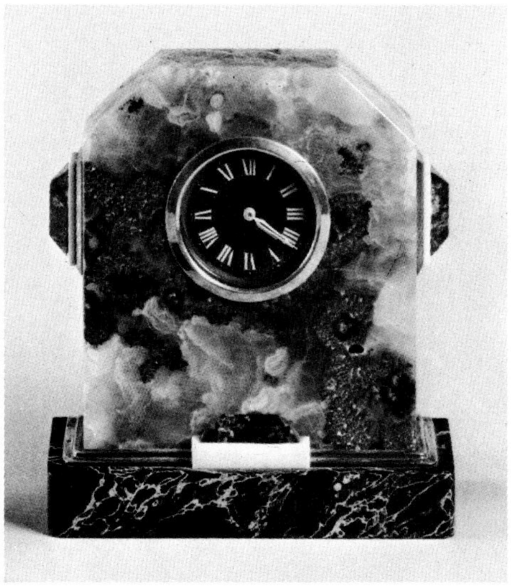

Boin-Taburet: 'milestone' clock in grey marble with cut-off corners and lapis cabochons, mounted on ivory and silver, signed. Etude Couturier–Nicolay.

Goupy: small clock in crystal and translucent enamels, put into production by Géo Rouard, reproduced in Art et Décoration, July 1921.

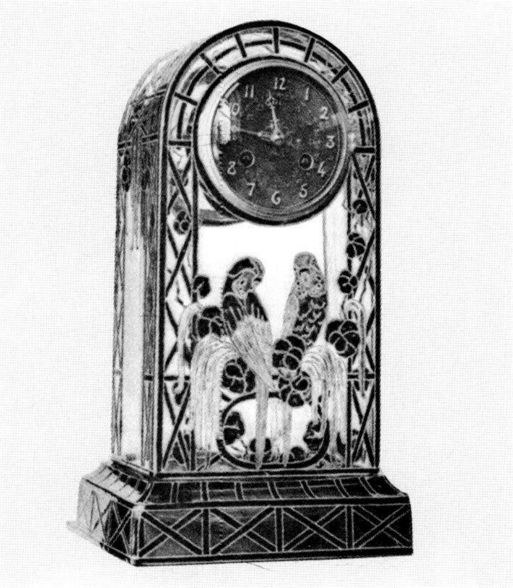

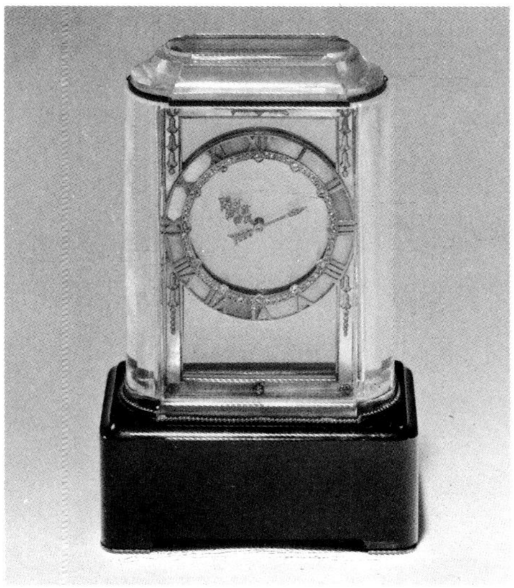

Cartier: 'mystery' clock in rock crystal, diamonds, onyx and mother-of-pearl. Christie's, New York.

Lalique: small clock in engraved and enamelled glass, reproduced in Art et Décoration, July 1921.

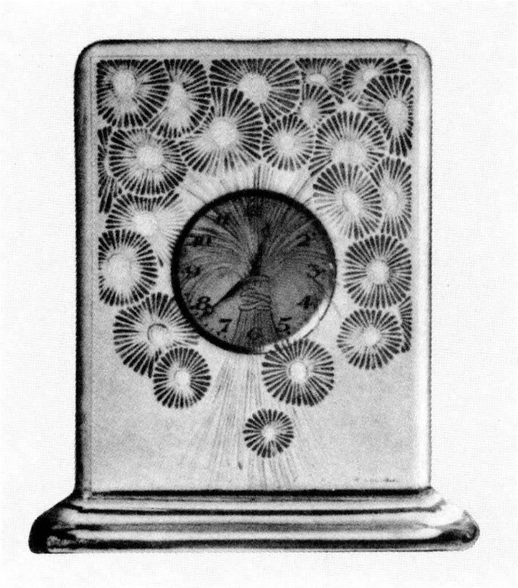

Lalique: small clock in engraved and enamelled glass, reproduced in Art et Décoration, July 1921.

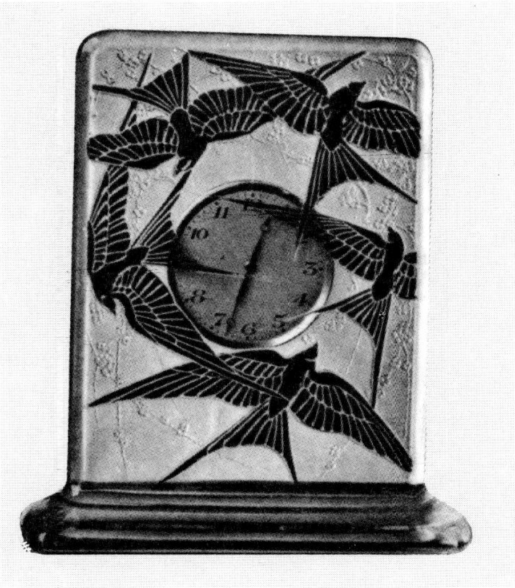

Van Cleef & Arpels: small clock in black lacquer, onyx, enamels and engraved crystals. Clockcase in jade, onyx, coral and crystal; numerals in red enamel; hands in gold. Christie's, New York.

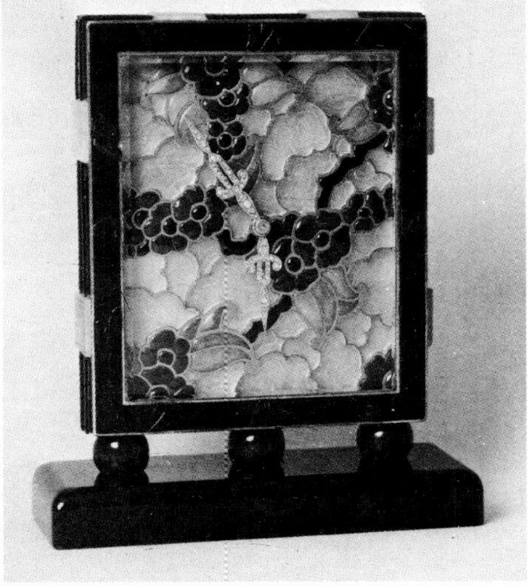

Following pages: Jean Fouquet: cigarette case in silver, black, dark-blue and light-blue lacquer, c. 1925, signed. H. 12.1 cm, W. 8.1 cm. Private Collection. Photo: T. Heuer and J.B. Rouault.

Gérard Sandoz: cigarette case in silver, black, blue and red lacquer, c. 1928, signed. H. 12.8 cm, W. 8.5 cm. Private Collection. Photo: T. Heuer and J.B. Rouault.

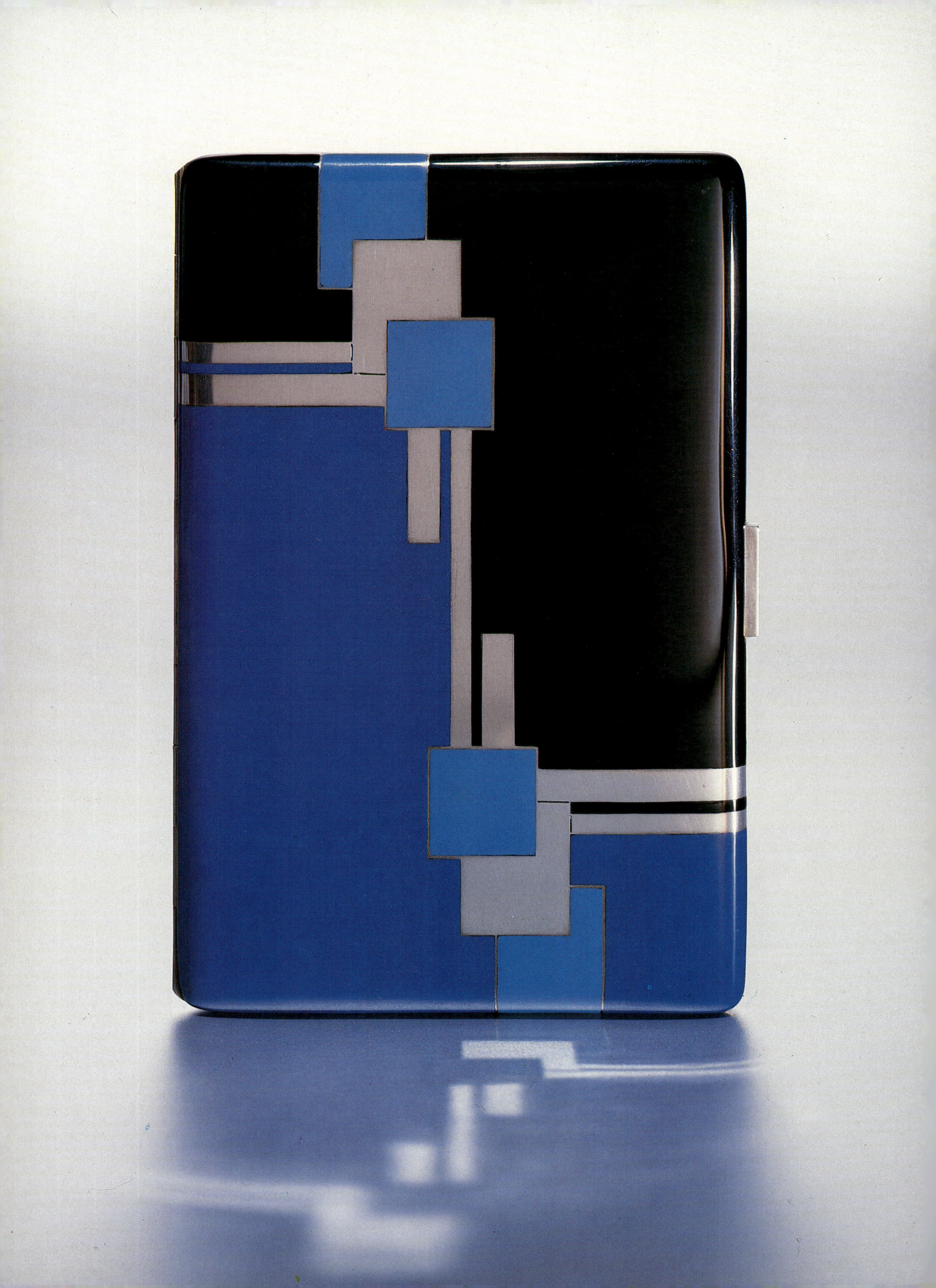

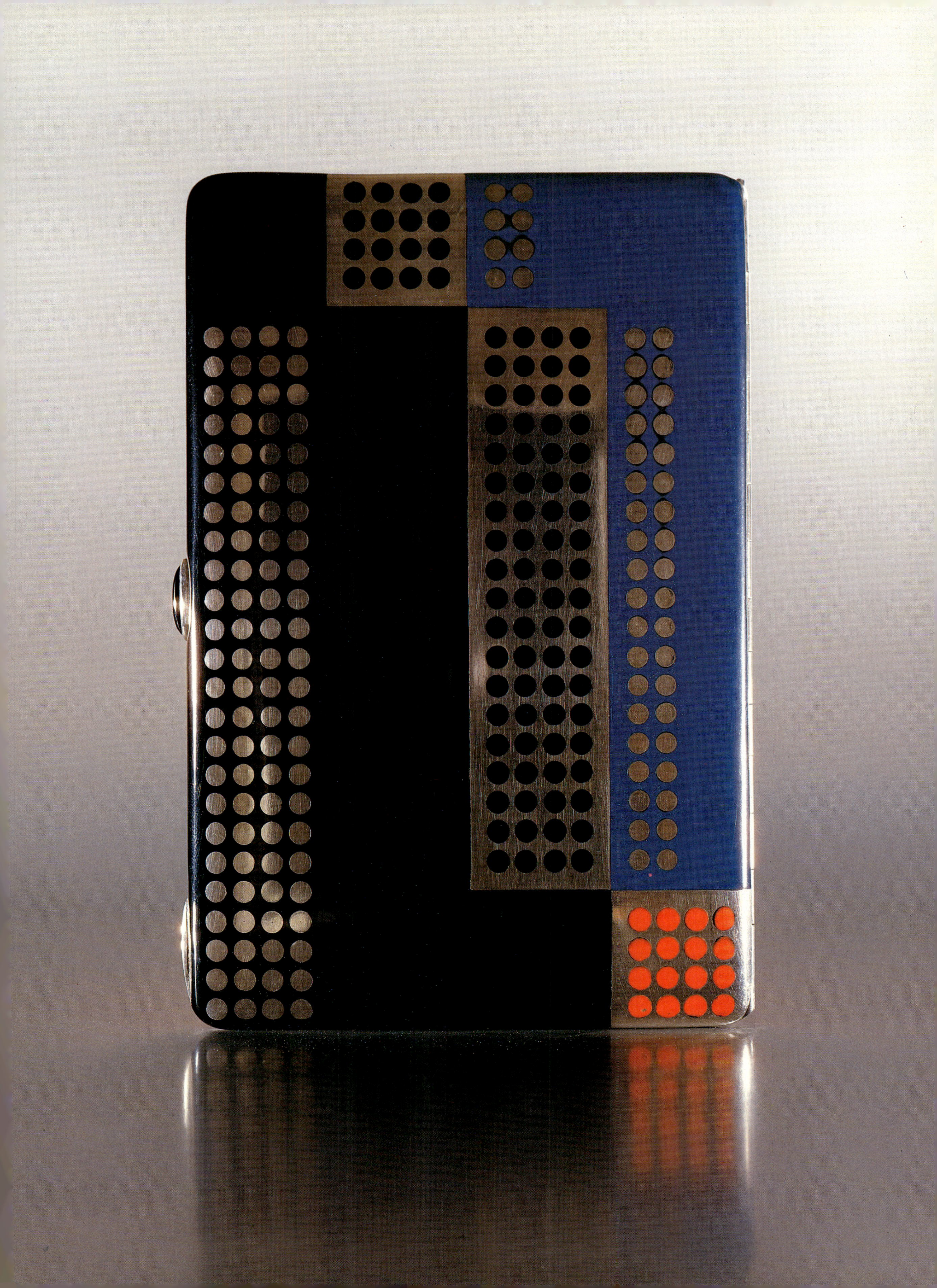

interior designers and clockmakers of their exclusive monopoly over the decoration of clocks, *pendulettes* (small travelling clocks) and alarm clocks. The clockmakers focused their efforts on desk clocks and the small clocks which one carried when travelling or which were attached to the interior of a car.

The models created by the interior designers Maurice Dufrêne, Léon Jallot, Paul Follot, Raymond Subes and Albert Cheuret, tended to be made of readily available materials such as marble, metal, ivory, glass, enamel, wood, porcelain and bronze. By contrast, the workshops of the *Haute Joaillerie* offered their monied clientele masterpieces of preciosity, which transformed the useful object into a piece of jewelry. All the jewelry firms turned their hand to producing clocks, but the Maison Cartier seems to have been the most prolific. The clockmakers of the Franche Comté or Switzerland, Vacheron et Constantin, Unic, Lip, Jaeger and Le Coultre made the movements, and the jewelers then took charge and handed the movements over to the metalworkers, watch case makers, enamellers, *guillocheurs* and stone setters.

The jewelers collaborated with the clock designers: one of the most famous, George Verger, son of Ferdinand Verger, worked for Van Cleef et Arpels, Janesich, Lacloche, Ostertag, Marzo, Boucheron, Chaumet, Gübelin in Lucerne, Black, Starr and Frost, Tiffany and Caldwell in the United States. Strongly defined shapes, simple lines and stylized decoration may have characterized the clocks generally available, but for their more demanding clientele the *Haute Joaillerie* created the most elaborate fancies of form and colour contrast.

Without doubt, the most spectacular of all were the 'mystery' clocks, the very symbol of the clock-as-jewel, counting off the hours and minutes for royalty and heads of state: Queen Eugenia of Spain, King Farouk of Egypt, and the Indian Maharajahs. The Maison Verger was the sole manufacturer and supplied Van Cleef et Arpels, Ostertag and Black, Starr and Frost. Cartier and Verger alone knew the secret of these clocks whose hands seemed to float in space, revealing no apparent connection with the movement. In fact, each hand was fixed to a rock crystal disc with a rim of notched metal, driven by worm-gears hidden in the base or in the frame of the clockcase. Sometimes citrine replaced rock crystal, a substance whose transparency created the illusion that the hands were imprisoned inside. The movement was housed in the base which took the form of sea monsters with Cartier or wild animals such as Van Cleef et Arpels' white bear with an emerald eye. Other models imitated the porticoes of Japanese or Egyptian temples, and in these the movement was lodged in the pediment.

The Maison Cartier holds the record for the sale of 'mystery' clocks: apparently more than ninety were created by them between 1913 and 1930. The designers generally preferred a combination of hardstones and precious stones (the mattness of lapis, coral, onyx and jade set against the sparkle of diamonds, emeralds, rubies or sapphires), but Lalique, Sabino and Daum, for their part,

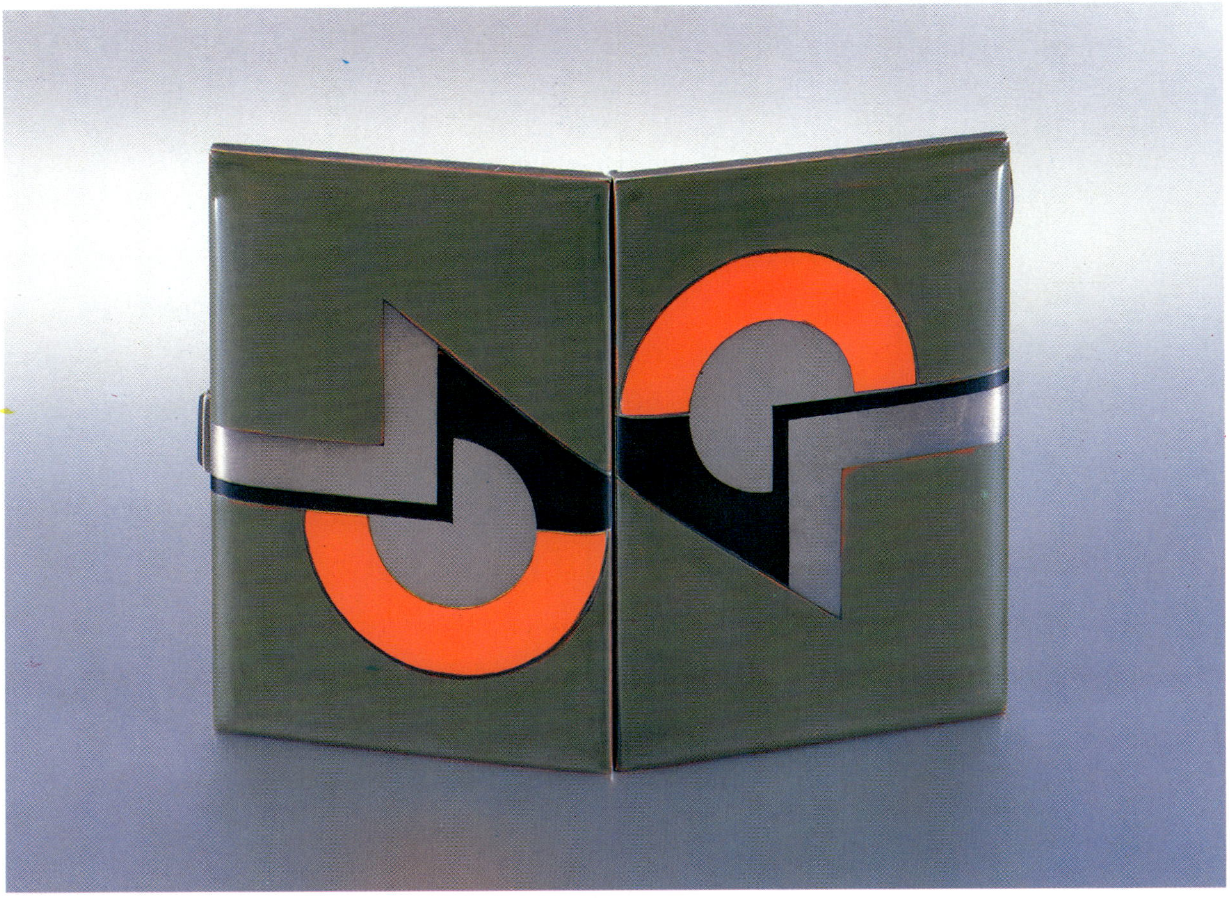

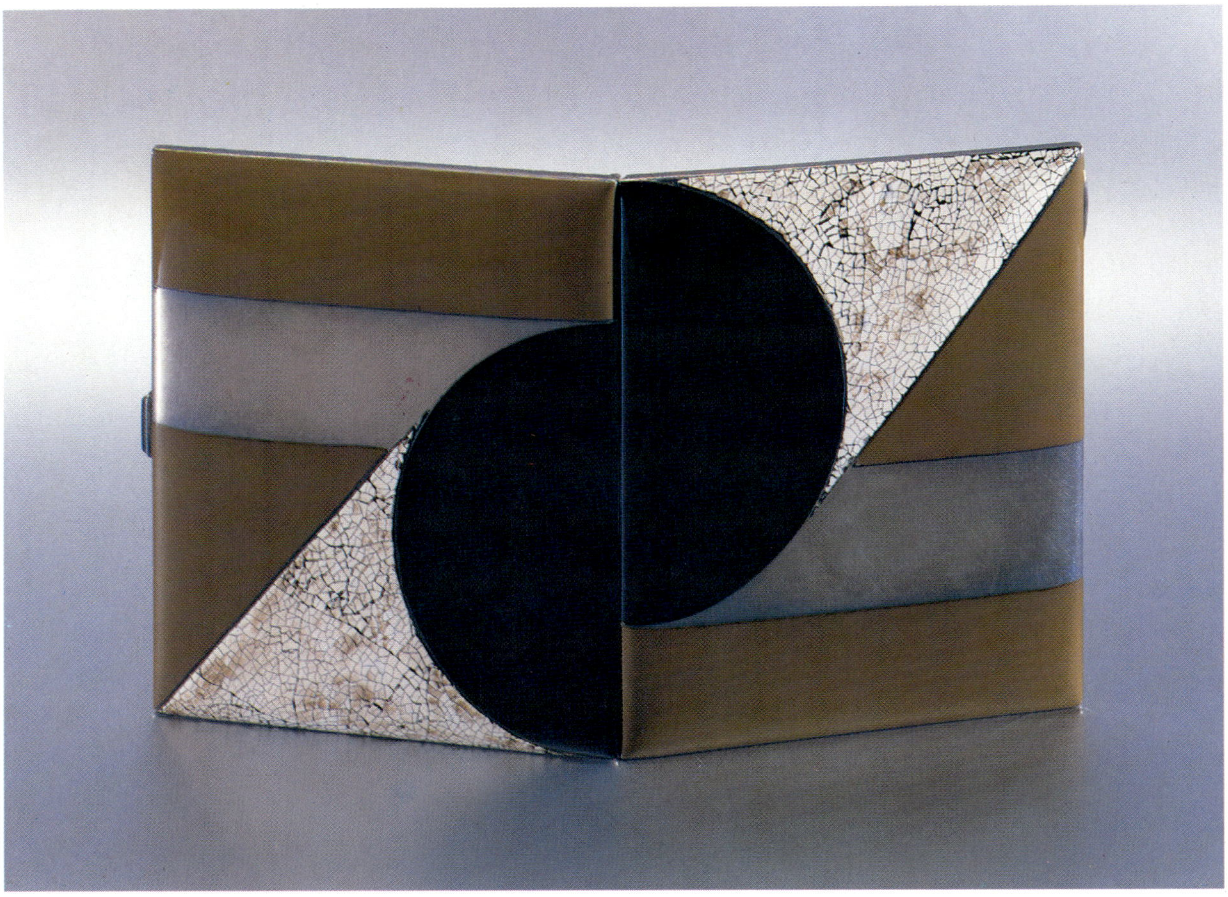

Raymond Templier: cigarette case in silver and green, red and black lacquer, 1928, signed. Private Collection. Photo: T. Heuer and J.B. Rouault.

Raymond Templier: cigarette case in silver, olive green and black lacquer and eggshell, 1928, signed. Private Collection. Photo: T. Heuer and J.B. Rouault.

Facing page: Gérard Sandoz: cigarette case in silver and blue and black lacquer, c. 1927, signed. H. 13 cm, W. 8.5 cm. Private Collection. Photo: T. Heuer and J.B. Rouault.

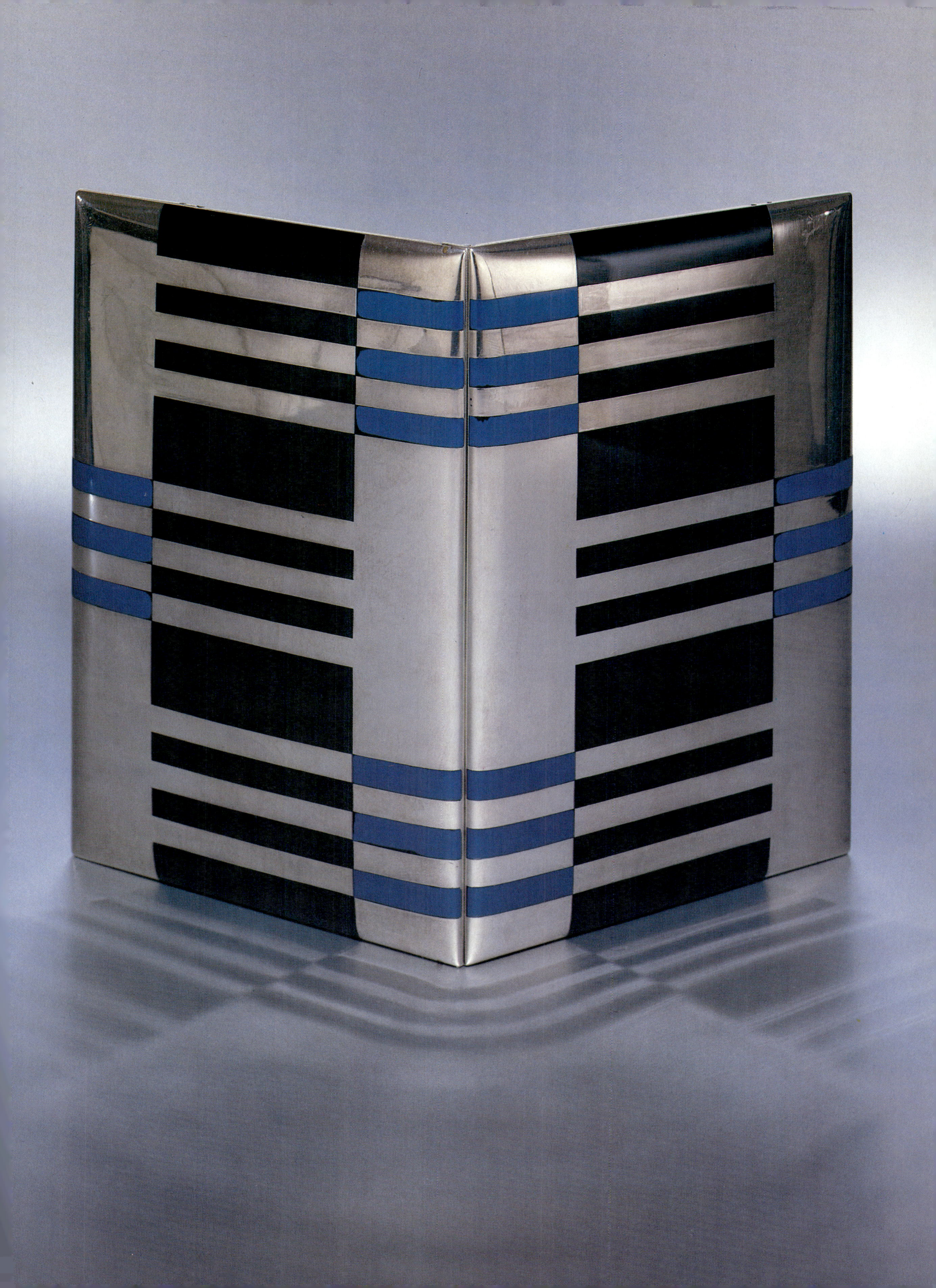

opted for the brilliance of crystal, which could be sculpted, engraved, frosted, patinated or translucent.

The clockmakers and jewelers brought all their ingenuity to bear on varying the form of the dial, the hands and the numerals. They preferred a rectangular, square or octagonal dial to the circular one. Cartier even went to twelve sides. The hands of the most gorgeous clocks – the 'mystery' clocks – were wrought and chased into miniature works of art: with Cartier they became diamond covered snakes or a fire-breathing dragon uncoiling in the centre of the dial, its head marking the hours, its tail the minutes. Other less extravagant ones took the form of arrows which narrowed until they were no more than two black lines, or were decorated with stylized floral motifs. Mélik Minassiantz did away with the hands altogether, substituting rotating metal balls in plain or coloured enamel, fixed to circular plates.

Roman numerals, in spite of their graphic sobriety, were rejected by the designer-creators in favour of Arabic numerals. In a geometric design, a detail which is not geometric plays the role of counterpoint and enhances the whole. Sometimes plain, neat strokes or large metal dots replaced the numerals. The creators of the Japanese portico clock at Van Cleef et Arpels executed the unusual idea of replacing the numerals with the twelve signs of the zodiac, painted on grisaille enamel on a black ground, in imitation of old-fashioned agate cameos.

The dials were covered with the rarest and most refined materials: enamel on a ground of *guilloché* gold, iridescent mother-of-pearl inlay, satin-finished crystal, either plain or sculpted in bas relief with floral motifs for Van Cleef et Arpels' portico clock, or blue-green kingfisher feathers for Cartier.

Prosperity raised the art of the accessory to its most perfect expression, and the Twenties and Thirties brought to the mundane objects of the everyday an almost unprecedented sophistication and preciosity.

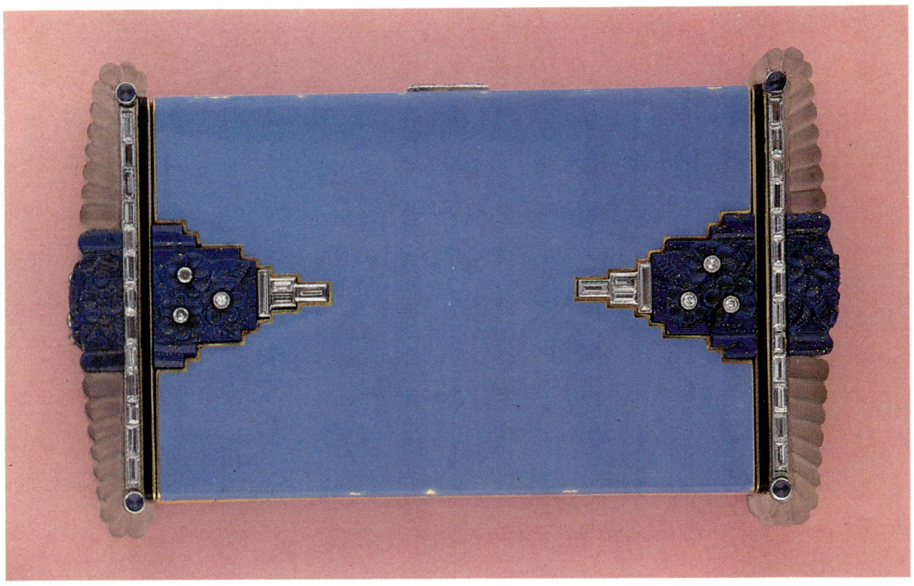

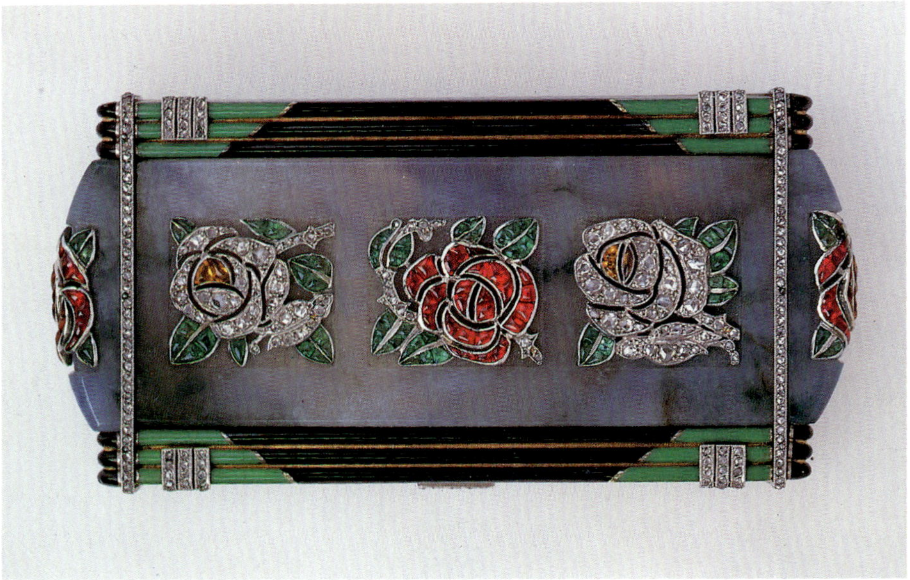

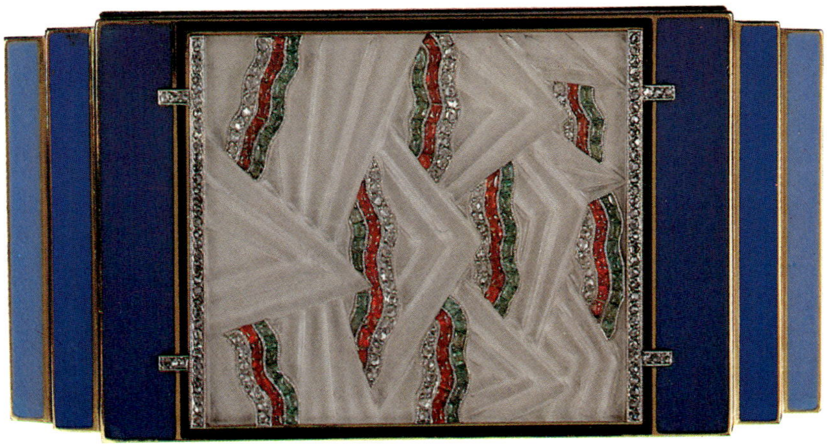

Janesich: vanity case in gold and lavender enamel with floral motifs in engraved lapis set with round diamonds, edged on two sides with baguette diamonds and fluted and frosted rock crystal, signed. Sotheby's.

Van Cleef & Arpels: vanity case in gold and mauve jade with floral motifs in rubies, emeralds and rose-cut diamonds, edged with green and black enamel, 1926. Van Cleef & Arpels Archives.

Van Cleef & Arpels: vanity case in gold and blue enamel with a plaque of engraved rock crystal, set with emeralds, calibré *rubies and rose-cut diamonds, 1927. Private Collection.*

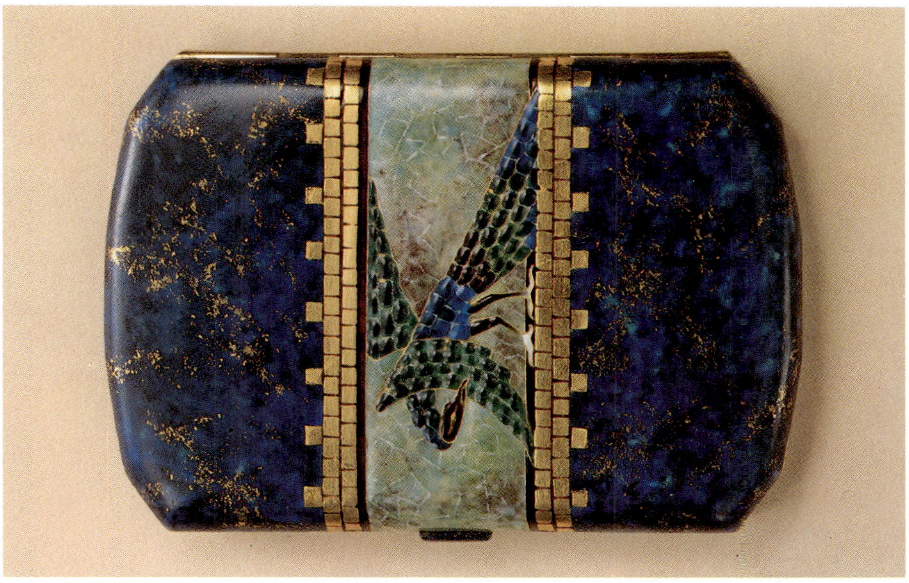

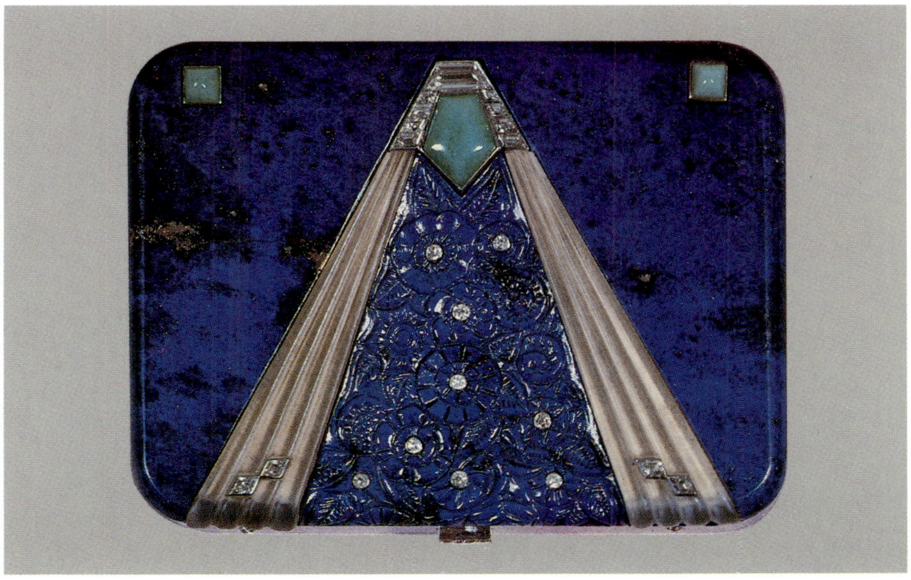

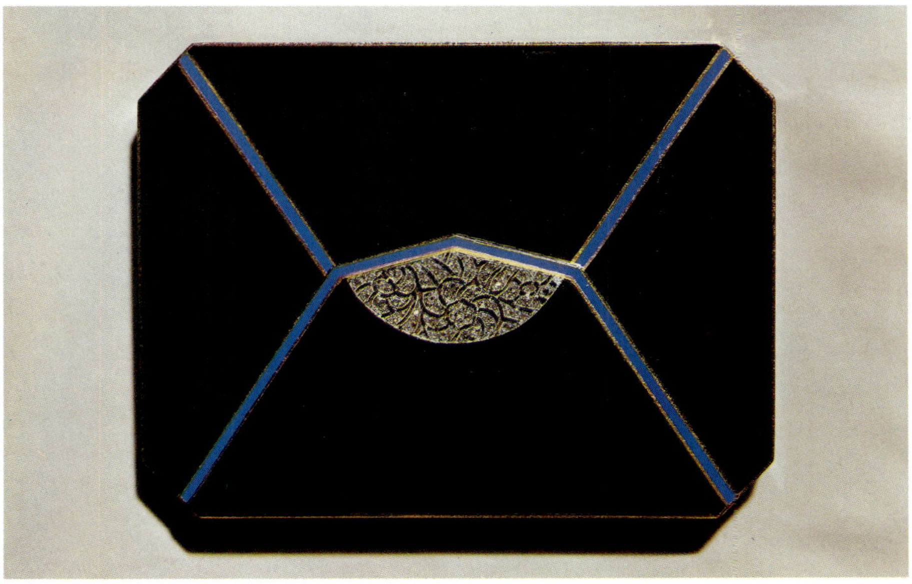

Van Cleef & Arpels: cigarette case decorated on two sides in lapis-like enamel and gold, with a centre panel showing a blue and green enamel bird on a pale-green mosaic ground. Private Collection. Van Cleef & Arpels Archives.

Van Cleef & Arpels: powder compact in polished lapis engraved with floral motifs, and bearing a triangular design in fluted rock crystal, turquoise cabochons and diamonds. Private Collection. Van Cleef & Arpels Archives.

Van Cleef & Arpels: envelope-shaped vanity case in gold and black enamel outlined in blue enamel, with motif in rose-cut diamonds and cut-off corners. Private Collection. Van Cleef & Arpels Archives.

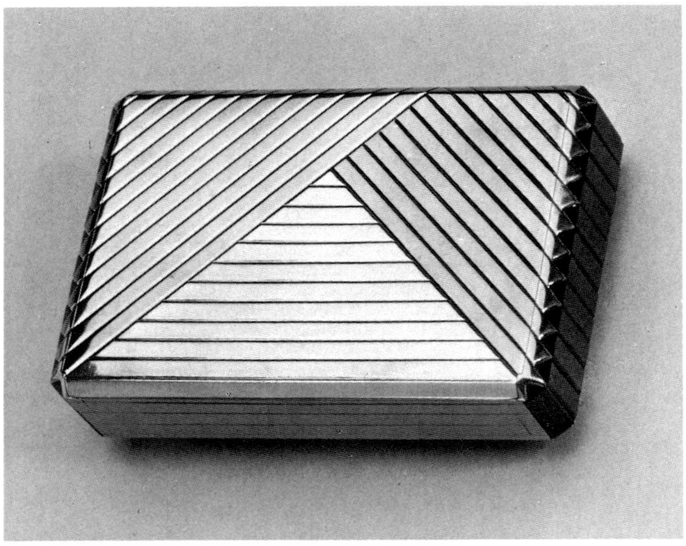

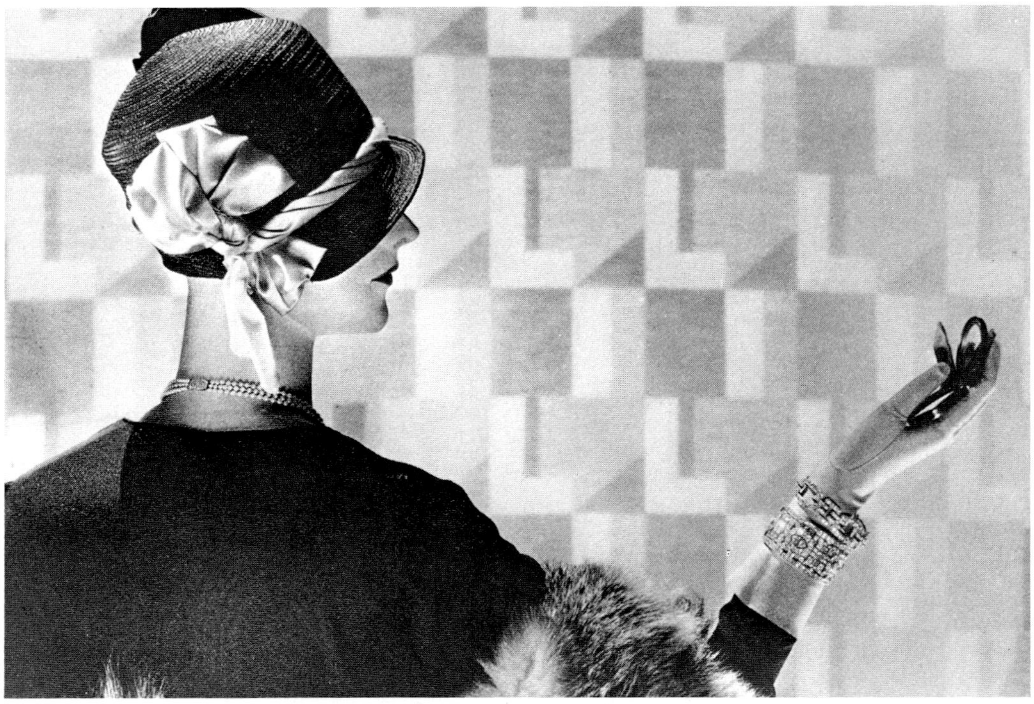

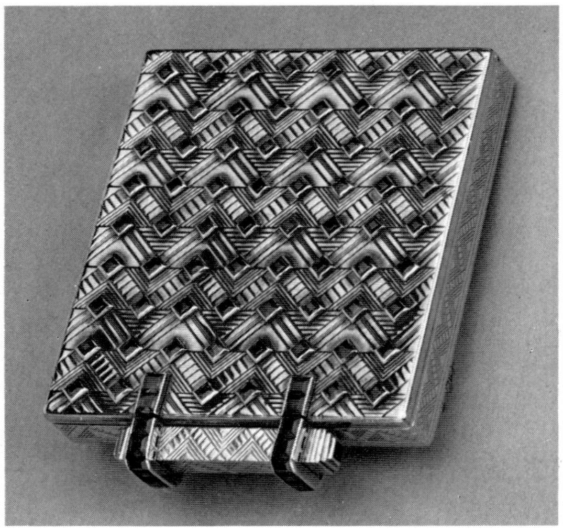

Anonymous: cigarette case in gold in three colours, flanked with fantaisie-cut sapphires, c. 1920. Sotheby's, Geneva.

Siegel mannequin wearing Mauboussin jewelry, hat by Rose Valois, silver fox fur and dress by Yteb. Photo: Hoyningen-Huene.

Ostertag: powder compact in gold and sapphires in a geometric design. Sotheby's.

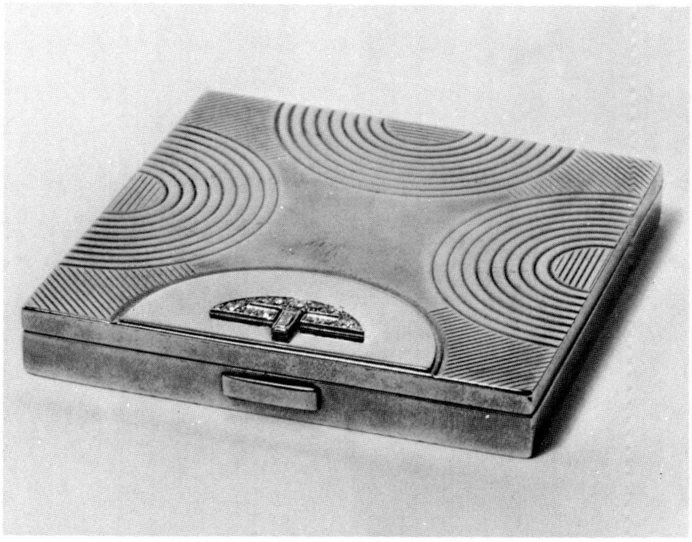

Lacloche: powder compact in white gold with a design of semicircles on three sides and a yellow gold semicircle on one side, set with diamonds in the form of a stylized mask, c. 1930. Sotheby's.

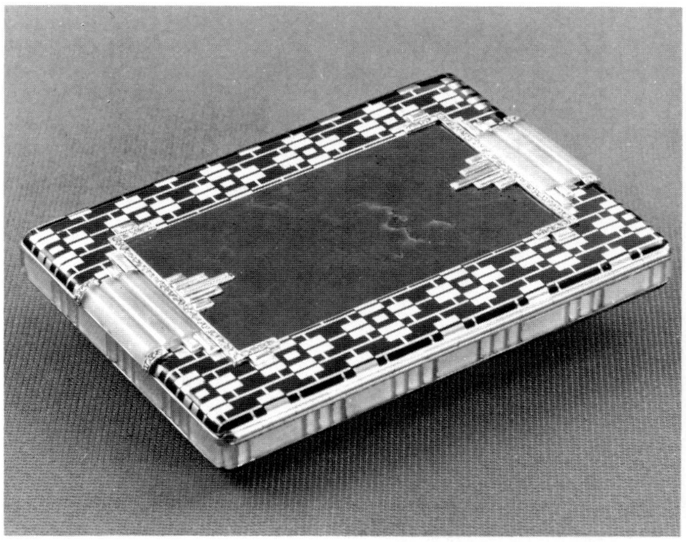

Boucheron: cigarette case in gold and black enamel with a jade plaque set with baguette-cut and rose-cut diamonds and grey agate, 1928. Boucheron Archives.

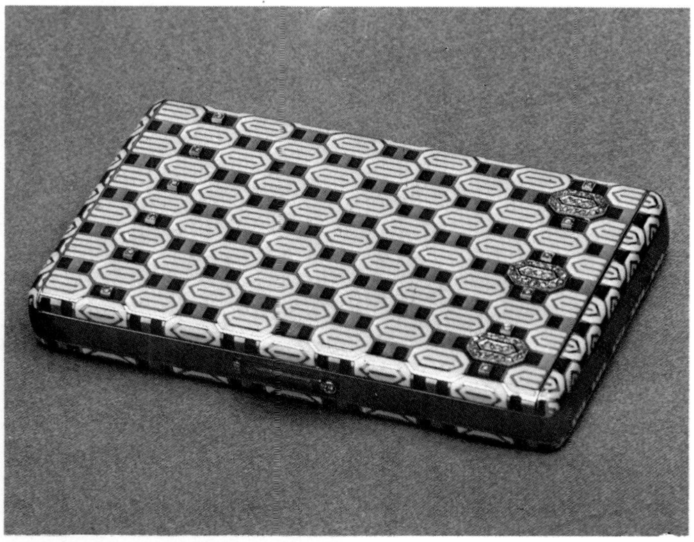

Van Cleef & Arpels: vanity case in gold, white, green and lilac enamel, set with rose-cut diamonds. Private Collection. Van Cleef & Arpels Archives.

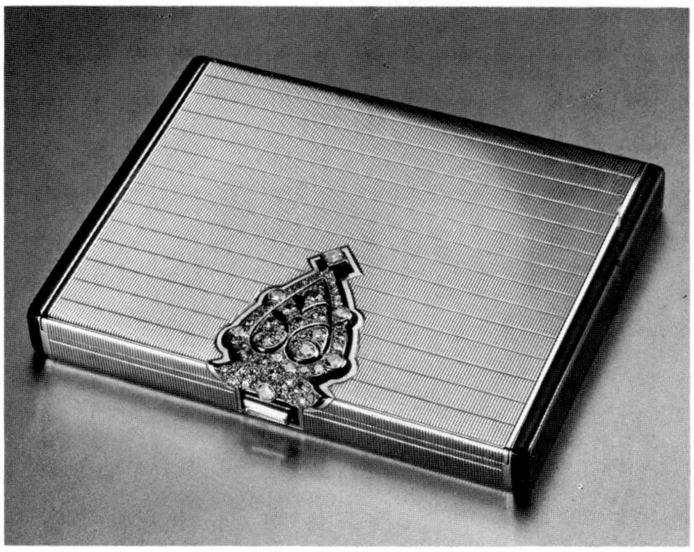

Cartier: cigarette case in guilloché *gold, flanked with black lacquer, and bearing a diamond motif edged with black lacquer and a baton-shaped diamond catch, 1930.*

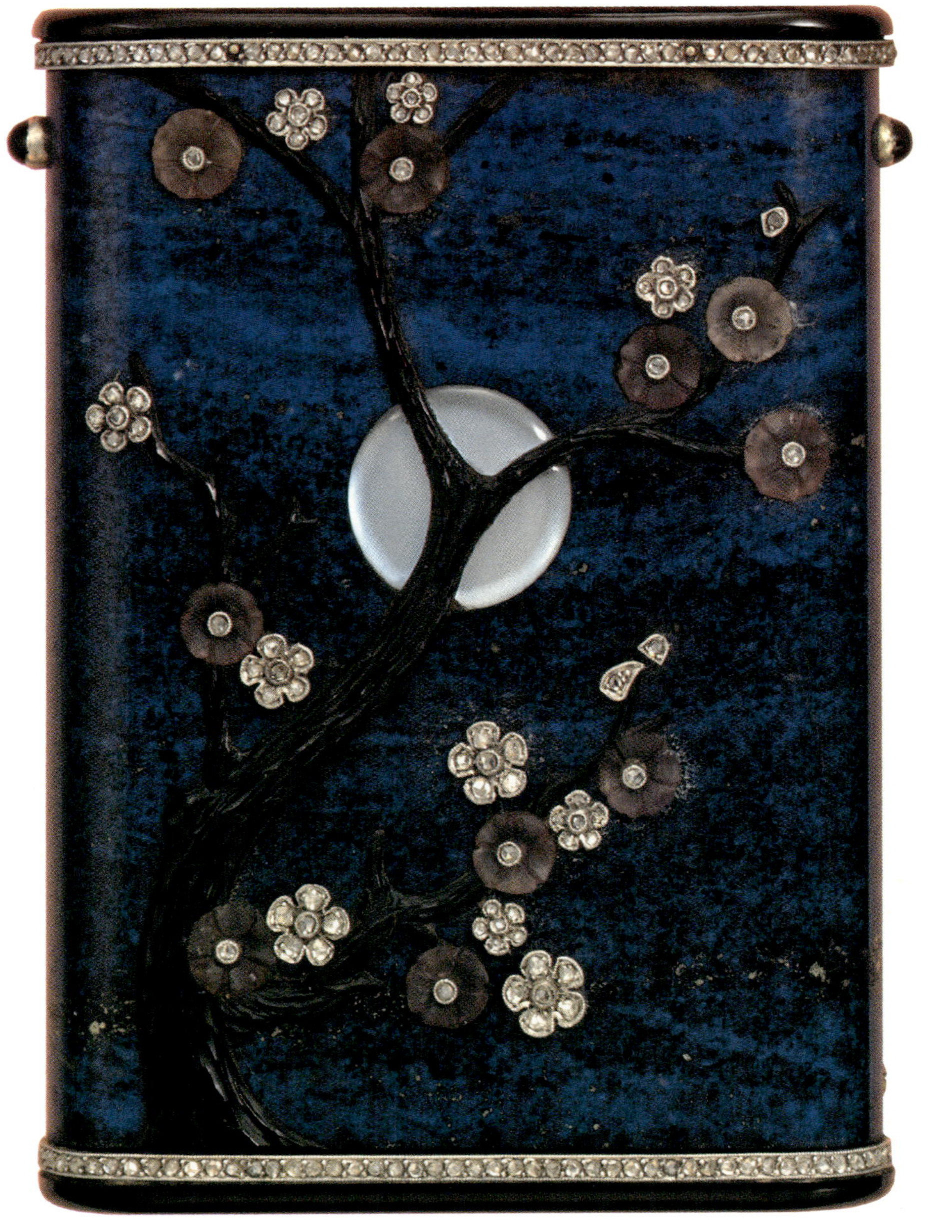

Janesich: card case in lapis with the design of a flowering tree and moon in hardstones, rose-cut diamonds and precious stones, edged on two sides with onyx and rose-cut diamonds, signed. Christie's, Geneva.

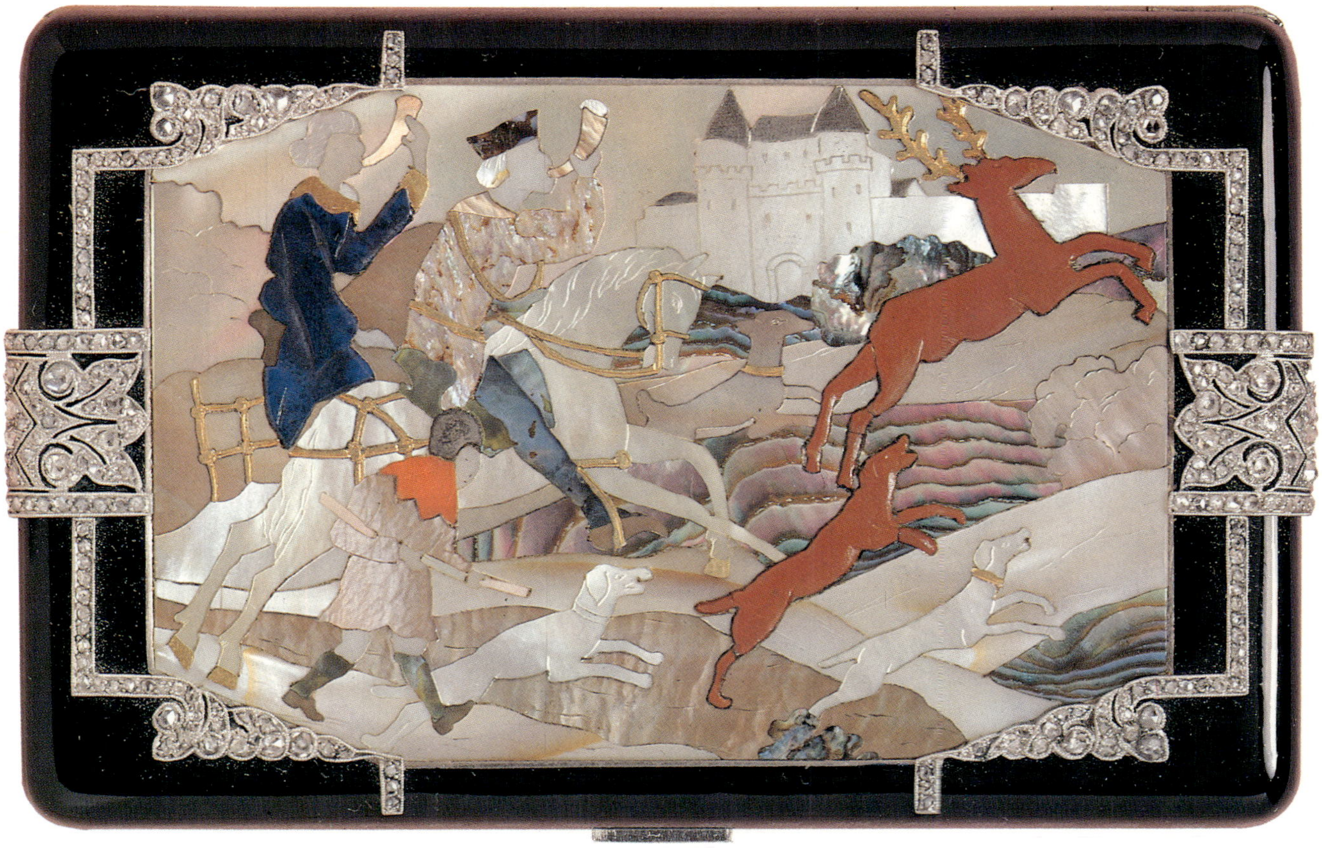

Van Cleef & Arpels: vanity case in gold and black enamel with a hunting scene in mother-of-pearl and enamel inlay and motifs in rose-cut diamonds, 1926. Private Collection. Van Cleef & Arpels Archives.

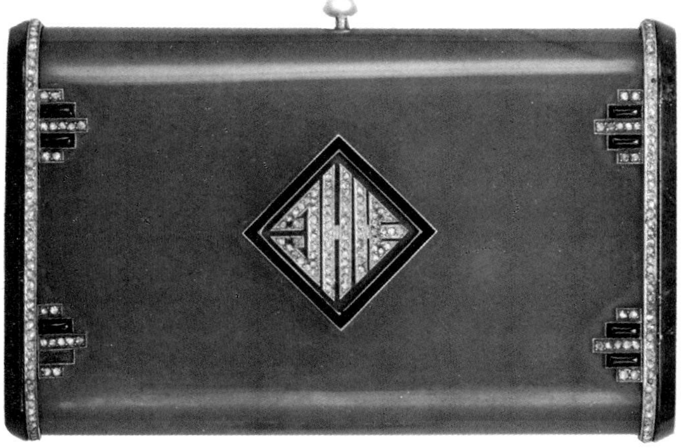

Lacloche: cigarette case in tortoiseshell edged with lapis, diamonds and onyx baguettes, with monogram at the centre in rose-cut diamonds.

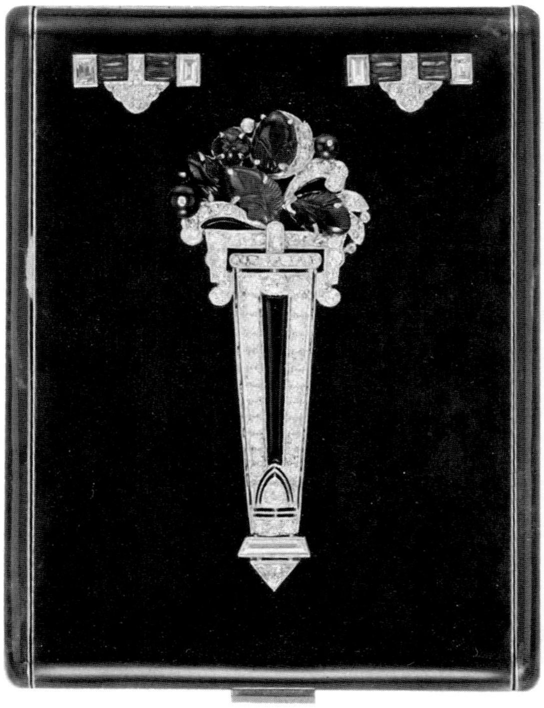

Charlton: vanity case in lapis-like blue enamel and jade-like green enamel, with a vase of flowers in diamonds, onyx, engraved ruby cabochon, sapphires and emeralds. Christie's, New York.

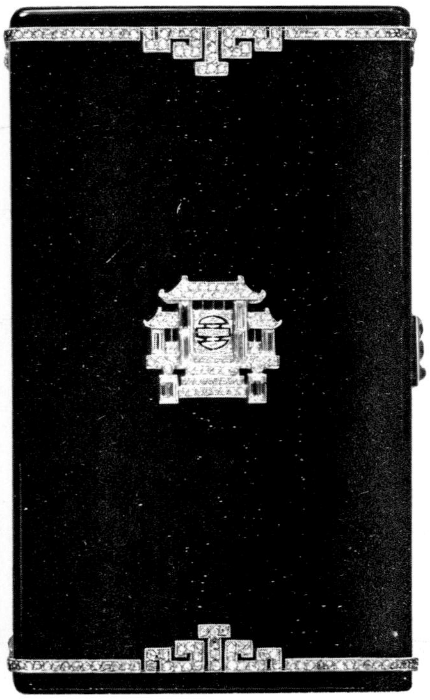

Cartier: vanity case in black enamel with the motif of a Japanese temple in baguette-cut and rose-cut diamonds, borders in rose-cut diamonds and rose-cut diamond catch, signed. Christie's, Geneva.

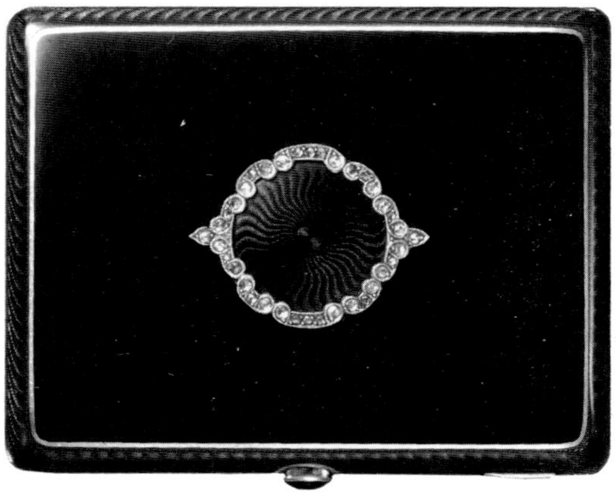

Tiffany: cigarette case in gold and black enamel with a border and central motif in green guilloché *enamel and diamonds. Sotheby's.*

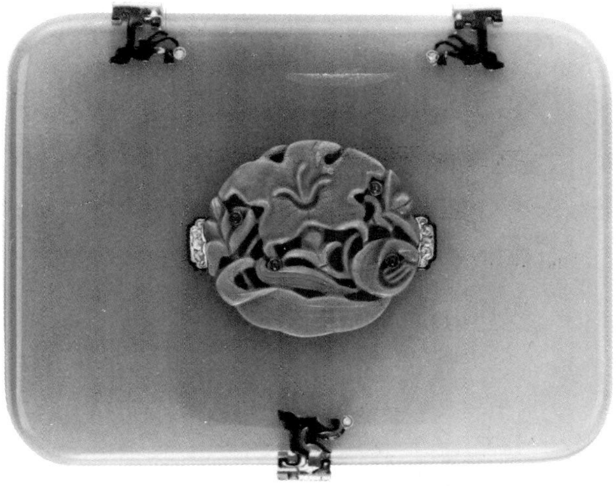

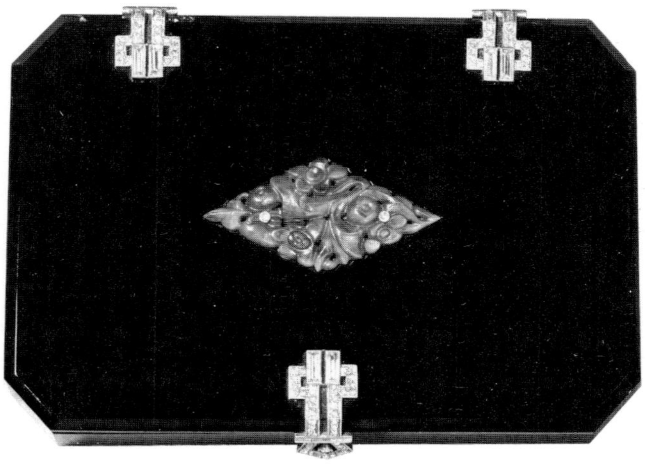

Anonymous: agate vanity case with a Chinese motif depicting a stylized iris in engraved coral set with emerald cabochons and rose-cut diamonds, the hinges and catch in black enamel and diamonds, c. 1925.

Boucheron: cigarette case in black onyx with a Chinese motif in engraved jade, hinges and catch in diamonds.

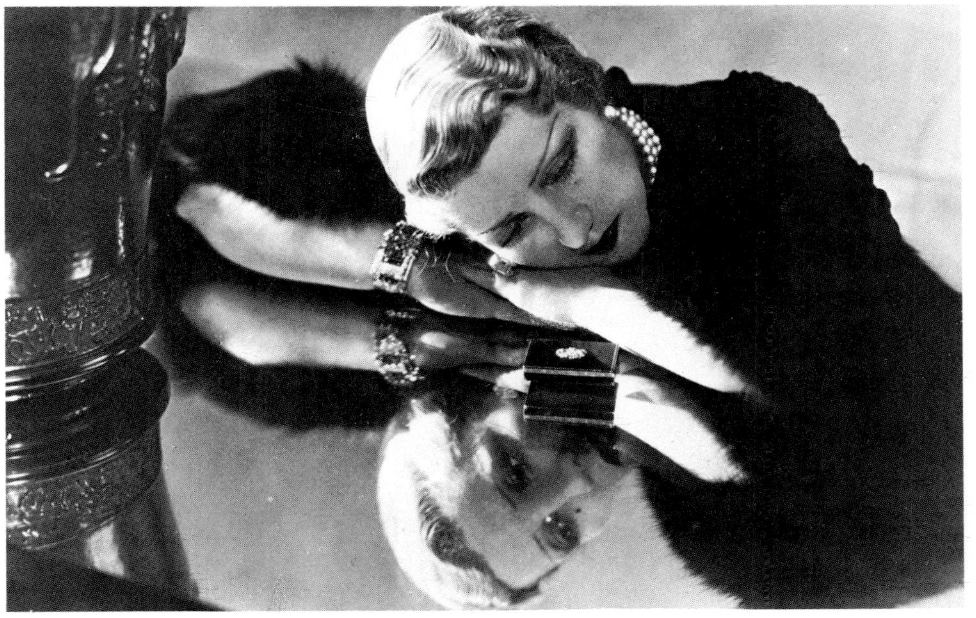

Photograph of Florence Gould, who was the inspiration behind Van Cleef & Arpels' minaudière.

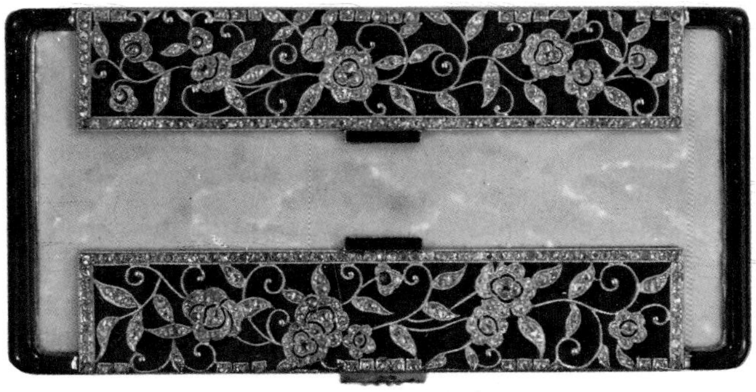

Van Cleef & Arpels: vanity case in gold, black and marbled 'old rose' enamel, with floral motifs in rose-cut diamonds, 1925. Musée Van Cleef & Arpels, Paris.

Following pages: Ostertag: vanity case in pâte de verre, enamel and gold. Private Collection.

Anonymous: vanity case in blue and green enamel with stylized floral decoration, suspended by a chain from a lipstick case and mounted on gold, France, 1925. Private Collection.

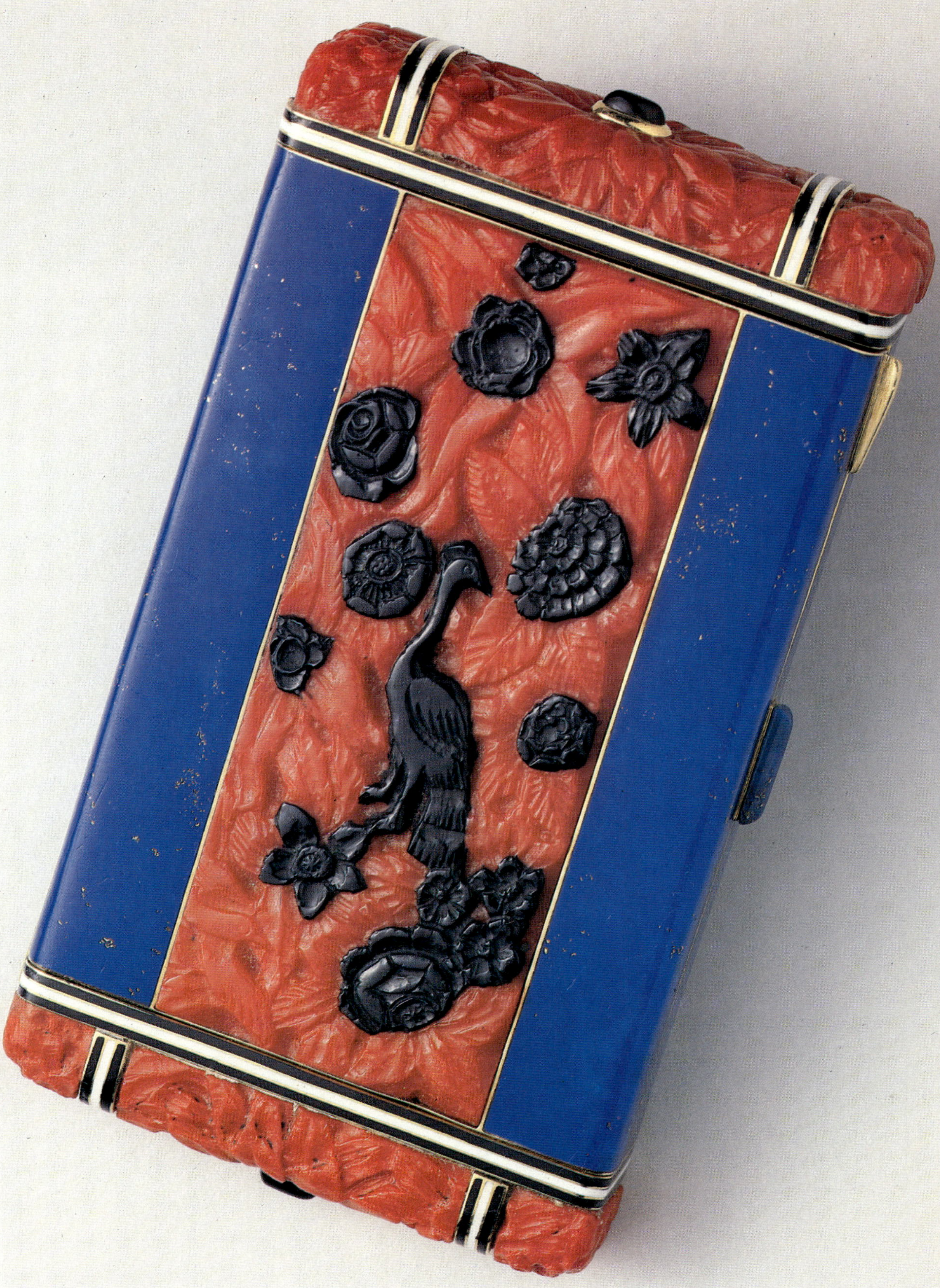

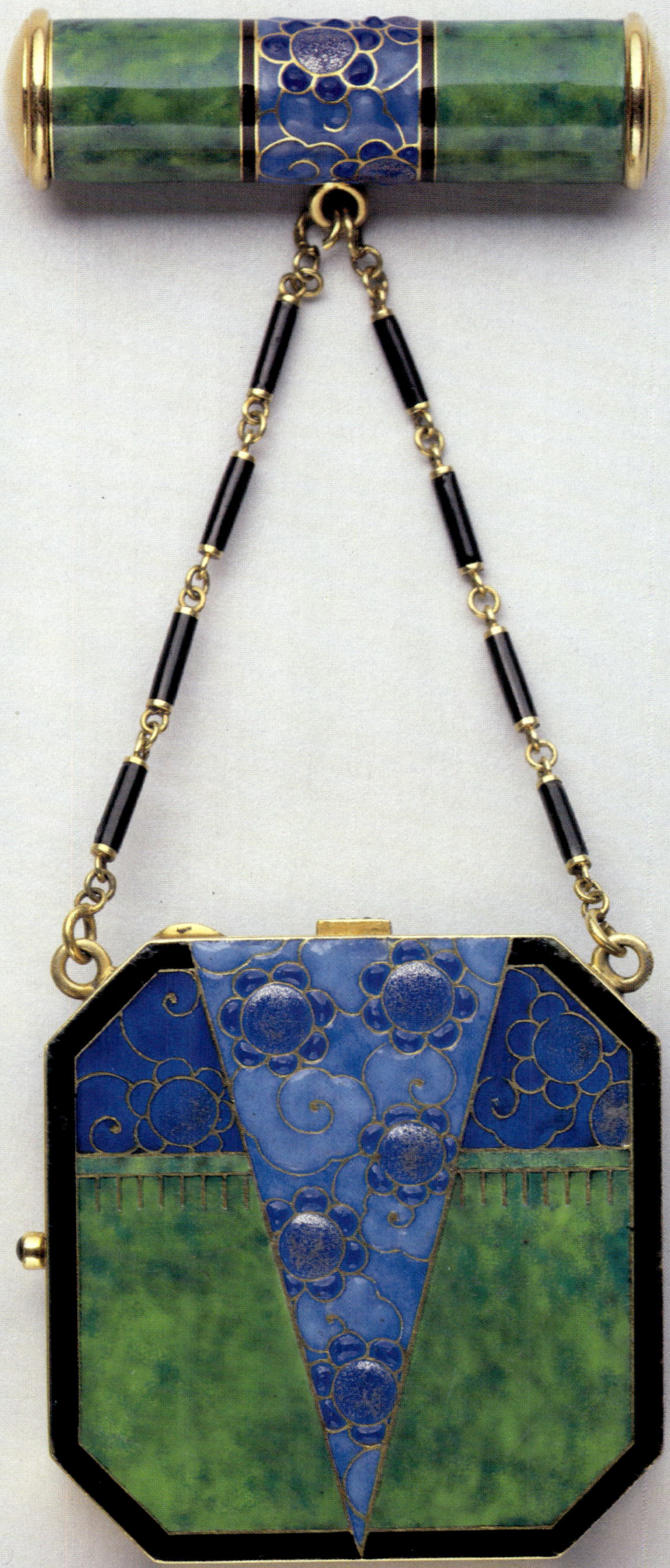

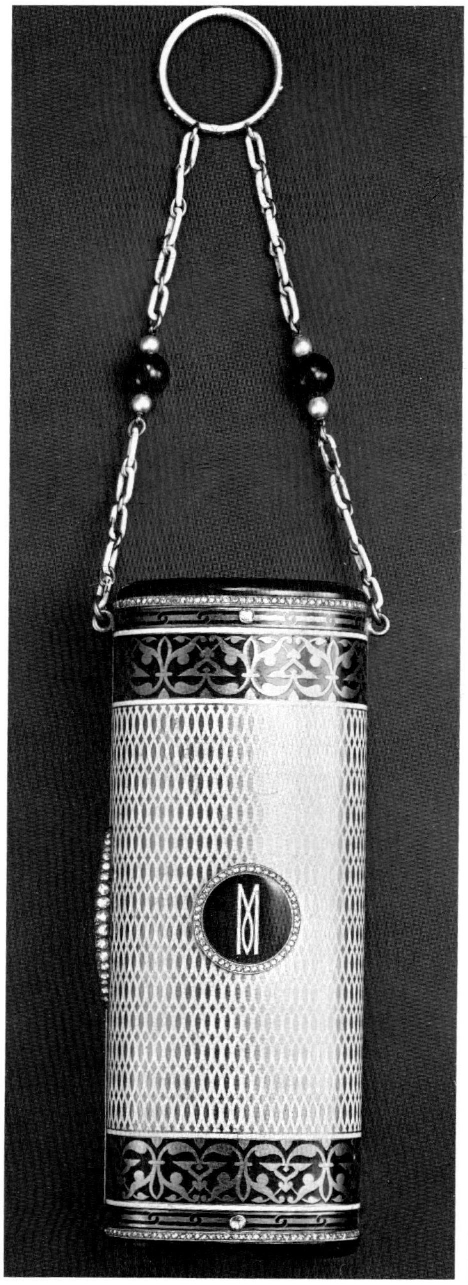

Cartier: gold vanity case in the form of an oval cylinder with oriental motifs and onyx lid, 1914. Christie's, Geneva.

Van Cleef & Arpels: vanity case in the form of an oval cylinder in black enamel with an ornamental border of rose-cut diamonds and lateral catch in the form of a sapphire cabochon and rose-cut diamonds, signed. Christie's, New York.

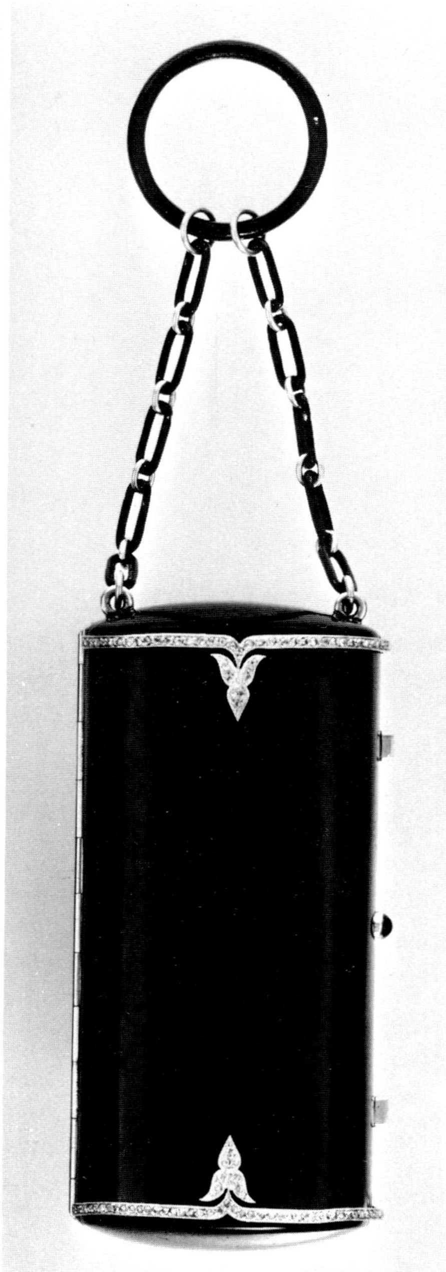

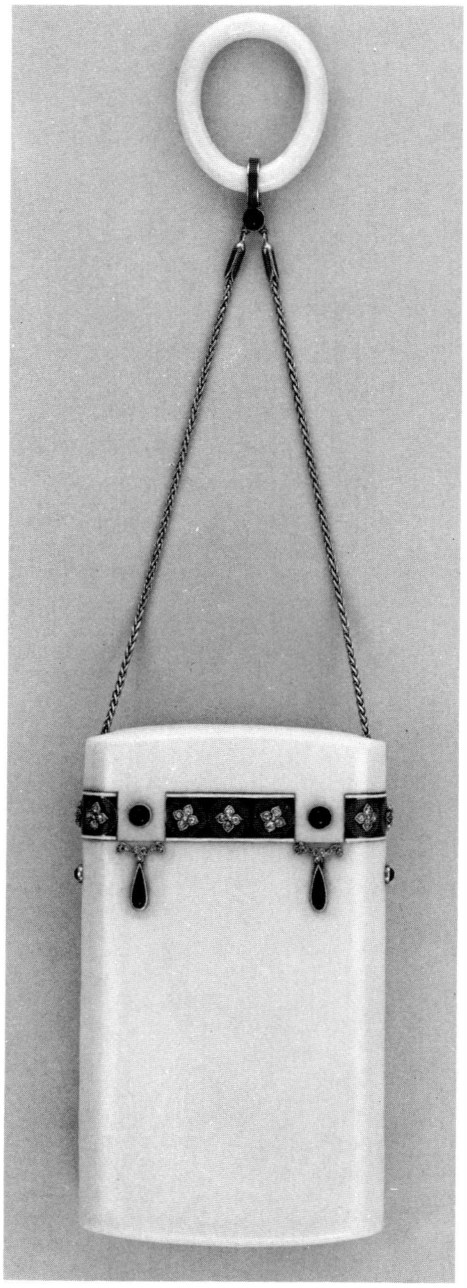

Ghiso: card case in the form of an oval cylinder in polished ivory with rose-cut diamonds in a four-leaved clover motif on a green, black and white enamel ground, and onyx cabochons and drops, signed. Christie's, New York.

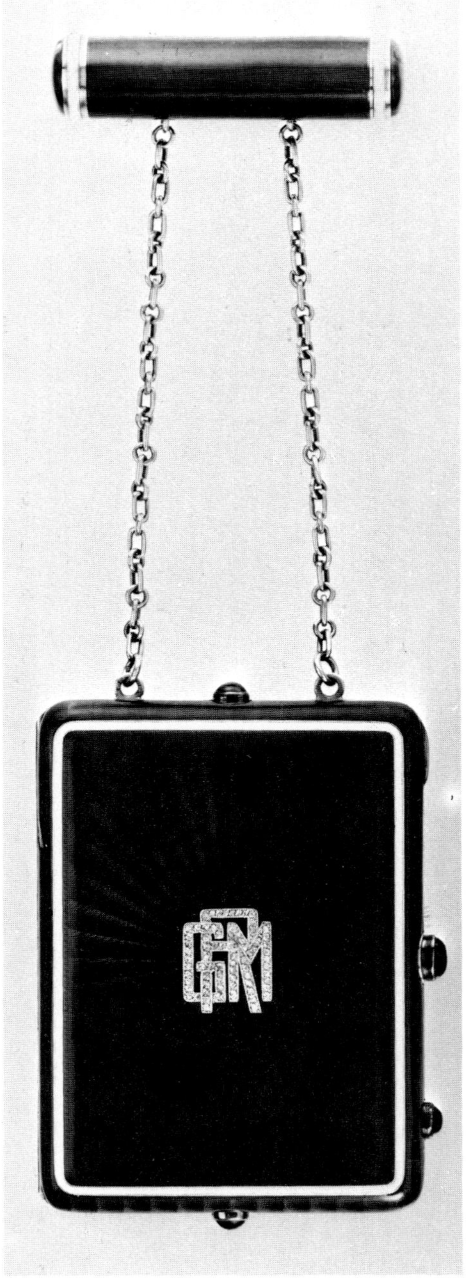

Anonymous: vanity case in blue guilloché *enamel with a white enamel border and a diamond monogram, the clasp consisting of four sapphire cabochons. Mounted on yellow gold and attached by chains to a lipstick case. Christie's.*

Boucheron: vanity case in black and coloured enamel with onyx cabochons, from which a black silk tassel is suspended. Boucheron Archives.

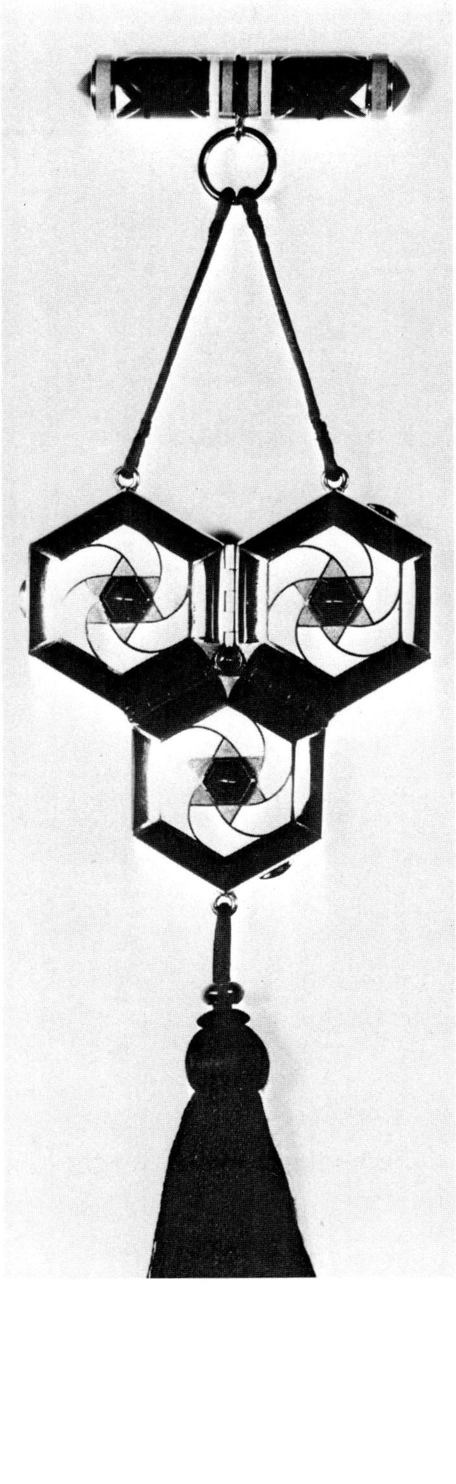

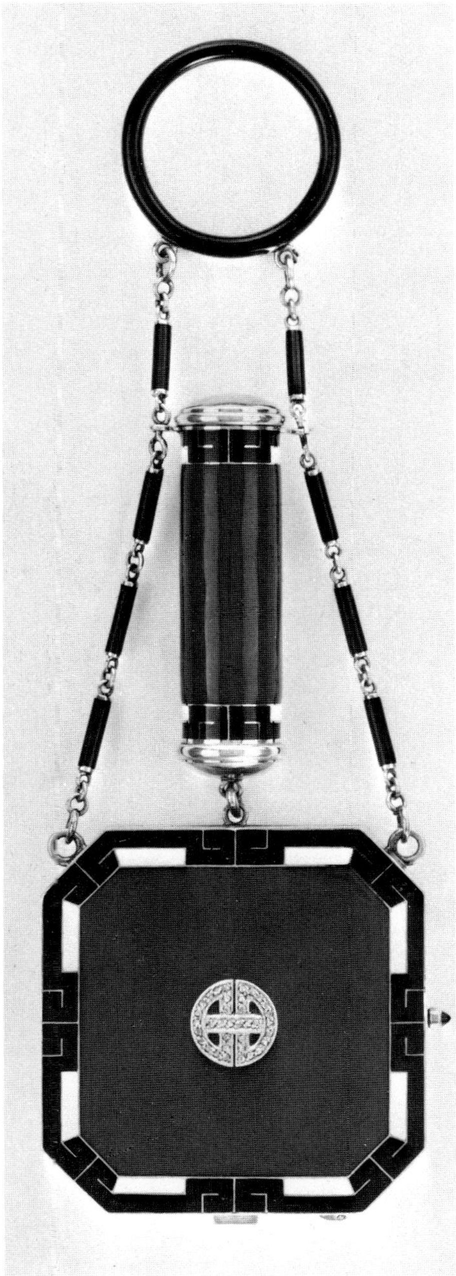

Anonymous: vanity case in red enamel bordered with white and black enamel, with a central motif in diamonds and a lipstick case attached between the two chains, c. 1927. Christie's.

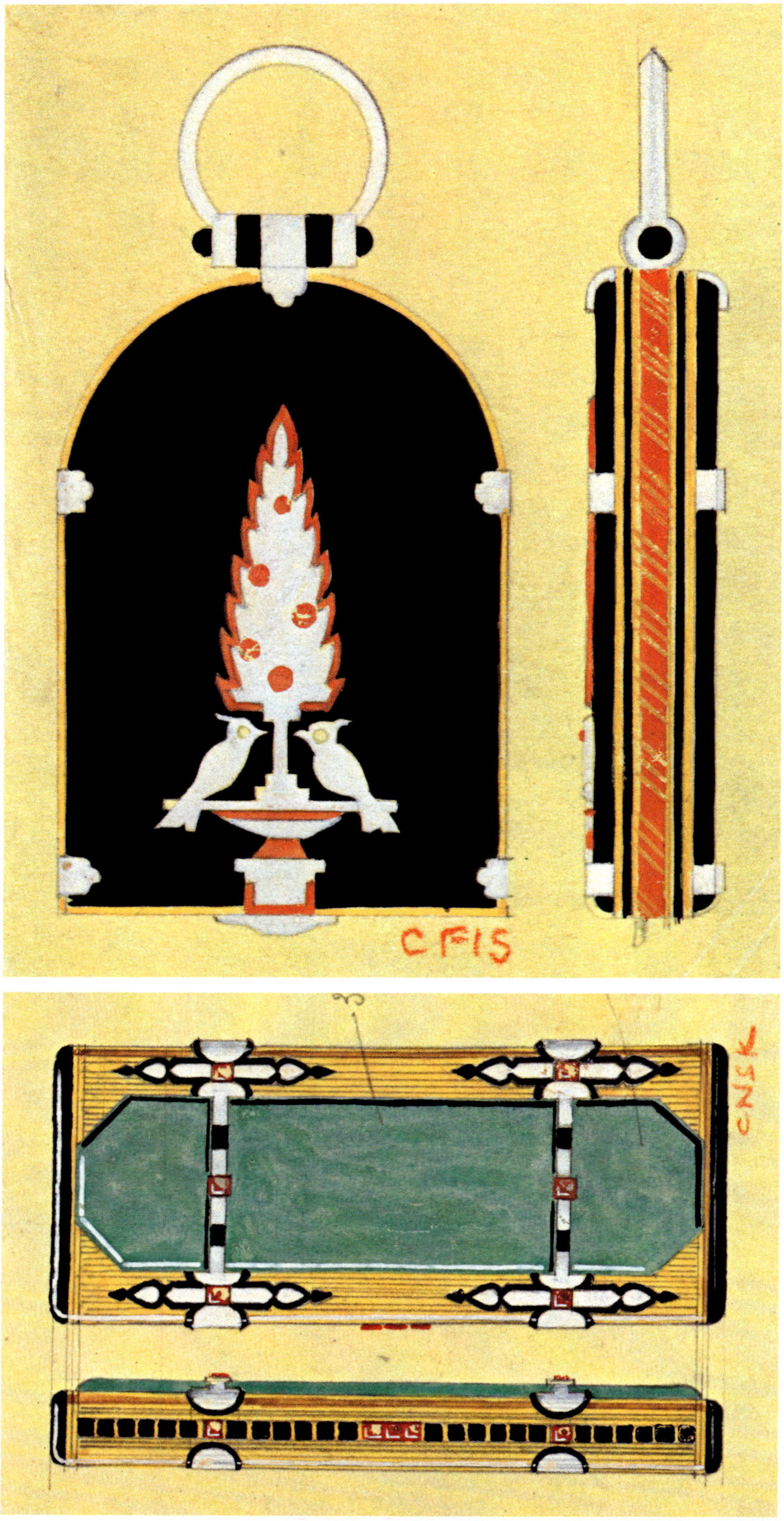

Gouache studies for vanity cases executed by designer-craftsmen for the Haute Joaillerie. *M. Souillac Archives.*

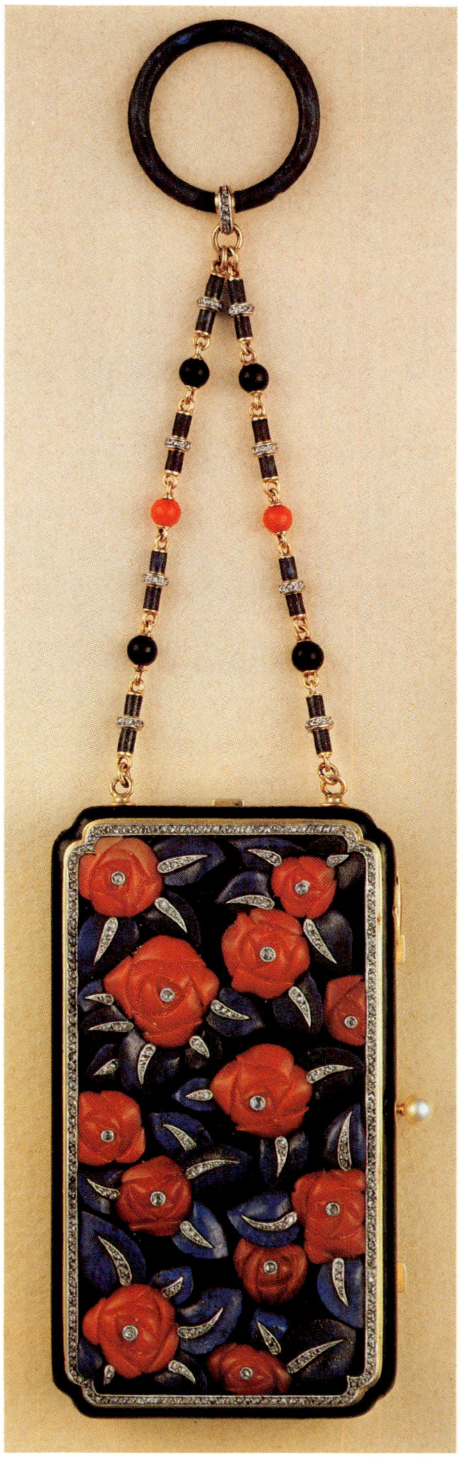

Chaumet: vanity case with stylized flowers in coral and lapis, edged with rose-cut diamonds, on a black enamel ground; pearl catch. Sotheby's, Saint Moritz.

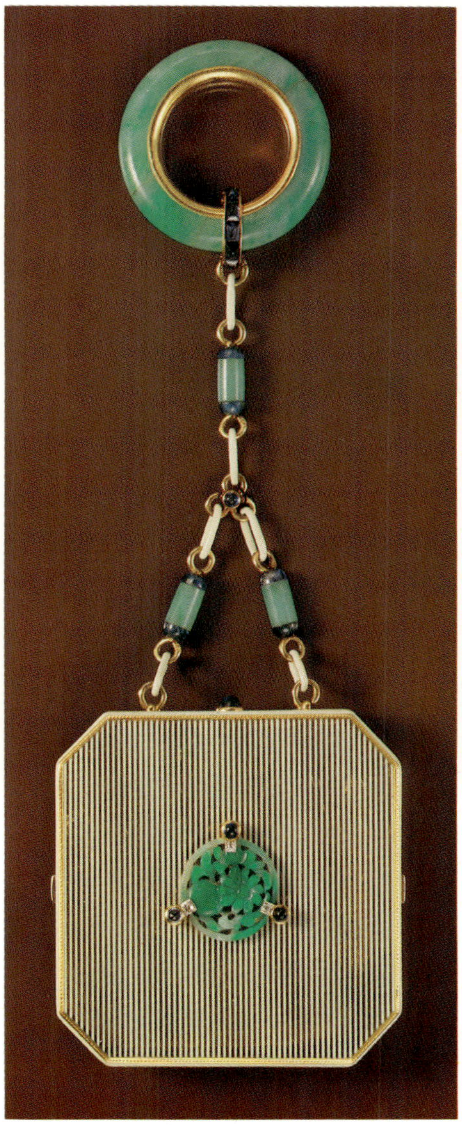

Cartier: square vanity case with cut-off corners, in ivory enamel with stripes in gold, a central motif on both sides in engraved jade, sapphires and diamonds. Attached to a jade ring by chains decorated with sapphire, jade and enamel. Sotheby's.

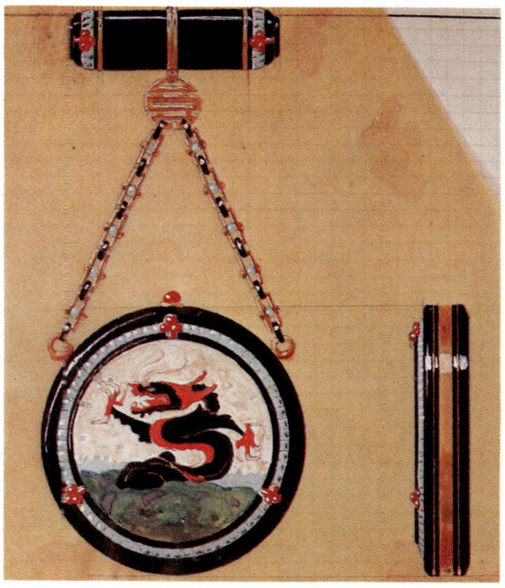

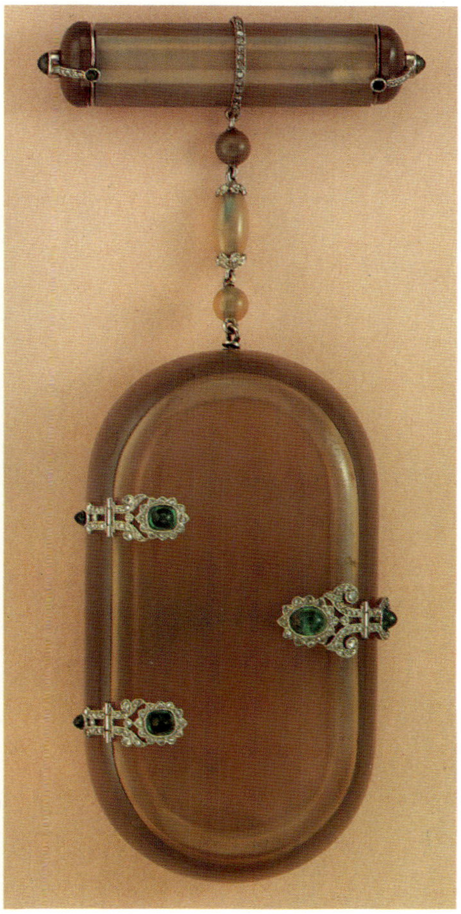

Cartier: gouache study for a powder compact attached by two chains to a lipstick case, in pink gold, enamelled black, with a Chinese dragon motif inlaid on ivory and a border of turquoise batons and ruby cabochons, 1925.

Anonymous: agate vanity case with, on the hinges and catch, floral motifs composed of emerald cabochons and rose-cut diamonds. A chain, composed of three agate beads set with diamonds, links the case to an agate lipstick case. Mounted on platinum and gold. Christie's, New York.

Da Silva Bruhns: evening bag in salmon pink, copper and pale-pink beads, with a geometric design, c. 1925. Sotheby's, Monte Carlo.

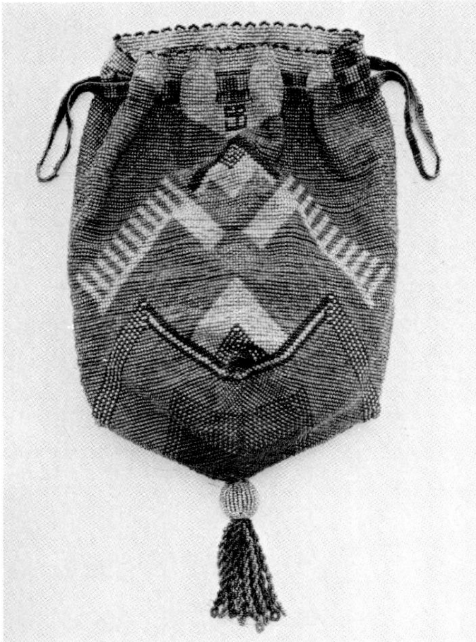

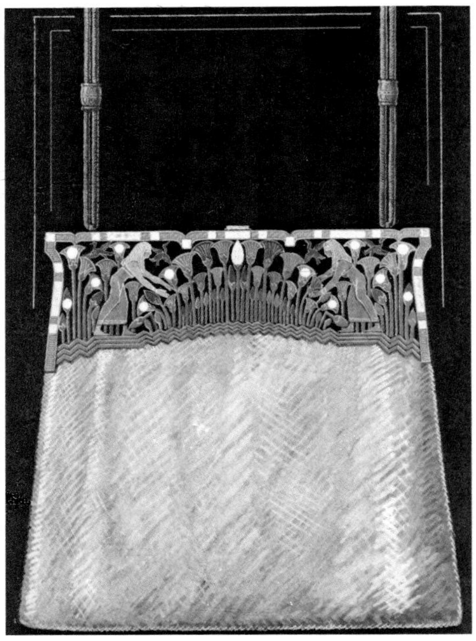

Cartier: design for an evening bag in enamelled gold and diamonds with Pharaonic Egyptian motifs. Cartier Archives.

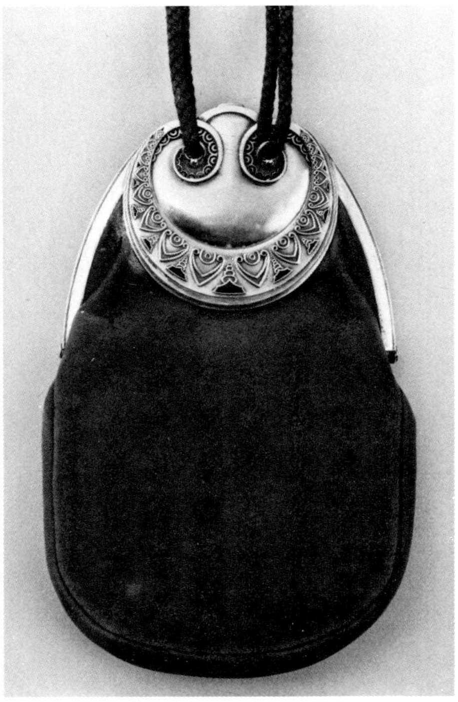

Raymond Templier: bag in silver and velvet, 1912. A. Lesieutre Collection. Photo: L. Sully-Jaulmes.

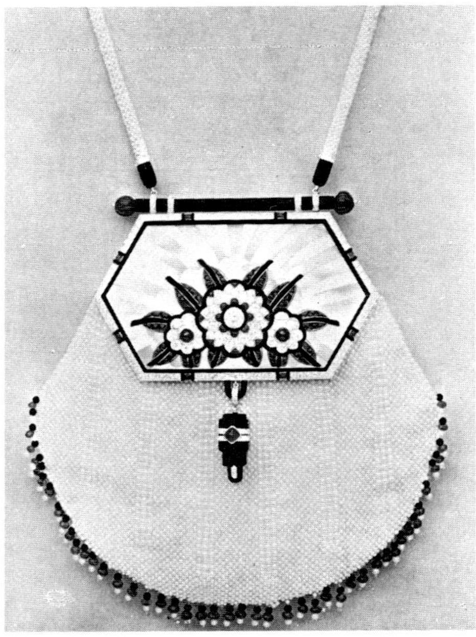

Dusausoy: evening bag in seed pearls, onyx and precious stones.

Facing page: Cartier: evening bag in cultured pearls, set with diamonds, engraved emeralds, rubies and sapphires; fringes of pearls and coloured stone beads, signed. H. 15.5 cm, W. 14 cm.

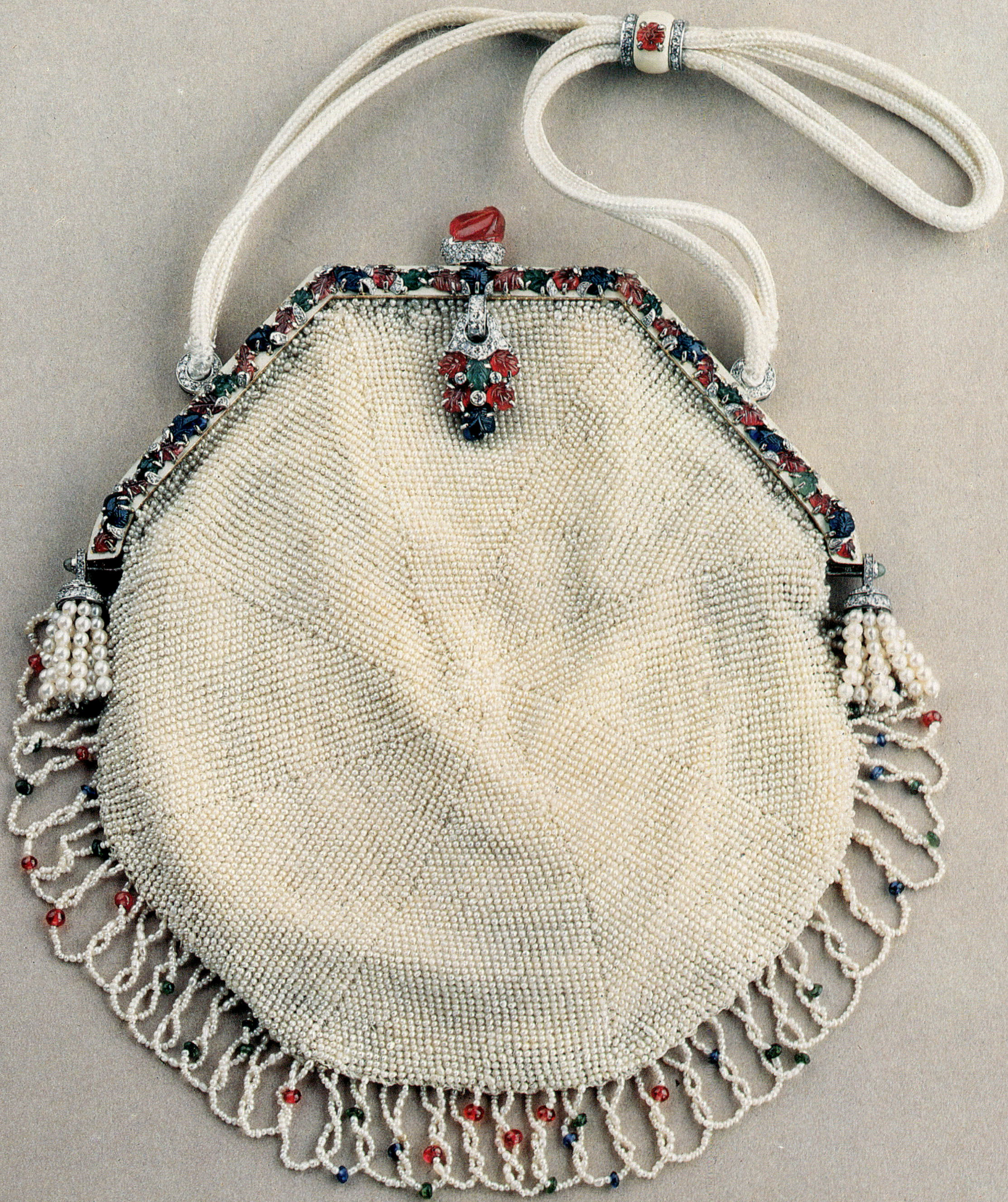

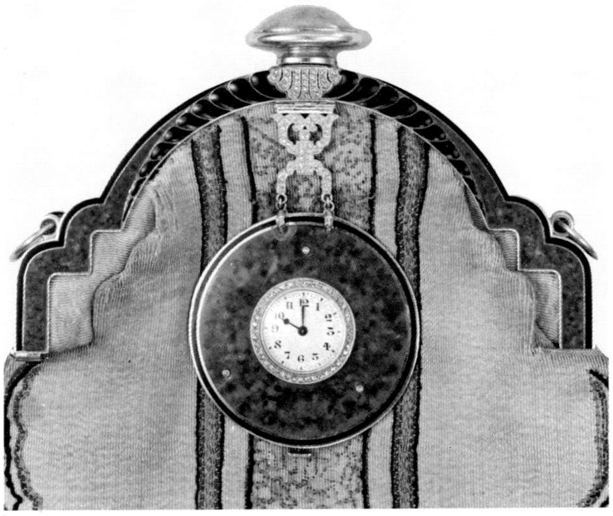

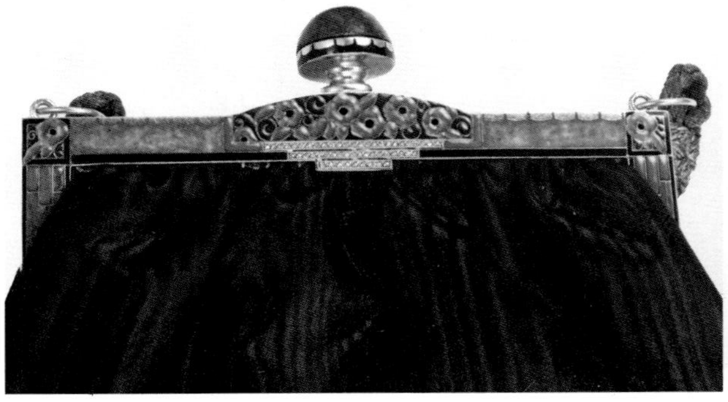

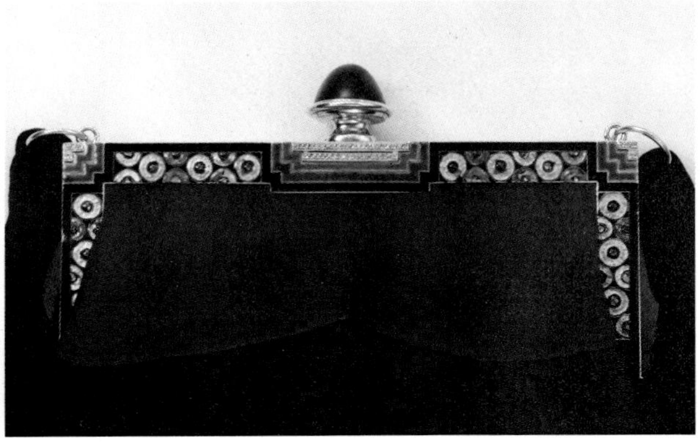

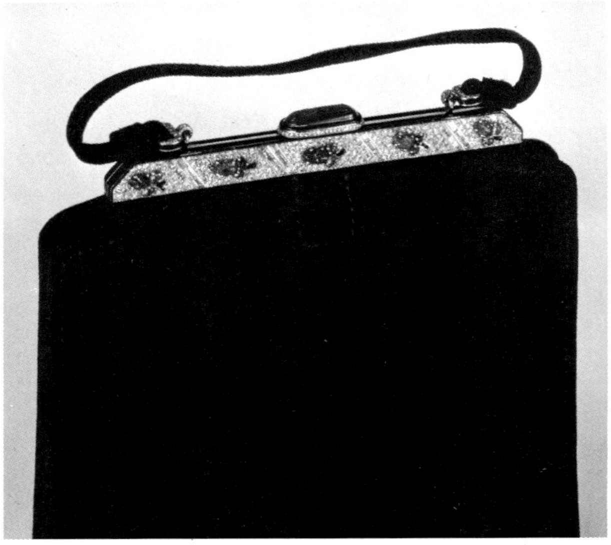

Anonymous: evening bag decorated with gold and green and black enamel, from which a round watch, set in a green marbled disc and bordered with rose-cut diamonds, is suspended. Sotheby's, Geneva.

Anonymous: evening bag in black moiré silk, with a geometric and stylized floral design in coloured enamel set with diamonds; catch in gold with a lapis cabochon. Sotheby's, Geneva.

Lacloche: silk evening bag, with green and mauve enamel and an amethyst cabochon catch. Christie's.

Cartier: evening bag in blue reindeer hide with diamonds, engraved emeralds and rubies, edged with black enamel, the catch comprising an engraved ruby on platinum. Cartier Archives.

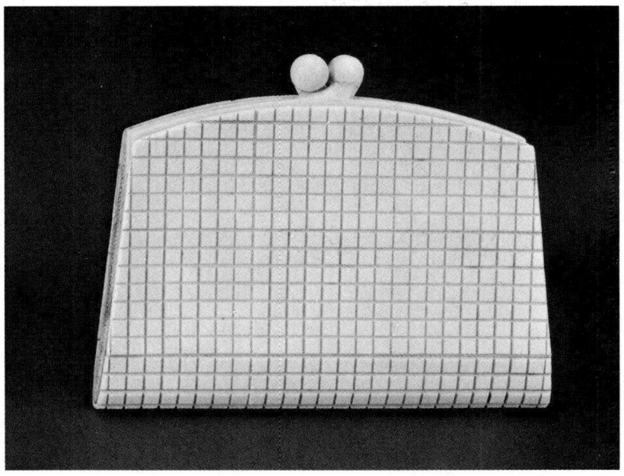

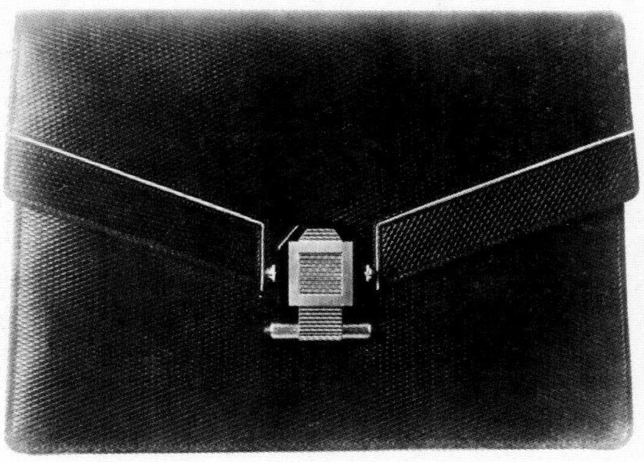

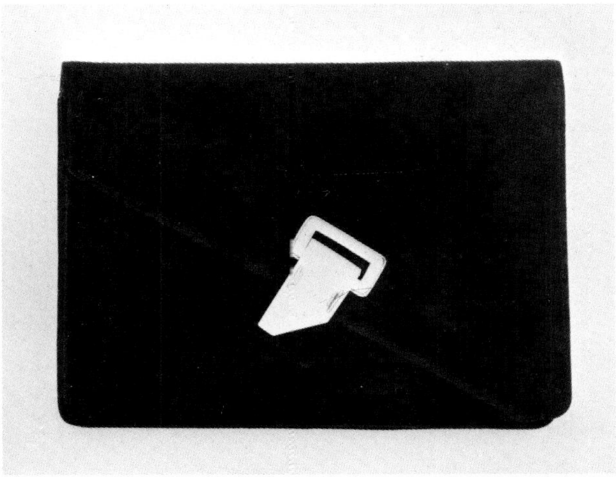

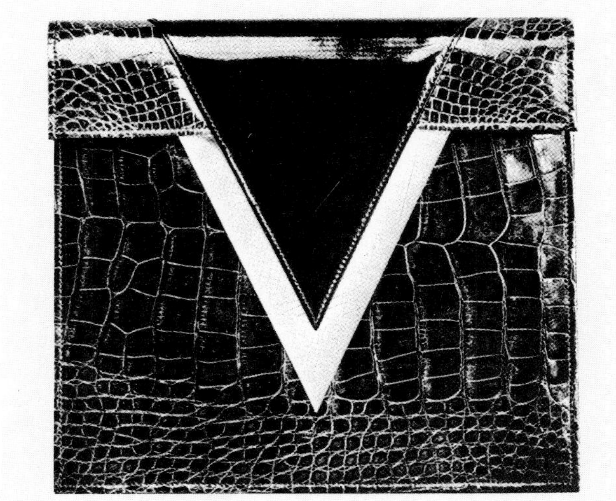

Anonymous: pochette in white Bakelite.
M. Souillac Collection. Photo: J.B. Rouault.

Boucheron: pochette in grained leather with a catch in precious metal and black onyx. Boucheron Archives.

Van Cleef & Arpels: evening pochette in black suède with an ivory and gold clasp, c. 1930. Sotheby's.

Jean Fouquet: pochette in crocodile-skin and coloured leather.

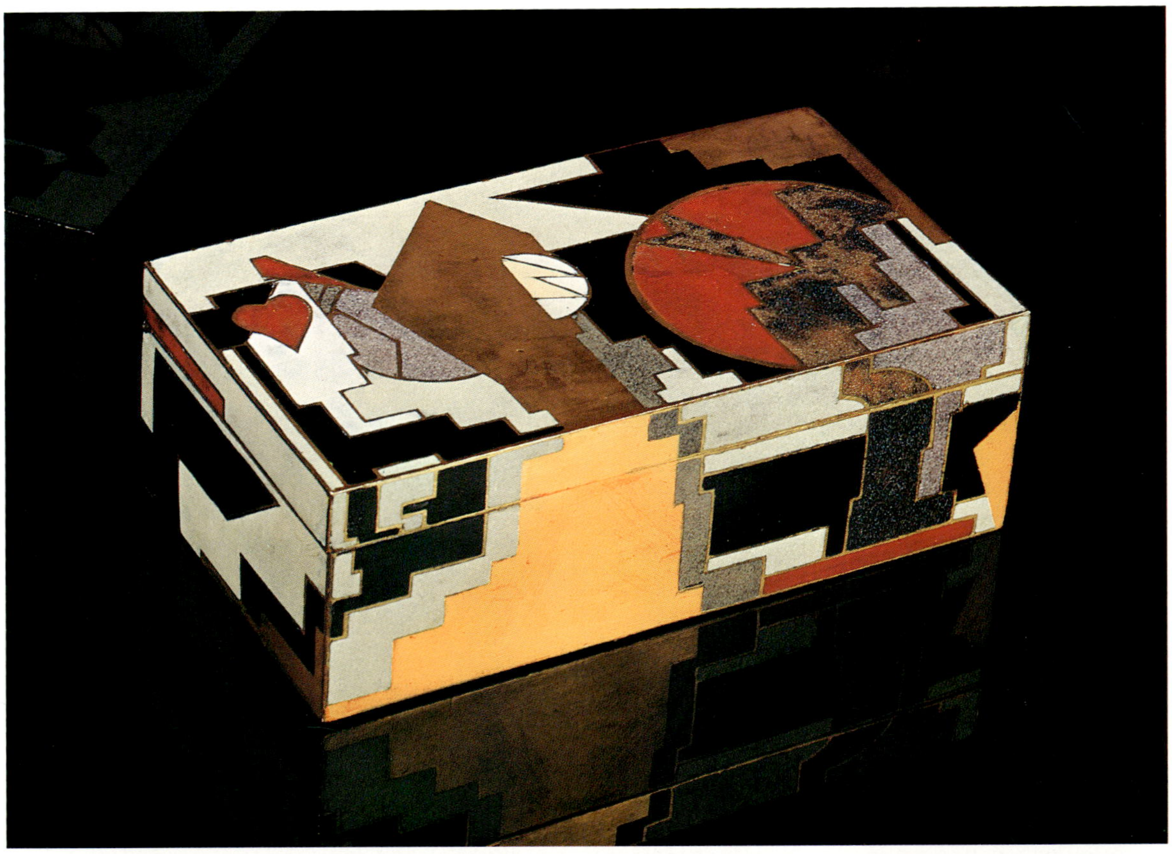

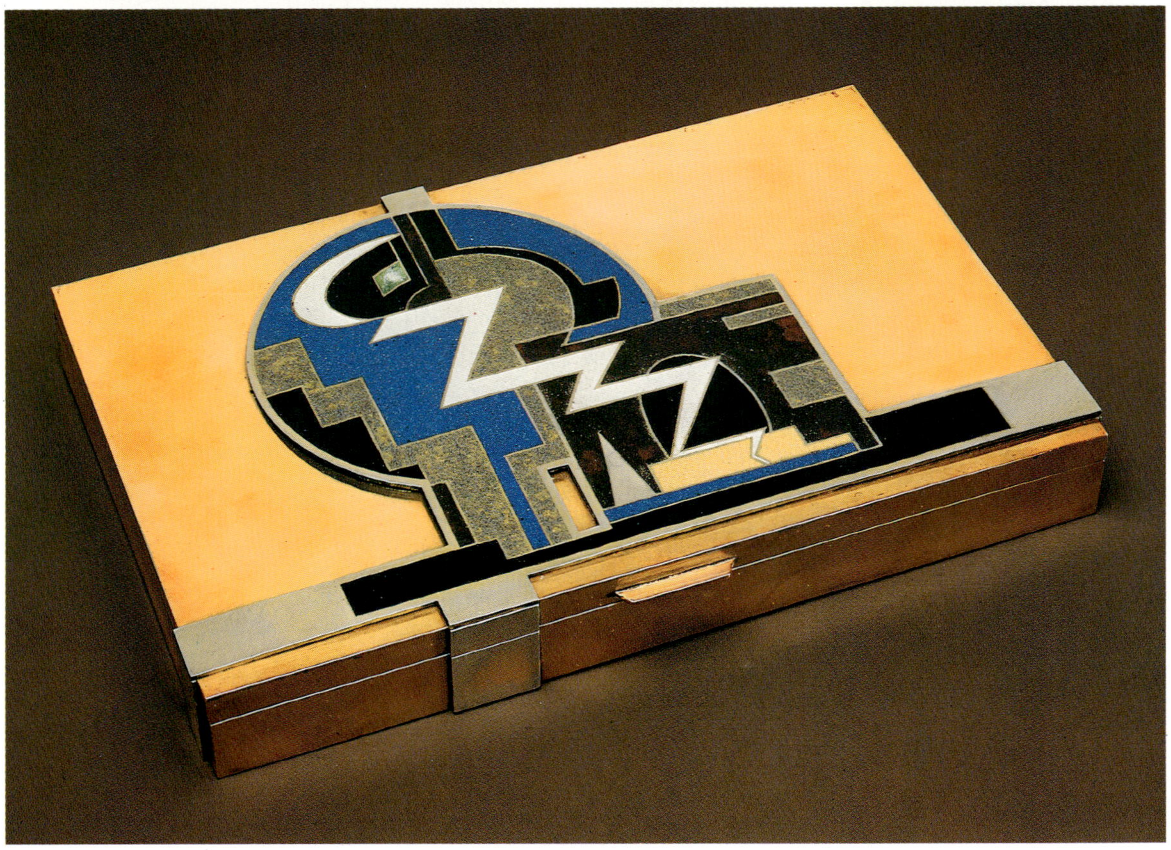

Jean Goulden: casket in copper and champlevé enamel, 1925, signed. Photo: L. Sully-Jaulmes.

Jean Goulden: casket in copper, silver and champlevé enamel. Galerie Vallois. Photo: Vénus Mercenaire.

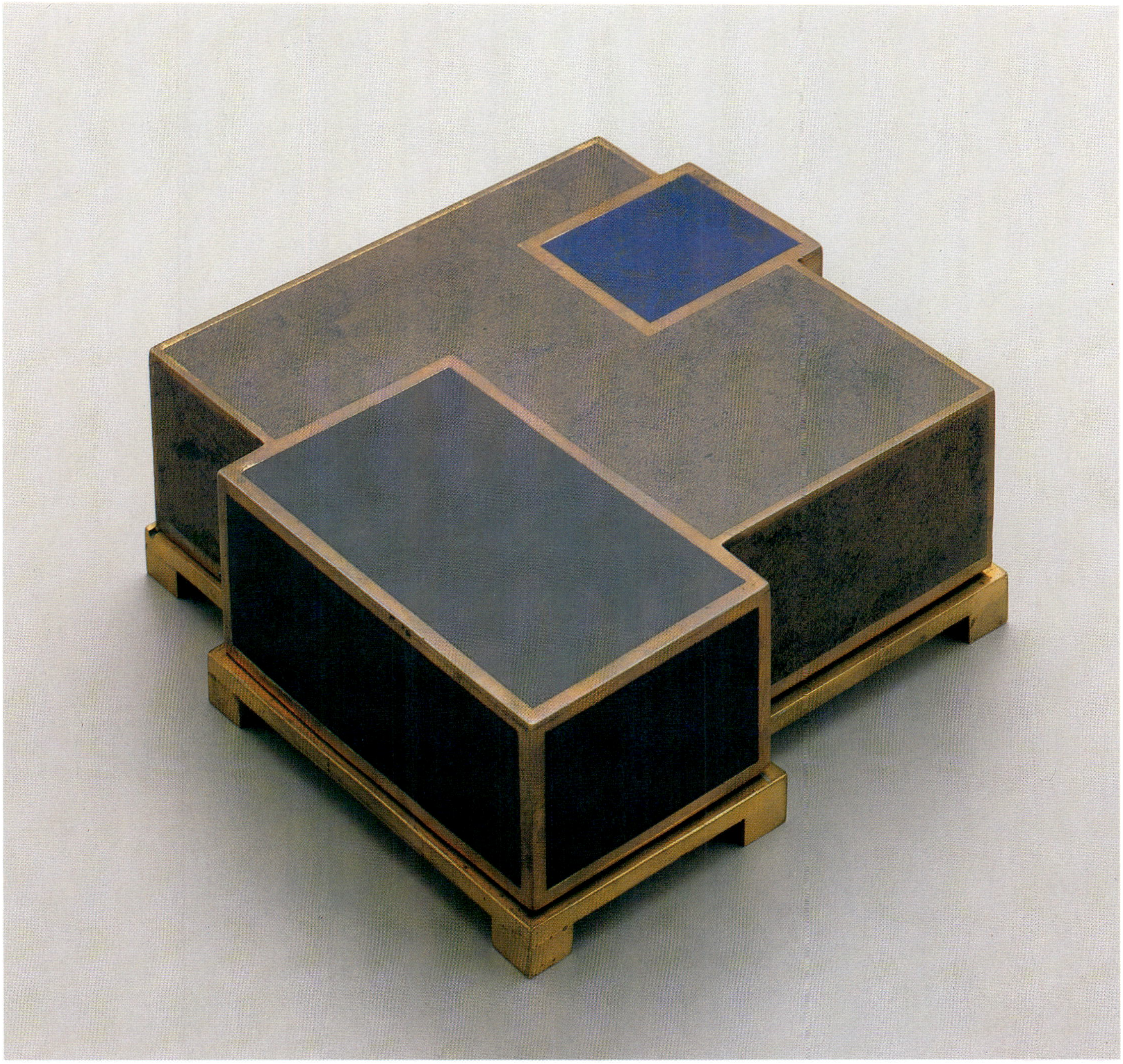

Jean Goulden: box in copper, silver and champlevé *enamel. Private Collection.*

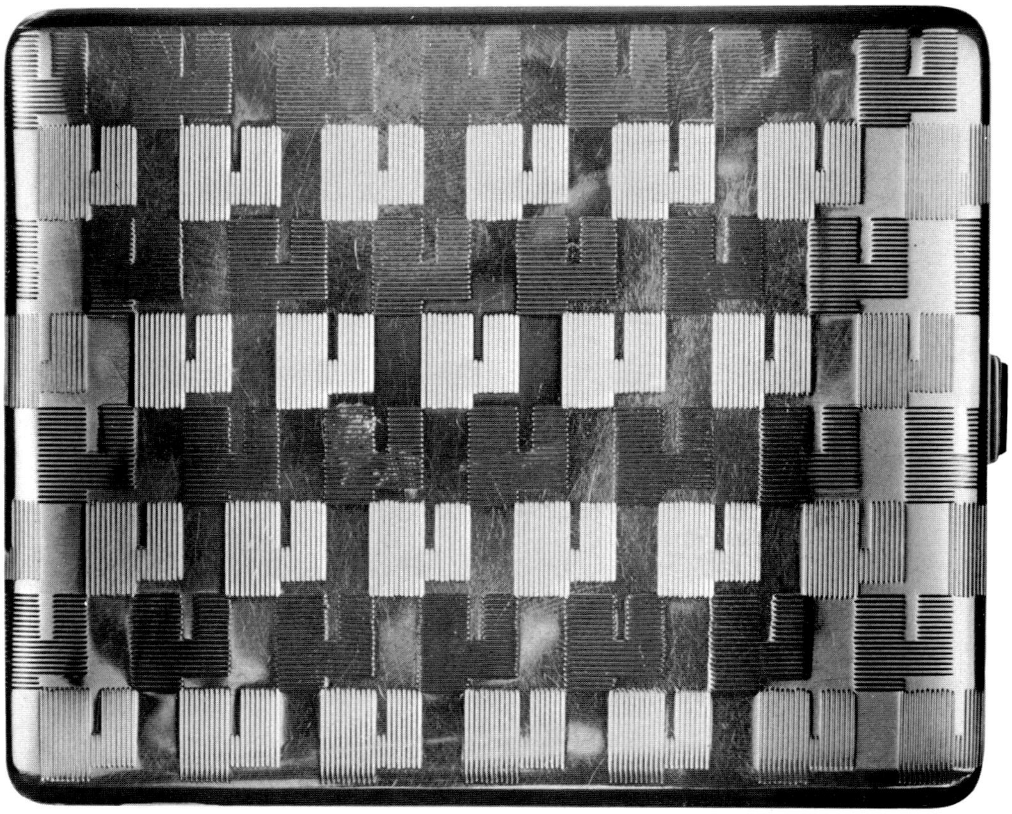

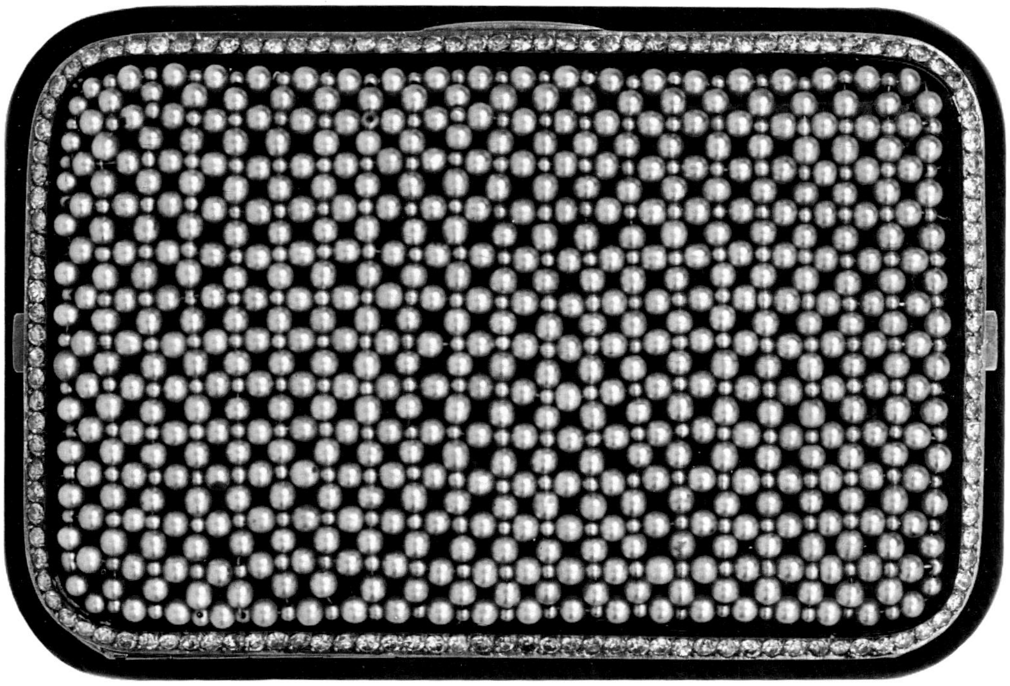

Raymond Templier: cigarette case in guilloché gold, edged with lacquered shell, with a repeated motif of initials, made for Marcel l'Herbier, 1929, signed. Sotheby's, Monte Carlo.

Van Cleef & Arpels: vanity case in gold, black enamel, pearls and diamonds, 1927. Van Cleef & Arpels Archives.

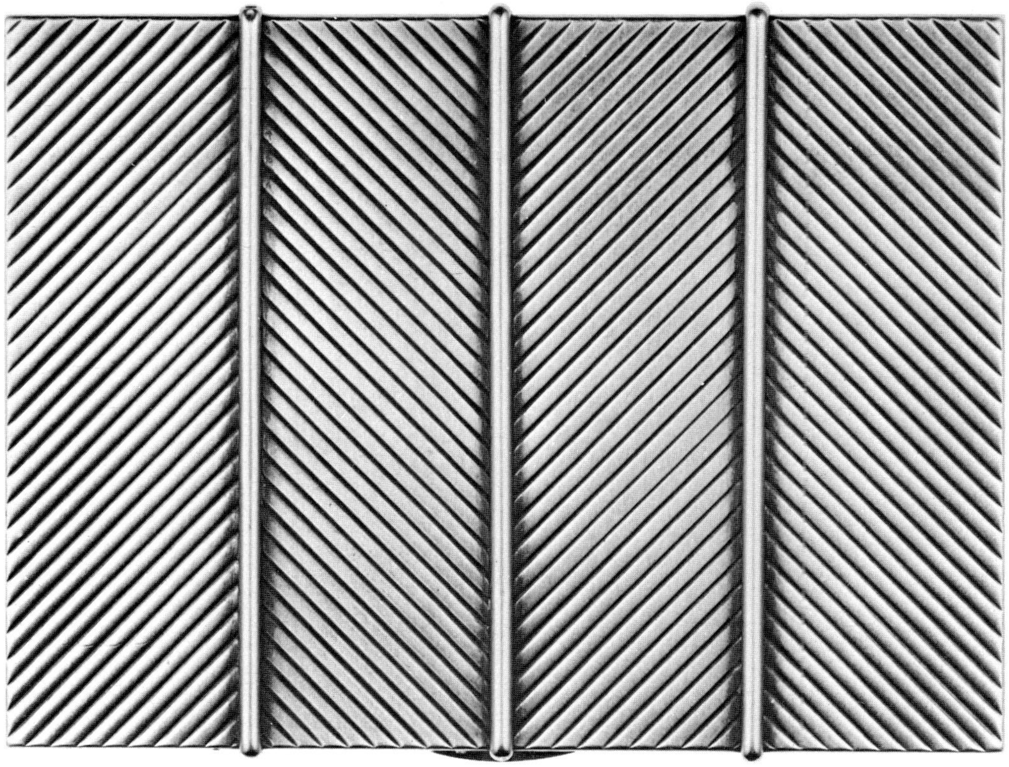

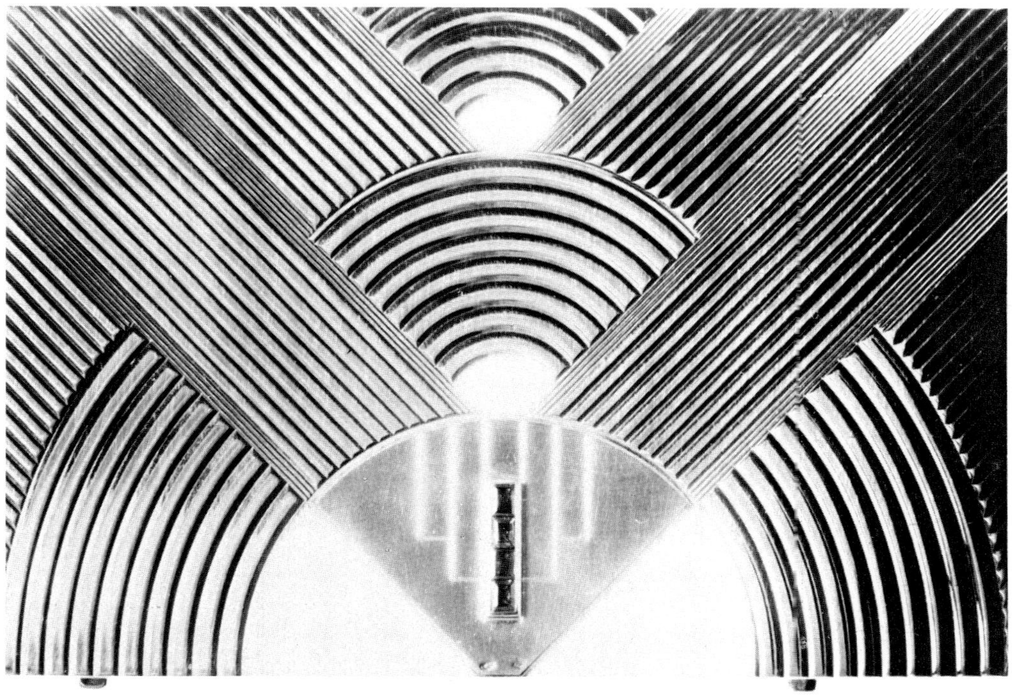

Tiffany: powder compact in silver and gold with chevron design and three gold bands, c. 1925, signed. Sotheby's, Monte Carlo.

Boucheron: powder compact in silver and gold with fluted chevrons; catch of calibré *sapphires, c. 1925. Boucheron Archives.*

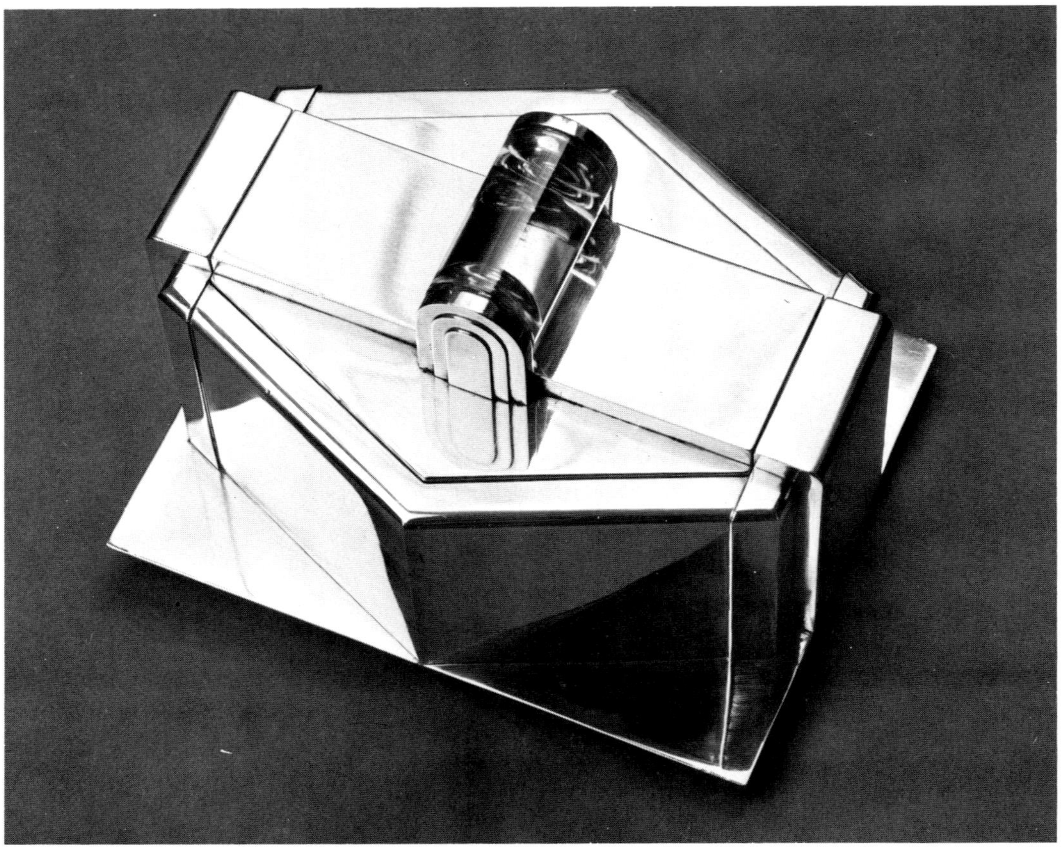

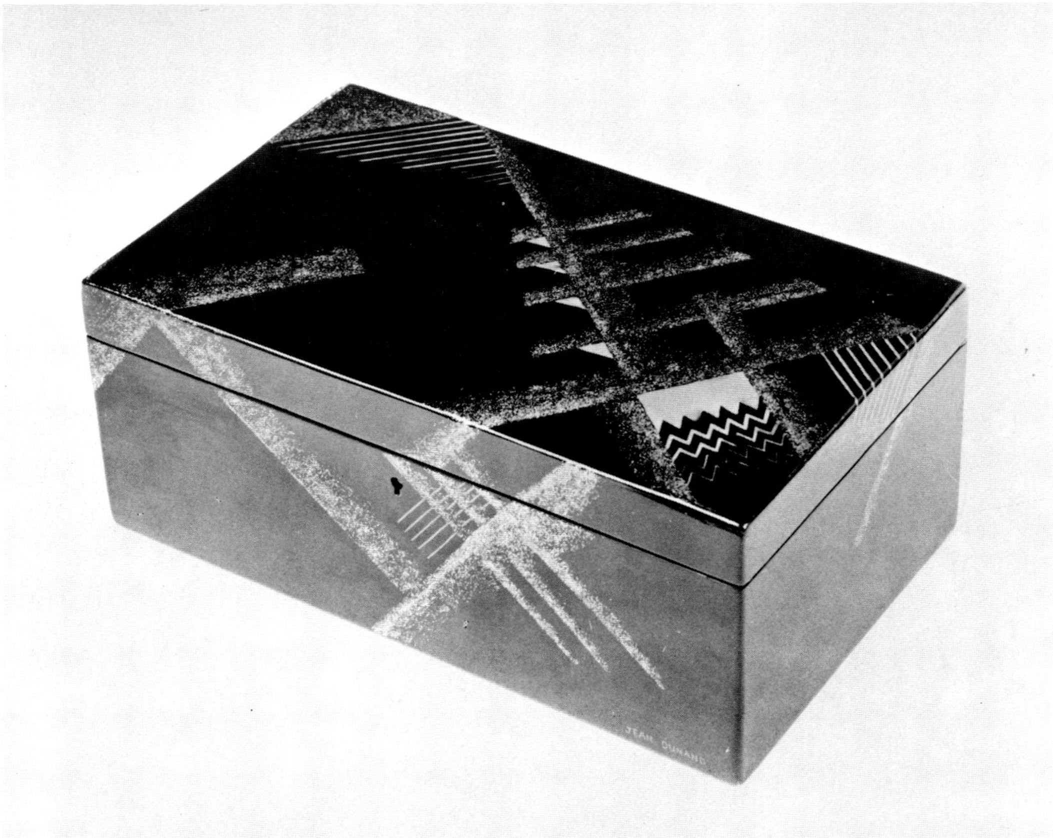

Jean Puiforcat: silver box with cut-off corners and crystal handle, presented at the 1925 Paris Exposition. Private Collection. Photo: L. Sully-Jaulmes.

Jean Dunand: box in black lacquer with eggshell. A. Lesieutre Collection. Photo: L. Sully-Jaulmes.

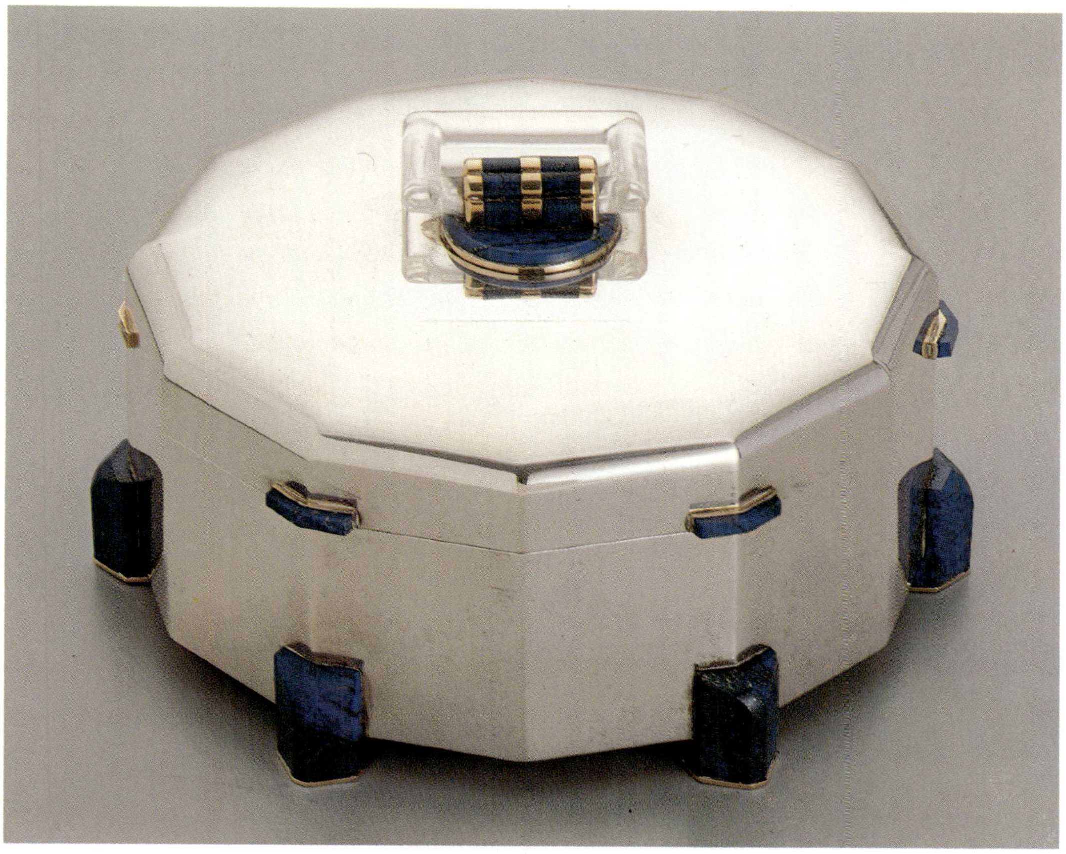

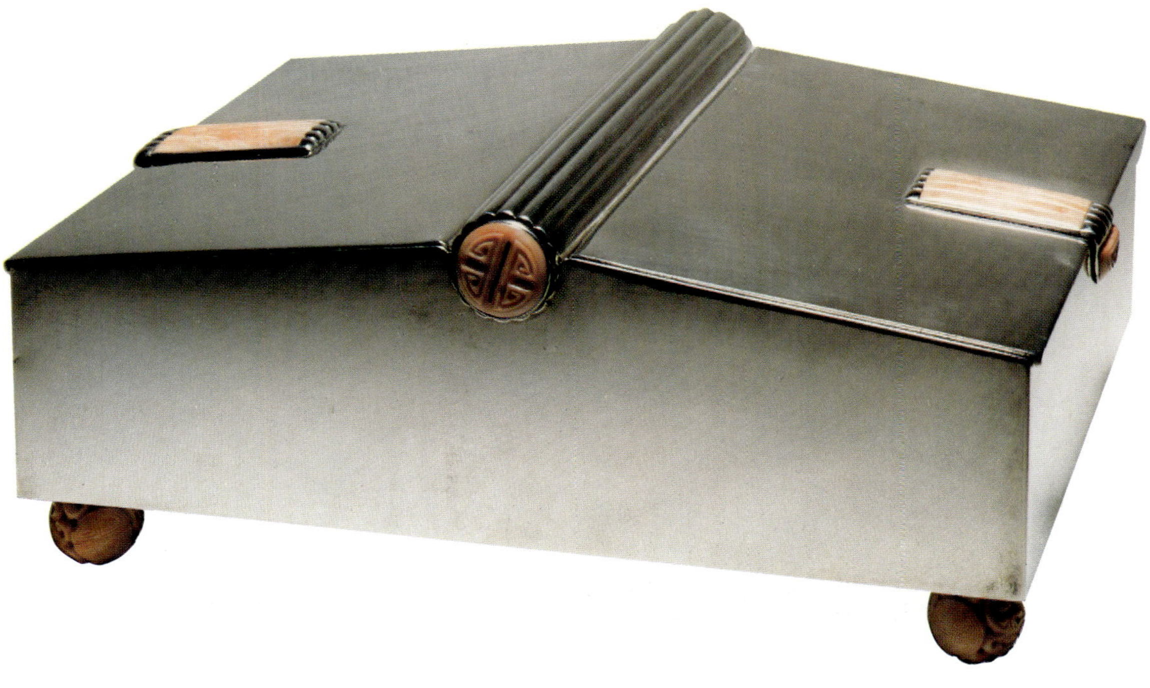

Cartier: box in silver, lapis and rock crystal, signed.

Boucheron: box in silver and coral, 1930.

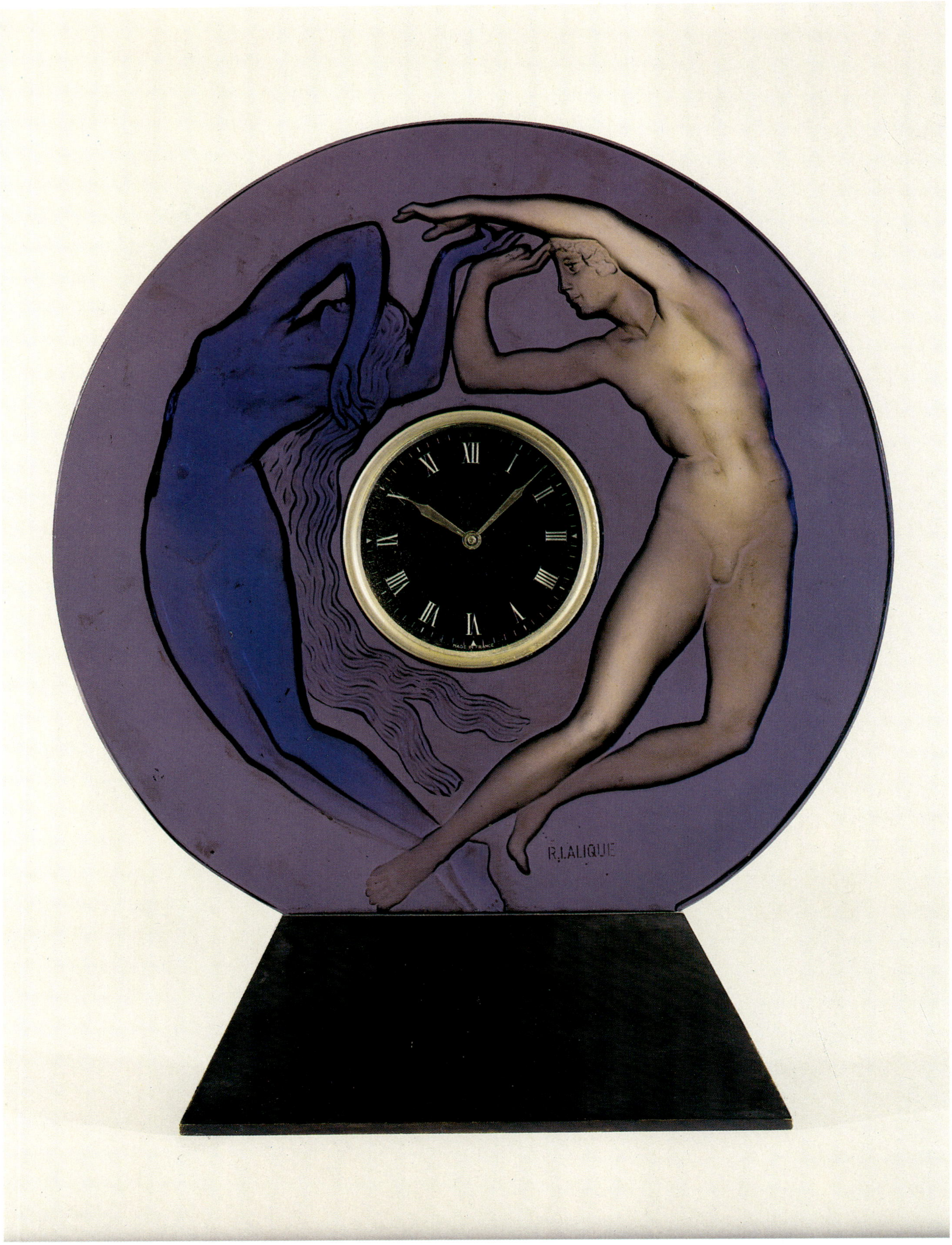

Lalique: 'night and day' clock composed of a circular slab of smoked glass and dark amber, with a pyramidal base of patinated bronze, signed. Etude Couturier–Nicolay.

Facing page: Jean Goulden: clock in silvered bronze and champlevé enamel with black marble base, dial in champlevé enamel and lacquered hands, signed, 1929. Private Collection. Photo: L. Sully-Jaulmes.

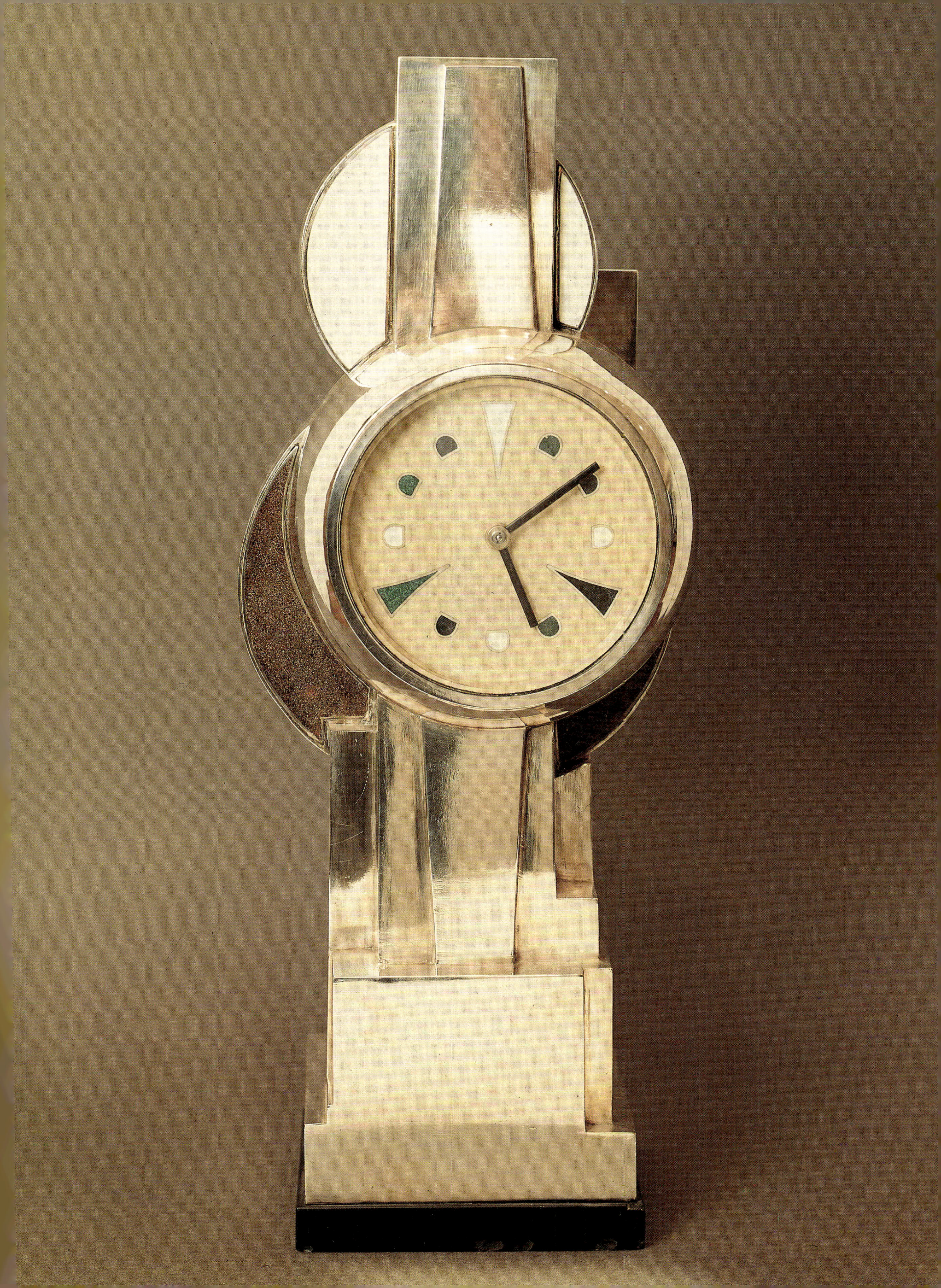

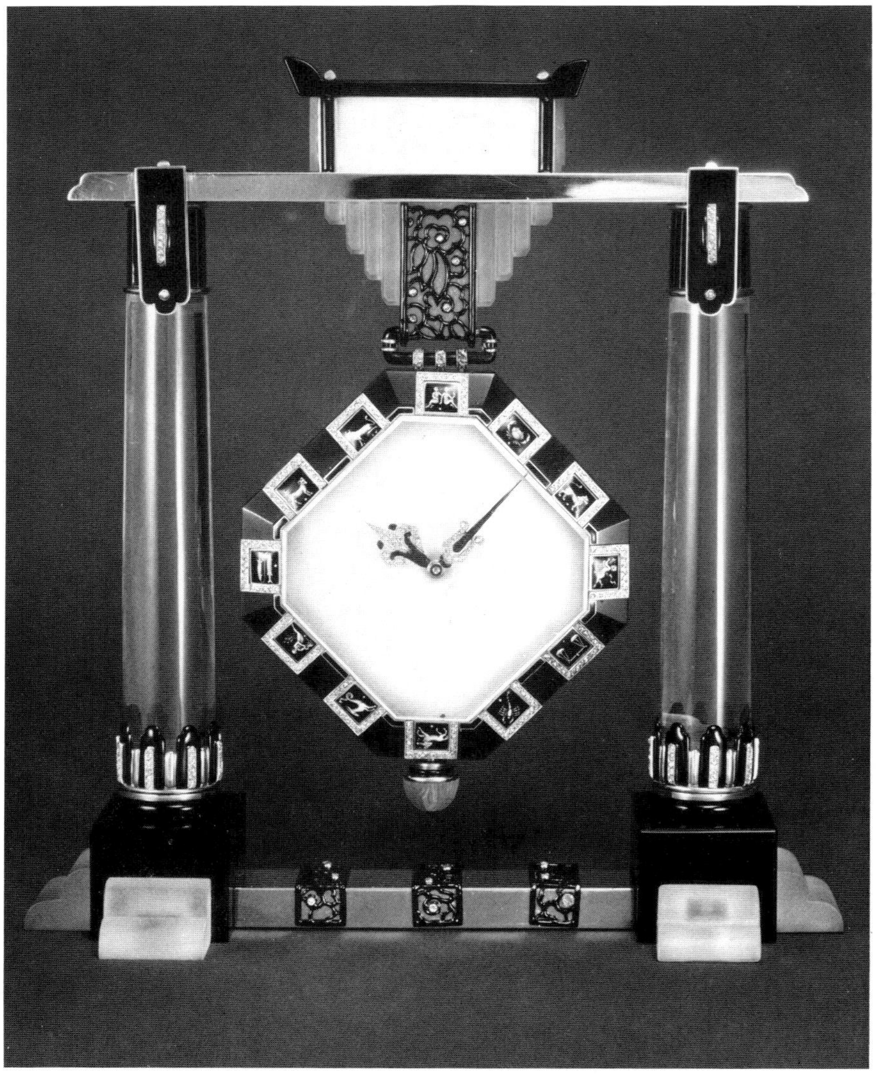

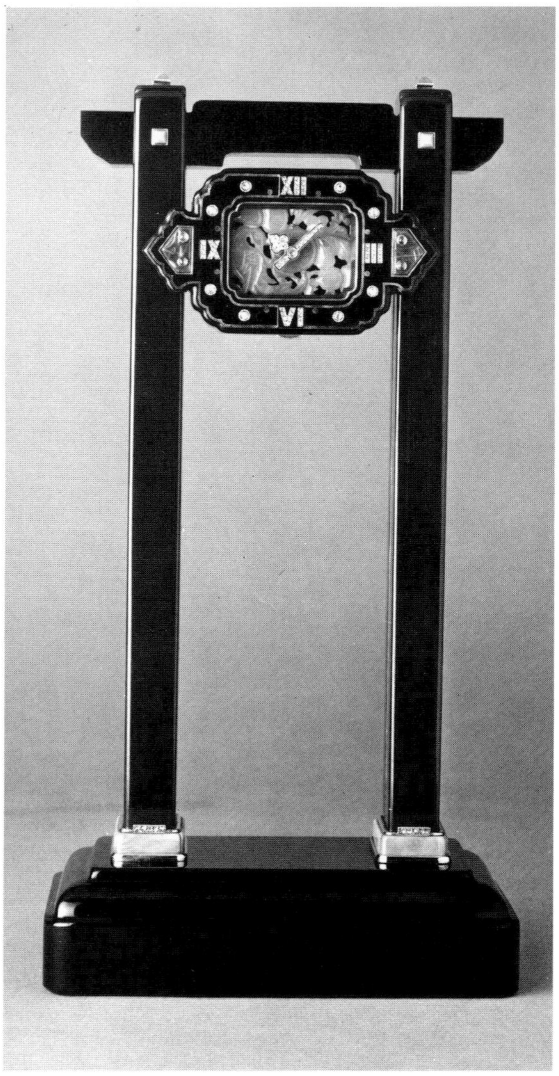

Van Cleef & Arpels: clock in the form of a Japanese temple portico. Two rock crystal columns, with pedestal and base in black onyx and satin-finished crystal, support a gold cross-bar from which an irregular octagonal clockcase in onyx is suspended. The satin-finished crystal dial is sculpted in bas relief with floral motifs; the numerals have been replaced by the twelve signs of the zodiac and the hands are set with diamonds, 1926. Van Cleef & Arpels Archives.

Cartier: clock comprising two columns and a cross-bar in nephrite and onyx set with coral, to which is fixed a black enamel clockcase decorated with jade and rubies surrounding an engraved jade dial. Roman numerals and hands set with diamonds, 1927. Sotheby's.

Facing page: Cartier: 'mystery' clock comprising two rock crystal columns supporting a black onyx architrave surmounted by a squat figure in rock crystal and two coral cabochons. The base is in crystal, gold and enamel and the hands and Roman numerals on the twelve-sided dial are set with diamonds. Signed, 1924.

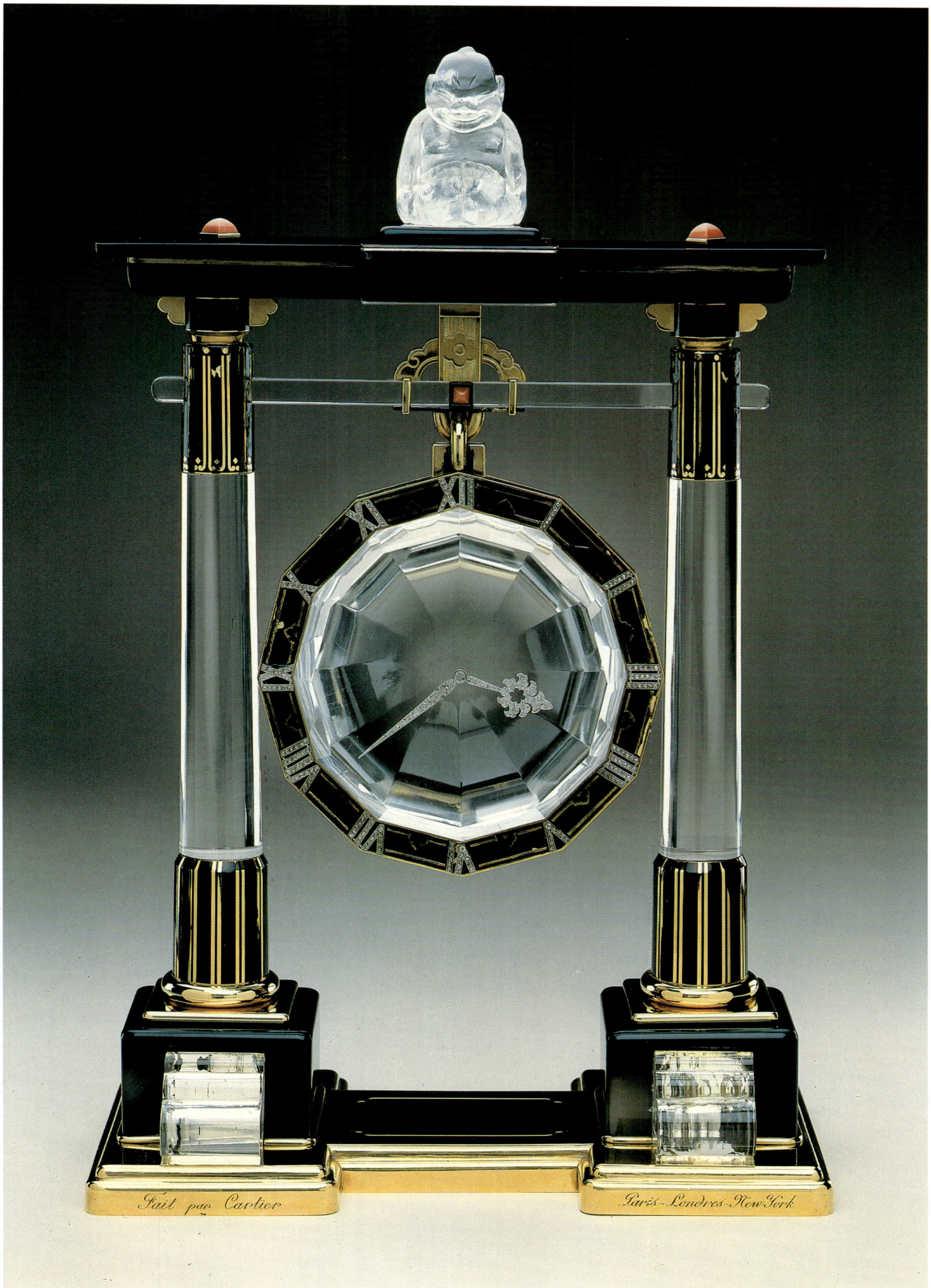
Fait par Cartier
Paris-Londres-New-York

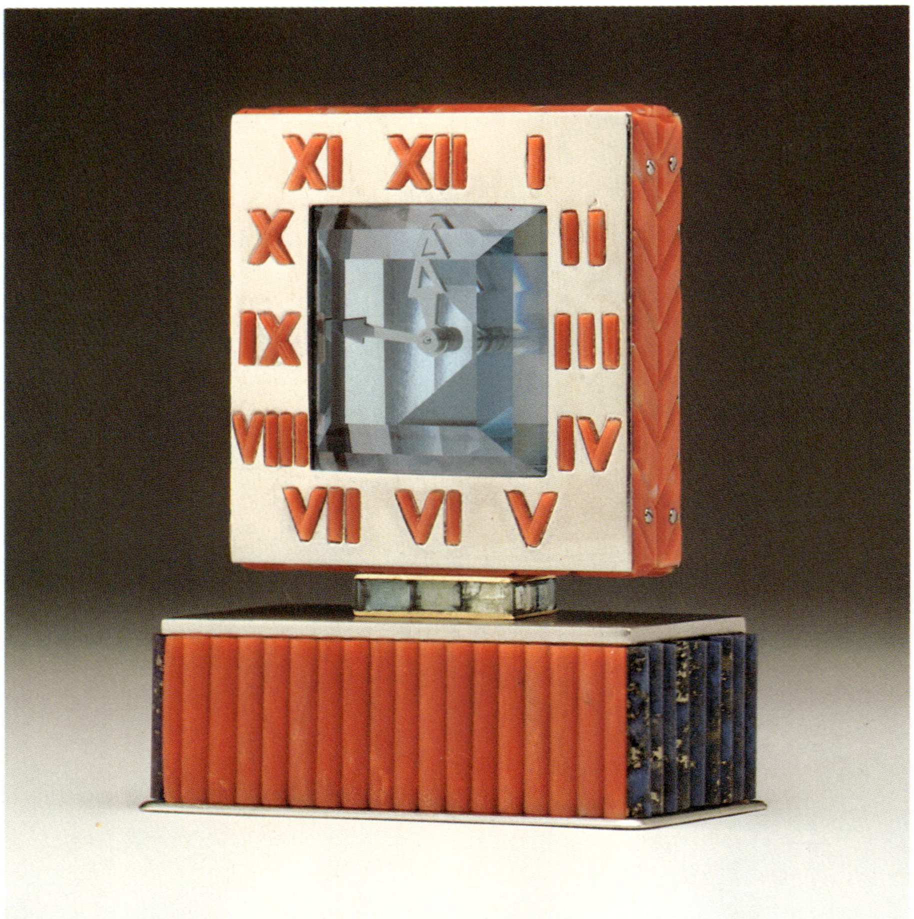

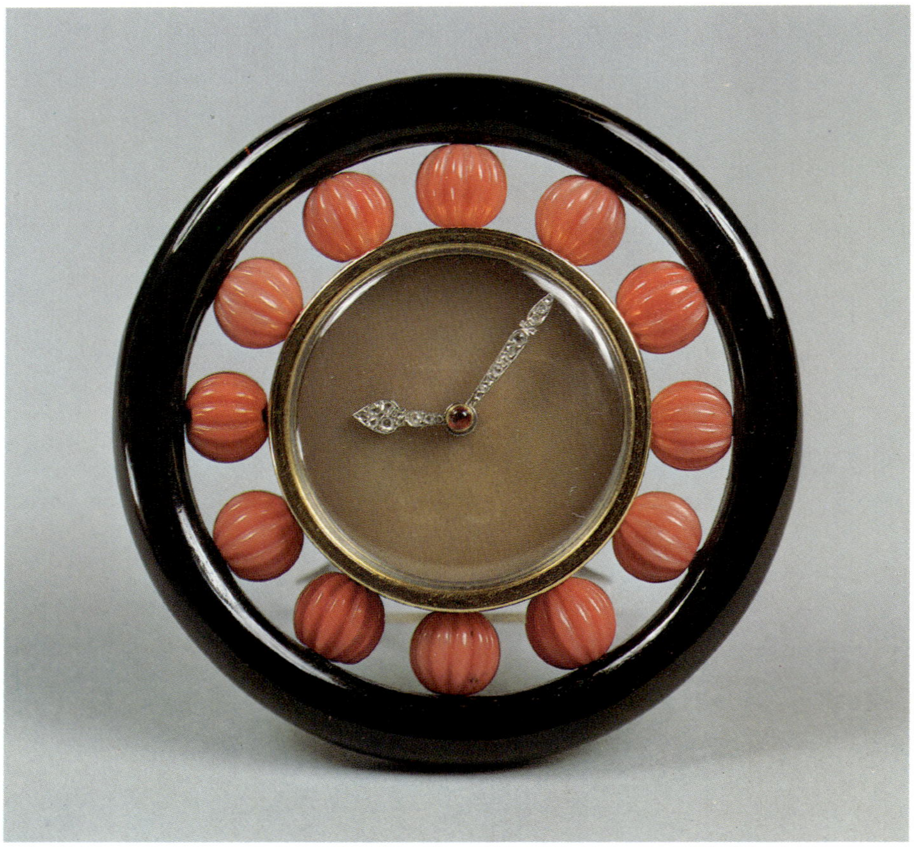

Cartier: 'mystery' clock comprising an aquamarine dial in a platinum frame with Roman numerals in coral. A diamond attachment joins the clock to the base which is in platinum with coral and lapis batons at the sides. Sotheby's, Geneva.

Cartier: small clock comprising an onyx ring, twelve fluted coral beads in place of numerals and an agate and gold dial; hands set with rose-cut diamonds and joined by a ruby cabochon; rock crystal support, signed. Etude Couturier–Nicolay.

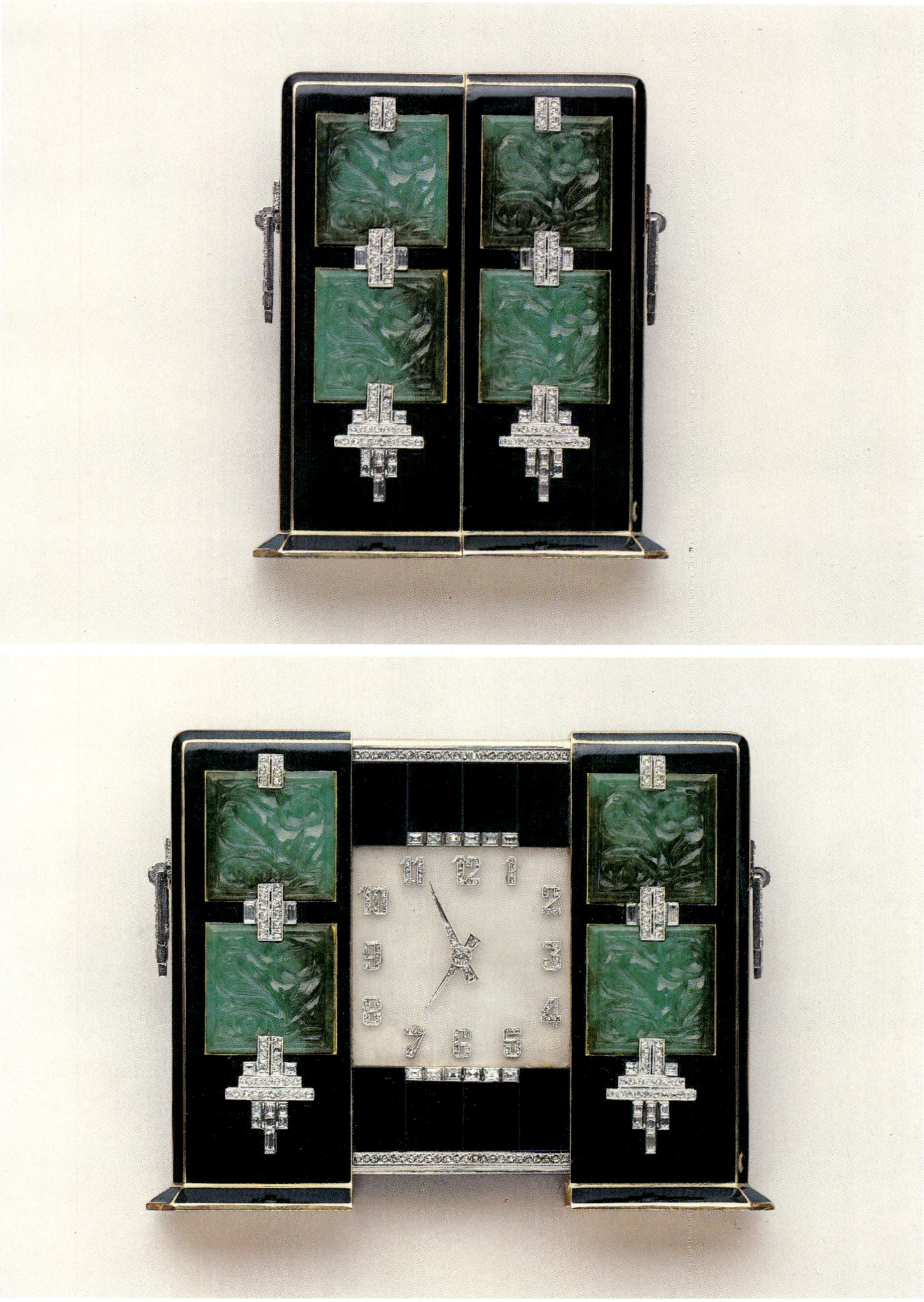

Chaumet: clock in engraved jade, diamonds and black enamel, 1925. Private Collection.

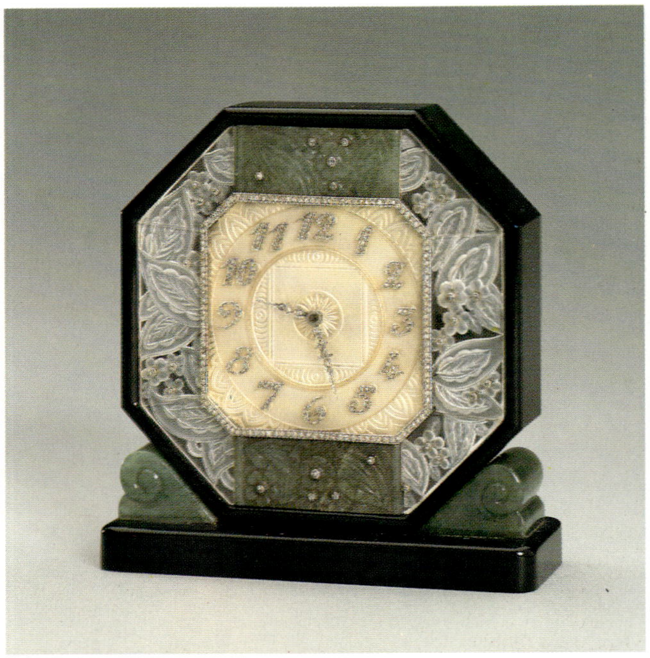

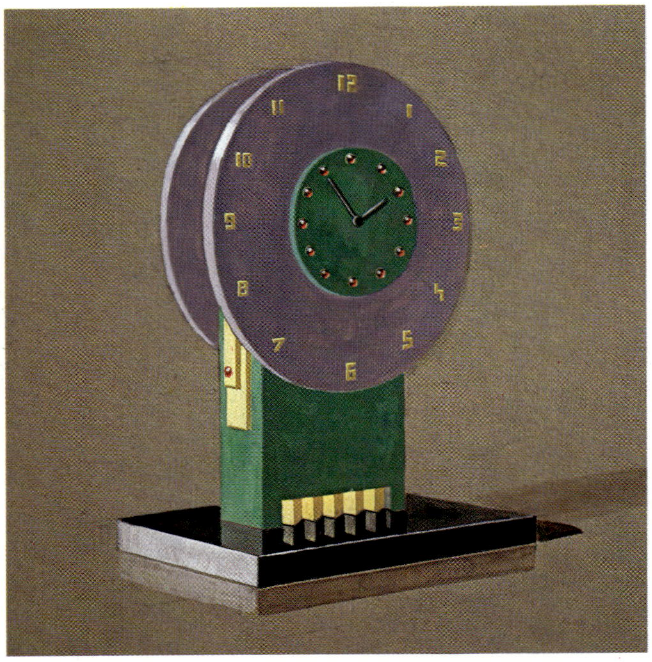

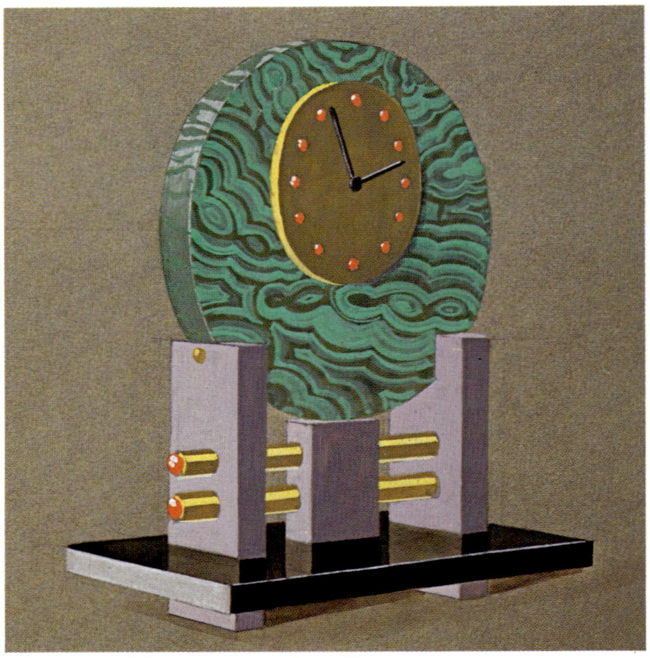

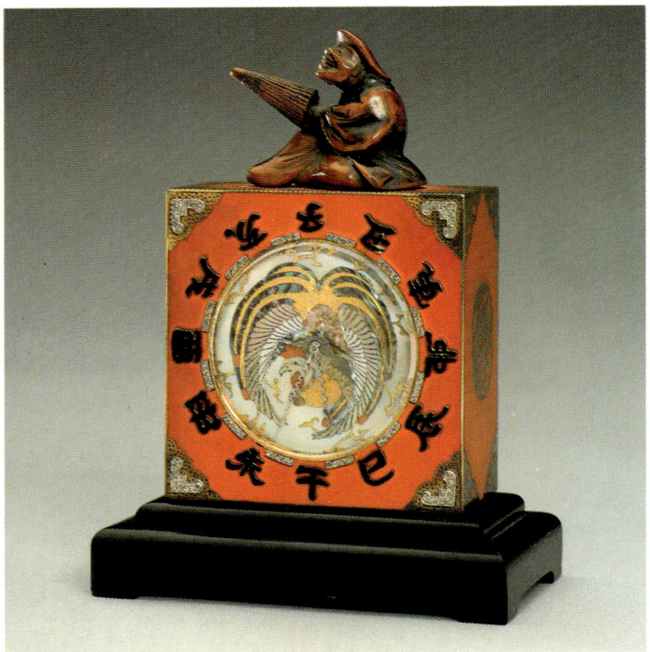

Janesich: small clock comprising an engraved crystal and jade dial; hands and Arabic numerals set with diamonds; base in jade and onyx. Sotheby's, Geneva.

Mauboussin: gouache study for a small clock. Mauboussin Archives.

Mauboussin: gouache study for a small clock. Mauboussin Archives.

Anonymous: small clock in the Chinese style comprising a dial with mother-of-pearl inlay depicting a cockerel, in a red enamel clockcase surmounted by a Chinese figure in carved wood. Chinese numerals in black enamel, base in onyx. Sotheby's, Geneva.

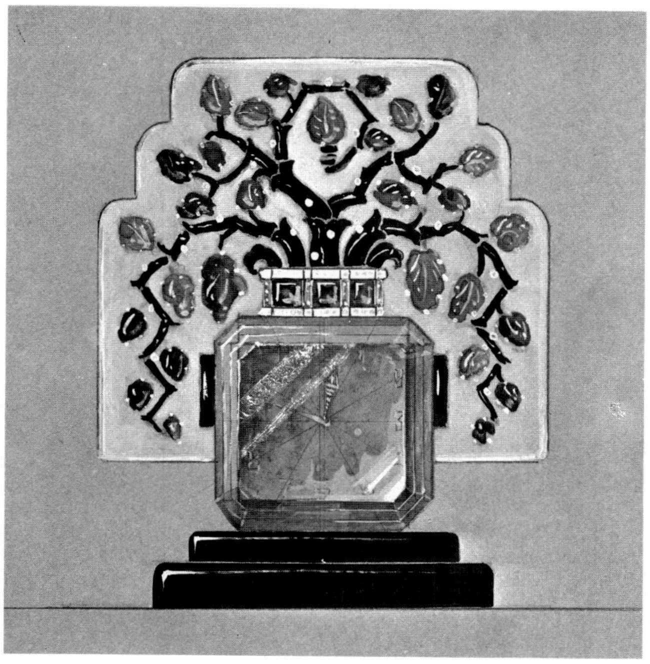

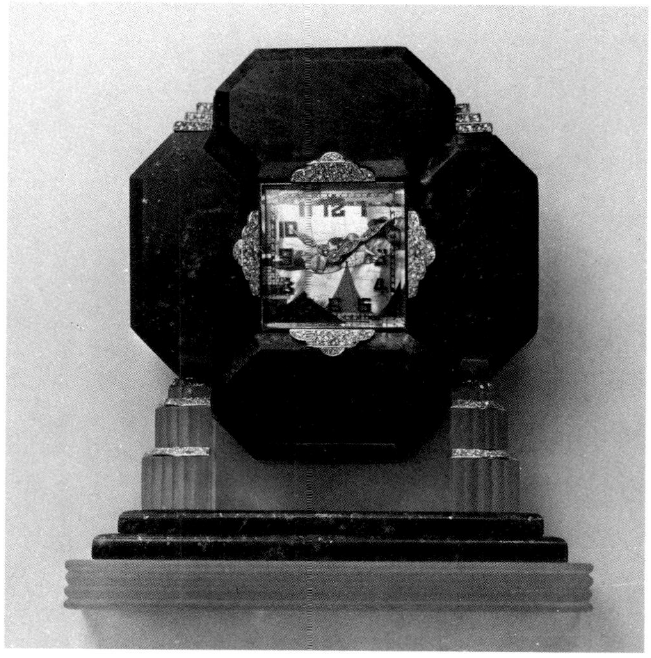

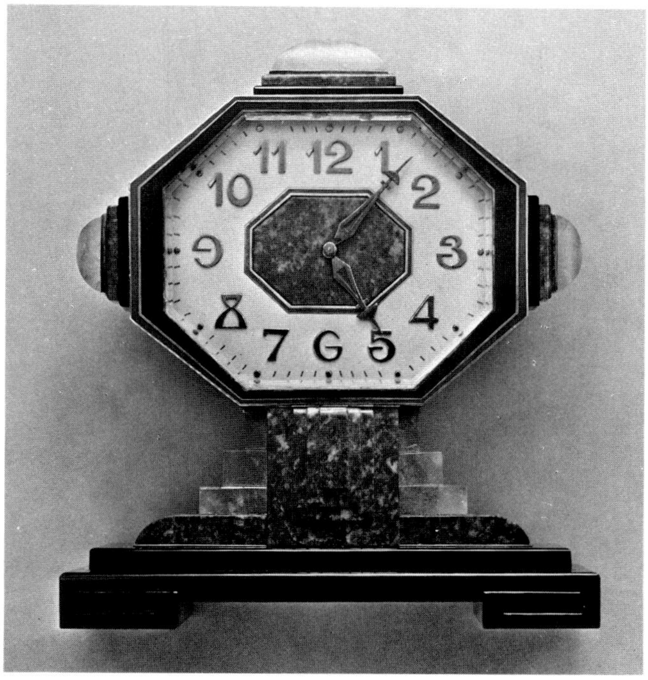

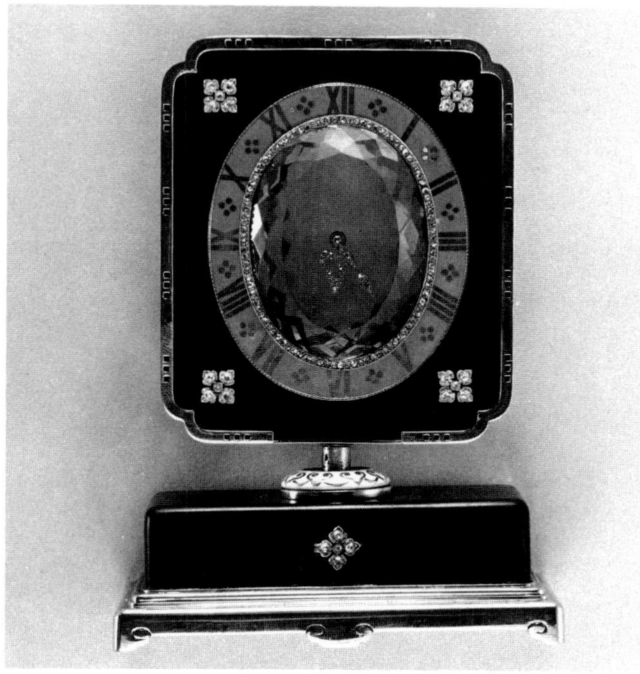

Mauboussin: gouache study for a clock comprising an agate screen decorated with onyx and engraved coloured stones. Mauboussin Archives.

Anonymous: clock comprising a lapis and sky-blue enamel dial, silver and black enamel clockcase with three rose quartz cabochons and rectangular lapis motifs. Numerals and hands in gold. Base in lapis, rose quartz and onyx. Sotheby's, Geneva.

Anonymous: clock comprising a dial in mother-of-pearl inlay depicting pyramids, framed with lapis petals and supported by fluted and frosted rock crystal columns. Lapis and rock crystal base.

Cartier: 'mystery' clock comprising a citrine dial edged with rose-cut diamonds and a blue enamel circle bearing Roman numerals in gold, on an ebony clockcase set with stylized flowers in rose-cut diamonds. Ebony and gold base, 1924. Christie's.

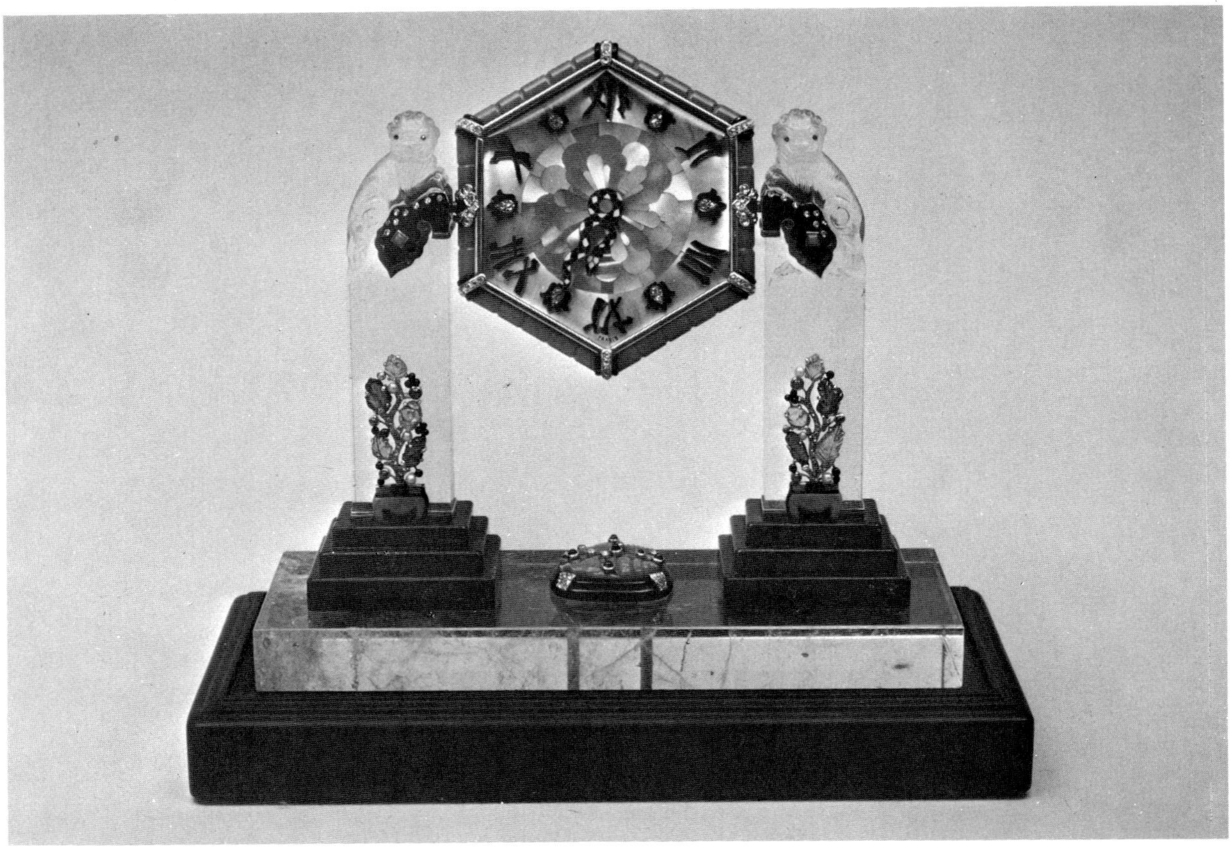

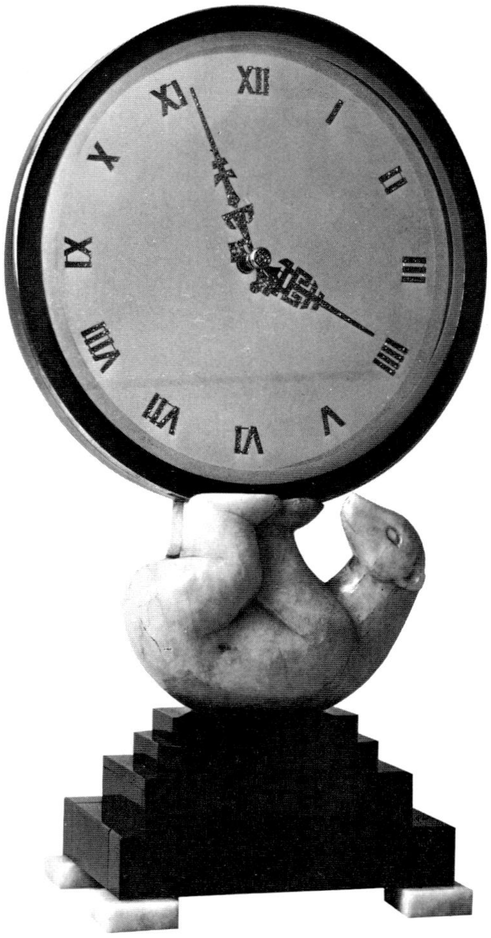

Above: Cartier: clock comprising a dial in mother-of-pearl, engraved coral, rose-cut diamonds and black enamel, pivoting on an axis attached to two rock crystal columns. The columns are surmounted by dogs of Fo and decorated at the base with bouquets of flowers in coral, rubies, emeralds and sapphires. Lapis base, 1926. Cartier Archives.

Van Cleef & Arpels: small 'mystery' clock comprising an onyx base supporting a white jade bear with an emerald eye, its paws holding up a rock crystal dial edged with black lacquer. Numerals and hands set with diamonds, 1926. Van Cleef & Arpels Archives.

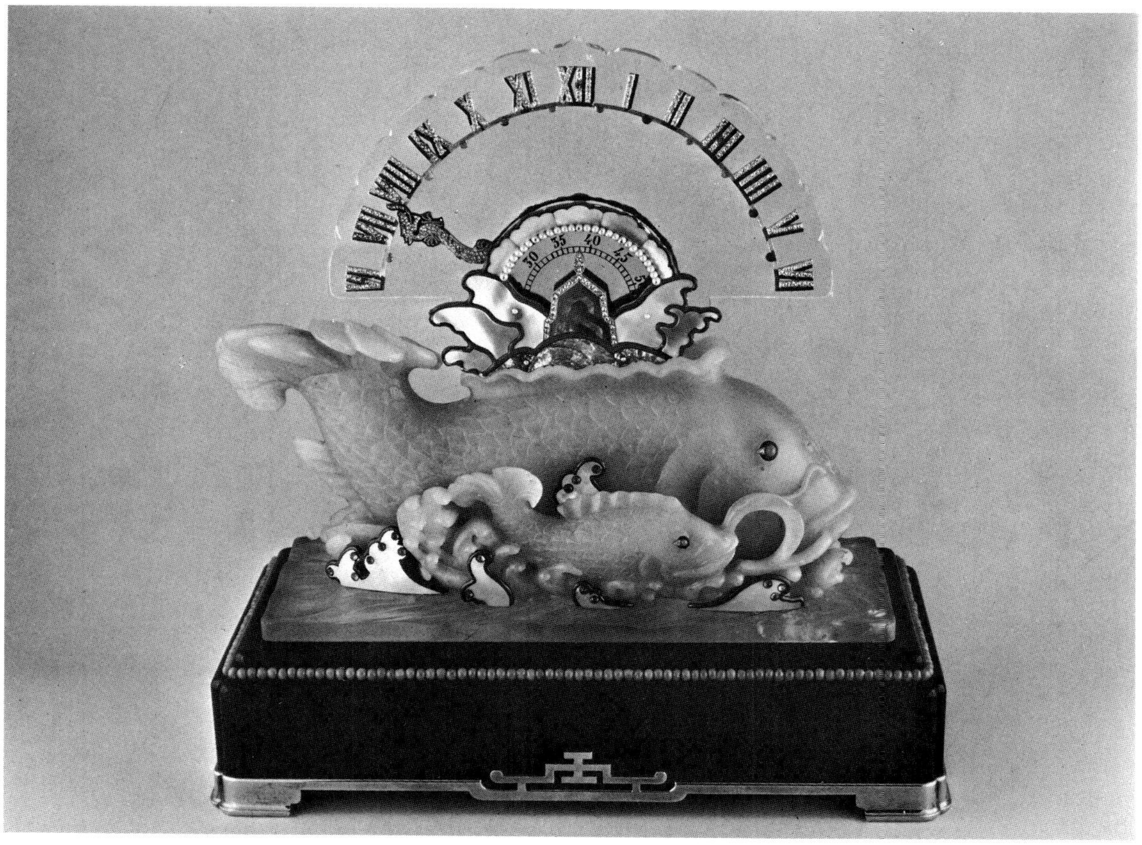

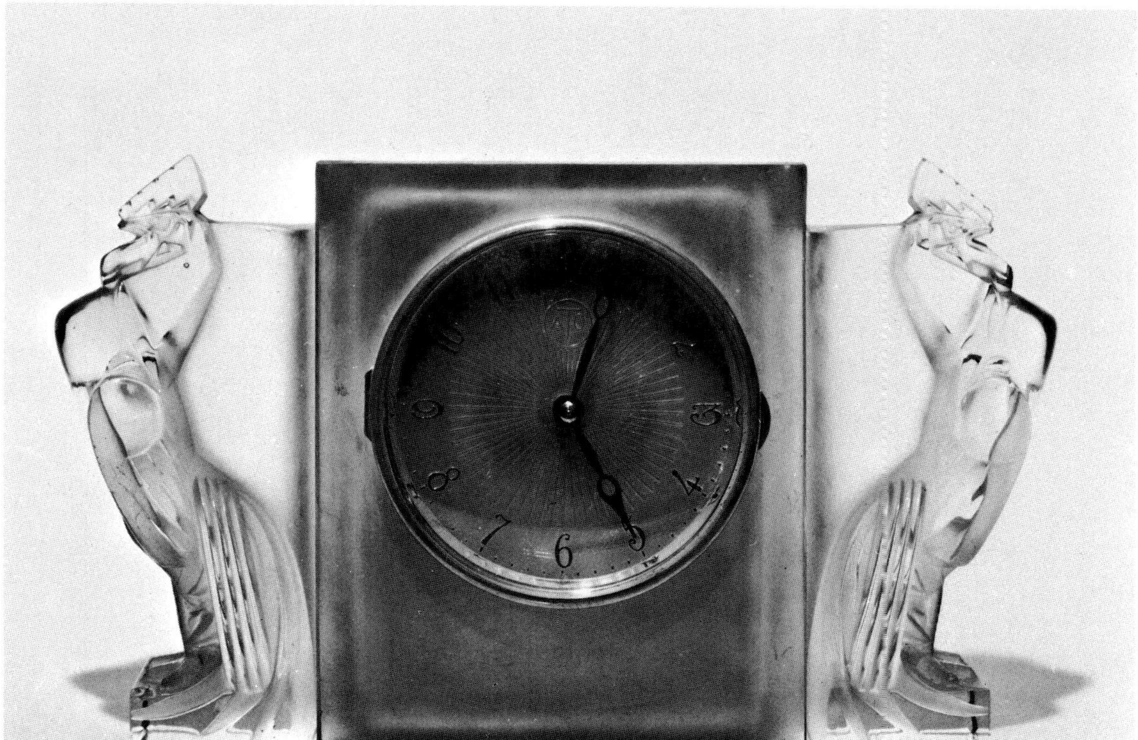

Cartier: clock comprising a jade carp and its young with mother-of-pearl and ruby inlay, supporting a fan-shaped rock crystal dial; obsidian base decorated with gold and coral beads, with a rock crystal slab representing waves. Numerals and hands set with diamonds, c. 1925.

Lalique: clock with two cockerels in colourless frosted glass, c. 1925. Sotheby's, Monte Carlo.

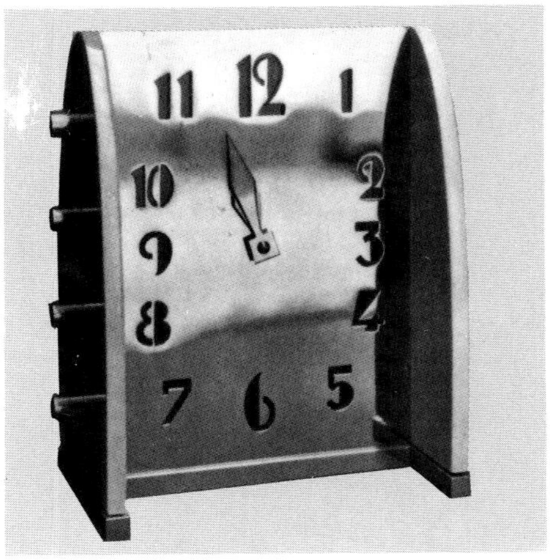

Hour Lavigne: small clock in metal, put into production by Monville Beaufils.

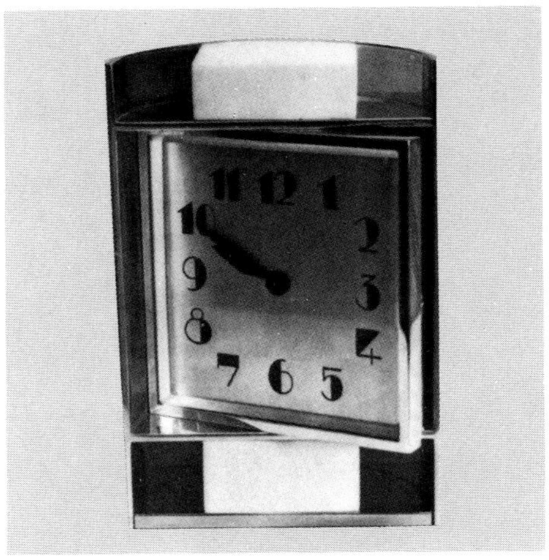

Paul Brandt: small clock in metal and ivory, put into production by Monville Beaufils.

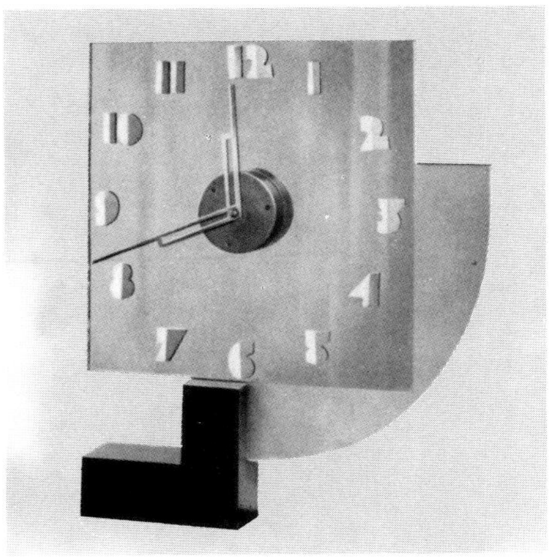

Jean Tranchant: small clock in clear and frosted glass; numerals in metal.

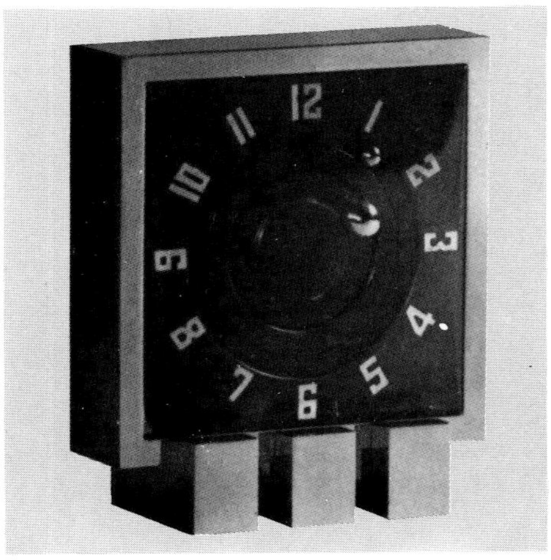

Mélik Minassiantz: small silver and lacquer clock.

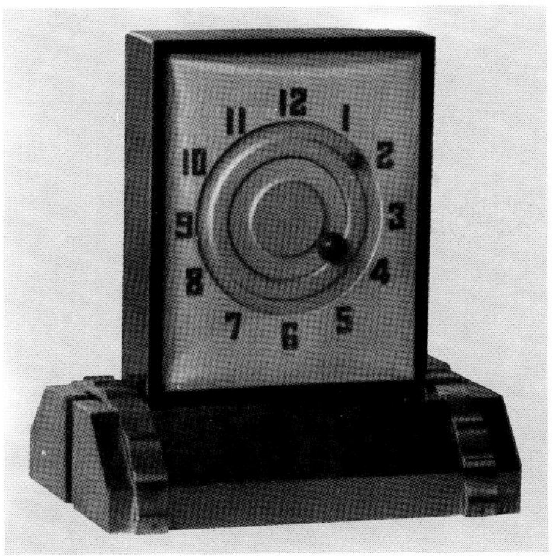

Mélik Minassiantz: small clock in silver and red lacquer. These clocks are reproduced in Art et Décoration, *December 1931.*

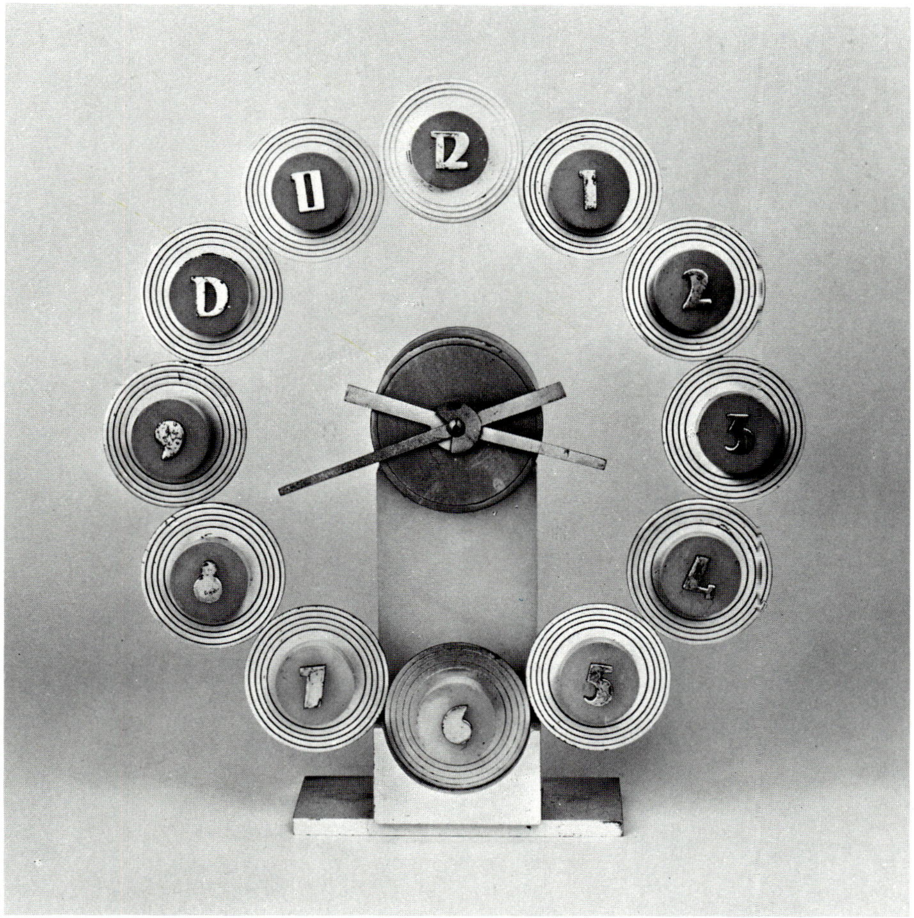

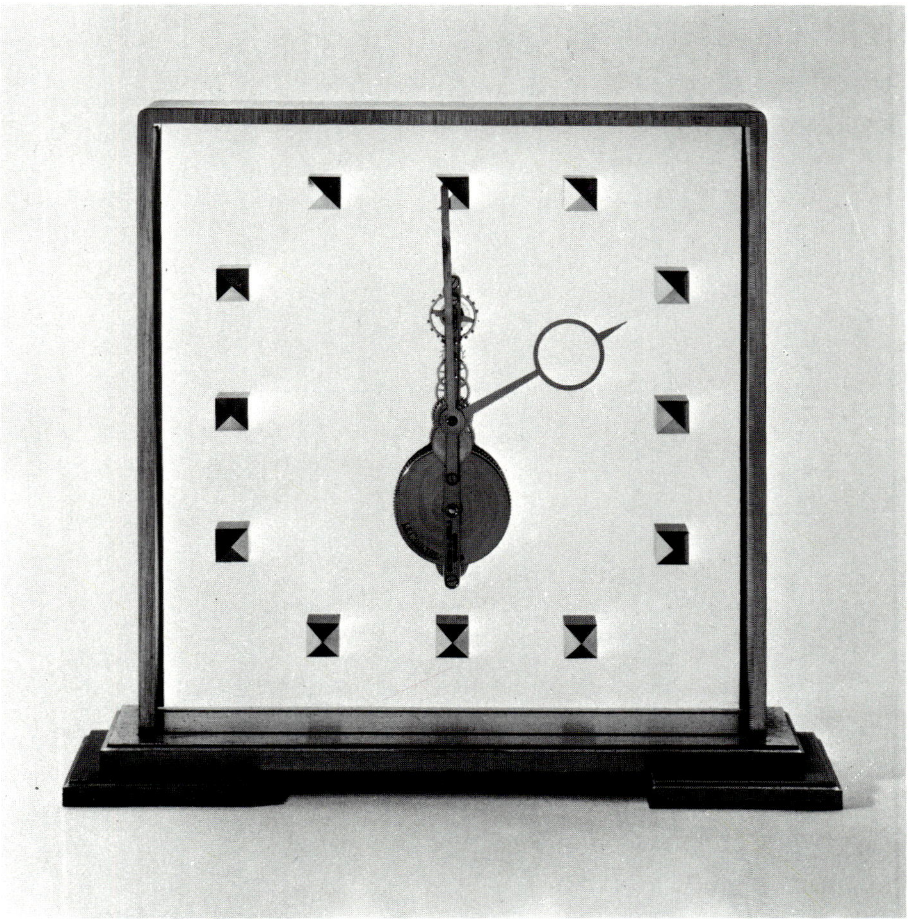

Puiforcat: 'modernist' clock in silvered metal and marble, comprising a cylindrical dial on a rectangular block of white marble. The numerals are mounted on marble cylinders decorated with silvered metal discs. Sotheby's, Monte Carlo.

Le Coultre: clock in gilded metal, the mechanism visible between two glass plates, c. 1930. Sotheby's, Monte Carlo.

CONCLUSION

'A FASHION', WROTE LA BRUYÈRE, 'has scarcely destroyed another fashion, when it is abolished by an even newer one, which gives way in turn to the one that follows it, and that one will not be the last; such is our fickleness. . . .' The Twenties were no exception to this rule. Cubism receded before the advance of figuration, and ornament, banished at the beginning of the century, redeployed its curves, sustained by the fashion magazines which delighted in repeating that the taste for angularity and severity had gone. 'Romanticism', 'Grace', 'Fantasy' were the symbols of this new style. Elsa Schiaparelli emerged as fashion's new sacred idol and brought to clothes and accessories a spirit of mad eccentricity which stemmed from Surrealism and, in particular, from Dali. Dali collaborated in the creations of the Schiaparelli Maison, producing for them designs for chest-of-drawer ensembles, the telephone-handbag and even the shoe-hat.

A fascination with the baroque and a taste for the theatrical also took hold of the furniture designers and Dali's pink satin divan appeared, respresenting Mae West's lips; Kurt Seligman's *Ultra Meuble* (a piece of furniture composed of four female legs); and Robsjohn-Gittings' *jambe-table-console* (leg-table-console). Jewelry followed the same trend. The designer-creators' sketchbooks are revealing in this respect, showing the almost imperceptible variations which, year by year, were distancing jewelry from Art Deco. As the 'Exposition de Galliéra' announced in 1929, colour was losing ground; platinum was giving way to yellow gold; the sharp angles, the cut-off corners, the flat surfaces were being abandoned in favour of relief and curved lines; and, as an exhibition at Mauboussin's in 1930 predicted, the ruby took precedence over the diamond.

The value of its materials, far from preserving a piece of jewelry, tends to seal its fate. Too soon put to one side, it is dismantled long before its value as a work of art is recognized. One may suppose, along with Emile Sedeyn, that 'the most likely to last are not the showy pieces but those in which the metal is combined with raw materials – such as aquamarine, topaz, amethyst, tourmaline, moonstone, turquoise, jade, lapis and coral – whose worth lies in their beauty rather than in their price. Art, which is timeless, will prolong the life of these pieces of jewelry and allow them their true character. No one will dismantle them in order to re-use the materials in other forms. They are works of art rather than valuable commodities' (in Georges Fouquet *et al*, *La Bijouterie, la Joaillerie . . .*, 1934, p. 151). Numerous pieces of jewelry, often the creations of the pioneers, have nevertheless disappeared. In 1969, a pendant by Raymond Templier, incorporating a valuable aquamarine, was sold for scrap at auction.

The Twenties, once disparaged, then forgotten, are again entering the limelight. Georges Fouquet, predicting in 1929 the fate of Art Deco, said: 'There can be no doubt that, in a couple of hundred years, our jewelry will be sought after for collections and museums where it will have its own specially allotted place' (in *Le Figaro, supplément artistique*,

13 June 1929). But Art Deco did not have to wait that long: the exhibition at the Musée des Arts Décoratifs in 1966, which was followed by other large exhibitions in museums abroad, announced the brilliant come back of this epoch. Today, the prices for Art Deco jewelry soar at the huge sales by auction in the markets of London, Paris, Monte Carlo, Geneva and New York, where speculators rub shoulders with art lovers. Numerous contemporary jewelers, moreover, are busy creating models in the Art Deco style: what better proof do we need of its modernity and inventive richness?

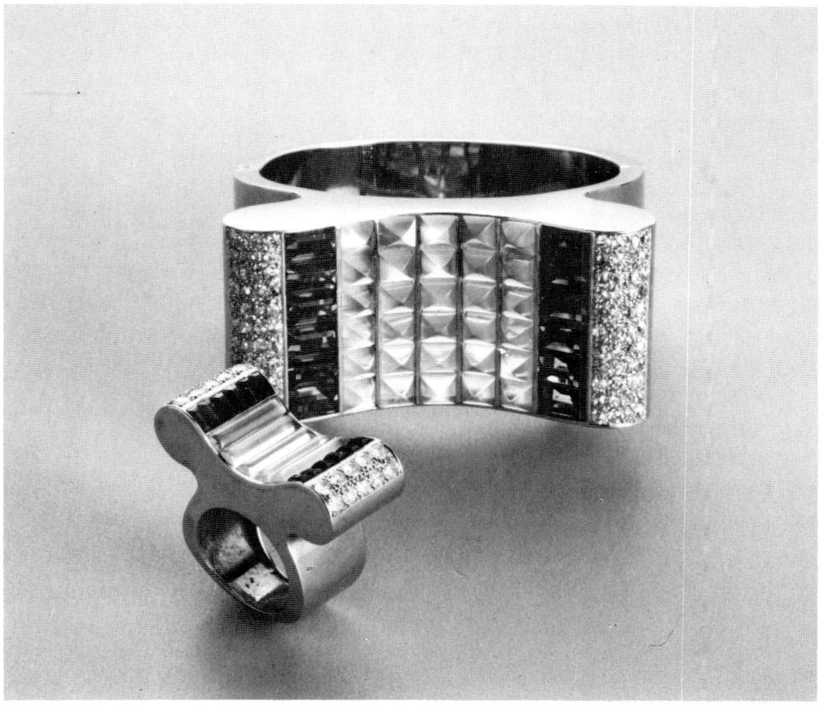

Jean Fouquet: bangle and ring in white gold, platinum, amethysts, moonstones and diamonds, 1937, signed. Photo: Musée des Arts Décoratifs, Paris.

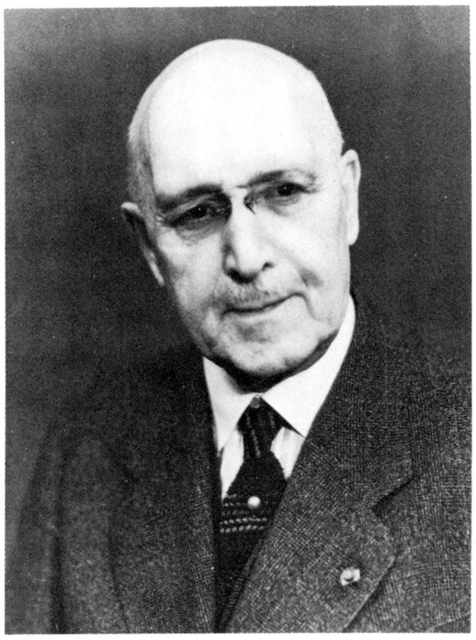

Georges Fouquet

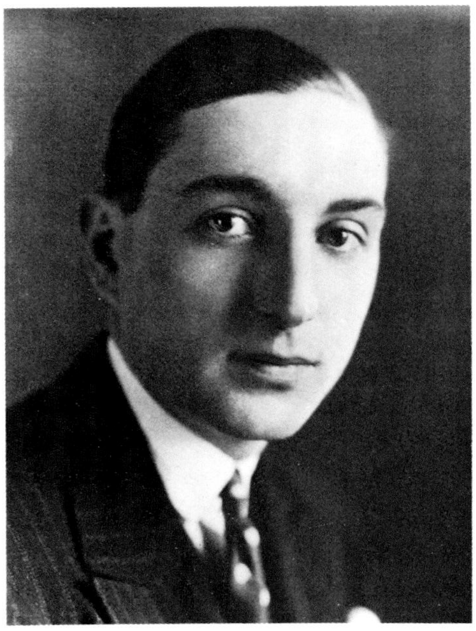

Jean Fouquet

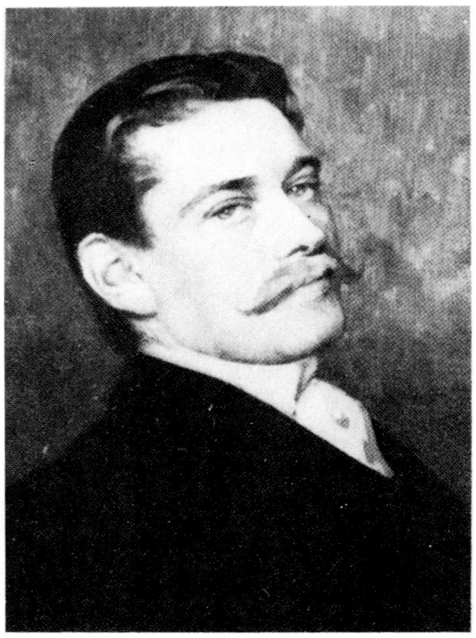

Louis Cartier

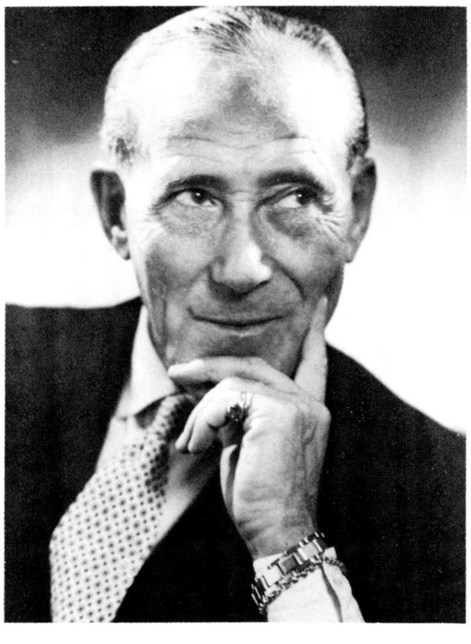

Louis Arpels

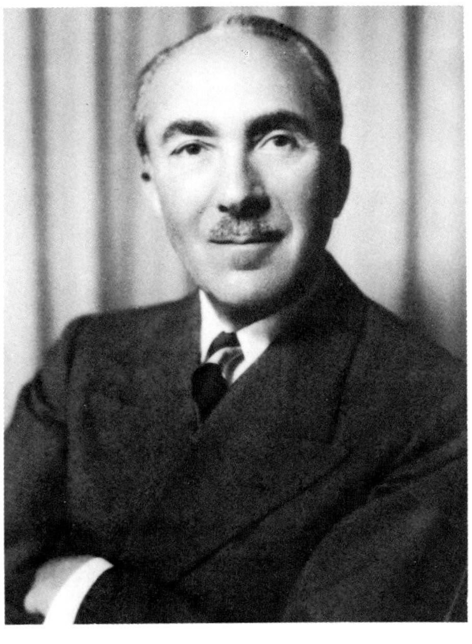

Julien Arpels

BIOGRAPHIES

ARGY-ROUSSEAU, Gabriel
Born at Meslay-le-Vidame in 1885, died in Paris in 1953.
After training at the Manufacture de Sèvres under the direction of Jean Cros whose father, Henri Cros, had revived the technique of pâte de verre, he exhibited his first works in this material in 1914. After his marriage, he signed his work Argy-Rousseau, not simply Rousseau as previously. In 1921 he entered into partnership with G.G. Moser-Millot who opened a boutique on Paris' boulevard des Italiens and financed his workshop. His works were usually composed of opaque pâte de verre, which was coloured by means of an oxide powder, then fixed by a second firing at a low temperature. The motifs were usually animals or human figures, but evolved progressively towards more abstract forms. He also produced enamel bottles. In 1938, he executed a series of sculptures in crystal from designs by Bouraine.

BABLET, Paul
Born in 1889, lives in Paris.
His jewelry was exhibited at the 'Salon d'Automne' as early as 1912, then at the 'Salon des Artistes Décorateurs' in 1914. He also exhibited in New York, Zagreb and Madrid, as well as in Belgium and Holland, and again in Paris in 1925, 1931 and 1937.

BAGGE, Eric
Born in Antony, near Paris, in 1890, died in 1978.
After embarking on a career as an architect, he went on to design wallpapers and fabrics, then became titular Director of the Ecole Pratique of the Chambre Syndicale de la Bijouterie, Orfèvrerie, Joaillerie. He exhibited at the 'Salon des Artistes Décorateurs' from the time of its inception and in 1925, after winning a competition whose jury was led by Georges Fouquet, he designed the architecture of the Bijouterie-Joaillerie hall at the 'Exposition Internationale des Arts Décoratifs'. In 1929, he was once again put in charge of designing the exhibition organized by the profession at the Musée Galliéra. Subsequently, he executed various official commissions including the design of a boudoir and a bathroom for a French embassy, as well as exhibition halls for the Manufacture des Gobelins and the Manufacture de Beauvais.

BASTARD, Georges
Born in Anderville (Oise) in 1881, died in 1939.
Born into a family of fanmakers established in Paris since the seventeenth century, he attended a course at the Ecole Nationale des Arts Décoratifs and specialized in work with fine materials such as mother-of-pearl, ivory, shell, hardstones, jade and coral. He exhibited regularly at the 'Salon des Artistes Français' and the 'Salon d'Automne' (1910–12), as well as at the 'Salon des Tuileries' (1933 and 1934). He collaborated with Ruhlmann and Montagnac at the 'Salon des Arts Décoratifs' in 1925. In 1938, Bastard became Director of the Manufacture Nationale de Sèvres. The Musée des Arts Décoratifs devoted an exhibition to him in 1950.

BELPERRON, Suzanne
In the Twenties and Thirties, Suzanne Belperron designed pieces of jewelry which were among the most revolutionary of the period. She also opened a boutique in the rue Châteaudun in Paris under the name Herz-Belperron.

BLACK, STARR & FROST
This Maison was founded in 1810 in New York by Isaac Marquand on Lower Broadway but was transferred to 594 Fifth Avenue in 1912. After producing numerous commemorative articles, from the beginning of this century the firm specialized in jewelry and precious objects.

BOIVIN, René
Married to the sister of the couturier Paul Poiret, he opened a boutique with her in Paris, rue Sainte-Anastase. Here he displayed the creations in particular of Suzanne Belperron, with whom he collaborated for ten years. In 1931, the firm of René Boivin moved to the avenue de l'Opéra and Louis Girard took over the jewelry section. One of Girard's clients was Louise de Vilmorin, who helped to ensure his success. Juliette Moutard, and, following her, Germaine Boivin, one of René Boivin's two daughters, designed pieces which were to revolutionize the aesthetics of jewelry. Their works were shown at various exhibitions, including the 1937 'Exposition Universelle' and 1946 'Exposition des Arts Décoratifs'.

BOUCHERON
In 1858, Frédéric Boucheron founded his Paris Maison in the Palais Royal, the exclusive quarter of jewelers in the nineteenth century, and he exhibited successfully at numerous 'Expositions Universelles', including Philadelphia in 1875 and Paris in 1889 and 1900. In 1893, he left the Palais Royal for 26 Place Vendôme where the Comtesse de Castiglione, a favourite of the Emperor Napoleon III, was living. Boucheron was the first jeweler to move to this district which subsequently attracted a cosmopolitan and wealthy clientele. In the course of his career, he opened a branch in Moscow, which was closed down on the eve of the Revolution, and a shop in London. His son Louis succeeded him and, through his policy of promotion, confirmed the reputation and international fame of the name of Boucheron. Louis Boucheron was called the greatest expert in the world by Reza Shah Pahlavi who summoned him to Teheran in 1930 to value the treasure of the 'Thousand and One Nights'.

BRANDT, Paul-Emile
Born in La Chaux-de-Fonds (Switzerland)
A jeweler of Swiss origin, he moved to Paris and studied under the direction of Chaplain and Allard. He designed and made a significant number of pieces of jewelry and watches, usually with floral decoration in the Art Nouveau style, before turning to more geometric forms.

CARTIER
François Cartier, the son of Pierre Cartier, did his apprenticeship in Paris' rue Montorgueil under Maître Picard, an *orfèvre-joaillier*, whose business he took over in 1847. Cartier's fame was ensured during the Second Empire by the protection of Princess Mathilde, first cousin of Napoleon III. In 1859, he moved to the salons at 9 boulevard des Italiens where he attracted an international élite. In 1872, François Cartier took his son Alfred into partnership in the Maison. The latter was to do the same with his sons: his eldest, Louis (1875–1942), remained in Paris and moved to 13 rue de la Paix in 1898; his second, Pierre (1878–1964), took over the New York branch established in 1908; while the youngest, Jacques (1884–1941), was responsible for the London branch, opened in 1902. The 1925 Exposition confirmed the reputation of the Cartier Maison. Louis Cartier revived an art forgotten since the eighteenth century and created a range of clocks, vanity cases and desk sets, assisted by talented collaborators

such as Jeanne Toussaint who worked with him after 1923 and took charge of the *haute joaillerie* for the Maison Cartier in 1930.

CASSANDRE (Adolphe Mouron)
Born in 1901, died in 1968.
He moved to Paris with his family in 1915, after spending his childhood in Russia, and was a regular exhibitor at the Cormon studio, Ecole des Beaux Arts, and at the Académie Jullian. He became a poster designer and graphic artist. His first poster in the geometric style dates from 1923 and, after winning the Grand Prix de l'Affiche (Poster) at the 1925 Exposition, he produced a large number of maquettes whose lithographic execution he supervised himself. He also created jewelry designs which were executed by Georges Fouquet. He and Maurice Moyrand, later joined by Loupot, formed the 'Alliance Graphique', which lasted from 1921 to 1934. He produced a large number of posters and, after the death of his partner, took an interest in typographic work. Following a visit to the United States, he began designing sets for the stage.

CHAUMET
Etienne Nitot founded the Maison in 1780 and became jeweler to Napoleon I, for whom he created the consular sword carried at the latter's coronation. On Etienne Nitot's death, his son took over the business and made the parures which Napoleon offered to the future Empress Marie-Louise. Nitot chose Fossin as his successor. The fame of the Maison increased under the management of Prosper Morel: the firm exhibited at the 'Expositions Universelles', and established an important clientele in Russia. Morel's son-in-law and successor, Joseph Chaumet, opened a branch in London in 1875. The firm's participation in the great 'Expositions Internationales' was to confirm its fame in the first quarter of the twentieth century.

COURNAULT, Etienne
Born in Mazeville in 1891, died in 1948.
Painter, printer and illustrator, he was trained at the Ecole des Beaux Arts in Nancy, and, in 1920, moved to London, where he remained until 1930. He produced engraved mirrors for Jacques Doucet, collaborated with Pierre Legrain, and, following him, with Jean Desprès, in the field of jewelry. With Raymond Templier, Jean Fouquet and Gérard Sandoz, among others, he was one of the founder-members of the Union des Artistes Modernes.

CZESCHKA, Carl Otto
Born in Vienna in 1878, died in Hamburg in 1960.
Artist, painter and graphic designer and a member of the Wiener Werkstätte, he worked closely with, among others, Josef Hoffmann.

DESPRES, Jean
Born in Souvigny (Allier) in 1889, died in Avallon in 1980.
Orfèvre and *joaillier*, after the end of the First World War he regularly exhibited his creations in gold and silver (cigarette cases and table ornaments) as well as his jewelry. The latter was highly innovative and often included glass painted and engraved by Etienne Cournault.

DUNAND, Jean
Born in Lancy (Switzerland) in 1877, died in Paris in 1942.
After studying at the Ecole des Arts Industriels in Geneva, Jean Dunand moved to Paris in 1896 or 1897 in order to devote himself to sculpture. He did not produce his first vases until after 1905, but, nevertheless, remained greatly influenced by Art Nouveau

before moving towards more personal forms. In 1912, he learnt the technique of lacquerwork, and later opened several workshops which executed both lacquer- and copperwork. He worked closely with furniture designers such as Ruhlmann, Legrain and Printz. For the 1925 Exposition, he designed a smoking room for a French Embassy, simply using lacquer panels, and later contributed to the furnishing of a number of transatlantic liners. He also created pieces of jewelry on occasion, combining lacquer, silver and eggshell.

FOUQUET, Georges
Born in 1862, died in 1957.
After receiving a classical education, he succeeded his father, Alphonse Fouquet, as head of the family Maison which he was to bring in line with contemporary fashion, partly by collaborating with contemporary artists such as Mucha. Abandoning conventional floral motifs, Fouquet inclined towards more severe geometric forms and, after 1936, was to work closely with Jean Lambert-Rucki. He contributed to numerous international exhibitions and, in 1924, was a member of the selection committee for the 1925 'Exposition Internationale des Arts Décoratifs' where he presided over the *Bijouterie-Joaillerie* section. His archives and designs were bequeathed to the Musée des Arts Décoratifs in Paris.

FOUQUET, Jean
Born in Paris in 1899.
After receiving a classical education, he joined his father, Georges – a *joaillier* established at 6 rue Royale, Paris – as a jewelry designer. At the 1925 Exposition, his name appeared for the first time, alongside those of the other designer-creators of the Maison Fouquet. Between 1925 and 1937, he contributed to numerous international exhibitions. He exhibited under his own name at the 'Salons des Artistes Décorateurs' in 1926 and 1928. In 1928, he left the SAD to join the Union des Artistes Modernes with whom he exhibited in 1930, 1931 and 1932. After the closure of the family Maison in February 1936, he worked on commission for private clients.

HOFFMANN, Josef
Born in Pirnitz in Moravia in 1870, died in Vienna in 1956.
He studied architecture in Vienna under Otto Wagner whose disciple he became. A founder member of the Vienna Secession in 1897, he set up the Wiener Werkstätte with Koloman Moser in 1903. The Werkstätte were craft workshops whose work was distinguished by its simplicity and geometric design – in contrast to the undisciplined contemporary creations of Art Nouveau – prefiguring the style of the Twenties. While pursuing his activities as an architect, he produced jewelry designs in a highly coloured, geometric style.

JENSEN, Georg
Born in Raavad (Denmark) in 1866, died in Copenhagen in 1935.
After studying under Mogens Ballin and at the School of Fine Arts in Copenhagen, Jensen turned his hand to sculpture which he later abandoned in favour of silverwork. His venture into silverwork met with rapid success and he exhibited his work at the 'Salon d'Automne' in 1913 and at the San Francisco 'Panama-Pacific Exposition' in 1915, where he received first prize.

LACLOCHE
This Maison was founded in Madrid in 1875 by the Lacloche Brothers. Branches were opened in Saint-Sébastien, Biarritz and Paris. The firm took over Fabergé's London

shop in 1920 and met with considerable success in the Twenties through the production of clocks, cigarette cases and boxes.

LALIQUE, René
Born in Ay (Marne) in 1860, died in Paris in 1945.
René Lalique was apprenticed to Louis Aucoc and also attended courses at the Ecole des Beaux Arts. He did not exhibit under his own name until 1894. From 1902 onwards, he devoted himself to glass work and invented new techniques for moulding glass. After the war, he gave up producing unique pieces in favour of multiple production.

LAMBERT-RUCKI, Jean
Born in Cracow in 1888, died in 1967.
A sculptor and painter, he moved to Paris and exhibited at the most important salons. His style was influenced by Cubism and he frequently collaborated with Jean Dunand for whom he designed lacquerwork motifs. Attracted by the art of jewelry, Lambert-Rucki created designs for Georges Fouquet strongly influenced by African art.

LEVEILLE, André
Born in Lille in 1880, died in Paris in 1962.
After producing designs for the textile industry, he worked with Georges Fouquet for whom he designed strikingly original pieces of jewelry.

MAUBOUSSIN
The history of this Maison began shortly after 1810 in Paris' narrow rue Greneta, at no 64, where a jeweler's business was already established. M. Mauboussin, who had worked in the Maison since 1877, first as assistant, then partner to his uncle, M.B. Noury, and, finally, in 1903, as sole proprietor, in 1923 bought two adjoining premises between rue Saint Augustin, rue Choiseul and rue Monsigny. The Mauboussin Maison became increasingly famous with the years. The opening of branches in New York, Buenos Aires and Rio de Janeiro brought it international standing, as did its contribution to various international Expositions: in Milan in 1923 and 1924, New York in 1924 and Paris in 1925 and 1929.

NILSSON, Wiwen
Born in Lund (Sweden) in 1897.
After working with Georg Jensen in Paris, he set up his own workshop in Lund in 1927 and became an exponent of the geometric style of the Twenties and Thirties.

PECHE, Dagobert
Born in St Michael, near Salzburg, in 1887, died in Vienna in 1923.
An architect and painter, Peche studied at the Academy in Vienna. His work was greatly influenced by the Wiener Werkstätte.

PUIFORCAT, Jean
Born in Paris in 1897, died in 1945.
After receiving a classical education – interrupted by the war – Puiforcat entered his father's *orfèvrerie* workshop and also took sculpture lessons from Louis Lejeune. At the annual Salons from 1923 onwards, he exhibited original jewelry in precious metals combining lapis, ivory, jade and rock crystal with silver, and also made a number of pieces on commission. He was a member of the *Jury d'Admission* and the *Jury des Récompenses* (Selection and Prize-giving Committees) at the 1925 Exposition in Paris and exhibited at Ruhlmann's Hôtel du Collectionneur. Subscribing to the theory that

'beautiful is useful', he became, in 1929, a founder member of the Union des Artistes Modernes.

SANDOZ, Gérard
Born in Paris in 1902.
Gérard Sandoz was heir to a long line of clockmakers and *joailliers*, and his father's reputation among the other designer-houses of the period was considerable. He received a classical education and was instructed in modern decorative art by his uncle, Paul Follot. From a very early age, he contributed to the creations of the Maison Sandoz as a designer of jewelry and *orfèvrerie*, and was also a poster designer and painter. He took part in the 1925 Exposition and exhibited regularly at the 'Salon d'Automne' and the 'Salon des Artistes Décorateurs'. Recognized as one of the pioneers in the art of jewelry, he became a member of the Union des Artistes Modernes at its inception in 1928. Drawn to other forms of artistic expression, he finally closed down the Maison in the rue Royale in Paris in 1931 to devote his time to painting and the cinema.

SLUTZKY, Naum J.
Born in the Ukraine in 1898, a British national.
After pursuing his studies in Vienna, Slutzky worked as a freelance designer and was closely involved in the work of the Bauhaus until 1933. He established himself as a jewelry designer and moved to London.

TEMPLIER, Raymond
Born in 1891, died in 1968 in Paris.
Grandson of a *bijoutier-joaillier* who had founded the Maison in 1849, Templier was trained in the traditions of *joaillerie*. He studied at the Ecole Nationale Supérieure des Arts Décoratifs from 1909 to 1912, before joining his father and designing jewelry for him in the geometric style, favouring platinum, enamel, lacquer and semi-precious stones. He exhibited from 1911 onwards at the 'Salon des Artistes Décorateurs' and regularly contributed to exhibitions in France and abroad. Templier was strongly committed to simplicity and the geometric style and supported the Union des Artistes Modernes from its inception. In 1929, Marcel Percheron, a former student at the Ecole des Arts Décoratifs, joined the Maison as a designer. For thirty-six years Percheron was to produce minutely detailed designs for jewelry conceived by Raymond Templier. In 1935, Raymond Templier took over the management of the Maison from his father.

VAN CLEEF ET ARPELS
Julien, Louis and Charles Arpels came from a family of diamond merchants and, in 1904, with their brother-in-law, Alfred van Cleef, they took over a tiny shop in Paris' Place Vendôme and founded the Maison to which they gave their name. During the winter of 1924–25, they opened their first jewelry branch in Cannes, followed by branches in Deauville and Monte Carlo. They obtained a Grand Prix at the 1925 Exposition in Paris. The first *minaudière* was created in 1930 by Louis Arpels for Florence Gould. The word caused such a furore that every evening bag was given the name even though it was a registered trade mark of Van Cleef et Arpels. In 1935, the Maison launched the *serti mystérieux* or *serti invisible* (invisible setting), thereby revolutionizing the art of jewelry.

VERDURA, Duke Fulco of
Born in Palermo in 1900.
An amateur painter, he designed jewelry for Chanel from 1931, using semi-precious stones and enamel.

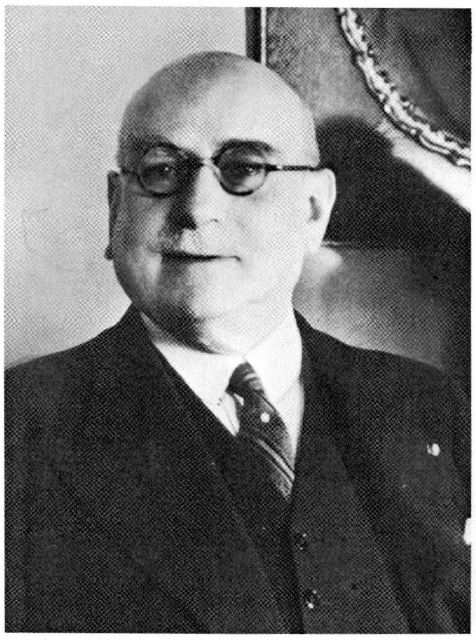

Paul Templier

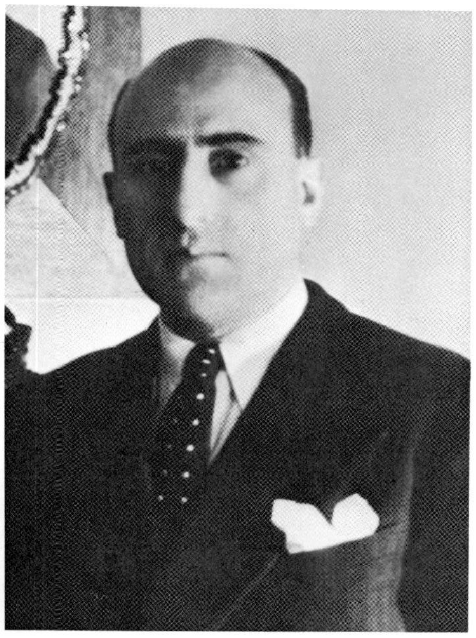

Raymond Templier

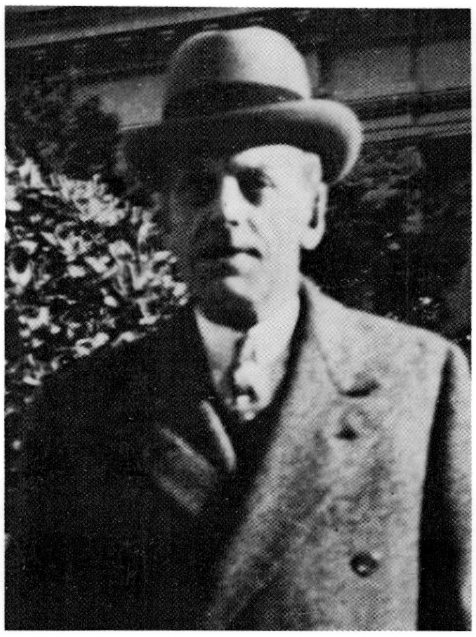

Alfred Van Cleef

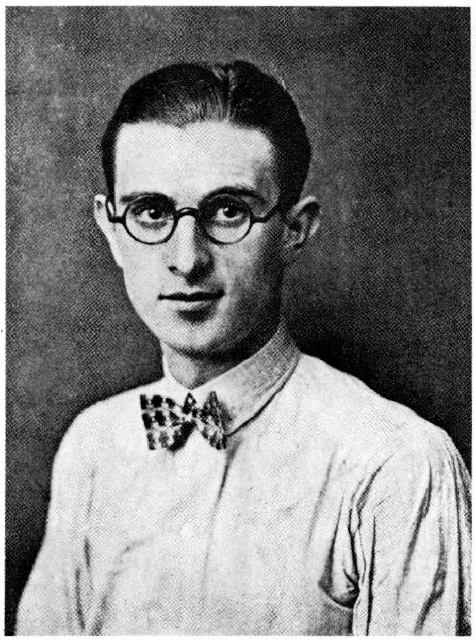

Gérard Sandoz

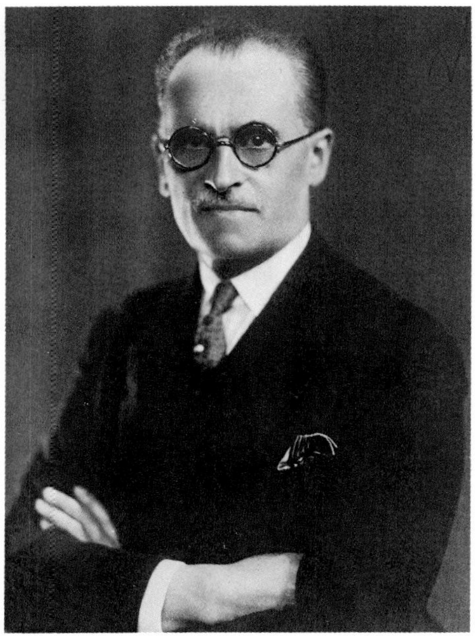

Georges Mauboussin

SELECT BIBLIOGRAPHY

Arwas, Victor. *Art Deco*, London and New York, 1980.

Battersby, Martin. *Art Deco Fashion*, London, 1974.

——. *The Decorative Thirties*, London and New York, 1971.

——. *The Decorative Twenties*, London, 1969.

Becker, Vivienne. *Antique and 20th Century Jewellery*, London, 1980, New York, 1982.

Black, Anderson. *Histoire des Bijoux*, Geneva and Paris, 1974.

Bossaglia, Rossana. *Il Deco Italiano*, Milan, 1975.

Brielle, Roger. 'Les verres gravés d'Etienne Cournault' in *Art et Décoration*, April 1931, pp. 121–28.

Brunhammer, Yvonne. *Art Deco Style*, London, 1984.

——. 'Jean Dunand. Jean Goulden' in the Exhibition Catalogue, Galerie du Luxembourg, 1973.

——. 'Les bijoux et la mode au 20e siècle' in *Métiers d'Art*, September 1983, pp. 95–101.

——. *1925. Les Presses de la Connaissance*, Paris, 1976.

Bury, Shirley. 'Jewellery Gallery Summary' in the Victoria and Albert Museum Catalogue, London, 1982.

Campagne, Jean-Marc. 'Les bijoux de René Robert' in *Art et Décoration*, September 1935, pp. 341–46.

Chavance, René. 'A l'Union des Artistes Modernes' in *Les Echos des Industries d'Art*, no 60, July 1930.

——. '17e Salon des Artistes Décorateurs' in *Les Echos des Industries d'Art*, no 23, June 1927, pp. 5–22.

——. '18e Salon des Artistes Décorateurs' in *Les Echos des Industries d'Art*, no 35, June 1928, pp. 9–30.

Chavance, René, and H. Verne. *Pour comprendre l'art décoratif moderne*, Paris, 1925.

Clouzot, Henri. *Les Arts Précieux à l'Exposition Coloniale*, Paris, 1931.

——. 'Le Bijou Moderne' in *Illustration*, December 1927.

——. 'L'Evolution de la Joaillerie depuis dix ans' in *L'Art Vivant*, no 147, April 1931, pp. 156–67.

——. 'La Parure à l'Exposition des Arts Décoratifs' in *La Renaissance de l'Art Français et des Industries de Luxe*, January 1926, pp. 17–46.

——. 'La Rue Royale' in *La Renaissance de l'Art Français et des Industries de Luxe*, June 1924, pp. 341–61.

——. 'Réflexions sur la Joaillerie de 1929' in *Le Figaro, supplément artistique*, 11 July 1929, pp. 685–88.

Cogniat, Raymond. 'Deuxième Exposition de l'Union des Artistes Modernes' in *Art et Décoration*, July 1931, pp. 1–37.

Contreau, Pierre. *Bijoux et Bijoutiers*, illustrated by René Robert, Besançon, 1932.

——. 'La Joaillerie et la Bijouterie à l'Exposition des Arts Décoratifs' in *Le Grand Négoce, Organe du Commerce de Luxe Français*, special number devoted to the 1925 Exposition of Decorative Arts, Paris, 1926.

——. 'Voici pour les étrennes les dernières créations des grands bijoutiers et joailliers' in *Les Echos des Industries d'Art*, no 17, December 1926.

Crespelle, Jean Paul. *La Folle Epoque*, Paris, 1968.

Derys, Gaston. 'Le décor moderne du bijou' in *Parures*, no 29, November 1928.

Deshairs, Léon. 'L'Exposition des Arts Décoratifs, Section Française' in *Art et Décoration*, July-December 1925, pp. 205–17.

Dewiel, Lydia L. *Les Bijoux*, Paris, 1980.

Fabre, Gladys C. 'Trois créateurs d'objets précieux (J. Fouquet, G. Sandoz, R. Templier)' in *L'oeil*, October 1969, pp. 43–48.

Falk, Fritz. '*Art Déco*, ein neuentdeckter Kunstbegriff' in *Blickpunkt Pforzheim*.

——. *Von der Antike zur Gegenwart*, Collection of the Pforzheim Museum, 1980.

Faveton. *Les Années 20*, Paris, 1982.

Fouquet, Georges. 'Jewellery and Goldsmith's work in France' in *The Studio*, tome IC, pp. 327–40.

——. 'La Bijouterie et la Joaillerie Modernes' in *Le Figaro, supplément artistique*, 13 June 1929, pp. 607–14.

——. 'La Bijouterie et la Joaillerie Modernes' in *L'Orfèvrerie, la Joaillerie*, Paris, 1942.

——. 'La Joaillerie et la Bijouterie à l'Exposition des Arts Décoratifs' in *Le Grand Négoce, Organe du Commerce de Luxe Français*, special number devoted to the 1925 Exposition of Decorative Arts, March 1926.

Fouquet, Georges, Emile Sedeyn, Jacques Guérin, Jean Lanllier, Paul Piel. (Preface by Paul Léon.) *La Bijouterie, la Joaillerie, la Bijouterie Fantaisie au 20e siècle*, Paris, 1934.

Fouquet, Jean. 'Bijoux et Orfèvrerie' in *Art International d'Aujourd'hui*, no 16, Paris, 1931.

Gallotti, Jean. 'L'Exposition de Joaillerie et d'Orfèvrerie au Musée Galliéra' in *Art et Décoration*, no 56, pp. 33–50.

Garner, Philippe. *Phaidon Encyclopedia of Decorative Arts: 1890–1940*, Oxford and New York, 1979.

Gary, Marie-Noel de (General Editor). *Les Fouquet, bijoutiers et joailliers à Paris 1860–1960*, Musée des Arts Décoratifs, Paris, 1983.

Georges, Waldemar. 'L'Exposition des Arts Décoratifs et Industriels de 1925' in *L'Amour de l'Art*, August 1925, pp. 283–91.

Heiniger, Ernst A. and Jeanne. *Le Grand Livre des Bijoux*, Paris, 1974.

Herbst, René. *25 années d'U.A.M.*, Paris, 1956.

Hillier, Bevis. *Art Deco of the 20s and 30s*, London, 1968.

——. *The World of Art Deco*, New York, 1981, London, 1984.

Hughes, Graham. *Modern jewellery. An international survey, 1890–1964*, London, 1964 (2nd Edition).

Kahn, Gustave. 'Charles Rivaud' in *Art et Décoration*, January 1924, pp. 13–18.

Lahalle, Pierre. 'Gérard Sandoz, orfèvre et joaillier moderne' in *Mobilier et Décoration d'Intérieur*, pp. 89–94.

Lanllier-Pini. *Cinq siècles de Joaillerie en Occident*, Freiburg, 1971.

Lenfant, Jacques. 'Bijouterie-Joaillerie' in *Encyclopédie contemporaine des métiers d'art*, Paris, 1979.

Léon, Paul. *Rapport Général de l'Exposition Internationale des Arts Décoratifs 1925*, Paris, volume IX, classes 20–24.

Lesieutre, Alain. *The Spirit and splendour of Art Deco*, New York, 1974.

Linzeler, Robert, 'La Joaillerie Française à l'Exposition' in *Vogue*, September 1925.

Martinie, H.A. 'Le XVIIIe Salon des Artistes et Décorateurs' in *Art et Décoration*, no 43, pp. 161–200.

Mazars, Pierre. 'Chronique de l'Amateur, Bijoux 1925' in *Jardin des Arts*, no 211, June 1972, pp. 70–71.

McClinton, Katherine Morrison. *Art Deco: A guide for collectors*, New York, 1972.

Menten, Théodore. *Art Deco Style in Household Objects, Architecture, Sculpture, Graphics, Jewellery*, New York, 1972, London, 1973.

Mundt, Barbara. *20er Jahr Neuerwerbungen*, Kunstgewerbemuseum, Berlin.

Nadelhoffer, Hans. *Cartier*, Paris, 1984.

Nalys, Roger. 'Gérard Sandoz' in *L'Officiel de la Couture*, 1927.

——. 'Jean Desprès' in *Art et Décoration*, September 1933, pp. 267–70.

——. 'Le Bijou compagnon de la grâce féminine' in *L'Officiel de la Couture*, June 1929, pp. 44–45.

Possémé, Evelyne. 'La Bijouterie Art Nouveau et Art Déco' in *Métiers d'Art*, September 1983, pp. 46–53.

Saffroy, Bernard. 'Cadeaux' in *Les Echos des Industries d'Art*, no 64, November 1930, pp. 7–16.

Scarlett, Frank, and Marjorie Townley. *A personal recollection of the Paris Exhibition*, London, 1975.

Sedyn, Emile. 'Des Bijoux Nouveaux' in *Art et Décoration*, no 43, pp. 143–52.

Sentenac, Paul. 'L'Art dans le bijou' in *La Renaissance des Arts Français et des Industries de Luxe*, March 1928.

——. 'Le carnet d'un curieux, les expositions' in *La Renaissance des Arts Français et des Industries de Luxe*, January 1929.

——. 'Les Arts de la Bijouterie-Joaillerie-Orfèvrerie au Musée Galliéra' in *La Renaissance de l'Art Français et des Industries de Luxe*, August 1929.

Siegel. *Catalogue de mannequins*, with photographs by Hoyningen-Huene, Paris, 1928.

Sterner, Gabrielle, and Albrecht Bangert. *Jugendstil Art Déco*, Munich, 1979.

Tardy and Dina Level. *Les pierres précieuses*, Paris, 1980.

Tisserand, Ernest. 'Art Décoratif et propagandes, quelques expositions privées' in *L'Art Vivant*, January 1927.

Tixier, Geneviève. *Les Arts Déco 20–30*, Société des Amis de la Bibliothèque Forney.

Varenne, Gaston. 'Raymond Templier et le bijou moderne' in *Art et Décoration*, no 57, February 1930, pp. 49–58.

Veronesi, Giulia. *Into the Twenties. Style and Design*, 1909–29, London, 1968.

Ward, Anne, John Cherry, Charlotte Gere, Barbara Cartlidge (based on an idea by Marielle Ernould Ganduet). *The Ring from Antiquity to the Twentieth Century*, London, 1981.

Werth, Léon. 'Le Premier Salon de l'Union des Artistes Modernes' in *Art et Décoration*, pp. 33–40.

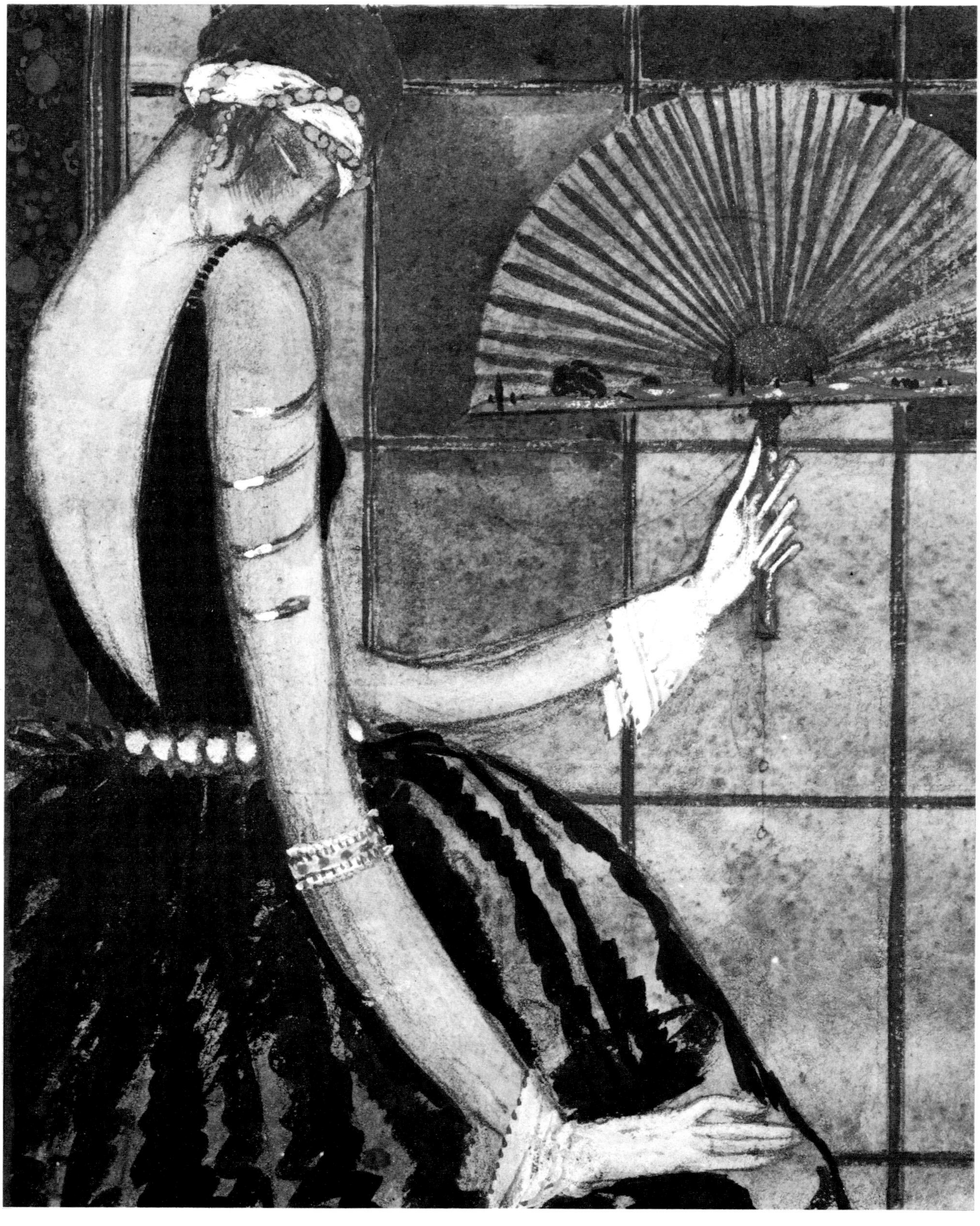

Georges Lepape: The Gold Fan, *Indian ink and gold. 17 × 14 cm. From* La Gazette du Bon Ton, *no 2, 1920.*

GLOSSARY

bijoutier: jeweler who makes jewelry using precious metals and gemstones, with the emphasis on design and craftsmanship. By contrast, the *joaillier* uses principally precious stones, the precious metal serving merely as a support. The *bijoutier-joaillier* combines both activities.

calibré (cut): style of cutting a gemstone in a shape, often oblong or elliptical, so that it and others cut in the same way will fit snugly together in clusters.

champlevé: technique of decoration by enamelling in which the design was made by lines or cells cut into the metal base which were filled with powdered enamel of various colours and then fired to fuse the enamels.

cloisonné: technique of decoration by enamelling in which a design is outlined on a metal plate with bent wire or metal strips and the spaces are filled in with coloured enamels that are then fused.

guilloché: style of engraved decoration made on metal by an engine-turning lathe having an eccentric motion that can cut a variety of patterns. The *guillocheur* is the craftsman responsible for such work.

Haute Joaillerie: the French jewelry establishment, comprising the best-known commercial jewelers such as Cartier, Mauboussin, Boucheron and Chaumet. It was from this establishment that the innovators of the Twenties and Thirties – names liked Raymond Templier, Jean Fouquet and Gérard Sandoz – aimed to break away.

horloger: clockmaker.

joaillier: see above under *bijoutier*.

orfèvre: jeweler who works in gold, silver and platinum.

parure: dress in its widest sense, including everything – clothing, jewelry and accessories – which goes to make up a woman's ensemble. A *parure* has been accepted into English in the sense of 'a matching set of jewelry'.

sablé: literally meaning 'sanded', this refers to a type of coarsely textured gold produced by lightly hammering the surface with a fine matting tool.

sautoir: long neck chain, worn loosely from the shoulders and usually extending down to below the waist; frequently with a jeweled pendant or tassel attached to it.

vermeil: gilded silver, i.e., sterling silver covered with a layer of gold by plating or some other process.

INDEX

Page numbers in *italic* refer to illustration captions.

ACKNOWLEDGMENTS

The publishers wish to thank Sylvie Raulet for her collaboration as author and adviser on the present work.

They would also like to express their gratitude to Mr Didier Grumbach, Mr Philippe Morane and Mrs Andrée Putman for their invaluable help.

Warmest thanks are due to Mr and Mrs Barlach Heuer for the confidence they have shown by placing their archives at the publishers' disposal.

Thanks also go to the following for their greatly appreciated assistance in the publication of this work: Mrs Stéphanie Aucoc, Galerie Günther, Paris; the Maison Boivin; Mr Jean Luc Bréant; Princess Jeanne Marie de Broglie, Christie's, Paris; Mr François Canavy, Van Cleef et Arpels; Etude Champin – Lombrail – Gautier, Enghien; Etude Couturier – Nicolay, Paris; Mr and Mrs Danenberg, Galerie Danenberg, Paris; Mrs Marie Odile Deutsch, Sotheby's, Paris; Mr Ralph Esmerian; Mrs Laure de Fels, Boucheron; Mrs Patricia Ferenczi, Christie's, New York; Mrs Audrey Friedman, Primavera Gallery, New York; Mr Philippe Garner, Sotheby's, London; Galerie Knut Günther; Miss Betty Jais, Cartier, Paris; the Maison Georg Jensen, Copenhagen; John Jesse and Irina Laski Ltd, London; the Maison Lalique; Mr Fred Leighton; Mr Jean Lepuil; Mr Alain Lesieutre; Mr Nicolas Manoukian; Mr Félix Marcilhac; the Maison Mellerio; Mrs Solange Morane; Mr Hans Nadelhoffer, Christie's, Geneva; Mrs Christine Ormes; Mrs Evelyne Possémé, Curator at the Musée des Arts Décoratifs, Paris; Mr Jean-Jacques Rioux; Mr Michel de Robert, Mauboussin; Mr Gérard-Julien Salvy; Mr Gérard Sandoz; Mrs Eliane Scali, Puiforcat; Mr Michel Souillac; Galerie Vallois, Paris.

Particular thanks are owed to Mrs Marie Noël de Gary, Curator at the Musée des Arts Décoratifs in Paris, for her great kindness and efficiency; and also to the following: Dr Fritz Falk, Schmuckmuseum, Pforzheim; Mrs Yvonne Deslandres, Curator at the Musée de la Mode, Paris; Dr Sigrid Barten, Curator at the Musée Bellerive, Zurich.